W9-BBO-787

Out There: Marginalization and Contemporary Cultures

Edited by

Russell Ferguson

Martha Gever

Trinh T. Minh-ha

Cornel West

Foreword by

Marcia Tucker

Out There: Marginalization and Contemporary Cultures

Images selected by

Félix González-Torres

The New Museum of Contemporary Art   New York, New York

The MIT Press   Cambridge, Massachusetts   London, England

The New Museum of Contemporary Art, New York
Documentary Sources in Contemporary Art
Series Editor: Marcia Tucker

Volume 1. *Art After Modernism: Rethinking Representation*
Edited by Brian Wallis

Volume 2. *Blasted Allegories: An Anthology of Writings by Contemporary Artists*
Edited by Brian Wallis

Volume 3. *Discourses: Conversations in Postmodern Art and Culture*
Edited by Russell Ferguson, William Olander, Marcia Tucker, and Karen Fiss

Volume 4. *Out There: Marginalization and Contemporary Cultures*
Edited by Russell Ferguson, Martha Gever, Trinh T. Minh-ha, and Cornel West

This volume is made possible through a generous grant from The Henry Luce
Fund for Scholarship in American Art.

Images selected by Félix González-Torres
Editorial Assistant: Alice Yang
Production Coordinator: Sowon Kwon
Typeset by Strong Silent Type, New York
Printed by Halliday Lithograph Corp., West Hanover, Massachusetts
Designed by Bethany Johns with Georgie Stout

Library of Congress Cataloging-in-Publication Data
Out there: marginalization and contemporary cultures /
edited by Russell Ferguson . . . [et al.].
    p.   cm.
ISBN 0-262-06132-5
1. Arts and society–History–20th century.   2. Ethnic arts.
3. Minorities in Art.   4. Marginality, Social–History–20th
century.   I. Ferguson, Russell.
NX 180.S6097 1990
700′.1′0308693–dc20   90-5562
Second printing, 1991   CIP

© 1990 The New Museum of Contemporary Art and Massachusetts Institute
of Technology

All rights reserved. No part of this book may be reproduced in any form by
any electronic or mechanical means (including photocopying, recording, or
information storage and retrieval) without written permission in writing
from the publisher.

Printed and bound in the United States of America.

The New Museum of Contemporary Art,
583 Broadway, New York, New York 10012

The MIT Press, Massachusetts Institute of Technology,
55 Hayward Street, Cambridge, Massachusetts, 02142

Contents

Marginalia: Displacement and Resistance

Director's Foreword

*We can train ourselves to respect our feelings and to transpose them
into a language so they can be shared.*
–Audre Lorde

Out There is a book about "marginalization," that complex and disputatious process by means of which certain people and ideas are privileged over others at any given time. It is a collection of essays that explore and ultimately, we hope, deconstruct the problematic binary notions of center and periphery, inclusion and exclusion, majority and minority, as they operate in artistic and social practice.

This book examines the process by which, through shifts in position, any given group can be ignored, trivialized, rendered invisible and unheard, perceived as inconsequential, de-authorized, "other," or threatening, while others are valorized.

The essays challenge the idea of identity as singular or monolithic, exploring instead the concept of a "multiple, shifting, and often self-contradictory identity . . . made up of heterogeneous and heteronomous representations of gender, race, and class."[1] Since art and culture are inseparable, these essays also challenge the strangely persistent idea that artists and the work they make come in only one gender, color or sexual preference.

The editors of this anthology, a team of four people from different cultural and racial backgrounds and positions, have had a difficult task, first of all in defining what constitutes the process of "marginalization" from the varied individual and collective points of view, and then arranging the material in a manner which might suggest issues beyond the specific ones addressed here. That they have done so is a tribute above all to their ability to listen to each other.

The book continues explorations which have long been in process among various groups and coalitions. But while women, people of color, gay men and lesbians, the physically handicapped, the aged (among others), have tried to address each other and examine these issues among themselves, it is only recently that attempts are being made to find our common ground.

None of us chooses our race, our gender, our age, or our country of origin, nor can we do anything to change them. But while these factors are outside our control, how we position ourselves in relation to them is very much a matter of choice. The approaches taken by these essays range from the confrontational to the seductive, from the theoretical to the personal. There are many voices, many points of view, and no single answer is offered. Through a variety of theoretical, critical and expository writings, we hope to begin to break down the Western, binary frame which, in critic Barbara Christian's words,

> *sees the rest of the world as minor and tries to convince the rest of the world that it is major, usually through force and then through language, even as it claims many of the ideas that we, its "historical" other, have known and spoken about for so long. For many of us have never conceived of ourselves only as somebody's other.*[2]

• • •

Out There is the fourth volume in our "Documentary Sources in Contemporary Art" series, funded by generous grants from The Henry Luce Fund for Scholarship in American Art. We are first and foremost grateful to the Henry Luce Foundation for the continuing intellectual and financial support which have made these volumes possible.

We are especially grateful to the four editors, Russell Ferguson, Martha Gever, Trinh T. Minh-ha and Cornel West, for undertaking this complex and important task, and for bringing their different views to a harmonious conclusion.

At the museum, Sowon Kwon, Production Coordinator, and Alice Yang, Editorial Assistant for the project, have worked extraordinarily hard to see it to completion. It is difficult to imagine the project without their skill and dedication to it.

Bethany Johns, who designed the book with Georgie Stout, and artist Félix González-Torres, who illustrated it, worked long and hard to translate its contents into visual terms; Janice Woo provided the indispensible index; Andrew Hunter, Miwon Kwon and Eleanor Martineau undertook the laborious task of proofreading, and Gillane Seaborne, the equally intensive job of word processing the manuscript. Thanks are due also to Terri Cafaro, who expertly copy-edited some of the original texts.

We would like to acknowledge as well the assistance of our many staff members, who solved minor and major problems throughout the production of this volume, copied thousands of pages of material for us, helped us raise the funds and organize its budget, and in general provided wisdom, guidance, advice, support and good humor throughout.

We are grateful to MIT Press and especially to Roger Conover for their cooperation in this endeavor; it has been, as always, a pleasure to work with them.

Last, but above all, our thanks to the authors for their generosity—not just in giving permission to print or reprint their essays, but for the generosity of spirit which prompted them to write in the first place.

1. Cheryl A. Wall, "Taking Positions and Changing Words," in *Changing Our Own Words: Essays on Criticism, Theory and Writing by Black Women*, ed. C. Wall (New Brunswick and London: Rutgers University Press, 1989), p. 10.

2. Barbara Christian, "The Race for Theory," *Feminist Studies*, vol. 14, no. 1 (1988); reprinted with revisions in *Cultural Critique* 6 (Spring 1987): 70.

• **Russell Ferguson**

Introduction: Invisible Center

When we say marginal, we must always ask, marginal to what? But this question is difficult to answer. The place from which power is exercised is often a hidden place. When we try to pin it down, the center always seems to be somewhere else. Yet we know that this phantom center, elusive as it is, exerts a real, undeniable power over the whole social framework of our culture, and over the ways that we think about it. Audre Lorde calls this center the mythical norm, defined as "white, thin, male, young, heterosexual, Christian and financially secure." Although each of these characteristics carries a somewhat different weight, their combination describes a status with which we are all familiar. It defines the tacit standards from which specific others can then be declared to deviate, and while that myth is perpetuated by those whose interests it serves, it can also be internalized by those who are oppressed by it. This unspoken structure is rejected by the writers in this volume. They don't allow themselves to be defined only relation to something else. They stand their own ground, and speak from there without apology.

But at the same time, they talk to each other. The juxtapositions made here set up resonances out of different but sometimes parallel exclusions. Too often the alternatives to dominant cultural power have been successfully segregated, so that many different bodies of marginalized creative production exist in uneasy isolation. Such isolation can only contribute to the security of a *political* power which implicitly defines itself as representative of a stable center around which everyone else must be arranged. The juxtapositions made in this book are intended to challenge that pattern. The anthology format itself is well suited to this project, since it consists of a series of discrete voices. It is always, inevitably, incomplete. There are many other essays, many other points of view, which could have been included alongside those we have chosen. Fragments from larger, continuing debates, the pieces collected here will perhaps leave the reader room to find a place for him or herself.

The essays are grouped in three sections. In the first, the critical context of contemporary cultural debates is explored in essays which draw on philosophy, literature, film, architecture, politics and art. The second addresses the questions of how to affirm cultural identities in a complex and often repressive society. The third deals with counter-movements of displacement and resistance to marginalization. Within this broad structure, however, themes and ideas reverberate throughout the book. The intent is not to create a new center of authority based on a spurious unity of the marginalized, but rather to open up spaces for new ways of thinking about the dynamics of cultural power. We also hope that the diversity of the voices we have included will help to disrupt the unified tone which can so easily become the commanding voice of authority, the voice which subsumes all difference under its cloak.

Since the 1960's the easy assumptions on which authority has been based in American society have been the subject to a continuing series of challenges, which have succeeded at least in making the real mechanisms of these norms much more clearly visible, and thus more insecure. The relaxed self-confidence of a TV patriarch like Ward Cleaver now seems to have slipped out of reach, replaced by the increasingly hysterical and ruthless campaigns of the last ten years to *enforce* "traditional family values." Such campaigns have cut a wide swath, ranging from attacks on the right of women to control their own bodies to the repeated implications that black poverty can be attributed to failures within the black family or that people with AIDS deserve their illness. The need to enforce values which are at the same time alleged to be "natural" demonstrates the insecurity of a center which could at one time take its own power much more for granted.[1]

As historically marginalized groups insist on their own identity, the deeper, structural invisibility of the so-called center becomes harder to sustain. The power of the center depends on a relatively unchallenged authority. If that authority breaks down, then there remains no point relative to which others can be defined as marginal. The perceived threat lies partly in the very process of becoming visible. It becomes increasingly obvious, for example, that white American men have their own specificity, and that it is from there that their power is exercised. No longer can whiteness, maleness or heterosexuality be taken as the ubiquitous paradigm, simultaneously center and boundary.[2]

The picture of a center which feels itself seriously challenged is also evident in the demands for a return to the teaching of the traditional canon of "great" works in the arts and humanities. In practice, of course, the great works under discussion almost all turn out to have been produced by white men. This is the corpus which we are expected to take as representing all of human culture. But the debate around the canon indicates some of the problematic elements which emerge alongside the opportunities offered by challenges to the center. Critiques which call only for the admission of a somewhat wider variety of voices to the canon tend to leave many of its most fundamental assumptions unchallenged. Despite the intensity of the polemic, the function of the canon is not deeply threatened by the demand that a particular "minority" artist be admitted to it. John Yau's essay on Wifredo Lam and the Museum of Modern Art demonstrates how even an artist such as Lam, whose ethnicity was central to his work, can be absorbed by the sophisticated apparatus of Eurocentric scholarship. The demand for admission to the canon remains a contradictory project, because it implies an acceptance of essential features of the existing structure. Real changes are impossible without a questioning of the master(piece) discourse which forms its foundation. As Toni Morrison points out, resistance could begin with a questioning of the unspoken assumption of white, male, heterosexual identity which underlies the concept of the "universal."

For artists and writers who have been brought up in a system entirely based on belief in great geniuses who produce great works, it is not easy to reject those concepts, even if that very system has consistently excluded works by members of their own race or sex. The broader attack on the canon can produce conflicted feelings of bitterness and anger in artists who have felt themselves on the edge of admittance: just when it seems that the canon might be opening up a little to include them, the whole process of canonization is being called into question. It seems that there can be no canon without exclusion. But at the same time, there is the nagging consciousness of working in a system which accepts only to recuperate. Edward Said writes, as a Palestinian, that

> . . . we can read ourselves against another people's pattern, but since it is not ours . . . we emerge as its effects, its errata, its counternarratives. Whenever we try to narrate ourselves, we appear as dislocations in their discourse.[3]

Counternarratives of all kinds do constantly enter "mainstream" culture. One of the great strengths of the existing structure is its capacity to absorb a constant flow of new elements. In any system based on consumption, new products and new styles must be perpetually supplied. Such a flow is essential to its health and survival. James Snead argues, in fact, that a salient characteristic of dominant Western culture is its denial of repetition in favor of the rhetoric of constant progress, growth and change. The vital, independent cultures of socially subordinated groups are constantly mined for new ideas with which to energize the jaded and restless mainstream of a political and economic system based on the circulation of commodities. The process depends on the delivery of continual novelty to the market while at the same time alternative cultural forms are drained of any elements which might challenge the system as a whole. But although this structure is strong and flexible, it is also inherently unstable. How much can the center really absorb without having its own authority called into question?

For artists, long participants in the process of mediation between the "exotic" and the "mainstream," the question of marginality poses special complexities. The tradition of the avant-garde has led many artists to identify with a kind of glamorized otherness; to see themselves as marginalized, and art by definition as a marginalized activity. Many have actively sought isolation from the rest of society, whether in bohemian garrets or ivory towers. This tradition inevitably creates an ambiguous relationship with those who have not chosen marginalization, but have had it thrust upon them. It is all too easy for a white, male artist to buy into the long-established myth of the outsider and, in the process, forget that his race and sex still confer on him privileges which are none the less real for having been forgotten.

We are thus returned to the invisibility of the center. In our society dominant discourse tries never to speak its own name. Its authority is based on absence. The absence is not just that of the various groups classified as "other," although members of these groups are routinely denied power. It is also the lack of any overt acknowledgment of the specificity of the dominant culture, which is simply assumed to be the all-encompassing norm. This is the basis of its power. When we see that a TV show is called *The History of White People in America* we know at once that the genre is comedy. The history of America and the history of white people are read as synonymous, so this program can't be serious. The joke is in the tautology.

Linda Peckham's discussion of the position of white intellectuals in South Africa outlines some of the problems inherent in trying to redefine a position which has historically taken its dominance for granted. Since the center of power always prefers to present itself as transparent, extreme situations such as that in South Africa, in which the question of white ethnicity is forced to the surface, are unusual. It is interesting to compare Peckham's essay with Simon Watney's analysis of Western press coverage of AIDS in Africa, in which he shows the whole battery of mechanisms, rhetorical and practical, that are deployed against a perceived threat to a white heterosexual norm that is never overtly acknowledged. In another context, Rosalyn Deutsche's essay reveals some of the hidden meanings and class relationships encoded in the concept of "public" space in the city. Such efforts to bring the invisible agenda of the dominant culture into the light help make it clear that definitions of the "other" are always relative, never absolute.

Richard Rodriguez's "Complexion," for example, is a reflection on all the real differences which can be hidden by an easy reliance on simple classifications. The distance which separates Rodriguez, a middle-class college student, from the Mexican day-laborers alongside whom he works one summer is a measure of how much is left out of schemas which rely on a single element for their structure. Rodriguez's ambivalence and inability to identify with *los pobres* graphically demonstrates how ethnicity can be complicated by the power conferred by class. Rodriguez is privileged by his economic status while remaining conscious of his race. That is his quandary.

Gilles Deleuze and Félix Guattari have argued that the invisibility of the dominant group in its own definitions means that the very concept of race has meaning only in terms of a system of oppression, and, further, that any concept of a "pure" race ignores this reality:

> . . . there is no race but inferior, minoritarian, there is no dominant race, a race is not defined by its purity but rather by the impurity conferred upon it by a system of domination. Bastard and mixed blood are the true names of race.[4]

In a self-consciously mythic way, Gerald Vizenor's "Socioacupuncture" addresses some of the issues raised by Deleuze and Guattari. He demonstrates how the dominant culture does not merely oppress a marginalized society, but actually reinvents it for its own purposes. Vizenor's allusive and poetic style steps outside the conventions of academic writing in an attempt to escape from language which can itself become a form of confinement: "linear methods of perception have denied a theater for tribal events in mythic time."

While Vizenor never posits the existence of a pure and unspoiled tribal identity which could potentially be freed from white cultural domination, he does assert the capacity of his culture to continue to (re)create itself outside the norms of that mainstream. Gloria Anzaldúa, bell hooks, Kobena Mercer and Teshome Gabriel also stress the role of independent cultural traditions in creating a positive self-identity, an identity not defined simply in terms of opposition, but one with its own traditions and values. The elements of such alternatives can be drawn from myth, history, language and form. But, equally, these writers recognize the impossibility of an absolute separation between any two cultures which exist in the same space. Perhaps now it is only the impure which might claim any kind of authenticity. This is the strategy identified by

Deleuze and Guattari in "What is a Minor Literature?": "To make use of the polylingualism of one's own language . . . to oppose the oppressed quality of this language to its oppressive quality." The mixed languages of Gloria Anzaldúa are the expression of a deterritorialization which she feels physically, in her mouth, her tongue, her teeth. It is out of precisely that experience, however, that she has created her own identity. To find one's own language today means to recognize an endless series of interpenetrations, while at the same time resisting dissolution into the dominant culture.

The specific role of language as an instrument of power is taken up in many of these essays. Homi Bhabha, Hélène Cixous and Monique Wittig all describe the oppression inherent in certain systems of language. One form of discourse repeatedly challenged here is the supposedly neutral, "objective" discourse of academia. It is challenged by some who have participated in it: "I tried writing a first version of this piece in the usual disinterested academic style," Gayatri Chakravorty Spivak begins. "I gave up after a few pages." By introducing her own personal voice, her feelings as well as her analysis, Spivak makes visible the hidden assumptions which set the context for conventional academic debate. She demonstrates the sophisticated way in which the academic system attempts to co-opt selected members of marginalized groups, subtly shaping the reception of their voices until they reproduce the discourse against which they were once raised.

The continuing struggle to find and maintain a genuine voice in a culture which can often seem suffocating is a theme which runs throughout the book. It is a theme echoed in the family snapshots among the images which Félix González-Torres has selected as illustrations. The snapshots show some of the writers and others involved in the making of the book. As children, we must all literally learn to speak for ourselves. As we enter into language we must simultaneously negotiate the crude classifications which are imposed upon us and create our own identities out of the twisted skeins of our backgrounds, families and environments.

We must do this in the face of the omnipresent center, the invisible center which claims universality without ever defining itself, and which exiles to its margins those who cannot or will not pay allegiance to the standards which it sets or the limits which it imposes. Part of the project of this anthology is to point to some of the places where these boundaries are stretched or porous, and thus to contribute to their destabilization. González-Torres's photographs of monumental inscriptions from the Museum of Natural History in New York express the power of these mythic classifications—here literally carved in stone—which press down on all of us and which have crushed many under their weight.

Perhaps it is not too much to hope for a future in which we can recognize differences without seizing them as levers in a struggle for power. But making this future must involve us all. Men cannot dissociate themselves from "women's issues," straight people cannot ignore the struggles of gay and lesbian people, and white people cannot declare themselves indifferent to racial politics. It is too easy for a "sympathetic" self-effacement to become another trick of quiet dominance.

Margin and center can draw their meanings only from each other. Neither can exist alone. This anthology, therefore, finds its place on the borderlines between shifting territories. It is not so much about the margins themselves, as it is about marginalization, and about the resistances to marginalization. Its subject is the process through which cultural margins are created, defined and enforced.

Out There was produced through a collaborative process of discussion, argument and analysis which took place over many months and which brought together many different approaches and points of view. That process opened up new insights for those who worked on the making of the book. We hope that the finished product will be useful to those who will continue the dialogue.

1. The language of advertising recognizes this insecurity: "It's as real as it gets"; "real taste for real people"; "It's the real thing." Such slogans, in their very insistence on an unproblematic, universalizing reality, acknowledge its potential disintegration.

2. See Richard Dyer, "White," *Screen*, vol. 29, no. 4 (Autumn 1988): 44-64.

3. Edward Said, *After the Last Sky: Palestinian Lives* (New York, Pantheon, 1986), p. 140.

4. Gilles Deleuze and Félix Guattari, *Nomadology: The War Machine* (New York: Semiotext[e], 1986), p. 49.

Other Questions: Critical Contexts

The New Cultural Politics of Difference

In these last few years of the 20th century, there is emerging a significant shift in the sensibilities and outlooks of critics and artists. In fact, I would go so far as to claim that a new kind of cultural worker is in the making, associated with a new politics of difference. These new forms of intellectual consciousness advance reconceptions of the vocation of critic and artist, attempting to undermine the prevailing disciplinary divisions of labor in the academy, museum, mass media and gallery networks, while preserving modes of critique within the ubiquitous commodification of culture in the global village. Distinctive features of the new cultural politics of difference are to trash the monolithic and homogeneous in the name of diversity, multiplicity and heterogeneity; to reject the abstract, general and universal in light of the concrete, specific and particular; and to historicize, contextualize and pluralize by highlighting the contingent, provisional, variable, tentative, shifting and changing. Needless to say, these gestures are not new in the history of criticism or art, yet what makes them novel—along with the cultural politics they produce—is how and what constitutes difference, the weight and gravity it is given in representation and the way in which highlighting issues like exterminism, empire, class, race, gender, sexual orientation, age, nation, nature, and region at this historical moment acknowledges some discontinuity and disruption from previous forms of cultural critique. To put it bluntly, the new cultural politics of difference consists of creative responses to the precise circumstances of our present moment—especially those of marginalized First World agents who shun degraded self-representations, articulating instead their sense of the flow of history in light of the contemporary terrors, anxieties and fears of highly commercialized North Atlantic capitalist cultures (with their escalating xenophobias against people of color, Jews, women, gays, lesbians and the elderly). The thawing, yet still rigid, Second World ex-communist cultures (with increasing nationalist revolts against the legacy of hegemonic party henchmen), and the diverse cultures of the majority of inhabitants on the globe smothered by international communication cartels and repressive postcolonial elites (sometimes in the name of communism, as in Ethiopia) or starved by austere World Bank and IMF policies that subordinate them to the North (as in free-market capitalism in Chile) also locate vital areas of analysis in this new cultural terrain.

The new cultural politics of difference are neither simply oppositional in contesting the mainstream (or *male*stream) for inclusion, nor transgressive in the avant-gardist sense of shocking conventional bourgeois audiences. Rather, they are distinct articulations of talented (and usually privileged) contributors to culture who desire to align themselves with demoralized, demobilized, depoliticized and disorganized people in order to empower and enable social action and, if possible, to enlist collective insurgency for the expansion of freedom, democracy and individuality. This perspective impels these cultural critics and artists to reveal, as an integral component of their production, the very operations of power within their immediate work contexts (i.e., academy, museum, gallery, mass media). This strategy, however, also puts them in an inescapable double bind—while linking their activities to the fundamental, structural overhaul of these institutions, they often remain financially dependent on them (so much for "independent" creation). For these critics of culture, theirs is a gesture that is simultaneously progressive *and* co-opted. Yet without social movement or political pressure from outside these institutions (extra-parliamentary and extra-curricular actions like the social movements of the recent past), transformation degenerates into mere accommodation or sheer stagnation, and the role of the "co-opted progressive"—no matter how fervent one's subversive rhetoric—is rendered more difficult. There can be no artistic breakthrough or social progress without some form of crisis in civilization—a crisis usually generated by organizations or collectivities that convince ordinary people to put their bodies and lives on the line. There is, of course, no guarantee that such pressure will yield the result one wants, but there is a guarantee that the status quo will remain or regress if no pressure is applied at all.

The new cultural politics of difference faces three basic challenges—intellectual, existential and political. The intellectual challenge—usually cast as methodological debate in these days in which academicist forms of expression have a monopoly on intellectual life—is how to think about representational practices in terms of history, culture and society. How does one understand, analyze and enact such practices today? An adequate answer to this question can be attempted only after one comes to terms with the insights and blindnesses of earlier attempts to grapple with the question in light of the evolving crisis in different histories, cultures and societies. I shall sketch a brief genealogy—a history that highlights the contingent origins and often ignoble outcomes—of exemplary critical responses to the question. This genealogy sets forth a historical framework that characterizes the rich yet deeply flawed Eurocentric traditions which the new cultural politics of difference build upon yet go beyond.

The Intellectual Challenge

An appropriate starting point is the ambiguous legacy of the Age of Europe. Between 1492 and 1945, European breakthroughs in oceanic transportation, agricultural production, state-consolidation, bureaucratization, industrialization, urbanization and imperial dominion shaped the makings of the modern world. Precious ideals like the dignity of persons (individuality) or the popular accountability of institutions (democracy) were unleashed around the world. Powerful critiques of illegitimate authorities—of the Protestant Reformation against the Roman Catholic Church, the Enlightenment against state churches, liberal movements against absolutist states and feudal guild constraints, workers against managerial subordination, people of color and Jews against white and gentile supremacist decrees, gays and lesbians against homophobic sanctions—were fanned and fuelled by these precious ideals refined within the crucible of the Age of Europe. Yet the discrepancy between sterling rhetoric and lived reality, glowing principles and actual practices loomed large.

By the last European century—the last epoch in which European domination of most of the globe was uncontested and unchallenged in a substantive way—a new world seemed to be stirring. At the height of England's reign as the major imperial European power, its exemplary cultural critic, Matthew Arnold, painfully observed in his "Stanzas From the Grand Chartreuse" that he felt some sense of "wandering between two worlds, one dead / the other powerless to be born." Following his Burkean sensibilities of cautious reform and fear of anarchy, Arnold acknowledged that the old glue—religion—that had tenuously and often unsuccessfully held together the ailing European regimes could not do so in the mid-19th century. Like Alexis de Tocqueville in France, Arnold saw that the democratic temper was the wave of the future. So he proposed a new conception of culture—a secular, humanistic one—that could play an integrative role in cementing and stabilizing an emerging bourgeois civil society and imperial state. His famous castigation of the immobilizing materialism of the declining aristocracy, the vulgar philistinism of the emerging middle classes and the latent explosiveness of the working-class majority was motivated by a desire to create new forms of cultural legitimacy, authority and order in a rapidly changing moment in 19th century Europe.

For Arnold, (in *Culture and Anarchy*, [1869]) this new conception of culture

. . . seeks to do away with classes; to make the best that has been thought and known in the world current everywhere; to make all men live in an atmosphere of sweetness and light . . .

This is the social idea and the men of culture are the true apostles of equality. The great men of culture are those who have had a passion for diffusing, for making prevail, for carrying from one end of society to the other, the best knowledge, the best ideas of their time, who have laboured to divest knowledge of all that was harsh, uncouth, difficult, abstract, professional, exclusive; to humanize it, to make it efficient outside the clique of the cultivated and learned, yet still remaining the best knowledge and thought of the time, and a true source, therefore, of sweetness and light.

As an organic intellectual of an emergent middle class—as the inspector of schools in an expanding educational bureaucracy, Professor of Poetry at Oxford (the first non-cleric and the first to lecture in English rather than Latin) and an active participant in a thriving magazine network—Arnold defined and defended a new secular culture of critical discourse. For him, this discursive strategy would be lodged in the educational and periodical apparatuses of modern societies as they contained and incorporated the frightening threats of an arrogant aristocracy and especially of an "anarchic" working-class majority. His ideals of disinterested, dispassionate and objective inquiry would regulate this new secular cultural production, and his justifications for the use of state power to quell any threats to the survival and security of this culture were widely accepted. He aptly noted, "Through culture seems to lie our way, not only to perfection, but even to safety."

This sentence is revealing in two ways. First, it refers to "our way" without explicitly acknowledging who constitutes the "we." This move is symptomatic among many bourgeois, male Eurocentric critics whose universalizing gestures exclude (by guarding a silence around) or explicitly degrade women and peoples of color. Second, the sentence links culture to safety—presumably the safety of the "we" against the barbaric threats of the "them," i.e., those viewed as different in some debased manner. Needless to say, Arnold's negative attitudes toward British working-class people, women and especially Indians and Jamaicans in the Empire clarify why he conceives of culture as, in part, a weapon for bourgeois male European "safety."

For Arnold the best of the Age of Europe—modeled on a mythological mélange of Periclean Athens, late Republican/early Imperial Rome and Elizabethan England—could be promoted only if there was an interlocking affiliation among the emerging middle classes, a homogenizing of cultural discourse in the educational and university networks, and a state advanced enough in its policing techniques to safeguard it. The candidates for participation and legitimation in this grand endeavor of cultural renewal and revision would be detached intellectuals willing to shed their parochialism, provincialism and class-bound identities for Arnold's middle-class-skewed project: ". . . Aliens, if we may so call them—persons who are mainly led, not by their class spirit, but by a general *humane* spirit, by the love of human perfection." Needless to say, this Arnoldian perspective still informs much of the academic practices and secular cultural attitudes today—dominant views about the canon, admission procedures and collective self-definitions of intellectuals. Yet Arnold's project was disrupted by the collapse of 19th century Europe—World War I. This unprecedented war brought to the surface the crucial role and violent potential not of the masses Arnold feared but of the state he heralded. Upon the ashes of this wasteland of human carnage—some of it the civilian European population—T.S. Eliot emerged as the grand cultural spokesman.

Eliot's project of reconstituting and reconceiving European highbrow culture—and thereby regulating critical and artistic practices—after the internal collapse of imperial Europe can be viewed as a response to the probing question posed by Paul Valéry in "The Crisis of the Spirit" after World War I,

This Europe, will it become what it is in reality, i.e., a little cape of the Asiatic continent? or will this Europe remain rather what it seems, i.e., the priceless part of the whole earth, the pearl of the globe, the brain of a vast body?

Eliot's image of Europe as a wasteland, a culture of fragments with no cementing center, predominated in postwar Europe. And though his early poetic practices were more radical, open and international than his Eurocentric criticism, Eliot posed a return to and revision of tradition as the only way of regaining European cultural order and political stability. For Eliot, contemporary history had become, as James Joyce's Stephen declared in *Ulysses* (1922), "a nightmare from which he was trying to awake"—"an immense panorama of futility and anarchy" as Eliot put it in his renowned review of Joyce's modernist masterpiece. In his influential essay, "Tradition and the Individual Talent," (1919) Eliot stated

Yet if the only form of tradition, of handing down, consisted in following the ways of the immediate generation before us in a blind or timid adherence to its successes, "tradition" should positively be discouraged. We have seen many such simple currents soon lost in the sand; and novelty is better than repetition. Tradition is a matter of much wider significance. It cannot be inherited, and if you want it you must attain it by great labour.

Eliot's fecund notion of tradition is significant in that it promotes a historicist sensibility in artistic practice and cultural reflection. This historicist sensibility—regulated in Eliot's case by a reactionary politics—produced a powerful assault on existing literary canons (in which for example Romantic poets were displaced by the Metaphysical and Symbolist ones) and unrelenting attacks on modern Western civilization (such as the liberal ideas of democracy, equality and freedom). Like Arnold's notion of culture, Eliot's idea of tradition was part of his intellectual arsenal, to be used in the battles raging in European cultures and societies.

Eliot found this tradition in the Church of England, to which he converted in 1927. Here was a tradition that left room for his Catholic cast of mind, Calvinistic heritage, puritanical temperament and rebellient patriotism for the old American South (the place of his upbringing). Like Arnold, Eliot was obsessed with the idea of civilization and the horror of barbarism (echoes of Joseph Conrad's Kurtz in *Heart of Darkness*) or more pointedly, the notion of the decline and decay of European civilization. With the advent of World War II, Eliot's obsession became a reality. Again unprecedented human carnage (50 million dead)—including an indescribable genocidal attack on Jewish people—throughout Europe as well as around the globe, put the last nail in the coffin of the Age of Europe. After 1945, Europe consisted of a devastated and divided continent, crippled by a humiliating dependency on and deference to the USA and USSR.

The second historical coordinate of my genealogy is the emergence of the USA as *the* world power. The USA was unprepared for world power status. However, with the recovery of Stalin's Russia (after losing 20 million dead), the USA felt compelled to make its presence felt around the globe. Then with the Marshall plan to strengthen Europe against Russian influence (and provide new markets for U.S. products), the 1948 Russian takeover of Czechoslovakia, the 1948 Berlin blockade, the 1950 beginning of the Korean War and the 1952 establishment of NATO forces in Europe, it seemed clear that there was no escape from world power obligations.

The post-World War II era in the USA, or the first decades of what Henry Luce envisioned as "The American Century," was not only a period of incredible economic expansion but of active cultural ferment. In the classical Fordist formula, mass production required mass consumption. With unchallenged hegemony in the capitalist world, the USA took economic growth for granted. Next to exercising its crude, anti-communist, McCarthyist obsessions, buying commodities became the primary act of civic virtue for many American citizens at this time. The creation of a mass middle class—a prosperous working class with a bourgeois identity—was countered by the first major emergence of subcultures of American non-WASP intellectuals: the so-called New York intellectuals in criticism, the Abstract Expressionists in painting and the BeBop artists in jazz music. This emergence signaled a vital challenge to an American male WASP elite loyal to an older and eroding European culture.

The first significant blow was dealt when assimilated Jewish Americans entered the higher echelons of the cultural apparatuses (academy, museums, galleries, mass media). Lionel Trilling is an emblematic figure. This Jewish entree into the anti-Semitic and patriarchal critical discourse of the exclusivistic institutions of American culture initiated the slow but sure undoing of the male WASP cultural hegemony and homogeneity. Lionel Trilling's project was to appropriate Matthew Arnold for his own political and cultural purposes—thereby unraveling the old male WASP consensus, while erecting a new post-World War II liberal academic consensus around cold war, anti-communist renditions of the values of complexity, difficulty, variousness and modulation. In addition, the post-war boom laid the basis for intense professionalization and specialization in expanding institutions of higher education—especially in the natural sciences that were compelled to somehow respond to Russia's successful ventures in space. Humanistic scholars found themselves searching for new methodologies that could buttress self-images of rigor and scientific seriousness. For example, the close reading techniques of New Criticism (severed from their conservative, organicist, anti-industrialist ideological roots), the logical precision of reasoning in analytic philosophy and the jargon of Parsonian structural-functionalism in sociology helped create such self-images. Yet towering cultural critics like C. Wright Mills, W.E.B. DuBois, Richard Hofstadter, Margaret Mead and Dwight MacDonald bucked the tide. This suspicion of the academicization of knowledge is expressed in Trilling's well-known essay "On the Teaching of Modern Literature"

> . . . can we not say that, when modern literature is brought into the classroom, the subject being taught is betrayed by the pedagogy of the subject? We have to ask ourselves whether in our day too much does not come within the purview of the academy. More and more, as the universities liberalize themselves, turn their beneficent imperialistic gaze upon what is called life itself, the feeling grows among our educated classes that little can be experienced unless it is validated by some established intellectual discipline. . . .

Trilling laments the fact that university instruction often quiets and domesticates radical and subversive works of art, turning them into objects "of merely habitual regard." This process of "the socialization of the anti-social, or the acculturation of the anti-cultural, or the legitimization of the subversive" leads Trilling to "question whether in our culture the study of literature is any longer a suitable means for developing and refining the intelligence." Trilling asks this question not in the spirit of denigrating and devaluing the academy but rather in the spirit of highlighting the possible failure of an Arnoldian conception of culture to contain what he perceives as the philistine and anarchic alternatives becoming more and more available to students of the 60's—namely, mass culture and radical politics.

This threat is partly associated with the third historical coordinate of my genealogy—the decolonization of the Third World. It is crucial to recognize the importance of this world-historical process if one wants to grasp the significance of the end of the Age of Europe and the emergence of the USA as a world power. With the first defeat of a western nation by a non-western nation—in Japan's victory over Russia (1905), revolutions in Persia (1905), Turkey (1908), China (1912), Mexico (1911-12) and much later the independence of India (1947) and China (1948) and the triumph of Ghana (1957)—the actuality of a decolonized globe loomed large. Born of violent struggle, consciousness-raising and the reconstruction of identities, decolonization simultaneously brings with it new perspectives on that long festering underside of the Age of Europe (of which colonial domination represents the *costs* of "progress," "order" and "culture"), as well as requiring new readings of the economic boom in the USA (wherein the Black, Brown, Yellow, Red, female, elderly, gay, lesbian and White working class live the same *costs* as cheap labor at home as well as in US-dominated Latin American and Pacific rim markets).

The impetuous ferocity and moral outrage that motors the decolonization process is best captured by Frantz Fanon in *The Wretched of the Earth* (1961).

> *Decolonization, which sets out to change the order of the world, is obviously, a program of complete disorder . . . Decolonization is the meeting of two forces, opposed to each other by their very nature, which in fact owe their originality to that sort of substantification which results from and is nourished by the situation in the colonies. Their first encounter was marked by violence and their existence together—that is to say the exploitation of the native by the settler—was carried on by dint of a great array of bayonets and cannons . . .*

> *In decolonization, there is therefore the need of a complete calling in question of the colonial situation. If we wish to describe it precisely, we might find it in the well-known words: "The last shall be first and the first last." Decolonization is the putting into practice of this sentence.*

> *The naked truth of decolonization evokes for us the searing bullets and bloodstained knives which emanate from it. For if the last shall be first, this will only come to pass after a murderous and decisive struggle between the two protagonists.*

Fanon's strong words, though excessively Manichean, still describe the feelings and thoughts between the occupying British Army and colonized Irish in Northern Ireland, the occupying Israeli Army and subjugated Palestinians on the West Bank and Gaza Strip, the South African Army and oppressed Black South Africans in the townships, the Japanese Police and Koreans living in Japan, the Russian Army and subordinated Armenians and others in the Southern and Eastern USSR. His words also partly invoke the sense many Black Americans have toward police departments in urban centers. In other words, Fanon is articulating century-long heartfelt human responses to being degraded and despised, hated and hunted, oppressed and exploited, marginalized and dehumanized at the hands of powerful xenophobic European, American, Russian and Japanese imperial countries.

During the late '50s, '60s and early '70s in the USA, these decolonized sensibilities fanned and fueled the Civil Rights and Black Power movements, as well as the student anti-war, feminist, gray, brown, gay, and lesbian movements. In this period we witnessed the shattering of male WASP cultural homogeneity and the collapse of the short-lived liberal consensus. The inclusion of African Americans, Latino/a Americans, Asian Americans, Native Americans and American women into the culture of critical discourse yielded intense intellectual polemics and inescapable ideological polarization that focused principally on the exclusions, silences and blindnesses of male WASP cultural homogeneity and its concomitant Arnoldian notions of the canon.

In addition, these critiques promoted three crucial processes that affected intellectual life in the country. First is the appropriation of the theories of post-war Europe–especially the work of the Frankfurt school (Marcuse, Adorno, Horkheimer), French/Italian Marxisms (Sartre, Althusser, Lefebvre, Gramsci), structuralisms (Lévi-Strauss, Todorov) and post-structuralisms (Deleuze, Derrida, Foucault). These diverse and disparate theories–all preoccupied with keeping alive radical projects after the end of the Age of Europe–tend to fuse versions of transgressive European modernisms with Marxist or post-Marxist left politics and unanimously shun the term "post-modernism." Second, there is the recovery and revisioning of American history in light of the struggles of white male workers, women, African Americans, Native Americans, Latino/a Americans, gays and lesbians. Third is the impact of forms of popular culture such as television, film, music videos and even sports, on highbrow literate culture. The Black-based hip-hop culture of youth around the world is one grand example.

After 1973, with the crisis in the international world economy, America's slump in productivity, the challenge of OPEC nations to the North Atlantic monopoly of oil production, the increasing competition in hi-tech sectors of the economy from Japan and West Germany and the growing fragility of the international debt structure, the USA entered a period of waning self-confidence (compounded by Watergate) and a nearly contracting economy. As the standards of living for the middle classes declined, owing to runaway inflation, and the quality of living fell for most, due to escalating unemployment, underemployment and crime, religious and secular neo-conservatism emerged with power and potency. This fusion of fervent neo-nationalism, traditional cultural values and "free market" policies served as the ground work for the Reagan-Bush era.

The ambiguous legacies of the European Age, American preeminence and decolonization continue to haunt our postmodern moment as we come to terms with both the European, American, Japanese, Soviet, and Third World *crimes against* and *contributions to* humanity. The plight of Africans in the New World can be instructive in this regard.

By 1914 European maritime empires had dominion over more than half of the land and a third of the peoples in the world–almost 72 million square kilometers of territory and more than 560 million people under colonial rule. Needless to say, this European control included brutal enslavement, institutional terrorism and cultural degradation of Black diaspora people. The death of roughly seventy-five million Africans during the centuries-long transatlantic slave trade is but one reminder, among others, of the assault on Black humanity. The Black diaspora condition of New World servitude–in which they were viewed as mere commodities with production value, who had no proper legal status, social standing or public worth–can be characterized as, following Orlando Patterson, natal alienation. This state of perpetual and inheritable domination that diaspora Africans had at birth produced the *modern Black diaspora problematic of invisibility and namelessness.* White supremacist practices–enacted under the auspices of the prestigious cultural authorities of the churches, printed media and scientific academics– promoted Black inferiority and constituted the European background against which

Black diaspora struggles for identity, dignity (self-confidence, self-respect, self-esteem) and material resources took place.

An inescapable aspect of this struggle was that the Black diaspora peoples' quest for validation and recognition occurred on the ideological, social and cultural terrains of other non-Black peoples. White supremacist assaults on Black intelligence, ability, beauty and character required persistent Black efforts to hold self-doubt, self-contempt and even self-hatred at bay. Selective appropriation, incorporation and re-articulation of European ideologies, cultures and institutions alongside an African heritage—a heritage more or less confined to linguistic innovation in rhetorical practices, stylizations of the body in forms of occupying an alien social space (hair styles, ways of walking, standing, hand expressions, talking) and means of constituting and sustaining comraderie and community (e.g. antiphonal, call-and-response styles, rhythmic repetition, risk-ridden syncopation in spectacular modes in musical and rhetorical expressions)—were some of the strategies employed.

The modern Black diaspora problematic of invisibility and namelessness can be understood as the condition of *relative lack of Black power to represent themselves to themselves and others as complex human beings, and thereby to contest the bombardment of negative, degrading stereotypes put forward by White supremacist ideologies.* The initial Black response to being caught in this whirlwind of Europeanization was to resist the misrepresentation and caricature of the terms set by uncontested non-Black norms and models and fight for self-representation and recognition. Every modern Black person, especially cultural disseminators, encounters this problematic of invisibility and namelessness. The initial Black diaspora response was a mode of resistance that was *moralistic in content* and *communal in character.* That is, the fight for representation and recognition highlighted moral judgments regarding Black "positive" images over and against White supremacist stereotypes. These images "re-presented" monolithic and homogeneous Black communities, in a way that could displace past misrepresentations of these communities. Stuart Hall has talked about these responses as attempts to change "the relations of representation."

These courageous yet limited Black efforts to combat racist cultural practices uncritically accepted non-Black conventions and standards in two ways. First, they proceeded in an *assimilationist manner* that set out to show that Black people were really like White people—thereby eliding differences (in history, culture) between Whites and Blacks. Black specificity and particularity was thus banished in order to gain White acceptance and approval. Second, these Black responses rested upon a *homogenizing impulse* that assumed that all Black people were really alike—hence obliterating differences (class, gender, region, sexual orientation) between Black peoples. I submit that there are elements of truth in both claims, yet the conclusions are unwarranted owing to the basic fact that non-Black paradigms set the terms of the replies.

The insight in the first claim is that Blacks and Whites are in some important sense alike—i.e., in their positive capacities for human sympathy, moral sacrifice, service to others, intelligence and beauty, or negatively, in their capacity for cruelty. Yet the common humanity they share is jettisoned when the claim is cast in an assimilationist manner that subordinates Black particularity to a false universalism, i.e., non-Black rubrics or prototypes. Similarly, the insight in the second claim is that all Blacks are in some significant sense "in the same boat"–that is, subject to White supremacist abuse. Yet this common condition is stretched too far when viewed in a *homogenizing* way that overlooks how racist treatment vastly differs owing to class, gender, sexual orientation, nation, region, hue and age.

The moralistic and communal aspects of the initial Black diaspora responses to social and psychic erasure were not simply cast into simplistic binary oppositions of positive/negative, good/bad images that privileged the first term in light of a White norm so that Black efforts remained inscribed within the very logic that dehumanized them. They were further complicated by the fact that these responses were also advanced principally by anxiety-ridden, middle-class Black intellectuals, (predominantly male and heterosexual) grappling with their sense of double-consciousness–namely their own crisis of identity, agency and audience–caught between a quest for White approval and acceptance and an endeavor to overcome the internalized association of Blackness with inferiority. And I suggest that these complex anxieties of modern Black diaspora intellectuals partly motivate the two major arguments that ground the assimilationist moralism and homogeneous communalism just outlined.

Kobena Mercer has talked about these two arguments as the *reflectionist* and the *social engineering* arguments. The reflectionist argument holds that the fight for Black representation and recognition must reflect or mirror the real Black community, not simply the negative and depressing representations of it. The social engineering argument claims that since any form of representation is constructed–i.e., selective in light of broader aims–Black representation (especially given the difficulty of Blacks gaining access to positions of power to produce any Black imagery) should offer positive images of themselves in order to inspire achievement among young Black people, thereby countering racist stereotypes. The hidden assumption of both arguments is that we have unmediated access to what the "real Black community" is and what "positive images" are. In short, these arguments presuppose the very phenomena to be interrogated, and thereby foreclose the very issues that should serve as the subject matter to be investigated.

Any notions of "the real Black community" and "positive images" are value-laden, socially-loaded and ideologically-charged. To pursue this discussion is to call into question the possibility of such an uncontested consensus regarding them. Stuart Hall has rightly called this encounter "the end of innocence or the end of the innocent notion of the essential Black subject . . . the recognition that 'Black' is essentially a politically and culturally *constructed* category." This recognition–more and more pervasive among the postmodern Black diaspora intelligentsia–is facilitated in part by the slow but sure dissolution of the European Age's maritime empires, and the unleashing of new political possibilities and cultural articulations among ex-colonialized peoples across the globe.

One crucial lesson of this decolonization process remains the manner in which most Third World authoritarian bureaucratic elites deploy essentialist rhetorics about "homogeneous national communities" and "positive images" in order to repress and regiment their diverse and heterogeneous populations. Yet in the diaspora, especially among First World countries, this critique has emerged not so much from the Black male component of the left but rather from the Black women's movement. The decisive push of postmodern Black intellectuals toward a new cultural politics of difference has been made by the powerful critiques and constructive explorations of Black diaspora women (e.g. Toni Morrison). The coffin used to bury the innocent notion of the essential Black subject was nailed shut with the termination of the Black male monopoly on the construction of the Black subject. In this regard, the Black diaspora womanist critique has had a greater impact than the critiques that highlight exclusively class, empire, age, sexual orientation or nature.

This decisive push toward the end of Black innocence–though prefigured in various degrees in the best moments of W.E.B. DuBois, Anna Cooper, C.L.R. James, James Baldwin, Claudia Jones, the later Malcolm X, Frantz Fanon, Amiri Baraka and others–forces Black diaspora cultural workers to encounter what Hall has called the "politics of representation." The main aim now is not simply access to representation in order to produce positive images of homogeneous communities–though broader access remains a practical and political problem. Nor is the primary goal here that of contesting stereotypes–though contestation remains a significant though limited venture. Following the model of the Black diaspora traditions of music, athletics and rhetoric, Black cultural workers must constitute and sustain discursive and institutional networks that deconstruct earlier modern Black strategies for identity-formation, demystify power relations that incorporate class, patriarchal and homophobic biases, and construct more multi-valent and multi-dimensional responses that articulate the complexity and diversity of Black practices in the modern and postmodern world.

Furthermore, Black cultural workers must investigate and interrogate the other of Blackness–Whiteness. One cannot deconstruct the binary oppositional logic of images of Blackness without extending it to the contrary condition of Blackness/Whiteness itself. However, a mere dismantling will not do–for the very notion of a deconstructive social theory is oxymoronic. Yet social theory is what is needed to examine and *explain* the historically specific ways in which "Whiteness" is a politically constructed category parasitic on "Blackness," and thereby to conceive of the profoundly hybrid character of what we mean by "race," "ethnicity," and "nationality." For instance, European immigrants arrived on American shores perceiving themselves as "Irish," "Sicilian," "Lithuanian," etc. They had to learn that they were "White" principally by adopting an American discourse of positively-valued Whiteness and negatively-charged Blackness. This process by which people define themselves physically, socially, sexually and even politically in terms of Whiteness or Blackness has much bearing not only on constructed notions of race and ethnicity but also on how we understand the changing character of u.s. nationalities. And given the Americanization of the world, especially in the sphere of mass culture, such inquiries–encouraged by the new cultural politics of difference–raise critical issues of "hybridity," "exilic status" and "identity" on an international scale. Needless to say, these inquiries must traverse those of "male/female," "colonizer/colonized," "heterosexual/homosexual," et al., as well.

In light of this brief sketch of the emergence of our present crisis–and the turn toward history and difference in cultural work–four major historicist forms of theoretical activity provide resources for how we understand, analyze and enact our representational practices: Heideggerian *destruction* of the western metaphysical tradition, Derridean *deconstruction* of the western philosophical tradition, Rortian *demythologization* of the western intellectual tradition and Marxist, Foucaultian, feminist, anti-racist or anti-homophobic *demystification* of western cultural and artistic conventions.

Despite his abominable association with the Nazis, Martin Heidegger's project is useful in that it discloses the suppression of temporality and historicity in the dominant metaphysical systems of the West from Plato to Rudolph Carnap. This is noteworthy in that it forces one to understand philosophy's representational discourses as thoroughly historical phenomena. Hence, they should be viewed with skepticism as they are often flights from the specific, concrete, practical and particular. The major problem with Heidegger's project—as noted by his neo-Marxist student, Herbert Marcuse—is that he views history in terms of fate, heritage and destiny. He dramatizes the past and present as if it were a Greek tragedy with no tools of social analyses to relate cultural work to institutions and structures or antecedent forms and styles.

Jacques Derrida's version of deconstruction is one of the most influential schools of thought among young academic critics. It is salutary in that it focuses on the political power of rhetorical operations—of tropes and metaphors in binary oppositions like white/black, good/bad, male/female, machine/nature, ruler/ruled, reality/appearance—showing how these operations sustain hierarchal world views by devaluing the second terms as something subsumed under the first. Most of the controversy about Derrida's project revolves around this austere epistemic doubt that unsettles binary oppositions while undermining any determinate meaning of a text, i.e., book, art-object, performance, building. Yet, his views about skepticism are no more alarming than those of David Hume, Ludwig Wittgenstein or Stanley Cavell. He simply revels in it for transgressive purposes, whereas others provide us with ways to dissolve, sidestep or cope with skepticism. None, however, slide down the slippery, crypto-Nietzschean slope of sophomoric relativism as alleged by old-style humanists, be they Platonists, Kantians or Arnoldians.

The major shortcoming of Derrida's deconstructive project is that it puts a premium on a sophisticated ironic consciousness that tends to preclude and foreclose analyses that guide action with purpose. And given Derrida's own status as an Algerian-born, Jewish leftist marginalized by a hostile French academic establishment (quite different from his reception by the youth in the American academic establishment), the sense of political impotence and hesitation regarding the efficacy of moral action is understandable—but not justifiable. His works and those of his followers too often become rather monotonous, Johnny-one-note rhetorical readings that disassemble texts with little attention to the effects and consequences these dismantlings have in relation to the operations of military, economic and social powers.

Richard Rorty's neo-pragmatic project of demythologization is insightful in that it provides descriptive mappings of the transient metaphors—especially the ocular and specular ones—that regulate some of the fundamental dynamics in the construction of self-descriptions dominant in highbrow European and American philosophy. His perspective is instructive because it discloses the crucial role of narrative as the background for rational exchange and critical conversation. To put it crudely, Rorty shows why we should speak not of History, but histories, not of Reason, but historically constituted forms of rationality, not of Criticism or Art, but of socially constructed notions of criticism and art—all linked but not reducible to political purposes, material interests and cultural prejudices.

Rorty's project nonetheless leaves one wanting owing to its distrust of social analytical explanation. Similar to the dazzling new historicism of Stephen Greenblatt, Louis Montrose and Catherine Gallagher—inspired by the subtle symbolic-cum-textual anthropology of Clifford Geertz and the powerful discursive materialism of Michel Foucault—Rorty gives us mappings and descriptions with no explanatory accounts for change and conflict. In this way, it gives us an aestheticized version of historicism in which the provisional and variable are celebrated at the expense of highlighting who gains, loses or bears what costs.

Demystification is the most illuminating mode of theoretical inquiry for those who promote the new cultural politics of difference. Social structural analyses of empire, exterminism, class, race, gender, nature, age, sexual orientation, nation and region are the springboards—though not landing grounds—for the most desirable forms of critical practice that take history (and herstory) seriously. Demystification tries to keep track of the complex dynamics of institutional and other related power structures in order to disclose options and alternatives for transformative praxis; it also attempts to grasp the way in which representational strategies are creative responses to novel circumstances and conditions. In this way, the central role of human agency (always enacted under circumstances not of one's choosing)—be it in the critic, artist or constituency and audience—is accented.

I call demystificatory criticism "prophetic criticism"—the approach appropriate for the new cultural politics of difference—because while it begins with social structural analyses it also makes explicit its moral and political aims. It is partisan, partial, engaged and crisis-centered, yet always keeps open a skeptical eye to avoid dogmatic traps, premature closures, formulaic formulations or rigid conclusions. In addition to social structural analyses, moral and political judgments, and sheer critical consciousness, there indeed is evaluation. Yet the aim of this evaluation is neither to pit art-objects against one another like racehorses nor to create eternal canons that dull, discourage or even dwarf contemporary achievements. We listen to Ludwig Beethoven, Charlie Parker, Luciano Pavarotti, Laurie Anderson, Sarah Vaughan, Stevie Wonder or Kathleen Battle, read William Shakespeare, Anton Chekhov, Ralph Ellison, Doris Lessing, Thomas Pynchon, Toni Morrison or Gabriel García Márquez, see works of Pablo Picasso, Ingmar Bergman, Le Corbusier, Martin Puryear, Barbara Kruger, Spike Lee, Frank Gehry or Howardena Pindell—not in order to undergird bureaucratic assents or enliven cocktail party conversations, but rather to be summoned by the styles they deploy for their profound insight, pleasures and challenges. Yet all evaluation—including a delight in Eliot's poetry despite his reactionary politics, or a love of Zora Neale Hurston's novels despite her Republican party affiliations—is inseparable from, though not identical or reducible to, social structural analyses, moral and political judgments and the workings of a curious critical consciousness.

The deadly traps of demystification—and any form of prophetic criticism—are those of reductionism, be it of the sociological, psychological, or historical sort. By reductionism I mean either one factor analyses (i.e., crude Marxisms, feminisms, racialisms, etc.) that yield a one-dimensional functionalism, or a hyper-subtle analytical perspective that loses touch with the specificity of an art work's form and the context of its reception. Few cultural workers of whatever stripe can walk the tightrope between the Scylla of reductionism and the Charybdis of aestheticism—yet demystificatory (or prophetic) critics must.

The Existential Challenge

The existential challenge to the new cultural politics of difference can be stated simply: how does one acquire the resources to survive and the cultural capital to thrive as a critic or artist? By cultural capital (Pierre Bourdieu's term), I mean not only the high-quality skills required to engage in critical practices but, more important, the self-confidence, discipline and perseverance necessary for success without an undue reliance on the mainstream for approval and acceptance. This challenge holds for all prophetic critics, yet it is especially difficult for those of color. The widespread modern European denial of the intelligence, ability, beauty and character of people of color puts a tremendous burden on critics and artists of color to "prove" themselves in light of norms and models set by white elites whose own heritage devalued and dehumanized them. In short, in the court of criticism and art—or any matters regarding the life of the mind—people of color are guilty, i.e., not expected to meet standards of intellectual achievement, until "proven" innocent, i.e., acceptable to "us."

This is more a structural dilemma than a matter of personal attitudes. The profoundly racist and sexist heritage of the European Age has bequeathed to us a set of deeply-ingrained perceptions about people of color including, of course, the self-perceptions that people of color bring. It is not surprising that most intellectuals of color in the past exerted much of their energies and efforts to gain acceptance and approval by "white normative gazes." The new cultural politics of difference advises critics and artists of color to put aside this mode of mental bondage, thereby freeing themselves to both interrogate the ways in which they are bound by certain conventions and to learn from and build on these very norms and models. One hallmark of wisdom in the context of any struggle is to avoid knee-jerk rejection and uncritical acceptance.

Self-confidence, discipline and perseverance are not ends-in-themselves. Rather they are the necessary stuff of which enabling criticism and self-criticism are made. Notwithstanding inescapable jealousies, insecurities and anxieties, one telling characteristic of critics and artists of color linked to the new prophetic criticism should be their capacity for and promotion of relentless criticism and self-criticism—be it the normative paradigms of their white colleagues that tend to leave out considerations of empire, race, gender and sexual orientation or the damaging dogmas about the homogeneous character of communities of color.

There are four basic options for people of color interested in representation—if they are to survive and thrive as serious practitioners of their craft. First, there is the Booker

T. Temptation, namely the individual preoccupation with the mainstream and its legitimizing power. Most critics and artists of color try to bite this bait. It is nearly unavoidable, yet few succeed in a substantive manner. It is no accident that the most creative and profound among them—especially those with staying power beyond mere flashes in the pan to satisfy faddish tokenism—are usually marginal to the mainstream. Even the pervasive professionalization of cultural practitioners of color in the past few decades has not produced towering figures who reside within the established White patronage system that bestows the rewards and prestige for chosen contributions to American society.

It certainly helps to have some trustworthy allies within this system, yet most of those who enter and remain tend to lose much of their creativity, diffuse their prophetic energy and dilute their critiques. Still, it is unrealistic for creative people of color to think they can sidestep the White patronage system. And though there are indeed some White allies conscious of the tremendous need to rethink identity politics, it's naive to think that being comfortably nested within this very same system—even if one can be a patron to others—does not affect one's work, one's outlook and, most important, one's soul.

The second option is the Talented Tenth Seduction, namely, a move toward arrogant group insularity. This alternative has a limited function—to preserve one's sanity and sense of self as one copes with the mainstream. Yet it is, at best, a transitional and transient activity. If it becomes a permanent option it is self-defeating in that it usually reinforces the very inferior complexes promoted by the subtly racist mainstream. Hence it tends to revel in a parochialism and encourage a narrow racialist and chauvinistic outlook.

The third strategy is the Go-It-Alone option. This is an extreme rejectionist perspective that shuns the mainstream and group insularity. Almost every critic and artist of color contemplates or enacts this option at some time in their pilgrimage. It is healthy in that it reflects the presence of independent, critical and skeptical sensibilities toward perceived constraints on one's creativity. Yet it is, in the end, difficult if not impossible to sustain if one is to grow, develop and mature intellectually; as some semblance of dialogue with a community is necessary for almost any creative practice.

The most desirable option for people of color who promote the new cultural politics of difference is to be a critical organic catalyst. By this I mean a person who stays attuned to the best of what the mainstream has to offer—its paradigms, viewpoints and methods—yet maintains a grounding in affirming and enabling subcultures of criticism. Prophetic critics and artists of color should be exemplars of what it means to be intellectual freedom-fighters, that is, cultural workers who simultaneously position themselves within (or alongside) the mainstream while clearly aligned with groups who vow to keep alive potent traditions of critique and resistance. In this regard, one can take clues from the great musicians or preachers of color who are open to the best of what other traditions offer yet are rooted in nourishing subcultures that build on the grand achievements of a vital heritage. Openness to others—including the mainstream—does not entail wholesale co-optation, and group autonomy is not group insularity. Louis Armstrong,

W.E.B. DuBois, Ella Baker, Jose Carlos Mariatequi, M.M. Thomas, Wynton Marsalis, Martin Luther King, Jr., and Ronald Takaki have understood this well.

The new cultural politics of difference can thrive only if there are communities, groups, organizations, institutions, subcultures and networks of people of color who cultivate critical sensibilities and personal accountability–without inhibiting individual expressions, curiosities and idiosyncrasies. This is especially needed given the escalating racial hostility, violence and polarization in the USA. Yet this critical coming-together must not be a narrow closing-ranks. Rather it is a strengthening and nurturing endeavor that can forge more solid alliances and coalitions. In this way, prophetic criticism–with its stress on historical specificity and artistic complexity–directly addresses the intellectual challenge. The cultural capital of people of color–with its emphasis on self-confidence, discipline, perseverance and subcultures of criticism–also tries to meet the existential requirement. Both are mutually reinforcing. Both are motivated by a deep commitment to individuality and democracy–the moral and political ideals that guide the creative response to the political challenge.

The Political Challenge

Adequate rejoinders to intellectual and existential challenges equip the practitioners of the new cultural politics of difference to meet the political ones. This challenge principally consists of forging solid and reliable alliances of people of color and white progressives guided by a moral and political vision of greater democracy and individual freedom in communities, states and transnational enterprises, e.g. corporations, information and communications conglomerates.

Jesse Jackson's Rainbow Coalition is a gallant yet flawed effort in this regard–gallant due to the tremendous energy, vision and courage of its leader and followers, yet flawed because of its failure to take seriously critical and democratic sensibilities within its own operations. In fact, Jackson's attempt to gain power at the national level is a symptom of the weakness of U.S. progressive politics, and a sign that the capacity to generate extra-parliamentary social motion or movements has waned. Yet given the present organizational weakness and intellectual timidity of left politics in the USA, the major option is that of multi-racial grass-roots citizens' participation in credible projects in which people see that their efforts can make a difference. The salutary revolutionary developments in Eastern Europe are encouraging and inspiring in this regard. Ordinary people organized can change societies.

The most significant theme of the new cultural politics of difference is the agency, capacity and ability of human beings who have been culturally degraded, politically oppressed and economically exploited by bourgeois liberal and communist illiberal status quos. This theme neither romanticizes nor idealizes marginalized peoples. Rather it accentuates their humanity and tries to attenuate the institutional constraints on their life-chances for surviving and thriving. In this way, the new cultural politics of difference shuns narrow particularisms, parochialisms and separatisms, just as it rejects false universalisms and homogeneous totalisms. Instead, the new cultural politics of difference affirms the perennial quest for the precious ideals of individuality and democracy by digging deep in the depths of human particularities and social specificities in order to construct new kinds of connections, affinities and communities across empire, nation, region, race, gender, age and sexual orientation.

The major impediments of the radical libertarian and democratic projects of the new cultural politics are threefold: the pervasive processes of objectification, rationalization and commodification throughout the world. The first process—best highlighted in Georg Simmel's *The Philosophy of Money* (1900)—consists of transforming human beings into manipulable objects. It promotes the notion that people's actions have no impact on the world, that we are but spectators not participants in making and remaking ourselves and the larger society. The second process—initially examined in the seminal works of Max Weber—expands bureaucratic hierarchies that impose impersonal rules and regulations in order to increase efficiency, be they defined in terms of better service or better surveillance. This process leads not only to disenchantment with past mythologies but also to deadening, flat, banal ways of life. The third and most important process—best examined in the works of Karl Marx, Georg Lukács and Walter Benjamin—augments market forces in the form of oligopolies and monopolies that centralize resources and powers and promote cultures of consumption that view people as mere spectatorial consumers and passive citizens.

These processes cannot be eliminated, but their pernicious effects can be substantially alleviated. The audacious attempt to lessen their impact—to preserve people's agency, increase the scope of their freedom and expand the operations of democracy—is the fundamental aim of the new cultural politics of difference. This is why the crucial questions become: What is the moral content of one's cultural identity? And what are the political consequences of this moral content and cultural identity?

In the recent past, the dominant cultural identities have been circumscribed by immoral patriarchal, imperial, jingoistic and xenophobic constraints. The political consequences have been principally a public sphere regulated by and for well-to-do White males in the name of freedom and democracy. The new cultural criticism exposes and explodes the exclusions, blindnesses and silences of this past, calling from it radical libertarian and democratic projects that will create a better present and future. The new cultural politics of difference is neither an ahistorical Jacobin program that discards tradition and ushers in new self-righteous authoritarianisms nor a guilt-ridden leveling anti-imperialist liberalism that celebrates token pluralism for smooth inclusion. Rather, it acknowledges the uphill struggle of fundamentally transforming highly objectified, rationalized and commodified societies and cultures in the name of individuality and democracy. This means locating the structural causes of unnecessary forms of social misery (without reducing all such human suffering to historical causes), depicting the plight and predicaments of demoralized and depoliticized citizens caught in market-driven cycles of therapeutic release—drugs, alcoholism, consumerism—and projecting alternative visions, analyses and actions that proceed from particularities and arrive at moral and political connectedness. This connectedness does not signal a homogeneous unity or monolithic totality but rather a contingent, fragile coalition building in an effort to pursue common radical libertarian and democratic goals that overlap.

In a world in which most of the resources, wealth and power are centered in huge corporations and supportive political elites, the new cultural politics of difference may appear to be solely visionary, utopian and fanciful. The recent cutbacks of social service programs, business takebacks at the negotiation tables of workers and management, speedups at the workplace and buildups of military budgets reinforce this perception. And surely the growing disintegration and decomposition of civil society—of shattered families, neighborhoods and schools—adds to this perception. Can a civilization that evolves more and more around market activity, more and more around the buying and selling of commodities, expand the scope of freedom and democracy? Can we simply bear witness to its slow decay and doom—a painful denouement prefigured already in many poor black and brown communities and rapidly embracing all of us? These haunting questions remain unanswered yet the challenge they pose must not remain unmet. The new cultural politics of difference tries to confront these enormous and urgent challenges. It will require all the imagination, intelligence, courage, sacrifice, care and laughter we can muster.

The time has come for critics and artists of the new cultural politics of difference to cast their nets widely, flex their muscles broadly and thereby refuse to limit their visions, analyses and praxis to their particular terrains. The aim is to dare to recast, redefine and revise the very notions of "modernity," "mainstream," "margins," "difference," "otherness." We have now reached a new stage in the perennial struggle for freedom and dignity. And while much of the First World intelligentsia adopts retrospective and conservative outlooks that defend the crisis-ridden present, we promote a prospective and prophetic vision with a sense of possibility and potential, especially for those who bear the social costs of the present. We look to the past for strength, not solace; we look at the present and see people perishing, not profits mounting; we look toward the future and vow to make it different and better.

To put it boldly, the new kind of critic and artist associated with the new cultural politics of difference consists of an energetic breed of New World *bricoleurs* with improvisational and flexible sensibilities that sidestep mere opportunism and mindless eclecticism; persons from all countries, cultures, genders, sexual orientations, ages and regions with protean identities who avoid ethnic chauvinism and faceless universalism; intellectual and political freedom-fighters with partisan passion, international perspectives, and, thank God, a sense of humor that combats the ever-present absurdity that forever threatens our democratic and libertarian projects and dampens the fire that fuels our will to struggle. Yet we will struggle and stay, as those brothers and sisters on the block say, "out there"—with intellectual rigor, existential dignity, moral vision, political courage and soulful style.

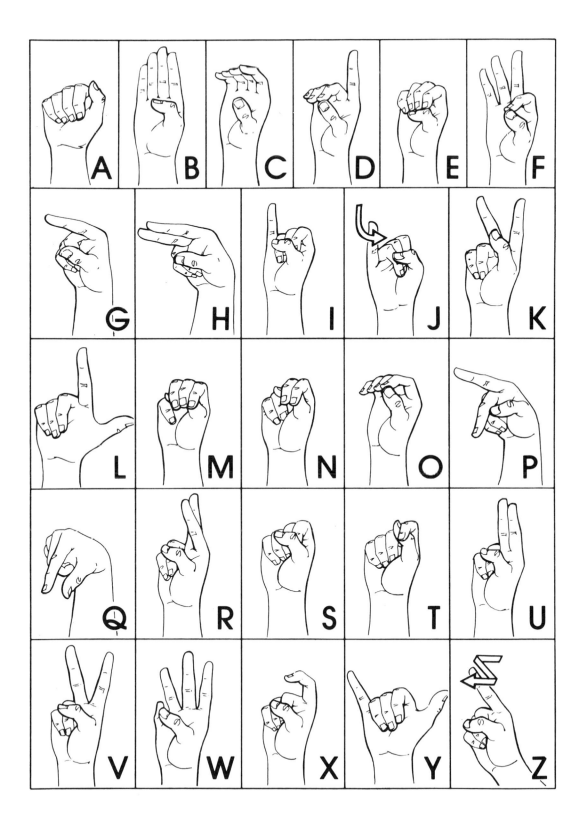

EATING DISORDER

they'll consume all
that you do and despise
what you are

• **Michele Wallace**

Modernism, Postmodernism and the Problem
of the Visual in Afro-American Culture

In 1954 in the case of Brown vs. The Board of Education, the Supreme Court ruled that segregated schools were inherently unequal, discriminatory and illegal. The case made by the NAACP included the findings of Kenneth and Mamie Clark, black Ph.D.s. in social psychology who had been using a doll test and a coloring test to measure how racism and segregation damaged the self-esteem of black children, ranging in age from three to seven. They found, among other things, that black children–I don't know how many of them were girls or if anyone thought about the fact that only girls generally play with dolls–preferred white dolls to black dolls, and that black children had a tendency to use a white or yellow crayon to color both a same-sex figure said to be themselves and an opposite sex figure said to be a friend.[1]

There has been much debate within the fields of psychology and sociology about the meaning of the Clarks' research, most of it focused upon the scientific validity of the testing methods.[2] However, it is not at all unusual for the media to refer back to this research as evidence that racism is an unambiguously deprivational experience, while completely ignoring what the visual implications of such findings might be. In fact, just this summer, there was a TV special called *Blacks In White America*, entirely produced by black journalists at ABC.[3] The documentary opened with a present day reenactment of the Clarks' research showing small black children choosing a white doll over a black one, and interpreting a stereotypical line drawing of a blond little white girl as prettier or cleaner or nicer. It closed with the narrator's voice–a black female journalist–telling us that she had been one of the little girls who had participated in the Clarks' original research in the early fifties. She confessed that she, too, had preferred the white doll over the black one.

The documentary interpreted this information as corroboration of the fact that blacks are still comparatively poor and disenfranchised in comparison to whites. Profiles of a black regiment of fighter pilots in World War II and of the newly appointed black Chairman of the Joint Chiefs of Staff, Colin L. Powell, were offered as correctives. Amazingly, neither art nor beauty nor aesthetics nor high culture nor pop culture nor media were raised as significant precipitating factors in this process.

Of course, poverty and powerlessness feed a child's perception of what it means to have black skin, but this process is much more complex than a direct correlation could encompass. Rather, it is society's always already operative evaluation of images, further inscribed by skin color (dark or light, white or black or yellow or red) that would most affect a child's opinion of race. Not only the presence of "negative" black stereotypes in schoolbook illustrations, posters, religious imagery, advertising images, as well as movie and television images, but the absence of black images in mass media in general is the crucial dynamic never accounted for.

The power of the image–as well as of the word–seems to be the very thing addressed so well by Toni Morrison's use of the Dick and Jane text in order to characterize white hegemony in *The Bluest Eye*.[4] After all, this was an elementary school reader whose illustrations were at least as unforgettably repetitive and stifling to the imagination as its text. The absence of black images in the reflection of the social mirror, which such programmatic texts (from "Dick and Jane," to Disney movies, to "The Weekly Reader") invariably construct, could and did produce the void and the dread of racial questions that the Clarks found in the '50s, particularly in Northern black children who were already attending integrated schools. Their studies related how these children sometimes cried when asked to identify the doll that was "Negro" or that was the same race as them. On the other hand, Southern children who attended segregated schools displayed less ambivalence, which the Clarks interpreted as a cynicism inappropriate to childhood: "'Oh, yeah, that's me there–that's a nigger,' they'd say. 'I'm a nigger.'"[5]

We all know in our hearts, as any mere child in our midst today must know, that "nigger," "black," and "schwartze" are often used interchangeably in our language to mean an abject "other," and yet we persist in denying it, just as Kenneth and Mamie Clark, the NAACP and the Supreme Court denied it in 1954. In 1979, when Donald Neuman designated his exhibition of charcoal drawings at Artist Space as "Nigger Drawings," and in 1989 when Jackie Mason called mayoral candidate David Dinkins a "schwartze," sizable downtown New York controversies followed precisely in order to continue this charade, which has become one of the principal tenets of bourgeois humanism, that color is an innately trivial matter, which does not signify.

• • •

How one is seen (as black) and, therefore, what one sees (in a white world) is always already crucial to one's existence as an Afro-American. The very markers that reveal you to the rest of the world, your dark skin and your kinky/curly hair, are visual. However, *not* being seen by those who don't want to see you because they are racist, what Ralph Ellison called "invisibility," often leads racists to the interpretation that *you are unable* to see.

This has meant, among other things, that Afro-Americans have not produced (because they've been prevented from doing so by intra-racial pain and outside intervention) a tradition in the visual arts as vital and compelling to other Americans as the Afro-American tradition in music.[6] Moreover, the necessity, which seems to persist of its own volition in Afro-American Studies, for drawing parallels or alignments between Afro-American music and everything else cultural among Afro-Americans, stifles and represses most of the potential for understanding the visual in Afro-American culture. For if the positive scene of instruction between Africans and Europeans in the

U.S.[7] is located in what is now triumphantly called the "tradition" of Afro-American music, the negative scene of instruction is in its visual tradition.[8] This "negative scene of instruction" (so much more common in Afro-American experience) was one in which white teachers refused to teach black students who were in turn just as reluctant to learn from them. As even the smallest child seems to instinctively understand, institutionalized education has always been, first and foremost, a means of transmitting social values, not knowledge or power.

It appears that the only reason black artists aren't as widely accepted as black writers (and this is far from widely enough) is because shifts in art historical judgment result in extraordinary economic contingencies. Consequently, the closed economic nepotism of the art world perpetuates a situation in which, as Howardena Pindell has pointed out, "artists of color face an industry-wide 'restraint of trade,' limiting their ability to show and sell their work."[9]

If black writers had had to rely on the kinds of people and developments that determine the value of art, if writing had to be accepted into rich white people's homes and into their investment portfolios in the manner of the prized art object, I suspect that none of us would have ever heard of Langston Hughes, Richard Wright, Zora Neale Hurston, Ralph Ellison, Amiri Baraka, Sonia Sanchez, John Edgar Wideman, Ishmael Reed, Alice Walker, Adrienne Kennedy, Toni Morrison, Ntozake Shange, August Wilson, George Woolfe and Trey Ellis. Indeed, we are lucky to have heard of Jacob Lawrence, Betye Saar, Romare Bearden, Richard Hunt, Sam Gilliam, Daniel Johnson, Mel Edwards and Faith Ringgold.

• • •

I was two years old in 1954. And perhaps because my mother was pursuing a Master's in Art Education until I was nine, I grew up being aware of the Clarks' research. I also grew up watching a television on which I rarely saw a black face, reading Archie and Veronica comics, Oz and Nancy Drew stories and *Seventeen* magazine, in which "race" was unmentionable. At the same time, I always had black dolls and I was always given a brown crayon to take to school as an encouragement to color my people brown as I did at home.

In the spring of 1961 my mother, who wanted to be an artist, graduated from City College of New York with her Master's in Art Education. That summer my mother planned and carried out an elaborate tour of the art treasures of Italy and France with my grandmother, my sister and myself in tow. I remember the virtually endless streams of white faces not only in paintings and sculpture but also in the operas, film, theater and television we saw that summer. I can also remember a French saleswoman being asked by my mother to find a black doll at the Galleries Lafayette in Paris, and being relieved when she succeeded in producing one. I can still recall that doll, which was blacker than most American black dolls.

"Race" was frequently discussed in my family's home, although "racism" was not. As far as I know, no such word had entered common parlance. Moreover, and more personally, any discussion of "race" in the presence of people who were not black embarrassed me. I can remember giving a report on the "races of the world" in my seventh grade class and being so embarrassed by my subject matter that I could hardly speak. I said "colored" to refer to my own people. A black boy in my class corrected me by saying "Negro." I was mortified, for "Negro" was then considered to be the more militant word. My grandmother never used "Negro" at all, although my mother and her friends did. Of course, "black," as a description of race, was still the ultimate and virtually unspeakable insult.

So you can see I come by my fascination with the visual quite automatically. Visual production has always been an obsession in my life, because I was a child of the 1954 Supreme Court decision, a child of Kenneth Clark's research, Dr. Kenneth Clark who taught at CCNY where my mother was a graduate student, and, together with his wife, ran the Northside Psychological Testing Service, which shared a building with the private school I attended from the seventh grade on.

I saw Kenneth and Mamie Clark often. If I didn't actually know them, I felt as though I did, was enormously proud of them as was everyone in my family. For they were part of this whole business of being a Negro, I well knew, this whole self-conscious business of something that would later be called "The Black Aesthetic" but which, for right now confined itself to this problem of not liking dolls of the same color as yourself unless carefully educated to do so. This I understood even then for I was also a child of television, comic books and magazines, although I was carefully instructed by parents and teachers to know that the pleasure these gave was counterfeit, not to be taken seriously.

Moreover, my mother and my grandmother were artists. My paternal grandmother, Momma T from Jamaica, West Indies, was a Sunday landscape painter. My maternal grandmother, Momma Jones, was a fashion designer. I modeled in all her fashion shows while growing up, and was constantly being photographed by the two or three black photographers she always had on hand to document even the most trivial events. Later she would collaborate on quilts and other kinds of fabric art with my mother, the "fine" artist.

In the work of the women in my family, it is actually in the career of my mother, Faith Ringgold, that fashion and fine art were finally conjoined. But for quite a long time before she became interested in the questions of a black aesthetic and a feminist aesthetic, she was a painter who tried to take seriously her relationship to the tradition of Western painting, particularly its culmination in Cubism. Our home revolved around the tension this challenge created in her and in her work. I remember in particular when I was very young, a very bad (Postmodern?), often wet Picasso-esque "study" that contained a *mise en abime* effect of endless doors within doors, which occupied in our home the space which should have been occupied by a dining room table and chairs.

• • •

According to Raymond Williams in *Marxism and Literature*, hegemony is a process that relies upon the mechanisms of traditions and canons of Old Masters in order to waylay the utopian desires that are potentially embodied in cultural production.[10] The underly-

ing structure of the very concept of "tradition" lies in wait behind contemporary variations on "tradition"—whether they are named feminist, Afro-American or Eskimo—in
that they are inevitably radically selective in favor of maintaining the dominance of a
brutal status quo despite their best intentions to subvert it.

I cannot recall a time during which I didn't perceive Western art and Western culture
as a problem in ways that seem to me now akin to the manner in which Modernism,
Postmodernism and feminism raise such problems. On the other hand, thanks to my
mother's unrelenting ambition to be a successful artist and her political interpretation of
the continuing frustration of that ambition, I can't remember a time during which I
didn't know that artmaking and visual production were also deeply problematic in
Afro-American culture. For these reasons and more, James Baldwin's statement in *Notes
of a Native Son* that he "despised" black people "possibly because they failed to produce
Rembrandt,"[11] had a profound resonance as I was growing up.

More specifically it was Picasso (not Rembrandt) and Modernism, in general, that
epitomized the art historical moment of greatest fascination. The debate was precisely
situated in the paradox that Picasso, Cubism and subsequent Modernists had borrowed
heavily from African Art. In other words, as it was widely interpreted among a black
middle-class intelligentsia in the '50s and '60s, "they," or white Euro-American high
Modernism, had borrowed from "us," the African peoples of the world, even if "they"
were incapable of admitting it.

My interest in Modernism only accelerated once I had become knowledgeable
enough about the visual and literary production of both Afro-Americans and white Europeans and Americans in this century (no small task) to know that Modernism actually
took place in the Afro-American as well as in the white American-European milieu.
Afro-American Modernism is both the same and different, as imitative as it is original,
which is consistent with Henry Louis Gates's notion of "critical signification," an
attempt to describe the mechanical relationship between Afro-American culture
and Euro-American culture. According to Gates—and he has employed "critical
signification" almost exclusively in the context of literature and the question of Afro-
American literacy—Afro-American culture imitates and reverses the terms of Euro-
American culture. This relationship can also usefully be described as dialogical, or
as one of intertextuality.[12]

But the problem remains the unilateral unwillingness of Euro-American culture to
admit and acknowledge its debt, or even its relationship, to African and Afro-American
culture. In fact, this problem—which lies at the heart of the problem of the visual in
Afro-American culture—has such a long and convoluted history that its enunciation has
become one of the telling features of Afro-American Modernism. One of the early
practitioners of Afro-American literary Modernism, Ralph Ellison, even gave it a
name: invisibility.

In *Invisible Man* (1951), Ellison catalogues the dilemma. According to the myth of
blackness, it is the opposite of whiteness, or it is so much "the same" that it is "invisible." Both dynamics are, in fact, aspects of this "invisibility's" inevitable and structural
binary opposition. On the one hand, there is no black difference. On the other, the difference is so vast as to be unspeakable and indescribable. Invisibility, a visual metaphor,

is then employed as a way of presenting a variety of responses to racism and cultural apartheid: there is the problem of translating a musical/oral Afro-American tradition into a written history and literature; there is the problem of Eurocentrism; and there is the problem of not being seen, in all its various connotations.

There is also the problem of being viewed as an object whose subjectivity is considered as superfluous as that of the dancing, grinning Sambo doll that the formerly political Clifton sells on the street corner in downtown New York. And finally, there is the problem of being the patriarch of a black family whose role must be defined in opposition to that of the patriarch of the white family. Therefore, myth constructs the black family on a model contrasting with the Freudian/Oedipal/Modernist drama of individuation, so that, early in the novel, the illiterate storyteller/farmer, Trueblood, impregnates both his wife and his daughter, and thereby gains cachet in the white community which pays him, again and again, to tell them the story of how it happened.[13] However, perhaps the most psychologically damaging residual of this story is that in the process of its unfolding, the subjectivity of the black woman becomes entirely unimaginable.

In *Invisible Man*, "women" are generally "white" and while the text is not especially sympathetic or kind to white women, it seems entirely engaged by the assumption that from a white male progressive point-of-view, or from the perspective of Euro-American Modernism (I am not suggesting that these are necessarily synonymous), the problem of the female (white) "other" and the problem of the black (male) "other" are easily interchangeable. In Euro-American Modernism, and in Afro-American modernism, as well, for that matter, the position of the "other" is as unitary and as incapable of being occupied by categories more diverse than "women and blacks" as was the formerly unified, omniscient subject from which it split.

It seems to me not entirely irrelevant to mention here that Ellison's prediction wasn't at all accurate, in that it is a handful of black women writers who follow in the tradition of Trueblood, in being well paid by a white (Postfeminist?) audience to tell the stories of the Oedipal transgressions of black men. I don't mean to suggest that either black men or black women are doing anything wrong, for the Oedipal transgressions of the black male are as inevitable as the black woman's need to break her silence about them (and I am not referring only to incest). But the motives of the whites who are ostensibly being entertained by this story-telling are not necessarily much different from those whites who paid Trueblood to tell his tale, or who stood on the corner watching Clifton's grinning, dancing Sambo dolls. The difference in the motivation is only a function of the extent to which the performance and consumption of these texts are interrogated by a critical discourse emanating from white, black (and brown) feminist and Afro-Americanist discourses. The relative scarcity of such interrogation in the media and in academia is as telling as the relative scarcity of a multicultural "other" presence in the various fields of visual production, from museum administration to films. It is telling us, in fact, that the fabric of invisibility has not altered, that it makes little difference in our hegemonic arrangements if Trueblood is now a woman.

But if we move now from the Afro-American Modernist novel par excellence to the Afro-American Postmodernist novel par excellence, Ishmael Reed's *Mumbo Jumbo*, there is an interesting black female character who comes into view.[14] It is the dancer, vaudevillian and Folies Bergère star Josephine Baker, who shares with African art, and with Picasso and the Cubists, a mutual location in the Paris of the '20s. Reed's novel brings all of these variables into dramatic dialogue or juxtaposition with each other during the Harlem Renaissance.[15] Yet the "idea" of Josephine Baker in *Mumbo Jumbo*, and in most of what has been written about her, remains the old-fashioned one wherein she becomes the muse of the white man, whether that is resented as it is by Reed, or celebrated as it is by many others who have written about her.[16]

When one arrives at the Postmodern scene, marked as it is by reproduction and simulation, the rampant exploitation of international capitalism, not to mention much speculation regarding the death of the subject, the death of history and the total blurring of lines between pop culture and high culture, spin-offs of the Josephine Baker model proliferate. Tina Turner, Grace Jones, Jody Watley, Whitney Houston, Diana Ross and Donna Summer (as well as Michael Jackson?) all follow in her tracks. Baker's much photographed performances are not the only starting point, however, of this fascination with black women's bodies–the site upon which blackness was conceptualized as an aspect of the white personality and white Euro-American achievement. There was also the popularity in Europe of an ethnographic photography issuing from the process of the colonial/anthropological exploitation of a Third World Asia and Africa that proceeded and overlapped with a burgeoning interest in Europe in African and Oceanic art which was really about an interest in other ways of seeing and looking that had not before occurred to the West.

Sander L. Gilman points out that in the early decades of the 1800s, even before photography's ascendency, there was a general fascination in Europe with the "Hottentot Venus," as represented by series of black women who were imported from South Africa and exhibited in the major cities of Europe because of their large and fatty buttocks. In this way, representations of black women with large and fatty buttocks came to signify not only black women but all other categories of women, such as prostitutes, who were thought to be as sexually wanton as black women.

According to Gilman, Manet paints the white courtesan *Nana* with protruding buttocks for this reason, and in *Olympia*, the presence of the clothed buxom black female servant allows for the transgressive sexuality of Olympia. In 1901, Picasso painted a parody of *Olympia* in which she is a fat black woman with the huge thighs of the Hottentot Venus. Gilman describes this painting as a prolegomena to the intersection of issues of race and sexuality in *Les Demoiselles D'Avignon* of five years later.[17] *Les Demoiselles* might be seen as illustrating the occasional advantage of art over institutionalized history or science in that it seems to represent the desire to both reveal and repress the scene of appropriation as a conjunction of black/female bodies and white culture–a scene of negative instruction between black and white art or black and white culture.

Unlike the positive scene of instruction of Afro-American and Euro-American music, in which mutual influence and intertextuality is acknowledged (although not without struggles that further enrich the transmutation), in the negative scene of instruction of Afro-American art and Euro-American art the exchange is disavowed and disallowed–no one admits to having learned anything from anyone else. Subsequently,

Euro-American Postmodernism emerges as the lily white pure blooded offspring of an inbred and dishonest (in the sense of not acknowledging its mixed blood) Modernism and Poststructuralism. And, more or less simultaneous with this subtle but effective metamorphosis, the Black Aesthetic emerges as the unambivalent, uncompromised link-up between Africa and the "New World" in which Euro-American influences are superfluous and negligible.

• • •

Griselda Pollock, following Julia Kristeva's lead in "Woman's Time," has proposed that there is a third position in feminist discourse beyond the simplistic mechanics of the struggle for equality for (white) women and the celebration of (white) female difference.[18] This third position is the most difficult to describe because it encompasses many positions and strategies still *in potentia*. Its goal, however, is to deconstruct the discursive formations which define the hegemonic process and which define, as well, the subversive limitations of previous feminist approaches. Herein lies my opportunity to usher forth "new knowledge," as Pollock names it, in conceptualizations of the visual in Afro-American culture that would consider the interdependency in issues of ethnicity and sex. This "new knowledge" would be constituted in the excavation of the black artistic versus the white artistic experience under the historic headings of Modernism and Postmodernism—on the theory that this is, in fact, the genuinely counter-hegemonic thing to explore at this particular art historical moment. The purpose of this would be to subvert the most persistent arrangement of present day cultural hegemony, with its cultural apartheid and "separate development" as Trinh Minh-ha has described it.[19] Instead of being concerned with commonalities in the developments of Afro- and European American communities in the '20s (or in subsequent periods), each camp of canonizers, whether white or black, male or female, is only interested in claiming autonomous achievement. What gives "Modernist Primitivism" any critical import in this cultural revisioning of the visual is the fact that it appears to be an ongoing category in Modernist, Postmodernist and feminist discourses, a fundamental way of discounting the "blackness" of the occasional black artist who is accepted within its ranks (as in the case of Jean-Michel Basquiat and Martin Puryear), while rejecting the category of black artist in general.[20]

This said, there also exists in this Postmodern moment the problems encountered, for example, by black British filmmaker Isaac Julien, who has experienced the opposition of the Langston Hughes estate for his counter-historical and counter-hegemonic vision of the Harlem Renaissance in his most recent film *Looking for Langston*. Ostensibly the estate objects to the implication that Hughes was gay, but the film is really about the erasure of the gay black subject, and in the process, the erasure of the body and of sexuality in the dominant discourse. This film made me aware, as I had not been before, of how disembodied cultural figures of the Harlem Renaissance generally are made to appear within black critical discourses, compared with those black artists, such as Louis Armstrong, Bessie Smith and Josephine Baker, who have been cast in "primitivist" or neoprimitivist terms and who, as such, have always been of more interest to white criticism.

This disembodiment, with its attendant desexualization of black literature and high culture, occurs in response to the over-sexualization of black images in white mass culture. It is an effort, in part, to block the primitivization of the black subject by white critics (this is particularly relevant in Afro-American literary criticism), resulting in the not surprising though still devastating outcome of, once again, marginalizing or erasing as irrelevant or unworthy the female subject. If this process of desexualization and deprimitivization had not been assimilated in the consolidation of black high culture within Afro-American Studies, many more black female artists, writers and blues singers–whose gender seems of paramount importance here–would figure in the discussion of black culture. To focus on the intersections of gender and sexuality would be to bring into relief the terms not only of the sexual victimization of black women (rape, etc.) but of black men (lynchings, etc.) in the South in the '20s, and evidence how the dread of such scenarios fed into the literary and visual production and the modernist aspirations of the artists, writers and intellectuals of the Harlem Renaissance.

• • •

On the other hand, the absence of black voices in the debate over the Primitivism show at The Museum of Modern Art in 1984 was no accident. William Rubin, the curator of the show, would have us think that Modernism is the culmination of universal aesthetic values and standards. Therefore, it should come as no surprise that, in a few isolated instances, so called primitive art would be as good as Western art, for the people who made these objects are people too.[21] Thomas McEvilley, his respondent in *Artforum* would have us shed Western aesthetics for Western anthropology,[22] although, as James Clifford points out in his contribution to the debate, both discourses assume a primitive world in need of preservation, or, in other words, no longer vital and needless to say, incapable of describing itself.

Clifford is right when he says, "The fact that rather abruptly, in the space of a few decades, a large class of non-Western artifacts came to be redefined as art is a taxonomic shift that requires critical historical discussion, not celebration."[23] Yet I am not convinced that "minority" artists of color in the West, who are, in some sense, along with African and Third World artists, the rightful heirs to the debate around "Primitivism," will ever surface up in the discussion.

Black criticism was blocked from the discussions of Modernism, which are defined as exclusively white by an intricate and insidious cooperation of art galleries, museums and academic art history, and also blocked from any discussion of "primitivism," which has been colonized beyond recognition in the space of the international and now global museum. At this juncture one is compelled to ask, "Is multiculturalism, as it is being institutionally defined, occupying the same space as 'primitivism' in relationship to Postmodernism?" For me, a response to such a question would need to include a careful scrutiny of the history of black popular culture and race relations, and account for the sexualization of both, thus defining the perimeters of a new knowledge which I can only name, at this point, as the problem of the visual in Afro-American culture.

For this reason, more suggestive to me is Hal Foster's reading of the stakes of the debate on Primitivism in his book of essays *Recodings* in which he describes *Les Demoiselles* as the landmark of a crisis in phallocentric culture. Primitivism becomes the "magical commodity" whereby white European art will appropriate the ritual function of tribal art and resist the process, which the museum space makes inevitable, of being reduced to a lifeless commodity. "On the one hand, then," Foster writes,

> *the primitive is a modern problem, a crisis in cultural identity, which the west moves to resolve: hence the modernist construction "primitivism," the fetishistic recognition-and-disavowal of the primitive difference. This ideological resolution renders it a "nonproblem" for us. On the other hand, this resolution is only a repression: delayed into our political unconscious, the primitive returns uncannily at the moment of its potential eclipse. The rupture of the primitive, managed by the moderns, becomes our postmodern event."*[24]

And yet finally there is only an implied entry way here for the artist or the critic of color who is not a member of a postcolonial intellectual elite, because we who are subject to internal colonization, we who are called "minorities" suffer the problems of the modern and of cultural identity, perhaps more than anyone, and the unified, unmarked subject of this and so far most other analyses of the Postmodern, never mind the Modern, continues to render us "invisible" and silent.

Gayatri Spivak ventures the point in "Who Claims Alterity?" that postcolonial intellectuals have the advantage over minorities subject to "internal colonization" because of the tendency for those who control theory to conflate the two spheres.[25] To me the potential difference for white intellectuals is between one's somewhat dark past and one's absolutely dark future. While a white art world may debate the nature of the relationship between "primitive" art and modern art, black artists and intellectuals widely assume that a white world is simply unable to admit that art from Africa and elsewhere in the Third World had a direct and profound influence on Western art because of an absolutely uncontrollable racism, xenophobia and ethnocentrism.

The so-called discovery of tribal objects by Modernism is analogous to an equally dubious discovery of the new world by European colonization. What was there was not, in fact, "discovered" but rather appropriated and/or stolen. But more to the point, the dynamic that emerged was born not only from the probability that European civilization would first repudiate and deny, then revise and reform that which they would eventually label "tribal" or "primitive," but from the even greater probability of a new kind of civilization or art, no longer strictly European, which would be revitalized by its proximity to and contact with an internal alternative. In other words, both European and non-European cultures were transformed by their "new" and closer relationship to one another in the "New World." For the most part, the relationship was one of exploitation, appropriation, oppression and repression. But it is also true that something came into and is coming into being: something neither "primitive/tribal" nor European modern.

While the most concrete sign of that something new is generally referred to as Postmodernism, unfortunately this move usually carries along with it the reinscription of Modernism's apartheid. Although the negation of their former powers to explain the world is potentially useful to counter-hegemonic strategies, invariably European influenced theorists are so preoccupied with the demise of the Hegelian dialectic that they never really get to anything or anyone other than white men who share similar feelings. Moreover, there is another sign just as indicative of novelty which is best represented by the cultural contributions of Afro-Americans to popular culture.

The temptation is great to subsume and reify this contribution under the heading of "Primitivism," or Neo-Primitivism, following the pattern of Modernist criticism. But it is the kind of development that will only occur because white males continue to absolutely dominate and control all aspects of Postmodern criticism. In other words, it is not the kind of choice that black critics or black feminist cultural critics are likely to endorse.

1. Richard Kluger, *Simple Justice*, Vol. 1 (New York: Knopf, 1979), pp. 398-403.

2. Ibid., pp. 446-448.

3. Scott Minerbrook, "At ABC: Black Journalists Make News," *Emerge* (October 1989): 33.

4. Toni Morrison, *The Bluest Eye* (New York: Holt, Rinehart and Winston, 1970), p. 7: "Here is the house. It is green and white. It has a red door. It is very pretty. Here is the family. Mother, Father, Dick, and Jane live in the green-and-white house They are very happy. See Jane. She wants to play. Who will play with Jane? . . ."

5. Kluger, *Simple Justice*, p. 448.

6. Cornel West, "Black Culture and Postmodernism," in *Remaking History*, eds. Barbara Kruger, and Phil Mariani (Seattle: Bay Press, 1989), p. 274.

7. Lawrence Levine, *Black Culture and Black Consciousness: Afro-American Folk Thought from Slavery to Freedom* (New York: Oxford University Press, 1977); and Amiri Baraka (Leroi Jones), *Blues People: Negro Music in White America* (New York: Grove Press, 1963).

8. Howardena Pindell, "Art (World) & Racism," *Third Text*, vol. 3/4 (Spring/Summer 1988): 161: "I have learned over my 20 years in New York not to 'romanticize' white artists, expecting them to be liberal, open, or necessarily supportive because they are creative people. Pests, a group of non-white artists, had hung a poster in Soho on Broome and Broadway last spring which read, 'There are 11,000 artists of color in New York. Why don't you see us?' Someone had written on the poster, 'Because you do poor work.' "

9. Ibid., p. 160.

10. Raymond Williams, *Marxism and Literature* (Oxford: Oxford University Press, 1977), pp. 115-117.

11. James Baldwin, *Notes of A Native Son* (New York: Beacon Press, 1955), p. 7.

12. Henry Louis Gates, Jr., "Figures in Black: Words, Signs and the 'Racial' Self," and Robert Stam, "Mikhail Bakhtin and Left Cultural Critique" in *Postmodernism and Its Discontents*, ed. E. Ann Kaplan (London and New York: Verso, 1988). Not only does Gates tend to use interchangeably the terms signifying, intertextuality and the dialogic, Stam points out in his essay that the term "intertextuality" was first introduced into critical discourse as Julia Kristeva's translation of Bakhtin's concept of the dialogic. Of course, Gates draws heavily upon Bakhtin's notion of the dialogic in order to describe how critical signification works.

13. Ralph Ellison, *The Invisible Man* (New York: Random House, 1952).

14. Of course there are many other relevant black female figures in Black Modernism (Bessie Smith and Zora Neale Hurston, for instance) but my attention here is on how a perspective which focuses on the Afro-American "other" of Euro-American Modernism and Postmodernism must necessarily exclude (black) female subjectivity in some crucial ways.

15. Josephine Baker is on the cover of *Mumbo Jumbo* by Ishmael Reed (Garden City: Doubleday, 1972).

16. Phyllis Rose, *Jazz Cleopatra: Josephine Baker in Her Time* (New York: Doubleday, 1989); Brian

Hammond, and Patrick O'Connor, *Josephine Baker* (London: Jonathan Cape, 1988).

17. Sander L. Gilman, "Black Bodies, White Bodies: Toward an Iconography of Female Sexuality in Late 19th Century Art, Medicine and Literature," in *"Race," Writing and Difference*, ed. Henry Louis Gates, Jr. (Chicago: University of Chicago Press, 1986), pp. 251-253.

18. Griselda Pollock, "Differencing the Canon," paper delivered at CAA "Firing the Canon" panel, Hilton Hotel, New York City, February 16, 1990.

19. Trinh T. Minh-ha, *Woman Native Other* (Bloomington: Indiana University Press, 1989), p. 80.

20. Peter Schjeldahl, "Paint the Right Thing," *Elle* (November 1989): 214-216; Michael Brenson, "A Sculptor's Struggle to Fuse Culture and Art," *New York Times*, Arts and Leisure Section (October 29, 1989): 37.

21. William Rubin, ed., *"Primitivism" in 20th Century Art: Affinity of the Tribal and the Modern*, 2 Vols. (New York: The Museum of Modern Art, 1984).

22. Thomas McEvilley, "Doctor Lawyer Indian Chief: '"Primitivism" in 20th Century Art' at The Museum of Modern Art," *Artforum* (November 1984): 54-60.

23. James Clifford, *The Predicament of Culture: Twentieth Century Ethnography, Literature and Art* (Cambridge: Harvard University Press, 1988), p. 196.

24. Hal Foster, *Recodings: Art, Spectacle, and Cultural Politics* (Port Townsend, WA: Bay Press, 1985), p. 204.

25. Gayatri Spivak, "Who Claims Alterity?" in *Remaking History*, eds. Barbara Kruger, and Phil Mariani (Seattle: Bay Press, 1989), p. 274.

The Straight Mind

In recent years in Paris, language as a phenomenon has dominated modern theoretical systems and the social sciences, and has entered the political discussions of the lesbian and women's liberation movements. This is because it relates to an important political field where what is at play is power, or more than that, a network of powers, since there is a multiplicity of languages which constantly act upon the social reality. The importance of language as such as a political stake has only recently been perceived.[1] But the gigantic development of linguistics, the multiplication of schools of linguistics, the advent of the sciences of communication, and the technicality of the metalanguages that these sciences utilize, represent the symptoms of the importance of that political stake. The science of language has invaded other sciences, such as anthropology through Lévi-Strauss, psychoanalysis through Lacan, and all the disciplines which have developed from the basis of structuralism.

The early semiology of Roland Barthes nearly escaped from linguistic domination to become a political analysis of the different systems of signs, to establish a relationship between this or that system of signs—for example, the myths of the petit bourgeois class—and the class struggle within capitalism that this system tends to conceal. We were almost saved, for political semiology is a weapon (a method) that we need to analyze what is called ideology. But the miracle did not last. Rather than introducing into semiology concepts which are foreign to it in this case Marxist concepts—Barthes quickly stated that semiology was only a branch of linguistics and that language was its only object.

Thus, the entire world is only a great register where the most diverse languages come, to have themselves recorded, such as the language of the Unconscious,[2] the language of fashion, the language of the exchange of women where human beings are literally the signs which are used to communicate. These languages, or rather these discourses, fit into one another, interpenetrate one another, support one another, reinforce one another, auto-engender, and engender one another. Linguistics engenders semiology and structural linguistics, structural linguistics engenders structuralism which engenders the Structural Unconscious. The ensemble of these discourses produces a confusing static for the oppressed, which makes them lose sight of the material cause of their oppression and plunges them into a kind of ahistoric vacuum.

For they produce a scientific reading of the social reality in which human beings are given as invariants, untouched by history and unworked by class conflicts, with a psyche identical for each one of them because genetically programmed. This psyche, equally untouched by history and unworked by class conflicts, provides the specialists, from the beginning of the twentieth century, with a whole arsenal of invariants: the symbolic language which very advantageously functions with very few elements, since like digits (0-9) the symbols "unconsciously" produced by the psyche are not very numerous. Therefore, these symbols are very easy to impose, through therapy and theorization, upon the collective and individual unconscious. We are taught that the unconscious, with perfectly good taste, structures itself upon metaphors, for example, the name-of-the-father, the Oedipus complex, castration, the murder-or-death-of-the-father, the exchange of women, etc. If the unconscious, however, is easy to control, it is not just by anybody. Similar to mystical revelations, the apparition of symbols in the psyche demands multiple interpretations. Only specialists can accomplish the deciphering of the unconscious. Only they, the psychoanalysts, are allowed (authorized?) to organize and interpret psychic manifestations which will show the symbol in its full meaning. And while the symbolic language is extremely poor and essentially lacunary, the languages or metalanguages which interpret it are developing, each one of them, with a richness, a display, that only logical exegeses (?) have equalled.

Who gave the psychoanalysts their knowledge? For example, for Lacan, what he calls the "psychoanalytical discourse," or the "analytical experience," both "teach" him what he already knows. And each one teaches him what the other one taught him. But who will deny that Lacan scientifically acknowledged, through the "analytical experience" (somehow an experiment) the structures of the Unconscious? Who will be irresponsible enough to disregard the discourses of the psychoanalyzed people lying on their couches? In my opinion, there is no doubt that Lacan found in the unconscious the structures he said he found there, since he had previously put them there. People who did not fall into the power of the psychoanalytical institution may experience an immeasurable feeling of sadness in front of the degree of oppression (of manipulation) that the psychoanalyzed discourses show. In the analytical experience there is an oppressed person, the psychoanalyzed, whose need for communication is exploited and who (in the same way as witches could, under torture, only repeat the language that the inquisitors wanted to hear) has no other choice, (if s/he does not want to destroy the implicit contract which allows her/him to communicate and which s/he needs), than to attempt to say what s/he is supposed to say. They say that this can last for a lifetime–cruel contract which constrains a human being to display her/his misery to an oppressor who is directly responsible for it, who exploits her/him economically, politically, ideologically and whose interpretation reduces this misery to a few figures of speech.

But can the need to communicate that this contract implies only be satisfied in the psychoanalytical situation, in being cured or "experimented" with? If we believe recent testimonies by lesbians, feminists, and gay men, this is not the case.[3] All their testimonies emphasize the political significance of the impossibility that lesbians, feminists, and gay men face in the attempt to communicate in heterosexual society, other than with a psychoanalyst. When the general state of things is understood (one is not sick or to be cured, one has an enemy) the result is for the oppressed person to break the psychoanalytical contract. This is what appears in the testimonies along with the teaching that the psychoanalytical contract was not a contract of consent but a forced one.

The discourses which particularly oppress all of us, lesbians, women, and homosexual men, are those discourses which take for granted that what founds society, any society, is heterosexuality.[4] These discourses speak about us and claim to say the truth in an apolitical field, as if anything of that which signifies could escape the political in this moment of history, and as if, in what concerns us, politically insignificant signs could exist. These discourses of heterosexuality oppress us in the sense that they prevent us from speaking unless we speak in their terms. Everything which puts them into question is at once disregarded as elementary. Our refusal of the totalizing interpretation of psychoanalysis makes the theoreticians say that we neglect the symbolic dimension. These discourses deny us every possibility of creating our own categories. But their most ferocious action is the unrelenting tyranny that they exert upon our physical and mental selves.

When we use the overgeneralizing term "ideology" to designate all the discourses of the dominating group, we relegate these discourses to the domain of Irreal Ideas, we forget the material (physical) violence that they directly do to the oppressed people, a violence produced by the abstract and "scientific" discourses as well as by the discourses of the mass media. I would like to insist on the material oppression of individuals by discourses, and I would like to underline its immediate effects through the example of pornography.

Pornographic images, films, magazine photos, publicity posters on the walls of the cities, constitute a discourse, and this discourse covers our world with its signs, and this discourse has a meaning: it signifies that women are dominated. Semioticians can interpret the system of this discourse, describe its disposition. What they read in that discourse are signs whose function is not to signify and which have no *raison d'être* except to be elements of a certain system or disposition. But for us this discourse is not divorced from the real as it is for semioticians. Not only does it maintain very close relations with the social reality which is our oppression (economically and politically), but also it is in itself real since it is one of the aspects of oppression, since it exerts a precise power over us. The pornographic discourse is part of the strategies of violence which are exercised upon us: it humiliates, it degrades, it is a crime against our "humanity." As a harassing tactic it has another function, that of a warning. It orders us to stay in line and it keeps those who would tend to forget who they are in step; it calls upon fear. These same experts in semiotics, referred to earlier, reproach us for confusing, when we demonstrate against pornography, the discourses with the reality. They do not see that this discourse *is* reality for us, one of the facets of the reality of our oppression. They believe that we are mistaken in our level of analysis.

I have chosen pornography as an example, because its discourse is the most symptomatic and the most demonstrative of the violence which is done to us through discourses, as well as in the society at large. There is nothing abstract about the power that sciences and theories have, to act materially and actually upon our bodies and our minds, even if the discourse that produces it is abstract. It is one of the forms of domination, its very expression, as Marx said. I would say, rather, one of its exercises. All of the oppressed know this power and have had to deal with it. It is the one which says: you do not have the right to speech because your discourse is not scientific and not theoretical, you are on the wrong level of analysis, you are confusing discourse and reality, your discourse is naive, you misunderstand this or that science.

If the discourse of modern theoretical systems and social science exert a power upon us, it is because it works with concepts which closely touch us. In spite of the historic advent of the lesbian, feminist, and gay liberation movements, whose proceedings have already upset the philosophical and political categories of the discourses of the social sciences, their categories (thus brutally put into question) are nevertheless utilized without examination by contemporary science. They function like primitive concepts in a conglomerate of all kinds of disciplines, theories, and current ideas that I will call the straight mind. (See *The Savage Mind* by Claude Lévi-Strauss). They concern "woman," "man," "sex," "difference," and all of the series of concepts which bear this mark, including such concepts as "history," "culture," and the "real." And although it has been accepted in recent years that there is no such thing as nature, that everything is culture, there remains within that culture a core of nature which resists examination, a relationship excluded from the social in the analysis—a relationship whose characteristic is ineluctability in culture, as well as in nature, and which is the heterosexual relationship. I will call it the obligatory social relationship between "man" and "woman." (Here I refer to Ti-Grace Atkinson and her analysis of sexual intercourse as an institution.[5]) With its ineluctability as knowledge, as an obvious principle, as a given prior to any science, the straight mind develops a totalizing interpretation of history, social reality, culture, language, and all the subjective phenomena at the same time. I can only underline the oppressive character that the straight mind is clothed in in its tendency to immediately universalize its production of concepts into general laws which claim to hold true for all societies, all epochs, all individuals. Thus one speaks of *the* exchange of women, *the* difference between the sexes, *the* symbolic order, *the* Unconscious, desire, *jouissance*, culture, history, giving an absolute meaning to these concepts when they are only categories founded upon heterosexuality or thought which produces the difference between the sexes as a political and philosophical dogma.

The consequence of this tendency toward universality is that the straight mind cannot conceive of a culture, a society where heterosexuality would not order not only all human relationships but also its very production of concepts and all the processes which escape consciousness, as well. Additionally, these unconscious processes are historically more and more imperative in what they teach us about ourselves through the instrumentality of specialists. The rhetoric which expresses them (and whose seduction I do not underestimate) envelops itself in myths, resorts to enigma, proceeds by accumulating metaphors, and its function is to poeticize the obligatory character of the "you-will-be-straight-or-you-will-not-be."

In this thought, to reject the obligation of coitus and the institutions that this obligation has produced as necessary for the constitution of a society, is simply an impossibility, since to do this would mean to reject the possibility of the constitution of the other and to reject the "symbolic order," to make the constitution of meaning impossible, without which no one can maintain an internal coherence. Thus lesbianism, homosexuality, and the societies that we form cannot be thought of or spoken of, even though they have always existed. Thus, the straight mind continues to affirm that incest, and not homosexuality, represents its major interdiction. Thus, when thought by the straight mind, homosexuality is nothing but heterosexuality.

Yes, straight society is based on the necessity of the different/other at every level. It cannot work economically, symbolically, linguistically, or politically without this concept. This necessity of the different/other is an ontological one for the whole conglomerate of sciences and disciplines that I call the straight mind. But what is the different/other if not the dominated? For heterosexual society is the society which not only oppresses lesbians and gay men, it oppresses many different/others, it oppresses all women and many categories of men, all those who are in the position of the dominated. To constitute a difference and to control it is an "act of power, since it is essentially a normative act. Everybody tries to show the other as different. But not everybody succeeds in doing so. One has to be socially dominant to succeed in it."[6]

For example, the concept of difference between the sexes ontologically constitutes women into different/others. Men are not different, whites are not different, nor are the masters. But the blacks, as well as the slaves, are. This ontological characteristic of the difference between the sexes affects all the concepts which are part of the same conglomerate. But for us there is no such thing as being-woman or being-man. "Man" and "woman" are political concepts of opposition, and the copula which dialectically unites them is, at the same time, the one which abolishes them.[7] It is the class struggle between women and men which will abolish men and women.[8] The concept of difference has nothing ontological about it. It is only the way that the masters interpret a historical situation of domination. The function of difference is to mask at every level the conflicts of interest, including ideological ones.

In other words, for us, this means there cannot any longer be women and men, and that as classes and as categories of thought or language they have to disappear, politically, economically, ideologically. If we, as lesbians and gay men, continue to speak of ourselves and to conceive of ourselves as women and as men, we are instrumental in maintaining heterosexuality. I am sure that an economic and political transformation will not dedramatize these categories of language. Can we redeem *slave*? Can we redeem *nigger, negress*? How is *woman* different? Will we continue to write *white, master, man*? The transformation of economic relationships will not suffice. We must produce a political transformation of the key concepts, that is of the concepts which are strategic for us. For there is another order of materiality, that of language, and language is worked upon from within by these strategic concepts. It is at the same time tightly connected to the political field where everything that concerns language, science and thought refers to the person as subjectivity and to her/his relationship to society.[9] And we cannot leave this within the power of the straight mind or the thought of domination.

If among all the productions of the straight mind I especially challenge structuralism and the Structural Unconscious, it is because: at the moment in history when the domination of social groups can no longer appear as a logical necessity to the dominated, because they revolt, because they question the differences, Lévi-Strauss, Lacan and their epigones call upon necessities which escape the control of consciousness and therefore the responsibility of individuals.

They call upon unconscious processes, for example, which require the exchange of women as a necessary condition for every society. According to them, that is what the unconscious tells us with authority, and the symbolic order, without which there is no meaning, no language, no society, depends on it. But what does women being exchanged mean if not that they are dominated? No wonder then that there is only one unconscious, and that it is heterosexual. It is an unconscious which looks too consciously after the interests of the masters in whom it lives for them to be dispossessed of their concepts so easily.[10] Besides, domination is denied; there is no slavery of women, there is difference. To which I will answer with this statement made by a Rumanian peasant at a public meeting in 1848: "Why do the gentlemen say it was not slavery, for we know it to have been slavery, this sorrow that we have sorrowed." Yes, we know it, and this science of oppression cannot be taken away from us.

It is from this science that we must track down the "what goes-without-saying" heterosexual, and (I paraphrase the early Roland Barthes) we must not bear "seeing Nature and History confused at every turn."[11] We must make it brutally apparent that structuralism, psychoanalysis, and particularly Lacan have rigidly turned their concepts into myths–Difference, Desire, the Name-of-the-father, etc. They have even "over-mythified" the myths, an operation that was necessary for them in order to systematically heterosexualize that personal dimension which suddenly emerged through the dominated individuals into the historical field, particularly through women, who started their struggle almost two centuries ago. And it has been done systematically, in a concert of interdisciplinarity, never more harmonious than since the heterosexual myths started to circulate with ease from one formal system to another, like sure values that can be invested, in anthropology as well as in psychoanalysis and in all the social sciences.

This ensemble of heterosexual myths is a system of signs which uses figures of speech, and thus it can be politically studied from within the science of our oppression; "for-we-know-it-to-have-been-slavery" is the dynamic which introduces the diachronism of history into the fixed discourse of eternal essences. This undertaking should somehow be a political semiology, although with "this sorrow that we have sorrowed" we work also at the level of language/manifesto, of language/action, that which transforms, that which makes history.

In the meantime in the systems that seemed so eternal and universal that laws could be extracted from them, laws that could be stuffed into computers, and in any case for the moment stuffed into the unconscious machinery, in these systems, thanks to our action and our language, shifts are happening. Such a model, as for example, the exchange of women, reengulfs history in so violent and brutal a way that the whole system, which was believed to be formal, topples over into another dimension of knowledge. This dimension belongs to us, since somehow we have been designated, and since, as Lévi-Strauss said, we talk, let us say that we break off the heterosexual contract.

So, this is what lesbians say everywhere in this country and in some others, if not with theories at least through their social practice, whose repercussions upon straight culture and society are still unenvisionable. An anthropologist might say that we have to wait for fifty years. Yes, if one wants to universalize the functioning of these societies and make their invariants appear. Meanwhile the straight concepts are undermined. What is woman? Panic, general alarm for an active defense. Frankly, it is a problem that the lesbians do not have because of a change of perspective, and it would be incorrect to say that lesbians associate, make love, live with women, for "woman" has meaning only in heterosexual systems of thought and heterosexual economic systems. Lesbians are not women.[12]

Translated by Mary Jo Lakeland and Susan Ellis Wolf. This text was first read in New York at the Modern Language Association Convention in 1978 and dedicated to the American lesbians.

1. However, the classical Greeks knew that there was no political power without mastery of the art of rhetoric, especially in a democracy.
2. Throughout this paper when Lacan's use of the term "the unconscious" is referred to it is capitalized, following his style.
3. For example see Karla Jay, and Allen Young, eds., *Out of the Closets* (New York: Links Books, 1972).
4. Heterosexuality: a word which first appears in the French language in 1911.
5. Ti-Grace Atkinson, *Amazon Odyssey* (New York: Links Books, 1974), pp. 13-23.
6. Claude Faugeron, and Philippe Robert, *La Justice et son public et les représentations sociales du système pénal* (Paris: Masson, 1978).
7. See for her definition of "social sex" Nicole-Claude Mathieu, "Notes pour une définition sociologique des categories de sexe," *Epistemologie Sociologique* 11 (1971); translated in Nicole-Claude Mathieu, *Ignored by Some, Denied by Others: The Social Sex Category in Sociology* (pamphlet), Explorations in Feminism 2 (London: Women's Research and Resources Centre Publications, 1977), pp. 16-37.
8. In the same way as for every other class struggle where the categories of opposition are "reconciled" by the struggle whose goal is to make them disappear.
9. See Christine Delphy, "Pour un Féminisme Matérialiste," *l'Arc* 61, *Simone de Beauvoir et la lutte des femmes.*
10. Are the millions of dollars a year made by the psychoanalysts symbolic?
11. Roland Barthes, *Mythologies* (New York: Hill and Wang, 1972), p. 11.
12. No more is any woman who is not in a relation of personal dependency with a man.

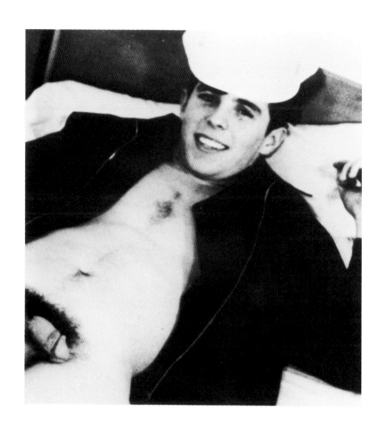

JOIN

What Is a Minor Literature?

A minor literature doesn't come from a minor language; it is rather that which a minority constructs within a major language. But the first characteristic of minor literature in any case is that in it language is affected with a high coefficient of deterritorialization. In this sense, Kafka marks the impasse that bars access to writing for the Jews of Prague and turns their literature into something impossible—the impossibility of not writing, the impossibility of writing in German, the impossibility of writing otherwise.[1] The impossibility of not writing because national consciousness, uncertain or oppressed, necessarily exists by means of literature ("The literary struggle has its real justification at the highest possible levels"). The impossibility of writing other than in German is for the Prague Jews the feeling of an irreducible distance from their primitive Czech territoriality. And the impossibility of writing in German is the deterritorialization of the German population itself, an oppressive minority that speaks a language cut off from the masses, like a "paper language" or an artificial language; this is all the more true for the Jews who are simultaneously a part of this minority and excluded from it, like "gypsies who have stolen a German child from its crib." In short, Prague German is a deterritorialized language, appropriate for strange and minor uses. (This can be compared in another context to what blacks in America today are able to do with the English language.)

The second characteristic of minor literatures is that everything in them is political. In major literatures, in contrast, the individual concern (familial, marital, and so on) joins with other no less individual concerns, the social milieu serving as a mere environment or a background; this is so much the case that none of these Oedipal intrigues are specifically indispensable or absolutely necessary but all become as one in a large space. Minor literature is completely different; its cramped space forces each individual intrigue to connect immediately to politics. The individual concern thus becomes all the more necessary, indispensable, magnified, because a whole other story is vibrating within it. In this way, the family triangle connects to other triangles—commercial, economic, bureaucratic, juridical—that determine its values. When Kafka indicates that one of the goals of a minor literature is the "purification of the conflict that opposes father and son and the possibility of discussing that conflict," it isn't a question of an Oedipal phantasm but of a political program. "Even though something is often thought through calmly, one still does not reach the boundary where it connects up with similar things, one reaches the boundary soonest in politics, indeed, one even strives to see it before it is there, and often sees this limiting boundary everywhere . . . What in great literature goes on down below, constituting a not indispensable cellar of the structure, here takes place in the full light of day, what is there a matter of passing interest for a few, here absorbs everyone no less than as a matter of life and death."[2]

The third characteristic of minor literature is that in it everything takes on a collective value. Indeed, precisely because talent isn't abundant in a minor literature, there are no possibilities for an individuated enunciation that would belong to this or that "master" and that could be separated from a collective enunciation. Indeed, scarcity of talent is in fact beneficial and allows the conception of something other than a literature of masters; what each author says individually already constitutes a common action, and what he or she says or does is necessarily political, even if others aren't in agreement. The political domain has contaminated every statement *(énoncé)*. But above all else, because collective or national consciousness is "often inactive in external life and always in the process of break-down," literature finds itself positively charged with the role and function of collective, and even revolutionary, enunciation. It is literature that produces an active solidarity in spite of skepticism; and if the writer is in the margins or completely outside his or her fragile community, this situation allows the writer all the more the possibility to express another possible community and to forge the means for another consciousness and another sensibility; just as the dog of "Investigations" calls out in his solitude to *another science*. The literary machine thus becomes the relay for a revolutionary machine-to-come, not at all for ideological reasons but because the literary machine alone is determined to fill the conditions of a collective enunciation that is lacking elsewhere in this milieu: *literature is the people's concern.*[3] It is certainly in these terms that Kafka sees the problem. The message doesn't refer back to an enunciating subject who would be its cause, no more than to a subject of the statement *(sujet d'énoncé)* who would be its effect. Undoubtedly, for a while, Kafka thought according to these traditional categories of the two subjects, the author and the hero, the narrator and the character, the dreamer and the one dreamed of.[4] But he will quickly reject the role of the narrator, just as he will refuse an author's or master's literature, despite his admiration for Goethe. Josephine the mouse renounces the individual act of singing in order to melt into the collective enunciation of "the immense crowd of the heros of [her] people." A movement from the individuated animal to the pack or to a collective multiplicity—seven canine musicians. In "The Investigations of a Dog," the expressions of the solitary researcher tend toward the assemblage *(agencement)* of a collective enunciation of the canine species even if this collectivity is no longer or not yet given. There isn't a subject; *there are only collective assemblages of enunciation,* and literature expresses these acts insofar as they're not imposed from without and insofar as they exist only as diabolical powers to come or revolutionary forces to be constructed. Kafka's solitude opens him up to everything going on in history today. The letter K no longer designates a narrator or a character but an assemblage that becomes all the more machine-like, an agent that becomes all the more collective because an individual is locked into it in his or her solitude (it is only in connection to a subject that something individual would be separable from the collective and would lead its own life).

The three characteristics of minor literature are the deterritorialization of language, the connection of the individual to a political immediacy, and the collective assemblage of enunciation. We might as well say that minor no longer designates specific literatures but the revolutionary conditions for every literature within the heart of what is called great (or established) literature. Even he who has the misfortune of being born in the country of a great literature must write in its language, just as a Czech Jew writes in German, or an Ouzbekian writes in Russian. Writing like a dog digging a hole, a rat digging its burrow. And to do that, finding his own point of underdevelopment, his own *patois*, his own third world, his own desert. There has been much discussion of the questions "What is a marginal literature?" and "What is a popular literature, a proletarian literature?" The criteria are obviously difficult to establish if one doesn't start with a more objective concept–that of minor literature. Only the possibility of setting up a minor practice of major language from within allows one to define popular literature, marginal literature, and so on.[5] Only in this way can literature really become a collective machine of expression and really be able to treat and develop its contents. Kafka emphatically declares that a minor literature is much more able to work over its material.[6] Why this machine of expression, and what is it? We know that it is in a relation of multiple deterritorializations with language; it is the situation of the Jews who have dropped the Czech language at the same time as the rural environment, but it is also the situation of the German language as a "paper language." Well, one can go even farther; one can push this movement of deterritorialization of expression even farther. But there are only two ways to do this. One way is to artificially enrich this German, to swell it up through all the resources of symbolism, of oneirism, of esoteric sense, of a hidden signifier. This is the approach of the Prague school, Gustav Meyrink and many others, including Max Brod.[7] But this attempt implies a desperate attempt at symbolic reterritorialization, based in archetypes, Kabbala, and alchemy, that accentuates its break from the people and will find its political result only in Zionism and such things as the "dream of Zion." Kafka will quickly choose the other way, or, rather, he will invent another way. He will opt for the German language of Prague as it is and in its very poverty. Go always farther in the direction of deterritorialization, to the point of sobriety. Since the language is arid, make it vibrate with a new intensity. Oppose a purely intensive usage of language to all symbolic or even significant or simply signifying usages of it. Arrive at a perfect and unformed expression, a materially intense expression. (For these two possible paths, couldn't we find the same alternatives, under other conditions, in Joyce and Beckett? As Irishmen, both of them live within the genial conditions of a minor literature. That is the glory of this sort of minor literature–to be the revolutionary force for all literature. The utilization of English and of every language in Joyce. The utilization of English and French in Beckett. But the former never stops operating by exhilaration and overdetermination and brings about all sorts of worldwide reterritorializations. The other proceeds by dryness and sobriety, a willed poverty, pushing deterritorialization to such an extreme that nothing remains but intensities.)

How many people today live in a language that is not their own? Or no longer, or not yet, even know their own and know poorly the major language that they are forced to serve? This is the problem of immigrants, and especially of their children, the problem of minorities, the problem of a minor literature, but also a problem for all of us: how to tear a minor literature away from its own language, allowing it to challenge the language and making it follow a sober revolutionary path? How to become a nomad and an immigrant and a gypsy in relation to one's own language? Kafka answers: steal the baby from its crib, walk the tightrope.

Rich or poor, each language always implies a deterritorialization of the mouth, the tongue, and the teeth. The mouth, tongue, and teeth find their primitive territoriality in food. In giving themselves over to the articulation of sounds, the mouth, tongue, and teeth deterritorialize. Thus, there is a certain disjunction between eating and speaking, and even more, despite all appearances, between eating and writing. Undoubtedly, one can write while eating more easily than one can speak while eating, but writing goes further in transforming words into things capable of competing with food. Disjunction between content and expression. To speak, and above all to write, is to fast. Kafka manifests a permanent obsession with food, and with that form of food *par excellence*, in other words, the animal or meat—an obsession with the mouth and with teeth and with large, unhealthy, or gold-capped teeth.[8] This is one of Kafka's main problems with Felice. Fasting is also a constant theme in Kafka's writings. His writings are a long history of fasts. The Hunger Artist, surveyed by butchers, ends his career next to beasts who eat their meat raw, placing the visitors before an irritating alternative. The dogs try to take over the mouth of the investigating hound by filling it with food so that he'll stop asking questions, and there too there is an irritating alternative: "[T]hey would have done better to drive me away and refuse to listen to my questions. No, they did not want to do that; they did not indeed want to listen to my questions, but it was because I asked these questions that they did not want to drive me away." The investigating hound oscillates between two sciences, that of food—a science of the Earth and of the bent head ("Whence does the Earth procure this food?")—and that of music which is a science of the air and of the straightened head, as the seven musical dogs of the beginning and the singing dog of the end well demonstrate. But between the two there is something in common, since food can come from high up and the science of food can only develop through fasting, just as the music is strangely silent.

Ordinarily, in fact, language compensates for its deterritorialization by a reterritorialization in sense. Ceasing to be the organ of one of the senses, it becomes an instrument of Sense. And it is sense, as a correct sense, that presides over the designation of sounds (the thing or the state of things that the word designates) and, as figurative sense, over the affectation of images and metaphors (those other things that words designate under certain situations or conditions). Thus, there is not only a spiritual reterritorialization of sense, but also a physical one. Similarly, language exists only through the distinction and the complementarity of a subject of enunciation, who is in connection with sense, and a subject of the statement, who is in connection, directly or metaphorically, with the designated thing. This sort of ordinary use of language can be called extensive or representative—the reterritorializing function of language (thus, the singing dog at the end of the "Investigations," forces the hero to abandon his fast, a sort of re-Oedipalizaton).

Now something happens: the situation of the German language in Czechoslovakia, as a fluid language intermixed with Czech and Yiddish, will allow Kafka the possibility of invention. Since things are as they are ("it is as it is, it is as it is," a formula dear to

Kafka, marker of a state of facts), he will abandon sense, render it no more than implicit; he will retain only the skeleton of sense, or a paper cutout.

Since articulated sound was a deterritorialized noise but one that will be reterritorialized in sense, it is now sound itself that will be deterritorialized irrevocably, absolutely. The sound or the word that traverses this new deterritorialization no longer belongs to a language of sense, even though it derives from it, nor is it an organized music or song, even though it might appear to be. We noted Gregor's warbling and the ways it blurred words, the whistling of the mouse, the cough of the ape, the pianist who doesn't play, the singer who doesn't sing and gives birth to her song out of her nonsinging, the musical dogs who are musicians in the very depths of their bodies since they don't emit any music. Everywhere, organized music is traversed by a line of abolition—just as a language of sense is traversed by a line of escape—in order to liberate a living and expressive material that speaks for itself and has no need of being put into a form.[9] This language torn from sense, conquering sense, bringing about an active neutralization of sense, no longer finds its value in anything but an accenting of the word, an inflection: "I live only here or there in a small word in whose vowel . . . I lose my useless head for a moment. The first and last letters are the beginning and end of my fishlike emotion."[10] Children are well skilled in the exercise of repeating a word, the sense of which is only vaguely felt, in order to make it vibrate around itself (at the beginning of *The Castle*, the schoolchildren are speaking so fast that one cannot understand what they are saying). Kafka tells how, as a child, he repeated one of his father's expressions in order to make it take flight on a line of non-sense: "end of the month, end of the month."[11] The proper name, which has no sense in itself, is particularly propitious for this sort of exercise. *Milena*, with an accent on the *i*, begins by evoking "a Greek or Roman gone astray in Bohemia, violated by Czech, cheated of its accent," and then, by a more delicate approximation, it evokes " a woman whom one carries in one's arms out of the world, out of the fire," the accent marking here an always possible fall or, on the contrary, "the lucky leap which you yourself make with your burden."[12]

It seems to us that there is a certain difference, even if relative and highly nuanced, between the two evocations of the name Milena: one still attaches itself to an extensive, figurative scene of the fantasmatic sort; the second is already much more intensive, marking a fall or a leap as a threshold of intensity contained within the name itself. In fact, we have here what happens when sense is actively neutralized. As Wagenbach says, "The word is master; it directly gives birth to the image." But how can we define this procedure? Of sense there remains only enough to direct the lines of escape. There is no longer a designation of something by means of a proper name, nor an assignation of metaphors by means of a figurative sense. But *like* images, the thing no longer forms anything but a sequence of intensive states, a ladder or a circuit for intensities that one can make race around in one sense or another, from high to low, or from low to high. The image is this very race itself; it has become becoming—the becoming-dog of the man and the becoming-man of the dog, the becoming-ape or the becoming-beetle of the man and vice versa. We are no longer in the situation of an ordinary, rich language where the word dog, for example, would directly designate an animal and would apply metaphorically to other things (so that one could say "like a dog").[13] *Diaries*, 1921:

"Metaphors are one of the things that makes me despair of literature." Kafka deliberately kills all metaphor, all symbolism, all signification, no less than all designation. Metamorphosis is the contrary of metaphor. There is no longer any proper sense or figurative sense, but only a distribution of states that is part of the range of the word. The thing and other things are no longer anything but intensities overrun by deterritorialized sound or words that are following their line of escape. It is no longer a question of a resemblance between the comportment of an animal and that of a man; it is even less a question of a simple wordplay. There is no longer man or animal, since each deterritorializes the other, in a conjunction of flux, in a continuum of reversible intensities. Instead, it is now a question of a becoming that includes the maximum of difference as a difference of intensity, the crossing of a barrier, a rising or a falling, a bending or an erecting, and accent on the word. The animal does not speak "like" a man but pulls from the language tonalities lacking in signification; the words themselves are not "like" the animals but in their own way climb about, bark and roam around, being properly linguistic dogs, insects, or mice.[14] To make the sequences vibrate, to open the word onto unexpected internal intensities—in short, an asignifying *intensive utilization* of language. Furthermore, there is no longer a subject of the enunciation, nor a subject of the statement, It is no longer the subject of the statement who is a dog, with the subject of the enunciation remaining "like" a man; it is no longer the subject of enunciation who is "like" a beetle, the subject of the statement remaining a man. Rather, there is a circuit of states that forms a mutual becoming, in the heart of a necessarily multiple or collective assemblage.

How does the situation of the German language in Prague—a withered vocabulary, an incorrect syntax—contribute to such a utilization? Generally, we might call the linguistic elements, however varied they may be, that express the "internal tensions of a language" *intensives* or *tensors*. It is in this sense that the linguist Vidal Sephiha terms intensive "any linguistic tool that allows a move toward the limit of a notion or a surpassing of it," marking a movement of language toward its extremes, toward a reversible beyond or before.[15] Sephiha well shows the variety of such elements which can be all sorts of master-words, verbs, or prepositions that assume all sorts of senses; prenominal or purely intensive verbs as in Hebrew; conjunctions, exclamations, adverbs; and *terms that connote pain.*[16] One could equally cite the accents that are interior to words, their discordant function. And it would seem that the language of a minor literature particularly develops these tensors or these intensives. In the lovely pages where he analyzes the Prague German that was influenced by Czech, Wagenbach cites as the characteristics of this form of German the incorrect use of prepositions; the abuse of the pronominal; the employment of malleable verbs (such as *Giben*, which is used for the series "put, sit, place, take away" and which thereby becomes intensive); the multiplication and succession of adverbs; the use of pain-filled connotations; the importance of the accent as a tension internal to the word; and the distribution of consonants and vowels as part of an internal discordance. Wagenbach insists on this point: all these marks of the poverty of a language show up in Kafka but have been taken over by a creative utilization for the purposes of a new sobriety, a new expressivity, a new flexibility, a new intensity.[17] "Almost every word I write jars up against the next, I hear the consonants rub leadenly against each other and the vowels sing an accompaniment like Negroes in a minstrel show."[18] *Language stops being representative in order to now move toward its extremities or its limits.* The connotation of pain accompanies this metamorphosis, as in the words that become a painful warbling with Gregor, or in Franz's cry "single and irrevocable." Think about the utilization of French as a spoken language in the films of Godard. There too is an accumulation of stereotypical adverbs and conjunctions that form the base of all the phrases—a strange poverty that makes French a minor language within French; a creative process that directly links the word to the image; a technique that surges up at the end of sequences in connection with the intensity of the limit "that's enough, enough, he's had enough," and a generalized intensification, coinciding with a panning shot where the camera pivots and sweeps around without leaving the spot, making the image vibrate.

Perhaps the comparative study of images would be less interesting than the study of the functions of language that can work in the same group across different languages—bilingualism or even multilingualism. Because the study of the functions in distinct languages alone can account for social factors, relations of force, diverse centers of power, it escapes from the "informational" myth in order to evaluate the hierarchic and imperative system of language as a transmission of orders, an exercise of power or of resistance to this exercise. Using the research of Ferguson and Gumperz, Henri Gobard has proposed a tetralinguistic model: vernacular, maternal, or territorial language, used in rural communities or rural in its origins; a vehicular, urban, governmental, even worldwide language, a language of businesses, commercial exchange, bureaucratic transmission, and so on, a language of the first sort of deterritorialization; referential language, language of sense and of culture, entailing a cultural reterritorialization; mythic language, on the horizon of cultures, caught up in a spiritual or religious reterritorialization. The spatiotemporal categories of these languages differ sharply: vernacular language is *here*; vehicular language is *everywhere*; referential language is *over there*; mythic language is *beyond*. But above all else, the distribution of these languages varies from one group to the next and, in a single group, from one epoch to the next (for a long time in Europe, Latin was a vehicular language before becoming referential, then mythic; English has become the worldwide vehicular language for today's world).[19] What can be said in one language cannot be said in another, and the totality of what can and can't be said varies necessarily with each language and with the connections between these languages.[20] Moreover, all these factors can have ambiguous edges, changing borders, that differ for this or that material. One language can fill a certain function for one material and another function for another material. Each function of a language divides up in turn and carries with it multiple centers of power. A blur of languages, and not at all a system of languages. We can understand the indignation of integrationists who cry when Mass is said in French, since Latin is being robbed of its mythic function. But the classicists are even more behind the times and cry because Latin has even been robbed of its referential cultural function. They express regret in this way for the religious or educational forms of powers that this language exercised and that have now been replaced by other forms. There are even more serious examples that cross over between groups. The revival of regionalisms, with a reterritorialization through dialect or patois, a vernacular language—how does that serve a worldwide or transnational technocracy? How can that contribute to revolutionary movements, since they are also filled with archaisms that they are trying to impart a contemporary sense to? From Servan-Schreiber to the Breton bard to the Canadian singer. And that's not really how the borders divide up, since the Canadian singer can also bring about the most reactionary, the most Oedipal of reterritorializations, oh mamma, oh my native land, my cabin, olé, olé. We would call this a blur, a mixed-up history, a political situation, but linguists don't know about this, don't want to know about this, since, as linguists, they are "apolitical," pure scientists. Even Chomsky compensated for his scientific apoliticism only by his courageous struggle against the war in Vietnam.

Let's return to the situation in the Hapsburg empire. The breakdown and fall of the empire increases the crisis, accentuates everywhere movements of deterritorialization, and invites all sorts of complex reterritorializations—archaic, mythic, or symbolist. At random, we can cite the following among Kafka's contemporaries: Einstein and his deterritorialization of the representation of the universe (Einstein teaches in Prague, and the physicist Philipp Frank gives conferences there with Kafka in attendance); the Austrian dodecaphonists and their deterritorialization of musical representation (the cry that is Marie's death in *Wozzeck*, or Lulu's, or the echoed *si* that seems to us to follow a musical path similar in certain ways to what Kafka is doing); the expressionist cinema and its double movement of deterritorialization and reterritorialization of the image (Robert Wiene, who has Czech background; Fritz Lang, born in Vienna; Paul Wegener and his utilization of Prague themes). Of course, we should mention Viennese psychoanalysis and Prague school linguistics.[21] What is the specific situation of the Prague Jews in relation to the "four languages?" The vernacular language for these Jews who have come from a rural milieu is Czech, but the Czech language tends to be forgotten and repressed; as for Yiddish, it is often disdained or viewed with suspicion—it *frightens*, as Kafka tells us. German is the vehicular language of the towns, a bureaucratic language of the state, a commercial language of exchange (but English has already started to become indispensable for this purpose). The German language—but this time, Goethe's German—has a cultural and referential function (as does French to a lesser degree). As a mythic language, Hebrew is connected with the start of Zionism and still possesses the quality of an active dream. For each of these languages, we need to evaluate the degrees of territoriality, deterritorialization, and reterritorialization. Kafka's own situation: he is one of the few Jewish writers in Prague to understand and speak Czech (and this language will have a great importance in his relationship with Milena). German plays precisely the double role of vehicular and cultural language, with Goethe always on the horizon (Kafka also knows French, Italian, and probably a bit of English). He will not learn Hebrew until later. What is complicated is Kafka's relation to Yiddish; he sees it less as a sort of linguistic territoriality for the Jews than as a nomadic movement of deterritorialization that reworks German language. What fascinates him in Yiddish is less a language of a religious community than that of a popular theater (he will become patron and impresario for the travelling theater of Isak Lowy).[22] The manner in which Kafka, in a public meeting, presented Yiddish to a rather hostile Jewish bourgeois audience is completely remarkable: Yiddish is a language that frightens more than it invites disdain, "dread mingled with a certain fundamental distaste"; it is a language that is lacking a grammar and that is filled with vocables that are fleeting, mobilized, emigrating, and turned into nomads that interiorize "relations of force." It is a language that is grafted onto Middle-High German and that so reworks the German language from within that one cannot translate it into German without destroying it; one can understand Yiddish only by "feeling it" in the heart. In short, it is a language where minor utilizations will carry you away: "Then you will come to feel the true unity of Yiddish and so strongly that it will frighten you, yet it will no longer be fear of Yiddish but of yourselves. Enjoy this self-confidence as much as you can!"[23]

Kafka does not opt for a reterritorialization through the Czech language. Nor toward a hypercultural usage of German with all sorts of oneiric or symbolic or mythic flights (even Hebrew-ifying ones), as was the case with the Prague school. Nor toward an oral, popular Yiddish. Instead, using the path that Yiddish opens up to him, he takes it in such a way as to convert it into a unique and solitary form of writing. Since Prague German is deterritorialized to several degrees, he will always take it farther, to a greater degree of intensity, but in the direction of a new sobriety, a new and unexpected modification, a pitiless rectification, a straightening of the head. Schizo politeness, a drunkenness caused by water.[24] He will make the German language take flight on a line of escape. He will feed himself on abstinence; he will tear out of Prague German all the qualities of underdevelopment that it has tried to hide; he will make it cry with an extremely sober and rigorous cry. He will pull from it the barking of the dog, the cough of the ape, and the bustling of the beetle. He will turn syntax into a cry that will embrace the rigid syntax of this dried-up German. He will push it toward a deterritorialization that will no longer be saved by culture or by myth, that will be an absolute deterritorialization, even if it is slow, sticky, coagulated. To bring language slowly and progressively to the desert. To use syntax in order to cry, to give syntax to the cry.

There is nothing that is major or revolutionary except the minor. To hate all languages of masters. Kafka's fascination for servants and employees (the same thing in Proust in relation to servants, to their language). What interests him even more is the possibility of making of his own language—assuming that it is unique, that it is a major language or has been—a minor utilization. To be a sort of stranger *within* his own language; this is the situation of Kafka's Great Swimmer.[25] Even when it is unique, a language remains a mixture, a schizophrenic mélange, a Harlequin costume in which very different functions of language and distinct centers of power are played out, blurring what can be said and what can't be said; one function will be played off against the other, all the degrees of territoriality and relative deterritorialization will be played out. Even when major, a language is open to an intensive utilization that makes it take flight along creative lines of escape which, no matter how slowly, no matter how cautiously, can now form an absolute deterritorialization. All this inventiveness, not only lexically, since the lexical matters little, but sober syntactical invention, simply to write like a dog (but a dog can't write—exactly, exactly). It's what Artaud did with French—cries, gasps; what Celine did with French, following another line, one that was exclamatory to the highest degree. Celine's syntactic evolution went from *Voyage* to *Death on the Credit*

Plan, then from *Death on the Credit Plan* to *Guignol's Band*. (After that, Celine had nothing more to talk about except his own misfortunes; in other words, he had no longer any desire to write, only the need to make money. And it always ends like that, language's lines of escape: silence, the interrupted, the interminable, or even worse. But until that point, what a crazy creation, what a writing machine! Celine was so applauded for *Voyage* that he went even further in *Death on the Credit Plan* and then in the prodigious *Guignol's Band* where language is nothing more than intensities. He spoke with a kind of "minor music." Kafka, too, is a minor music, a different one, but always made up of deterritorialized sounds, a language that moves head over heels and away.) These are the true minor authors. An escape for language, for music, for writing. What we call pop—pop music, pop philosophy, pop writing—Worterflucht. To make use of the polylingualism of one's own language, to make a minor or intensive use of it, to oppose the oppressed quality of this language to its oppressive quality, to find points of nonculture or underdevelopment, linguistic Third World zones by which a language can escape, an animal enters into things, an assemblage comes into play. How many styles or genres or literary movements, even very small ones, have only one single dream: to assume a major function in language, to offer themselves as a sort of state language, an official language (for example, psychoanalysis today, which would like to be a master of the signifier, of metaphor, of wordplay). Create the opposite dream: know how to create a becoming-minor. (Is there a hope for philosophy, which for a long time has been an official, referential genre? Let us profit from this moment in which antiphilosophy is trying to be a language of power.)

Translated by Dana Polan.

1. See letter to Brod, Franz Kafka, *Letters to Friends, Family and Editors*, trans. Richard and Clara Winston (New York: Schocken Books, 1977), p. 289, and commentaries in Wagenbach, *Franz Kafka, Années de Jeunesse* (Paris: Mercure, 1967), p. 84.
2. *The Diaries of Franz Kafka*, trans. Joseph Kresh (New York: Schocken Books, 1948), p. 194.
3. Ibid., p. 193: "[L]iterature is less a concern of literary history, than of the people."
4. See "Wedding Preparations in the Country," in Franz Kafka, *Complete Stories*, (New York: Schocken Books, 1971): "And so long as you say 'one' instead of 'I,' there's nothing in it" (p. 53). And the two subjects appear several pages later: "I don't even need to go to the country myself, it isn't necessary. I'll send my clothed body," while the narrator stays in bed like a bug or a beetle (p. 55). No doubt, this is one of the origins of Gregor's becoming-beetle in "The Metamorphosis" (in the same way, Kafka will give up going to meet Felice and will prefer to stay in bed). But in "The Metamorphosis," the animal takes on all the value of a

true becoming and no longer has any of the stagnancy of a subject of enunciation.
5. See Michel Ragon, *Histoire de la littérature prolétarienne en France* (Paris: Albin Michel, 1974) on the difficulty of criteria and on the need to use a concept of a "secondary zone literature."
6. Kafka, *Diaries*, December 25, 1911, p. 193: "A small nation's memory is not smaller than the memory of a large one and so can digest the existing material more thoroughly."
7. See the excellent chapter "Prague at the turn of the century," in Wagenbach, *Franz Kafka,* on the situation of the German language in Czechoslovakia and on the Prague school.
8. Constancy of the theme of teeth in Kafka. A grandfather-butcher; a streetwise education at the butcher-shop; Felice's jaws; the refusal to eat meat except when he sleeps with Felice in Marienbad. See Michel Cournot's article, "Toi qui as de si grandes dents," *Nouvel Observateur* (April 17, 1972). This is one of the most beautiful texts on Kafka. One can find a similar opposition between eating and speaking in Lewis Carroll, and a comparable escape into non-sense.
9. Franz Kafka, *The Trial*, trans. Willa and Edwin

Muir (New York: Schocken Books, 1956): "[H]e noticed that they were talking to him, but he could not make out what they were saying, he heard nothing but the din that filled the whole place, through which a shrill unchanging note like that of a siren seemed to sing."

10. Kafka, *Diaries*, August 20, 1911, pp. 61-62.

11. Kafka, *Diaries*: "Without gaining a sense, the phrase 'end of the month' held a terrible secret for me" especially since it was repeated every month–Kafka himself suggests that if this expression remained shorn of sense, this was due to laziness and "weakened curiosity." A negative explication invoking lack or powerlessness, as taken by Wagenbach. It is well-known that Kafka makes this sort of negative suggestion to present or to hide the objects of his passion.

12. Kafka, *Letters to Milena*, p. 58. Kafka's fascination with proper names, beginning with those that he invented: see Kafka, *Diaries*, February 11, 1913 (à propos of the names in *The Verdict*).

13. Kafka commentators are at their worst in their interpretations in this respect when they regulate everything through metaphors: thus, Marthe Roberts reminds us that the Jews are *like* dogs or, to take another example, that "since the artist is treated as someone starving to death Kafka makes him into a hunger artist; or since he is treated as a parasite, Kafka makes him into an enormous insect" (*Oeuvres complètes*, Cercle du livre precieux, 5:311). It seems to us that this is a simplistic conception of the literary machine–Robbe-Grillet has insisted on the destruction of all metaphors in Kafka.

14. See, for example, the letter to Pollak in Kafka, *Letters*, February 4, 1902, pp. 1-2.

15. See H. Vidal Sephiha, "Introduction à l'étude de l'intensif," in *Langages* 18 (June 1970): 104-20. We take the term *tensor* from J.F. Lyotard who uses it to indicate the connection of intensity and libido.

16. Sephiha, "Introduction," p. 107 ("We can imagine that any phrase conveying a negative notion of pain, evil, fear, violence can cast off the notion in order to retain no more than its limit-value–that is, its intensive value": for example, the German word *sehr*, which comes from the Middle High German word, *Ser* meaning "painful").

17. Wagenbach, *Franz Kafka*, pp. 78-88 (especially 78, 81, 88).

18. Kafka, *Diaries*, December 15, 1910, p. 33.

19. Henri Gobard, "De la vehicularité de la langue anglaise," *Langues modernes* (January 1972) (and *L'Alienation linguistique: analyse tetraglossique* [Paris: Flammarion, 1976]).

20. Michel Foucault insists on the importance of the distribution between what can be said in a language at a certain moment and what cannot be said (even if it can be *done*). Georges Devereux (cited by H. Gobard) analyzes the case of the young Mohave Indians who speak about sexuality with great ease in their vernacular language but who are incapable of doing so in that vehicular language that English constitutes for them; and this is so not only because the English instructor exercises a repressive function, but also because there is a problem of languages (see *Essais d'ethnopsychiatrie générale* [Paris: Gallimard, 1970], pp. 125-126).

21. On the Prague Circle and its role in linguistics, see *Change*, no. 3 (1969) and no. 10 (1972). (It is true that the Prague circle was only formed in 1925. But in 1920, Jakobson came to Prague where there was already a Czech movement directed by Mathesius and connected with Anton Marty who had taught in the German university system. From 1902 to 1905, Kafka followed the courses given by Marty, a disciple of Brentano, and participated in Brentanoist meetings.)

22. On Kafka's connections to Lowy and Yiddish theater, see Brod, *Franz Kafka*, pp. 110-116, and Wagenbach, *Franz Kafka*, pp. 163-167. In this mime theater, there must have been many bent heads and straightened heads.

23. "An Introductory Talk on the Yiddish Language," trans. Ernst Kaiser and Eithne Wilkins in Franz Kafka, *Dearest Father* (New York: Schocken Books, 1954), pp. 381-386.

24. A magazine editor will declare that Kafka's prose has "the air of the cleanliness of a child who takes care of himself" (see Wagenbach, *Franz Kafka*, p. 82).

25. "The Great Swimmer" is undoubtedly one of the most Beckett-like of Kafka's texts: "I have to well admit that I am in my own country and that, in spite of all my efforts, I don't understand a word of the language you are speaking."

• **Homi K. Bhabha**

The Other Question: Difference, Discrimination and the Discourse of Colonialism

The genesis of this essay is diverse and discontinuous; its long march of critical contestation tracks my attempts to clear a space for the "other" question. To pose the colonial question is to realize that the problematic representation of cultural and racial difference cannot simply be read off from the signs and designs of social authority that are produced in the analyses of class and gender differentiation. As I was writing in 1982, the conceptual boundaries of the west were being busily reinscribed in a clamor of counter-texts—transgressive, semiotic, semanalytic, deconstructionist—none of which pushed those boundaries to their colonial periphery; to that limit where the west must face a peculiarly displaced and decentered image of itself "in double duty bound," at once a civilizing mission and a violent subjugating force. It is there, in the colonial margin, that the culture of the west reveals its *différance*, its limit-text, as its practice of authority displays an ambivalence that is one of the most significant discursive and psychical strategies of discriminatory power—whether racist or sexist, peripheral or metropolitan.

It is the force of ambivalence that gives the colonial stereotype its currency: ensures its repeatability in changing historical and discursive conjunctures; informs its strategies of individuation and marginalization; produces that effect of probabilistic truth and predictability which, for the stereotype, must always be in *excess* of what can be empirically proved or logically construed. The absence of such a perspective has its own history of political expediency. To recognize the stereotype as an ambivalent mode of knowledge and power demands a theoretical and political response that challenges deterministic or functionalist modes of conceiving of the relationship between discourse and politics, and questions dogmatic and moralistic positions on the meaning of oppression and discrimination. My reading of colonial discourse suggests that the point of intervention should shift from the *identification* of images as positive or negative, to an understanding of the *processes of subjectification* made possible (and plausible) through stereotypical discourse.

My essay is indebted to traditions of post-structuralist and psychoanalytic theory, especially in their feminist formulation. Equally important is its theoretical reorientation, effected through my reading of the work of Frantz Fanon and Edward Said. Fanon's insights into the language of the unconscious, as it emerges in the grotesque psychodrama of everyday life in colonial societies, demands a rethinking of the forms and forces of "identification" as they operate at the edge of cultural authority. Said's work—especially *Orientalism* (1978) and *The Question of Palestine* (1980)—dramatically shifts the locus of contemporary theory from the Left Bank to the West Bank and beyond, through a profound meditation on the myths of western power and knowledge which confine the colonized and dispossessed to a half-life of misrepresentation and migration. For me, Said's work focused the need to quicken the half-light of western history with the disturbing memory of its colonial texts that bear witness to the trauma that accompanies the triumphal art of Empire.

Edward Said concludes his essay "Orientalism Reconsidered" with a perspective on the state of the art, which is both informative and interdisciplinary.[1] Three recent publications which are representative of developments in the analysis of "otherness" are: *Europe and Its Others*; "*'Race,' Writing and Difference*"; and *Black Literature and Literary Theory*.[2]

To describe the racist discourse of colonial power as constructed around a "boundary dispute" is not merely to pun the political with the psychoanalytic. It is the object of my essay to suggest that the construction of the colonial subject in discourse, and the exercise of colonial power through discourse demands an articulation of forms of difference—racial and sexual. Such an articulation becomes crucial if it is held that the body is always simultaneously inscribed in both the economy of pleasure and desire and the economy of discourse, domination and power. I do not wish to conflate, unproblematically, two forms of the marking—and splitting—of the subject nor to globalize two forms of representation. I want to suggest, however, that there is a theoretical space and a political space for such an articulation—in the sense in which that word itself denies an "original" identity or a "singularity" to objects of difference, sexual or racial. If such a view is taken, as Feuchtwang argues in a different context,[3] it follows that the epithets racial or sexual come to be seen as modes of differentiation, realized as multiple, crosscutting determinations, polymorphous and perverse, always demanding a specific and strategic calculation of their effects. Such is, I believe, the moment of colonial discourse. It is the most theoretically underdeveloped form of discourse, but crucial to the binding of a range of differences and discriminations that inform the discursive and political practices of racial and cultural hierarchization.

Before turning to the construction of colonial discourse, I want briefly to discuss the process by which forms of racial/cultural/historical otherness have been marginalized in theoretical texts committed to the articulation of *différance*, *signifiance*, in order, it is claimed, to reveal the limits of western metaphysical discourse. Despite the differences (and disputes) between grammatology and semiology, both practices share an anti-epistemological position that impressively contests western modes of representation predicated on an episteme of presence and identity. In facilitating the passage "from work to text" and stressing the arbitrary, differential and systemic construction of social and cultural signs, these critical strategies unsettle the idealist quest for meanings that are, most often, intentionalist and nationalist. So much is not in question. What does need to be questioned, however, is the *mode of representation of otherness*, which depends crucially on how the "west" is deployed within these discourses.

The anti-ethnocentric stance is a strategy which, in recognizing the spectacle of otherness, conceals a paradox central to these anti-epistemological theories. For the critique of western idealism or logocentrism requires that there is a constitutive discourse of lack imbricated in a philosophy of presence, which makes the differential or deconstructionist reading possible, "between the lines." As Mark Cousins says, the *desire* for presence which characterizes the western episteme and its regimes of representation, "carries with it as the condition of its movement and of the regulation of its economy, a destiny of non-satisfaction."[4] This could lead, as he goes on to say, "to an endless series of playful deconstructions which manifest a certain sameness in the name of difference." If such repetitiousness is to be avoided, then the strategic failure of logocentrism would have to be given a displacing and subversive role. This requires that the "non-satisfaction" should be specified *positively* which is done by identifying an anti-west. Paradoxically, then, cultural otherness functions as the moment of *presence* in a theory of *différance*. The "destiny of non-satisfaction" is fulfilled in the recognition of otherness as a *symbol* (not sign) of the presence of *significance* or *différance*: otherness is the point of equivalence or identity in a circle in which what needs to be proved (the limits of logocentricity) is assumed (as a destiny or economy of lack/desire). What is denied is any knowledge of cultural otherness as a differential *sign*, implicated in specific historical and discursive conditions, requiring construction in different practices or reading. The place of otherness is fixed in the west as a subversion of western metaphysics and is finally appropriated by the west as its limit-text, anti-west.

Derrida, for example, in the course of his *Positions* interview,[5] tends to fix the problem of ethnocentricity repeatedly at the limits of logocentricity, the unknown territory mapped neatly on to the familiar, as presuppositions inseparable from metaphysics, merely another limitation of metaphysics. Such a position cannot lead to the construction or exploration of other discursive sites from which to investigate the differential materiality and history of colonial culture. The interiority and immediacy of voice as "consciousness itself," central to logocentric discourse, is disturbed and dispersed by the imposition of a foreign tongue which differentiates the gentleman from the native, culture from civilization. The colonial discourse is always at least twice-inscribed and it is in that process of *différance* that denies "originality," that the problem of the colonial subject must be thought.

To address the question of ethnocentricity in Derrida's terms, one could explore the exercise of colonial power in relation to the violent hierarchy between written and aural cultures. One might examine, in the context of a colonial society, those strategies of normalization that play on the difference between an "official" normative language of colonial administration and instruction and an unmarked, marginalized form–pidgin, creole, vernacular–which becomes the site of the native subject's cultural dependence and resistance, and as such a sign of surveillance and control.

Finally, where better to raise the question of the subject of racial and cultural difference than in Stephen Heath's masterly analysis of the chiaroscuro world of Orson Welles' classic *A Touch of Evil*. I refer to an area of its analysis which has generated the least comment, that is, Heath's attention to the structuration of the border Mexico/USA that circulates through the text affirming and exchanging some notion of "limited being." Heath's work departs from the traditional analysis of racial and cultural differences, which identifies stereotype and image, and elaborates them in a moralistic or nationalistic discourse that affirms the *origin* and *unity* of national identity. Heath's attentiveness to the contradictory and diverse sites within the textual system which *construct* national/cultural differences in their deployment of the semes of "foreignness," "mixedness," "impurity," as transgressive and corrupting, is extremely relevant. His attention to the turnings of this much neglected subject, as sign (not symbol or stereotype) disseminated in the codes (as "partition," "exchange," "naming," "character," etc.), gives us a welcome sense of the circulation and proliferation of racial and cultural otherness. Despite the awareness of the multiple or cross-cutting determinations in the construction of modes of sexual and racial differentiation, there is a sense in which Heath's analysis marginalizes otherness. Although I shall argue that the problem of the border Mexico/USA is read too singularly, too exclusively under the sign of sexuality, it is not that I am unaware of the many proper and relevant reasons for that "feminist" focus. The "entertainment" operated by the realist Hollywood film of the 1950s was always also a containment of the subject in a narrative economy of voyeurism and fetishism. Moreover, the displacement that organizes any textual system, within which the display of difference circulates, demands that the play of "nationalities" should participate in the sexual positioning, troubling the law and desire. There is, nevertheless, a singularity and reductiveness in concluding that:

> *Vargas is the position of desire, its admission and its prohibition. Not surprisingly he has two names: the name of desire is Mexican, Miguel . . . that of the Law American Mike . . . The film uses the border, the play between American and Mexican . . . at the same time it seeks to hold that play finally in the opposition of purity and mixture which in turn is a version of Law and desire.*[6]

However liberatory it is from one position to see the logic of the text traced ceaselessly between the Ideal Father and the Phallic Mother, in another sense, in seeing only one possible articulation of the differential complex "race-sex" it half colludes with the proffered images of marginality. For if the naming of Vargas is crucially mixed and split in the economy of desire, then there are other mixed economies which make naming and positioning equally problematic "across the border." For to identify the "play" on the border as purity and mixture and to see it as an allegory of law and desire reduces the articulation of racial and sexual difference to what is dangerously close to becoming a circle rather than a spiral of différance. On that basis, it is not possible to construct the polymorphous and perverse collusion between racism and sexism as a *mixed economy*—for instance, the discourses of American cultural colonialism and Mexican dependency, the fear/desire of miscegenation, the American border as cultural signifier of a pioneering, male "American" spirit always under threat from races and cultures beyond the border. If the death of the Father is the interruption on which the narrative is initiated, it is through that death that miscegenation is both possible and deferred; if, again, it is the purpose of the narrative to restore Susan as "good object," it also becomes its project to deliver Vargas from his racial "mixedness." It is all there in Heath's splendid scrutiny of the text, revealed as he brushes against its grain. What is missing is the taking up of these positions as also the *object(ives)* of his analysis.

The difference of other cultures is other than the excess of signification, the *différance* of the trace or the trajectory of desire. These are theoretical strategies that may be necessary to combat "ethnocentrism" but they cannot, of themselves, unreconstructed, represent that otherness. There can be no inevitable sliding from the semiotic or deconstructionist activity to the unproblematic reading of other cultural and discursive systems. There is in such readings a will to power and knowledge that, in failing to specify the limits of their own field of enunciation and effectivity, proceed to individualize otherness as the discovery of their own assumptions.

What is meant by colonial discourse as an apparatus of power will emerge more fully as a critique of specific, historical texts. At this stage, however, I shall provide what I take to be the minimum conditions and specifications of such a discourse. It is an apparatus that turns on the recognition and disavowal of racial/cultural/historical differences. Its predominant strategic function is the creation of a space for a "subject peoples" through the production of knowledges in terms of which surveillance is exercised and a complex form of pleasure/unpleasure is incited. It seeks authorization for its strategies by the production of knowledges of colonizer and colonized which are stereotypical but antithetically evaluated. The objective of colonial discourse is to construe the colonized as a population of degenerate types on the basis of racial origin, in order to justify conquest and to establish systems of administration and instruction. Despite the play of power within colonial discourse and the shifting positionalities of its subjects (e.g. effects of class, gender, ideology, different social formations, varied systems of colonization, etc.), I am referring to a form of governmentality that in marking out a "subject nation," appropriates, directs and dominates its various spheres of activity. Therefore, despite the play in the colonial system which is crucial to its exercise of power, I do not consider the practices and discourses of revolutionary struggle as the under/other side of "colonial discourse." They may be historically co-present with it and intervene in it, but can never be "read-off" merely on the basis of their opposition to it. Anti-colonialist discourse requires an alternative set of questions, techniques and strategies in order to construct it.

Through this paper I shall move through forms of colonial discourse or descriptions of it, written from the late nineteenth century to the present. I have referred to specific historical texts in order to construct three theoretical problems which I consider crucial. In Temple's work the circulation of power as knowledge; in Said's the fixation/fetishization of stereotypical knowledge as power; and in Fanon's the circulation of power and knowledge in a binding of desire and pleasure.

The social Darwinist problematic of Charles Temple's "The Native Races and Their Rulers"[7] (1918) enacts the tension between "the free and continual circulation" that natural selection requires and the effects of colonial power which claims to assist natural selection by controlling racial degeneracy but, through that intervention, must necessarily impede free circulation. The colonial system then requires some justification other than mere material necessity; and if justification is understood as both vindication and correction, then we can see in this text a crucial adjustment in the exercise of colonial power. In the face of an ambitious native "nationalist" bourgeois, Temple's text marks the shift in the form of colonial government, from a juridical sovereign exercise of power as punitive and restrictive–as harbinger of death–to a disciplinary form of power.

Disciplinary power is exercised through indirection on the basis of a knowledge of the subject-races as "abnormal." They are not merely degenerate and primitive but, Temple claims, they also require the "abnormality" of imperialist intervention to hasten the process of natural selection. If "normalization" can imply even the faint possibility of an absorption or incorporation of the subject-races then, like mass rule at home, this must be resisted in the colonies. The natives are therefore "individualized," through the racist testimony of "science" and colonialist administrative wisdom, as having such divergent ethical and mental outlooks that integration or independence is deemed impossible. Thus marginalized or individualized, the colonial subject as bearer of racial typologies and racist stereotypes is reintroduced to the circulation of power as a "productive capacity" within that form of colonial government called "indirect rule."

The co-option of traditional elites into the colonial administration is then seen to be a way of harnessing the ambitious life-instinct of the natives. This sets up the native subject as a site of productive power, both subservient and always potentially seditious. What is increased is the visibility of the subject as an object of surveillance, tabulation, enumeration, and indeed, paranoia and fantasy. When the upward spiral of natural selection encounters differences of race, class and gender as potentially contradictory and insurrectionary forces, whose mobility may fracture the closed circuit of natural selection, social Darwinism invokes what Temple calls "the decrees of all-seeing Providence." This agency of social control appeals in desperation to God instead of Nature to fix the colonized at that point in the social order from which colonial power will, in Foucault's specification, be able simultaneously to increase the subjected forces and to improve the force and efficacy of that which subjects them.

Colonial power produces the colonized as a fixed reality which is at once an "other" and yet entirely knowable and visible. It resembles a form of narrative in which the productivity and circulation of subjects and signs are bound in a reformed and recognizable totality. It employs a system of representation, a regime of truth, that is structurally similar to realism. And it is in order to intervene within that system of representation that Edward Said proposes a semiotic of "Orientalist" power, which in raising the problem of power as a question of narrative introduces a new topic in the territory of colonial discourse.

> *Philosophically, then, the kind of language, thought, and vision that I have been calling Orientalism very generally is a form of radical realism; anyone employing Orientalism, which is the habit for dealing with questions, objects, qualities and regions deemed Oriental, will designate, name, point to, fix what he is talking or thinking about with a word or phrase, which is then considered either to have acquired, or more simply to be, reality . . . The tense they employ is the timeless eternal; they convey an impression of repetition and strength . . . For all these functions it is frequently enough to use the simple copula is.*[8]

But the syllogism, as Kristeva once said, is that form of western rationalism that reduces heterogeneity to two-part order so that the *copula* is the point at which this binding preserves the boundaries of sense for an entire tradition of philosophical thinking. Of this, too, Said is aware when he hints continually at a polarity or division at the very center of Orientalism.[9] It is, on the one hand, a topic of learning, discovery, practice; on the other it is the site of dreams, images, fantasies, myths, obsessions and requirements. It is a static system of "synchronic essentialism," a knowledge of "signifiers of stability" such as the lexicographic and the encyclopedic. However, this site is continually under threat from diachronic forms of history and narrative, signs of instability. And, finally, this line of thinking is given a shape analogical to the dream-work, when Said refers explicitly to a distinction between "an unconscious positivity" which he terms *latent* Orientalism, and the stated knowledges and views about the Orient which he calls *manifest* Orientalism.

Where the originality of this account loses some of its interrogative power is in Said's inadequate engagement with alterity and ambivalence in the articulation of these two economies which threaten to split the very object of Orientalist discourse as a knowledge and the subject positioned therein. He contains this threat by introducing a binarism within the argument which, in initially setting up an opposition between these two discursive scenes, finally allows them to be correlated as a congruent system of representation that is unified through a political-ideological *intention* which, in his words, enables Europe to advance securely and *unmetaphorically* upon the Orient.

This seems to be a rather peremptory resolution to a problem posed with remarkable insight. It is compounded by a psychologistic reduction when, in describing Orientalism through the nineteenth century, Said identifies the *content* of Orientalism as the unconscious repository of fantasy, imaginative writings and essential ideas; and the *form* of manifest Orientalism as the historically and discursively determined, diachronic aspect.

To develop a point made above, the division/correlation structure of manifest and latent Orientalism leads to the effectivity of the concept of discourse being undermined by what I will call the polarities of intentionality. This is a problem fundamental to Said's use of the terms *power* and *discourse*. The productivity of Foucault's concept of power/knowledge is its refusal of an epistemology which opposes form/content, ideology/science, essence/appearance. "Pouvoir/Savoir" places subjects in a relation of power and recognition that is not part of a symmetrical or dialectical relation—self/other, Master/Slave—which can then be subverted by being inverted. Subjects are always disproportionately placed in opposition or domination through the symbolic decentering of multiple power-relations which play the role of support as well as target or adversary. It becomes difficult, then, to conceive of the *historical* enunciations of colonial discourse without them being either functionally overdetermined or strategically elaborated or displaced by the *unconscious* scene of latent Orientalism. Equally, it is difficult to conceive of the process of subjectification as a placing *within* orientalist or colonial discourse for the dominated subject without the dominant being strategically placed within it too. There is always, in Said, the suggestion that colonial power and discourse is possessed entirely by the colonizer, which is a historical and theoretical simplification. The terms in which Said's Orientalism are unified—which is, the intentionality and undirectionality of colonial power—also unifies the subject of colonial enunciation.

This is a result of Said's inadequate attention to representation as a concept that articulates the historical and fantasy (as the scene of desire) in the production of the "political" effects of discourse. He rightly rejects a notion of Orientalism as the misrepresentation of an Oriental essence. However, having introduced the concept of "discourse" he does not attend adequately to the problems it makes for the instrumentalist use of power/knowledge that he sometimes seems to require. This problem is summed up by his ready acceptance of the view that

> Representations are formations, or as Roland Barthes has said of all the operations of language, they are deformations.[10]

This brings me to my second point, that the closure and coherence attributed to the unconscious pole of colonial discourse, and the unproblematized notion of the subject, restricts the effectivity of both power and knowledge. This makes it difficult to see how power could function productively both as incitement and interdiction. Nor would it be possible without the attribution of ambivalence to relations of power/knowledge to calculate the traumatic impact of the return of the oppressed—those terrifying stereotypes of savagery, cannibalism, lust and anarchy which are the signal points of identification and alienation, scenes of fear and desire, in colonial texts. It is precisely this function of the stereotype as phobia and fetish that, according to Fanon, threatens the closure of the racial/epidermal schema for the colonial subject and opens the royal road to colonial fantasy.

If Said's theory disavows that *mise-en-scène*, his metaphoric language somehow prefigures it. There is a forgotten, under-developed passage which, in cutting across the body of the text, articulates the question of power and desire that I now want to take up. It is a process that has the power to reorientate our representation and recognition of colonial "otherness."

> Altogether an internally structured archive is built up from the literature that belongs to these experiences. Out of this comes a restricted number of typical encapsulations: the journey, the history, the fable, the stereotype, the polemical confrontation. These are the lenses through which the Orient is experienced, and they shape the language, perception, and form of the encounter between East and West. What gives the immense number of encounters some unity, however, is the vacillation I was speaking about earlier. Something patently foreign and distant acquires, for one reason or another, a status more rather than less familiar. One tends to stop judging things either as completely novel or as completely well-known; a new median category emerges, a category that allows one to see new things, things seen for the first time, as versions of a previously known thing. In essence such a category is not so much a way of receiving new information as it is a method of controlling what seems to be a threat to some established view of things . . . The threat is muted, familiar values impose themselves, and in the end the mind reduces the pressure upon it by accommodating things to itself as either "original" or "repetitious" . . . The Orient at large, therefore, vacillates between the West's contempt for what is familiar and its shivers of delight in—or fear of—novelty.[11]

What is this other scene of colonial discourse played out around the "median-category?" What is this theory of encapsulation or fixation which moves between the recognition of cultural and racial difference and its disavowal, by affixing the unfamiliar to something established, in a form that is repetitious and vacillates between delight and fear? Is it not analogous to the Freudian fable of fetishism (and disavowal) that circulates within the discourse of colonial power, requiring the articulation of modes of differentiation–sexual and racial–as well as different modes of discourse–psychoanalytic and historical?

The strategic articulation of "co-ordinates of knowledge"–racial and sexual–and their inscription in the play of colonial power as modes of differentiation, defense, fixation, hierarchization, is a way of specifying colonial discourse which would be illuminated by reference to Foucault's post-structuralist concept of the *dispositif* or apparatus. In displacing his earlier search for discursive regularity as *episteme*, Foucault stresses that the relations of knowledge and power within the apparatus are always a strategic response to an *urgent need* at a given historical moment–much as I suggested at the outset, that the force of colonial discourse as a theoretical and political intervention was the *need*, in our contemporary moment, to contest singularities of difference and to articulate modes of differentiation. Foucault writes:

> the apparatus is essentially of a strategic nature, which means assuming that it is a matter of a certain manipulation of relations of forces, either developing them in a particular direction, blocking them, stabilizing them, utilizing them, etc. The apparatus is thus always inscribed in a play of power, but it is always also linked to certain coordinates of knowledge which issue from it but, to an equal degree, condition it. This is what the apparatus consists in: strategies of relations of forces supporting and supported by, types of knowledge.[12]

In this spirit I argue for the reading of the stereotype in terms of fetishism. The myth of historical origination–racial purity, cultural priority–production in relation to the colonial stereotype functions to "normalize" the multiple beliefs and split subjects that constitute colonial discourse as a consequence of its process of disavowal. The scene of fetishism functions similarly as, at once, a reactivation of the material of original fantasy–the anxiety of castration and sexual difference–as well as a normalization of that difference and disturbance in terms of the fetish object as the substitute for the mother's penis. Within the apparatus of colonial power, the discourses of sexuality and race relate in a process of *functional overdetermination*, "because each effect . . . enters into resonance or contradiction with the others and thereby calls for a re-adjustment or re-working of the heterogeneous elements that surface at various points."[13]

There is both a structural and functional justification for reading the racial stereotype of colonial discourse in terms of fetishism.[14] My rereading of Said establishes the *structural* link. Fetishism, as the disavowal of difference, is that repetitious scene around the problem of secondary castration. The recognition of sexual difference–as the precondition for the circulation of the chain of absence and presence in the realm of the symbolic–is disavowed by the fixation on an object that masks that difference and restores an original presence. The functional link between the fixation of the fetish and the stereotype (or the stereotype as fetish) is even more relevant. For fetishism is always a "play" or vacillation between the archaic affirmation of wholeness/similarity–in Freud's terms: "All men have penises"; in ours: "All men have the same skin/race/culture; and the anxiety associated with lack of difference"–again, for Freud: "Some do not have penises"; for us: "Some *do not* have the same skin/race/culture." Within discourse, the fetish represents the simultaneous play between metaphor as substitution (making absence and difference) and metonymy (which contiguously registers the perceived lack). The fetish or stereotype gives access to an "identity" which is predicated as much on mastery and pleasure as it is on anxiety and defense, for it is a form of multiple and contradictory belief in its recognition of difference and disavowal of it. This conflict of pleasure/unpleasure, mastery/defense, knowledge/disavowal, absence/presence, has a fundamental significance for colonial discourse. For the scene of fetishism is also the scene of the reactivation and repetition of primal fantasy—the subject's desire for a pure origin that is always threatened by its division, for the subject must be gendered to be engendered, to be spoken. The stereotype, then, as the primary point of subjectification in colonial discourse, for both colonizer and colonized, is the scene of a similar fantasy and defense—the desire for an originality which is again threatened by the differences of race, color and culture. My contention is splendidly caught in Fanon's title *Black Skin White Masks* where the disavowal of difference turns the colonial subject into a misfit—a grotesque mimicry or "doubling" that threatens to split the soul and whole, undifferentiated skin of the ego. The stereotype is not a simplification because it is a false representation of a given reality. It is a simplification because it is an arrested, fixated form of representation that, in denying the play of difference (that the negation through the other permits), constitutes a problem for the *representation* of the subject in significations of psychic and social relations.

When Fanon talks of the positioning of the subject in the stereotyped discourse of colonialism, he gives further credence to my point. The legends, stories, histories and anecdotes of a colonial culture offer the subject a primordial Either/Or.[15] *Either* he is fixed in a consciousness of the body as a solely negating activity *Or* as a new kind of man, a new genus. What is denied the colonial subject, both as colonizer and colonized, is that form of negation which gives access to the recognition of difference in the symbolic. It is that possibility of difference and circulation which would liberate the signifier of skin/culture from the signifieds of racial typology, the analytics of blood, ideologies of racial and cultural dominance or degeneration. "Wherever he goes," Fanon despairs, "the negro remains a negro"—his race becomes the ineradicable sign of negative difference in colonial discourse. For the stereotype impedes the circulation and articulation of the signifier of "race" as anything other than its *fixity* as racism. We always already know that blacks are licentious, Asiatics duplicitous...

There are two "primal scenes" in Fanon's *Black Skin White Masks*: two myths of the origin of the marking of the subject within the racist practices and discourses of a colonial culture. On one occasion a white girl fixes Fanon in look and word as she turns to identify with her mother. It is a scene which echoes endlessly through his essay "The Fact of Blackness": "Look, a negro... Mamma, *see* the Negro! I'm frightened. Frightened." "What else could it be for me," Fanon concludes, "but an amputation, an excision, a hemorrhage that splattered my whole body with black blood."[16] Equally, he stresses the primal moment when the child encounters racial and cultural stereotypes in children's fictions, where white heroes and black demons are proffered as points of ideological and psychical identification. Such dramas are enacted *every day* in colonial societies, says Fanon, employing a theatrical metaphor—the scene—which emphasizes the visible–the seen. I want to play upon both these senses which refer at once to the site of fantasy and desire and to the site of subjectification and power.

The drama underlying these dramatic "everyday" colonial scenes is not difficult to discern. In each of them the subject turns around the pivot of the "stereotype" to return to a point of total identification. The girl's gaze returns to her mother in the recognition and disavowal of the negroid type; the black child turns away from himself, his race, in his total identification with the positivity of whiteness which is at once color and no color. In the act of disavowal and fixation the colonial subject is returned to the narcissism of the Imaginary and its identification of an ideal-ego that is white and whole. For what these primal scenes illustrate is that looking/hearing/reading as sites of subjectification in colonial discourse are evidence of the importance of the visual and auditory imaginary for the *histories* of societies.[17]

My anatomy of colonial discourse remains incomplete until I locate the stereotype as an arrested, fetishistic mode of representation within its field of identification, which I have identified in my description of Fanon's primal scenes, as the Lacanian scheme of the Imaginary. The Imaginary[18] is the transformation that takes place in the subject at the formative mirror phase, when it assumes a discrete image which allows it to postulate a series of equivalences, samenesses, identities, between the objects of the surrounding world. However, this positioning is itself problematic, for the subject finds or recognizes itself through an image which is simultaneously alienating and hence potentially confrontational. This is the basis of the close relation between the two forms of identification complicit with the Imaginary–narcissism and aggressivity. It is precisely these two forms of "identification" that constitute the dominant strategy of colonial power exercised in relation to the stereotype which, as a form of multiple and contradictory belief, gives knowledge of difference and simultaneously disavows or masks it. Like the mirror-phase "the fullness" of the stereotype–its image *as* identity–is always threatened by "lack."

The construction of colonial discourse is then a complex articulation of the tropes of fetishism–metaphor and metonymy–and the forms of narcissistic and aggressive identification available to the Imaginary. Stereotypical racial discourse is then a four-term strategy. There is a tie-up between the metaphoric or masking function of the fetish and the narcissistic object-choice and an opposing alliance between the metonymic figuring of lack and the aggressive phase of the Imaginary. One has then a repertoire of conflictual positions that constitute the subject in colonial discourse. The taking up of any one position, within a specific discursive form in a particular historical conjuncture, is then always problematic–the site of both fixity and fantasy. It provides a colonial identity that is played out–like all fantasies of originality and origination–in the face and space of the disruption and threat from the heterogeneity of other positions. As a form of splitting and multiple belief, the stereotype requires, for its successful signification, a continual and repetitive chain of other stereotypes. This is the process by which the metaphoric "masking" is inscribed on a lack which must then be concealed, that gives the stereotype both its fixity and its phantasmatic quality–the same old stories of the negro's animality, the coolie's inscrutability or the stupidity of the Irish which *must* be told (compulsively) again and afresh and is differently gratifying and terrifying each time.

In any specific colonial discourse the metaphoric/narcissistic and metonymic/aggressive positions will function simultaneously, but always strategically poised in relation to each other; similar to the moment of alienation which stands as a threat to Imaginary plenitude and "multiple belief" which threatens fetishistic disavowal. Caught in the Imaginary as they are, these shifting positionalities will never seriously threaten the dominant power relations, for they exist to exercise them pleasurably and productively. They will always pose the problem of difference as that between the pre-constituted, "natural" poles of black and white with all its historical and ideological ramifications. The *knowledge of the construction* of that "opposition" will be denied the colonial subject. He is constructed within an apparatus of power which *contains*, in both senses of the word, an "other" knowledge–a knowledge that is arrested and fetishistic and circulates through colonial discourse as that limited form of otherness, that fixed form of difference, that I have called the stereotype.

My four-term strategy of the stereotype tries tentatively to provide a structure and a process for the "subject" of colonial discourse. I now want to take up the problem of discrimination as the political effect of such a discourse and relate it to the question of "race" and "skin." To that end it is important to remember that the multiple belief that accompanies fetishism does not only have disavowal value; it also has "knowledge value" and it is this that I shall now pursue. In calculating this knowledge value it is crucial to try and understand what Fanon means when he says that:

> There is a quest for the Negro, the Negro is a demand, one cannot get along without him, he
> is needed, but only if he is made palatable in a certain way. Unfortunately the Negro knocks
> down the system and breaks the treaties.[19]

What this demand is, and how the native or negro is made palatable requires that we acknowledge some significant differences between the general theory of fetishism and its specific uses for an understanding of racist discourse. First, the fetish of colonial discourse–what Fanon calls the epidermal schema–is not, like the sexual fetish, a secret. Skin, as the key signifier of cultural and racial difference in the stereotype, is the most visible of fetishes, recognized as common knowledge in a range of cultural, political, historical discourses, and plays a public part in the racial drama that is enacted every day in colonial societies. Second, it may be said that the sexual fetish is closely linked to the "good object"; it is the prop that makes the whole object desirable and lovable, facilitates sexual relations and can even promote a form of happiness. The stereotype can also be seen as that particular "fixated" form of the colonial subject which *facilitates* colonial relations, and sets up a discursive form of racial and cultural opposition in terms of which colonial power is exercised. If it is claimed that the colonized are most often objects of hate, then we can reply with Freud that

> affection and hostility in the treatment of the fetish–which run parallel with the disavowal and
> acknowledgment of castration–are mixed in unequal proportions in different cases, so that the
> one or the other is more clearly recognizable.[20]

What this statement recognizes is the wide range of the stereotype, from the loyal servant to Satan, from the loved to the hated; a shifting of subject positions in the circulation of colonial power which I tried to account for through the mobility of the metaphoric/narcissistic and metonymic/aggressive system of colonial discourse. What remains to be examined, however, is the construction of the signifier "skin/race" in those regimes of visibility and discursivity—fetishistic, scopic, imaginary—within which I have located the stereotypes. It is only on that basis that we can construct its "knowledge-value" which will, I hope, enable us to see the place of fantasy in the exercise of colonial power.

My argument relies upon a particular reading of the problematic of representation which, Fanon suggests, is specific to the colonial situation. He writes:

> the originality of the colonial context is that the economic substructure is also a superstruc-
> ture . . . you are rich because you are white, you are white because you are rich. This is why
> Marxist analysis should always be slightly stretched every time we have to do with the colo-
> nial problem.[21]

Fanon could either be seen as adhering to a simple reflectionist or determinist notion of cultural/social signification or, more interestingly, he could be read as taking an "anti-repressionist" position (attacking the notion that ideology as miscognition, or misrepresentation, is the repression of the real). For our purposes I tend towards the latter reading which then provides a visibility to the exercise of power; gives force to the argument that skin, as a signifier of discrimination, must be produced or processed as visible. As Paul Abbott says, in a very different context:

> whereas repression banishes its object into the unconscious, forgets and attempts to forget the
> forgetting, discrimination must constantly invite its representations into consciousness, reinforc-
> ing the crucial recognition of difference which they embody and revitalizing them for the
> perception on which its effectivity depends . . . It must sustain itself on the presence of the very
> difference which is also its object.[22]

What "authorizes" discrimination, Abbott continues, is the occlusion of the pre-construction of working-up of difference:

> this repression of production entails that the recognition of difference is procured in an inno-
> cence, as a "nature"; recognition is contrived as primary cognition, spontaneous effect of the
> "evidence of the visible."[23]

This is precisely the kind of recognition, as spontaneous and visible, that is attributed to the stereotype. The difference of the object of discrimination is at once visible and natural—color as the cultural/political sign of inferiority or degeneracy, skin as its natural "identity."

Although the "authority" of colonial discourse depends crucially on its location in narcissism and the Imaginary, my concept of stereotype-as-suture is a recognition of the *ambivalence* of that authority and those orders of identification. The role of fetishistic identification, in the construction of discriminatory knowledges that depend of the *presence of difference*, is to provide a process of splitting and multiple/contradictory belief at the point of enunciation and subjectification. It is this crucial splitting of the ego which is represented in Fanon's description of the construction of the colonial subject as effect of sterotypical discourse: the subject primordially fixed and yet triply split between the incongruent knowledges of body, race, ancestors. Assailed by the stereotype

> *The corporeal schema crumbled, its place taken by a racial epidermal scheme . . . It was no longer a question of being aware of my body in the third person but a triple person . . . I was not given one, but two, three places.*[24]

This process is best understood in terms of the articulation of multiple-belief that Freud proposes in the essay "Fetishism." It is a non-repressive form of knowledge that allows for the possibility of simultaneously embracing two contradictory beliefs, one official and one secret, one archaic and one progressive, one that allows the myth of origins, the other that articulates difference and division. Its knowledge-value lies in its orientation as a defense towards external reality, and provides, in Metz's words

> *the lasting matrix, the effective prototype of all those splittings of belief which man will hence-forth be capable of in the most varied domains, of all the infinitely complex unconscious and occasionally conscious interactions which he will allow himself between believing and not-believing.*[25]

It is through this notion of splitting and multiple belief that, I believe, it becomes easier to see the bind of knowledge and fantasy, power and pleasure, that informs the particular regime of visibility deployed in colonial discourse. The visibility of the racial/colonial other is at once a *point* of identity "Look at a negro" and at the same time a *problem* for the attempted closure within discourse. For the recognition of difference as "imaginary" points of identity and origin—such as black and white—is disturbed by the representation of splitting in the discourse. What I called the play between the metaphoric/narcissistic and metonymic/aggressive moments in colonial discourse—that four-part strategy of the stereotype—crucially recognizes the prefiguring of desire as a potentially conflictual, disturbing force in all those regimes of the "originary" that I have brought together. In the objectification of the scopic drive there is always the threatened return of the look; in the identification of the Imaginary relation there is always the alienating other (or mirror) which crucially returns its image to the subject; and in that form of substitution and fixation that is fetishism there is always the trace of loss, absence. To put it succinctly, the recognition and disavowal of "difference" is always disturbed by the question of its re-presentation or construction. The stereotype is, in fact, an impossible object. For that very reason, the exertions of the "official knowledges" of colonialism—pseudo-scientific, typological, legal-administrative, eugenicist—are imbricated at the point of their production of meaning and power with the fantasy that dramatizes the impossible desire for a pure, undifferentiated origin. Not itself the object of desire but its setting; not an ascription of prior identities but their production in the syntax of the scenario of racist discourse; colonial fantasy plays a crucial part in those everyday scenes of subjectification in a colonial society that Fanon refers to repeatedly. Like fantasies of the origins of sexuality, the productions of colonial desire mark the discourse as *a favored spot for the most primitive defensive reactions such a turning against oneself, into an opposite, projection, negation.*[26]

The problem of origin as the problematic of racist, stereotypical knowledge is a complex one and what I have said about its construction will come clear in this illustration from Fanon. Stereotyping is not the setting up of a false image which becomes the scapegoat of discriminatory practices. It is a much more ambivalent text of projection and introjection, metaphoric and metonymic strategies, displacement, overdetermination, guilt, aggressivity; the masking and splitting of "official" and fantasmatic knowledges to construct the positionalities and oppositionalities of racist discourse:

> *My body was given back to me sprawled out, distorted, recolored, clad in mourning in that white winter day. The Negro is an animal, the Negro is bad, the Negro is mean, the Negro is ugly; look, a nigger, it's cold, the nigger is shivering because he is cold, the little boy is trembling because he is afraid of the nigger, the nigger is shivering with cold, that cold that goes through your bones, the handsome little boy is trembling because he thinks that the nigger is quivering with rage, the little white boy throws himself into his mother's arms: Mama the nigger's going to eat me up.*[27]

It is the scenario of colonial fantasy which, in staging the ambivalence of desire, articulates the demand for the negro which the negro disrupts. For the stereotype is at once a substitute and a shadow. By acceding to the wildest fantasies (in the popular sense) of the colonizer, the stereotyped other reveals something of the fantasy (as desire, defense) of that position of mastery. For if "skin" in racist discourse is the visibility of darkness, and a prime signifier of the body and its social and cultural correlates, then we are bound to remember what Karl Abraham says in his seminal work on the scopic drive.[28] The pleasure-value of darkness is a withdrawal in order to know nothing of the external world. Its symbolic meaning, however, is thoroughly ambivalent. Darkness signifies at once birth and death; it is in all cases a desire to return to the fullness of the mother, a desire for an unbroken and undifferentiated line of vision and origin.

But surely there is another scene of colonial discourse; where the subverting "split" is recuperable within a strategy of social and political control. It is recognizably true that the chain of stereotypical signification is curiously mixed and split, polymorphous and perverse. The black is both savage (cannibal) and yet the most obedient and dignified of servants (the bearer of food); he is the embodiment of rampant sexuality and yet innocent as a child; he is mystical, primitive, simple-minded and yet the most worldly and accomplished liar, and manipulator of social forces. In each case what is being dramatized is a separation−*between* races, cultures, histories, *within* histories−a separation between *before* and *after* that repeats obsessively the mythical moment of disjunction. Despite the structural similarities with the play of need and desire in primal fantasies, the colonial fantasy does not try to cover up that moment of separation. It is more ambivalent. On the one hand, it proposes a teleology−under certain conditions of colonial domination and control the native is progressively reformable. On the other, however, it effectively displays the "separation," makes it more visible. It is the visibility of this separation which, in denying the colonized capacities of self-government, independence, western modes of civility, lends authority to the official version and mission of colonial power. Colonial fantasy is the continual dramatization of emergence—of difference, freedom—as the beginning of a history which is repetitively denied. Such a denial is the clearly voiced demand of colonial discourse as the legitimization of a form of rule that is facilitated by the racist fetish. In concluding, I would like to develop a little further my working definitions of colonial discourse given at the start of this paper.

Racist stereotypical discourse, in its colonial moment, inscribes a form of governmentality that is informed by a productive splitting in its constitution of knowledge and exercise of power. Some of its practices recognize the differences of race, culture, history as elaborated by stereotypical knowledges, racial theories, administrative colonial experience, and on that basis institutionalize a range of political and cultural ideologies that are prejudicial, discriminatory, vestigial, archaic, "mythical" and, crucially, are recognized as being so. By knowing the native population in these terms, discriminatory and authoritarian forms of political control are considered appropriate. The colonized population is then deemed to be both the cause and effect of the system, imprisoned in the circle of interpretation. What is visible is the *necessity* of such rule which is justified by those moralistic and normative ideologies of amelioration recognized as the "civilizing mission" or the "white man's burden." However, there coexists within the same apparatus of colonial power, modern systems and sciences of government, progressive western forms of social and economic organization which provide the manifest justification for the project of colonialism—an argument which, in part, impressed Karl Marx. It is on the site of this coexistence that strategies of hierarchization and marginalization are employed in the management of colonial societies. And if my deduction from Fanon about the peculiar visibility of colonial power is acceptable to you, then I would extend it to say that it is a form of governmentality in which the ideological space functions in more openly collaborative ways with political and economic exigencies. The barracks stand by the church which stands by the schoolroom; the cantonment stands hard by the "civil lines." Such visibility of the institutions and apparatuses of power is possible because the exercise of colonial power makes their *relationship* obscure, produces them as fetishes, spectacles of a naturalized racial preeminence. Only the seat of government is everywhere—alien and separate by that distance upon which surveillance depends for its strategies of objectification, normalization and discipline.

1. Edward Said, "Orientalism Reconsidered," in *Literature, Politics and Theory: Papers from the Essex Conference 1976-84*, eds. Francis Barker, et al.(New York: Methuen, 1986), pp. 210-229.
2. Francis Barker, et al., eds., *Europe and Its Others*, 2 vols. (Colchester: University of Essex Press, 1985); "'Race,' Writing and Difference," *Critical Inquiry*, no. XII (1985); and Henry Louis Gates, ed., *Black Literature and Literary Theory* (New York: Methuen, 1984).

3. Stephan Feuchtwang, "Socialist, Feminist and Anti-racist Struggles" *m/f*, no. 4 (1980): 41.
4. Mark Cousins, "The Logic of Deconstruction," in *The Oxford Literary Review*, no. 3 (1978): 76.
5. Jacques Derrida, *Positions*, trans. Alan Bass (London, 1981).
6. Stephen Heath, "Film and System, Terms of Analysis," *Screen*, vol. XVI, no. 1/2 (1975): 93.
7. Charles Temple, "The Native Races and Their

Rulers," excerpted in P.D. Curtin, *Imperialism* (London, 1971), pp. 93-104.

8. Edward Said, *Orientalism* (London, 1978), p. 72.

9. Ibid., p. 206.

10. Ibid., p. 273.

11. Ibid., p. 58-59.

12. Michel Foucault, *Power/Knowledge: Selected Interviews and Other Writings 1972-1977*, ed. Colin Gordon (Brighton, 1980), p. 196.

13. Ibid., p. 195

14. See Sigmund Freud, "Fetishism," in *On Sexuality* (Harmondsworth, 1981), p. 345; for fetishism and "the Imaginary Signifier" see Christian Metz, *Psychoanalysis and Cinema* (London, 1982), ch. 5. See also Steve Neale, "The Same Old Story: Stereotypes and Differences," *Screen Education* (1979/80): 32-33, 33-37.

15. Frantz Fanon, *Black Skin White Masks*, trans. Charles Lam Markmann (London, 1970), pp. 78-82.

16. Fanon, *Black Skin White Masks*, p. 69.

17. Metz, "The Imaginary Signifier," pp. 56-60.

18. For the best account of Lacan's concept of the Imaginary see Jacqueline Rose, "The Imaginary," in *The Talking Cure: Essays in Psychoanalysis and Language*, ed. Colin MacCabe (London, 1981), pp. 132-61.

19. Fanon, *Black Skin White Masks*, p. 114

20. Freud, "Fetishism," pp. 357.

21. Frantz Fanon, *The Wretched of the Earth*, trans. Constance Farrington (Harmondsworth, 1969), p. 31.

22. Paul Abbott, "On Authority," *Screen*, vol. XX, no. 2 (1979): 15-16.

23. Ibid., p. 16.

24. Fanon, *Black Skin White Masks*, p. 79.

25. Metz, "The Imaginary Signifier," p. 70.

26. J. Laplanche and J.B. Pontalis, "Phantasy (or fantasy)," *The Language of Psychoanalysis* (London, 1980), p. 318.

27. Fanon, *Black Skin White Masks*, p. 80.

28. Karl Abraham, "Transformations of Scopophilia," in *Selected Papers in Psychoanalysis* (London, 1978), pp. 169-234.

• **Simon Watney**

Missionary Positions: AIDS, "Africa," and Race

The discursive regularities of Western AIDS commentary are nowhere more apparent than in the construction of "African AIDS."[1] In *Newsweek* in 1986 a French doctor was quoted as saying: "It's difficult using these words, but (in Africa) we risk an apocalypse."[2] A year later *The Guardian* described a "leading doctor" in Uganda who "believes that next year will be apocalyptic."[3] Again in 1986, *Newsweek* informed its readers that in Kinshasa: "Some joke that the French acronym for AIDS, SIDA (Syndrome d'Immune-Déficitaire Acquis), stands for Syndrome Imaginaire pour Décourager les Amoureux."[4] In the same year Thomson Prentice reported back to readers of *The Times* that the citizens of Kinshasa joke that: "the French acronym for the illness, Sida, actually stood for Syndrome Imaginaire pour Décourager les Amoureux."[5] And as recently as July 1988, Alex Shoumatoff flew all the way back from Zaire to reveal in *Vanity Fair* that: "there is a joke in Kinshasa that Sida stands for Syndrome Imaginaire pour Décourager les Amoureux."[6]

Such repetitions already suggest something of the "mise en discours" of "African AIDS," and its potential for fomenting displacements. In a three-part series of reports entitled "*Africa's New Agony*," Prentice set the familiar stage: "young men suddenly grown old . . . haggard mothers with sickly children clinging to their backs . . . For the foreseeable future, they will be confronted by a hideous, unimaginable disaster."[7] A doctor in Burundi states that: "Telling people that they could die from a sexually transmitted disease is unlikely to have much impact. They think it's just the church preaching at them. But if we tell women that they may give birth to infected children who will die because of parental promiscuity, there may be a chance of changing their behavior." The situation in "Africa" is offered as a premonitory image of "our" future in Europe and the United States, as planes fly out carrying away "the seeds of infection, to be planted on foreign soil."

In the third article, headlined "Nightmare of a Raddled City," Kinshasa is the central focus, with its "unenviable name of the AIDS capital of Africa," where, "even today, donor blood is not comprehensively screened for the AIDS virus. Tragic but predictable then, that 31 percent of children with AIDS in a city hospital have a history of blood transfusions. Tragic, too, that a fatal flaw in the maternal instincts of most African women leads them to choose injections rather than pills for sick babies." According to Prentice, "many men, if not most, have numerous liaisons with different women, including prostitutes, who have been clearly identified in Kinshasa and elsewhere as reservoirs of AIDS infection . . . Promiscuity and lack of medical resources have made Kinshasa the AIDS capital of the world." The sudden leap from being "AIDS capital of Africa" to "AIDS capital of the world" is strongly indicative of the anxieties which inform and motivate such commentary, which need to be unpicked in some detail.

It is evident that Prentice's narrative and iconography operate within a long discursive tradition which finds perhaps its most complete description in Joseph Conrad's *Heart of Darkness*.[8] The former's "young men suddenly grown old" are indistinguishable from the latter's dying man who "seemed young–almost a boy–but you know with them it's hard to tell."[9] The image of "hideous, unimaginable disaster" also speaks directly of an Africa constituted in inscrutability, a "treacherous" domain of "lurking death" and "hidden evil." Its people are so hopelessly sunk in depravity and licentiousness that education is impossible, unthinkable. These "people" can only be frightened into measures which supposedly will save their lives. Yet these measures amount to only one thing–monogamy, understood as the only effective prophylactic against HIV infection. Two points immediately stand out. First, if "Africa" is as saturated with HIV as is suggested, monogamy as such is unlikely to provide any protection against transmission. The text is telling us that these "people" can and must die, but they should at least have the "decency" to do so within the moral conventions of Christian marriage. Second, the text concedes that these "people" are only too well aware of the missionary imperative: "They think it's just the church preaching at them." What we actually learn here is that the population of Burundi operates a highly sophisticated de-coding of Western "information," understanding its motives only too clearly. Any seeming concern for the lives of the populations described is entirely secondary to the larger ideological imperatives of Western AIDS commentary, as it redraws the epidemic in the likeness of older colonial beliefs and values, targeted at the assumed (white) reader. I use the term "AIDS commentary" to refer to the complex discursive field in which AIDS is used to signify the interests of many different institutions, from government to the press: commentary that may be characterized by: "its repetitions, its slippages, its omissions, its emphases, its 'no-go' areas, its narrative patterns, and so on."[10]

Rather than acknowledge the actual diversity and complexity of human sexuality, this commentary exhorts us all to reduce the numbers of our sexual partners, rather than address the potentially embarrassing question of sexual behavior. Such commentary is far more interested in stopping "promiscuity" than it is in stopping the transmission of HIV. Committed in advance to the hypothesis that HIV originated somewhere in Central or Eastern Africa, such journalism wreaks its own sadistic "revenge." Hence the otherwise frankly extraordinary picture of "a fatal flaw in the maternal instincts of African women," who somehow are supposed to have understood the modes of transmission of HIV long before the research teams at the C.D.C. and the Pasteur Institute in Paris. The maternal fecundity of this imaginary "Africa" becomes the target for particular hatred. Thus any woman whose sexuality cannot immediately be classified within the terms of Christian monogamy becomes a "prostitute" and, as such, deserves to die. Moreover, she is the author of her own destruction, rather than someone who has herself been infected by a man. "Africa" emerges, as in Conrad, in "a wild and gorgeous apparition of a woman." A woman moreover whose fascination speaks too much of

Western sexuality, and its ever attendant poles of disgust and attraction, contempt and desire.

A year later Peter Murtagh wrote a similar three-part series entitled "AIDS in Africa" for *The Guardian*. Each section begins with the image of a woman–a prostitute, a woman with AIDS, and a nurse. The opening lines prepare us for the familiar genre of AIDS-safari reportage: "The best time to observe the Nairobi hooker is at dusk when the tropical sun dips beneath the Rift Valley and silhouettes the thorn trees against the African skyline."[11] According to Murtagh, East African truck drivers "like nothing better than to round off a day's work by visiting a prostitute." Prostitutes, truck drivers and their respective families are all carefully distinguished from "the general population." Writing of British soldiers stationed in Kenya, he describes how: "The futility of trying to keep the soldiers and women apart was evident last week by the numbers of men from the 2nd. Battalion of the Parachute Regiment in the bars and discos of Nairobi." This certainly gives the lie to his report in the same newspaper a month later, where he claimed that "prostitutes, who are regarded as the main potential AIDS carriers likely to have contact with soldiers, follow the troops to wherever they take their leave."[12] One cannot avoid asking who is following whom.

In his second article, "Death is Simply a Fact of Life," Murtagh introduces Josephine Nnagingo, who "lives in a mud and wattle farmhouse in the middle of her family's field of banana trees not far from Kyotera, a few miles from the shores of Lake Victoria in southern Uganda." She is dying from AIDS, and "the wasting of her shrunken body has made her head appear outsized, and her dress is now too big for her. Her arms and legs are desperately thin, and she moves only with pain." In some districts "deaths in the houses have prompted survivors to flee in the belief that the buildings themselves are in some way responsible for the illness." Recourse to witch-doctors, herbal remedies and talismans are all detailed, together with the warning that because hospitals are overwhelmed, and patients prefer to live at home in their villages, "figures for the numbers of AIDS deaths may not be accurate."

His series ended with a final article entitled "Sickening of a Continent," in which one doctor concludes that "if we do not beat AIDS it will be the end of a continent." This sits ironically beside a description of a Catholic nurse, Sister Miriam, who "cannot bring herself to advocate the use of condoms. 'Church teaching is one man, one woman and no sex before marriage. I'm not going to go against theology,' she said." Another nurse can identify people with HIV "by the way they look. They have a kind of listlessness." Yet we already always know these scenes, from a host of sources which, like Conrad, depict the spectacle of black Africans "dying slowly . . . nothing but black shadows of disease and starvation . . . The black bones reclined at full length . . . and slowly the eyelids rose and the sunken eyes looked up at me, enormous and vacant."[13] It is as if HIV were a disease of "African-ness," the viral embodiment of a long legacy of colonial imagery which naturalizes the devastating economic and social effects of European colonialism in the likeness of starvation–bodies reduced to "bundles of acute angles."[14] Hence the significance of a recent advertising campaign on behalf of the British charity, the National Campaign for the Prevention of Cruelty to Children (NCPCC), which shows the emaciated body of a small child with the accompanying caption: "Four years old. Seriously underweight for her age. Scavenging for food where she can find it. And she's English." For "English" read "white." Whilst such advertisements evidently derive from very different institutional sources, they none the less draw upon presumed long-standing "knowledge" concerning the supposedly correct relations between England and "Africa," between whites and blacks. This "knowledge" is constituted in the complex discursive legacy of British colonial history, sedimented over the course of many centuries, and centrally involved in the formation of British national cultural identities, as much in their acceptance as in their contestation. Hence the need to understand that the language of metaphor that informs so much African AIDS commentary carries a very specific ideological cargo, and nowhere more so than in talk of the "heart of Africa."

Alex Shoumatoff's lengthy *Vanity Fair* article "In Search of the Source of AIDS" begins with a piece of typical scene-setting: "The heart of Africa is stricken. The 'AIDS belt' is spreading, and the disease that has already claimed the lives of thousands of men, women, and children will claim millions more. *Vanity Fair* sent Alex Shoumatoff on a journey of exploration along the equator; where he met the fatalistic bar-girls of Kinshasa, the exhausted doctors of war-shattered Uganda, the folk-healers of Guinea-Bissau, and the plague-ridden smugglers of Lake Victoria. Is this a nightmare vision of our own future?" And set against a photograph of a vast expanse of water we read the caption: "Lake Victoria, deep in the heart of darkest Africa, is on some level, perhaps only mythical, the font of AIDS."

"How curious it would be," thinks Shoumatoff idly to himself, "if the source of the Nile and the source of AIDS prove to be one and the same, that huge teeming lake in the dangerous heart of darkest Africa." He asks about the number of local cases, but "having been through this several times before in the Third World, I know it is futile to expect reliable figures." The Ugandans he talks to think that HIV is transmitted "mainly by sex but sometimes by witchcraft against debt welshers." They are thus set up as authentic "natives"–unreliable, superstitious, in a word, primitive. Arriving in Bissau he notes: "There were no whores on the premises, as there usually are in African hostelries." There is a striking parallel here to the earlier observation by an American doctor describing the situation in Kigali in Rwanda where: "The small number of prostitutes who are inconspicuously present on the streets are believed to be a prime source of spreading AIDS."[15] The figure of the prostitute is necessary, as presence or absence. The local Director of Public Health informs Shoumatoff that "the patients and their families were not being told what they had. Most of the public did not know that nasty little microbes were on the loose, threatening to kill them. They still believed that irãs, the spirits, were the cause of sickness and death. In some ways [he] observed, the viruses had a lot in common with the irãs: they were invisible, their existence had to be taken on faith, and one was powerless against them."

Quite apart from Shoumatoff's evident inability to distinguish between microbes and viruses, we should immediately note the infantalizing tone. In the logic of racism, it stands to reason that one talks to child-like black Africans about "nasty little microbes" rather than modes of transmission. Yet countless surveys demonstrate that irrational beliefs concerning the (non-existent) threat of miasmatic contagion from HIV are at least as prevalent in the West as any Ugandan faith in irãs. It is particularly unpleasant to find people's lay beliefs held up for mockery in a context in which they have evidently been systematically denied access to any other sources of information–they "were not being told what they had." The complete failure to recognize this double-standard is hardly surprising from a writer who casually wonders if the local "weaseloid carnivores" had been tested for retroviruses. Shoumatoff also casually accepts the notion of a Simian origin for HIV, six months after the definitive rejection of the theory by the same Harvard scientists who first proposed it in 1985.[16] Such a cavalier attitude towards virological evidence is entirely in keeping with the belief that the current crisis of public health and health care provision may be attributed to the "withdrawal" (as he curiously puts it) of Belgian colonial authority in 1960, rather than to the long-term effects of colonialism itself. This is rather like attributing the current economic crisis in Vietnam to the "withdrawal" of American troops, rather than the Vietnam wars and the subsequent punitive denial of Western funding.

However, as we have seen, Shoumatoff "knows" his Africa, just as he "knows" that "the Western gays who participated in la ronde of bar sex and promiscuity were in fact suffering from an infectious-disease burden very similar to the Africans." Once the notion of "promiscuity" has been medicalized in this way, a Royal Road of analogy is opened up between the different groups first affected by HIV. Already regarding black Africans and gay men as effectively interchangeable, a convenient "intestinal-parasite co-factor theory" can be invoked, claiming that "Africans, Haitians, and many Western homosexual men are riddled with amoebas." Thus Africa becomes a "deviant" continent, just as Western gay men are effectively Africanized. Returning to Masaka, in Uganda, our intrepid hero finds that "the only place still open is a bar, where we wash down chapatis with Bell beer. It is the most degenerate scene, the closest thing to Sodom I have ever seen. Guys completely bombed, with girls on their laps etc. Obviously nobody cares about getting AIDS." Everything here hangs upon the unelaborated "etc.," for if getting drunk with a girl on one's knee is Sodom, then Sodom is an extensive province indeed. According to *Newsweek* in 1986 it undoubtedly extends well into Tanzania, where the town of Kashenye in the Kagera region "was like Sodom and Gomorrah" with "wild parties, orgies."[17]

Equatorial Africa is so primitive ("unreliable") that "most tribes . . . don't even seem to have a word for homosexual," although "homosexuality is very taboo." This observation is strikingly similar to that of an anthropologist from Berkeley who recently commented in *The Guardian* that in Brazil "a great many men who engage in same-sex interactions simply don't identify themselves as homosexuals or bisexuals."[18] It is clear that the relatively recent emergence of the classificatory system of Western sexuality is by now as completely taken for granted and de-historicized as Linnaean taxonomy.

Shoumatoff concludes his article with a familiar valedictory slip-stream of *de riguer* anxieties. "I thought how HIV must have become airborne–airplane-borne–moving . . . from continent to continent: tens of thousands of revelers flying down to Rio for Carnival for instance . . . I imagined this archetypal communicable disease travelling along the mutually manipulative interface of the First and Third Worlds in countless copulations," through the Far East and on into "the Arab world, where the predilection for buggery will provide a brisk amplification system." He also ponders mightily on "the unprecedented merging and mixing and growing together of the world's population in the last four decades," and it struck him that "for a microcosm of the melting-pot process, one had to look no further than this completely booked and waitlisted Rome-New York jumbo 747. Among the four hundred passengers winging their way to the great land whose politically admirable but epidemiologically lamentable motto is *E Pluribus Unum* were Indians and Arab, Venezuelans, Poles, Africans, Israelis, Italians, Turks and Bulgarians, not to mention Americans of assorted hues and stripes—a rich cross section of the human cornucopia. . . . Statistically three people aboard ought to be carrying the virus."

All of this might seem a good case for international HIV screening, if one is not aware of the World Health Organization's detailed statistical analysis of the problems of sensitivity and specificity (accuracy in identifying true HIV positives and true negatives) which are inseparable from large-scale HIV testing.[19] As the WHO consultation points out, "HIV screening programmes for international travellers would, at best and at *great cost*, retard *only briefly* the dissemination of HIV both globally and with respect to any particular country." Besides, the imagery of "airborne" HIV only serves to draw attention sooner or later to profound unacknowledged fears concerning the (non-existent) miasmatic transmission of the virus, which are rationalized and displaced across the field of international travel. This in turn seems to be closely connected to an equally deep-seated fear of racial miscegenation. How else should we account for the patently absurd fantasy that international travel is a function of jet propulsion? The "forgetting" that is going on here concerns a far simpler mode of transport in a far earlier period—the galleys and galleons of the international slave trade, which carried another "cross section of the human cornucopia" across from Africa to the Americas. It is the power of disease to effect such displacements and "forgettings" to which we should now turn our attention.

AIDS in "Africa" versus "African AIDS"

The rising rates of HIV infection and AIDS in central and eastern Africa have been widely recognized since the early 1980's, with the highest cumulative numbers of cases in descending order from Uganda, Tanzania, Kenya, The Congo, Burundi, Rwanda, Zambia, and Malawi, to Zaire. It is important to recognize that every country affected by HIV has its own epidemic, shaped by a multitude of variable local factors, amongst which the circumstances of the population groups affected first by the virus are the most important. In this respect the notion of "African AIDS" already obscures the specific characteristics of the different AIDS epidemics in these countries, constructing them in the spurious unity of an "Africa" which is immediately denied any of the cultural, social, economic and ethnic diversity which are taken for granted in Europe and North or South America.

As a cultural and psychic construction, "African AIDS" exhibits at least five consistent aspects. First, it speaks of a peculiar and special affinity between a virus and a continent. Second, it reads the modes of transmission of HIV as signs of a generalized and homogenous African "primitiveness," whether sexual or medical. Third, it singles out the alleged "mis-reporting" of African HIV and AIDS statistics as further evidence of "backwardness" and "unreliability." Fourth, it equates black Africans and Western gay men as willful "perverts" who are equally threatening to "family values." Fifth, it regards "Africa" as the source of the HIV infection in the sense of origin and of *cause*. Whilst none of these aspects are individually specific to the issue of AIDS, their collective configuration is, I believe, unprecedented. The construction of "African AIDS" tells us much about the West, and its major strategies of self-knowledge, rooted in systems of difference and Otherness. But even more importantly, it serves to justify and validate the continued, genocidal indifference to the long-term consequences of HIV infection amongst people of color. It is here that we can map out the complex relations between racial and sexual boundaries which legitimate and make possible the casual contemplation of the virtual extinction of all black Africans and all gay men.[20]

1. *The Infectious Continent*

Patrick Brantlinger has acutely observed how "racism often functions as a displaced or surrogate class system, growing more extreme as the domestic class alignments it reflects are threatened or eroded. As a rationalization for the domination of 'inferior' peoples, imperialist discourse is inevitably racist; it treats race and class terminology as covertly interchangeable or at least analogous. Both a hierarchy of classes and a hierarchy of races exist; both are the results of evolution or of the laws of nature; both are simpler than but similar to species; and both are developing but are also, at any given moment, fixed, inevitable, not subject to political manipulation."[21]

"African AIDS" emerges with a similar effect of inevitability, condensing the distinct issues of a virus with clearly established modes of transmission, and a syndrome of more than forty distinct opportunistic conditions which may appear in the wake of HIV's progressive weakening of the body's immunological defenses. Hence the relentless misclassification of "African AIDS" as a *disease*, a seemingly "natural" result of sexual "treachery" which is also aspective of the "treachery" of Africa itself. The symptoms of this *ideological* "African AIDS disease" are also immediately identifiable as evidence of some innate "African-ness"—lassitude, extreme weight-loss, huge staring eyes—the only too familiar signs of famine, but in this instance supposedly "caused" by excessive (sexual) appetite. The identification "African" thus slides directly into the diagnosis, "AIDS." An entire continent may be infected because its peoples and its physical geography are held as one. "African AIDS" thus legitimates and "proves" the fantasy of intrinsic correspondences between environment, character, and physical health—constructing "Africa" as an undifferentiated domain of rot, slime, filth, decay, disease, and naked "animal" blackness. This infernal and unhygienic territory is the perfect imaginary swamp in which a new virus might "percolate," as Shoumatoff so revealingly speculates—a virus which eventually kills by transforming all its "victims" into "Africans," and which threatens to "Africanize" the entire world . . .

2. *AIDS and "The Primitive"*

Writing of Africa, *Newsweek* recently reported that: "Today, in the zones of highest infestation, AIDS pervades everyday life."[22] It is highly unlikely that the same journalist would ever describe London or New York as "infested" with AIDS. The heads of the poor may be infested with lice, and a rotting corpse may be infested with maggots. Thus First World cities are merely "affected" by AIDS, though black or Hispanic or gay communities within them may be "devastated." The rhetoric of infestation is reserved for a continent which is always known in advance to be polluted and pestilential. The images of liquidity and putrefaction which are so indispensable to "African AIDS" commentary speak of a coital condensation in which Africa, understood as the font of human life, is confused with Africa the supposed "font of AIDS."[23] This *maternal* Africa is subject to the phantasmatic projections of her Western "sons," locked in the double difference of race and gender—white and male, repulsed and desiring. The flow of Africa is the flow of the mother's body, the atavistic source of life *and* death.

It is clear that the evolutionary model of the social sciences which was established in the second half of the nineteenth century grounded a narrowly restrictive picture of "higher" human nature in a series of contrasts with "the primitive." To leave Africa is to be purified, to return to "the light," which is also repression. "African AIDS" must, therefore, always be presented as *sui generis*, a completely different disease from AIDS in the First World. Indeed, most commentators have preferred almost *any* explanation for the 1:1 AIDS ratio of men to women in most African countries, rather than that of heterosexual transmission. These "explanations" including cannibalism, bestiality, ritual scarification, violent sex and so on, bear a striking similarity to the "weird customs" catalogued by Rider Haggard and his contemporaries. As long ago as 1985 Dr. Angus Dalgleish reported on behalf of an extensive field survey conducted by researchers from the London Institute of Cancer Research, that: "We investigated and ruled out all other factors in the disease's spread—except heterosexual activity."[24] Yet the cultural logic remains: "primitive" Africa generates "African AIDS"—"civilized" Europeans and Americans (white, heterosexual) are safe.

3. *Fun With Figures*

"Primitive" Africa is also inscribed in the field of epidemiology. The "under-reporting" of HIV and AIDS statistics from African nations has long been a familiar trope in "African AIDS" commentary, generally attributed either to "poor facilities" or the mendacity of individual governments. Yet it should be recognized that by their nature, such figures can *never* be precise, and further, that their relative accuracy is no more characteristic of Zaire or Uganda than they are of Texas or the United Kingdom.

For example, there are strong social and economic disincentives to HIV antibody testing in Britain, where ignorance and prejudice abound against those known to be infected. Nor is there any legislation (or hope of legislation) to protect the most fundamental rights to employment or housing or insurance for infected individuals or members of the social constituencies in which HIV was widely transmitted before its existence was known or even suspected. We should also recognize that most people at high potential risk of infection have long since taken measures to minimize any chance of viral transmission. Hence the dramatic fall in new infections among gay men in Britain and elsewhere in recent years. In such circumstances the principal reason for testing would be to obtain drug treatments, in the form of anti-virals, immune-stimulants, or prophylaxes against individual opportunistic conditions. Sadly, financial cuts in the National Health Service have made such treatment drugs unequally available in Britain, and government White Papers on the future of the NHS have made a difficult situation worse.

Doctors also frequently fail to diagnose AIDS, since they mistakenly assume that it is only to be found in the inner cities, or because their acceptance of sexual stereotypes means that they simply don't realize that their patients are at risk. In both circumstances the larger cultural climate surrounding the epidemic affects HIV and AIDS statistics by reinforcing highly misleading notions about "the promiscuous" or "gay men" or "injecting drug users," as if these were all instantly identifiable. The widespread shaming of people with AIDS in the First World, together with their families, lovers and friends, has also led many doctors to attribute deaths to individual opportunistic conditions, rather than naming the syndrome on death certificates, in order to "spare" the bereaved. This is entirely understandable, and moreover, is clinically correct. But it does not serve to clarify the epidemiological profile of the British AIDS epidemic. A recent report that "doctors should no longer assume the elderly do not get AIDS" only further reinforces the extraordinary ignorance and naivety among many doctors concerning the actual complexity of sexual and drug using behavior, across all social barriers of class, race, age and gender.[25] In such circumstances the repeated emphasis on the "under-reporting" or "mis-reporting" of "African AIDS" statistics only serves to reinforce prevailing notions of African "primitiveness," whilst masking the brutal forces which constantly skew European and American figures concerning the incidence and prevalence of both HIV and AIDS.

"Primitive" Africa also emerges in relation to countless anecdotes concerning "dirty" hospitals, "out of date" medical equipment, the sharing of syringes, and so on. What is at stake here, however, is not the fact of poverty or the effects of post-colonial disruption throughout central Africa, but the implication that "African AIDS" can be explained away as a by-product of "African medicine," with the assumption that Western medicine is invariably "better" and more "advanced." Everything in this distinction depends upon the value we place on the *look* of high technology. Whilst experimental drug trials take place widely in the United States, they are restricted to those who can either afford them, or who are fortunate enough to be insured. The fundamental injustice of American private medicine is thus erased by the image of gleaming chromium. This is particularly regrettable since it also obscures the fact that health insurance is unavailable to those categorized as members of "high-risk groups." In this manner, *demographic* factors such as gender, marital status, and even postal localities, has been substituted for actual risk factors, which include the possible sharing of needles, and the question of whether individuals are having Safer Sex or not. In the meantime, fears that the US public health system may collapse under the strain of the epidemic will continue to reflect the originating mythology of "African AIDS," rather than the prior structural inadequacies of American health care provision.

4. *Monstrous Passions*

In 1897 the missionary Joseph Johnston noted that he had been "increasingly struck with the rapidity with which such members of the white race as are not of the best class, can throw over the restraints of civilization and develop into savages of unbridled lust and abominable cruelty."[26] Another missionary "believed that merely witnessing heathen customs could be dangerous: 'Can a man touch pitch and not be defiled?' "[27] The narrator in Conrad's *Heart of Darkness* struggles to explain: "You can't understand. How could you?—with solid pavements under your feet, surrounded by kind neighbors ready to cheer you or to fall on you . . . how can you imagine what particular region of the first ages of a man's untrammelled feet may take him into by the way of solitude."[28] In all these texts, and countless like them, we may identify "the heavy, mute spell of the wilderness," drawing white men "to its pitiless breast by the awakening of forgotten and brutal instincts, by the memory of gratified and monstrous passions."[29]

These passions, too monstrous to name, are outwardly sanctioned in the projective image of Africa as the "wild and gorgeous apparition of a woman."[30] As early as 1758 Linnaeus had contrasted the "caprice" of Africans to the "customs" of Europeans.[31] Lacking "restraint," like Conrad's Mr. Kurtz, or merely deprived of neighborly "customs," the white man is uniquely vulnerable to the temptation to "go native." Yet this temptation is always ambiguous, since it is at once a return to Nature and the Unnatural. Moreover, the "monstrous passions" which Africa awakes, have evidently already been "gratified." A series of complex analogies thus become possible in colonial discourse. For the child-like "primitive" is immediately identified as a sexual adult *and* as a sexually active child. There is also a close parallel between the anthropological attention to African sexuality, illustrated in the lantern-light of eugenic theory, and the equally spectacular inventory of "the perversions," so painstakingly catalogued by the early sexologists. Blacks and "perverts" alike were held to share the characteristics of unbridled sexual rapacity and low cunning. They might also, however, be led to at least the semblance of normality—the former as a result of missionary zeal, and the latter by "therapeutic" initiatives.

In spite of the widespread acceptance of more pluralistic models of both human societies and sexuality in the twentieth century, the national-popular of the West remains strongly influenced by the notion of a single, linear model of human cultural evolution, and an equally over-simplified picture of normative psycho-sexual "development." At many levels of popular culture, including folklore, children's fiction, cinema, the press, and gossip and jokes, blacks and gay men remain curiously linked—the two great indispensable Others in the operations of postmodern governmentality.[32] Given the widespread revival of evangelical Christian and "pro-family" currents in contemporary Anglo-American political culture, we may fairly detect significant parallels between the hystericized anxieties concerning the "threat" of white colonialists "going native," and modern fears about the possibility of "innocent" heterosexuals "going gay." At a time when homosexuality in Western societies is once more regarded as a critical "problem," AIDS has been widely used to reinforce the boundaries of object-choice. Hence the widespread tendency of Western governments to emphasize the "threat" of HIV "leaking" from the social constituencies affected most severely by AIDS, into the newly designated "heterosexual community."[33] The recent emergence of this extraordinary category is only comprehensible as an expression of the cultural paranoia which still regards HIV as an innately black or gay condition, the scourge of "perverts," against which only "the family" can prevail.

Ronald Hyams has argued that "the willingness of Victorian Britons to endure the deprivations involved in working overseas probably depended quite crucially on the easy availability of a range of sexual consolations."[34] It is only too easy to identify the psychic structures of denial and defence which register transgression on such a scale—the "horror" of "going native," which is in turn closely paralleled in our times by excessive responses to the intrinsically unremarkable fact of sexual diversity. Just as the figure of "the prostitute" is habitually regarded as a source rather than a victim of disease, so we may trace out the pattern of displacements which offer us a carnal Africa as the "source" of AIDS, transported home to the bosom of the white Western family via the "monstrous passions" of "perverts" and "the promiscuous." Anything which threatens this fantasy must be ruthlessly denied. Anything which suggests the actual complexity and diversity of human sexuality must be censored. Hence the discursive necessity for a non-Western point of origin for AIDS, and the requirement that "perverts" be held responsible as culpable intermediaries.

5. Fons et origen

Infectious disease has long provided the fundamental epistemological model for Western medicine, with its familiar narrative of identification/diagnosis, treatment, and cure. Indeed, it is precisely this model that historians have already used to "explain" the history of AIDS, which is frequently compared to the earlier histories of syphilis and cholera in such a way that the specific dimensions of racism, misogyny, and homophobia are entirely erased from consideration.[35] With the gradual recognition that environmental change has improved life-expectancy and general public health more effectively than medical interventions, this model has been faced with something of a crisis. This has been reinforced by the parallel recognition that the major threats to late twentieth-century Western health have not been infectious diseases. In this respect HIV has proved something of a Godsend, being widely used to reinstate the authority of a particular medical model of treatment, together with its attendant doctor/patient relations, calculations of risk, and so on. This in turn has tended to deflect attention away from questions of preventative medicine to the possibility of developing a vaccine. It is of course important to recognize that if virologists were able to prove that HIV "mutated from an ancestor virus that caused little harm in humans, or is derived from a closely related virus in animals, then a theoretical chance exists that the ancestor virus might be used to develop a vaccine to protect humans."[36] This is not, however, how "African AIDS" commentary has dealt with the question of the possible origins of HIV. By the late 1980's "many researchers are agreed that the evidence for AIDS originating in Africa is weak."[37] Robert Biggar of the U.S. National Cancer Institute has pointed out that there is no conclusive evidence that HIV "originated in Africa, since the epidemic seemed to start at approximately the same time as in America and Europe."[38] However, as Cindy Patton explains: "The unconscious belief that a strange new virus could not have arisen from the germ-free West led researchers on a fantastic voyage in search of the origin of HIV in Haiti and then in Africa."[39]

Sander Gilman has also argued that: "We need to locate the origin of a disease, since its source, always distant from ourselves in the fantasy land of our fears, gives us assurance that we are not at fault, that we have been invaded from without, that we have been polluted by some external agents."[40] Whilst it is possible to disarticulate the tangled web of racism and homophobia which work to resist or obscure acknowledgement of the intrinsically unremarkable modes of transmission of HIV, we should certainly not conclude that AIDS is not a real and terrible epidemic throughout Central and Eastern Africa. The analysis of the social and psychic construction of "African AIDS" has unfortunately led some commentators to deny the actual scale of AIDS in Africa.[41] At present it seems unlikely that the origins of HIV will ever be precisely established. Yet even if they were, we should not make the absurd mistake of blaming the people of that cultural and geographical locality for its emergence. Indeed, we should constantly be on our guard against any such attempts to blame those affected first by any infectious disease, as if the *source* of a virus were somehow its *cause*.

Conclusion

The construction of "African AIDS" tells us little or nothing of AIDS in Africa, but a very great deal about the changing organization of sexual and racial boundaries in the West, where AIDS has been widely harnessed to the interests of a new hygienic politics of intense moral purity. This new politics aspires to realign national-popular identities, replacing the vulnerable barriers of class identities which can no longer be easily policed, with strongly pathologized distinctions between sexual "normality" and "perversion." As Europe draws together in the likeness of a federation, and as the Soviet Union embarks on the complex road of wholesale democratization, Africa has been effectively demonized, in a post-colonial discourse of perpetual catastrophe and *unnatural* disasters. This undifferentiated apocalyptic Africa has proved an ideal site in which to find and "see" disease. "African AIDS" thus condenses ancient fears concerning contagious disease, together with vengeful fantasies concerning "excessive" sexuality, understood in essentially pre-modern terms as both the *source* and the *cause* of AIDS.

Besides the callous insult which such commentary adds to the tragic injuries of HIV-related disease and human suffering, this reconstitution of "African AIDS" sadly only serves to increase the likelihood of HIV transmission in the West, by deflecting perceptions of risk away from the domestic sphere of white heterosexuals. The racism and homophobia which Western culture has visited on racial and sexual minorities for millennia now threaten to turn back on heterosexuals themselves, in their seeming refusal and inability to acknowledge the realities of HIV infection and disease.[42] It would appear that we are witnessing a fundamental reorganization of Western racism, as the constitutive colonial analogy between race and class is dissolved, and African blackness is reconceptualized as an analogue of the sexually perverse. The relations which emerge between First and Third World blacks is one of the many instabilities which this new alignment opens up. The role of black gay men in this emergent configuration may well prove to be of decisive importance, for they occupy a space of maximum contradiction, since the majority of black and Hispanic American men with AIDS are gay, whilst in

Africa black men who only have sex with one another should be regarded as a low-risk population group for HIV.

The recent insistence by the Primate of Kenya, the Most Rev. Manesses Kuria, that AIDS "is a disease from the sin of homosexuality" suggests a regrettable reaction to the implications of "African AIDS" commentary. This ironically only further serves the interests of Western principles of governmentality. Imposing the restrictive categories of Western sexuality on a global scale threatens to obliterate cultural alternatives which, equally, provide secure social and individual identities.[43] The picture of "African AIDS" is also largely responsible for the climate of increasing hostility and violence to Western lesbians and gay men, of which the notorious "Helms Amendment" and Section 28 of the British 1988 Local Government are the most extreme examples.[44] Cindy Patton has described the "Queer paradigm," according to the logic of which "AIDS has such power as a supposedly 'gay disease' that anyone who gets it becomes 'queer' by association."[45] Yet "African AIDS" is a two-way street, presenting black Africans and gay men as mutual surrogates, whilst steadfastly refusing ever to consider AIDS from the actual lived positions of either group. As "official" state racism directed against the black populations of the First World is slowly delegitimized, AIDS is evidently being used to validate the drawing of new lines of power and popular consent which require the fabrication of new Others, to bolster "healthy" familial identies. The British government already feels sufficiently confident in these strategies to legislate binding distinctions between supposedly "pretended" and "real" families. How Western gay men and Africans can respond to this crisis in both their cultural representation and their objective circumstances remains to be seen. But we should all note as a matter of considerable urgency that when supposedly "democratic" governments feel free to criminalize the so-called "promotion" of homosexuality, they are equally at liberty to prosecute the "promotion" of anything which might be construed as inimical to "public health" or "family values," or "tradition," which may be rewritten daily. In such circumstances it is salutary to recall how Joseph Conrad reversed the terms and values of an earlier moment in the history of racism when, at the beginning of *Heart of Darkness* he invited his readers to imagine the Romans arriving in Britain two thousand years ago, at "the very end of the world, a sea the color of lead, a sky the color of smoke . . . and going up this river with stores, or orders, or what you like. Sand-banks, marshes, forests, savages—precious little to eat fit for a civilized man, nothing but Thames water to drink . . . They must have been dying like flies here."[46] All the evidence suggests that people with AIDS in Africa are treated with all the care and support that their communities can provide. There can be few more starkly telling contrasts in the modern world than between the way in which black African societies treat their sick and dying, and the spectacle of the tens of thousands of Americans with AIDS, few of whom can afford such drug treatments as are available—many of whom are homeless and living out on the streets of New York, Los Angeles, and every major city in the United States. In August 1989 the World Health Organization reported that the Americas constitute 67% of diagnosed cases of AIDS, whilst Africa contains 18% and Europe 14% respectively. Yet the United States government continues to discriminate against foreign nationals with HIV wishing to visit the USA, although it is perfectly clear that the US is the worst affected country in the world.

Such legislation however demonstrates the continued refusal of the US government to acknowledge its democratic responsibilities to US citizens living with HIV and AIDS, or to recognize that visitors to America are far more at risk of contracting HIV from Americans, than Americans are at risk from foreign nationals. By projecting AIDS as an overseas issue the US government and media legitimate a form of ideological isolationism that is only likely to persuade large numbers of US citizens that they are not in fact at risk of HIV if they have unprotected sex with fellow Americans. In Britain, changes in the Social Security Act (1986) have reduced the income of people living with AIDS by up to two thirds, whilst treatment drugs are frequently unavailable, and standards of personal care are highly uneven. In all of this it seems that people with HIV and AIDS are entirely dependent on the limited resources of private charity, rather than the fundamental estimation of needs and rights to adequate health care provisions that obtain elsewhere in the National Health Service.[47] Who in this picture are the "primitives?" Who are the "barbarians?"

This article is dedicated to Paula A. Treichler, whose work on HIV/AIDS provides continual inspiration. Her article "AIDS and HIV Infection In The Third World: A First World Chronicle," in Remaking History, *eds. Barbara Kruger, and Phil Mariani (Seattle: Bay Press, 1989), pp. 31-86, appeared too late for me to refer to in this article. I strongly recommend it to anyone interested in the complex, tragic subject of "African AIDS."*

1. I am indebted to Cindy Patton for the concept of "African AIDS," which she has elaborated in "Inventing African AIDS," *City Limits*, no. 363 (September 15-22, 1988).
2. Rod Nordland, et al., "Africa in the Plague Years," *Newsweek* (December 1, 1986): 44.
3. Peter Murtagh, "AIDS in Africa: A Present from Buffalo Bill," *The Guardian* (February 3, 1987).
4. Nordland, "Africa in the Plague Years," p. 46.
5. Thomson Prentice, "Africa's New Agony: Dark Future," *The Times* (October 29, 1986).
6. Alex Shoumatoff, "In Search of the Source of AIDS," *Vanity Fair*, vol. 51, no. 7 (July 1988): 105.
7. Thomson Prentice, "Africa's New Agony: A Continent Under Seige," *The Times* (October 27, 1986).
8. Joseph Conrad, *Heart of Darkness*, Oxford: Oxford Paperbacks, 1984).
9. Ibid., p. 67.
10. Simon Watney, *Policing Desire: Pornography, AIDS and the Media*, (Minneapolis: University of Minnesota Press, 1987 and 1989), p. 4.
11. Murtagh, "AIDS in Africa."
12. Peter Murtagh, "Highlanders Get All Clear After Kenya AIDS Alarm," *The Guardian* (March 25, 1987).

13. Conrad, *Heart of Darkness*, p. 66.
14. Ibid., p. 67.
15. Lawrence K. Altman, "AIDS in Africa: A Pattern of Mystery," *New York Times* (November 8, 1985): A8.
16. see Renée Sabatier, *Blaming Others: Prejudice, Race and Worldwide AIDS* (London: The Panos Institute, 1988), p. 54.
17. Nordland, "Africa in the Plague Years," p. 46.
18. Andrew Veitch, "The Cruel March of AIDS," *The Guardian* (February 16, 1988), p. 32.
19. See World Health Organization, *Report of the Consultation on International Travel and HIV Infection* (Geneva, April 1987).
20. see Watney, *Policing Desire*.
21. Patrick Brantlinger, "Victorians and Africans: The Genealogy of the Myth of the Dark Continent," *Critical Inquiry*, vol. 12, no. 1 (Autumn 1985): 181.
22. Nordland, "Africa in the Plague Years," p 45.
23. Shoumatoff, "In Search of the Source of AIDS," p. 95.
24. Robin McKie, "Straight Sex Link in AIDS Epidemic," *The Observer* (November 10, 1985): 15.
25. Nicholas Timmins, "Old People are Getting AIDS, Doctors Reveal," *The Independent* (September 16, 1988): 1.
26. Brantlinger, "Victorians and Africans," p. 194.
27. Ibid.
28. Conrad, *Heart of Darkness*, p. 116.
29. Ibid., p. 144.
30. Ibid., p. 135.
31. Stephen Jay Gould, *The Mismeasure of Man* (Harmondsworth: Penguin, 1981), p. 35.
32. See Michel Foucault, "On Governmentality,"

Ideology & Consciousness, no. 6 (Autumn 1979): 5-23.

33. The notion of "leakage" has been a central term in British and American discussion concerning the epidemiology of HIV.

34. Ronald Hyam, "Empire and Sexual Opportunity," *The Journal of Imperial and Commonwealth History*, vol. 14, no. 2 (January 1986): 75. I would like to thank Michael Budd for drawing this article to my attention.

35. For example, see Susan Sontag, *AIDS and Its Metaphors* (London: Allen Lane, 1989); and Elizabeth Fee and Daniel M. Fox, eds., *AIDS: The Burdens of History* (Berkeley: University of California Press, 1989). I would except the work of Paula A. Treichler and Allan M. Brandt from my judgment of the latter book.

36. Altman, "AIDS in Africa," p. A14.

37. Steve Connor, and Sharon Kingman, *The Search for the Virus: The Scientific Discovery of AIDS and the Quest for a Cure* (London: Penguin, 1988), p. 204.

38. Ibid., p. 196.

39. Patton, "Inventing African AIDS," p. 85.

40. Sander Gilman, *Disease and Representation: Images of Illness from Madness to AIDS* (Ithaca: Cornell University Press, 1988), p. 262.

41. See Richard C. Chirimuuta, and Rosalind J. Chirimuuta, *AIDS, Africa and Racism* (Burton-on-Trent: R. Chirimuuta, 1987).

42. See Simon Watney, "Psychoanalysis, Sexuality & AIDS" in *Homosexuality, Politics and Culture*, eds. M. Wallis, and S. Shepherd (London: Unwin-Heinneman, 1989).

43. Andrew Brown, "Africans Attack 'Sin of Homosexuality,'" *The Independent* (August 5, 1988).

44. Subsection 2A. of Section 28 of the 1988 Local Government Act states, "A local authority shall not (a) intentionally promote homosexuality or publish material with the intention of promoting homosexuality; (b) promote the teaching in any maintained school of the acceptability of homosexuality as a pretended family relationship."

45. Cindy Patton, "Safer Sex and Lesbians: Becoming Queer," *The Pink Paper*, issue 14 (February 25, 1988): 2.

46. Conrad, *Heart of Darkness*, p. 49.

47. See Alex Brazier, *A Double Deficiency?: A Report on the Social Security Act 1986 and People with Acquired Immune Deficiency Syndrome (AIDS), AIDS Related Complex (ARC), and HIV Infection* (London: The Terrence Higgins Trust, 1989); see also Erica Carter, and Simon Watney, eds., *Taking Liberties: AIDS and Cultural Politics* (London: Serpent's Tail Press, 1989).

• **Rosalyn Deutsche**

Uneven Development: Public Art in New York City

> *The true issue is not to make beautiful cities or well-managed cities, it is to make a work of life. The rest is a by-product. But, making a work of life is the privilege of historical action. How and through what struggles, in the course of what class action and what political battle could urban historical action be reborn? This is the question toward which we are inevitably carried by our inquiry into the meaning of the city.*
> –Raymond Ledrut, "Speech and the Silence of the City"

Beauty and Utility: Weapons of Redevelopment

By now it is clear to most observers that the visibility of masses of homeless people obstructs belief in positive images of New York, constituting a crisis in the city's official representation. Dominant responses to the crisis assume two principal, often complementary, forms. They treat homelessness as an individual social problem isolated from the realm of urban politics or, as Peter Marcuse contends, "attempt to neutralize the outrage homelessness produces in those who see it."[1] Because substantial efforts to deal with homelessness itself would require at least a partial renunciation of its immediate causes—the commodification of housing, existing patterns of employment, the social service policies of today's austerity state—those committed to preserving the status quo try, instead, through strategies of isolation and neutralization, to cope with the legitimation problems that homelessness raises.

Exemplary of the "social problem" approach is a widely circulated report issued in June 1987 by the Commission on the Year 2000. Obedient to its governmental mandate to forecast New York City's future, the panel defined New York as "ascendant," sustaining this image by pointing to the city's "revitalized" economy and neighborhoods. Conspicuous poverty and patent stagnation in other neighborhoods compelled the commission, nonetheless, to remark on the unequal character of this rise: "We see that the benefits of prosperity have passed over hundreds of thousands of New Yorkers."[2] But the group's recommendations—prescribing the same pro-business and privatizing policies that are largely responsible for homelessness in the first place—failed to translate this manifest imbalance into a recognition that uneven economic and geographical development is a structural, rather than incidental, feature of New York's present expansion. The panelists' own expansive picture required, then, a certain contraction of their field of vision. Within its borders, social inequities appear as random disparities and disappear as linked phenomena. An optical illusion fragments the urban condition: "growth"–believed to occur in different locations at varying paces of cumulative development, but ultimately to unfold its advantages to all–emerges as a remedy for urban decay, obscuring a more integrated reality that is also inscribed across the city's surface. For in the late capitalist city, growth, far from a uniform process, is driven by the hierarchical differentiation of social groups and territories. Residential components of prosperity–gentrification and luxury housing–are not distinct from, but in fact depend upon, residential facets of poverty–disinvestment, eviction, displacement, homelessness. Together, they comprise only one aspect of the city's comprehensive redevelopment, itself part of more extensive social, economic, and spatial changes, all marked by uneven development. Consequently, redevelopment proceeds, not as an embracing benefit, but according to social *relations* of ascendancy, that is, of domination. Consensus-oriented statements such as *New York Ascendant* disavow these relations, impressionistically offering proof of growth side-by-side with proof of decline; both pieces of evidence acquire the appearance of discrete entities. But today there is no document of New York's ascendancy which is not *at the same time* a document of homelessness. Whether such documents are municipal reports, landmark buildings, or what we call public spaces, they exhibit an ambiguity as to their meaning.

Faced with the instability pervading New York's urban images, the second major response to homelessness–the neutralization of its effects on viewers–attempts to restore to the city a surface calm that belies underlying contradictions. To legitimate the city, this response delegitimates the homeless. In the spring of 1988, Mayor Koch demonstrated the neutralizing approach while speaking, fittingly, before a group of image makers, the American Institute of Architects, convened in New York to discuss, even more appropriately, "Art in Architecture." Answering a question about Grand Central Station–landmark building and public place–Koch, too, underscored the dual signification of New York's urban spaces by directing his listeners' attention to the presence of the homeless who now reside in the city's train stations:

> These homeless people, you can tell who they are. They're sitting on the floor, occasionally defecating, urinating, talking to themselves–many, not all, but many–or panhandling. We thought it would be reasonable for the authorities to say, "You can't stay here unless you're here for transportation." Reasonable, rational people would come to that conclusion, right? Not the Court of Appeals.[3]

The mayor was denigrating the state court's reversal of an antiloitering law under which police would have been empowered to remove the homeless from the public areas they currently inhabit. Deprived of repressive powers, however, Koch could only protect the space by ideological means, proclaiming its transparency, in the eyes of reasonable people, to an objective function–transportation.

To assert in the language of commonsense that an urban space refers unequivocally to intrinsic uses is to claim that the city itself speaks. Such a statement makes it seem that individual locations within the city and the spatial organization of the city as a whole contain an inherent meaning determined by the imperative to fulfill needs that are presupposed to be natural, simply practical. Instrumental function is the only meaning signified by the built environment. What this essentialist view systematically obstructs—an obstruction that is actually its principal function—is the perception that the organization, shape, and meaning of space is social. Seen through the lens of function, however, spatial order appears instead to be controlled by natural, mechanical, or organic laws. It is recognized as social only in the sense that it meets the purportedly unified needs of aggregated individuals. The functionalization of the city, which presents space as politically neutral, merely utilitarian, is, then, filled with politics. For the notion that the city speaks for itself conceals the identity of those who speak through the city.

This effacement has two interrelated functions. In the service of those groups whose interests dominate decisions about the organization of space, it holds that the exigencies of human social life provide a single meaning which necessitates proper uses of the city—proper places for its residents. The prevailing goals of the existing spatial structure are regarded as, by definition, beneficial to all. Correlatively, the ideology of function obscures the conflictual manner in which cities are actually defined and used, repudiating the very existence of those groups who counter dominant uses of space. For these reasons, critical evaluations of the relations of domination materialized in space pivot on the recognition that the production and use of the city is a conflictual process. As the urban critic Raymond Ledrut observes, "The city is not an object produced by a group in order to be bought or even used by others. *The city is an environment formed by the interaction and the integration of different practices.* It is maybe in this way that the city is truly the city."[4]

Ledrut's definition of the city as the product of social practice, negating its hypostatization as a physical object, strongly opposes the technocratic definition of the city as the product of experts. The city, Ledrut insists, is not a spatial framework external to its users, but is produced by them. Deceptively simple, Ledrut's formulation has far-reaching implications. Not only does it explicitly acknowledge the participation of diverse social groups in the production of the environment, it argues against an environment imposed from above by state institutions or private interests, one that is dictated by the necessities of control and profit but legitimized by concepts of efficiency or beauty. Delineating the city as a social form rather than a collection and organization of neutral physical objects implicitly affirms the right of presently excluded groups to have access to the city—to make decisions about the spaces they use, to be attached to the places they live, to refuse marginalization. It describes a concrete social reality suppressed by dominant urban spaces, sketches the terms of resistance to those spaces, and envisions the liberation of the environment in what Henri Lefebvre calls a "space of differences."[5] In place of the image of a "well-managed city," it proposes the construction of a "work of life," suggesting that such a vital work is extinguished by a discourse that separates people endowed with "eternal" needs from an environment supposedly built to meet them. It restores the subject to the city. The struggle to establish the validity of Ledrut's definition of the city is, then, irrevocably fused to other controversies about the city's form and use. "The definition of urban meaning," Manuel Castells maintains, describing the inscription of political battles in space,

> will be a process of conflict, domination, and resistance to domination, directly linked to the dynamics of social struggle and not to the reproductive spatial expression of a unified culture. Furthermore, cities and space being fundamental to the organization of social life, the conflict over the assignment of certain goals to certain spatial forms will be one of the fundamental mechanisms of domination and counter-domination in the social structure.[6]

Koch's assignment of a directing purpose–transportation–to Grand Central Station in order to prevail over what he portrays as a parasitic function–shelter for homeless people–encapsulates this means of domination. First, it sequesters a single place from the totality of spatial organization. But the real efficacy of the functionalization of the city as a weapon of power in struggles over the use of urban space rests on its ability to deny the reality that such struggles are productive of spatial organization in the first place. Yet the presence in public places of the homeless–the very group that Koch invokes–represents the most acute symptom of a massive and disputed transformation in the uses of the broader city. Far from a natural or mechanical adjustment, this reorganization is determined in all its facets by prevailing power relations. It includes a transformation of New York into a center for international corporations and business services with attendant changes in the nature of employment. The shift in manufacturing jobs elsewhere, frequently overseas, is accompanied by a loss of traditional blue-collar jobs and the rise of poverty-level wages in low-echelon service sector or new manufacturing jobs. Since land and housing are commodities to be exploited for profit, the marginalization of large numbers of workers engenders a loss of housing for the poor as New York devotes more space to profit-maximizing real estate development–high-rent office towers, luxury condominiums, corporate headquarters–that also provides the physical conditions to meet the needs of the new economy. Today's homeless, therefore, are refugees from evictions, secondary and exclusionary displacement–the conversion of their neighborhoods into areas they can no longer afford.[7] More broadly, they are the products of wage and property relations and of governmental policies allocating spatial resources to the uses of big business and real estate while withdrawing them from social services such as public housing. And the homeless are produced by technical decisions made by state and municipal planning agencies about land uses, decisions that increasingly reinforce an economically and racially segregated spatial structure by directing low-income groups toward the city's periphery. To elucidate the specific historical, rather than mythical, reasons, for the presence of today's homeless, they should, more accurately, be called "the evicted." Koch's attempt, exemplified in his address to the architects' convention, to extract New York's urban space from the very social relations that create it further marginalizes the poor. Having first been expelled from their apartments and neighborhoods, they are now denied, by means of what the French situationists termed "a blackmail of utility,"[8] a right to the city at all.

Exhortations to the authority of objective use are considered in situationist pronouncements to be one of two mechanisms shielding the capitalist conquest of the urban environment from challenge. The other is aesthetics, characterized, along with urban planning, as "a rather neglected branch of criminology."[9] This appraisal retains its pertinence in New York today, where, in unison, notions of beauty and utility comprise the ideological alibi for redevelopment. Under its protection, the conditions of daily life for hundreds of thousands of residents are destroyed. The reciprocity between discourses of beauty and utility is evidenced by the fact that Koch's question and answer session at the architects' meeting, where he made his remarks about utility, replaced, at the last minute, a prepared speech he was to deliver on the subject not of the well-managed city but of the beautiful one. The substitution does not indicate a reversal of priorities. Both urban images are equally instrumental for the redevelopment process no matter how much it is supported by a postmodern architecture that claims to have renounced a functionalist aesthetic. In the name of needs and corresponding functions, Koch engaged in narrow problem-solving about the uses of public spaces. But his espousal of the city that speaks for itself permits a remarkable silence to prevail about the incompatibility between true functionality and a social system in which production "is accomplished not for the fulfillment of needs in general, but for the fulfillment of one particular need: profit."[10] Within such a system—indeed, as Baudrillard warns, within *any* system of productivist growth—if a person eats, drinks, lives somewhere, reproduces himself, it is because the system requires his self-production in order to reproduce itself: it needs men.[11] In bourgeois society, when people such as today's evicted are redundant in the economy—or needed to cheapen labor costs—they are converted from residents of the city into predators on the "fundamental" needs of New Yorkers. No longer required as productive forces, the homeless themselves have no requirements.

The stunning reversals enacted in the name of utility—invoking for the purpose of demonstrating natural needs the very group whose existence testifies to the social construction of needs—occur also in the name of beauty. Koch's prepared speech on the topic of government's relation to aesthetics celebrated the city's preservation of historical landmarks, architectural heterogeneity, and neighborhood context, mobilizing a protectionist discourse of permanence and continuity under whose aegis patterns of development progressively threaten historical action, diversity, and entire communities with elimination. Such inversions are possible because, presupposed to lie outside of socio-material conditions, commitments to beauty and utility present themselves as incontrovertible evidence of public accountability. Thus, as further proof of the advantages of New York's "ascendancy," Koch's planned speech stressed his administration's interest in the aesthetics of the city—its revitalization of the municipal art commission, programs of flexible zoning regulations, planning controls, design review panels, and public art. "Once again," the speech asserted, "public art has become a priority."[12]

Redeveloping "the Public"

It is not difficult to understand why an increase in public art commissions attends New York's "ascendancy." As a practice within the built environment, public art participates in the production of meanings, uses, and forms for the city. In this capacity, it can help secure consent to redevelopment and to the restructuring that makes up the historical form of late capitalist urbanism. It is also not unexpected that along with demonstrations of the new city's beauty and utility, intensified talk of "the public" should accompany the accelerating privatization and bureaucratization of land-use decisions in New York. Wholescale appropriations of land by private interests, massive state interventions that de-territorialize huge numbers of residents, and inequitable distribution of spatial resources by government agencies insulated from public control: these acts governing the shape of New York's landscape require a legitimating front. Citing "the public," whether this word is attached to art, space, or any number of other objects, ideas, and practices is one means of providing the uneven development of New York with democratic legitimacy. Discourse about "the public" is frequently cast as a commitment made by the principal actors in the real estate market—developers, financial institutions, landlords, corporations, politicians—to rescue, for New Yorkers, a significant quantity of "public space" from the ravages of "overdevelopment." Routinely, for instance, public areas, paid for with public funds, furnish private redevelopment projects with the amenities necessary to maximize profits.[13] In other cases, city regulations require corporations, in exchange for increased density allowances, to build privately owned atriums or plazas. The resulting locations are designated "public" spaces. These phenomena mirror each other as facets of the privatization of public space. Private public space is most frequently acclaimed as an innovative partnership between the public and private sectors—falsely supposed to be distinct spheres. Such an alliance, we are told, if extended to the entire configuration of the city, would benefit all New York residents. Yet the provision of space for "the public" testifies, under present circumstances, to the wholesale withdrawl of space from social control. Clearly, the local state can meet with only limited and precarious success in harmonizing its goals of meeting captial's demands and maintaining democratic legitimacy, since the two goals are, objectively, in conflict. Not surprisingly, therefore, New York's new public spaces, materializations of attempts at reconciliation, are the objects of contests over uses and, moreover, are hardly designed for accessibility to all. Rather, they permit, through a multitude of legal, physical, or symbolic means, access by certain social groups for selected purposes while excluding others.

When disputes do arise that threaten to expose the political implications of such exclusions, an ideology of "the public" justifies particular exclusions as natural. Because "the public" is conceived either as a unity or, what amounts to the same thing, as a field composed of essential divisions, dilemmas plaguing the use of public spaces can be attributed to the inevitable disruptions attendant on the need to harmonize the "natural" differences and diverse interests characteristic of any society. Heightened diversity is viewed, even further, as a distinctive feature of modern urban life, whose problems, in turn, are understood to result from the inevitable technological evolution of human society. Neutralizing concepts of diversity form part of the urban ideology and are wielded to defeat genuine diversity. "The public," employed as an imprecise and embracing rubric, substitutes for analysis of specific spatial contests, ascribing discord to quasi-natural origins. Exclusions enacted to homogenize public space by expelling specific differences are dismissed as deeds necessary to restore social harmony. This perspective disavows the social relations of domination that such deeds make possible.

Exclusions and homogenization, operations undertaken in the name of "the public," distinguish what German filmmaker Alexander Kluge has called the "pseudo-public sphere." With Oskar Negt, Kluge has theorized various permutations in the bourgeois public sphere and, especially, its transformation in the interests of profit-maximization. The pseudo-, or, as variously labeled, the representative, classical, or traditional, public sphere, conventionally deemed to be a spatial and temporal arena where citizens participate in political dialogue and decision-making, is, according to Negt and Kluge, an arena that in practice represses debate. This repression, a hallmark of the bourgeois public sphere, results from its origins in the false demarcation drawn in bourgeois society between the private and public realms. Because economic gain, protected from public accountability by its seclusion within the private domain, actually depends on conditions that are publicly provided, the bourgeois public sphere developed as a means by which private interests seek to control public activity. But since capitalism requires the preservation of the illusion that a well-defined boundary divides the public and private realms, the contradictions that gave birth to the public sphere are perpetuated and "reconciled" in its operations. Conflicts between groups are obfuscated by transmuting differential interests into an abstract equality based on universal reason and by privatizing certain realms of experience. Homogenization of divergent concerns can, however, only be effected through exclusions: "A representative public sphere," Kluge argues, "is representative insofar as it involves exclusions." It "only represents parts of reality, selectively and according to certain value systems. . ."[14] Negt and Kluge describe how, increasingly, the pseudo-public sphere has yielded to a public sphere that is privately owned, determined by profit motives, and characterized by the transformation of the conditions of all aspects of everyday life into objects of production. Within this public sphere, "the public" is defined as a mass of consumers and spectators.[15] Against the pseudo–and private public spheres, grounded in relations of exclusion and private property, Negt and Kluge conceptualize the construction of an oppositional public sphere—an arena of political consciousness and articulation of social experience which would challenge these relations.

Recently, artists and critics have sought to initiate such a challenge within art practice by constructing what has been termed a cultural public sphere. The ideas that art cannot assume the preexistence of a public but must help produce one and that the public sphere is less a physical space than a practice, nullify, to a considerable extent, accepted divisions between public and nonpublic art. Potentially, any exhibition venue is a public sphere and, conversely, the location of artworks outside privately owned galleries, in parks and plazas or, simply, outdoors, hardly guarantees that they will constitute a public. But while, in these ways, the concept of a public sphere shatters the category of public art, it also raises unique questions for art that has been conventionally so categorized and, especially, for work commissioned to occupy New York's public spaces. Given the proliferation of pseudo–and private public spaces, how can public art counter the functions of its "public" sites in constructing the dominant city? We can at least begin to answer this question by discarding the simplifications that pervade mainstream aesthetic discourse about "the public." Rather than a real category, the definition of "the public," like the definition of the city, is an ideological artifact, a contested and fragmented terrain. "'The public,'" as Craig Owens observes, "is a discursive formation susceptible to appropriation by the most diverse–indeed, opposed–ideological interests."[16] But crucial as this perception is, significant challenges to dominant interests will continue to elude us unless this basic understanding prompts inquiries into the precise identity of those interests and the concrete mechanisms of their power. Unless we seriously respond to Owens' subsequent query–"who is to define, manipulate and profit from 'the public'" today?[17]–critical interventions will remain inchoate and directionless. Paramount among the issues confronting all urban practices is the present appropriation of public space and of the city itself for use by the forces of redevelopment. Public art shares this plight. Although its current predicament is not without historical precedent, the complexities of the present conjuncture necessitate a new framework for analyzing the social functions of public art.

Public Art and Its Uses

Interrogating the conditions of public art's existence requires that we dislodge public art from its ghettoization within the parameters of aesthetic discourse, even critical aesthetic discourse, and resituate it, at least partially, within critical urban discourse. More precisely, such a shift in perspective erodes the borders between the two fields, disclosing the existence of crucial interfaces between art and urbanism in the subject of public art. The need for criticism to conceptualize this meeting ground is especially pressing now, since neoconservative forces are appropriating that task in order to promote a type of public art that complies with the demands of redevelopment. Indeed, when Koch's speechwriters for his talk before the American Institute of Architects stated that "once again, public art has become a priority," they were not only drawing attention to an increase in the number of public commissions, but also to enhanced support for a qualitatively different kind of public art. And even though their reference to art was contained within a speech on aesthetics–the beautiful city–it could equally have supported Koch's later remarks about utility–the well-managed city. In fact, the new public art illustrates the marriage of the two images in the redevelopment process.

What distinguishes the "new" public art in the eyes of its proponents, and, further, what renders it more socially accountable than the old, is precisely its "usefulness." "What is the new public art?" asked an art journalist in one of the earliest articles reporting on the new phenomenon:

> *Definitions differ from artist to artist, but they are held together by a single thread:* It is art plus function, *whether the function is to provide a place to sit for lunch, to provide water drainage, to mark an important historical date, or to enhance and direct a viewer's perceptions.*[18]

From this indiscriminate list of functions it is difficult to ascertain precisely how the new public sculpture differs from previous types. Nineteenth-century war memorials, after all, commemorate important events, while Richard Serra's *Tilted Arc*, against which the new art opposes itself, directs a viewer's perception. Yet advocates do specify, albeit confusedly, a quality that distinguishes the work of new public artists:

> *All share a dedication to extra-aesthetic concerns. Use—not as in criticality but as in seating and tables, shade and sunlight—is a primary issue.*[19]

> *We are putting function back into art again.*[20]

> *This architectural art has a functional basis. Unlike most traditionally modern works of painting and sculpture, which modern artists were careful to define as "useless" in comparison to other objects of daily life, recent architectural art is often very much like a wall, a column, a floor, a door or a fence.*[21]

Scott Burton—whose work, primarily pieces of furniture designed for public places, epitomizes the phenomenon—repeatedly declared that "utility" is the principal yardstick for measuring the value of public art.[22]

The new art, then, is promoted as useful in the reductive sense of fulfilling "essential" human and social needs. Just as Koch designated Grand Central Station a place for travel, this art designates places in the city for people to sit, to stand, to play, to eat, to read, even to dream. Building on this foundation, the new art claims to unify successively a whole sequence of divided spheres, offering itself in the end as a model of integration. Initially setting up a polarization between the concerns of art and those of utility, it then transcends the division by making works that are both artworks and usable objects. Further, it claims to reconcile art, through its usefulness, with society and with the public benefit. Use, we are told, ensures relevance. Just as function is limited to utilitarianism, social activity is constricted to narrow problem-solving, so that the provision of "useful" objects automatically collapses into a social good. "The social questions interest me more than the art ones," said Scott Burton, describing his furnishings for the Equitable Assurance Building, whose function in raising real estate values remained thoroughly unexamined. "I hope that people will love to eat their lunch there."[23] And, he continued, "Communal and social values are now more important than my pushing the limits of my self-expression."[24]

The conflation of utility with social benefit has a distinctly moralistic cast: "All my work is a rebuke to the art world,"[25] Burton has stated. Critics agree: "[Scott Burton] challenges the art community with neglect of its social responsibility. . . . Carefully calculated for use, often in public spaces, Burton's furniture clearly has a social function."[26] All these purported acts of unification, predicated as they are on prior separations, conceal underlying processes of dissociation. Each element of the formula—art, use, society—first isolated from the others, has individually undergone a splitting operation in which it is rationalized and objectified. Art possesses an aesthetic essence; utilitarian objects serve universal needs; society is a functional ensemble. They surmount specific histories, geographies, values, relations to subjects and social groups, to be reconstituted as abstract categories. Individually and as a whole, they are severed from social relations, fetishized as external objects. This is the real social function of the new public art: to reify as natural the conditions of the late capitalist city into which it hopes to integrate us.

The supreme act of unification with which the new public art is credited, however, is its interdisciplinary cooperation with other professions shaping the physical environment.

> *The new public art invariably requires the artist to collaborate with a diverse group of people, including architects, landscape architects, other artists and engineers. So far, most of the public artists have had few problems adjusting to the collaborative process; indeed, many have embraced it with enthusiasm.*[27]

"Few might have guessed that these collaborations would so seriously affect the art, design and planning professions in such a short time,"[28] writes one critic with surprise. Yet, given the fact that the new public art rallies all the notions that currently inform the planning of redevelopment, it is hardly surprising, if not in fact completely predictable, that such work should be fully integrated into the process of designing New York's redeveloped spaces.

Since their emergence in the late 1970s, as part of the acceleration of urban restructuring, public art collaborations have grown to such an extent that they now dominate accounts of public art. "This is a season," writes Michael Brenson,

> *that is bringing the issue of artistic collaboration to a head. Over the past few years a great deal of hope has been invested in the partnership between sculptors and architects, and between sculptors and the community. There is a widespread feeling that this is the future for public sculpture and perhaps for sculpture in general.*[29]

The consistent invocation of "the community" in passages such as these typifies the terminological abuses pervading discussions of public art and endowing the new type with an aura of social accountability. That John Beardsley's 1981 survey *Art in Public Places*, consistently describes government-funded art as "community-sponsored" is especially ironic, since the "new initiatives within cities" and "major building programs" the author identifies as the impetus for collaborations frequently comprise state interventions in the environment, interventions that destroy minority and working-class communities and disperse their residents.[30]

Inaccuracies of language, demonstrating indifference to the issues of urban politics, resemble other distortions pervading discourse about public art collaborations, distortions that confuse the issues of aesthetic politics as well. Like the appropriation of the language of urban studies, these misrepresentations try to invest the recent marriage of art and urban planning with a social justification, using the vocabulary of radical art practice. The new public art is described as anti-individualist, contextualist, and site-specific. Collaborative artists frequently display a lack of concern with private self-expression and, thereby, an opposition to the autonomy and privilege of art. As part of urban design teams, they also reject notions of public art as "decoration," because, as they contend, they are not merely placing objects in urban spaces but creating the spaces themselves. If writers such as Beardsley single out "new initiatives within cities" as one

factor contributing to the growth of public art collaborations, they see the second crucial factor to be developments within contemporary art itself.

But to say that the new public art is born of recent tendencies within urbanism and
art practice tells us very little. Genuine explanation hinges on understanding the nature
of each of these developments and of their interaction. The new art's promoters misunderstand both sources of the new public art. The difference between their version of
site-specificity and its original meaning is obvious and needs only to be summarized
here.

Commitment to developing an art that neither diverts attention from nor merely
decorates the spaces of its display originated from the imperative to challenge the neu-
trality of those spaces and of art objects themselves. Contexualist art intervened in its
spatial context critically by making the social relations of that space visible. The new
public art, in contrast, moves "beyond decoration" into the field of spatial design in
order to affirm, rather than question, its space, to conceal its constitutive social relations. It moves from a notion of art that is "in" but independent of its spaces to one that
views art as integrated with its spaces and users but in which all three are independent of
urban politics. It simply combines twin fetishisms. One critic, delineating "a right way
and a wrong way to insert art in public places," wrote about a collaborative art project
in New York exemplifying the "right way" that it

> represents the gentrification of site art—it's been successfully, even brilliantly, tamed, its sting
> removed. You can sometimes miss the good old days when artists were fierce individualists
> wrestling the wilderness to its knees, like Dan'l Boone with the bear; the "otherness" of art
> out on the American desert touched some mythic nerve. But times have changed. The two
> traditions—the gentrified and the wild—can't be mixed.[31]

The statement constructs false dualisms that contain genuine differences. What has been
eliminated from the new "site-specific" art is not "individualism," as opposed to team-
work, but political resistance in favor of collaboration with the forces of power. The real
measure of just how depoliticized this art has become—and how political it actually is—
under the guise of being "environmentally sensitive" is the author's assumption that
gentrification is a positive metaphor. As anyone genuinely sensitive to New York's
social landscape realizes, however, the prior symbolization of gentrification as the
domestication of wild frontiers profoundly misapprehends the nature of the phenomenon. Gentrification only appears to result from the heroic conquest of hostile
environments by individual "pioneers"; in truth, as Neil Smith writes,

> it is apparent that where the "urban pioneers" venture, the banks, real-estate companies, the
> state or other collective economic actors have generally gone before. In this context it may be
> more appropriate to view the James Rouse Company not as the John Wayne but as the Wells
> Fargo of gentrification.[32]

The depiction of gentrification—a process which replaces poor, usually minority,
residents of frequently well-established neighborhoods with white middle-class residents—as a beneficial activity taming uncivilized terrains is not only naive about
economics, it is an ethnocentric and racist conceit as well. The use of this conceit in

art criticism epitomizes the arrogance inherent in aesthetic practices claiming to respond to urban environments while lacking any commitment to comprehend them.

Instead, proponents of the new public art respond to urban questions by constructing images of well-managed and beautiful cities. Theirs is a technocratic vision. Insofar as it discerns a real problem—the loss of people's attachment to the city—it reacts by offering solutions that can only perpetuate alienation: a belief that needs and pleasures can be gratified by expertly produced, "humanized" environments. The incapacity to appreciate that the city is a social rather than technical form, renders this perspective helpless to explain a situation in which the same system that produces, for the purposes of profit and control, a city dissociated from its users, today for the same reasons, literally detaches people from their living space through eviction and displacement. Under these circumstances, the technocratic view is left with limited options: encouragement of these actions, disavowal, or dismissal of homelessness as an example of how the system fails rather than, more accurately, how it currently works. To fashion the mental and physical representations of New York's ascendency, interdisciplinary urban design teams—including public artists—must suppress the connection between redeveloped spaces and New York's homelessness.

The Social Uses of Space

Public artists seeking to reveal the contradictions underlying images of well-managed or beautiful cities also explore relations between art and urbanism. Their interdisciplinary ventures differ, however, from the new collaborative and useful ones. Instead of extending the idealist conception of art to the surrounding city, they combine materialist analyses of art as a social product with materialist analyses of the social production of space. As a contribution to this work, urban studies has much to offer, since it analyzes the concrete mechanisms by which power relations are perpetuated in spatial forms and identifies the precise terms of spatial domination and resistance. Over the last twenty years, the "social production of space" has become the object of an impressive body of literature generated by urbanists in many fields—geography, sociology, urban planning, political economy. Critical spatial theories share a key theme with critical aesthetic thought, and the two have unfolded along a similar trajectory. Initially, critical urban studies questioned mainstream idealist perspectives on urban space.[33] "The dominant paradigm," as sociologist Marc Gottdiener summarizes it,

> *loosely identified as urban ecology, explains settlement space as being produced by an adjustment process involving large numbers of relatively equal actors whose interaction is guided by some self-regulating invisible hand. This "organic" growth process—propelled by technological innovation and demographic expansion—assumes a spatial morphology which, according to ecologists, mirrors that of lower life forms within biological kingdoms. Consequently, the social organization of space is accepted by mainstreamers as inevitable, whatever its patterns of internal differentiation.*[34]

The ecological perspective views forms of metropolitan social life in terms of the adaptation of human populations to environments in which certain processes tend to remain constant and invariable. Employing biologistic analogies, it attributes patterns of urban growth to "laws" of competition, dominance, succession, and invasion, and thus explains the form of the city as a product of semi-natural processes. Even when the ecological legacy of environmental determinism has been complicated or discarded altogether, many tendencies within urban studies continue to view space as an objective entity against which subjectivities are measured and therefore to marginalize the wider social system as cause of urban spatial form. But just as critical art practice in the late 1960s and 1970s sought to de-fetishize the ideological art object, critical urban studies did the same with the ideological spatial object—the city as an ecological form—investigating the ways in which social relations produce the city.

Having insisted, however, on the relationship between society and space, this critique rejected the return of idealism to spatial discourse in the formulation that space simply "reflects" social relations. "Two things can only interact or reflect each other if they are defined in the first place as separate," observes urban geographer Neil Smith.

> *Even having taken the first step of realization, then, we are not automatically freed from the burden of our conceptual inheritance; regardless of our intentions, it is difficult to start from an implicitly dualistic conception of space and society and to conclude by demonstrating their unity.*[35]

Indeed, by means of such separations, not only is space endowed with an identity as a discrete entity, but social life appears to be *unsituated*, to exist apart from its material forms. Space (like art) can be rescued from further mystification only by being grasped as a socially produced category in the first instance, as an arena where social relations are reproduced and as, itself, a social relation.

Both critical aesthetics and urban studies attempt to reveal the depoliticizing effects of the hegemonic perspectives they criticize and, conversely, share an imperative to politicize the production of space and art. These comparable goals do not merely present an interesting academic parallel. Nor, as in the standard conception of interdisciplinary endeavors, do they simply enrich each other. Rather, they converge in producing a new object of study—public art, which, under current circumstances functions as a spatial activity. Understanding the fusion of urban space with prevailing social relations reveals the extent to which the predominant tendency within public art to design the landscape of redevelopment fully implicates art in spatial politics.

Such a statement only makes sense, however, in light of a theory of spatial organization as a terrain of political struggle. Urban theories, far from monolithic, are characterized by debates that are much too complex to receive justice within the scope of this essay.[36] Still, it is necessary to outline, however briefly, why space is on the political agenda as it has never been before. Henri Lefebvre, originator of the phrase "the production of space," attributes the significance of space, in part, to changes in the organization of production and accumulation under late capitalism. New spatial arrangements assure captialism's very survival by permitting its penetration into all aspects of everyday life and by facilitating conditions of profitable growth via uneven development. Because production is no longer isolated in independent units within space but, instead, takes place across vast spatial networks, "the production of things in space" gives way to "the production of space."[37] Due to this growth and to revolutions in telecommunications and information technology, "the planning of the modern economy tends to become spatial planning."[38] The implications of this fundamental premise are clear. Individual cities cannot be defined apart from the spatial totality–the relations of spaces to one another within and between various geographic levels: global, regional, urban. The spatial restructuring of New York–a process at the urban level–can only be comprehended within the global context: the internationalization of capital, new international division of labor, and new international urban hierarchy.[39] Cities such as New York, occupying the upper ranks of the hierarchy, function within the division of labor as centers for decision-making and administrative control of finance capital and global corporations. Productive activities and, now, low-level clerical jobs are exported, permitting savings on labor costs along with enhanced flexibility and control. But the corporate center itself materializes not only because of global restructuring but also through a restructuring within the city. Concentrations of luxury housing, office buildings, and high-status entertainment and recreational facilities serve the new workforce and destroy physical conditions of survival for blue-collar workers. This restructuring is paradoxical, entailing as it does simultaneous processes of deindustrialization and reindustrialization, decentralization and recentralization, internationalization and peripheralization. Crucial to grasping the character of New York, however, is the key insight that within the finance and service center, as on the global level, individual spaces have no intrinsic substance; their character and condition can only be explained in relation to other city spaces.

Specific spatial relations within the city also correspond to the circumstances of accumulation under late capitalism. Today the accumulation process occurs not by absolute expansion but through the internal differentiation of space. It is, then, a process of uneven development, "the hallmark of the geography of capitalism."[40] While urban geographers and sociologists routinely include uneven development among the features distinguishing the production of late capitalist space, Neil Smith has extensively analyzed it as a structural process governing spatial patterns at all scales. Smith's work is essential to a comprehension of the spatial restructuring of New York since it explains phenomena such as gentrification and redevelopment as manifestations of the broad, yet specific, underlying process of uneven development affecting land use in the city.

Smith theorizes two factors responsible for uneven development at the urban scale. Following David Harvey, he applies to explanations of urban space theories maintaining that overaccumulation crises prompt capital, in an attempt to counteract falling rates of profit, to switch its investment from crisis-ridden spheres of the economy into the built environment. Gentrification and redevelopment represent this attempt. But uneven development in the city operates not only in response to such broad economic cycles; it functions because of corresponding conditions within metropolitan land markets. According to Smith, the profitability of investment in the built environment depends on the creation of what he calls a "rent gap."[41] The rent gap describes the difference between the present value of land and its potential value. The devalorization of real estate, through blockbusting, redlining, and abandonment of buildings, creates a situation in which investment by real estate and finance capital for "higher" land uses can produce a profitable return. In Smith's analysis, redevelopment results from both the uneven development of capital in general and of urban land in particular. Whether or not one agrees that the creation of a rent gap is sufficient to produce redevelopment, Smith's thesis discloses the concealed relation between processes such as gentrification and those of abandonment. The decline of neighborhoods, rather than being corrected by gentrification, is its precondition. Smith's theorization of uneven urban development offers, as well, a key to understanding the construction of the image of the redeveloped city. The identity of redeveloped spaces as symbols of beneficial and uniform growth requires that declining spaces be constituted as separate categories. Growth as redifferentiation is disavowed. Consequently, the repressed "other" of spaces of ascendancy has a concrete identity in deteriorating areas and immiserated city residents.

Uncovering the economic determinations of spatial redifferentiation in New York does not, however, illuminate the operations of space as a determining weight on social life or as ideology. For urbanists such as Lefebvre, advanced capitalism creates a distinctive and multivalent space that reproduces all social relations. "It is not only supported by social relations, but it also is producing and produced by social relations."[42] Capitalist space, which Lefebvre, among other, calls abstract space, serves many functions. It is, at once, a means of production, an object of consumption, and a property relation. Abstract space is also a vehicle for state domination, subordination, and surveillance. According to Lefebvre, it possesses a distinctive combination of three features. Abstract space is homogeneous or uniform so that it can be used, manipulated, controlled, and exchanged. Within the homogeneous whole, which spreads over vast areas, it is fragmented into interchangeable parts, so that, as a commodity, it can be bought and sold. Abstract space is, further, hierarchically ordered, divided into centers and peripheries, upper- and lower-status spaces, spaces of the governing and governed. All three features require that space be objectified and universalized, submitted to an abstract measure. But above all else, numerous contradictions haunt this space. As a global productive force, space is universalized, but it is also, as Lefebvre describes it, "pulverized" by relations of private property that demand its fragmentation into units. This conflict expresses a broader contradiction in the asymmetrical development of the forces of production–geographical space in this case–and the social relations of production–here the economic ownership and control of space. The universalization/pulverization contradiction embodies still another conflict–that between homogenized space serving as a tool of state domination and the fragmentation of space required by economic relations. Abstract space can serve as a space of control because it is generalized from specificity and diversity, from its relation to social subjects and their uses of space. But while abstract space homogenizes differences, it causes them at the same time to assert themselves. This contradiction emerges as cities–which Lefebvre defines as arenas for the encounter between differences–are homogenized, by means of exclusion, into centers of wealth, decision-making, and power. "The dominant space, that of the spaces of richness and power, is forced to fashion the dominated spaces, that of the periphery."[43] The relegation of groups of people and particular uses of space to enclosed areas outside the center produces an "explosion of spaces." Thus, through homogenization, a multitude of differences become available to perception as abstract space imposes itself on the space of everyday life. This process embodies a further contradiction, that between the production of space for profit and control—abstract space—and for social reproduction—the space of everyday life, which is both created by and yet escapes the generalizations of exchange. Abstract space represents, then, the *unstable* subordination of integrated social space by a centralized space of power. Because space is essential to daily life, the space of domination is resisted by what Lefebvre terms the "appropriation" of space for individual and social purposes. It follows that society's essential spatial conflict entails the appropriation of space from its alienation in capitalist spatial organization. This reparative goal is what Lefebvre refers to as "the right to the city,"[44] and it includes the struggle of the marginalized to occupy and control space.

Lefebvre's intricate formulations about the preeminence of space in social conflicts have provoked extensive criticism, including charges of "spatial fetishism," "vagueness," and "reproductionism." Largely untranslated from the French, they originally became familiar to English-speaking readers in Manuel Castells' *The Urban Question*, where the author opposed Lefebvre in a debate on the theory of space.[45] Although Lefebvre's ideas have since been advanced by numerous English-speaking urbanists, his emphasis on social reproduction rather than production has made him vulnerable to criticism from those who continue to privilege production as the primary locus of political activity. Surely Lefebvre's rejection of reformist measures to ameliorate urban problems and his refusal to propound doctrinaire solutions frustrate those who are searching for single explanatory factors or new systems. Yet, Lefebvre's analysis of the spatial exercise of power as a construction and conquest of difference, although it is thoroughly grounded in Marxist thought, rejects economism and predictability, opening up possibilities for advancing analysis of spatial politics into realms of feminist and anti-colonialist discourse and into the theorization of radical democracy. More successfully than anyone of whom I am aware, Lefebvre has specified the operations of space as ideology and built the foundation for cultural critiques of spatial design as a tool of social control. For Lefebvre, space is broadly ideological because it reproduces existing social relations. Through the auspices of coherent spatial order, efforts are made to control the contradictions inherent in abstract space. "One of the most crying paradoxes of abstract space," Lefebvre observes,

> is that it can be simultaneously the birthplace of contradictions, the milieu in which they are worked out and which they tear up, and finally, the instrument which allows their suppression and the substitution of an apparent coherence. All of which confers on space a function previously assumed by ideology.[46]

Professions such as urban planning and design—and now, public art—assume the job of imposing such coherence, order, and rationality on space. They can be regarded as disciplinary technologies in Foucault's sense insofar as they attempt to pattern space so that docile and useful bodies are created by and deployed within it. Consequently, urban practitioners who view planning as a technical problem and politics as a foreign substance to be eliminated from spatial structures mask spatial politics.

The contours of New York's redevelopment cannot be conceptually manipulated to fit exactly within the mold of Lefebvre's depiction of late capitalist space. Yet the concepts of abstract space, and of uneven geographic development, specify the terms, distilled from concrete events, of urban spatial struggle. Materialist analyses of space enable us to evaluate the consequences of cultural practices, such as the new public art, engaged in that struggle on the side of real estate and state domination. They also indicate the points where public art can enter the arena of urban politics in order to resist that domination, perhaps facilitating the expression of social groups excluded by the current organization of the city. Participation in urban design and planning enmeshes public art, unwittingly or not, in spatial politics. But public art can also appropriate the city, organized to repress contradictions, as a vehicle for illuminating them. It can transform itself into a spatial praxis, which Edward Soja has clarified as "the active and informed attempt by spatially conscious social actors to reconstitute the embracing spatiality of social life."[47] Against aesthetic movements that design the spaces of redevelopment, interventionist aesthetic practice might–as it does with other spaces– redesign these sites. For if official public art creates the redeveloped city, art as spatial praxis approaches this city in the cautious manner of the cultural critic described by Walter Benjamin. Confronted with "cultural treasures"–"documents of civilization"– Benjamin's critic unveils the barbarism underlying their creation by brushing their history "against the grain."[48] Likewise, we can brush New York's spatial documents of ascendancy against the grain, revealing them to be, at the same time, documents of homelessness.

A Beautiful and Useful Weapon

In the winter of 1988, Koch ordered that the evicted living in public places be examined by authorities and, if judged mentally incompetent, forcibly hospitalized. Coinciding with these events, occuring in the middle of a season that is always the most difficult for the evicted, the Clocktower, a city-owned exhibition space in lower Manhattan, displayed a proposal for a public artwork entitled the *Homeless Vehicle Project*. The exhibition included several elements combined in a format that resembled the presentational modes by which urban planning and architecture proposals are regularly unveiled to the public. Its nucleus was a prototype of a stark, industrial-looking object–a vehicle designed by public artist Krzysztof Wodiczko in consultation with several evicted men. Constructed of aluminum, steel mesh, sheet metal, and plexiglass, the vehicle aims to facilitate the survival activities of one segment of the evicted population–individuals who live on the streets and survive by collecting, sorting, storing, and returning cans and bottles to supermarkets in exchange for deposits. The device would enable this group of residents to circulate more easily through the city, a mobility necessitated by their lack of permanent housing and their mode of subsistence. Besides easing the job of scavenging, the cart offers a degree of shelter. Engineered so that it can expand or fold into a variety of positions, it furnishes, minimally, facilities for eating, sleeping, washing, defecating, and sitting. Sketches of the vehicle demonstrating different aspects of its operation were displayed at the Clocktower along with the model itself. Also shown

were preliminary drawings revealing alterations made during the evolution of the design as the artist responded to requests from the consultants. In a separate section of the
gallery, Wodiczko simulated an outdoor urban landscape by projecting onto the walls
slides depicting public spaces in New York City–Tompkins Square, City Hall Park, and
the area directly outside the Municipal Building. Employing montage techniques, he
then infiltrated the scenes with ghostly images, enlarged from sketches, of the vehicle
being maneuvered through the municipal spaces by its potential users. The figures' spec-
tral aspect materialized from two procedures: the drawings were printed white on black,
and blown up, their outlines became slightly blurred. By visualizing the vehicle in civic
spaces, the slides thematically related homelessness to the action and inaction of local
government, accusing the city not only of failing to cure the problem but, in fact, of
producing it. Wodiczko's slide images also, more obliquely, associated homelessness
with dispersed apparatuses of power in the city. The artist's presentation adopted an
institutionalized form that embodies architecture, city planning, and urban design
discourses: the visual projection of proposed objects and spatial alterations into the existing urban context in order to demonstrate their positive, benign, or, at the very least,
unobtrusive effect on potential physical sites. By modifying this convention and projecting images that merged physical and social sites, Wodiczko's panorama commented on
and established its divergence from the official role of environmental disciplines in New
York today. Such practices engineer redevelopment, ejecting people from their homes
and banishing the evicted. They also suppress the evidence of rupture by assigning social functions and groups to designated zones within the spatial hierarchy. Wodiczko's
presentations, in contrast, symbolically lodged the evicted in the urban center, concretizing memories of social disruption and imagining the impact of the evicted on the city.

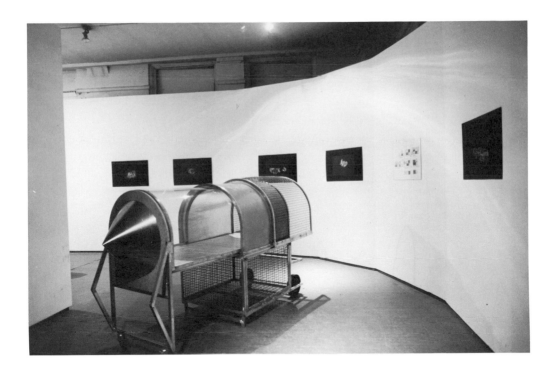

In this sense, the vehicle becomes, to adopt a phrase from Deleuze and Guattari, "a machine against the apparatus." Taped conversations between Wodiczko and evicted people, in which they discussed the vehicle's design, played continuously during the exhibition, and the gallery distributed a text containing transcripts of the conversations as well as an essay about the project, coauthored by Wodiczko and David Lurie.

Dictated by the practical needs and direct requests of men who live and work on the streets, the *Homeless Vehicle Project* implicitly expressed support for those people who, deprived of housing, choose against official coercion to resist relegation to dangerous and dehumanizing shelters. In no way offering itself as a solution, the Homeless Vehicle challenges the city's present "solution"—the proliferation of a shelter system not simply as a temporary adjunct to, but in lieu of, substantive construction of decent permanent housing. Questioning government housing and shelter policies does not obviate support for the construction of low income housing. It simply means that advocacy of housing and even shelters must be framed within a broad critique that voices the terms of substantive change—social ownership of housing, opposition to the rights of private property, resistance to the homogenized city—and comprehends how policies offered as solutions frequently exacerbate or merely regulate the problem. Currently, government emphasizes "temporary" shelters, which, given the lack of new public housing construction, tacitly become permanent. Or it manufactures cumbersome financing schemes by which a grossly inadequate number of low-income units are provided without direct public expenditure, as a means of facilitating redevelopment and, frequently, for private gain. At the same time, the city continues to channel large subsidies to business and developers. Thus, it perpetuates and disavows the relation between homelessness and the city's economic transformation. Described by one critic as "an in-

sidious form of institutionalized displacement purporting to be humane while incarcer-
ating thousands whose only 'crime' is poverty,"[49] the shelter system is, however, not
only necessitated by restructuring and real estate development, but itself participates in
New York's spatial division into core and periphery areas. By increasing the visibility
of the evicted, who, in reality, already inhabit urban space, the Homeless Vehicle
dramatizes the right of the poor not to be isolated and excluded. Heightened visibility,
however, is only the necessary, but not the sufficient, condition for this dramatization.
Indeed, visibility can also be used, as it is by conservatives, to support demands for the
removal of the evicted. But the Homeless Vehicle positions the evicted as active New
York residents whose means of subsistence form a legitimate element of the urban social
structure. It thus focuses attention on that structure and, in so doing, not only challenges the economic and political systems that evict people but also subverts the modes
of perception that exile them as well.

The Homeless Vehicle is, then, both practical object and symbolic articulation. In the
gallery and, potentially, on the streets, it alters the image of the city. It is precisely the
tension between its two functions that raises and openly confronts a troubling question,
one that informs debates among the homeless and their advocates about the shelter system. Cultural practices addressing New York's environment face a similar problem:
How is it possible to recognize and respond to homelessness and still not foster, as do
some proposals designing equipment for the homeless, an acceptance of current conditions and concealment of their causes? The dilemma presents art with a seemingly
paradoxical solution. In the very act of referring to a practical function, it must reaffirm
its status as a signifying object. Yet this oscillation simply illustrates the truth, concealed
by functionalist ideology, about all urban objects. Without recognizing the social construction of function—and without indicting the forces producing homelessness—
practical plans to help the evicted survive on the streets are likely, no matter how well-
intentioned, to be tools for redevelopment. Openly complicitous, of course, are those
plans sponsored by redevelopment associations themselves, groups who proffer charita-
ble projects as evidence of redevelopment's benefits or of corporate philanthropy. A
sleekly presented proposal sponsored by the Community Redevelopment Agency (CRA)
of Los Angeles, exhibited in 1986 at the New York Storefront for Art and Architecture's
Homeless at Home exhibition, epitomizes this tactic. Observing that Los Angeles' skid
row lies within the CRA's 1,500 acre Central Business District Redevelopment Project,
the CRA announced a plan to direct a portion of the tax revenues generated from new
development and rising property values for programs to aid the inhabitants of skid
row, "recognizing," as the proposal's text phrased it, "that skid rows will always exist"
and seeking to "reduce the impact of Skid Row on the adjacent downtown area." Primarily, these projects try to shelter the redeveloped city from the adverse effects of the
homelessness it causes and, simultaneously, to counteract the system's legitimation crisis
by presenting homelessness as a transhistorical problem.

The *Homeless Vehicle Project* also proposes a way to alleviate some of the worst aspects of evicted peoples' lives, but in doing so, it strengthens, rather than reduces, their
impact on the central business district. The project's critical force, then, springs from the
interaction between its practical and signifying purposes, a reciprocity emblematized in

the design of the vehicle, which, on the one hand, recalls Bauhaus functionalism and, on the other, resembles a weapon. It thus becomes a tool used against redevelopment. Instead of rendering the evicted invisible or reinforcing an image of them as servile beings, the Homeless Vehicle illuminates their mobile existence. Instead of severing or cosmeticizing the link between homelessness and redevelopment, the project visualizes the connection through its active insertion into the transformed city. It facilitates the seizing of space by evicted subjects rather than containing them in prescribed locations. Consequently, instead of restoring a surface calm to the "ascendant" city, as reformist plans struggle to do, it disrupts the coherent urban image, which today is only constructed by neutralizing homelessness. As a result, the Homeless Vehicle legitimates the homeless rather than the dominant spaces that exclude them, symbolically countering the city's own ideological campaign against the poor. In a minor, yet exemplary, gesture in this crusade, Koch, as we have seen, tried to eject the evicted from Grand Central Station by aiming against them the weapon of functionalization. The station's objective function, he insisted, is to serve the needs of travel, and it is impeded by the stationary homeless. The Homeless Vehicle retaliates by announcing a different function for the urban environment—the fulfillment of the travel needs of the evicted. Yet the vehicle does not simply pit one use or group against another. It subverts the ideology of utility, silencing the city that seems to speak for itself—the instrumental city—by disrupting the city's silence on the subject of social needs. For the Homeless Vehicle's function, far from general or inevitable, is clearly a socially created scandal. The work strikes at the heart of the well-managed city, an image which today functions for the needs of profit and control.

Collaborative public art helps build this image under the guises of utility, beauty, social responsibility—a rapprochement between art and life. But the Homeless Vehicle, too, is useful and collaborative. For this project, a skilled professional has applied sophisticated design principles to an object of everyday life, which, intruding upon space, practices a mode of urban design. Whereas "the new public art" employs design to enforce dominant social organization, converting social reality into design, the Homeless Vehicle uses design for counter-organization, rearranging the transformed city. A vehicle for organizing the interests of the dominated classes into a group expression, it employs design to illuminate social reality, supporting the right of these groups to refuse marginalization.

In the essay accompanying the exhibition of the *Homeless Vehicle Project*, Wodiczko and Lurie stress the significance of collaborative relationships between professional designers and users of the vehicle. "Direct participation of users in the construction of the vehicle," they explain, "is the key to developing a vehicle which belongs to its users, rather than merely being appropriated by them."[50] Countering the technocracy of design, they seem to be referring to the distinction between a vehicle planned specifically by and for the evicted and the adaptation by the evicted of supermarket shopping carts. It is only through the collective production of objects by their users, Lurie and Wodiczko suggest, that people might resist the domination of their lives by abstract forces. Yet the Homeless Vehicle's substitution of an actively produced object for an appropriated one suggests the need for a more sweeping change—the possession by users of their living space. Just as it negates the abstraction of function from specific social relations, the project challenges the abstraction of the city from its inhabitants. At the same time, foregrounding a collateral system already built by the evicted to support their daily lives, it suggests that even under current circumstances the act of production is, in fact, not confined to those who manufacture the city, but already includes those who use and appropriate it.

Appropriating the space of the city–reclaiming space for the social needs of residents against space organized for profit and control–and diverting it, in a manner similar to what the situationists called *détournement*, from its prescribed functions, the Homeless Vehicle responds to ordinary needs and horrifying realities, yet, in a mixture of fantasy and reality that some critics find "disturbing," it offers a vision of the emancipation of the environment. Such a possibility will not, of course, be realized in isolated acts of *détournement*. Still, in the present, by upholding the "right to the city," the *Homeless Vehicle Project* corroborates Ledrut's definition of the city–"an environment formed by the interaction and the integration of different practices"–and thus anticipates the construction, not simply of beautiful or well-managed cities–they are, after all, by-products–but of a "work of life." Through this imaginative act, the project participates as well in the construction of an oppositional public sphere, one that counters the dominant relations organizing public space and permits the expression of social experience. The production of such a public art is, in fact, inseparable from the production of New York City as a living work. Yet the *Homeless Vehicle Project* also attests to the degree of knowledge about urbanism and the astuteness, even stealth, of operation required by public art if it is to accomplish these goals. For given its reliance on corporate and civic approval, public art, like New York itself, will, no doubt, develop unevenly.

I am grateful to Robert Ubell for countless conversations during which many of the ideas in this article were discussed and to Lynne Tillman who made valuable suggestions that were incorporated into the revised version of the essay.

1. Peter Marcuse, "Neutralizing Homelessness," *Socialist Review*, vol. 18, no. 1 (January/March 1988): 83. Marcuse's premise–that the sight of homeless people is shocking to viewers and that this initial shock is, subsequently, counteracted by ideological portrayals–assumes that responses to the presence of the homeless in New York today are simple, direct, almost "natural." It thus fails to recognize that current experience of beggars and "vagrants" by other city residents is always mediated by already-existing representations, including the naming of such people as "the homeless" in the first place. The form and iconography of such representations not only produce complex, even contradictory, meanings about the homeless–the object of the representation–but also, in the act of constituting the homeless as an image, construct positions in social relations. It is necessary to alter these relationships as well as the content of representations of the homeless. Despite its limited understanding of representation–a subject which, however, it importantly raises–Marcuse's description of official attempts to neutralize the effects of homelessness and the author's own, largely successful, efforts to counteract these neutralizations are extremely valuable. This is especially true *now*, when, encouraged by the final years of the Koch administration, the mass media seems determined to depict the homeless as predators, to encourage New Yorkers to refuse donations to street beggars, and to create the impression that city services exist to serve the needs of the poor and homeless.
2. *New York Ascendant*, report of the Commission of the Year 2000 (New York: Harper and Row, 1988), p. 167.
3. David W. Dunlap, "Koch, the 'Entertainer,'

Gets Mixed Review," *New York Times* (May 19, 1988): B4.

4. Raymond Ledrut, "Speech and the Silence of the City," in *The City and the Sign: An Introduction to Urban Semiotics*, eds. M. Gottdiener, and Alexandros Ph. Lagopoulos (New York: Columbia University Press, 1986), p. 122.

5. Henri Lefebvre, "Space: Social Product and Use Value," in *Critical Sociology: European Perspectives*, ed. J.W. Freiberg (New York: Irvington Publishers, 1979), p. 293.

6. Manuel Castells, *The City and the Grassroots: A Cross-Cultural Theory of Urban Social Movements* (Berkeley and Los Angeles: University of California Press, 1983), p. 302.

7. For a more complete definition of "exclusionary displacement," see Peter Marcuse, "Abandonment, Gentrification, and Displacement: The Linkages in New York City," in *Gentrification of the City*, eds. Neil Smith, and Peter Williams (Boston: Allen & Unwin, 1986), pp. 153-177.

8. Attila Kotányi, and Raoul Vaneigem, "Elementary Program of the Bureau of Unitary Urbanism," in *Situationist International Anthology*, ed. Ken Knabb (Berkeley: Bureau of Public Secrets, 1981), p. 65.

9. Ibid.

10. Neil Smith, *Uneven Development: Nature, Capital and the Production of Space* (Oxford: Basil Blackwell, 1984), p. 54.

11. Jean Baudrillard, "The Ideological Genesis of Needs," in *For a Critique of the Political Economy of the Sign* (St. Louis: Telos Press, 1981).

12. "Remarks by Mayor Edward I. Koch at Awards Luncheon of the American Institute of Architects" (May 18, 1988): 7.

13. For a discussion of one example of this process, see Rosalyn Deutsche, "Krzysztof Wodiczko's *Homeless Projection* and the Site of Urban 'Revitalization,'" *October*, no. 38 (Fall 1986): 63-98.

14. Alexander Kluge, "On Film and the Public Sphere," *New German Critique*, nos. 24-25 (Fall/Winter 1981-82): 212.

15. An especially patronizing depiction of the public as consumers of mass spectacle appeared in a 1980 *New York Times* editorial about New York's public space. "New Yorkers," the editorial began, "love parades, festivals, celebrations, demonstrations and entertainments, particularly when such occasions bring large numbers of them together outdoors." The conflation of political demonstrations (rallies in Union Square were cited as a historical example) and patriotic celebrations (the 1976 Bicentennial celebration, for one) and the reduction of both to an opportunity to enjoy the weather ("The finer the weather, the greater the urge to gather, the sweeter the siren call of causes")

were employed to support the use of public funds to create public parks for a luxury redevelopment project Battery Park City. Needless to say, by the end of the editorial any reference to political demonstrations had been dropped. "What better place for New Yorkers to do *their public thing?*" the editorial concluded ("A Public Plaza for New York," *New York Times* [June 16, 1980]: A22, emphasis added).

16. Craig Owens, "The Yen for Art," contribution to a discussion entitled "The Birth and Death of the Viewer: On the Public Function of Art," in *Discussions in Contemporary Culture*, ed. Hal Foster (Seattle: Bay Press, 1987), p. 18.

17. Ibid., p. 23.

18. Douglas C. McGill, "Sculpture Goes Public," *New York Times Magazine* (April 27, 1986): 45.

19. Nancy Princenthal, "On the Waterfront: South Cove Project at Battery Park City," *Village Voice* (June 7, 1988): 99.

20. Nancy Holt, quoted in McGill, "Sculpture Goes Public."

21. Robert Jensen, "Commentary," in *Architectural Art: Affirming the Design Relationship* (New York: American Craft Museum, 1988): 3.

22. See Gibson, "Public Art and the Public Realm."

23. Quoted in McGill, "Sculpture Goes Public," p. 63.

24. Ibid., p. 67.

25. Quoted in Nancy Princenthal, "Social Seating," *Art in America*, vol. 75, no. 6 (June 1987): 131.

26. Ibid.

27. McGill, p. 66.

28. Diane Shamash, "The A Team, Artists and Architects: Can They Work Together," *Stroll: The Magazine of Outdoor Art and Street Culture*, nos. 6-7 (June 1988): 60.

29. Michael Brenson, "Outdoor Sculptures Reflect Struggles of Life in the City," *New York Times* (July 15, 1988): C1, C28.

30. John Beardsley, *Art in Public Places: A Survey of Community-Sponsored Projects Supported by The National Endowment for the Arts* (Washington, DC: Partners for Livable Places, 1981), p. 81.

31. Kay Larson, "Combat Zone," *New York* (May 13, 1985): 118.

32. Neil Smith, "Gentrification, the Frontier, and the Restructuring of Urban Space," in *Gentrification of the City*, eds. Smith and Williams, pp. 18-19.

33. For critiques of traditional urban studies, see, among others, Manuel Castells, *The Urban Question: A Marxist Approach* (Cambridge: MIT Press, 1977); M. Gottdiener, *The Social Production of Urban Space* (Austin: University of Texas Press, 1985); Peter Saunders, *Social Theory and the Urban Question* (London: Hutchinson, 1981); Edward W.

Soja, "The Spatiality of Social Life: Towards a Transformative Retheorization," in *Social Relations and Spatial Structures*, eds. Derek Gregory and John Urry (New York: St. Martin's Press, 1985).

34. Gottdiener, *The Social Production of Urban Space*, p. 264.

35. Smith, *Uneven Development*, p. 77.

36. Summaries of these debates and of the history of spatial theories are included in Gottdiener, *The Social Production of Urban Space*; Edward W. Soja, "The Socio-spatial Dialectic," *Annals of the Association of American Geographers*, vol. 70 (1980): 207-25; Saunders, *Social Theory and the Urban Question*.

37. Lefebvre, "Space: Social Product and Use Value," p. 285.

38. Ibid., p. 286.

39. For a discussion of the international urban hierarchy, see R.B. Cohen, "The New International Division of Labor, Multinational Corporations and Urban Hierarchy," in *Urbanization and Urban Planning in Capitalist Society*, eds. Michael Dear and Allen J. Scott (London and New York: Methuen, 1981), pp. 287-315.

40. Smith, *Uneven Development*, p. xi.

41. For explanations of the "rent gap," see Neil Smith and Michele LeFaivre, "A Class Analysis of Gentrification," in *Gentrification, Displacement and Neighborhood Revitalization*, eds. J. John Palen, and Bruce London (Albany: State University of New York Press, 1984), pp. 43-63; and Smith, "Gentrification, the Frontier and the Restructuring of Urban Space."

42. Lefebvre, "Space: Social Product and Use Value," p. 286.

43. Ibid., p. 290.

44. Henri Lefebvre, *Le droit à la ville* (Paris: Anthropos, 1968).

45. Manuel Castells, "From Urban Society to Urban Revolution," in *The Urban Question*.

46. Henri Lefebvre, *La production de l'espace* (Paris: Anthropos, 1974), p. 420. Translated in M. Gottdiener, "Culture, Ideology, and the Sign of the City," in *The City and the Sign*, eds. Gottdiener and Lagopoulos, p. 215.

47. Edward W. Soja, "The Spatiality of Social Life: Towards a Transformative Retheorization," in *Social Relations and Spatial Structures*, eds. Gregory and Urry.

48. Walter Benjamin, "Theses on the Philosophy of History," in *Illuminations*, trans. Harry Zohn (New York: Schocken, 1969), p. 257.

49. Theresa Funiciello, reply to letters, *The Nation* (June 18, 1988): 876.

50. David Lurie and Krzysztof Wodiczko, "Homeless Vehicle Project," The Clocktower, 1988; reprinted in *October*, no. 47 (Winter 1988): 53-67.

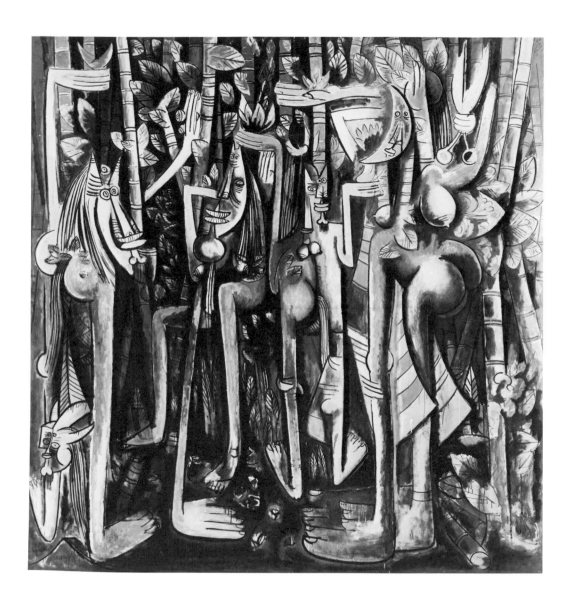

Wifredo Lam, *The Jungle*, 1943

Please Wait By the Coatroom

I.

Wifredo Lam's *The Jungle* hangs in the hallway leading to the coatroom of the Museum of Modern Art. Its location is telling. The artist has been allowed into the museum's lobby, but, like a delivery boy, has been made to wait in an inconspicuous passageway near the front door. By denying Lam the possibility of going upstairs and conversing with Paul Cézanne, Pablo Picasso, Jackson Pollock, and Frank Stella (their works are carefully arranged on the walls of the main galleries), the museum relegates *The Jungle* to a secondary status. This action is the result of numerous assumptions nearly everyone in today's mainstream art world takes for granted. In fact, such assumptions are an integral aspect of the art world's institutions (museums, galleries, and magazines), as well as of its individuals (curators, editors, critics, dealers, and collectors). However, nearing the end of the century and in a country whose demographics are rapidly changing, perhaps it is time that these assumptions be re-examined.

II.

Wifredo Lam (1902–82) was born in Cuba, the son of a Chinese father and Afro-Cuban mother. During his childhood, Lam's mother told him that one of her ancestors was José Castilla, who had been nicknamed *Mano Cortada* (Chopped Hand). Castilla was a half-caste who had to go into hiding. In doing so, he became a *cimarrón*, a runaway slave.

The other major influence on Lam during this period was his Yoruba priestess godmother, Mantonica Wilson. Because of her reputation as a sorcerer and healer, Lam was able to participate in various religious ceremonies. She also introduced him to such figures as Shangô, the mythical ancestor of the Yorubas and master of thunder.

In 1918, he sailed to Spain, where he attended art school and began gaining a reputation as an artist. Later, he fought and was wounded in the Spanish Civil War. In 1938, after recovering from his wound, he went to Paris and met Picasso. In 1940, due to France's defeat and the German occupation of Paris, he set out for Marseilles. Once there, he reacquainted himself with such friends as André Breton, Victor Brauner, and Oscar Dominguez. In 1941, he embarked with Breton, Claude Lévi-Strauss and more than three hundred others on the *Capitaine Paul-Merle*.

Lam's odyssey lasted more than seven months, and during that time he was detained on Martinique for more than a month. While he was incarcerated, he met and formed a lasting relationship with the poet Aimé Césaire, one of the founders of the Negritude movement. Before leaving Martinique, Lam provided the illustrations for Césaire's *Cahier d'un Retour au Pays Natal* (Notebook of a Return to the Native Land). It is in this long poem/journal that the word *negritude* probably appears for the first time: "My negritude is not a stone, its deafness hurled against the clamor of the day/ my negritude is not a leukoma of dead liquid over the earth's dead eye/ my negritude is neither tower nor cathedral."[1] For both Lam and Césaire, their return to a native land was both a symbolic journey and an actual one.

In an interview with Max-Pol Fouchet, Lam describes the Cuba he returned to in the early 1940's:

> *Poetry in Cuba then was either political and committed, like that of Nicolás Guillén and a few others, or else written for the tourists. The latter I rejected, for it had nothing to do with an exploited people, with a society that crushed and humiliated its slaves. No, I decided that my painting would never be the equivalent of that pseudo-Cuban music for nightclubs. I refused to paint cha-cha-cha. I wanted with all my heart to paint the drama of my country, but by thoroughly expressing the negro spirit, the beauty of the plastic art of the blacks. In this way I could act as a Trojan horse that would spew forth hallucinating figures with the power to surprise, to disturb the dreams of the exploiters. I knew I was running the risk of not being understood by either the man in the street or by the others. But a true picture has the power to set the imagination to work, even if it takes time.*[2]

Here, Lam outlines his aesthetic/social mission. He wants to become a Trojan horse inside the world of "the exploiters." The Museum of Modern Art, on the other hand, has redefined him as a delivery boy. And in doing so, they have rejected his message.

III.

The Museum of Modern Art's placement of *The Jungle* is influenced by William Rubin's estimation of Wifredo's Lam's achievement. In *Dada, Surrealism, and Their Heritage*, William S. Rubin, who was the director of the Department of Painting and Sculpture at MOMA from 1973 to 1988, wrote a six sentence entry on Lam:

> *Wifredo Lam was the first Surrealist to make primitive and ethnic sources central to his art. Though we see iconographical traces of such magical imagery from time to time in the work of Ernst, it counted for surprisingly little among the Surrealist painters in general. This despite the fact that many Surrealists were avid collectors of primitive art, which appealed to them especially because it stood outside an aesthetic tradition. Such pictures as Lam's* Antillean Parade *contain a fusion of influences as diverse as Haitian voodoo figures and African masks. From the penumbra of bamboo and palm frond forests that form Lam's primal landscape, emerge hybrid personages whose presences seem to be discovered in the very defining of the flora. Picasso was one of the earliest and continuous influences on Lam, and many of his forests reflect the shallow space and hybrid iconography of* Les Demoiselles d'Avignon, *but the fac-*

ture is less aggressive, attaining sometimes, as in Song of the Osmosis, *a transparency and delicacy that rather recalls Cézanne's watercolors.*[3]

IV.

Rubin begins his six sentence entry on Wifredo Lam's paintings with a profile: "He was the first Surrealist to make primitive and ethnic sources central to his art." On the surface, Rubin's statement appears to be a complimentary description of Lam's achievement within the continuous tradition of Western Art; and his words are a way of locating the artist within one of history's chapters. However, if one were to uncover the aesthetic agenda behind this sentence and the ones that follow it, it would become apparent that Rubin's judgments are both misleading and insensitive.

According to Rubin's line of thinking, Lam is not the first artist to use primitive sources, but he is the first member of a specific group to extend its stylistic parameters. Thus, Rubin believes that Lam is an important member of a group rather than a unique individual. The reason he is unwilling to confer the status of unique individual upon Lam is because he doesn't perceive the artist to be a groundbreaker. Instead of inventing a new way of making space, which Rubin judges to be the central issue an artist must successfully address in order to be considered a candidate for canonization, Lam expanded the boundaries of a particular style. Within Rubin's hierarchy of connoisseurship, Lam is able to rise to the rank of minor artist.

In the second sentence of this entry, Rubin shifts his attention from Lam to the group to which the artist supposedly belonged: "Though we see iconographical traces of such magical imagery from time to time in the work of Ernst, it counted for surprisingly little among the Surrealists in general." By acting surprised at their failure to use primitive art, Rubin is able to isolate Lam's achievement against the backdrop of the Surrealists. In his opinion, Lam is a minor artist who belonged to a minor group, a one-eyed man in the kingdom of the blind.

Rubin's third sentence is a continuation of his analysis of the Surrealists: "This, despite the fact that many Surrealists were avid collectors of primitive art, which appealed to them especially because it stood outside an aesthetic tradition." Here, he not only underscores his judgment that Lam is a one-eyed ruler, but he also names the form of blindness afflicting the Surrealists. At the same time, he deftly avoids addressing Surrealism's avowed goal, which was to overthrow the rational structures of Western Civilization, by using the bland term, "aesthetic tradition."

Rubin's deafness to the Surrealists' call to revolution allows him to demonstrate the clarity of his hindsight. From his secure vantage point in history, he can point to Surrealism's failure; they were unable to take advantage of the formal possibilities afforded them by primitive art. By embedding his opinion in the guise of a factual disclosure, Rubin sets up the framework of his hierarchical view of art.

In his fourth and fifth sentences, Rubin describes Lam's paintings: "Such pictures as Lam's *Antillean Parade* contain a fusion of influences as diverse as Haitian voodoo figures and African masks. From the penumbra of bamboo and palm frond forests that form Lam's primal landscapes, emerge hybrid personages whose presences seem to be discovered in the very defining of the flora." It is worth noting that "forest" is a misrepresentation of Lam's intentions. As he said to Max-Pol Fouchet:

> *In any case, the title has nothing to do with the real countryside of Cuba, where there is no jungle but woods, hills and open country, and the background of the picture is a sugar-cane plantation. My painting was intended to communicate a psychic state."*[4]

Secure in his aesthetic judgment of Lam's achievement, Rubin has proceeded to misread his paintings in order to make them conform to his hierarchy.

In the sixth and last sentence of his entry, Rubin outlines the terms of his aesthetic judgment: "Picasso was one of the earliest and continuous influences on Lam, and many of his forests reflect the shallow space and hybrid iconography of *Les Demoiselles d'Avignon*, but the facture is less aggressive, attaining sometimes, as in *Song of the Osmosis*, a transparency and delicacy that rather recalls Cézanne's watercolors." Here, Rubin places Lam in a subservient position to Picasso and Cézanne, the acknowledged inventors of the spatially flat, all-over composition he considers to be the cornerstone of Formalism's version of Modernism. By evoking *Les Demoiselles d'Avignon* (the first Cubist painting to incorporate primitive iconography), Rubin suggests that all of Lam's paintings are diluted descendents of this groundbreaking composition. He further emphasizes their diluted achievement by citing another precedent, Cézanne's watercolors (a minor aspect of this artist's oeuvre).

V.

Rubin's judgment of Lam is based on a centrist, linear reading of art history. It is a reading shaped by such prejudices as a belief in the importance of formal innovation and the de-emphasis of subject matter. In his approach to art, Rubin values formal innovation over style, and style over iconography. In his opinion, subject matter, which might be defined as the translation of the hybrid ingredients of consciousness into visual evidence, is of little consequence, since the aesthetic tradition of Western Art can only be renewed when an individual makes a formal breakthrough.

VI.

William S. Rubin derived much of his highly encoded understanding of contemporary art from the writings and theories of Clement Greenberg. In fact, it can be said that Rubin chose to be marked by Greenberg's theories because he believed they endowed him with a discerning eye, as well as an intellectually precise attitude. In choosing Greenberg as an authority, Rubin aligned himself with the tradition of critics that begins, in this century, with Clive Bell. Bell's primary contribution to aesthetic theory was his invention of the phrase "Significant Form" to define certain aesthetic elements within painting and sculpture. By equating formal effectiveness with aesthetic significance, Bell is able to propose a neat circular argument. The most obvious benefit of this centrist argument is a connoisseur's lens with which one can scan all art. Bell's highly refined lens looks for something rather than at something. It brings into focus a predetermined topological area of painting and sculpture.

Greenberg refined Bell's argument one step further by shifting his focus from "Significant Form," the aesthetic elements within a composition, to the picture plane, the painting's objecthood. According to Greenberg's line of thinking, the two dimensional picture plane was the only aspect of a painting that was simultaneously irreducible and essential. Within the hierarchy of his construct, the physical field of the painting was more important than what the field contained.

Influenced by Bell and Greenberg, Rubin (along with a number of other critics and curators who came to prominence in the 1960s) arrived at the seemingly inevitable conclusion that the goal of painting was to invent definitions of its irreducible, material identity. Since then, Rubin has based all of his decisions and developed all of his insights in accordance with his belief that the entire tradition of Western Art, particularly as it occurs in the 20th century, can be judged by its visible linear progress (an unbroken string of formal accomplishments) towards an invisible goal.

However, by outlining the profile an artist must fill in order to achieve the status of unique individual, Rubin also determines the issues in advance. His narrow reading of the past limits the future. In effect, he dangles a carrot from a stick, and then sits back and waits to see who is both hungry and savvy enough to snap it up. In turn, the artist who embraces this aesthetic agenda stands a good chance of being singled out by the discerning curator. Rubin's circular argument establishes the rules of conduct to be followed by the charter members of a mutual admiration society.

VII.

By designating Lam as "the first Surrealist to make primitive and ethnic sources central to his art," Rubin deprives the artist of his birthright. Instead of addressing the issues raised by Lam's response to his hybrid cultural background, Rubin writes about him as if he were a generic caucasian artist who appropriated primitive iconography. Had Rubin been sensitive to cultural differences, oppositional stances, and an individual's attempt to define the hybrid ingredients of their cross cultural identity, he might have written: *Born in Cuba, which is part of the Americas, Wifredo Lam is the first Modernist artist to emphasize his African descent by transforming his personal awareness of primitive sources into a contemporary mode of expression.* Such a sentence would have suggested that an artist of African descent could recover his heritage. Such a sentence would have revealed an awareness of the dominant culture's need to change. Such a sentence would have enlarged the continually shifting geo-political, social, and aesthetic boundaries of Western Art, as well as introduced Lam into the canon as a unique individual.

VIII.

Rubin's writing is an act of transgression. He sees in Lam only what is in his own eyes: colorless or white artists. For Lam to have achieved the status of unique individual, he would have had to successfully adapt to the conditions of imprisonment (the aesthetic standards of a fixed tradition) Rubin and others both construct and watch over. To enter this prison, which takes the alluring form of museums, art history textbooks, galleries, and magazines, an individual must suppress his cultural differences and become a colorless ghost. The bind every hybrid American artist finds themself in is this: should they try and deal with the constantly changing polymorphous conditions effecting identity, tradition, and reality? Or should they assimilate into the mainstream art world by focusing on approved of aesthetic issues? Lam's response to this bind sets an important precedent. Instead of assimilating, Lam infiltrates the syntactical rules of "the exploiters" with his own specific language. He becomes, as he says, "a Trojan horse."

IX.

America is a country where people of different races and cultures have transplanted themselves (after arriving here willingly or unwillingly). However, in their concern with aesthetic issues, the art world's institutions have consistently ignored and suppressed how hybrid American artists have transplanted the polymorphous process of their cross-cultural experiences into visual evidence. Although Wifredo Lam was a black artist from the Americas who addressed this issue, Rubin's color blind response is typical of the art world's insensitivity.

X.

Rubin's six sentence entry on Wifredo Lam is a miniscule portion of everything he has ever written. And yet, might not his gross misrepresentation of Lam suggest the fallibility inherent in his approach to art? And might not an awareness of this fallibility raise certain questions which the institutions of the art world (museums, magazines, textbooks, and galleries) have consistently failed to address? In fact, might not the entire process of determining which artists have made a significant contribution to culture be questionable?

XI.

For Lam, Surrealism was an aid in recovering his African heritage. Certainly, Césaire was as important an influence on Lam as was Breton and Picasso. Rubin's writings reverse Lam's intentions. They place him back in the diaspora. This reversal is doubled by the museum's placement of *The Jungle* in the lobby.

1. Aimé Césaire, *The Collected Poetry*, trans. Clayton Eshleman (Berkeley: University of California Press, 1983), p. 67.

2. Max-Pol Fouchet, *Wifredo Lam* (Barcelona: Ediciones Poligrafa, S.A., 1976), pp. 188-189.

3. William S. Rubin, *Dada, Surrealism, and Their Heritage* (New York: Museum of Modern Art, 1977), p. 171.

4. Ibid., p. 198.

• **James Clifford**

On Collecting Art and Culture

There is a Third World in every First World, and vice versa.
–Trinh T. Minh-ha

This essay is composed of four loosely connected parts, each concerned with the fate of tribal artifacts and cultural practices once they are relocated in Western museums, exchange systems, disciplinary archives and discursive traditions. The first part proposes a critical, historical approach to collecting, focusing on subjective, taxonomic, and political processes. It sketches the "art-culture system" through which in the last century exotic objects have been contextualized and given value in the West. This ideological and institutional system is further explored in the second part, where cultural description is presented as a form of collecting. The "authenticity" accorded to both human groups and their artistic work is shown to proceed from specific assumptions about temporality, wholeness, and continuity. The third part focuses on a revealing moment in the modern appropriation of non-Western works of "art" and "culture," a moment portrayed in several memoirs of Claude Lévi-Strauss of his wartime years in New York. A critical reading makes explicit the redemptive metahistorical narrative these memoirs presuppose. The general art-culture system supported by such a narrative is contested throughout the essay and particularly in the fourth part, where alternative "tribal" histories and contexts are suggested.

Collecting Ourselves

Entering
You will find yourselves in a climate of nut castanets,
A musical whip
From the Torres Straits, from Mirzapur a sistrum
Called Jumka, "used by Aboriginal
Tribes to attract small game
On dark nights," coolie cigarettes
And mask of Saagga, the Devil Doctor,
The eyelids worked by strings.[1]

James Fenton's poem "The Pitt Rivers Museum, Oxford" from which this stanza is taken, rediscovers a place of fascination in the ethnographic collection. For this visitor even the museum's descriptive labels seem to increase the wonder ("... attract small game / on dark nights") and the fear. Fenton is an adult-child exploring territories of danger and desire, for to be a child in this collection ("Please sir, where's the withered / Hand?") is to ignore the serious admonitions about human evolution and cultural diversity posted in the entrance hall. It is to be interested instead by the claw of a condor, the jaw of a dolphin, the hair of a witch, or "a jay's feather worn as a charm / in Buckinghamshire." Fenton's ethnographic museum is a world of intimate encounters with inexplicably fascinating objects: personal fetishes. Here collecting is inescapably tied to obsession, to recollection. Visitors "find the landscape of their childhood marked out / Here in the chaotic piles of souvenirs ... boxroom of the forgotten or hardly possible."

> Go
> As a historian of ideas or a sex-offender,
> For the primitive art,
> As a dusty semiologist, equipped to unravel
> The seven components of that witch's curse
> Or the syntax of the mutilated teeth. Go
> In groups to giggle at curious finds.
> But do not step into the kingdom of your promises
> To yourself, like a child entering the forbidden
> Woods of his lonely playtime.

Do not step in this tabooed zone "laid with snares of privacy and fiction / And the dangerous third wish." Do not encounter these objects except as *curiosities* to giggle at, *art* to be admired, or *evidence* to be understood scientifically. The tabooed way, followed by Fenton, is a path of too-intimate fantasy, recalling the dreams of the solitary child "who wrestled with eagles for their feathers" or the fearful vision of a young girl, her turbulent lover seen as a hound with "strange pretercanine eyes." This path through the Pitt Rivers Museum ends with what seems to be a scrap of autobiography, the vision of a personal "forbidden woods"–exotic, desired, savage, and governed by the (paternal) law:

> He had known what tortures the savages had prepared
> For him there, as he calmly pushed open the gate
> And entered the wood near the placard: "TAKE NOTICE MEN
> MEN-TRAPS AND SPRING-GUNS ARE SET ON THESE
> PREMISES."
> For his father had protected his good estate.

Fenton's journey into otherness leads to a forbidden area of the self. His intimate way of engaging the exotic collection finds an area of desire, marked off and policed. The law is preoccupied with *property*.

    C.B. Macpherson's classic analysis of Western "possessive individualism" traces the seventeenth-century emergence of an ideal self as owner: the individual surrounded by accumulated property and goods.[2] The same ideal can hold true for collectivities making and remaking their cultural "selves." For example Richard Handler analyzes the making of a Québécois cultural "patrimoine," drawing on Macpherson to unravel the assumptions and paradoxes involved in "having a culture," selecting and cherishing an authentic collective "property."[3] His analysis suggests that this identity, whether cultural or personal, presupposes acts of collection, gathering up possessions in arbitrary systems of value and meaning. Such systems, always powerful and rule governed, change historically. One cannot escape them. At best, Fenton suggests, one can transgress ("poach" in their tabooed zones) or make their self-evident orders seem strange. In Handler's subtly perverse analysis a system of retrospection–revealed by a Historic Monuments Commission's selection of ten sorts of "cultural property"–appears as a taxonomy worthy of Borges' "Chinese Encyclopedia": "(1) commemorative monuments; (2) churches and chapels; (3) forts of the French Regime; (4) windmills; (5) roadside crosses; (6) commemorative inscriptions and plaques; (7) devotional monuments; (8) old houses and manors; (9) old furniture; (10) 'les choses disparues.' "[4] In Handler's discussion the collection and preservation of an authentic domain of identity cannot be natural or innocent. It is tied up with nationalist politics, with restrictive law, and with contested encodings of past and future.

• • •

Some sort of "gathering" around the self and the group–the assemblage of a material "world," the marking-off of a subjective domain that is not "other"–is probably universal. All such collections embody hierarchies of value, exclusions, rule-governed territories of the self. But the notion that this gathering involves the accumulation of possessions, the idea that identity is a kind of wealth (of objects, knowledge, memories, experience), is surely not universal. The individualistic accumulation of Melanesian "big men" is not possessive in Macpherson's sense, for in Melanesia one accumulates not to hold objects as private goods but to give them away, to redistribute. In the West, however, collecting has long been a strategy for the deployment of a possessive self, culture, and authenticity.

Children's collections are revealing in this light: a boy's accumulation of miniature cars, a girl's dolls, a summer-vacation "nature museum" (with labelled stones and shells, a hummingbird in a bottle), a treasured bowl filled with the bright shavings of crayons. In these small rituals we observe the channelings of obsession, an exercise in how to make the world one's own, to gather things around oneself tastefully, appropriately. The inclusions in all collections reflect wider cultural rules–of rational taxonomy, of gender, of aesthetics. An excessive, sometimes even rapacious need to *have* is transformed into rule-governed, meaningful desire. Thus the self that must possess but cannot have it all learns to select, order, classify in hierarchies–to make "good" collections.[5]

Whether a child collects model dinosaurs or dolls, sooner or later she or he will be encouraged to keep the possessions on a shelf or in a special box or to set up a doll house. Personal treasures will be made public. If the passion is for Egyptian figurines, the collector will be expected to label them, to know their dynasty (it is not enough that they simply exude power or mystery), to tell "interesting" things about them, to distinguish copies from originals. The good collector (as opposed to the obsessive, the miser) is tasteful and reflective.[6] Accumulation unfolds in a pedagogical, edifying manner. The collection itself—its taxonomic, aesthetic structure—is valued, and any private fixation on single objects is negatively marked as fetishism. Indeed a "proper" relation with objects (rule-governed possession) presupposes a "savage" or deviant relation (idolatry or erotic fixation).[7] In Susan Stewart's gloss, "The boundary between collection and fetishism is mediated by classification and display in tension with accumulation and secrecy."[8]

Stewart's wide-ranging study *On Longing* traces a "structure of desire" whose task is the repetitious and impossible one of closing the gap that separates language from the experience it encodes. She explores certain recurrent strategies pursued by Westerners since the sixteenth century. In her analysis the miniature, whether a portrait or doll's house, enacts a bourgeois longing for "inner" experience. She also explores the strategy of gigantism (from Rabelais and Gulliver to earthworks and the billboard), the souvenir, and the collection. She shows how collections, most notably museums—create the illusion of adequate representation of a world by first cutting objects out of specific contexts (whether cultural, historical, or intersubjective) and making them "stand for" abstract wholes—a "Bambara mask," for example, becoming an ethnographic metonym for Bambara culture. Next a scheme of classification is elaborated for storing or displaying the object so that the reality of the collection itself, its coherent order, overrides specific histories of the object's production and appropriation.[9] Paralleling Marx's account of the fantastic objectification of commodities, Stewart argues that in the modern Western museum "an illusion of a relation between things takes the place of a social relation."[10] The collector discovers, acquires, salvages objects. The objective world is given, not produced, and thus historical relations of power in the work of acquisition are occulted. The *making* of meaning in museum classification and display is mystified as adequate *representation*. The time and order of the collection erase the concrete social labor of its making.

Stewart's work, along with Phillip Fisher, Krzysztof Pomian, James Bunn, Daniel Defert, Johannes Fabian, and Rémy Saisselin, among others, brings collecting and display sharply into view as crucial processes of Western identity formation.[11] Gathered artifacts—whether they find their way into curio cabinets, private living rooms, museums of ethnography, folklore, or fine art—function within a developing capitalist "system of objects."[12] By virtue of this system a world of *value* is created and a meaningful deployment and circulation of artifacts is maintained. For Baudrillard collected objects create a structured environment that substitutes its own temporality for the "real time" of historical and productive processes: "The environment of private objects and their possession—of which collections are an extreme manifestation—is a dimension of our life that is both essential and imaginary. As essential as dreams."[13]

* * *

A history of anthropology and modern art needs to see in collecting both a form of

Western subjectivity and a changing set of powerful institutional practices. The history of collections (not limited to museums) is central to an understanding of how those social groups that invented anthropology and modern art have *appropriated* exotic things, facts, and meanings. (*Appropriate*: "to make one's own," from the Latin *propius*, "proper," "property.") It is important to analyze how powerful discriminations made at particular moments constitute the general system of objects within which valued artifacts circulate and make sense. Far-reaching questions are thereby raised.

What criteria validate an authentic cultural or artistic product? What are the differential values placed on old and new creations? What moral and political criteria justify "good," responsible, systematic collecting practices? Why, for example, do Leo Frobenius' wholesale acquisitions of African objects around the turn of the century now seem excessive?[14] How is a "complete" collection defined? What is the proper balance between scientific analysis and public display? (In Santa Fe a superb collection of Native American art is housed at the School of American Research in a building constructed, literally, as a vault, with access carefully restricted. The Musée de l'Homme exhibits less than a tenth of its collections; the rest is stored in steel cabinets or heaped in corners of the vast basement.) Why has it seemed obvious until recently that non-Western objects should be preserved in European museums, even when this means that no fine specimens are visible in their country of origin? How are "antiquities," "curiosities," "art," "souvenirs," "monuments," and "ethnographic artifacts" distinguished—at different historical moments and in specific market conditions? Why have many anthropological museums in recent years begun to display certain of their objects as "masterpieces?" Why has tourist art only recently come to the serious attention of the anthropologists?[15] What has been the changing interplay between natural-history collecting and the selection of anthropological artifacts for display and analysis? The list could be extended.

The critical history of collecting is concerned with what from the material world specific groups and individuals choose to preserve, value, and exchange. Although this complex history, from at least the Age of Discovery, remains to be written, Baudrillard provides an initial framework for the deployment of objects in the recent capitalist West. In his account it is axiomatic that all categories of meaningful objects—including those marked off as scientific evidence and as great art—function within a ramified system of symbols and values.

To take just one example: the *New York Times* of December 8, 1984, reported the widespread illegal looting of Anasazi archaeological sites in the American Southwest. Painted pots and urns thus excavated in good condition could bring as much as $30,000 on the market. Another article in the same issue contained a photograph of Bronze Age pots and jugs salvaged by archaeologists from a Phoenician shipwreck of the coast of Turkey. One account featured clandestine collecting for profit, the other scientific collecting for knowledge. The moral evaluations of the two acts of salvage were sharply opposed, but the pots recovered were all meaningful, beautiful and old. Commercial, aesthetic, and scientific worth in both cases presupposed a given system of value. This system finds intrinsic interest and beauty in objects from a past time, and it assumes that collecting everyday objects from ancient (preferably vanished) civilizations will be more *rewarding* than collecting, for example, decorated thermoses from modern China or customized T-shirts from Oceania. Old objects are endowed with a sense of "depth" by their historically minded collectors. Temporality is reified and salvaged as origin, beauty, and knowledge.

This archaizing system has not always dominated Western collecting. The curiosities of the New World gathered and appreciated in the sixteenth century were not necessarily valued as antiquities, the products of primitive or "past" civilizations. They frequently occupied a category of the marvelous, of a present "Golden Age."[16] More recently the retrospective bias of Western appropriations of the world's cultures has come under scrutiny.[17] Cultural or artistic "authenticity" has as much to do with an inventive present as with a past, its objectification, preservation or revival.

•   •   •

Since the turn of the century objects collected from non-Western sources have been classified in two major categories: as (scientific) cultural artifacts or as (aesthetic) works of art.[18] Other collectibles—mass produced commodities, "tourist art," curios, and so on—have been less systematically valued; at best they find a place in exhibits of "technology" or "folklore." These and other locations within what may be called the "modern art-culture system" can be visualized with the help of a (somewhat procrustian) diagram.

A.J. Greimas' "semiotic square" shows us "that any initial binary opposition can, by the operation of negations and the appropriate syntheses, generate a much larger field of terms which, however, all necessarily remain locked in the closure of the initial system."[19] Adapting Greimas for the purposes of cultural criticism, Fredric Jameson uses the semiotic square to reveal "the limits of a specific ideological consciousness, [marking] the conceptual points beyond which that consciousness cannot go, and between which it is condemned to oscillate."[20] Following his example, I offer the following map (see diagram) of a historically specific, contestible field of meanings and institutions.

Beginning with an initial opposition, by a process of negation four terms are generated. This establishes horizontal and vertical axes and between them four semantic zones : (1) the zone of authentic masterpieces, (2) the zone of authentic artifacts, (3) the zone of inauthentic masterpieces, (4) the zone of inauthentic artifacts. Most objects—old and new, rare and common, familiar and exotic—can be located in one of these zones or ambiguously, in traffic, between two zones.

The system classifies objects and assigns them relative value. It establishes the "contexts" in which they properly belong and between which they circulate. Regular movements toward positive value proceed from bottom to top and from right to left. These movements select artifacts of enduring worth or rarity, their value normally guaranteed by a "vanishing" cultural status or by the selection and pricing mechanisms of the art market. The value of Shaker crafts reflects the fact that Shaker society no longer exists: the stock is limited. In the art world work is recognized as "important" by connoisseurs and collectors according to criteria that are more than simply aesthetic.[21] Indeed, prevailing definitions of what is "beautiful" or "interesting" sometimes change quite rapidly.

THE ART–CULTURE SYSTEM
A Machine for Making Authenticity

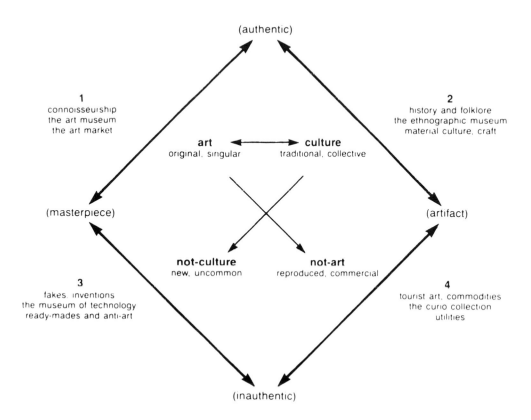

(authentic)

1
connoisseurship
the art museum
the art market

2
history and folklore
the ethnographic museum
material culture, craft

art ⟷ **culture**
original, singular   traditional, collective

(masterpiece)

(artifact)

not-culture   **not-art**
new, uncommon   reproduced, commercial

3
fakes, inventions
the museum of technology
ready-mades and anti-art

4
tourist art, commodities
the curio collection
utilities

(inauthentic)

An area of frequent traffic in the system is that linking zones 1 and 2. Objects move in two directions along this path. Things of cultural or historical value may be promoted to the status of fine art. Examples of movement in this direction, from ethnographic "culture" to fine "art," are plentiful. Tribal objects located in art galleries (the Rockefeller Wing at the Metropolitan Museum in New York) or displayed anywhere according to "formalist" rather than "contextualist" protocols move in this way.[22] Crafts (Shaker work collected in the Whitney Museum in 1986), "folk art," certain antiques, "naive" art all are subject to periodic promotions. Movement in the inverse direction occurs whenever art masterworks are culturally and historically "contextualized," something that has been occurring more and more explicitly. Perhaps the most dramatic case has been the relocation of France's great impressionist collection, formerly at the Jeu de Paume, to the new Museum of the Nineteenth Century at the Gare d'Orsay. Here art masterpieces take their place in the panorama of a historical-cultural "period." The panorama includes an emerging industrial urbanism and its triumphant technology, "bad" as well as "good" art. A less dramatic movement from zone 1 to zone 2 can be seen in the routine process within art galleries whereby objects become "dated," of interest less as immediately powerful works of genius than as fine examples of a period style.

Movement also occurs between the lower and upper halves of the system, usually in an upward direction. Commodities in zone 4 regularly enter zone 2, becoming rare period pieces and thus collectibles (old green glass coke bottles). Much current non-Western work migrates between the status of "tourist art" and creative cultural-artistic strategy. Some current productions of Third World peoples have entirely shed the stigma of modern commercial inauthenticity. For example Haitian "primitive" painting—commercial and of relatively recent, impure origin—has moved fully into the art-culture circuit. Significantly this work entered the art market by association with zone 2, becoming valued as the work not simply of individual artists but of *Haitians*. Haitian painting is surrounded by special associations with the land of voodoo, magic and negritude. Though specific artists have come to be known and prized, the aura of "cultural" production attaches to them much more than, say, to Picasso, who is not in any essential way valued as a "Spanish artist." The same is true, as we shall see, of many recent works of tribal art, whether it is from Sepik or the American Northwest Coast. Such works have largely freed themselves from the tourist or commodity category to which, because of their modernity, purists had often relegated them; but they cannot move directly into zone 1, the art market, without trailing clouds of authentic (traditional) culture. There can be no direct movement from zone 4 to zone 1.

Occasional travel occurs between zones 4 and 3, for example when a commodity or technological artifact is perceived to be a case of special inventive creation. The object is selected out of commercial or mass culture, perhaps to be featured in a museum of technology. Sometimes such objects fully enter the realm of art: "technological" innovations or commodities may be contextualized as modern "design," thus passing through zone 3 into zone 1 (for example the furniture, household machines, cars, and so on displayed at the Museum of Modern Art in New York).

There is also regular traffic between zones 1 and 3. Exposed art forgeries are demoted (while nonetheless preserving some of their original aura). Conversely various forms of "anti-art" and art parading its unoriginality or "inauthenticity" are collected and valued (Warhol's soup can, Sherrie Levine's photo of a photo by Walker Evans, Duchamp's urinal, bottle rack, or shovel). Objects in zone 3 are all potentially collectible within the general domain of art: they are uncommon, sharply distinct from or blatantly cut out of culture. Once appropriated by the art world, like Duchamp's readymades, they circulate within zone 1.

The art-culture system I have diagramed excludes and marginalizes various residual and emergent contexts. To mention only one: the categories of art and culture, technology and commodity are strongly secular. "Religious" objects can be valued as great art (an altarpiece by Giotto), as folk art (the decorations on a Latin American popular saint's shrine), or as cultural artifact (an Indian rattle). Such objects have no individual "power" or mystery—qualities once possessed by "fetishes" before they were reclassified in the modern system as primitive art or cultural artifact. What "value," however, is stripped from an altarpiece when it is moved out of a functioning church (or when its church begins to function as a museum)? Its specific power or sacredness is relocated to a general aesthetic realm.[23]

• • •

It is important to stress the historicity of this art-culture system. It has not reached its final form: the positions and values assigned to collectible artifacts have changed and will continue to do so. Moreover a synchronic diagram cannot represent zones of contest and transgression except as movements or ambiguities among fixed poles. As we shall see at the end of this essay, much current "tribal art" participates in the regular art-culture traffic *and* in traditional spiritual contexts not accounted for by the system.[24] Whatever its contested domains, though, generally speaking the system still confronts any collected exotic object with a stark alternative between a second home in an ethnographic or an aesthetic milieu. The modern ethnographic museum and the art museum or private art collection have developed separate, complementary modes of classification. In the former a work of "sculpture" is displayed along with other objects of similar function or in proximity to objects from the same cultural group, including utilitarian artifacts such as spoons, bowls, or spears. A mask or statue may be grouped with formally dissimilar objects and explained as part of a ritual or institutional complex. The names of individual sculptors are unknown or suppressed. In art museums a sculpture is identified as the creation of an individual: Rodin, Giacometti, Barbara Hepworth. Its place in everyday cultural practices (including the market) is irrelevant to its essential meaning. Whereas in the ethnographic museum the object is culturally or humanly "interesting," in the art museum it is primarily "beautiful" or "original." It was not always thus.

Elizabeth Williams has traced a revealing chapter in the shifting history of these discriminations.[25] In nineteenth-century Paris it was difficult to conceive of pre-Columbian artifacts as fully "beautiful." A prevailing naturalist aesthetic saw *ars Americana* as grotesque or crude. At best pre-Columbian work could be assimilated into the category of the antiquity and appreciated through the filter of Viollet-le-Duc's medievalism. Williams shows how Mayan and Incan artifacts, their status uncertain, migrated between the Louvre, the Bibliothèque Nationale, the Musée Guimet, and (after 1878) the Trocadéro, where they seemed at last to find an ethnographic home in an institution that treated them as scientific evidence. The Trocadéro's first directors, Ernest-Théodore Hamy and Rémy Verneau, showed scant interest in their aesthetic qualities.

The "beauty" of much non-Western "art" is a recent discovery. Before the twentieth century many of the same objects were collected and valued, but for different reasons. In the early modern period their rarity and strangeness were prized. The "cabinet of curiosities" jumbled everything together, with each individual object standing metonymically for a whole region or population. The collection was a microcosm, a "summary of the universe."[26] The eighteenth century introduced a more serious concern for taxonomy and for the elaboration of complete series. Collecting was increasingly the concern of scientific naturalists, and objects were valued because they exemplified an array of systematic categories: food, clothing, building materials, agricultural tools, weapons (of war, of the hunt), and so forth.[27] E. F. Jomard's ethnographic classifications and A.H.L.F. Pitt Rivers' typological displays were mid-nineteenth-century culminations of this taxonomic vision.[28] Pitt Rivers' typologies featured developmental sequences. By the end of the century evolutionism had come to dominate arrangements of exotic artifacts. Whether objects were presented as antiquities, arranged geographically or by society, spread in panoplies, or arranged in realistic "life groups" and dioramas, a story of human development was told. The object had ceased to be primarily an exotic "curiosity" and was now a source of information entirely integrated in the universe of Western Man.[29] The value of exotic objects was their ability to testify to the concrete reality of an earlier stage of human Culture, a common past confirming Europe's triumphant present.

With Franz Boas and the emergence of relativist anthropology an emphasis on placing objects in specific lived contexts was consolidated. The "cultures" thus represented could either be arranged in a modified evolutionary series or dispersed in synchronous "ethnographic presents." The latter were times neither of antiquity nor of the twentieth century but rather representing the "authentic" context of the collected objects, often just prior to their collection or display. Both collector and salvage ethnographer could claim to be the last to rescue "the real thing." Authenticity, as we shall see, is produced by removing objects and customs from their current historical situation—a present-becoming-future.

With the consolidation of twentieth-century anthropology, artifacts contextualized ethnographically were valued because they served as objective "witnesses" to the total multidimensional life of a culture.[30] Simultaneously with new developments in art and literature, as Picasso and others began to visit the "Troca" and to accord its tribal objects a nonethnographic admiration, the proper place of non-Western objects was again thrown in question. In the eyes of a triumphant modernism some of these artifacts at least could be seen as universal masterpieces. The category of "primitive art" emerged.

This development introduced new ambiguities and possibilities in a changing taxonomic system. In the mid-nineteenth century pre-Columbian or tribal objects were grotesques or antiquities. By 1920 they were cultural witnesses and aesthetic masterpieces. Since then a controlled migration has occurred between these two institutionalized domains. The boundaries of art and science, the aesthetic and anthropological, are not permanently fixed. Indeed anthropology and fine arts museums have recently shown signs of interpenetration. For example the Hall of Asian Peoples at the New York Museum of Natural History reflects the "boutique" style of display, whose objects could never seem out of place as "art" on the walls or coffee tables of middle class living rooms. In a complementary development downtown the Museum of Modern Art has expanded its permanent exhibit of cultural artifacts: furniture, automobiles, home appliances, and utensils—even hanging from the ceiling, like a Northwest Coast war canoe, a much-admired bright green helicopter.

· · ·

While the object systems of art and anthropology are institutionalized and powerful, they are not immutable. The categories of the beautiful, the cultural, and the authentic have changed and are changing. Thus it is important to resist the tendency of collections to be self-sufficient, to suppress their own historical, economic, and political processes of production.[31] Ideally the history of its own collection and display should be a visible aspect of any exhibition. It had been rumored that the Boas Room of Northwest Coast artifacts in the American Museum of Natural History was to be refurbished, its style of display modernized. Apparently (or so one hopes) the plan has been abandoned, for this atmospheric, dated hall exhibits not merely a superb collection but a moment in the history of collecting. The widely publicized Museum of Modern Art show of 1984, "'Primitivism' in Twentieth Century Art," made apparent (as it celebrated) the precise circumstance in which certain ethnographic objects suddenly became works of universal art.[32] More historical self-consciousness in the display and viewing of non-Western objects can at least jostle and set in motion the ways in which anthropologists, artists, and their publics collect themselves and the world.

At a more intimate level, rather than grasping objects only as cultural signs and artistic icons, we can return to them, as James Fenton does, their lost status as fetishes—not specimens of a deviant or exotic "fetishism" but *our own* fetishes.[33] This tactic, necessarily personal, would accord to things in collections the power to fixate rather than simply the capacity to edify or inform. African and Oceanian artifacts could once again be *objets sauvages*, sources of fascination with the power to disconcert. Seen in their resistance to classification they could remind us of our *lack* of self-possession, of the artifices we employ to gather a world around us.

Culture Collecting

Found in *American Anthropologist*, n.s. 34 (1932): 740:

> Note from New Guinea
> Aliatoa, Wiwiak District, New Guinea
>
> April 21, 1932
>
> We are just completing a culture of a mountain group here in the lower Torres Chelles. They have no name and we haven't decided what to call them yet. They are a very revealing people in spots, providing a final basic concept from which all the mother's brothers' curses and father's sisters' curses, etc. derive, and having articulate the attitude toward incest which Reo [Fortune] outlined as fundamental in his Encyclopedia article. They have taken the therapeutic measures which we recommended for Dobu and Manus—having a devil in addition to the neighbor sorcerer, and having got their dead out of the village and localized. But in other ways they are annoying: they have bits and snatches of all the rag

tag and bob tail of magical and ghostly belief from the Pacific, and they are somewhat like the Plains in their receptivity to strange ideas. A picture of a local native reading the index to *The Golden Bough* just to see if they had missed anything, would be appropriate. They are very difficult to work, living all over the place with half a dozen garden houses, and never staying put for over a week at a time. Of course this offered a new challenge in method which was interesting. The difficulties incident upon being two days over impossible mountains have been consuming and we are going to do a coastal people next.

> Sincerely yours,
> Margaret Mead

"Cultures" are ethnographic collections. Since Tylor's founding definition of 1871 the term has designated a rather vague "complex whole" including everything that is learned group behavior, from body techniques to symbolic orders. There have been recurring attempts to define culture more precisely or, for example, to distinguish it from "social structure."[34] But the inclusive use persists. For there are times when we still need to be able to speak holistically of Japanese or Trobriand or Moroccan culture in the confidence that we are designating something real and differentially coherent. It is increasingly clear, however, that the concrete activity of representing a culture, subculture, or indeed any coherent domain of collective activity is always strategic and selective. The world's societies are too systematically interconnected to permit any easy isolation of separate or independently functioning systems.[35] The increased pace of historical change, the common recurrence of stress in the systems under study, forces a new self-consciousness about the way cultural wholes and boundaries are constructed and translated. The pioneering *élan* of Margaret Mead "completing a culture" in highland New Guinea, collecting a dispersed population, discovering its key customs, naming the result–in this case "the Mountain Arapesh"–is no longer possible.

To see ethnography as a form of culture collecting (not, of course, the *only* way to see it) highlights the ways that diverse experiences and facts are selected, gathered, detached from their original temporal occasions, and given enduring value in a new arrangement. Collecting–at least in the West, where time is generally thought to be linear and irreversible–implies a rescue of phenomena from inevitable historical decay or loss. The collection contains what "deserves" to be kept, remembered, and treasured. Artifacts and customs are saved out of time.[36] Anthropological culture collectors have typically gathered what seems "traditional"–what by definition is opposed to modernity. From a complex historical reality (which includes current ethnographic encounters) they select what gives form, structure, and continuity to a world. What is hybrid or "historical" in an emergent sense has been less commonly collected and presented as a system of authenticity. For example in New Guinea Margaret Mead and Reo Fortune chose not to study groups that were, as Mead wrote in a letter, "badly missionized"[37]; and it had been self-evident to Malinowski in the Trobriands that what most deserved scientific attention was the circumscribed "culture" threatened by a host of modern "outside" influences. The experience of the Melanesians becoming Christians for their own reasons—learning to play, and play with, the outsiders' games—did not seem worth salvaging.

Every appropriation of culture, whether by insiders or outsiders, implies a specific temporal position and form of historical narration. Gathering, owning, classifying, and valuing are certainly not restricted to the West; but elsewhere these activities need not be associated with accumulation (rather than redistribution) or with preservation (rather than natural or historical decay). The Western practice of culture collecting has its own local genealogy, enmeshed in distinct European notions of temporality and order. It is worth dwelling for a moment on this genealogy, for it organizes the assumptions being arduously unlearned by new theories of practice, process, and historicity.[38]

A crucial aspect of the recent history of the culture concept has been its alliance (and division of labor) with "art." Culture, even without a capital *c*, strains toward aesthetic form and autonomy. I have already suggested that modern culture ideas and art ideas function together in an "art-culture system." The inclusive twentieth-century culture category—one that does not privilege "high" or "low" culture—is plausible only within this system, for while in principle admitting all learned human behavior, this culture with a small *c* orders phenomena in ways that privilege the coherent, balanced, and "authentic" aspects of shared life. Since the mid-nineteenth century, ideas of culture have gathered up those elements that seem to give continuity and depth to collective existence, seeing it whole rather than disputed, torn, intertextual, or syncretic. Mead's almost postmodern image of "a local native reading the index to *The Golden Bough* just to see if they had missed anything" is not a vision of authenticity.

Mead found Arapesh receptivity to outside influences "annoying." *Their* culture collecting complicated hers. Historical developments would later force her to provide a revised picture of these difficult Melanesians. In a new preface to the 1971 reprint of her three-volume ethnography *The Mountain Arapesh* Mead devotes several pages to letters from Bernard Narokobi, an Arapesh then studying law in Sydney, Australia. The anthropologist readily admits her astonishment at hearing from him: "How was it that one of the Arapesh—a people who had had such a light hold on any form of collective style—should have come further than any individual among the Manus, who had moved as a group into the modern world in the years between our first study of them, in 1928, and the beginning of our restudy, in 1953?"[39] She goes on to explain that Narakobi, along with other Arapesh men studying in Australia, had "moved from one period in human culture to another" as "individuals." The Arapesh were "less tightly bound within a coherent culture" than Manus.[40] Narokobi writes, however, as a member of his "tribe," speaking with pride of the values and accomplishments of his "clansfolk." (He uses the name Arapesh sparingly.) He articulates the possibility of a new multiterritorial "cultural" identity: "I feel now that I can feel proud of my tribe and at the same time feel I belong not only to Papua-New Guinea, a nation to be, but to the world community at large."[41] Is not this modern way of being "Arapesh" already prefigured in Mead's earlier image of a resourceful native paging through *The Golden Bough*? Why must such behavior be marginalized or classed as "individual" by the anthropological culture collector?

Expectations of wholeness, continuity, and essence have long been built into the linked Western ideas of culture and art. A few words of recent background must suffice, since to map the history of these concepts would lead us on a chase for origins back at least to the Greeks. Raymond Williams provides a starting point in the early nineteenth century—a moment of unprecented historical and social disruption. In *Culture and Society*, *Keywords*, and elsewhere Williams has traced a parallel development in usage for the words *art* and *culture*. The changes reflect complex responses to industrialism, to the specter of "mass society," to accelerated social conflict and change.[42]

According to Williams in the eighteenth century the word *art* meant predominantly "skill." Cabinetmakers, criminals, and painters were each in their way artful. *Culture* designated a tendency to natural growth, its uses predominantly agricultural and personal: both plants and human individuals could be "cultured." Other meanings also present in the eighteenth century did not predominate until the nineteenth. By 1820s *art* increasingly designated a special domain of creativity, spontaneity, and purity, a realm of refined sensibility and expressive "genius." The "artist" was set apart from, often against, society—whether "mass" or "bourgeois." The term *culture* followed a parallel course, coming to mean what was most elevated, sensitive, essential, and precious—most uncommon—in society. Like art, culture became a general category; Williams calls it a "final court of appeal" against threats of vulgarity and leveling. It existed in essential opposition to perceived "anarchy."

Art and culture emerged after 1800 as mutually reinforcing domains of human *value*, strategies for gathering, marking off, protecting the best and most interesting creations of "Man."[43] In the twentieth century the categories underwent a series of further developments. The plural, anthropological definition of culture (lower-case *c* with a possibility of a final *s*) emerged as a liberal alternative to racist classifications of human diversity. It was a sensitive means for understanding different and dispersed "whole ways of life" in a high colonial context of unprecedented global interconnection. *Culture* in its full evolutionary richness and authenticity, formerly reserved for the best creations of modern Europe, could now be extended to all the world's populations. In the anthropological vision of Boas' generation "cultures" were of equal value. In their new plurality, however, the nineteenth-century definitions were not entirely transformed. If they became less elitist (distinctions between "high" and "low" culture were erased) and less Eurocentric (every human society was fully "cultural"), nevertheless a certain body of assumptions were carried over from the older definitions. George Stocking shows the complex interrelations of nineteenth-century humanist and emerging anthropological definitions of culture.[44] He suggests that anthropology owes as much to Matthew Arnold as to its official founding father, E.B. Tylor. Indeed much of the vision embodied in *Culture and Anarchy* has been transferred directly into relativist anthropology. A powerful structure of feeling continues to see culture, wherever it is found, as a coherent *body* that lives and dies. Culture is enduring, traditional, structural (rather than contingent, syncretic, historical). Culture is a process of ordering, not of disruption. It changes and develops like a living organism. It does not normally "survive" abrupt alterations.

In the early twentieth century, as *culture* was being extended to all the world's functioning societies, an increasing number of exotic, primitive, or archaic objects came to be seen as "art." They were equal in aesthetic and moral value with the greatest Western masterpieces. By midcentury the new attitude toward "primitive art" had been accepted by large numbers of educated Europeans and Americans. Indeed from the standpoint of the late twentieth century it becomes clear that the parallel concepts of art and culture did successfully, albeit temporarily, comprehend and incorporate a plethora of non-Western artifacts and customs. This was accomplished through two strategies. First, objects re-classified as "primitive art" were admitted to the imaginary museum of human creativity and, though more slowly, to the actual fine arts museums of the West. Second, the discourse and institutions of modern anthropology constructed comparative and synthetic images of Man drawing evenhandedly from among the world's authentic ways of life, however strange in appearance or obscure in origin. Art and culture, categories for the best creations of Western humanism, were in principle extended to all the world's peoples.

It is perhaps worth stressing that nothing said here about the historicity of these cultural or artistic categories should be construed as claiming that they are false or denying that many of their values are worthy of support. Like any successful discursive arrangement the art-culture authenticity system articulates considerable domains of truth and scientific progress as well as areas of blindness and controversy. By emphasizing the transience of the system I do so out of a conviction (it is more a feeling of the historical ground moving underfoot) that the classifications and generous appropriations of Western art and culture categories are now much less stable than before. This instability appears to be linked to the growing interconnection of the world's populations and to the contestation since the 1950s of colonialism and Eurocentrism. Art collecting and culture collecting now take place within a changing field of counterdiscourses, syncretisms, and reappropriations originating both outside and inside "the West." I cannot discuss the geopolitical causes of these developments. I can only hint at their transforming consequences and stress that the modern genealogy of culture and art that I have been sketching increasingly appears to be a local story. "Culture" and "art" can no longer be simply *extended* to non-Western peoples and things. They can at worst be *imposed*, at best *translated*—both historically and politically contingent operations.

Before I survey some of the current challenges to Western modes of collection and authentication, it may be worth portraying the still-dominant form of art and culture collecting in a more limited, concrete setting. The system's underlying historical assumptions will then become inescapable. For if collecting in the West salvages things out of non-repeatable time, what is the assumed direction of this time? How does it confer rarity and authenticity on the varied productions of human skill? Collecting presupposes a story; a story occurs in a "chronotope."

A Chronotope for Collecting

> *Dans son effort pour comprendre le monde, l'homme dispose*
> *donc toujours d'un surplus de signification.* —Claude Lévi-Strauss

The term *chronotope*, as used by Bakhtin, denotes a configuration of spatial and temporal indicators in a fictional setting where (and when) certain activities and stories *take place*.[45] One cannot realistically situate historical detail—putting something "in its time"—without appealing to explicit or implicit chronotopes. Claude Lévi-Strauss's pointed, nostalgic recollections of New York during the Second World War can serve as a chronotope for modern art and culture collecting. The setting is elaborated in an essay whose French title, "New York post-et préfiguratif," suggests its underlying spatio-temporal predicament more strongly than the published English translation, "New York in 1941."[46] The essay falls within a microgenre of Lévi-Strauss's writing, one he developed with virtuosity in *Tristes tropiques*. Specific places—Rio, Fire Island, new Brazilian cities, Indian sacred sites—appear as moments of intelligible human order and transformation surrounded by the destructive, entropic currents of global history.

In what follows I have supplemented the essay on New York with passages from other texts written by Lévi-Strauss either during the war years or in recollection of them. In reading them as a unified chronotrope, one ought to bear in mind that these are not historical records but complex literary commemorations. The time-space in question has been retrospectively composed by Lévi-Strauss and recomposed, for other purposes, by myself.

• • •

A refugee in New York during the Second World War, the anthropologist is bewildered and delighted by a landscape of unexpected juxtapositions. His recollections of those seminal years, during which he invented structural anthropology, are bathed in a magical light. New York is full of delightful incongruities. Who could resist

> *the performances that we watched for hours at the Chinese opera under the first arch of the Brooklyn Bridge, where a company that had come long ago from China had a large following. Every day, from mid-afternoon until past midnight, it would perpetuate the traditions of classical Chinese opera. I felt myself going back in time no less when I went to work every morning in the American room of the New York Public Library. There, under its neo-classical arcades and between walls paneled with old oak, I sat near an Indian in a feather headdress and a beaded buckskin jacket—who was taking notes with a Parker pen.*[47]

As Lévi-Strauss tells it, the New York of 1941 is an anthropologist's dream, a vast selection of human culture and history.[48] A brief walk or a subway ride will take him from a Greenwich Village reminiscent of Balzac's Paris to the towering skyscrapers of Wall Street. Turning a corner in this jumble of immigrants and ethnic groups, the stroller suddenly enters a different world with its own language, customs, cuisine. Everything is available for consumption. In New York one can obtain almost any treasure. The anthropologist and his artistic friends André Breton, Max Ernst, André Masson, Georges Duthuit, Yves Tanguy, and Matta find masterpieces of pre-Colombian, Indian, Oceanic, or Japanese art stuffed in dealers' closets or apartments. Everything somehow finds its way here. For Lévi-Strauss New York in the 1940s is a wonderland of sudden openings to other times and places, of cultural matter out of place:

> *New York (and this is the source of its charm and peculiar fascination) was then a city where anything seemed possible. Like the urban fabric, the social and cultural fabric was riddled with holes. All you had to do was pick one and slip through it if, like Alice, you wanted to get to the other side of the looking glass and find worlds so enchanting that they seemed unreal.*[49]

The anthropological *flâneur* is delighted, amazed, but also troubled by the chaos of simultaneous possibilities. This New York has something in common with the early-century dada-surrealist flea market–but with a difference. Its *objets trouvés* are not just occasions for reverie. This they surely are, but they are also signs of vanishing worlds. Some are treasures, works of great art.

Lévi-Strauss and the refugee surrealists were passionate collectors. The Third Avenue art dealer they frequented and advised, Julius Carlebach, always had several Northwest Coast, Melanesian, or Eskimo pieces on hand. According to Edmund Carpenter, the surrealists felt an immediate affinity with these objects' predilection for "visual puns"; their selections were nearly always of a very high quality. In addition to the art dealers another source for this band of primitive-art connoisseurs was the Museum of the American Indian. As Carpenter tells it: "The Surrealists began to visit the Bronx warehouse of that Museum, selecting for themselves, concentrating on a collection of magnificent Eskimo masks. These huge visual puns, made by the Kuskokwim Eskimo a century or more ago, constituted the greatest collection of its kind in the world. But the Museum Director, George Heye, called them "jokes" and sold half for $38 and $54 each. The Surrealists bought the best. Then they moved happily through Heye's Northwest Coast collection, stripping it of one masterwork after another."[50] In 1946 Max Ernst, Barnett Newman, and several others mounted an exhibit of Northwest Coast Indian Painting at the Betty Parsons Gallery. They brought together pieces from their private collections and artifacts from the American Museum of Natural History. By moving the museum pieces across town, "the Surrealists declassified them as scientific specimens and reclassified them as art."[51]

The category of primitive art was emerging, with its market, its connoisseurship, and its close ties to modernist aesthetics. What had begun with the vogue for *l'art nègre* in the twenties would become institutionalized by the fifties and sixties; but in wartime New York the battle to gain widespread recognition for tribal objects was not yet won. Lévi-Strauss recalls that as cultural attaché to the French Embassy in 1946 he tried in vain to arrange a trade: for a massive collection of American Indian art a few Matisses and Picassos. But "the French authorities turned a deaf ear to my entreaties, and the Indian collections wound up in American museums."[52] The collecting of Lévi-Strauss and the surrealists during the forties was part of a struggle to gain aesthetic status for these increasingly rare masterworks.

· · ·

New York seemed to have something unusual, valuable, and beautiful for everyone. Franz Boas liked to tell his European visitors about a Kwakiutl informant who had come to work with him in the city. As Roman Jakobson recalls:

> Boas loved to depict the indifference of this man from Vancouver Island toward Manhattan sky-scrapers ("we built houses next to one another, and you stack them on top of each other"), toward the Aquarium, ("we throw such fish back in the lake") or toward the motion pictures which seemed tedious and senseless. On the other hand, the stranger stood for hours spellbound in the Times Square freak shows with their giants and dwarfs, bearded ladies and fox-tailed girls, or in the Automats where drinks and sandwiches appear miraculously and where he felt transferred to the universe of Kwakiutl fairy-tales.[53]

In Lévi-Strauss's memory brass balls on staircase bannisters also figure in the collection of fascinating phenomena.[54]

• • •

For a European New York's sheer space is vertiginous:

> I strode up and down miles of Manhattan avenues, those deep chasms over which loomed skyscrapers' fantastic cliffs. I wandered randomly into cross streets, whose physiognomy changed drastically from one block to the next: sometimes poverty-stricken, sometimes middle-class or provincial, and most often chaotic. New York was decidedly not the ultra-modern metropolis I had expected, but an immense, horizontal and vertical disorder attributable to some spontaneous upheaval of the urban crust rather than to the deliberate plans of builders.[55]

Lévi-Strauss's New York is a juxtaposition of ancient and recent "strata," chaotic remnants of former "upheavals." As in *Tristes tropiques* metaphors from geology serve to transform empirical surface incongruities or faults into legible history. For Lévi-Strauss the jumble of Manhattan becomes intelligible as an overlay of past and future, legible as a story of cultural development. Old and new are side by side. The European refugee encounters scraps of his past as well as a troubling prefiguration of common destiny.

New York is a site of travel and reverie unlike the oneiric city of Breton's *Najda* or Aragon's *Paysan de Paris*. For Parisian emigrés finding their feet on its streets and avenues it is never a known place, something to be made strange by a certain surrealist and ethnographic attention. Instead they are ambushed by the familiar—an older Paris in Greenwich Village, glimpses of the European world in immigrant neighborhoods, medieval buildings reassembled at the Cloisters. But these reminders are masks, survivals, mere collectibles. In New York one is permanently away from home, *dépaysé*, both in space and in time. Post- and pre-figurative New York is fantastically suspended between a jumble of pasts and a uniform future.

> Whoever wanted to go hunting needed only a little culture, and flair, for doorways to open in the wall of industrial civilization and reveal other worlds and other times. Doubtless nowhere more than in New York at that time were there such facilities for escape. Those possibilities seem almost mythical today when we no longer dare to dream of doors: at best we may wonder

about niches to cower in. But even these have become the stake in a fierce competition among those who are not willing to live in a world without friendly shadows or secret shortcuts known only to a few initiates. Losing its old dimensions one after another, this world has pushed us back into the one remaining dimension: one will probe it in vain for secret loopholes.[56]

The resigned "entropologist" of *Tristes tropiques* remembers New York as the final glow and prophetic disintegration of all real cultural differences. Soon even the loopholes will be gone. Millennia of human diversity and invention seem to have been shipwrecked here, remnants and broken shards, good to evoke in escapist reveries, good to collect as art (or antiques), and "good to think with" in salvaging the cultural structures of a trans-historical *esprit humain*. The chronotope of New York prefigures anthropology.

Structuralist anthropology at least was conceived and written there. It is hard to imagine a better setting. Among New York's jumble of cultures, arts, and traditions, as a professor at the Ecole Libre des Hautes Etudes, Lévi-Strauss attended Roman Jakobson's celebrated lectures on sound and meaning. On many occasions he has testified to their revolutionary impact. Jakobson's demonstration that the bewildering di-versity of meaningful human sounds could be reduced to discrete differential systems through the application of phonemic analysis offered an immediate model for studying the plethora of human kinship systems. More generally Jakobson's approach suggested a research program—that of discovering elementary cognitive structures behind the many "language-like" productions of human culture. Amid the cultural-historical jumble of wartime New York—too much in the same place at the same time—Lévi-Strauss glimpsed an underlying order.

The Elementary Structures of Kinship was researched in the New York Public Library reading room, where, beside what seemed to be a parody of a feathered Indian with a Parker pen, Lévi-Strauss pored over accounts of tribal marriage rules. The founding text of structural anthropology was drafted in a small, dilapidated studio in Greenwich Village, down the street from Yves Tanguy and a few yards (through the walls) from Claude Shannon, who, unknown to his neighbor, "was creating cybernetics."[57]

• • •

Uptown at the American Museum of Natural History Lévi-Strauss could wander and wonder among the intimate, hyperreal dioramas of African animal species. Or he could marvel in the Hall of Northwest Coast Indians, where Kwakiutl and Tlingit masks in their glass cases whispered to him of Baudelairean *correspondences*.[58] Indeed by the 1940s a deep correspondence between primitive and modern art was widely assumed in avant-garde milieux. The anthropologist friend of the surrealists saw these magical, archaic objects as luminous examples of human creative genius. He wrote in 1943 for the *Ga-zette des beaux arts*:

These objects—beings transformed into things, human animals, living boxes—seem as remote as possible from our own conception of art since the time of the Greeks. Yet even here one would err to suppose that a single possibility of the aesthetic life had escaped the prophets and virtuosos of the Northwest Coast. Several of those masks and statues are thoughtful portraits

*which prove a concern to attain not only physical resemblance but the most subtle spiritual es-
sence of the soul. The sculptor of Alaska and British Columbia is not only the sorcerer who
confers upon the supernatural a visible form but also the creator, the interpreter who translates
into eternal chefs d'oeuvre the fugitive emotions of man.*[59]

Human artistic creation transcends location and time. To communicate the incredible inventiveness he sees in the Northwest Coast Hall, Lévi-Strauss finds a revealing comparison: "This incessant renovation, this sureness which in no matter what direction guarantees definite and overwhelming success, this scorn of the beaten path, this ceaseless driving toward new feats which infallibly ends in dazzling results—to know this our civilization had to await the exceptional destiny of a Picasso. It is not futile to emphasize that the daring ventures of a single man which have left us breathless for thirty years, were known and practiced during one hundred and fifty years by an entirely indigenous culture."[60] The passage is undoubtedly adapted to its occasion: the need to promote tribal works for an art-world public. (Elsewhere Lévi-Strauss would stress the systems limiting and making possible inventions by any local group or individual creator.) Here he insists only that tribal works are as inventive as that modern paragon of creativity, Picasso. Implicit in the conceit was a vision of human cultures as comparable to creative artists. As I have already argued, the twentieth-century categories of art and culture presupposed each other.

The categories were, however, institutionally separated. If the surrealists could reclassify tribal objects by moving them across town from an anthropology museum to an art gallery, the end points of the traffic were not thereby undermined. The discourses of anthropology and art were developing on separate but complimentary paths. Their evolving relationship may be seen in a legendary surrealist journal of 1942-43 edited by David Hare and dominated by its "editorial advisors" André Breton, Max Ernst, and Marcel Duchamp. *vvv*, according to its subtitle, aspired to cover the fields of "poetry, plastic arts, anthropology, sociology, psychology." In fact it did justice to the first two, with a sprinkling of the third. (Only four issues of *vvv* appeared in four years.) Number 1 contained two short articles by Lévi-Strauss, one on Kaduveo Indian face painting, the other an obituary for Malinowski. The following number contained a note by Alfred Métraux on two ancestral figurines from Easter Island. And in the final issue Robert Allerton Parker fancifully interpreted complex line drawings from the New Hebrides (extracted from A. B. Deacon's ethnography) under the title "Cannibal Designs." In general material from non-Western cultures was included as exoticism or naive art. There were occasional photos of an Alaskan mask or a kachina.

In *vvv* anthropology was part of the décor of avant-garde art and writing. Serious cultural analysis made no real inroads into what were by now canonical surrealist notions of genius, inspiration, the irrational, the magical, the exotic, the primitive. Few of those around Breton (with the possible exception of Max Ernst) had any systematic interest in ethnological science. Lévi-Strauss's contributions to *vvv* seem out of place. Essentially a journal of art and literature, *vvv* was preoccupied with dreams, archetypes, genius, and apocalyptic revolution. It engaged in little of the unsettling, reflexive ethnography practiced by the dissidents of the earlier journal *Documents*.[61]

"Mainstream" surrealism did not typically bring cultural analysis to bear on its own categories.

Surrealist art and structural anthropology were both concerned with the human spirit's "deep" shared springs of creativity. The common aim was to transcend–not, as in *Documents,* to describe critically or subvert–the local orders of culture and history. Surrealism's subject was an international and elemental humanity "anthropological" in scope. Its object was Man, something it shared with an emerging structuralism. But a conventional division of labor was solidifying. Within the project of probing and extending humanity's creative esprit, the two methods diverged, one playing art to the other's science.

· · ·

Modern practices of art and culture collecting, scientific and avant-garde, have situated themselves at the end of a global history. They have occupied a place–apocalyptic, progressive, revolutionary, or tragic–from which to gather the valued inheritances of Man. Concretizing this temporal set up, Lévi-Strauss's "post- and prefigurative" New York anticipates humanity's entropic future and gathers up its diverse pasts in de-contextualized, collectible forms. The ethnic neighborhoods, the provincial reminders, the Chinese Opera Company, the feathered Indian in the library, the works of art from other continents and eras that turn up in dealers' closets: all are survivals, remnants of threatened or vanished traditions. The world's cultures appear in the chronotope as shreds of humanity, degraded commodities, or elevated great art but always functioning as vanishing "loopholes" or "escapes" from a one-dimensional fate.

In New York a jumble of humanity has washed up in one vertiginous place and time, to be grasped simultaneously in all its precious diversity and emerging uniformity. In this chronotope the pure products of humanity's pasts are rescued by modern aesthetics only as sublimated art. They are salvaged by modern anthropology as consultable archives for thinking about the range of human invention. In Lévi-Strauss's setting the products of the present-becoming-future are shallow, impure, escapist, and "retro" rather than truly different–"antiques" rather than genuine antiquities. Cultural invention is subsumed by a commodified "mass culture."[62]

The chronotope of New York supports a global allegory of fragmentation and ruin. The modern anthropologist, lamenting the passing of human diversity, collects and values its survivals, its enduring works of art. Lévi Strauss's most prized acquisition from a marvelous New York where everything seemed available was a nearly complete set of volumes 1 through 48 of the *Annual Reports* of the Bureau of American Ethnology. These were, he tells us in another evocation of the war years, "sacrosanct volumes, representing most of our knowledge about the American Indians . . . It was as though the American Indian cultures had suddenly come alive and become almost tangible through the physical contact that these books, written and published before these cultures' definite extinction, established between their times and me."[63] These precious records of human diversity had been recorded by an ethnology still in what he calls its "pure" rather than "diluted" state.[64] They would form the authentic ethnographic material from which structuralism's metacultural orders were constructed.

Anthropological collections and taxonomies, however, are constantly menaced by temporal contingencies. Lévi-Strauss knows this. It is a disorder he always holds at bay. For example in *Tristes tropiques* he is acutely aware that focusing on a tribal past necessarily blinds him to an emergent present. Wandering through the modern landscape of New York, far from encountering less and less to know, the anthropologist is confronted with more and more—a heady mix-and-match of possible human combinations. He struggles to maintain a unified perspective; he looks for order in deep "geological" structures. But in Lévi-Strauss's work generally, the englobing "entropological" narrative barely contains a current history of loss, transformation, invention, and emergence.

Toward the end of his brilliant inaugural lecture at the Collège de France, "The Scope of Anthropology," Lévi-Strauss evokes what he calls "anthropological doubt," the inevitable result of ethnographic risktaking, the "buffetings and denials directed at one's most cherished ideas and habits by other ideas and habits best able to rebut them."[65] He poignantly recalls Boas's Kwakiutl visitor, transfixed by the freaks and automats of Times Square, and he wonders whether anthropology may not be condemned to equally bizarre perceptions of the distant societies and histories it seeks to grasp. New York was perhaps Lévi-Strauss's only true "fieldwork": for once he stayed long enough and mastered the local language. Aspects of the place, such as Boas's Kwakiutl, have continued to charm and haunt his anthropological culture collecting.

But one New York native sits with special discomfort in the chronotope of 1941. This is the feathered Indian with the Parker pen working in the Public Library. For Lévi-Strauss the Indian is primarily associated with the past, the "extinct" societies recorded in the precious Bureau of American Ethonology *Annual Reports*. The anthropologist feels himself "going back in time."[66] In modern New York an Indian can appear only as a survival or a kind of incongruous parody.

Another historical vision might have positioned the two scholars in the library differently. The decade just preceding Lévi-Strauss's arrival in New York had seen a dramatic turnaround in federal policy. Under John Collier's leadership at the Bureau of Indian Affairs a "New Indian Policy" actively encouraged tribal reorganization all over the country. While Lévi-Strauss studied and collected their pasts, many "extinct" Native American groups were in the process of reconstituting themselves culturally and politically. Seen in this context, did the Indian with the Parker pen represent a "going back in time" or a glimpse of another future? That is a different story.[67]

Other Appropriations

To tell these other stories, local histories of cultural survival and emergence, we need to resist deep-seated habits of mind and systems of authenticity. We need to be suspicious of an almost-automatic tendency to relegate non-Western peoples and objects to the pasts of an increasingly homogeneous humanity. A few examples of current invention and contestation may suggest different chronotopes for art and culture collecting.

Anne Vitart-Fardoulis, a curator at the Musée de l'Homme, has published a sensitive account of the aesthetic, historical, and cultural discourses routinely used to explicate individual museum objects. She discusses a famous intricately painted animal skin (its present name: M.H.34.33.5), probably originating among the Fox Indians of North America. The skin turned up in Western collecting systems some time ago in a "cabinet of curiosities"; it was used to educate aristocratic children and was much admired for its aesthetic qualities. Vitart-Fardoulis tells us that now the skin can be decoded ethnographically in terms of its combined "masculine" and "feminine" graphic styles and understood in the context of a probable role in specific ceremonies. But the meaningful contexts are not exhausted. The story takes a new turn:

> The grandson of one of the Indians who came to Paris with Buffalo Bill was searching for the [painted skin] tunic his grandfather had been forced to sell to pay his way back to the United States when the circus collapsed. I showed him all the tunics in our collection, and he paused before one of them. Controlling his emotion, he spoke. He told the meaning of this lock of hair, of that design, why this color had been used, the meaning of that feather . . . This garment, formerly beautiful and interesting but passive and indifferent, little by little became meaningful, active testimony to a living moment through the mediation of someone who did not observe and analyze but who lived the object and for whom the object lived. It scarcely matters whether the tunic is really his grandfather's.[68]

Whatever is happening in this encounter, two things are clearly *not* happening. The grandson is not replacing the object in its original or "authentic" cultural context. That is long past. His encounter with the painted skin is part of a modern recollection. And the painted tunic is not being appreciated as art, as an aesthetic object. The encounter is too specific, too enmeshed in family history and ethnic memory.[69] Some aspects of "cultural" and "aesthetic" appropriation are certainly at work, but they occur within a *current tribal history*, a different temporality from that governing the dominant systems I diagrammed earlier. In the context of a present-becoming-future the old painted tunic becomes newly, traditionally meaningful.

The currency of "tribal" artifacts is becoming more visible to non-Indians. Many new tribal recognition claims are pending at the Department of the Interior. And whether or not they are formally successful matters less than what they make manifest: the historical and political reality of Indian survival and resurgence, a force that impinges on Western art and culture collections. The "proper" place of many objects in museums is now subject to contest. The Zuni who prevented the loan of their war god to the Museum of Modern Art[70] were challenging the dominant art-culture system, for in traditional Zuni belief war god figures are sacred and dangerous. They are not ethnographic artifacts, and they are certainly not "art." Zuni claims on these objects specifically reject their "promotion" (in all senses of the term) to the status of aesthetic or scientific treasures.

I would not claim that the only true home for the objects in question is in "the tribe"—a location that, in many cases, is far from obvious. My point is just that the dominant, interlocking contexts of art and anthropology are no longer self-evident and uncontested. There are other contexts, histories, and futures in which non-Western objects and cultural records may "belong." The rare Maori artifacts that in 1984-85 toured museums in the United States normally reside in New Zealand museums. But they are controlled by the traditional Maori authorities, whose permission was required for them to leave the country. Here and elsewhere the circulation of museum collections is significantly influenced by resurgent indigenous communities.

What is at stake is something more than conventional museum programs of community education and "outreach."[71] Current developments question the very status of museums as historical-cultural theaters of memory. Whose memory? For what purposes? The Provincial Museum of British Columbia has for some time encouraged Kwakiutl carvers to work from models in its collection. It has lent out old pieces and donated new ones for use in modern potlatches. Surveying these developments, Michael Ames, who directs the University of British Columbia Museum, observes that "Indians, traditionally treated by museums only as objects and clients, add now the role of patrons." He continues: "The next step has also occurred. Indian communities establish their own museums, seek their own National Museum grants, install their own curators, hire their own anthropologists on contract, and call for repatriation of their own collections."[72] The Quadra Island Kwakiutl Museum located in Quathraski Cove, British Columbia, displays tribal work returned from the national collections in Ottawa. The objects are exhibited in glass cases, but arranged according to their original family ownership. In Alert Bay, British Columbia, the U'mista Cultural Centre displays repatriated artifacts in a traditional Kwakiutl "big house" arranged in the sequence of their appearance at the potlatch ceremony. The new institutions function both as public exhibits and as cultural centers linked to ongoing tribal traditions. Two Haida museums have also been established in the Queen Charlotte Islands, and the movement is growing elsewhere in Canada and the United States.

Resourceful Native American groups may yet appropriate the Western museum—as they have made their own another European institution, the "tribe." Old objects may again participate in a tribal present-becoming-future. Moreover, it is worth briefly noting that the same thing is possible for written artifacts collected by salvage ethnography. Some of these old texts (myths, linguistic samples, lore of all kinds) are now being recycled as local history and tribal "literature."[73] The objects of both art and culture collecting are susceptible to other appropriations.

This disturbance of Western object systems is reflected in a recent book by Ralph Coe, *Lost and Found Traditions: Native American Art: 1965-1985*.[74] Coe's work is a collector's tour de force. Once again a white authority "discovers" true tribal art—but with significant differences. Hundreds of photographers document very recent works, some made for local use, some for sale to Indians or white outsiders. Beautiful objects—many formerly classified as curios, folk art, or tourist art—are located in ongoing, inventive traditions. Coe effectively questions the widespread assumption that fine tribal work is disappearing, and he throws doubt on common criteria for judging purity and authenticity. In his collection among recognizably traditional kachinas, totem poles, blankets, and plaited baskets we find skillfully beaded tennis shoes and baseball caps, articles developed for the curio trade, quilts, and decorated leather cases (peyote kits modeled on old-fashioned toolboxes).

Since the Native American Church, in whose ceremonies the peyote kits are used, did not exist in the nineteenth century, their claim to traditional status cannot be based on age. A stronger historical claim can in fact be made for many productions of the curio trade, such as the beaded "fancies" (hanging birds, mirror frames) made by Matilda Hill, a Tuscarora who sells at Niagra Falls:

> *"Just try telling Matilda Hill that her 'fancies' are tourist curios," said Mohawk Rick Hill, author of an unpublished paper on the subject. "The Tuscarora have been able to trade pieces like that bird or beaded frame at Niagara since the end of the War of 1812, when they were granted exclusive rights, and she wouldn't take kindly to anyone slighting her culture!"*

"Surely," Coe adds, "a trade privilege established at Niagara Falls in 1816 should be acceptable as tradition by now."[75] He drives the general point home: "Another misconception derives from our failure to recognize that Indians have always traded both within and outside their culture; it is second nature to the way they operate in all things. Many objects are, and always have been, created in the Indian world without a specific destination in mind. The history of Indian trading predates any white influence, and trading continues today unabated. It is a fascinating instrument of social continuity, and in these modern times its scope has been greatly enlarged."[76]

Coe does not hesitate to commission new "traditional" works, and he spends considerable time eliciting the specific meaning of objects both as individual possessions and as tribal art. We see and hear particular artists; the coexistence of spiritual, aesthetic, and commercial forces is always visible. Overall Coe's collecting project represents and advocates ongoing art forms that are both related to and separate from dominant systems of aesthetic-ethnographic value. In *Lost and Found Traditions* authenticity is something produced, not salvaged. Coe's collection, for all its love of the past, gathers futures.

A long chapter on "tradition" resists summary, for the diverse statements quoted from practice artists, old and young, do not reproduce prevailing Western definitions. "Whites think of our experience as the past," says one group of students discussing the topic. "We know it is right here with us."[77]

> *"We always begin our summer dances with a song that repeats only four words, over and over. They don't mean much of anything in English, 'young chiefs stand up.' To us those words demonstrate our pride in our lineage and our happiness in always remembering it. It is a happy song. Tradition is not something you gab about . . . It's in the doing."*

> *"Your tradition is 'there' always. You're flexible enough to make of it what you want. It's always with you. I pray to the old pots at the ruins and dream about making pottery. I tell them I want to learn it. We live for today, but never forget the past."*

> *"Our job as artists is to go beyond, which implies a love of change, [always accomplished with] traditions in mind, by talking to the elders of the tribe and by being with your grandparents. The stories they tell are just amazing. When you become exposed to them, everything becomes a reflection of those events. There's a great deal of satisfaction being an artist of traditions."*

> *"We've always had charms: everything that's new is old with us."*[78]

1. James Fenton, *Children in Exile: Poems 1963-1984* (New York: Random House, 1984), pp. 81-84.

2. C.B. Macpherson, *The Political Theory of Possessive Individualism* (New York: Oxford University Press, 1962).

3. Richard Handler, "On Having a Culture: Nationalism and the Preservation of Quebec's Patrimoine," in *History of Anthropology*, Vol. 3, *Objects and Others*, ed. George Stocking (Madison: University of Wisconsin Press, 1985), pp. 192-217.

4. Ibid., p. 199.

5. On collecting as a strategy of desire see the highly suggestive catalogue by Jacques Hainard, and Rolland Kaehr, eds. *Collections passion* (Neuchâtel: Musée d' Ethnographie, 1982). This analytic collection of collections was a tour de force of reflexive museology. On collecting and desire see also Donna Haraway's brilliant analysis of the American Museum of Natural History, American manhood, and the threat of decadence between 1908 and 1936. (Donna Haraway, "Teddy Bear Patriarchy: Taxidermy in the Garden of Eden, New York City, 1908-1936," *Social Text* [Winter 1985]: 20-63.) Her work suggests that the passion to collect, preserve, and display is articulated in gendered ways that are historically specific. Pierre Beaucage, Jacques Gomilia, and Lionel Vallée offer critical meditations on the ethnographer's complex experience of objects in *L'expérience anthropologique* (Montreal: Presses de l'Université de Montreal, 1976), pp. 71-133.

6. Walter Benjamin's essay "Unpacking My Library" in *Illuminations*, ed. Hannah Arendt, trans. Harry Zohn (New York: Schocken Books, 1969), pp. 59-68, provides the view of a reflective devotee. Collecting appears as an art of living intimately allied with memory, with obsession, with the salvaging of order from disorder. Benjamin sees (and takes a certain pleasure in) the precariousness of the subjective space attained by the collection. "Every passion borders on the chaotic, but the collector's passion borders on the chaos of memories. More than that: the chance, the fate, that suffuse the past before my eyes are conspicuously present in the accustomed confusion of these books. For what else is this collection but a disorder to which habit has accommodated itself to such an extent that it can appear as order? You have all heard of people whom the loss of their books has turned into invalids, of those who in order to acquire them became criminals. These are the very areas in which any order is a balancing act of extreme precariousness." (p.60)

7. My understanding of the role of the fetish as a mark of otherness in Western intellectual history—from DeBrosses to Marx, Freud, and Deleuze—owes a great deal to the largely unpublished work of William Pietz; see "The Problem of the Fetish, I" *Res* 9 (Spring 1985): 5-17.

8. Susan Stewart, *On Longing: Narratives of the Miniature, the Giagantic, the Souvenir, the Collection* (Baltimore: Johns Hopkins University Press, 1984), p. 163.

9. Ibid., pp. 162-165.

10. Ibid., p. 165.

11. Philip Fisher, "The Future's Past," *New Literary History* 6, no. 3 (1975): 587-606; Krzysztof Pomian, "Entre l'invisible et le visible: La collection," *Libre* 78, no. 3 (1978): 3-56; James Bunn, "The Aesthetics of British Mercantilism," *New Literary History* II (1980): 303-321; Daniel Defert, "The Collection of the World: Accounts of Voyages from the Sixteenth to the Eighteenth Centuries," *Dialectical Anthropology* 7 (1982): 11-20; Johannes Fabian, *Time and Other: How Anthropology Makes Its Object* (New York: Columbia University Press, 1983); Remy Saisselin, *The Bourgeois and the Bibelot* (New Brunswick: Rutgers University Press, 1984).

12. Jean Baudrillard, *Le systeme des objets* (Paris: Gallimard, 1968).

13. Ibid., p. 135.

14. See also Douglas Cole, *Captured Heritage: The Scramble for Nothwest Coast Artifacts* (Seattle: University of Washington Press, 1985), and Michael Pye, "Whose Art Is It Anyway?" *Connoisseur* (March 1987): 78-85.

15. See Nelson Graburn, ed. *Ethnic and Tourist Arts* (Berkeley: University of California Press, 1976), and Benetta Jules-Rosette, *The Message of Tourist Art* (New York: Plenum, 1984).

16. Hugh Honour, *The New Golden Land* (New York: Pantheon, 1975); Steven Mullaney, "Strange Things, Gross Terms, Curious Customs: The Rehearsal of Cultures in the Late Renaissance," *Representations* 3 (1983): 40-67; Jose Rabasa, "Fantasy, Errancy, and Symbolism in New World Motifs: An Essay on Sixteenth Century Spanish Historiography," Ph.D. dissertation (Santa Cruz: University of California Press, 1985).

17. Fabian, *Time and Other*; James Clifford, "On Ethnographic Allegory," in *Writing Culture*, eds. J. Clifford and George Marcus (Berkeley: University of California Press, 1986), pp. 98-121.

18. For "hard" articulations of ethnographic culturalism and aesthetic formalism see Roy Sieber, "The Aesthetics of Traditional African Art," in *Art and Aesthetics in Primitive Societies*, ed. Carol R. Jopling (New York: Dutton), pp. 127-145; Sally Price, and Richard Price, *Afro-American Arts of the Suriname Rain Forest* (Berkeley: University of California Press, 1980); Susan Vogel, *African Masterpieces from the Musée de l'Homme* (New York: Abrams, 1985), pp. 10-11; and William Rubin, ed., *'Primitivism' in Modern Art: Affinity of the Tribal and*

the *Modern* (New York: Museum of Modern Art, 1984). The first two works argue that art can be understood (as opposed to merely appreciated) only in its original context. Vogel and Rubin assert that aesthetic qualities transcend their original local articulation, that "masterpieces" appeal to universal or at least transcultural sensibilities. For a glimpse of how the often incompatible categories of "aesthetic excellence," "use," "rarity," "age," and so on are debated in the exercise of assigning authentic value to tribal works, see the richly inconclusive symposium organized by the journal *African Arts* (Frank Willet et al., "Authenticity in African Art" *African Arts* 9, no. 3 (1976): 6-74).

19. A.J. Greimas, and Francois Rastier, "The Interpretation of Semiotic Constraints," *Yale French Studies*, no. 41 (1968): 86-105.

20. Fredric Jameson, *The Political Unconscious: Narrative as a Socially Symbolic Act* (Ithaca: Cornell University Press, 1981), p. 62, 47.

21. See Howard Becker, *Art Worlds* (Berkeley: University of California Press, 1982).

22. Michael Ames, *Museums, the Public, and Anthropology* (Vancouver: University of British Columbia Press, 1986), pp. 39-42.

23. See James Clifford, "Histories of the Tribal and Modern," in *The Predicament of Culture* (Cambridge: Harvard University Press, 1988), p. 209, n. 11.

24. Ralph Coe, *Lost and Found Traditions: Native American Art: 1965-1985* (Seattle: University of Washington Press, 1986).

25. Elizabeth Williams, "Art and Artifact at the Trocadero," in *History of Anthropology*, ed. Stocking, pp. 145-166.

26. Pomian, "Entre l'invisible et le visible."

27. Christian Feest, "From North America," in *'Primitivism' in Twentieth Century Art*, ed. Rubin, p. 90.

28. William Chapman, "Arranging Ethnology: A.H.L.F. Pitt Rivers and the Typological Tradition," in *History of Anthropology*, ed. Stocking, pp. 24-25.

29. Nelia Dias, "La fondation du Musée d'Ethnographie du Trocadero (1879-1900): Un aspect de l'histoire institutionelle de l'anthropologie française," Thesis, troisième cycle (Paris: Ecole des Hautes Etudes en Sciences Sociale, 1985), pp. 378-379.

30. Jean Jarmin, "Objets trouvés la Mission Dakar-Djibouti," in *Collections passion*, eds. J. Hainard and R. Kaehr, pp. 89-95; J. Jamin, "Les objets ethnographiques sont-ils des choses perdues?" in *Temps perdu, temps retrouvé: Voir les choses du passe au present*, eds. Hainard and Kaehr (Neuchâtel: Musée d'Ethnographie, 1985), pp. 51-74.

31. Hans Haacke, *Framing and Being Framed* (Halifax: Nova Scotia College of Art and Design, 1975); Susan Hiller, "Sacred Circles: 2000 Years of North American Art," *Studio International* (December 1979): 8-15.

32. See Clifford, *The Predicament of Culture*, pp. 189-214.

33. Remo Guidieri, and Francesco Pellizzi, Editorial, *Res* 1 (1981): 3-6. For a post-Freudian positive sense of the fetish see Michel Leiris, "Alberto Giacometti," *Documents* 1, no. 4 (1929): 209-211, trans. J. Clifford in *Sulfur* 15 (1986): 38-41; Leiris, *L'age d'homme* (Paris: Gallimard), trans. Richard Howard as *Manhood* (Berkeley: North Point Press, 1985); for fetish theory's radical possibilities see Pietz, "The Problem of the Fetish," which draws on Deleuze; and for a repentant semiologist's perverse sense of the fetish (the "punctum") as a place of strictly personal meaning unformed by cultural codes (the "studium") see Roland Barthes, *La chambre claire*, trans. Richard Howard as *Camera Lucida* (New York: Hill and Wang, 1981). Jacques Gomila rethinks ethnographic material culture from some of these surrealist-psychoanalytical perspectives ("Objectif, objectal, objecteur, objecte," in Beaucage, Gomila, and Vallée, *L'experience anthropologique*, pp. 71-133).

34. See A.L. Kroeber, and Clyde Kluckhohn, *Culture: A Critical Review of Concepts and Definitions* (New York: Vintage, 1952).

35. George Marcus, "Contemporary Problems of Ethnography in the Modern World System," in *Writing Culture*, eds. Clifford and Marcus, pp. 165-193.

36. An exhibition, "Temps perdu, temps retrouvé," held during 1985 at the Musée d'Ethnographie of Neuchâtel systematically interrogated the temporal predicament of the Western ethnographic museum. Its argument was condensed in the following text, each proposition of which was illustrated museographically: "Prestigious places for locking things up, museums give value to things that are outside of life: in this way they resemble cemeteries. Acquired by dint of dollars, the memory-objects participate in the group's changing identity, serve the powers that be, and accumulate into treasures, while personal memory fades. Faced with the aggressions of everyday life and the passing of phenomena, memory needs objects—always manipulated through aesthetics, selective emphasis, or the mixing of genres. From the perspective of the future, what from the present should be saved?" (Jacques Hainard, and Roland Kaehr, "Temps perdu, temps retrouvé. Du côte de l'ethno . . . ," *Gradhiva* 1 (Autumn 1986): 33; also Hainard and Kaehr, *Temps perdu, temps retrouvé: Voir les choses du passe au present*, in *Temps perdu*, eds. Hainard and Kaehr.)

37. Margaret Mead, *Letters from the Field: 1925-1975* (New York: Harper and Row, 1977), p. 123.
38. Pierre Bourdieu, *Outline of a Theory of Practice* (Cambridge: Cambridge University Press, 1977); Anthony Giddens, *Central Problems in Social Theory: Action, Structure and Contradiction in Social Analysis* (Berkeley: University of California Press, 1979); Sherry Ortner, "Theory in Anthropology since the Sixties," *Comparative Studies in Society and History* 26 (1984): 126-166; Marshall Sahlins, *Islands of History* (Chicago: University of Chicago Press, 1985).
39. Margaret Mead, *The Mountain Arapesh*, Vol. 3 (Garden City: Natural History Press, 1971), p. ix.
40. Ibid., pp. ix-x.
41. Ibid., p. xiii.
42. Although Williams' analysis is limited to England, the general pattern applies elsewhere in Europe, where the timing of modernization differed or where other terms were used. In France for example, the words *civilisation* or, for Durkheim, *société* stand in for *culture*. What is at issue are general qualitative assessments of collective life.
43. As Virginia Dominguez has argued, the emergence of this new subject implies a specific historicity closely tied to ethnology. Drawing on Michel Foucault's *Order of Things* (New York: Random House, 1966) and writing of the scramble for ethnographic artifacts during the "Museum Age" of the late nineteenth century, she cites Douglas Cole's summation of the prevailing rationale: "It is necessary to use the time to collect before it is too late." (Cole, *Captured Heritage*, p. 50) "Too late for what?" Dominguez asks. "There is a historical consciousness here of a special sort. We hear an urgency in the voices of the collectors, a fear that we will no longer be able to get our hands on these objects, and this would amount to an irretrievable loss of the means of preserving our own historicity. There is a twofold displacement here. Objects are collected no longer because of their intrinsic value but as metonyms for the people who produced them. And the people who produced them are the objects of examination not because of their intrinsic value but because of their perceived contribution to our understanding of our own historical trajectory. It is a certain view of 'man' and a certain view 'history' that makes this double displacement possible." (Virginia Dominguez "The Marketing of Heritage," *American Ethnologist* 13, no. 3 (1986): 546-555.)
44. George Stocking, "Arnold Taylor and the Uses of Invention," in *Race, Culture and Evolution* (New York: The Free Press, 1968), pp. 69-90.
45. *Chronotope*: literally "time-space" with no priority to either dimension (Mikhail Bakhtin, "Forms of Time and Chronotope in the Novel," in *The Dialogic Imagination*, ed. Michael Holquist [Austin: University of Texas Press, 1981], pp. 84-258). The chronotope is a fictional setting where historically specific relations of power become visible and certain stories can "take place" (the bourgeois salon in the nineteenth-century social novels, the merchant ship in Conrad's tales of adventure and empire). As Bakhtin puts it: "In the literary artistic chronotope, spatial and temporal indicators are fused into one carefully thought-out, concrete whole. Time, as it were, thickens, takes on flesh, becomes artistically visible; likewise space becomes charged and responsive to the movements of time, plot and history." (p. 84)
46. Claude Lévi-Strauss, "New York post-et préfiguratif," in *Le regard éloigné* (Paris: Plon, 1983), pp. 345-356; and Claude Lévi-Strauss, "New York in 1941," in *The View from Afar* (New York: Basic Books, 1985), pp. 258-267.
47. Lévi-Strauss, "New York in 1941," p. 266.
48. It still is. Returning to the neighborhood where I grew up on the Upper West Side and walking between 116th and 86th Streets, I invariably encounter several races, cultures, languages, a range of exotic smells, "Cuban-Chinese" restaurants, and so on. It is enough to seriously smudge at least the spatial distinction between the First and Third Worlds, center and periphery in the modern world system.
49. Lévi-Strauss, "New York in 1941," p. 261.
50. Edmund Carpenter, "Collecting Northwest Coast Art," in Bill Holm, and Bill Reid, *Indian Art of the Northwest Coast* (Seattle: University of Washington Press, 1975), p. 10.
51. Ibid., p. 11.
52. Lévi-Strauss, "New York in 1941," p. 262.
53. Roman Jakobson, "Boas' view of Grammatical Meaning," in *The Anthropology of Franz Boas*, ed. Walter Goldschmidt (San Francisco: American Anthropology Association, 1959), p. 142.
54. "Scope of Anthropology," in *Structural Anthropology*, Vol. 2 (New York: Basic Books, 1976), p. 27.
55. Lévi-Strauss, "New York in 1941," p. 258.
56. Ibid., p. 262.
57. Ibid., p. 260.
58. Claude Lévi-Strauss, "The Art of the Northwest Coast at the American Museum of Natural History," *Gazette des beaux arts* (September 1943): 180.
59. Ibid., p. 181.
60. Ibid., p. 175.
61. See Clifford, *The Predicament of Culture*, pp. 117-151.
62. Lévi-Strauss, "New York in 1941." pp. 264-267.

63. Claude Lévi-Strauss, "The Work of the Bureau of American Ethnology," in *Structural Anthropology*, p. 50.

64. Lévi-Strauss, "Leçon inaugurale," p. 26.

65. Ibid., p. 26.

66. Lévi-Strauss, "New York in 1941," p. 266.

67. See Clifford, *The Predicament of Culture*, pp. 277-346.

68. Anne Virtart-Fardoulis, "L'objet interrogé: Ou comment faire parler une collection d'ethnographie," *Gradhiva* 1 (Autumn 1986): 12.

69. In his wide-ranging study "Ethnicity and the Post-Modern Arts of Memory" in *Writing Culture*, ed. Clifford and Marcus, pp. 194-233, Michael Fischer identifies general processes of cultural reinvention, personal search, and future-oriented appropriations of tradition. The specificity of some Native American relations with collected "tribal" objects is revealed in a grant proposal to the National Endowment for the Humanities by the Oregon Art Institute (Dan Monroe, "Northwest Coast Native American Art Reinstallation Planning Grant," Application for NEH funding on behalf of the Oregon Art Institute, Portland, Oregon). In preparation for a reinstallation of the Rasmussen Collection of Northwest Coast works at the Portland Art Museum a series of consultations is envisioned with the participation of Haida and Tlingit elders from Alaska. The proposal makes clear that great care must be given "to matching specific groups of objects in the collection to the clan membership and knowledge base of specific elders. Northwest Coast Natives belong to specific clans who have extensive oral traditions and histories over which they have ownership. Elders are responsible for representing their clans as well as their group." The reinstallation "will present *both the academic interpretation of an object or objects and the interpretation of the same material as viewed and understood by Native elders and artists."* (p. 5; original emphasis.)

70. See Clifford, *The Predicament of Culture*, pp. 189-214.

71. Edward Alexander, *Museums in Motion: An Introduction to the History and Functions of Museums* (Nashville: American Association for State and Local History, 1979), p. 215.

72. Ames, "Museums, the Public and Anthropology," p. 57.

73. The archives of James Walker, produced before 1910, have become relevant to the teaching of local history by Sioux on the Pine Ridge Reservation (see Clifford, *The Predicament of Culture*, p. 53, note 15; and Clifford, "Partial Truths," in *Writing Culture*, eds. Clifford and Marcus, pp. 15-17). Also a corpus of translated and untranslated Tolowa tales and linguistic texts collected by A.L. Kroeber and P.E. Goddard are important evidence in a planned petition for tribal recognition. The texts were gathered as "salvage ethnography" to record the shreds of a purportedly vanishing culture. But in the context of Tolowa persistence, retranslated and interpreted by Tolowa elders and their Native American lawyer, the texts yield evidence of tribal history, territorial limits, group distinctness, and oral tradition. They are Tolowa "literature" (Logan Slagle, *Tribal Recognition and the Tolowa*, Lecture presented at conference on the Nature and Function of Minority Literature, University of California, Berkeley, May 25, 1986).

74. On inventive tribal work see also Peter McNair, Alan Hoover, and Kevin Neary, *The Legacy: Tradition and Innovation in Northwest Coast Indian Art* (Vancouver: Douglass and McIntyre, 1984); Jan Steinbright, ed., *Alaskameut '86: An Exhibition of Contemporary Alaska Native Masks* (Fairbanks: Institute of Alaska Native Arts, 1986); Barbara Babcock, Guy Monthan, and Doris Monthan, *The Pueblo Storyteller: Development of a Figurative Ceramic Tradition* (Tuscon: University of Arizona Press, 1986).

75. Coe, *Lost and Found Traditions*, p. 17.

76. Ibid., p. 16. The common presumption that tribal art is *essentially* noncommercial ("sacred," "spiritual," "environmental," and so on) is of questionable value everywhere. A revealing case is the New Guinea Sepik region, where customary objects and lore have long been traded, bought, and sold. To a significant degree the involvement of local groups in the art markets of a wider world can be "traditional." Indigenous commodity systems interact with outside capitalist forces; they do not simply give way to them. The world system is thus dynamically and locally organized. A persistent tendency to see non-Western societies as lacking historical agency is corrected by a growing number of academic studies; for example Renato Rosaldo, *Ilongot Headhunting 1833-1974: A Study in Society and History* (Stanford: Stanford University Press, 1980), and Marshall Sahlins, *Islands of History* (Chicago: University of Chicago Press, 1985). These works undermine the binary ("Orientalist") division of human groups into historical and mythical, "hot" and "cold," diachronic and synchronic, modern and archaic. Sally Price draws attention to the diverse *historical divisions* of non-Western, "tribal" peoples and to the role of art in articulation of these visions ("L'esthetique et le temps: Commentaire sur l'histoire orale de l'art," *L'ethnographie* 82 (1986): 215-225.)

77. Ibid., p. 49.

78. Ibid., p. 46, 47, 79.

Wild Tongues: Affirming Identities

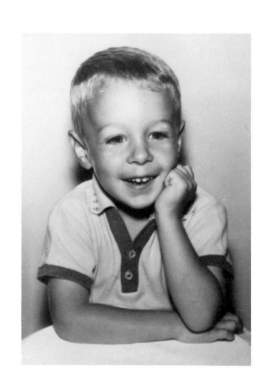

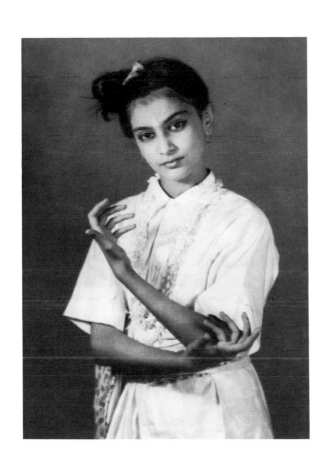

• **Martha Gever**

The Names We Give Ourselves

What attracts me to questions about how cultural identities are produced is the same as what repels me: ambivalence about being a member of a caste which is regularly and ritualistically derided and denied. Having marched on various Gay Pride Days and felt exhilarated by those events, having enjoyed the camaraderie of friends and strangers in lesbian bars, at poetry readings and dinner parties, having stayed up all night reading maudlin lesbian romance novels, having watched innumerable lesbian-produced films and videotapes, having written articles and lectured on lesbian culture, read lesbian scholarly literature and followed lesbian political debates, I still find myself ambivalent. And I find every effort to define a "lesbian sensibility" or a "lesbian community" untenable. And this more than fifteen years after assuming my lesbian identity.

My experience has taught me a few things. Above all, it has taught me that to *be* a lesbian means engaging in a complex, often treacherous, system of cultural identities, representations and institutions, and a history of sexual regulation. This is not a unique status nor a form of privileged consciousness; everyone is implicated in these systems. But being a lesbian tests the meanings of sexual identity in ways that evoke intense, sometimes violent, social disapproval, while being straight is taken for granted as a neutral position from which gay folks deviate. Deviant, pervert, invert, queer—the names describe twists, turns, and distortions in whole, true sexualities, embodied in "real" women and "real" men. Throughout the twentieth century, in Europe and North America the liberal argument against criminalization and other forms of overt punishment for being classified as a "homosexual" was, "They can't help it." Of course, if "they" could, "they" should. So, in these cultures where sexuality and power are intricately intertwined, lesbianism requires an explanation. Unrepentant lesbians are suspect. Very often, we demand such explanations of ourselves and speculate about the sources of our sexual desires, how we came to be "that way," whereas "being straight" is never accompanied by similar fits of self-examination or public inquiry into sexual histories.

At the same time that the freakish, pathological character of lesbian identity troubles me, lesbian cultures—and, I should add, lesbian participation in more generalized gay cultures—fascinate me. Partly this stems from an opposition to the tyranny of straight sexuality in all sectors of Western culture. More importantly, the emergence of international lesbian cultures replaces systems of subterfuge and apology with imaginative, often disturbing challenges to this tyranny, contradicting its absolute authority. Such challenges, however, are not issued from another planet—Uranus perhaps[1]—but are marked by many of the same tensions and contradictions I encounter as a writer on these topics. Rather than roaming around in a general survey of lesbian cultures in an attempt to tease out the implications of these dynamics, I prefer to concentrate on the involvement of lesbians and gay men in one set of cultural institutions–those that comprise "cinema" and related mass media.

Mass cultural forms are relevant here, because they highlight certain questions about the circulation of representations and, specifically, the positions occupied by lesbians and gay men within public discourse: Must we applaud the appearance in mass media of characters who "happen to be gay," as is frequently advocated? Or is it preferable to support work that portrays distinctly different sexual practices and cultures? To what extent must a gay or lesbian film or videomaker allay the homophobic fears of straight viewers, not to mention distributors and exhibitors? Are lesbian and gay film or television screenings, which are announced as such, regressive, forestalling the recognition of lesbian and gay sexualities as components of "human sexuality." Or do these events help create solidarity? And does inclusion in such an event attach a stigma to the work or its maker that will limit its reception beyond these venues? How does one defend the process of selection for these kinds of events determined by identity, especially when the terms of identification are recognized as contingent, not eternal or universal?

Although it may be tempting to offer opinions on each of these topics, there is far too much disagreement among those of us who are affected to pretend that the task is so simple. Better yet, more voices should be introduced into the discussion.

> *There is an implicit understanding in gay cinema that homosexuality is not a sexual preference . . . that homosexuals are born homosexual and that homosexuality is not a chosen activity but a state of being.*
> –Vito Russo, in *Film Comment*[2]

> *The [gay] New Wave abandons the myth of an innate gay identity, focussing instead on the particularities of sexuality in a given culture.*
> –Richard Goldstein, in the *Village Voice*[3]

> *Perhaps it's time to discard lesbianism–and homosexuality–as a subject. Offhandedness may be the most progressive politics of the day . . .*
> –Marcia Pally, in *Film Comment*[4]

In the spring of 1986, when the articles cited above appeared, several independently produced feature films with central gay and lesbian characters involved in romantic plots–*Desert Hearts, My Beautiful Laundrette* and *Parting Glances* in particular–had recently achieved broad theatrical distribution and garnered modest profits at the box office. These developments prompted the three articles, all assessments of the state of gay and lesbian filmmaking and cinematic representations of intimate relationships. All three authors described a proliferation of mass media productions where lesbian and gay sexual relations are portrayed as neither tragic nor camp, less stigmatized and stereotypical than in most films. But, interestingly, they disagreed radically in their interpretations of the political factors at work in these films and their popular reception. Most interestingly, what they had to say in this regard concisely replicates many of the longstanding arguments about lesbian and gay identities.

I clipped and saved these articles and have periodically added material to the file. One of the most recent additions begins by posing questions: "If a gay filmmaker makes a film about something that has nothing to do with being gay, is that a gay film? If a straight filmmaker makes a film with lesbians in it is that a lesbian film?"[5] Critic Maria Maggenti, whose subject in this piece is the work of Canadian filmmaker Midi Onodera, goes on to register her "boredom and disappointment" with Onodera's *The Displaced View*, mainly because the film concentrates on the filmmaker's cultural identity in relation to her mother and her aging Japanese-Canadian grandmother. "[N]owhere in the film does [Onodera] say she is a lesbian," complains Maggenti, who screened the work at the New York Festival of Lesbian and Gay Film.[6] Although I disagree with this assessment of *The Displaced View*, I still find Maggenti's confusion about what constitutes a lesbian film indicative of the urgency that the imprecise boundaries of lesbian identity seem to provoke. For the most part, these questions have been pursued by journalists writing both in the gay press and in other progressive publications—as well as in conversations and political discussions—a reflection perhaps of the extremely tentative and dynamic character of this particular aspect of individual and cultural identity and the representations related to it.

Although lesbian and gay historians and political theorists have methodically studied the formations of lesbian communities, as well as the lives of lesbians within cultures at large, and a great deal of work has been done on the medical and legal definitions of homosexuality and homosexuals, the most provocative thinking about cultural identity has been produced in other contexts. For example, in his essay "Cultural Identity and Cinematic Representation" Stuart Hall outlines "two different ways of thinking about 'cultural identity.'" The first, he explains,

> *defines cultural identity in terms of the idea of one, shared culture, a sort of collective "one true self," hiding inside the many other, more superficial or artificially imposed "selves" which people with a shared culture and ancestry hold in common. Within the terms of this definition, our cultural identities reflect the common historical experiences and shared cultural codes which provide us, as "one people," with stable, unchanging and continuous frames of reference and meaning, beneath the shifting divisions and vicissitudes of our actual history.[7]*

The second mode Hall sees as qualifying, "if it does not replace, the first":

> *[Cultural identity] is not something which already exists, transcending place, time, history and culture…. Far from being eternally fixed in some essentialized past, [cultural identities] are subject to the continual play of history, culture and power. Far from being grounded in a mere "recovery" of the past, which is waiting to be found, and which, when found, will secure our sense of ourselves into eternity, identities are the names we give to the different ways we are positioned by, and position ourselves within, the narratives of the past.[8]*

Hall's distinctions suggest insightful, pertinent strategies for taking the question of lesbian identities beyond reportage or reviews of cultural activities. However, the application of these ideas to lesbian cultural identities cannot merely reiterate his analysis, since the emphasis in his essay is on national cultural identities and post-colonial Afro-Caribbean cultural identities in particular. To posit analogies between national (or diaspora) cultures informed by a colonial past, forced relocations, and/or enslavement and gay cultures in the United States (or other Western countries) both trivializes the oppressive operations of national and racial hierarchies and ignores different cultural formations of sexuality in various national cultures.

Caution about conflating or equating cultural differences should also be exercised in the realm of definitive statements about lesbian cultures, where these differences are also significant. Naming oneself never occurs divorced from other, contingent cultural identities. Black women in the U.S., for example, have questioned the white associations with the word "lesbian" and pointed out the reproduction of racial hierarchies in lesbian institutions and social relations. In a wide-ranging conversation with four other black women writers, which was transcribed and published in 1983, poet and critic Jewelle Gomez observes,

> *Words carry a certain amount of power—legitimate or not. And we need to acknowledge that about lesbianism. The word "lesbian" has taken on a negative power. So, it's very difficult to cleave to that negativeness. And for black women, "lesbian" has been a very white word. It connotes a kind of dabbling, aesthetic, frivolous something that I connect with a type of white cultural context that I never felt part of in my growing up and reading and looking desperately for something about women loving women.[9]*

Also, it has become common for white gay men and lesbians to remark upon homophobia in Latin American and black communities. Comments to this effect are often offered as a justification for the white bias of much gay/lesbian culture rather than examining that bias and the cultural practices that support it, even when confronted with the much more dangerous and destructive homophobia reproduced by white institutions and fostered in white communities.[10] Additionally, the gay-and-lesbian couplet falsely implies across-the-board parity in the amorphous "gay community," sidestepping the politics of gender that saturate every aspect of this coalition. I've summarized these instances of cultural differences because I don't want to perpetuate their oversight. But I also want to distinguish between what has been proposed as an unproblematic, unified "gay community"—or, at best two "communities," male and female—and lesbian and gay cultural identities, which, as Hall points out, neither preexist nor transcend history.

Although the courts and psychologists might be satisfied with empirical definitions, a lesbian cannot be described simply as an individual who engages in homosexual acts. Sexual desires and practices may form the basis for lesbian identities, but in late-twentieth-century Western societies the implications of such identities have become much more complex and subtle. For instance, the importance of coming out, announcing one's "gayness," became a primary tenet of the gay rights movement in the early seventies, invented as a political strategy based on the positive public assertion of sexual desire. Coming out has always meant more than an individual declaration; it is also a fundamentally social process that defies social disapprobation and infuses conventional representations of sexual deviance and moral degeneracy embodied by lesbians and gay men with new meanings—what Michel Foucault called "reverse discourse." In time, coming out also became conventionalized as a personal rite of passage, although from time to time the publicity surrounding the rumored or real gay relationships of a prominent cultural icon like Rock Hudson or Madonna may cause anxiety to ripple through the heterosexual assumptions of mass culture. Despite such relatively rapid historical shifts, however, the meanings attached to coming out remain a prominent factor in the construction of lesbian and gay cultural identities.

Perhaps the best barometer of how coming out inflects contemporary lesbian and gay cinema is the film *Word Is Out*, an archetypal gay rights advocacy film composed of first-person reflections on the consequences of asserting lesbian and gay identities, from electro-shock treatments to political organizing. Produced in 1977 by a collective of lesbians and gay men in San Francisco,[11] the city then seen as the gay capital of the Western world, the film initially played in movie theaters across the United States to excited and appreciative audiences made up largely of self-identified lesbians and gay men. I was among them, pleased to see an affirmation of the personal and political histories that congealed in the gay rights movement of the seventies.

As time went by, I became critical of *Word Is Out* as the prototypical lesbian/gay documentary, which intercuts various personal stories to construct representations of a cultural identity very like what Stuart Hall referred to as "the common historical experience and shared cultural codes which provide us, as 'one people,' with stable, unchanging and continuous frames of reference and meaning." But watching a broadcast of the film on television some years later, I was struck by the distinctly specific character of the various stories related, their separate contributions to the collage, which, by its thematic organization, emphasized their discontinuity and demanded a historical, not mythological, reading of the past. Heartened by this correction in my faulty memory, I was doubly surprised later when, comparing impressions of the broadcast with a few friends, I encountered criticism from another quarter. For these lesbian and gay viewers, the film was depressing and invoked a form of nervous self-consciousness. They were concerned that anyone prone to an opinion of lesbians or gay men as pathetic misfits would find their ideas upheld by the micro-portraits presented; too many of the people interviewed in the film told painful accounts about rejection and humiliation.

No one participating in our discussion advocated a redemptive counterproduction featuring cheerful, well-adjusted, unconflicted subjects. They just maintained that the sadness that pervades the film might provide ammunition for those who regard homosexuality as a pathological disorder to be "cured" or punished. Another friend and I responded very differently to the TV program. We allowed that the multiple-interview, direct-address-to-the-camera method used in *Word Is Out* implied an inclusive spectrum of unproblematic diversity, but we enjoyed watching how the group portrayed in the film described the difficult process of *constructing*–some flamboyantly, some very quietly–cultural identities resistant to mechanisms of sexual regulation. We were intrigued by the film because it's subject *is* identity.

Because of its structure, the history drawn upon, and its political significance as a sort of manifesto of gay rights, *Word Is Out* continues to function as a kind of blank slate upon which might be written the cultural positions occupied by lesbians and gay men in the United States in the latter part of the twentieth century. Although decidedly an attempt to project social visibility and positive identification for a social class rendered marginal by dicta governing sexual conduct, this film can serve as a reference point for the three disparate, potentially contradictory critical stances cited earlier, all of which were written as evaluations of the progress of the gay rights movement.

By asserting the intractability of sexual desires and attendant identities, *Word Is Out* can be taken as a refutation of the voluntary connotations of the concept of sexual *preference* (as opposed to *orientation*), which then can be used to support a theory of inherent tendencies like that advocated by Vito Russo. But it also clearly conveys "the peculiarities of sexuality in a given culture," which Richard Goldstein understands as contrary to an essentialist view like Russo's. And, although it seems to represent the opposite of Marcia Pally's recommendation that we "discard lesbianism—and homosexuality—as a subject," its TV broadcast places those subjects into the cultural mainstream and acts as a bridge between typical representations of gay characters as outsiders in a predominantly heterosexual society and an attitude of "offhandedness" that validates the subjectivity of lesbians and gay men.

Common to all three critics' remarks and their supporting arguments, as well as the text of *Word Is Out*, is an attempt to subvert or disarm oppressive categories of deviant sexuality. The task remains frustrating, though, since the project of classifying types and degrees of sexual deviance is produced by the same ideological system based on transcendent, individual identity that informs the films in question. In the case of *Word Is Out*, for instance, individual identity is the bedrock upon which the film builds a vision of full social recognition.

An insightful commentary on this approach occurs in the feature-length videotape *Bright Eyes*, produced by British artist Stuart Marshall in 1984 for Channel Four, a national broadcast outlet. The first third of Marshall's tape is devoted to an analysis of the elaborate interplay of visual representations and disease, specifically the pathological connotations of homosexuality in Western culture. In a scene that is obviously staged, a man whose face is obscured in shadow recounts a typical autobiographical story of psychiatric "treatment" imposed by his parents in the wake of his declaration of homosexual desires. His tale could easily have been included in *Word Is Out*, as it traces his assertion of identity in the face of his father's and his therapist's attempts to dissuade him from this course. However, the exaggerated lighting and stagey acting emphasize the artificiality of the performance and thus denaturalizes the scene, contrary to the methods employed to mask our awareness of contrivance in realist cinema (*Parting Glances, Desert Hearts,* and *My Beautiful Laundrette* all belong to this tradition, as do most documentaries). The vignette also immediately follows a historical survey of the exotic meanings assigned to pictures of "the homosexual," establishing the link between portraiture and personality. In this context, the coming out testimonial serves as a critique of the unwitting reproduction of this system of representation in films like *Word Is Out* and kindred works.

All of these propositions remain speculative, but I doubt that anyone would dispute that *Word Is Out* is a gay film. Still, it has managed to "cross over" into the realm of broadcast TV, found acceptable for an audience beyond the lesbian and gay film festival circuit because it predicates identity as a function of self-knowledge, an ideological position at the heart of Western systems of domination and regulation. In accordance with the melting pot myth of America, these are ideal citizens. The people interviewed belong to various social sectors—urban and rural, working-class laborers and middle-class professionals, black, Asian, white, Latina, young, middle-aged, and old—and all are intelligent and sensitive. Tellingly, all of the interviews are shot against the backdrop of the subject's home, where each one is shown alone or, in a few instances, with a lover. Distinctly absent from the film are any references to aspects of lesbian or gay subcultures that might be deemed degenerate: the bars, the baths, pornography, butch-fem roles, or, most notably, sexual practices of any kind. A political strategist might contend that it is the representations of exactly these sites of sexual promiscuity and deviance that promote disdain and incite hostility in the first place. Won't images of butch lesbians or drag queens merely confirm the insidious fantasies and persistent stereotypes used to justify homophobia? The point is moot, however, since, had the filmmakers included material of this sort, theirs or my friends' concern about popular perceptions of sexual perversity would have been unnecessary; the film would never have been allowed on the air.

The unspoken requirements of television executives demand that works with lesbian or gay references address what they perceive as reluctance by straight viewers to entertain these representations. And like the rules that guide theatrical distribution of motion pictures, a potential lesbian or gay audience is not considered significant. The anxiety that arises when these standards are questioned—both within specific works or in the context of an entire schedule—powerfully indicates the threat and ambivalence that animates this particular scene of cultural repression. The commercial broadcast and cable networks see the spectre of low ratings or outraged moralists. They may readily promote work that mobilizes sexual ambiguity as a titillating come on—a common enough advertising ploy—but they see overt, unapologetic recognition of lesbian or gay cultures as poison. The more high-minded practices of public television are governed by trickier criteria. Operating within a mandate to adhere to less crass motives and provide a more diverse menu, public television often appears to be more frightened than their market-driven counterparts. Two examples from recent history will illustrate their characteristic antipathy.

Although in 1986 PBS had scandalously ignored the need for public education about AIDS (airing only three hour-long programs dealing with what was then uniformly regarded as a gay issue during the first six years of the epidemic), they indicated interest in and then turned down *Chuck Solomon: Coming of Age*, a well-made documentary portrait of a gay playright and theater director with AIDS, which had already received a number of awards and been broadcast nationally in Great Britain and Spain and locally in San Francisco when it was submitted to PBS. They offered filmmakers Mark Huestis and Wendy Dallas no substantial explanation for declining the piece. But, given the film's formal and technical conformity to established documentary standards, it seems fair to surmise that PBS balked at the unproblematized depictions of drag queens, friends of Solomon's, who appear in lengthy scenes shot at a birthday party tribute in his honor. The decision to reject *Chuck Solomon* made at PBS headquarters bears all the earmarks of typical accession to unexamined ideas about what the public will accept. Less typical, but just as telling, was a 15-minute blackout during Los Angeles public TV station KCET's 1989 broadcast of Stuart Marshall's videotape *Bright Eyes*. An engineer working at the station pulled the plug, jeopardizing his job in order to register his repulsion with Marshall's historical analysis of the conflation of homosexuality and disease. Ironically, *Bright Eyes* includes a scene based on a newspaper item about a television technician in San Francisco who refused to remain in the studio when he discovered that a talk show guest was a man with AIDS.

Even as lesbians and gay men have exerted pressure to obtain recognition within established cultural institutions, another set of constraints, defined by the limits of liberal tolerance, have been put in motion. Just as the institutionalization of Black History Month has produced what painter Emma Amos has described as "ghetto-month shows that fulfill the funding needs of white institutions"[12] and precipitated the phenomenon videomaker Linda Gibson dubbed the "February film," gay culture now receives some attention during June in shows and television specials that coincide with the anniversary of the Stonewall Rebellion. The broadcast of *Word Is Out* that sparked the discussion I mentioned was shown on public TV as part of a special Gay History Week series during June 1987. Not only does the rationale that informs program design and scheduling indicate their exceptional status, thus confirming the rule of heterosexuality as the norm, but the work put on display is generally conventional in every respect save its gay themes or characters.[13]

The collective response to the severe censorship exercised by powerful cultural apparatuses has taken the institutional form of lesbian and gay film festivals, another kind of special event. This makes any festival organized according to thematic criteria, including the slippery concept of "lesbian and gay cinema," potentially a defense of absolute, ineffable identity. Unlike the practice of programming "ghetto-month shows," however, lesbian and gay film festivals generally give those who attend an opportunity to see works that otherwise hardly circulate. Since a film or videotape without exhibition, without a viewer, is incomplete, such events play an important role in the constitution of lesbian and gay culture. The appeal to a sympathetic community is evident in all aspects of program selection and promotion, even when concepts of a "gay community" remain questionable. In this milieu, film and video works that overstep the bounds of propriety and offer the less sanitized representations of lesbians and gay men play for crowds (temporarily) unconcerned about homophobic backlash.

Nevertheless, the difficulty of establishing the terms of inclusion and exclusion under the lesbian umbrella frequently spills over into the politics of these cultural forums, as the review of Midi Onodera's *The Displaced View* suggests. In my collection of clippings on lesbian film I've preserved another item that appeared in the *Village Voice* in late 1984, detailing the refusal of Belgian filmmaker Chantal Akerman to have her film *je tu il elle* screened at the New York Gay Film Festival. According to the article, she told the festival director, "This is not a business decision… but a moral and ethical one. I will not be ghettoized."[14] No artist wants her work "ghettoized," and Akerman's choice to withhold her film from a lesbian and gay festival is hardly unique. What is uncommon in this case is that Akerman's response was documented whereas most discussions along these lines are left unrecorded. The withdrawal of films from lesbian and/or gay events usually goes on behind the scenes, although most frequently distributors–not filmmakers–are the leery parties, arguing that a "lesbian" label will hamper potential screening opportunities and box office receipts.

Although not a coming out story, the Akerman/New York Gay Film Festival anecdote suggests many of the complicated issues entailed in assertions of or constraints imposed by lesbian identities. In defense of Akerman, it is conceivable that she was anticipating another kind of New York premiere for *je tu il elle*, one that would attract the all-too-important reviews in the *New York Times* and other power-brokering mass media publications which, in 1984, works in the Gay Film Festival never received but are necessary for the successful distribution of a feature film, even a risky, highly unconventional one like Akerman's. Similar sentiments are often expressed as the reasons behind the reluctance of many distributors and a few filmmakers to have work introduced to the public at explicitly lesbian events. But that rationale, even if accurate, reduces the question to economic terms, which may be relevant (a consideration that I will return to later) but remain inadequate to an investigation of the ambivalences of a cultural identity that is based on the concept of deviant sexuality. Also, Akerman clearly stated that hers was "not a business decision." Instead, her protest, "I will not be ghettoized," must be taken seriously.

On ethical grounds, Akerman's statement can be read as a principled repudiation of labelling which challenges any reductive idea of a fixed identity. Likewise, in *je tu il elle* (literally translated as *I you he she*) the central woman character, who is played by Akerman, enacts a series of intense engagements with the four pronouns of the title. As the film opens, the actress-director retreats to an almost unfurnished room, where she strips naked, sleeps, and obsessively eats sugar. Eventually she is seen in the same setting writing a lengthy letter to an unspecified lover. She then dons her clothes and takes to the road, shares a meal with a truck driver who gives her a lift, then gives him a blow job while he drives and recites his life story. Finally, she arrives unannounced at the door of another woman, arrogantly demands to be fed and, having eaten, engages in frenetic sex with her hostess, only to tiptoe out of the scene at dawn. It is the last segment that draws lesbians to the film, but given the resistance to identification in Akerman's film– none of the characters have names, for instance, and each of the segments lack motivation and resolution–her reluctance to have her work categorized as a lesbian film seems entirely consistent.[15]

Cultural critics who investigate the interplay of identity and ideology[16] have argued convincingly that identities are formed through representations. Akerman foregrounds that process in *je tu il elle* by stripping away the iconographic clutter of both cinematic space and narrative movement. In doing so, she has produced a minimalist film that seems particularly suited to an analysis of the components and effects of sexual identity. Unlike superficially similar declinings of invitations to participate in lesbian events because of their fears of alienating potential supporters who are straight or closeted, her decision may then be seen as a protest against concepts of identity based on theories that posit innate homosexuality. Yet, in removing the work from the arena where such ideas often hold sway, she may inadvertently lend credence to those who deny the ideological dimensions of sexual identification and campaign for entertainments showing people who merely "happen to be gay."

By and large, strategies aimed at achieving social integration—or, more pointedly, assimilation in liberal society where the "sexual orientations" or "lifestyles" of lesbians would be treated offhandedly—accept without question the dictates of consumer culture, equating cultural value with economic success. Audience numbers are frequently cited in the gay press and conversations as a fair measure of a work's significance. Likewise, lesbian and gay film critics are prone to overvaluation of work that looks like it could lead to a Hollywood studio deal. Operating within the same economic order, however, is a fundamental law of film distribution which maintains that work addressing gay or lesbian subjects by unproven directors won't make the grade. It's highly unlikely that major sources of production funds or the conservative distribution circuits that set the standards for popular appeal or "quality" will embrace work that presents gay or lesbian desires as anything other than a "problem." That's why the box office figures for *Parting Glances, My Beautiful Laundrette,* and *Desert Hearts* seemed to herald gay cinema's breakthrough into mass culture.

The rules of the game are not so quickly suspended or abandoned, though; subsequently we have seen few new movies with lesbian themes playing in multiplex theaters in shopping malls across the nation. In avant-garde artistic circles, achievement is similarly associated with recognition by prestigious institutions patronized by the rich. In these settings, homoerotic references may be tolerated as long as they are isolated from political purposes. While never losing sight of the importance of the resources controlled by powerful institutions that allow both the production and circulation of work, it is nevertheless possible to challenge rather than cater to the interests they uphold. Just as with sexual identities defined in the straight binary terms of masculinity and femininity, no one living within a capitalist social matrix escapes this system, which is also a powerful producer and product of representations.

My thoughts about the relationship between lesbian and gay cinema and the power exercised by mass cultural institutions is an attempt to introduce a dose of materialist thinking, along with analyses of the works that function as shared cultural references, into discussions of lesbian identities. This is by no means an automatic or particularly comfortable undertaking for a political movement founded on sexual identity. And it becomes even more difficult in the context of the gay rights movement as it has developed in the United States, which often downplays the domination by middle-class, white men that has nonetheless shaped many of its political platforms. This constituency fosters narratives of lesbian cultural identity reproduced in the image of consumer culture, a strategy that invariably feeds self-aggrandizing myths of possession and control.

Public lesbian cultures in the U.S., on the other hand, are historically rooted in the urban working classes, even if the most famous and revered forebears in the lesbian cultural pantheon are wealthy, white, sometimes reactionary artists, like Natalie Barney and her crowd. No wonder lesbian and gay film festivals which incorporate popular cultural forms, retain the character of a ghetto, where embattled people find pleasure without having to constantly look over our collective shoulder. Because self-identified lesbians approach these places with a presumption of community, no matter how fictional, these become cultural spaces that can change our relationship to the screen. Our identities are constituted as much in the event as in the images we watch. Reciprocally, what is on the screen will propose the lesbian public that it attracts—or doesn't.

The set of questions posed at the beginning of this article—the interrogation of the relationship between lesbian and gay cinema and identities, which has determined the critical vocabulary used to discuss lesbian cultural identities—if answered, promises a future where a lesbian identity can be assumed without ambivalence. But those questions and the responses they provoke presume an idealized future where either absolute sexual differences are clearly staked out or where lesbians are included in an undifferentiated mass audience. Both options ignore the various and often conflicted meanings at play in the arena of sexual identity and projections of community premised on identity.

To understand this relationship better, it seems more important to ask how lesbian narratives take shape, under what social conditions. What are the historical precedents in the institutions of cinema that engage and frustrate our imaginations? How did these works get on the screen? And, just as importantly, what is excluded? How did those who chose to show it anticipate our expectations? What were those expectations? What is this public that we actively seek out and join? How, in short, do these events, which call upon and catalyze our desires, position us and we position ourselves in narratives of the past. And in the present?

1. The adjective Uranian is one of the more fanciful nineteenth-century synonyms for "homosexual."
2. Vito Russo, "A State of Being," *Film Comment* (April 1986): 32.
3. Richard Goldstein, "The Gay New Wave," *Village Voice* (April 22, 1986): 52.
4. Marcia Pally, "Women in Love," *Film Comment* (April 1986): 39.
5. Maria Maggenti, "Midi Onodera Begs the Perennial Questions," *Gay Community News* (June 4-10, 1989): 9.
6. Ibid., p. 11. Maggenti's framing of the issues of identity echoes Daryl Chin's various writings about definitions of Asian American cinema, although Chin is more decisive, e.g.: "[I]f an Asian American made the movie, but the movie did not have specific Asian American content, was it still an Asian American movie? My answer is always, yes." (Daryl Chin, "After Ten Years: Some Notes on the Asian American International Film Festival," Asian American International Film Festival program [New York: Asian CineVision, 1988], p. 16).
7. Stuart Hall, "Cultural Identity and Cinematic Representation," *Framework*, no. 36 (1989): 69.
8. Ibid., p. 70.
9. Cheryl Clarke, Jewelle Gomez, Evelynn Hammonds, Bonnie Johnson, and Linda Powell, "Black Women on Black Women Writers: Conversations and Questions," *Conditions*, no. 9 (Spring 1983): 130. The various understandings and uses of "lesbian" is further complicated in this piece by a comment made by Clarke which follows Gomez's: "When I first came out I called myself 'gay' for a long time, because I did not care for the term 'lesbian.' But I do want to be known as a lesbian, as woman-affirming, black-woman affirming." (p. 131)
10. bell hooks discusses these myths in "Reflections on Homophobia in Black Communities," *Out/Look*, vol. 1, no. 2 (Summer 1988): 22-25.
11. *Word Is Out* was produced by the Mariposa Film Group, whose members were Peter Adair, Lucy Massie Phoenix, Rob Epstein, Veronica Selver, Nancy Adair, and Andrew Bowen.
12. Emma Amos, letter in the "Arts and Leisure" section of the *New York Times* (April 23, 1989): H3.
13. The exceptions to this rule are programs occasionally programmed by public TV stations in major cities with sizable lesbian and gay populations after 11 p.m.—usually in June.
14. Richard Goldstein, "Et Tu Chantal?" *Village Voice* (December 4, 1984): 51.

15. What's curiously inconsistent is that several of Akerman's films have subsequently been included in lesbian or gay programs, presumably with her consent.

16. In addition to Stuart Hall's essay cited above, many contemporary feminist film critics are concerned with the ideological operations of cinematic representation in relation to the construction of identities. And a general collection of articles dealing with such inquiries is Lisa Appignanesi, ed., *The Real Me: Post-Modernism and the Question of Identity* (London: Institute of Contemporary Arts, 1987).

How To Tame a Wild Tongue

"We're going to have to control your tongue," the dentist says, pulling out all the metal from my mouth. Silver bits plop and tinkle into the basin. My mouth is a motherlode.

The dentist is cleaning out my roots. I get a whiff of the stench when I gasp. "I can't cap that tooth yet, you're still draining," he says.

"We're going to have to do something about your tongue," I hear the anger rising in his voice. My tongue keeps pushing out the wads of cotton, pushing back the drills, the long thin needles. "I've never seen anything as strong or as stubborn," he says. And I think, how do you tame a wild tongue, train it to be quiet, how do you bridle and saddle it? How do you make it lie down?

> *Who is to say that robbing a people of its language is less violent than war?*
> –Ray Gwyn Smith[1]

I remember being caught speaking Spanish at recess–that was good for three licks on the knuckles with a sharp ruler. I remember being sent to the corner of the classroom for "talking back" to the Anglo teacher when all I was trying to do was tell her how to pronounce my name. "If you want to be American, speak 'American.' If you don't like it, go back to Mexico where you belong."

"I want you to speak English. *Pa' hallar buen trabajo tienes que saber hablar el inglés bien. Qué vale toda tu educación si todavía hablas inglés con un* 'accent,'" my mother would say, mortified that I spoke English like a Mexican. At Pan American University, I, and all Chicano students were required to take two speech classes. Their purpose: to get rid of our accents.

Attacks on one's form of expression with the intent to censor are a violation of the First Amendment. *El Anglo con cara de inocente nos arrancó la lengua.* Wild tongues can't be tamed, they can only be cut out.

Overcoming the Tradition of Silence

> *Ahogadas, escupimos el oscuro.*
> *Peleando con nuestra propia sombra*
> *el silencio nos sepulta.*

En boca cerrada no entran moscas. "Flies don't enter a closed mouth" is a saying I kept hearing when I was a child. *Ser habladora* was to be a gossip and a liar, to talk too much. *Muchachitas bien criadas*, well-bred girls don't answer back. *Es una falta de respeto* to talk back to one's mother or father. I remember one of the sins I'd recite to the priest in the confession box the few times I went to confession: talking back to my mother, *hablar pa' 'tras, repelar. Hocicona, repelona, chismosa,* having a big mouth, questioning, carrying tales are all signs of being *mal criada*. In my culture they are all words that are derogatory if applied to women–I've never heard them applied to men.

The first time I heard two women, a Puerto Rican and a Cuban, say the word *"nosotras,"* I was shocked. I had not known the word existed. Chicanas use *nosotros* whether we're male or female. We are robbed of our female being by the masculine plural. Language is a male discourse.

> And our tongues have become
> dry   the wilderness has
> dried out our tongues   and
> we have forgotten speech.
> –Irena Klepfisz[2]

Even our own people, other Spanish speakers *nos quieren poner candados en la boca.* They would hold us back with their bag of *reglas de academia.*

Oyé como ladra: el lenguaje de la frontera

> *Quien tiene boca se equivoca.*
> –Mexican saying

"*Pocho*, cultural traitor, you're speaking the oppressor's language by speaking English, you're ruining the Spanish language," I have been accused by various Latinos and Latinas. Chicano Spanish is considered by the purist and by most Latinos deficient, a mutilation of Spanish.

But Chicano Spanish is a border tongue which developed naturally. Change, *evolución, enriquecimiento de palabras nuevas por invención o adopción* have created variants of Chicano Spanish, *un nuevo lenguaje. Un lenguaje que corresponde a un modo de vivir.* Chicano Spanish is not incorrect, it is a living language.

For a people who are neither Spanish nor live in a country in which Spanish is the first language; for a people who live in a country in which English is the reigning tongue but who are not Anglo; for a people who cannot entirely identify with either standard (formal, Castillian) Spanish nor standard English, what recourse is left to them but to create their own language? A language which they can connect their identity to, one capable of communicating the realities and values true to themselves–a language with terms that are neither *español ni inglés,* but both. We speak a patois, a forked tongue, a variation of two languages.

Chicano Spanish sprang out of the Chicanos' need to identify ourselves as a distinct people. We needed a language with which we could communicate with ourselves, a secret language. For some of us, language is a homeland closer than the Southwest—for many Chicanos today live in the Midwest and the East. And because we are a complex, heterogeneous people, we speak many languages. Some of the languages we speak are:

1. Standard English
2. Working class and slang English
3. Standard Spanish
4. Standard Mexican Spanish
5. North Mexican Spanish dialect
6. Chicano Spanish (Texas, New Mexico, Arizona and California have regional variations)
7. Tex-Mex
8. *Pachuco* (called *caló*)

My "home" tongues are the languages I speak with my sister and brothers, with my friends. They are the last five listed, with 6 and 7 being closest to my heart. From school, the media and job situations, I've picked up standard and working class English. From Mamagrande Locha and from reading Spanish and Mexican literature, I've picked up Standard Spanish and Standard Mexican Spanish. From *los recién llegados*, Mexican immigrants, and *braceros*, I learned the North Mexican dialect. With Mexicans I'll try to speak either Standard Mexican Spanish or the North Mexican dialect. From my parents and Chicanos living in the Valley, I picked up Chicano Texas Spanish, and I speak it with my mom, younger brother (who married a Mexican and who rarely mixes Spanish with English), aunts and older relatives.

With Chicanas from *Nuevo México* or *Arizona* I will speak Chicano Spanish a little, but often they don't understand what I'm saying. With most California Chicanas I speak entirely in English (unless I forget). When I first moved to San Francisco, I'd rattle off something in Spanish, unintentionally embarrassing them. Often it is only with another Chicana *tejana* that I can talk freely.

Words distorted by English are known as anglicisms or *pochismos*. The *pocho* is an anglicized Mexican or American of Mexican origin who speaks Spanish with an accent characteristic of North Americans and who distorts and reconstructs the language according to the influence of English.[3] Tex-Mex, or Spanglish, comes most naturally to me. I may switch back and forth from English to Spanish in the same sentence or in the same word. With my sister and my brother Nune and with Chicano *tejano* contemporaries I speak Tex-Mex.

From kids and people my own age I picked up *Pachuco*. *Pachuco* (the language of the zoot suiters) is a language of rebellion, both against Standard Spanish and Standard English. It is a secret language. Adults of the culture and outsiders cannot understand it. It is made up of slang words from both English and Spanish. *Ruca* means girl or woman, *vato* means guy or dude, *chale* means no, *simón* means yes, *churro* is sure, talk is *periquiar*, *pigionear* means petting, *que gacho* means how nerdy, *ponte águila* means watch out, death is called *la pelona*. Through lack of practice and not having others who can speak it, I've lost most of the *Pachuco* tongue.

Chicano Spanish

Chicanos, after 250 years of Spanish/Anglo colonization have developed significant differences in the Spanish we speak. We collapse two adjacent vowels into a single syllable and sometimes shift the stress in certain words such as *maíz/maiz, cohete/cuete.* We leave out certain consonants when they appear between vowels: *lado/lao, mojado/mojao.* Chicanos from South Texas pronounce *f* as *j* as in *jue (fue).* Chicanos use "archaisms," words that are no longer in the Spanish language, words that have been evolved out. We say *semos, truje, haiga, ansina,* and *naiden.* We retain the "archaic" *j,* as in *jalar,* that derives from an earlier *h* (the French *halar* or the Germanic *halon* which was lost to standard Spanish in the 16th century), but which is still found in several regional dialects such as the one spoken in South Texas. (Due to geography, Chicanos from the Valley of South Texas were cut off linguistically from other Spanish speakers. We tend to use words that the Spaniards brought over from Medieval Spain. The majority of the Spanish colonizers in Mexico and the Southwest came from Extremadura–Hernán Cortés was one of them–and Andalucía. Andalucians pronounce *ll* like a *y,* and their *d*'s tend to be absorbed by adjacent vowels: *tirado* becomes *tirao.* They brought *el lenguaje popular, dialectos y regionalismos.*[4])

Chicanos and other Spanish speakers also shift *ll* to *y* and *z* to *s.*[5] We leave out initial syllables, saying *tar* for *estar, toy* for *estoy, hora* for *ahora* (*cubanos* and *puertorriqueños* also leave out initial letters of some words.) We also leave out the final syllable such as *pa* for *para.* The intervocalic *y,* the *ll* as in *tortilla, ella, botella* gets replaced by *tortia* or *tortiya, ea, botea.* We add an additional syllable at the beginning of certain words: *atocar* for *tocar, agastar* for *gastar.* Sometimes we'll say *lavaste las vacijas,* other times *lavates* (substituting the *ates* verb endings for the *aste*).

We use anglicisms, words borrowed from English: *bola* from ball, *carpeta* from carpet, *máchina de lavar* (instead of *lavadora*) from washing machine. Tex-Mex argot, created by adding a Spanish sound at the beginning or end of an English word such as *cookiar* for cook, *watchar* for watch, *parkiar* for park, and *rapiar* for rape, is the result of the pressures on Spanish speakers to adapt to English.

We don't use the word *vosotros/as* or its accompanying verb form. We don't say *claro* (to mean yes), *imagínate,* or *me emociona,* unless we picked up Spanish from Latinas, out of a book, or in a classroom. Other Spanish-speaking groups are going through the same, or similar, development in their Spanish.

Linguistic Terrorism

> Deslenguadas. Somos los del español deficiente. *We are your linguistic nightmare, your linguistic aberration, your linguistic* mestisaje, *the subject of your* burla. *Because we speak with tongues of fire we are culturally crucified. Racially, culturally and linguistically* somos huérfanos–*we speak an orphan tongue.*

Chicanas who grew up speaking Chicano Spanish have internalized the belief that we speak poor Spanish. It is illegitimate, a bastard language. And because we internalize how our language has been used against us by the dominant culture, we use our language differences against each other.

Chicana feminists often skirt around each other with suspicion and hesitation. For the longest time I couldn't figure it out. Then it dawned on me. To be close to another Chicana is like looking into the mirror. We are afraid of what we'll see there. *Pena*. Shame. Low estimation of self. In childhood we are told that our language is wrong. Repeated attacks on our native tongue diminish our sense of self. The attacks continue throughout our lives.

Chicanas feel uncomfortable talking in Spanish to Latinas, afraid of their censure. Their language was not outlawed in their countries. They had a whole lifetime of being immersed in their native tongue; generations, centuries in which Spanish was a first language, taught in school, heard on radio and TV, and read in the newspaper.

If a person, Chicana or Latina, has a low estimation of my native tongue, she also has a low estimation of me. Often with *mexicanas y latinas* we'll speak English as a neutral language. Even among Chicanas we tend to speak English at parties or conferences. Yet, at the same time, we're afraid the other will think we're *agringadas* because we don't speak Chicano Spanish. We oppress each other trying to out-Chicano each other, vying to be the "real" Chicanas, to speak like Chicanos. There is no one Chicano language just as there is no one Chicano experience. A monolingual Chicana whose first language is English or Spanish is just as much a Chicana as one who speaks several variants of Spanish. A Chicana from Michigan or Chicago or Detroit is just as much a Chicana as one from the Southwest. Chicano Spanish is as diverse linguistically as it is regionally.

By the end of this century, Spanish speakers will comprise the biggest minority group in the U.S., a country where students in high schools and colleges are encouraged to take French classes because French is considered more "cultured." But for a language to remain alive it must be used.[6] By the end of this century English, and not Spanish will be the mother tongue of most Chicanos and Latinos.

So, if you want to really hurt me, talk badly about my language. Ethnic identity is twin skin to linguistic identity—I am my language. Until I can take pride in my language, I cannot take pride in myself. Until I can accept as legitimate Chicano Texas Spanish, Tex-Mex and all the other languages I speak, I cannot accept the legitimacy of myself. Until I am free to write bilingually and to switch codes without having always to translate, while I still have to speak English or Spanish when I would rather speak Spanglish, and as long as I have to accommodate the English speakers rather than having them accomodate me, my tongue will be illegitimate.

I will no longer be made to feel ashamed of existing. I will have my voice: Indian, Spanish, white. I will have my serpent's tongue—my woman's voice, my sexual voice, my poet's voice. I will overcome the tradition of silence.

> My fingers
> move sly against your palm
> Like women everywhere, we speak in code . . .
> –Melanie Kaye/Kantrowitz[7]

"Vistas," corridos, y comida: My Native Tongue

In the 1960s, I read my first Chicano novel. It was *City of Night* by John Rechy, a gay Texan, son of a Scottish father and a Mexican mother. For days I walked around in stunned amazement that a Chicano could write and could get published. When I read *I Am Joaquín*[8] I was surprised to see a bilingual book by a Chicano in print. When I saw poetry written in Tex-Mex for the first time, a feeling of pure joy flashed through me. I felt like we really existed as a people. In 1971, when I started teaching High School English to Chicano students, I tried to supplement the required texts with works by Chicanos, only to be reprimanded and forbidden to do so by the principal. He claimed that I was supposed to teach "American" and English literature. At the risk of being fired, I swore my students to secrecy and slipped in Chicano short stories, poems, a play. In graduate school, while working toward a Ph.D., I had to "argue" with one advisor after the other, semester after semester, before I was allowed to make Chicano literature an area of focus.

Even before I read books by Chicanos or Mexicans, it was the Mexican movies I saw at the drive-in–the Thursday night special of $1.00 a carload–that gave me a sense of belonging. "*Vámonos a las vistas*," my mother would call out and we'd all–grandmother, brothers, sister and cousins–squeeze into the car. We'd wolf down cheese and bologna white bread sandwiches while watching Pedro Infante in melodramatic tearjerkers like *Nosotros los pobres*, the first "real" Mexican movie (that was not an imitation of European movies). I remember seeing *Cuando los hijos se van* and surmising that all Mexican movies played up the love a mother has for her children and what ungrateful sons and daughters suffer when they are not devoted to their mothers. I remember the singing-type "westerns" of Jorge Negrete and Miquel Aceves Mejía. When watching Mexican movies, I felt a sense of homecoming as well as alienation. People who were to amount to something didn't go to Mexican movies, or *bailes* or tune their radios to *bolero*, *rancherita*, and *corrido* music.

The whole time I was growing up, there was *norteño* music, sometimes called North Mexican border music, or Tex-Mex music, or Chicano music, or *cantina* (bar) music. I grew up listening to *conjuntos*, three- or four-piece bands made up of folk musicians playing guitar, *bajo sexto*, drums and button accordion, which Chicanos had borrowed from the German immigrants who had come to Central Texas and Mexico to farm and build breweries. In the Rio Grande Valley, Steve Jordan and Little Joe Hernández were popular, and Flaco Jiménez was the accordion king. The rhythms of Tex-Mex music are those of the polka, also adapted from the Germans, who in turn had borrowed the polka from the Czechs and Bohemians.

I remember the hot, sultry evenings when *corridos*–songs of love and death on the

Texas-Mexican borderlands—reverberated out of cheap amplifiers from the local *cantinas* and wafted in through my bedroom window.

Corridos first became widely used along the South Texas/Mexican border during the early conflict between Chicanos and Anglos. The *corridos* are usually about Mexican heroes who do valiant deeds against the Anglo oppressors. Pancho Villa's song, "*La cucaracha*," is the most famous one. *Corridos* of John F. Kennedy and his death are still very popular in the Valley. Older Chicanos remember Lydia Mendoza, one of the great border *corrido* singers who was called *la Gloria de Tejas*. Her "*El tango negro*," sung during the Great Depression, made her a singer of the people. The everpresent *corridos* narrated one hundred years of border history, bringing news of events as well as entertaining. These folk musicians and folk songs are our chief cultural mythmakers, and they made our hard lives seem bearable.

I grew up feeling ambivalent about our music. Country-western and rock-and-roll had more status. In the 50s and 60s, for the slightly educated and *agringado* Chicanos, there existed a sense of shame at being caught listening to our music. Yet I couldn't stop my feet from thumping to the music, could not stop humming the words, nor hide from myself the exhilaration I felt when I heard it.

There are more subtle ways that we internalize identification, especially in the forms of images and emotions. For me food and certain smells are tied to my identity, to my homeland. Woodsmoke curling up to an immense blue sky; woodsmoke perfuming my grandmother's clothes, her skin. The stench of cow manure and the yellow patches on the ground; the crack of a .22 rifle and the reek of cordite. Homemade white cheese sizzling in a pan, melting inside a folded *tortilla*. My sister Hilda's hot, spicy *menudo, chile colorado* making it deep red, pieces of *panza* and hominy floating on top. My brother Carito barbecuing *fajitas* in the backyard. Even now and 3,000 miles away, I can see my mother spicing the ground beef, pork and venison with *chile*. My mouth salivates at the thought of the hot steaming *tamales* I would be eating if I were home.

Si le preguntas a mi mamá, "¿Qué eres?"

> "*Identity is the essential core of who we are as individuals, the conscious experience of the self inside.*"
> —Kaufman[9]

Nosotros los Chicanos straddle the borderlands. On one side of us, we are constantly exposed to the Spanish of the Mexicans, on the other side we hear the Anglos' incessant clamoring so that we forget our language. Among ourselves we don't say *nosotros los americanos, o nosotros los españoles, o nosotros los hispanos.* We say *nosotros los mexicanos* (by *mexicanos* we do not mean citizens of Mexico; we do not mean a national identity, but a racial one). We distinguish between *mexicanos del otro lado* and *mexicanos de este lado.* Deep in our hearts we believe that being Mexican has nothing to do with which country one lives in. Being Mexican is a state of soul—not one of mind, not one of citizenship. Neither eagle nor serpent, but both. And like the ocean, neither animal respects borders.

> Dime con quien andas y te diré quien eres.
> (Tell me who your friends are and I'll tell you who you are.)
> —Mexican saying

Si le preguntas a mi mamá, "¿Qué eres?" te dirá, "Soy mexicana." My brothers and sister say the same. I sometimes will answer *"soy mexicana"* and at others will say *"soy Chicana" o "soy tejana."* But I identified as *"Raza"* before I ever identified as *"mexicana"* or "Chicana."

As a culture, we call ourselves Spanish when referring to ourselves as a linguistic group and when copping out. It is then that we forget our predominant Indian genes. We are 70-80% Indian.[10] We call ourselves Hispanic[11] or Spanish-American or Latin American or Latin when linking ourselves to other Spanish-speaking peoples of the Western hemisphere and when copping out. We call ourselves Mexican-American[12] to signify we are neither Mexican nor American, but more the noun "American" than the adjective "Mexican" (and when copping out).

Chicanos and other people of color suffer economically for not acculturating. This voluntary (yet forced) alienation makes for psychological conflict, a kind of dual identity—we don't identify with the Anglo-American cultural values and we don't totally identify with the Mexican cultural values. We are a synergy of two cultures with various degrees of Mexicanness or Angloness. I have so internalized the borderland conflict that sometimes I feel like one cancels out the other and we are zero, nothing, no one. *A veces no soy nada ni nadie. Pero hasta cuando no lo soy, lo soy.*

When not copping out, when we know we are more than nothing, we call ourselves Mexican, referring to race and ancestry; *mestizo* when affirming both our Indian and Spanish (but we hardly ever own our Black) ancestry; Chicano when referring to a politically aware people born and/or raised in the U.S.; *Raza* when referring to Chicanos; *tejanos* when we are Chicanos from Texas.

Chicanos did not know we were a people until 1965 when Cesar Chavez and the farmworkers united and *I Am Joaquín* was published and *La Raza Unida* party was formed in Texas. With that recognition, we became a distinct people. Something momentous happened to the Chicano soul—we became aware of our reality and acquired a name and a language (Chicano Spanish) that reflected that reality. Now that we had a name, some of the fragmented pieces began to fall together—who we were, what we were, how we had evolved. We began to get glimpses of what we might eventually become.

Yet the struggle of identities continues, the struggle of borders is our reality still. One day the inner struggle will cease and a true integration take place. In the meantime, *tenémos que hacer la lucha. ¿Quién está protegiendo los ranchos de mi gente? ¿Quién está tratando de cerrar la fisura entre la india y el blanco en nuestra sangre? El Chicano, si, el Chicano que anda como un ladrón en su propia casa.*

Los Chicanos, how patient we seem, how very patient. There is the quiet of the Indian about us.[13] We know how to survive. When other races have given up their tongue, we've kept ours. We know what it is to live under the hammer blow of the dominant *norteamericano* culture. But more than we count the blows, we count the days the weeks the years the centuries the eons until the white laws and commerce and customs will rot in the deserts they've created, lie bleached. *Humildes* yet proud, *quietos* yet wild, *nosotros los mexicanos-Chicanos* will walk by the crumbling ashes as we go about our business. Stubborn, persevering, impenetrable as stone, yet possessing a malleability that renders us unbreakable, we, the *mestizas* and *mestizos*, will remain.

1. Ray Gwyn Smith, *Moorland is Cold Country*, unpublished book.

2. Irena Klepfisz, "*Di rayze aheym*/The Journey Home," in *The Tribe of Dina: A Jewish Women's Anthology*, eds. Melanie Kaye/Kantrowitz, and Irena Klepfisz (Montpelier, VT: Sinister Wisdom Books, 1986), p. 49.

3. R.C. Ortega, *Dialectología Del Barrio*, trans. Hortencia S. Alwan (Los Angeles: R.C. Ortega Publisher & Bookseller, 1977), p. 132.

4. Eduardo Hernandéz-Chávez, Andrew D. Cohen, and Anthony F. Beltramo, *El Lenguaje de los Chicanos: Regional and Social Characteristics of Language Used by Mexican Americans* (Arlington, VA: Center for Applied Linguistics, 1975), p. 39.

5. Ibid., p. xvii.

6. Irena Klepfisz, "Secular Jewish Identity: Yidishkayt in America," in *The Tribe of Dina*, eds. Kaye/Kantrowitz and Klepfisz, p. 43.

7. Melanie Kaye/Kantrowitz, "Sign," in *We Speak in Code: Poems and Other Writings* (Pittsburgh: Motheroot Publications, 1980), p. 85.

8. Rodolfo Gonzales, *I Am Joaquín/Yo Soy Joaquín* (New York: Bantam Books, 1972). It was first published in 1967.

9. Gershen Kaufman, *Shame: the Power of Caring* (Cambridge: Schenkman Books, 1980), p. 68.

10. Hernandéz-Chávez, *El Lenguaje de los Chicanos*, pp. 88-90.

11. "Hispanic" is derived from *Hispanis* (*España*, a name given to the Iberian Peninsula in ancient times when it was a part of the Roman Empire) and is a term designated by the U.S. government to make it easier to handle us on paper.

12. The Treaty of Guadalupe Hidalgo created the Mexican-American in 1848.

13. Anglos, in order to alleviate their guilt for dispossessing the Chicano, stressed the Spanish part of us and perpetrated the myth of the Spanish Southwest. We have accepted the fiction that we are Hispanic, that is Spanish, in order to accommodate ourselves to the dominant culture and its abhorrance of Indians. Hernandéz-Chávez, pp. 88-91.

• **James A. Snead**

Repetition as a Figure of Black Culture

The Scope of Repetition in Culture

> *The world, as force, may not be thought of as unlimited, for it cannot be so thought of; we forbid ourselves the concept of an infinite force as incompatible with the concept "force." Thus–the world also lacks the capacity for eternal novelty.*
> –Nietzsche, *The Will to Power*

After all, people have by now had to make peace with the idea that the world is not inexhaustible in its combinations, nor life in its various guises. How we have come to terms with the discrepancy between our personal growth–the very model of linear development–and the physical plane upon which life unfolds, characterized by general recursiveness and repetition: this must be the concern of culture. "Coming-to-terms" may mean denial or acceptance, repression or highlighting, but in any case *transformation* is culture's response to its own apprehension of repetition.

Apart from revealing or secreting the repetitions of material existence, a third response is possible: to own that repetition has occurred, but that, given a "quality of difference" compared to what has gone before, it has become not a "repetition" but rather a "progression," if positive, or a "regression," if negative. This third response implies that one finds a scale of tendencies from culture to culture. In any case, let us remember that, whenever we encounter repetition in cultural forms, we are indeed not viewing "the same thing" but its transformation, not just a formal ploy but often the willed grafting onto culture of an essentially philosophical insight about the shape of time and history. But, even if not in intentional emulation of natural or material cyclicality, repetition would need to manifest itself. Culture as a reservoir of inexhaustible novelty is unthinkable. Therefore, repetition, first of all, would inevitably have to creep into the dimension of culture just as into that of language and signification because of the finite supply of elementary units and the need for recognizability. One may readily classify cultural forms according to whether they tend to admit or cover up the repeating constituents within them.

The important thing about culture is that it should not be dead. Or, if dead, then its transformations must continue to live on in the present. Culture must be both immanent and historical: something *there* and something to be studied in its present form and in its etiology. Our modern notion of "culture'" only arises early in this century, after an

500-year period of English usage as a noun of process rather than identification, referring rather to the tending of animals or crops than to types of music, literature, art and
temperament by which a group of people is aware of and defines itself for others and for
itself.[1] But this initial connotation may still be preserved. "Culture" in its present usage
always also means the *culture* of culture: a certain continuance in the nurture of those
concepts and experiences that have helped or are helping to lend self-consciousness and
awareness to a given group. Culture must not only be immanent now but also give the
promise of being *continuously* so. So the second way in which repetition enters the dimension of culture is in the necessity for every culture to maintain a sense of continuity
about itself: internal changes notwithstanding, a basic self-identity must not be altered.
Strangely enough, however, what recent Western or European culture repeats continuously is precisely the belief that there is *no* repetition in culture but only a difference,
defined as progress and growth.

It was Swift who said that "happiness . . . is a perpetual Possession of being well de-
ceived."[2] We are not far here from a proper definition of culture. At least a type of
"happiness" accrues through a perpetual repetition or apparent consensus and convention that provide a sense of security, identification and "rightness." Yet, however
fervently culture nurtures this belief, such a sense of security is also a kind of "coverage," both in the comforting sense of "insurance" against accidental and sudden
rupturing of a complicated and precious fabric, and in Swift's less favorable sense of a
"cover-up," or a hiding of otherwise unpleasant facts from the senses.[3] Like all insurance, this type of *coverage* does not prevent accidents but promises to be able to provide
the means to outlive them. Furthermore, this insurance takes full actuarial account of
the *most* and *least* likely points of intrusion or corruption to the self-image of the culture,
and covers them accordingly.

For example, most cultures seem quite willing to tolerate and often assimilate certain
foreign *games*—such as chess, imported to Europe from the Middle East as early as the
First or Second Crusade in the twelfth century, or lawn tennis developed and patented
in England in 1874 from an earlier form of tennis. The fate of foreign *words* in language,
however, has been frequently less happy, as witnessed in the *coverage* that European national languages institute against diluting "invasions of foreign words," exemplified in
England by the sixteenth-century "Cambridge School" (Ascham, Cheke and Wilson),
in seventeenth-century France by the purism of Boileau and the Académie Française (a
linguistic xenophobia which has by no means yet run its course) and by the recurrent attempts to expel foreignisms from the German language beginning with Leibnitz in the
seventeenth and Herder in the eighteenth century (most recently seen in the less innocu-
ous censorships of the National Socialists in the current century).[4]

Finally, as in all insurance, you pay a regular premium for *coverage*: culture has a
price. Might Swift's phrase "Flaws and Imperfections of Nature" not also include the
daunting knowledge that the apparently linear upward-striving course of human endeavor exists within nature's ineluctable circularity, and that birth and life end up in
death and decay?[5]

Cultures, then, are virtually all varieties of "long term" *coverage*, against both external and internal threats—self-dissolution, loss of identity; or repression, assimilation,

attachment (in the sense of legal "seizure"); or attack from neighboring or foreign cultures – with all the positive and negative connotations of the "cover-ups" thus produced. In this, black culture is no exception. Cultures differ among one another primarily in the tenacity with which the "cover-up" is maintained and the spacing and regularity of the intervals at which they cease to cover up, granting leeway to those ruptures in the illusion of growth which most often occur in the *déjà-vus* of exact repetition.

In certain cases, culture, in projecting an image *for others*, claims a radical difference *from others*, often further defined qualitatively as *superiority*. Already in this insistence on uniqueness and "higher" development we sense a linear, anthropomorphic drive. For centuries (and especially within the last three) Europe has found itself in hot contest internally over this very issue. Culture has been territorialized – and, with it, groups of its diverse adherents. Cultural wars have become territorial wars have become cultural wars again, and indeed into this maelstrom have been sucked concepts of "race," "virtue" and "nation," never to re-emerge.[6] What startles is not so much the content of these cross-cultural feuds as the vehemence and aggression with which groups of people wrangle over where one *coverage* ends and another begins. The incipient desire to define "race" and "culture" in the same breath as "identity" and "nationality" finally coincides with the great upheavals of the seventeenth and eighteenth centuries in Europe – among them, the overturning of the feudal monarchies of central Europe and the discovery and subjugation of black and brown masses across the seas. The word "culture" now gains two fateful senses: "that with which one whole group aggressively defines its superiority *vis-à-vis* another"; and a finer one, "that held at a level above the group or mass, for the benefit of the culture as a whole, by the conscious few (i.e. the distinction between *haute* and *basse culture*)."[7] At the same time as Europeans were defining themselves over against other European nations and even some of them against members of their own nations, they were also busy defining "European culture" as separate from "African culture," the ultimate otherness, the final *mass*. Only having now reached this stage can we make any sense whatever of the notion of "black culture" and what it might oppose.[8]

"Black culture" is a concept first created by Europeans and defined in opposition to "European culture." Hegel, for example, saw "black culture" as the lowest stage of that laudable self-reflection and development shown by European culture, whose natural outcome must be the state or nationhood. In his by no means untypical nineteenth-century view, Hegel said that black culture simply *did not exist* in the same sense as European culture did. Black culture (as one of several non-Western cultures) had no self-expression (i.e. no writing); there was no black *Volksgeist*, as in Europe, and not even particular tribes or groupings of Africans seemed in the least concerned to define themselves on the basis of any particular *Volksgeist*. Hegel (like most of Europe) was confused by the African: where did blacks fit into "the course of *world history*?"[9]:

> *In this main portion of Africa there can really be no history. There is a succession of* accidents and surprises.
>
> *There is* no goal, *no state there that one can follow, no subjectivity, but only a series of subjects who destroy each other. There has as yet been little comment upon* how strange a form of self-consciousness *this represents.*

These remarks give a rather fascinating definition of European culture (at least as Hegel introduces his countrymen in his "we") by inversion:

> We must forget all categories that lay at the bottom of our spiritual life and its subsumption under these forms; the difficulty [in such forgetting when examining Africa] lies in the fact that we repeatedly must bring along that which we have already imagined.

Because Hegel gives the first and still most penetratingly systematic definition by a European of the "African character" (and, consequently, of black culture), albeit in a severely negative tone, it is worth quoting him at length:

> In general it must be said that [African] consciousness has not yet reached the contemplation of a fixed objective, an objectivity. The fixed objectivity is called God, the Eternal, Justice, Nature, natural things . . . The Africans, however, have not yet reached this recognition of the General . . . What we name Religion, the State, that which exists in and for itself—in other words, all that is valid—all this is not yet at hand . . . Thus we find nothing other than man in his immediacy: that is man in Africa. As soon as Man as Man appears, he stands in opposition to Nature; only in this way does he become Man . . . The Negro represents the Natural Man in all his wildness and indocility: if we wish to grasp him, then we must drop all European conceptions.
>
> What we actually understand by "Africa" is that which is without history and resolution, which is still fully caught up in the natural spirit, and which here must be mentioned as being on the threshold of world history.

Hegel's African has an absolute alterity to the European. This fact conveniently enables us to re-read Hegel's criticism as an insightful classification and taxonomy of the dominant tendencies of both cultures. The written text of Hegel is a century and a half old, but its truth still prevails, with regard to the tendencies, in the present-day forms to be discussed later, of the cultures that Hegel describes.

What are the main characteristics that Hegel finds to distinguish black culture from European culture? Interestingly, Hegel begins by implying that black culture is resilient because reticent, or by nature of its very backwardness untouchable: it is totally *other* and incomprehensible to the European, whereas other cultures, such as the native American, have combated the European and have lost:

> the subjection of land has meant its downfall . . . as far as tribes of men are concerned, there are few of the descendants of the first Americans left, since close to seven million men have been wiped out . . . the entire [native] American world has gone under and been suppressed by the Europeans . . . They are perishing, so that no one sees that they do not have the strength to merge with the North Americans in the Free States. Such peoples of weak culture lose themselves more and more in contact with people of higher culture and more intensive cultural training. [10]

Noteworthy here is the persistent connection of physical and territorial suppression, attachment and extermination with cultural inadequacy.

Hegel's definition of black culture is simply negative: ever-developing European culture is the prototype for the fulfillment of culture in the future; black culture is the antitype, ever on the threshold. Black culture, caught in "historylessness" (*Geschicht-slosigkeit*), is none the less shielded from attack or assimilation precisely by its aboriginal intangibility (though particular blacks themselves may not be so protected). According to Hegel, the African, radical in his effect upon the European, is a "strange form of self-consciousness" unfixed in orientation towards transcendent goals and terrifyingly close to the cycles and rhythms of nature. The African, first, overturns all European categories of logic. Second, he has no idea of history or progress, but instead allows "accidents and surprises" to take hold of his fate. He is also not aware of being at a lower stage of development and perhaps even has no idea of what development is. Finally, he is "immediate" and intimately tied to nature with all its cyclical, non-progressive data. Having no self-consciousness, he is "immediate"–i.e. *always there*–in any given moment. Here we can see that, being there, the African is also *always already there*, or perhaps *always there before*, whereas the European is *headed there* or, better, *not yet there*.

Hegel was almost entirely correct in his reading of black culture, but what he could not have guessed was that in his very criticism of it he had almost perfectly described the "there" to which European culture was "headed." Like all models that insist on discrete otherness, Hegel's definition implicitly constituted elements of black culture that have only in this century become manifest. Only after Freud, Nietzsche, comparative and structural anthropology and the study of comparative religion could the frantic but ultimately futile coverings of repetition by European culture be seen as dispensable, albeit in limited instances of "uncovering." Moreover, the very aspects of black culture which had seemed to define its nonexistence for the phenomenologist Hegel may now be valued as positive terms, given a revised metaphysics of rupture and opening.[11]

The Types of Repetition: Their Cultural Manifestations

> *They are after themselves. They call it destiny. Progress. We call it*
> *Haints. Haints of their victims rising from the soil of Africa, South*
> *America, Asia . . .*
> –Ishmael Reed, *Mumbo Jumbo*

Hegel as a prophet of historical development was notorious but not unique. We may accept that his assumptions have long been and still are shared, particularly the view that culture in history occurs only when a group arrives at a state of self-consciousness sufficient to propel it to "their destination of becoming a state":

> *. . . formal culture on every level of intellectual development can and must emerge, prosper and*
> *arrive at a point of high flowering when it forms itself into a state and in this basic form of civi-*
> *lization proceeds to abstract universal reflection and necessarily to universal laws and forms.*[12]

The word "state" (*Staat*) is to be defined not as a strict political entity but as any coherent group whose culture progresses from the level of immediacy to self-awareness.

How, then, do European culture and black culture differ in their treatment of the inevitability of repetition, either in annual cycles or in artistic forms? The truly self-conscious culture resists all non-progressive views; it *develops*. Hegel admits the category of change, and even the fact of cyclical repetition in nature, but prefers not to look at it or, if at all, then not from a negative "oriental" but from a positive "occidental" standpoint. In such a view, Hegel states:

> Whatever development [*Bildung*] takes place becomes material upon which the Spirit elevates itself to a new level of development, proclaiming its powers in all the directions of its plenitude. [13]

Hence emerges the yet prevailing "third option" mentioned above as a response to repetition: the notion of progress within the cycle, "differentiation" within repetition.

So the first category where European culture separates itself from "oriental" and "African" cultures is in its treatment of physical and natural cycles. This separation into "occidental" and "oriental" must seem amusing to anyone familiar with–among other Western texts–Book XV of Ovid's *Metamorphoses*, where the "pessimistic" and "oriental" viewpoint appears in the lips of an "occidental" predecessor of Hegel, Pythagoras:

> *Nothing is constant in the whole world. Everything is in a state of flux, and comes into being as a transient appearance . . . don't you see the year passing through a succession of four seasons? . . . In the same way our own bodies are always ceaselessly changing . . . Time, the devourer, and all the jealous years that pass, destroy all things, and, nibbling them away, consume them gradually in a lingering death . . . Nor does anything retain its appearance permanently. Ever-inventive nature continually produces one shape from another . . . Though this thing may pass into that, and that into this, yet the sum of things remains unchanged.* [14]

The truth is that the cyclical views of history are not "oriental," but were widespread in Europe well before the inception of historicism, which began not with Hegel but long prior to the nineteenth century (and here one might mention as Hegel's precursors Bacon or Descartes in the Enlightenment, the progressive *consummatio* in the eschatology of Joachim of Floris, the Thomist orientation towards teleology, or even go back to the "final" triumph of the Heavenly City of St. Augustine of Hippo). The debate in Western culture over the question of the shape of history, for most of its course, has been pretty evenly waged, with the advantage perhaps initially even somewhat on the side of the cyclical view. Only with the coming of scientific progressivism (as predicted and formulated by Bacon in *The Advancement of Learning* in 1605) was the linear model able to attain pre-eminence, and then not for some 200 years. [15] The now suppressed (but still to be found) recognition of cycles in European culture has always resembled the beliefs that underlie the religious conceptions of black culture, observing periodic regeneration of biological and agricultural systems. [16]

Black culture highlights the observance of such repetition, often in homage to an original generative instance or act. Cosmogony, the origins and stability of things, hence prevails because it recurs, not because the world continues to develop from the archetypal moment. Periodic ceremonies are ways in which black culture comes to terms with its perception of repetition, precisely by highlighting that perception. Dance often accompanies those ritualistic occasions when a seasonal return is celebrated and the "rounds" of the dance (as of the "Ring Shout" or "Circle Dance") recapitulate the "roundings" of natural time: Christmas, New Year, funerals, harvest-time.[17] Weddings especially are a reenactment of the initial act of coupling that created mankind and are therefore particularly well suited as recognitions of recurrence. Conscious cultural observance of natural repetition no longer characterizes European culture. The German wedding festival, for example, the *Hochzeit*, is today fully divested of its original ties to the repeating New Year's festival *Hochgezit*, and the sense of an individual marriage as a small-scale image of a larger renewal and repetition is now gone.[18] Outside of the seasonal markings of farmers' almanacs, the sort of precise celebration of time's passage and return that we see in Spenser's *Shepheards Calendar* or in the cyclical mystery plays has been out of general favor in recent times (or simply consigned to the realm of the demonic as in the Mephisophelean "I've already buried heaps of them! / And always new blood, fresh blood, circulates again. / So it goes on . . . "[19]).

Yet the year does still go around: how does European culture deal with perceived cycles? Recurrent national and sacred holidays are still marked, but with every sense of a progression having taken place between them. The "New Year's Resolution" and its frequent unfulfillment precisely recalls the attempt and failure to impose a character of progression and improvement onto an often non-progressing temporal movement. Successive public Christmas celebrations and ornamental displays vie to show increase in size, splendor or brightness from previous ones (although, significantly, the realm of sacred ritual, while immediately coexisting with the commercial culture, still works to bar any inexact repetition of religious liturgy, such as in the Nativity service). Other contemporary cycles, such as the four-year intervals of the Olympic Games and presidential elections, fervently need to justify their obvious recurrence by some standard of material improvement or progress: a new or larger Olympic site or new Olympic records; a new or better political party or personality.

In European culture, financial and production cycles have largely supplanted the conscious sort of natural return of black culture. The financial year is the perfect example of this Hegelian subsumption of development within stasis. For repetition must be exact in all financial accounting, given that, globally, capital ultimately circulates within closed tautological systems (i.e. decrease in an asset is either an increase in another asset or a decrease in a liability, both within a corporate firm and in its relations with other firms). The "annual report" of a business concern, appearing cyclically in yearly or interim rhythm (always on the same "balance-sheet date"), contains ever the same kinds of symbols about the concern's health or decrepitude. It is only the properties of *difference* between $year_2$ and $year_1$ (as quantified by numerical changes in the symbols—say, in the cash-flow matrix) which determine how the essentially exact repetitions are to be evaluated and translated into a vocabulary of growth and development. Capital hence will not only necessarily *circulate* but must consequently also *accumulate or diminish*, depending on the state of the firm. Economics and business in their term "cyclicality," admit the existence and even the necessity of repetition of decline but continually overlay this rupture in the illusion of continuous growth with a rhetoric of "incremental" or "staged" development, which asserts that the repetition of decline in a cycle may occur, but occurs only within an overall upward or spiral tendency.[20]

The discourse used of capital in European economic parlance reveals a more general insight about how this culture differs from black culture in its handling of repetition. In black culture, repetition means that the thing *circulates* (exactly in the manner of any flow, including capital flows) there in an equilibrium. In European culture, repetition must be seen to be not just circulation and flow but accumulation and growth. In black culture, the thing (the ritual, the dance, the beat) is "there for you to pick it up when you come back to get it." If there is a goal (*Zweck*) in such a culture, it is always deferred; it continually "cuts" back to the start, in the musical meaning of "cut" as an abrupt, seemingly unmotivated break (an accidental *da capo*) with a series already in progress and a willed return to a prior series.[21]

A culture based on the idea of the "cut" will always suffer in a society whose dominant idea is material progress—but "cuts" possess their charm! In European culture, the "goal" is always clear: that which always is being worked towards. The goal is thus that which is reached only when culture "plays out" its history. Such a culture is never "immediate" but "mediated" and separated from the present tense by its own future-orientation. Moreover, European culture does not allow "a succession of accidents and surprises" but instead maintains the illusions of progression and control at all costs. Black culture, in the "cut," builds "accidents" into its *coverage*, almost as if to control their unpredictability. Itself a kind of cultural *coverage*, this magic of the "cut" attempts to confront accident and rupture not by covering them over but by making room for them inside the system itself.[22]

In one unexpected sphere of European consciousness, however, such an orientation towards the "cut" has survived: on the level of that psychological phenomenon which Freud fully details as the eruption of seemingly unwilled repetitions of the past into the individual's present life—*Wiederholungszwang* or *repetition compulsion*. On the individual psychic level, cultural prohibitions lose their validity. Hence in repetition compulsion, as Freud describes it, repetition—an idiosyncratic and immediate action—has replaced memory, the "normal" access to the past. Instead of a dialogue about a history already past, one has a restaging of the past. Instead of relating what happened in his or her history (Hegel's category of objectivity), the patient re-enacts it with all the precision of ritual.[23] This obsessive acting-out of the repressed past conflict brings the patient back to the original scene of drama. Repetition compulsion is an example of a "cut" or "seemingly fortuitous" (but actually motivated) repetition that appears in explicit contradiction to societal constraints and standards of behavior. Society would censure the act of unwilled repetition as much or even more than the original trespass: both are against custom (*Sitte*), or un-moral (*unsittlich*), but the lack of will in repetition compulsion makes it also uncanny (*unheimlich*). Jacques Lacan's fruitful idea of the *tuché*—the kind of repetition "that occurs *as if by chance*"—seems to complete the identification here of repetition compulsion as one further aspect of non-progressive culture to have been identified within the limits of the European individual consciousness.[24] By virtue of its accidence (or of its accidental way of showing through), the cycle of desire and repression that underlies repetition compulsion belongs together with the notion of the "cut."

Repetition in black culture finds its most characteristic shape in performance: rhythm in music, dance and language.[25] Whether or not one upholds the poet-politician-philosopher Léopold Senghor's attempts to fix the nature of black culture in a concept of *négritude*, it is true that he has well described the role that rhythm plays in it: "The organizing force which makes the black style is rhythm. It is the most perceptible and least material thing."[26] Where material is absent, dialectics is groundless. Repetitive words and rhythms have long been recognized as a focal constituent of African music and its American descendants—slave-songs, blues, spirituals and jazz.[27] African music normally emphasizes dynamic rhythm, organizing melody within juxtaposed lines of beats grouped into differing meters. The fact that repetition in some senses is the principle of organization shows the desire to rely upon "the thing that is there to pick up." Progress in the sense of "avoidance of repetition" would at once sabotage such an effort. Without an organizing principle of repetition, true improvisation would be impossible, since an improviser relies upon the ongoing recurrence of the beat.

Not only improvisation but also the characteristic "call and response" element in black culture (which already, in eliciting the general participation of the group at random, spontaneous "cuts," disallows any possibility of an *haute culture*) requires an assurance of repetition:

> While certain rhythms may establish a background beat, in almost all African music there is a dominant point of repetition developed from a dominant conversation with a clearly defined alternation, a swinging back and forth from solo to chorus or from solo to an emphatic instrumental reply.[28]

That the beat is there to pick up does not mean that it must have been metronomic, but merely that it must have been at one point begun and that it must be at any point "social"—i.e. amenable to restarting, interruption or entry by a second or third player or to response by an additional musician. The typical polymetry of black music means that there are at least two, and usually more, rhythms going on alongside the listener's own beat. The listener's beat is a kind of *Erwartungshorizont* (to use a term taken from a quite different area) or "horizon of expectations," whereby he or she knows where the constant beat must fall in order properly to make sense of the gaps that the other interacting drummers have let fall.[29] Because one rhythm always defines another in black music, and beat is an entity of relation, any "self-consciousness" or "achievement" in the sense of an individual participant working towards his or her own rhythmic or tonal climax "above the mass" would have disastrous results.

While repetition in black music is almost proverbial, what has not often been recognized in black music is the prominence of the "cut." The "cut" overtly insists on the repetitive nature of the music, by abruptly skipping it back to another beginning which we have already heard. Moreover, the greater the insistence on the pure beauty and value of repetition, the greater the awareness must also be that repetition takes place not on a level of musical development or progression, but on the purest tonal and timbric level.

James Brown is an example of a brilliant American practitioner of the "cut" whose skill is readily admired by African as well as American musicians.[30] The format of the Brown "cut" and repetition is similar to that of African drumming: after the band has been "cookin'" in a given key and tempo, a cue, either verbal ("Get down" or

"Mayfield"–the sax player's name–or "Watch it now") or musical (a brief series of rapid, percussive drum and horn accents), then directs the music to a new level where it stays with more "cookin' " or perhaps a solo–until a repetition of cues then "cuts" back to the primary tempo. The essential pattern, then, in the typical Brown sequence is recurrent: "ABA" or "ABCBA" or "ABC(B)A" with each new pattern set off (i.e. introduced and interrupted) by the random, brief hiatus of the "cut."[31] The ensuing rupture does not cause dissolution of the rhythm; quite to the contrary, it strengthens it, given that it is already incorporated into the format of that rhythm.

In jazz improvisation, the "cut"–besides uses similar to Brown's–is the unexpectedness with which the soloist will depart from the "head" or theme and from its normal harmonic sequence or the drummer from the tune's accepted and familiar primary beat. One of the most perfect exemplars of this kind of improvisation is John Coltrane, whose mastery of melody and rhythm was so complete that he and Elvin Jones, his drummer, often traded roles, Coltrane making rhythmic as well as melodic statements and "cutting" away from the initial mode of the playing.[32]

Black music sets up expectations and disturbs them at irregular intervals: that it will do this, however, is itself an expectation. This peculiarity of black music–that it draws attention to its own repetitions–extends to the way it does not hide the fact that these repetitions take place on the level of sound only. The extension of "free jazz," starting in the 1960s, into the technical practice of using the "material" qualities of sound–on the horns, for instance, using overtones, harmonics and subtones–became almost mandatory for the serious jazz musician and paralleled a similar movement on the part of European musicians branching out of the classical tradition. But black music has always tended to imitate the human voice, and the tendency to "stretch" the limits of the instrument may have been already there since the wail of the first blues guitar, the whisper of the first muted jazz trumpet or the growl of the first jazz trombonist.

The black church must be placed at the center of the manifestations of repetition in black culture, at the junction of music and language. Various rhetorics come into play here: the spoken black sermon employs a wide variety of strategies, such as particularly *epanalepsis* ("because His power brings you power, and your Lord is still the Lord") or *epistrophe* ("give your life to the Lord; give your faith to the Lord; raise your hands to the Lord"). Emphatic repetition most often takes the form of *anaphora*, where the repetition comes at the beginning of the clause (instead of at the beginning and at the end in the first example above, or at the end in the second case). Such a usage of repetition is not limited to the black church, however, and may even be derived in part from the uses of repetition in the key church text, the Bible, as in the following anaphora from the Psalms (29: 10-11): "The Lord remaineth a King forever. The Lord shall give strength unto his people. The Lord shall give his people the blessing of peace."

Both preacher and congregation employ the "cut." The preacher "cuts" his own speaking in interrupting himself with a phrase such as "praise God" (whose weight here cannot be at all termed denotative or imperative but purely sensual and rhythmic–an underlying "social" beat provided for the congregation). The listeners, in responding to the preacher's calls at random intervals, produce each time it "cuts" a slight shift in the texture of the performance. At various intervals a musical instrument such as the organ and often spontaneous dancing accompany the speaker's repetition of the "cut." When the stage of highest intensity comes, gravel-voiced "speaking in tongues" or the "testifying," usually delivered at a single pitch, gives credence to the hypothesis, that, all along, the very texture of the sound and nature of the rhythm—but not the explicit meaning—in the spoken words have been at issue.

Repetition in black literature is too large a subject to be covered here, but one may say briefly that it has learned from these "musical" prototypes in the sense that repetition of words and phrases, rather than being overlooked, is exploited as a structural and rhythmic principle. The sermon on the "Blackness of Blackness" which occurs early in Ralph Ellison's *Invisible Man* lifts the sermonic and musical repetitions (Ellison says he modeled this sequence on his knowledge of repetition in jazz music) directly into view in a literary text—and not just in the repetitions of its title.[33] The *ad hoc* nature of much black folklore and poetry, as well as its ultimate destination in song, tends to encourage the repeating refrain, as in this paean to the fighter Jack Johnson:

> Jack Johnson, he de champion of de worl'
> Jack Johnson, he de champion of de worl'
> Jack Johnson, he de champion
> Jack Johnson, he de champion
> Jack Johnson, he de champion of de worl'[34]

The "AABBA" repetitive format of so much black folklore and folk-lyric often finds its way into the black novel (as it does into the blues) in unaltered form. In Jean Toomer's *Cane*, the mixture of "fiction, songs, and poetry," presented against the theme of black culture in transition, provides a fine opportunity to view some typical (and not so typical) uses of repetition in the black novel. From the poem "Song of the Sun" to the very last page, the repetitive forms of black language and rhetoric are prominent until one notices that gradually the entire plot of the novel itself has all along been tending towards the shape of return—the circle:

> O land and soil, red soil and sweet-gum tree,
> So scant of grass, so profligate of pines
> Now just before an epoch's sun declines
> Thy son, in time, I have returned to thee,
> Thy son, I have in time returned to thee.[35]

Toni Morrison continues this use of repetition, particularly in *Song of Solomon*, with Sugarman's song and the final song of "Jake the only son of Solomon." In the latter song, where Morrison describes "the children, inexhaustible in their willingness to repeat a rhythmic, rhyming action game," and the will of black language to "perform in the round over and over again," she puts into words the essential component of her own written tradition. Leon Forrest (most notably in *There is a Tree more Ancient than Eden*) and Ishmael Reed are able to tap a long series of predecessors when they include folk-poems and folklore in their narratives, whose non-progressive form they need not feel constrained to justify.

But particularly in the work of Reed (mainly *Mumbo Jumbo*, but also quite noticeably in *The Free-Lance Pallbearers* and *Flight to Canada*) the kinds of repetition we have seen to have been derived from spoken discourse become only an emblem for much wider strategies of circulation and "cutting" in black writing and a model, or supplemental meter, for their future employment. The explicitly parodistic thrust of the title *Mumbo Jumbo* first of all rejects the need for making a definitive statement about the "black situation in America" and already implies, as all parody does, a comparison with, as well as regeneration of, what has come before and the return of a pre-logical past where, instead of words denoting sense, there was "mumbo jumbo." Jes Grew, the main "force" in the novel, besides being disembodied rhythm ("this bongo drumming called Jes Grew") or Senghor's "la chose la plus sensible et la moins matérielle," is ironically the essence of anti-growth, the avatar of a time "before this century is out" when, Reed predicts:

> . . . *men will turn once more to mystery, to wonderment; they will explore the vast reaches of space within instead of more measuring more "progress" more of this and more of that.*[36]

Jes Grew epidemics appear and reappear *as if by accident*: "So Jes Grew is seeking its words. Its text. For what good is a liturgy without a text?"[37] But there is no text to be found (besides Jes Grew's "rhythmic vocabulary larger than French or English or Spanish"), for the "text" is in fact the compulsion of Jes Grew to recur again and again—the "trace" of one such appearance is *Mumbo Jumbo*, the novel, but at the end of it we are left again with the text of the quest, which is the repetition of the seeking.

Reed elides the "cut" of black culture with the "cutting" used in cinema. Self-consciously filmable. *Mumbo Jumbo* ends with a "*freeze frame*" not only under-scoring its filmic nature, but also itself an example of a common cueing device for cinematic "cuts." Reed, also, in the manner of the jazz soloist, "cuts" frequently between the various subtexts in his novel (headlines, photographs, handwritten letters, italicized writing, advertisements) and the text of his main narrative. The linear narrative of the detective story and the feature film (*opening scenes, title, credits, story*, final *freeze frame*) also structures *Mumbo Jumbo*, but there is no progressive enterprise going on here, despite such evidence to the contrary. The central point remains clear right to Reed's very last words: "the 20s were back again. . . . Time is a pendulum. Not a river. More akin to what goes around comes around."[38] The film is in a loop.

The Return of Repetition

> *Repetition is reality and it is the seriousness of life. He who wills repetition is matured in seriousness. . . . Repetition is the new category which has to be brought to light.*
> –Kierkegaard, *Repetition*

In almost conscious opposition to Hegel's idea of "progressive" culture, European music and literature, perhaps realizing the limitations of innovation, have recently learned to "foreground" their already present repetitions, "cuts" and cyclical insights. As European music uses rhythm mainly as an aid in the construction of a sense of progression to a harmonic cadence, the repetition has been suppressed in favor of the fulfillment of the goal of harmonic resolution.[39] Despite the clear presence of consistent beat or rhythm in the common classical forms of the ostinato or the figured bass or any other continuo instrument, rhythm was scarcely a goal in itself and repetition seldom pleasurable or beautiful by itself.

Although the key role of "recapitulation" in the "ABA" or "AABBAA" sonata form (often within a movement itself, as in the so frequently ignored "second repeats" in Beethoven's major works) is undisputed in theory, in live performance these repetitions often are left out to avoid the undesirability of having "to be told the same thing twice." Repeating the exposition, as important as it no doubt is for the "classical style," is subsumed within and fulfilled by the general category called "development." By the time the music does return to the home tonic, in the final recapitulation, the sense is clearly one of repetition with a difference. The momentum has elevated the initial material to a new level rather than merely re-presenting it unchanged.[40] Even though the works of Wagner and his followers represent a break from this traditional formal model of development derived from the sonata form, the Wagnerian leitmotiv, for instance, is anything but a celebration of repetition in music. In the *Ring*, Wagner's consummate vehicle for the leitmotivic style of composition, the recurrent musical phrases are in fact a Hegelian progression or extended accumulation and accretion to an ultimate goal or expression that begins somewhere during the early part of the *Götterdämmerung*, or even starting late in *Siegfried*; the leitmotivs are invested in installments throughout *Das Rheingold* and *Die Walkure* and are then repaid with interest by the end of the *Götterdämmerung*.

In the pre-serial era, only Stravinsky took the already present expectations of concealed repetition in the classical tradition and uncovered them by highlighting them. In *Petrushka* (1911) and *Le Sacre du Printemps* (1913) particularly, the use of the "cut" and the unconcealed repetition is striking. In the First Tableau of *Petrushka*, an abbreviated fanfare and tattoo from snare drum and tambourine set off the first section (rehearsal numbers 1-29)–itself in ABACABA form–from the magic trick (30-32), which is the new, much slower tempo after the "cut." The magic trick concludes with a harp glissando and a brief unaccompanied piccolo figure–the next "cut"–leading to the famous "Danse russe" (33–46), overtly repetitive in its ABABA form, which then ends in a snare-drum "cut" (here, in 47, as well as elsewhere–at 62, 69 and 82). In *Le Sacre du Printemps* exact repetition within and across sections exceeds anything that had come before it. Moreover, Stravinsky had developed his use of the "cut," varying the cue-giving instrument.[41] Interestingly, both Stravinsky compositions resemble black musical forms not just in their relentless "foregrounding" of rhythmic elements and their use of the "cut" but also in being primarily designed for use in conjunction with dancers.[42]

In European literature, the recovery of repetition in this century is even more striking. Blatant repetitions of the folkloric, traditional or mnemonic sort that had characterized European oral poetry, medieval sagas and other forms of narrative right into late sixteenth-century baroque literature began to be transformed into the pretense of an external reality being depicted, culminating in *literary realism* in the late nineteenth century. The picaresque "cuts" found in the segmented narratives of *Lazarillo de Tormes*

(1554) or even *Don Quixote* (1605)—where a quite literal "cut" breaks off the manuscript before chapter 9—were soon becoming a thing of the past, aside from the rare extravagance of Sterne, whose *Tristram Shandy* (1760–7) was an outstanding exception. In a sense, all representational conventions such as literary realism suppress repetition and verbal rhythm in the telling in favor of the illusion of narrative verisimilitude. Thus they would portray an outside world, exhaustible in its manifestations, by the supposedly inexhaustible and ever-renewable resource of writing—hence evading the need for "repeated descriptions" of that world.

Until recently—particularly before the Dadaists, and their "cutting" practices; or the cinema-inspired "montagists," Joyce, Faulkner, Woolf, Yeats and Eliot—this practice had been dominant. Now its dominance has begun to ebb somewhat. With Joyce, most of all, we have realized that the incessant repetition of particular words (such as "pin" or "hat" in the early Bloom chapters of *Ulysses*) are not descriptions of objects seen repeatedly in the external environment and then described, but intentional repetitions of words scattered here and there in a text by its author as if by accident.

Narrative repetition tends to defuse the belief that any other meaning resides in a repeated signifier than the fact that it is being repeated.[43] Among European or American dramatists, Tom Stoppard, in *Travesties*, comes closest to understanding this insight. This play (in which Joyce plays a major role, along with Tristan Tzara and Lenin) not only refuses to cover up its repetitions but makes clear that there must be a definite "cut" between them. The "cut" is explained in the stage directions as a manifestation of the unreliable memory of the main character, Henry Carr:

> One result is that the story (like a toy train perhaps) occasionally jumps the rails and has to be restarted at the point where it goes wild . . . The scene has several of these "time slips," indicated by the repetitions of the exchange between BENNETT and CARR about the "newspapers and telegrams" . . . It may be desirable to mark these moments more heavily by using an extraneous sound or a light effect, or both. The sound of a cuckoo-clock, artificially amplified, would be appropriate since it alludes to time and to Switzerland.[44]

Underlying this notion of "time" is not just Freud's idea that repetition is a remedy for the failure of memory, but the related and necessary acceptance of rupture: in the smooth forward progress of the play; in the insistently forward motion of "time" on those occasions when history "jumps the rails and has to be restarted at the point where it goes wild."

The cuckoo-clock in *Travesties* (borrowed from the "Nausicaa" chapter of *Ulysses*, where it has a slightly different function) is the perfect signal for "cuts," being itself an emblem of time. When in Act I Tzara repeats the word "DADA" thirty-four times in response to Carr's homily "It is the duty of the artist to beautify existence," one begins to think that the word's meaning in the context, or even its etymology (interesting as it might be for "DADA"), are beside the point. A previous "cut" has made the point more clearly. Tzara (well known in real life for his "cut-ups," or poems stuck together at random), while trying to seduce Gwendolen, cuts up and tosses the words of Shakespeare's eighteenth sonnet (which she has been reciting) into a hat, shakes them up, and pulls the words one by one out of the hat. Instead of the expected random version of the original, a quite lewd poem, using the same words as the former sonnet emerges:

> Darling, shake thou thy gold buds
> the untrimmed but short fair shade
> shines —
> see, this lovely hot possession growest
> so long
> by nature's course —
> so . . . long — heaven!
> and declines,
> summer changing, more temperate complexion . . .[45]

What is the point of Stoppard's "travesty" of Shakespeare? The cutting of the sonnet should have produced only "mumbo jumbo," or at best "clever nonsense," as Carr had called Tzara's prior recitation of the word "DADA." But the emergence of the "new" poem is the emergence of the real: instead of poetry, lechery is Tzara's concern. The true message of the sonnet is not transcendent (about beauty) but immediate, in that it consists of words on paper that can be cut, but which signify only in the context of speaking, not by virtue of being masterfully arranged. Language — even Shakespeare's — here is shown to be, on the most obvious level, exactly what is there, not what is elsewhere: it is of desire, not of meaning.

The outstanding fact of twentieth-century European culture is its ongoing reconciliation with black culture. The mystery may be that it took so long to discern the elements of black culture already there in latent form, and to realize that the separation between the cultures was perhaps all along not one of nature, but one of force.

1. Raymond Williams, who calls the word *culture* "one of the two or three most complicated words in the English language," gives a thorough survey of the usage of the word in *Keywords* (London and Glasgow: Fontana, 1976), pp. 76-82.

2. Jonathon Swift, *A Tale of a Tub, and Other Satires* (1704; London: Dent, 1975), p. 108.

3. Throughout *A Tale of a Tub*, Swift (like Carlyle after him) employs images of undress and disrobing to denote death and pathology, while equating dress with the power of culture and language.

4. For the English examples, see Simeon Potter, *Our Language* (Harmondsworth: Penguin, 1976), pp. 59-61, 117-21. For the German attempts to expel foreign — especially French — words, see Robert Reinhold Ergang, *Herder and the Foundations of German Nationalism* (New York: Columbia University Press, 1931; repr. Octagon, 1966), pp. 131-132, 142-143, 163.

5. Contrast the Lenten admonition for the administering of ashes on Ash Wednesday, a statement of life as inevitable decay — "Memento, o homo, quod cines es, et in cinerem rivertaris" ("Remember, O man, that dust thou art and to dust thou shalt return") — with Pascal's use (in *Fragment d'un traité du vide*) of metaphors of human growth when speaking of the development of culture: "not only each man advances in the sciences day by day, but . . . all men, together make continual progress in them as the universe grows older." Quoted in *The Encyclopedia of Philosophy* (New York: Macmillan, 1967), p. 484.

6. Ergang, p. 7. See also Leo Weinstein, *Hippolyte Taine* (New York: Twayne, 1972), pp. 81–82.

7. That this separation between "culture" and "mass" is a "central concept of German fascist ideology" and directly leads to the identification of the "élite" army with the forces of national culture (and, conversely, the transformation of culture into a weapon) is most convincingly shown in Klaus Theweleit, *Mannerphantasien 2: Mannerkorper – zut Psychoanalyse des weissen Terrors* (Hamburg:

Rowohlt, 1980), pp. 47-64, in the chapter "Masse und Kultur–Der 'hochstehende Einzelne,'" and pp. 64-74, "Kultur und Heer." Goering is quoted as saying during the Nuremberg trials: "The Americans simply are not cultured enough to understand the German point of view," in ibid., p. 47.

8. I have chosen for the purpose of this essay to discuss "European culture" in contrast to "black culture" meaning the culture of both Africans and Afro-Americans, as the only usefully identifiable entities. I have refrained from any mention of "American culture," agreeing on the whole with Ralph Ellison when he states "I recognize no American culture which is not the partial creation of black people," and confident in the assertion that the terms "European" and "black" effectively exhaust the major manifestations of culture in contemporary America. See John Hersey, ed., *Ralph Ellison: A Collection of Critical Essays* (Englewood Cliffs, NJ: Prentice-Hall, 1974), p. 44.

9. Hegel's quote and those below it are from G. W. F. Hegel, *Die Vernunft in der Geschichte*, 5th revised edition (Hamburg: Felix Meiner, 1955), pp. 216-218; translation and italics are mine.

10. Ibid., pp. 200-201; translation and italics are mine.

11. I use the word "revised" advisedly here, since the proponents of the "new openness" never cease to point to historical benefactors going as far back as Plato. My tendency is to pick out Nietzsche as the principal "revisionist," but the key role of "rupture" in Freud, Heidegger and Husserl compels their mention here. For Jacques Derrida's views on Nietzsche, for instance, see *Spurs: Nietzsche's Styles*, trans. Barbara Harlow (Chicago: University of Chicago Press, 1979); French title *Épertons: Les styles de Nietzsche* (Venice: Corbo e Fiori, 1976). For the idea of "opening," see Derrida, *Of Grammatology*, trans. Gayatri Chakravorty Spivak (Baltimore: Johns Hopkins University Press, 1977). "The Hinge" ("La Brisure"), pp. 65-73; French title *De la grammatologie* (Paris: Minuit, 1967). See also Spivak's preface, pp. xxi-xxxviii, for a good introductory summary of the Derridian-Nietzschean critique of "the metaphysics of presence." See also Geoffrey Hartman's well-known essay "The Voice of the Shuttle: Language from the Point of View of Literature," in *Beyond Formalism* (New Haven: Yale University Press, 1970), pp. 337-355, and his more recent *Saving the Text: Literature, Derrida, Philosophy* (Baltimore: Johns Hopkins University Press, 1981).

12. Hegel, pp. 163, 173; translation is mine.

13. Ibid., pp. 35-36.

14. Ovid, *The Metamorphoses*, trans. Mary M. Innes (Harmondsworth: Penguin, 1970), pp. 339-341, II. 148-271. Pythagorean ideas on recurrence derive both from a belief in metempsychosis (transmigration of souls–see Plato's *Phaedrus*, 248e-249d) and from Pythagoras' likely belief in a periodic historical cycle (Great Year) of 9000 years of more, which involved an exact repetition in each phase. See J. A. Philip, *Pythagoras and Early Pythagoreanism* (Toronto: University of Toronto Press, 1966), p. 75.

15. The area of philosophy dealing with such issues–the philosophy of history–has been recently (approximately since Croce and Toynbee) rather neglected. The view of Hegel or Augustine on one side, being roughly opposed in their historical concept to Nietzsche or Vico on the other, may be said approximately to delimit the poles of Western discourse on the subject, although the opposition is more fluid than a simple counterposition. For fuller discussion of this broad and highly complex issue, consult: on Bacon, Benjamin Farrington, *Francis Bacon: Philosopher of Industrial Science* (London: Macmillan, 1973); on the general topic of the philosophy of history, Sir Isaiah Berlin, *Vico and Herder: Two Studies in the History of Ideas* (London: Hogarth Press, 1976); Manfred Buhr, *Zur Geschichte der klassischen bürgerlichen Philosophie: Bacon, Kant, Fichte, Schelling, Hegel* (Leipzig: Phillip Reclam, 1972); Kenneth Burke, *Permanence and Change: An Anatomy of Purpose*, 2nd revised edition, Library of Liberal Arts (Indianapolis: Bobbs-Merrill, 1965); Karl Löwith, *Meaning in History* (Chicago: University of Chicago Press, 1949); and G. A. Wells, *Herder and After: A Study in the Development of Sociology* (S-Gravenhage: Mouton, 1959). For a recent attempt, see Peter Munz, *The Shapes of Time: A New Look at The Philosophy of History* (Middletown: Wesleyan University Press, 1977). See also Sacvan Bercovitch, *Puritan Origins of the American Self* (New Haven: Yale University Press, 1975), on the idea of progress and growth in English and American thought in the seventeenth century.

16. See Mircea Eliade, *The Myth of the Eternal Return, or, Cosmos and History*, trans. Willard R. Trask (Princeton: Princeton University Press, 1974), in the chapters "Archetypes and Repetition" and "The Regeneration of Time," pp. 3-92; French title, *Le Mythe de l'eternel retour: archétypes et répétition* (Paris: Gallimard, 1949). See also Eliade, *Patterns in Comparative Religion*, trans. Rosemary Sheed (Cleveland: World, Meridian Books, 1963); French title, *Traité d'histoire des religions* (Paris: Gallimard, 1949). Indeed, it may be that black culture at its initial stages is rarely found outside such ritualistic employment, and that "African Art in Motion" (to use Robert F. Thompson's phrase) is closely linked to those cyclical events that speak of

228 • James A. Snead

the return and reproduction of a previous event, in which there can be no question of "progress."

17. Robert F. Thompson, in "An Aesthetic of the Cool," *African Forum*, vol. 2, no. 2 (Fall 1966): 85, refers to African religions as "danced faiths." See also Eileen Southern, ed., *Readings in Black American Music* (New York: Norton, 1971), pp. 41-47, for James Eights' description of the yearly "Pinckster" slave celebrations that originated in the Middle Colonies of early America, and pp. 50-51 for Latrobe's description of festival dances of African origin in New Orleans. For a precise listing of particular dances used in conjucnction with particular annual festivals, see Leonore Emery, *Black Dance in the United States, from 1619 to 1970*, University of Southern California, Ph. D. (Ann Arbor: University Microfilms, 1971), the section "Special Occasion Dances," pp. 50-102.

18. Eliade, *The Myth of the Eternal Return*, p. 26. Keith Thomas, *Religion and the Decline of Magic* (New York: Scribner, 1971), explains this transition in perhaps more unconventional terms.

19. Johann Wolfgang von Goethe, *Faust, Part One*, trans. Louis MacNeice (Oxford: Oxford University Press, 1952), p. 49; Goethe, *Faust*, kommentiert von Erich Trunz (München: Beck, 1972), p. 48, ll. 1371-73: "Wie viele hab' ich schon begraben!/Und immer zirkuliert ein neues, frisches Blut./So geht es fort . . . "

20. See Paul M. Sweezy, *The Theory of Capitalist Development* (Oxford: Oxford University Press, 1942), for a fuller—and for Marx's—analysis of this need for upward growth, Max Weber, *The Protestant Ethic and the Spirit of Capitalism* (New York: Scribner, 1958), chapters 2 and 5 illustrate the psychological ramifications of this need for growth.

21. The "cut" is most often signaled by a master drummer, as in the description of the Dagomba "Atwimewu" drum in John Miller Chernoff, *African Rhythm and African Sensibility: Aesthetics and Social Action in African Musical Idioms* (Chicago: University of Chicago Press, 1979), pp. 43-67. See also the cinematic definition of "*cutting, editing, or montage* which changes the picture all at once from one view to another," in Ralph Stephenson and J. R. Debrix, *The Cinema as Art* (Harmondsworth: Penguin, 1965), p. 238.

22. Examples of such systematization of accident are found in all cultures where oracles play a strong role. Two examples are the *sortes Virgilianae* in early European history, or the randomized systematology of the *I Ching*, or "Book of Changes," in China, which uses random entry into a fixed, stable system.

23. Sigmund Freud, "Erinnern, Wiederholen, und Durcharbeiten" (1914), in *Studienausgabe*, eds. A. Mitscherlich, A. Richards, J. Strachey, 11 Vols.

(Frankfurt: S. Fischer, 1969-), *Ergänzungsband: Schriften zur Behandlungstechnik*, pp. 210-211. The definitive statement on *Wiederholungszwang*, insofar as Freud was capable of making such statements, is to be found in "Jenseits des Lustprinzips" (1920), *Studeinausgabe*, Vol. 3, pp. 228-229. For the interesting and related phenomenon of *déjà raconté*, see Freud, "Uber fausse reconnaiseance [*déjà raconté*] während der psychoanalytischen Arbeit," (1914), *Studienausgabe, Ergänzungsband*, pp. 233-238.

24. Jacques Lacan, *The Four Fundamental Concepts of Psychoanalysis*, trans. Alan Sheridan (London: Hogarth, 1977), p. 54; French title, *Les Quatre Concepts fondamenteaux de la psychoanalyse: Le Séminaire, Livre XI* (Paris: Seuil, 1973).

25. Chernoff, p. 55: "In African music, the chorus or response is a rhythmic phrase which recurs regularly; the rhythms of a lead singer or musician vary and are cast against the steady repetition of the response . . . We [in the West] are not yet prepared to understand how people can find beauty in repetition." Chernoff puts it well in another passage: "The most important issues of improvisation, in most African musical idioms, are matters of repetition and change." (p. 111)

26. Quoted in ibid., p. 23: "Cette force ordinatrice qui fait le style nègre est le rythme. C'est la chose la plus sensible et la moins matérielle."

27. See Ibid., p. 29, on the continuity of African rhythmic forms in America. Also see Ruth Finnegan, *Oral Literature in Africa* (Oxford: Clarendon, 1976), and Southern, ed., *passim*. Also of interest in this regard is Janheinz Jahn, *A History of Neo-African Literature: Writing in Two Continents*, trans. Oliver Coburn and Ursula Lehrburger (London: Faber, 1968); German title, *Geschichte der neoafrikanischen Literatur* (Düsseldorf and Cologne: Eugen Diederichs Verlag, 1966).

28. Chernoff, p. 55. Although the beat need not have been begun and kept from a conductor's initial count (because it may have in the interim "cut" or changed to another meter), it must be there at every point to "pick up" or "follow."

29. The term as I use it derives from the work of H.R. Jauss, as in the article "Literatur als Provokation der Literatur-Wissenschaft," contained in the collection *Literaturgeschichte als Provokation* (Frankfurt: Suhrkamp, 1970).

30. Chernoff, p. 55.

31. Thompson, in his *African Art in Motion: Icon and Act in the Collection of Katherine Coryton White* (Los Angeles: University of California Press, 1974), pp. 10-13, takes Hegel's term *Aufheben*, meaning "a simultaneous suspension and preservation," and uses it of the African "cut" in the concept of "Afrikanische [sic] Aufheben."

Thompson's term must be mentioned here as a good approximation of the nature of the "cut," in which evey previous pattern that had first been "cut" away from still exists in suspended form until it is "cut" back to.

32. See Bill Cole, *John Coltrane* (New York: Macmillan, 1976), pp. 72-73 and *passim*.

33. See Ellison's interview with John Hersey in Hersey, ed., *Ralph Ellison*, pp. 2-3, 11.

34. Lawrence W. Levin, *Black Culture and Black Consciousness: Afro-American Folk Thought from Slavery to Freedom* (New York: Oxford University Press, 1977), p. 432.

35. Jean Toomer, *Cane* (New York: Boni and Liveright, 1923), p. 21. For the circular form of the novel, see Brian J. Benson and Mabel M. Dillard, *Jean Toomer* (New York: Twayne 1980), pp. 82-86. See also Addison Gayle, *The Way of the New World: The Black Novel in America* (Garden City: Doubleday, 1975), p. 98.

36. Ismael Reed, *Mumbo Jumbo* (New York: Bantam, 1972), pp. 247, 228.

37. Ibid., prologue, p. 5.

38. Ibid., p. 249.

39. Schenker's analyses present the extreme pole of the view that linear, descending cadential resolution is the aim of every tonal work. For discussion of this idea, see Maury Yeaston, ed., *Readings in Schenker Analysis and Other Approaches* (New Haven: Yale University Press, 1977).

40. For two splendid analyses of the role and consequence of repetition in the sonata, see Donald F. Tovey, *Essays in Musical Analysis*, Vol. 1: *Symphonies* (London: Oxford University Press, 1978), pp. 10-14; Charles Rosen, *The Classical Style: Hayden, Mozart, Beethoven* (London: Faber, 1977), pp. 30-34. Also see W.H. Hadow, *Sonata Form* (London: Novello, n.d.).

41. A fairly complete catalog of "cuts" in *Sacre* follows, with the instruments involved and practice numbers in brackets: violin (12); timpani and bass drum (37); clarinet and piccolo (48); piccolo and flute (54); viola, cello, double bass, tube, trumpet (57); bass drum (72); clarinet and violin (93); cornet and viola (100), addition of tuba, bassoons, timpani and bass drum (103-118); bass clarinet (141); piccolo, flute and timpani (201).

42. Chernoff, pp. 65-67, speaks very well on the essential inseparability of drumming and the dance. He quotes one African drummer (p. 101) as saying "every drumming has got its dance."

43. For a brief and fascinating philosophical speculation on one kind of narrative repetition, see Jacques Derrida, "Ellipsis," in *Writing and Difference*, trans. Alan Bass (Chicago: University of Chicago Press, 1978), pp. 294-300; French title, *L' Écriture et la différence* (Paris: Seuil, 1967). See also Daniel Giovannangeli, *Écriture et répétition: approche de Derrida* (Paris: Union Générale d'Éditions, 1979), for the effects upon the signifier/signified relationship of repetition.

44. See Tom Stoppard, *Travesties* (New York: Grove, 1975), p. 27, Act I.

45. Ibid., pp. 53-4.

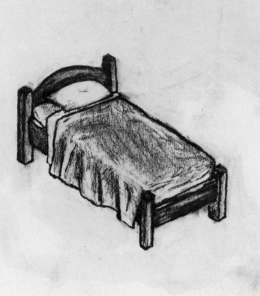

Mourning and Militancy

In a contribution to a special issue of *The South Atlantic Quarterly* on "Displacing Homophobia," Lee Edelman applies the lessons of Derridian deconstruction to the AIDS activist movement slogan Silence = Death. Claiming that our slogan calls for a discourse of facts marshalled against a demagogic rhetoric, Edelman concludes that the equation unknowingly produces the literal as a figure, and thereby betrays its ideological entanglement in the binary logic of Western discourse.

> *Precisely because the defensive appeal to literality in a slogan like Silence = Death must produce the literal as a figure of the need and desire for the shelter of certain knowledge, such a discourse is always necessarily a dangerously contaminated defense – contaminated by the Derridian logic of metaphor so that its attempt to achieve a natural or literal discourse beyond rhetoricity must reproduce the suspect ideology of reified (and threatened) identity marking the reactionary medical and political discourse it would counteract. The discursive logic of Silence = Death thus contributes to the ideologically motivated confusion of the literal and the figural, the proper and the improper, the inside and the outside, and in the process it recalls the biology of the human immunodeficiency virus as it attacks the mechanism whereby the body is able . . . to distinguish between "Self and Not-Self."*[1]

I do not think Edelman's deconstruction of the "text" of Silence = Death is necessarily wrong, but he seems to have very little sense of how the emblem functions for the movement. First, it is precisely as a figure that it does its work: as a striking image appearing on posters, placards, buttons, stickers, and T-shirts, its appeal is primarily graphic, and hardly therefore to be assimilated to a privileging of the logos. Second, it desires not a discourse of facts but direct action, the organized, militant enunciation of demands within a discursive field of *contested* facts. And finally, a question of address: for whom is this application of literary theory intended other than those within the academy who will find it, simply, interesting?[2] Silence = Death was produced and is employed for collective political struggle, and it entails altogether different problems for the community of AIDS activists. Taking our symbol literally holds for us a danger that goes unnoticed in Edelman's textual analysis: we ourselves are silent precisely on the subject of death, on how deeply it affects us.

I, too, will have something to say about the distinction between self and not-self, about the confusion of the inside and the outside, but I am impelled to do this *for us*, for my community of AIDS activists. Writing about mourning and militancy is for me both necessary and difficult, for I have seen that mourning troubles us; by "us" I mean gay men confronting AIDS. It should go without saying that it is not only gay men who confront AIDS, but because we face specific and often unique difficulties, and because I have some familiarity with them, I address them here exclusively. This paper is written for my fellow activists and friends, who have also informed it with their actions, their suggestions and encouragement–and in this I include many women as well.[3] The conflicts I address are also my own, which might account for certain of the paper's shortcomings.

I will begin then with an anecdote about my own ambivalent mourning, though not of an AIDS death. In 1977, while I was visiting my family in Idaho, my father died unexpectedly. He and I had had a strained and increasingly distant relationship, and I was unable to feel or express my grief over his death. After the funeral I returned to New York for the opening of an exhibition I'd organized and resumed my usual life. But within a few weeks a symptom erupted which to this day leaves a scar near my nose: my left tear duct became badly infected, and the resulting abscess grew to a golf-ball sized swelling that closed my left eye and completely disfigured my face. When the abscess finally burst, the foul-smelling pus oozed down my cheek like poison tears. I have never since doubted the force of the unconscious. Nor can I doubt that mourning is a psychic process that must be honored. For many AIDS activists, however, mourning is not respected; it is suspect:

> I look at faces at countless memorial services and cannot comprehend why the connection isn't made between these deaths and going out to fight so that more of these deaths, including possibly one's own, can be staved off. Huge numbers regularly show up in cities for Candlelight Marches, all duly recorded for the television cameras. Where are these same numbers when it comes to joining political organizations . . . or plugging in to the incipient civil disobedience movement represented in ACT UP?

These sentences are taken from a recent essay by Larry Kramer,[4] against whose sense of the quietism represented by AIDS candlelight marches I want to juxtapose the words of the organizer of this year's candlelight vigil on Christopher Street, addressed from the speaker's platform to the assembled mourners: "Look around!" he said, "This is the gay community, not ACT UP!"[5]

The presumption in this exhortation that no AIDS activists would be found among the mourners–whose ritual expression of grief is at the same time taken to be truer to the needs of the gay community–confidently inverts Kramer's rhetorical incomprehension, an incomprehension also expressed as antipathy: "I do not mean to diminish these sad rituals," Kramer writes, "though indeed I personally find them slightly ghoulish."[6]

Public mourning rituals may of course have their own political force, but they nevertheless often seem, from an activist perspective, indulgent, sentimental, defeatist–a perspective only reinforced, as Kramer implies, by media constructions of us as hapless victims. "Don't mourn, organize!"–the last words of labor movement martyr Joe Hill–is still a rallying cry, at least in its New Age variant, "Turn your grief to anger," which assumes not so much that mourning can be foregone as that the psychic process can simply be converted.[7] This move from prohibition to transformation only *appears*, however, to include a psychic component in activism's response, for ultimately both rallying cries depend on a definite answer to the question posed by Reich to Freud: "Where does the misery come from?" Activist antagonism to mourning hinges, in part, on how AIDS is interpreted, or rather, where the emphasis is laid, on whether the crisis is seen to be a natural, accidental catastrophe—a disease syndrome that has simply struck at this time and in this place—or as the result of gross political negligence or mendacity—an epidemic that was allowed to happen.

But leaving aside, only for the moment, the larger political question, I want to attend to the internal opposition of activism and mourning. That the two are incompatible is clear enough in Freud's description of the work of mourning, which he calls "absorbing." "Profound mourning," Freud writes in "Mourning and Melancholia," involves a *"turning away from every active effort* that is not connected with thoughts of the dead. It is easy to see that this inhibition and circumscription in the ego is the expression of an *exclusive* devotion to its mourning, *which leaves nothing over for other purposes or other interests."* [8] Although Freud's account of this process is well-known, I want to repeat it here in order to underscore its exclusive character:

> *The testing of reality, having shown that the loved object no longer exists, requires forthwith that all the libido shall be withdrawn from its attachments to this object. Against this demand a struggle of course arises—it may be universally observed that man never willingly abandons a libido-position, not even when a substitute is already beckoning to him. This struggle can be so intense that a turning away from reality ensues, the object being clung to through the medium of a hallucinatory wish-psychosis. The normal outcome is that deference for reality gains the day. Nevertheless its behest cannot be at once obeyed. The task is now carried through bit by bit, under great expense of time and cathectic energy, while all the time the existence of the lost object is continued in the mind. Each single one of the memories and hopes which bound the libido to the object is brought up and hyper-cathected, and the detachment of the libido from it accomplished.* [9]

In an important paper about mourning in the time of AIDS, which turns on a reading of Whitman's "Drum-Taps" poems, Michael Moon argues that Freud's view of mourning presents a difficulty for gay people, insofar as it promises a return to a normalcy that we were never granted in the first place: "As lesbians and gay men," Moon writes,

> *most of us are familiar with the experience of having been categorically excluded from "normalcy" at critical junctures in our lives. Having been through as much as most of us have in both our personal and collective struggles to get our own needs recognized, acknowledged, accepted, sometimes fulfilled, the Freudian model of mourning may well look fundamentally normalizing and consequently privative, diminishing the process and foreclosing its possible meaning rather than enriching it or making it more accessible to understanding.* [10]

Probably no gay man or lesbian can have an untroubled response to Freud, but we must nevertheless take care to maintain a crucial distinction: the ambition to normalize, to adapt, belongs not to Freud but to his later "egocentric" revisionists, to whom gay people owe a good portion of our oppression. This is not to say that there is no vision of normalcy in Freud, only that there is also no such thing as ever fully achieving it, *for anyone.* Freud *does* refer to mourning as a "grave departure from the normal attitude to life," [11] but what that normal attitude is in this context can be learned easily enough by reading his characterization of the state to which we return after the work of mourning is accomplished: very simply, "deference for reality gains the day," and "the ego becomes free and uninhibited again."[12]

So rather than looking beyond "Mourning and Melancholia" for other possibilities—Moon proposes fetishism, but a fetishism rescued from Freud's 1927 account by making it a *conscious* means of extending our homoerotic relations, even with the dead—I want to stay with Freud's earlier text, to read it in relation to the conflicts many of us now experience. First, two preliminary caveats: "Mourning and Melancholia" is not a theory of mourning as such, but of pathological mourning, that is, of melancholia. Moon is therefore right when he says that Freud's view of mourning only repeats conventional wisdom; it purports to do no more than describe mourning's dynamic process. Secondly, Freud can tell us very little about our grieving rituals, our memorial services and candlelight marches. Of our communal mourning, perhaps only the Names Project quilt displays something of the psychic work of mourning, insofar as each individual panel symbolizes—through its incorporation of mementos associated with the lost object—the activity of hyper-cathecting and detaching the hopes and memories associated with the loved one. But as against this often shared activity, mourning, for Freud, is a solitary undertaking. And our trouble begins here, for, from the outset, there is already a social interdiction of our private efforts. In the opening pages of *Policing Desire*, Simon Watney recounts a funeral service similar to those many of us have experienced, an event that made him decide "then and there" that he would write his book on AIDS.

> [Bruno's] funeral took place in an ancient Norman church on the outskirts of London. No mention was made of AIDS. Bruno had died, bravely, of an unspecified disease. In the congregation of some forty people there were two other gay men besides myself, both of whom had been his lover. They had been far closer to Bruno than anyone else present, except his parents. Yet their grief had to be contained within the confines of manly acceptability. The irony of the difference between the suffocating life of the suburbs where we found ourselves, and the knowledge of the world in which Bruno had actually lived, as a magnificently affirmative and life-enhancing gay man, was all but unbearable.[13]

Because Watney's anecdote is meant to explain his determination to write a polemic, it also suggests what has happened to mourning. It is not only that at this moment of society's demand for hypocrisy the three gay men had to conceal their grief, but also that their fond memories of Bruno as a gay man are thereby associated with the social opprobrium that attaches to them. When these memories are then recalled, hyper-cathexis may well be met with a defense, a need to preserve Bruno's world intact against the contempt in which it is commonly held. "My friend was not called Bruno," Watney adds.

> His father asked me not to use his real name. And so the anonymity is complete. The garrulous babble of commentary on AIDS constructs yet another "victim." It is this babble which is my subject matter, the cacophony of voices which sounds through every institution of our society on the subject of AIDS.[14]

Thus one of our foremost international AIDS activists became engaged in the struggle;

no further memories of Bruno are invoked. It is probably no exaggeration to say that each of us has a story like this, that during the AIDS crisis there is an all but inevitable connection between the memories and hopes associated with our lost friends and the daily assaults on our consciousness. Seldom has a society so savaged people during their hour of loss. "We look upon any interference with [mourning] as inadvisable or even harmful," warns Freud.[15] But for anyone living daily with the AIDS crisis, ruthless interference with our bereavement is as ordinary an occurrence as reading the *New York Times*.[16] The violence we encounter is relentless, the violence of silence and omission almost as impossible to endure as the violence of unleashed hatred and outright murder. Because this violence also desecrates the memories of our dead, we rise in anger to vindicate them. For many of us, mourning *becomes* militancy. Freud does not say what might happen if mourning is interfered with, but insofar as our conscious defenses direct us toward social action, they already show the deference to reality that Freud attributes to mourning's accomplishment. Nevertheless, we have to ask just how, against what odds, and with what unconscious effects this has been achieved.

The activist impulse may be reinforced by a second conflict within the process of mourning. "Reality," Freud explains, "passes its verdict–that the object no longer exists–upon each single one of the memories and hopes through which the libido was attached to the lost object, and the ego, confronted as it were with the decision whether it will share this fate, is persuaded by the sum of its narcissistic satisfactions in being alive to sever its attachment to the non-existent object."[17] But this confrontation with reality is especially fraught for gay men mourning now, since our decision whether we will share this fate is so unsure. For people with AIDS, the HIV-infected, and those at significant risk whose sero-status is unknown to them, narcissistic satisfactions in *still* being alive *today* can persuade us, will undoubtedly persuade us in our unconscious, to relinquish our attachments. But how are we to dissociate our narcissistic satisfactions in being alive from our fight to stay alive? And, insofar as we *identify* with those who have died, how can our satisfactions in being alive escape guilt at having survived?[18]

Upholding the memories of our lost friends and lovers and resolving that we ourselves shall live would seem to impose the same demand: resist! Mourning feels too much like capitulation. But we must recognize that our memories and our resolve also entail the more painful feelings of survivor's guilt, often exacerbated by our secret wishes, during our lovers' and friends' protracted illnesses, that they would just die and let us get on with our lives.

We can then partially revise our sense–and Freud's–of the incompatibility between mourning and activism and say that, for many gay men dealing with AIDS deaths, militancy might arise from conscious conflicts *within* mourning itself, the consequence, on the one hand, of "inadvisable and even harmful interference" with grief and, on the other, of the impossibility of deciding whether the mourner will share the fate of the mourned. But because mourning is a psychic process, conscious reactions to external interference cannot tell the whole story. What is far more difficult to determine is how these reactions are influenced by already-existing unconscious strife. Only by recognizing the role of the unconscious, however, will we be able to understand the relationship between the external obstacles to our grief and our own antagonism to mourning. But I want to be clear: It is because our impatience with mourning is burdensome for the movement that I am seeking to understand it. I have no interest in proposing a "psychogenesis" of AIDS activism. The social and political barbarism we daily encounter requires no explanation whatsoever for our militancy. On the contrary, what may require an explanation, as Larry Kramer's plaint suggested, is the quietism.

At the weekly ACT UP meetings in New York, regularly attended by about 400 people, I am struck by the fact that only a handful are of my generation, the Stonewall generation. The vast majority are post-Stonewall, born hardly earlier than the gay liberation movement itself, and their losses differ in one significant respect from ours. Last year one of these young men said something to me that said it all. A group of us had seen an early '70s film at the Gay and Lesbian Experimental Film Festival and went out for drinks afterwards. The young man was very excited about what seemed to me a pretty ordinary sex scene in the film; but then he said, "I'd give anything to know what cum tastes like, somebody else's that is." That broke my heart, for two different reasons: for him because he didn't know, for me because I do.

Freud tells us that mourning is the reaction not only to the death of a loved person, but also "to the loss of some abstraction which has taken the place of one, such as fatherland, liberty, an ideal. . . . "[19] Can we be allowed to include, in this "civilized" list, the ideal of perverse sexual pleasure itself rather than one stemming from its sublimation? Alongside the dismal toll of death, what many of us have lost is a culture of sexual possibility: back rooms, tea rooms, bookstores, movie houses, and baths; the trucks, the pier, the ramble, the dunes. Sex was everywhere for us, and everything we wanted to venture: golden showers and water sports, cocksucking and rimming, fucking and fist fucking. Now our untamed impulses are either proscribed once again or shielded from us by latex. Even Crisco, the lube we used because it was edible, is now forbidden because it breaks down the rubber. Sex toys are no longer added enhancements; they're safer substitutes.

For those who have obeyed civilization's law of compulsory genital heterosexuality, the options we've lost might seem abstract enough. Not widely acknowledged until the advent of the AIDS crisis, our sex lives are now publicly scrutinized with fascination and envy, only partially masked by feigned incredulity (William Dannemeyer, for example, entered into the *Congressional Record* of June 26, 1989 the list of pleasures I just enumerated). To say that we miss uninhibited and unprotected sex as we miss our lovers and friends will hardly solicit solidarity, even tolerance. But tolerance is, as Pasolini said, "always and purely nominal," merely "a more refined form of condemnation."[20] AIDS has further proved his point. Our pleasures were never tolerated anyway; we took them. And now we must mourn them too.

When, in mourning our ideal, we meet with the same opprobrium as when mourning our dead, we incur a different order of psychic distress, since the memories of our pleasures are already fraught with ambivalence. The abject repudiation of their sexual pasts by many gay men testifies to that ambivalence, even as the widespread adoption of safe sex practices vouches for our ability to work through it. Perhaps we may even think of safe sex as the substitute libido-position that beckoned to us as we mourned our lost sexual ideal. But here, I think, the difference between generations of gay men makes itself felt most sharply. For men now in their twenties, our sexual ideal is mostly just that—an ideal, the cum never swallowed. Embracing safe sex is for them an act of defiance, and its promotion is perhaps the AIDS activist movement's least inhibited stance. But, for many men of the Stonewall generation, who have also been the gay population thus far hardest hit by AIDS, safe sex may seem less like defiance than resignation, less like accomplished mourning than melancholia. I don't want to suggest that there is anything pathological about this disposition, but it does comprise many features of melancholia as Freud describes it, especially if considered in the context of its causes.

"The occasions giving rise to melancholia," Freud writes, "for the most part extend beyond the clear case of a loss by death, and include all those situations of being wounded, hurt, neglected, out of favor, or disappointed, which can . . . reinforce an already existing ambivalence."[21] Although Freud's theory concerns an object relationship, if we transpose these situations to the social sphere, they describe very perfectly the condition of gay men during the AIDS crisis, as regards both our rejection and our self-doubt. In Freud's analysis, melancholia differs from mourning in a single feature: "a fall in self-esteem":[22] "In grief the world becomes poor and empty; in melancholia it is the ego itself [which becomes poor and empty]."[23] And this lowering of self-esteem, Freud insists, is "predominantly moral";[24] it is a "dissatisfaction with the self on moral grounds."[25] "The patient represents his ego to us as worthless, incapable of any effort, and morally despicable; he reproaches himself, vilifies himself, and expects to be cast out and chastised."[26] "In his exacerbation of self-criticism he describes himself as petty, egoistic, dishonest, lacking in independence, one whose sole aim has been to hide the weaknesses of his own nature. . . . "[27] Moreover, the melancholiac "does not realize that any change has taken place in him, but extends his self-criticism back over the past and declares that he was never any better."[28]

This moralizing self-abasement is only too familiar to us in the response of certain gay men to AIDS—too familiar especially because the media have been so happy to give them voice as our spokesmen. Randy Shilts comes readily to mind, and though I've done with him elsewhere,[29] it is worth mentioning in this context that he was chosen as our representative to address the closing ceremonies of the Fifth International AIDS Conference in Montreal, where he obliged his hosts with an attack on the militancy of international AIDS activists attending the conference. But there is a recent example that is even more groveling: the book *After the Ball*, an aptly titled sequel to Shilts's *And the Band Played On*, whose authority it cites approvingly, and whose "Patient Zero" continues here to play his unhappy role. This flyleaf-described "gay manifesto for the nineties," published by Doubleday, is the dirty work of two Harvard-trained social scientists, one of whom now designs aptitude tests for people with high IQs, while the other is a Madison Avenue PR consultant whose specialty is creating "positive images" for what the two of them call " 'silent majority' gays." Informed by the latest trends in sociobiology, Marshall Kirk and Hunter Madsen have devised a program to eradicate homophobia—which they prefer to call homo-hatred so as to deny its unconscious force. Their proposal centers on a media campaign whose basis is the denial of difference. "A good beginning would be to take a long look at Coors beer . . . commercials," they suggest.[30] But copying Coors ads does not stop with creating "positive" images.

We have to "clean up our act," they say, and live up to those images.[31] This means purging our community of "'fringe' gay groups"—drag queens, radical fairies, pederasts, bull dykes, and other assorted scum.

Clearly we can take this book seriously only as a symptom of malaise—in its excoriation of gay culture, it bears every distinguishing characteristic of melancholia Freud specifies. Moreover, its accusations are also self-accusations: "*We*, the authors, are every bit as guilty of a lot of the nastiness we describe as are other gays," the Harvard boys confess. "This makes us not less qualified to inveigh against such evils but, if anything, even more so."[32] The authors' indictments of gay men are utterly predictable: we lie, deny reality, have no moral standards; we are narcissistic, self-indulgent, self-destructive, unable to love or even form lasting friendships; we flaunt it in public, abuse alcohol and drugs; and our community leaders and intellectuals are fascists.[33] Here are a few sample statements:

> *When we first delved into the gay urban* demimonde*, we assumed that they held, if not our values, at least some values. We were quickly disabused of this notion.*

> *As the works of many students of sociopathic personality assert, a surprisingly high percentage of pathological liars are, in fact, gay.*

> *The gay bar is the arena of sexual competition, and it brings out all that is most loathsome in human nature. Here, stripped of the facade of wit and cheer, gays stand nakedly revealed as single-minded, selfish sexual predators.*[34]

Therefore, "straights hate gays not just for what their myths and lies say we are, but also for what we *really* are."[35] This is the only line in the book with which I agree; and it is a statement which, if taken seriously, means that no sociological account of homophobia will explain or counteract it. Kirk and Madsen's reliance on homophobic myths to describe what we really are demonstrates, in any case, not their understanding of homophobia, but their complete identification with it.

Although melancholia, too, depends on the psychic process of identification and introjection, I will not press the point. No matter how extreme the self-hatred, I am loath for obvious reasons to accuse gay men of any *pathological* condition. I only want to draw an analogy between pathological mourning and the sorry need of some gay men to look upon our imperfectly liberated past as immature and immoral. But I will not resist a final word from Freud on melancholia, taken this time from "The Ego and the Id": "What is now holding sway in the super-ego is, as it were, a pure culture of the death-instinct."[36]

ACT UP, the AIDS Coalition to Unleash Power, was founded in March of 1987 in response to a speech at New York's Lesbian and Gay Community Services Center by Larry Kramer. In his inimitable manner of combining incomprehension and harangue, Kramer chided:

> *I sometimes think we have a death wish. I think we must want to die. I have never been able to understand why for six long years we have sat back and let ourselves literally be knocked off*

man by man—without fighting back. I have heard of denial, but this is more than denial; this is a death wish.[37]

Nearly two years later, in a mean-spirited, divisive attack on AIDS activism published by the *Nation,* Darrell Yates Rist accused ACT UP—entirely falsely—of ignoring any gay issue but AIDS. After recalling a visit to San Francisco's Tenderloin district, in which he encountered teen-age gay runaways and hustlers, Rist continued:

> *I had just spent a night among those abandoned adolescents when, at a dinner in the Castro, I listened to the other guests talk about nothing but AIDS, the dead, the dying—which to their minds included every gay man in the city: fashionable hysteria. "This," one of the them actually said, "is the only thing worth fighting for." Not long before, I'd heard Larry Kramer, playwright and AIDS activist, say something like that too, and had felt, in that suffocating moment, that finally we'd all gone suicidal, that we'd die of our own death wish.*[38]

It is between these two allegations of a death-wish—one because we were not yet AIDS activists, the other because we now are—that I want to frame the remainder of my discussion.

It might appear from what I've outlined so far that gay men's responses to the enormous losses suffered in the AIDS epidemic are predictable. This is far from the case, and is only the result of my schematic reading of "Mourning and Melancholia" against what I know of our experiences. I have accounted for neither the full depth and variety of our conflicts nor the multiplicity of their possible outcomes. What I offer to rectify this inadequacy is simply a list, to which anyone might add, of the problems we face.

Most people dying of AIDS are very young, and those of us coping with these deaths, ourselves also young, have confronted great loss entirely unprepared. The numbers of deaths are unthinkable: lovers, friends, acquaintances, and community members have fallen ill and died. Many have lost upwards of a hundred people. Apart from the deaths, we contend with the gruesome illness itself, acting as caretakers, often for very extended periods, making innumerable hospital visits, providing emotional support, negotiating our wholly inadequate and inhuman health care and social welfare systems, keeping abreast of experimental treatment therapies. Some of us have learned as much or more than most doctors about the complex medicine of AIDS. Added to the caretaking and loss of others is often the need to monitor and make treatment decisions about our own HIV illness, or face anxiety about our own health status.[39]

Through the turmoil imposed by illness and death, the rest of society offers little support or even acknowledgment. On the contrary, we are blamed, belittled, excluded, derided. We are discriminated against, lose our housing and jobs, and are denied medical and life insurance. Every public agency whose job it is to combat the epidemic has been slow to act, failed entirely, or been deliberately counterproductive. We have therefore had to provide our own centers for support, care, and education and even to fund and conduct our own treatment research. We have had to rebuild our devastated community and culture, reconstruct our sexual relationships, reinvent our sexual pleasure. Despite great achievements in so short a time and under such adversity, the dominant media still pictures us only as wasting deathbed victims; we have therefore had to wage a war of representation, too.

Frustration, anger, rage, and outrage, anxiety, fear, and terror, shame and guilt, sadness and despair—it is not surprising that we feel these things; what is surprising is that we often don't. For those who feel only a deadening numbness or constant depression, militant rage may well be unimaginable, as again it might be for those who are paralyzed with fear, filled with remorse, or overcome with guilt. To decry these responses—our own form of moralism—is to deny the extent of the violence we have all endured; even more importantly, it is to deny a fundamental fact of psychic life: violence is also self-inflicted.

The most contested theoretical concept in the later work of Freud is the drive to death, the drive that competes with the life instincts and comprises both aggression and self-aggression. It was over this concept that Reich broke with Freud, insisting that with the death drive Freud definitively side-stepped the social causes of human misery. But, against Reich's objection, and that of other early proponents of a political psychoanalysis, Jacqueline Rose argues that it is *only* through the concept of the death drive that we can understand the relationship between psychic and social life, as we seek to determine "where to locate the violence."[40] As opposed to Darrell Yates Rist's pop-psychology assertion that activists have a death wish, I want to suggest on the contrary that we do not acknowledge the death drive. That is, we disavow the knowledge that our misery comes from within as well as without, that it is the result of psychic as well as of social conflict—or rather, as Rose writes, our misery "is not something that can be located on the inside or the outside, in the psychic or the social . . . , but rather something that appears as the effect of the dichotomy itself."[41] By making all violence external, pushing it to the outside and objectifying it in "enemy" institutions and individuals, we deny its psychic articulation, deny that we are effected, as well as affected, by it.

Perhaps an example will clarify my point. The issue of HIV antibody testing has been a central concern for AIDS activists from the moment the movement was formed. We have insisted, against every attempt to implement mandatory or confidential testing, on the absolute right of voluntary *anonymous* testing. At the International AIDS Conference in Montreal last June, Stephen Joseph, health commissioner of New York City, called for confidential testing with mandatory contact tracing, based on the fact that immune-system monitoring and early treatment intervention for those who are HIV-positive could now prolong and perhaps save their lives. We immediately raised all the proper objections to his cynical proposal: that only if anonymity is guaranteed will people get tested, that New York has too few testing sites to accommodate the people wishing to be tested as it is, and that the services necessary to care for people who test positive cannot even accommodate the current caseload. Agreeing that testing, counselling, monitoring, and early treatment intervention are indeed crucial, we demanded instead an increase in the number of anonymous testing sites and a system of neighborhood walk-in HIV clinics for monitoring and treatment. We were entirely confident of the validity of our protests and demands. We know the history of Stephen Joseph's provocations, we know the city government's abysmal failure to provide health care for its huge infected population, and we know not only the advantages of early intervention but also exactly what the treatment options are. But with all this secure knowledge, we forget one thing: our own ambivalence about being tested, or, if seropositive, about making difficult treatment decisions. For all the hours of floor discussion about demanding wide availability of testing and treatment, we do not always avail *ourselves* of them, and we seldom discuss our anxiety and indecision.[42] Very shortly after Joseph's announcement in Montreal and our successful mobilization against his plan,[43] Mark Harrington, a member of ACT UP's Treatment and Data Committee, made an announcement at a Monday-night meeting: "I personally know three people in this group who recently came down with PCP," he said. "We have to realize that activism is not a prophylaxis against opportunistic infections; it may be synergistic with aerosolized pentamidine, but it won't on its own prevent you from getting AIDS."

By referring to Freud's concept of the death drive, I am not saying anything so simple as that a drive to death directly prevents us from protecting ourselves against illness. Rather I am saying that by ignoring the death drive, that is, by making all violence external, we fail to confront ourselves, to acknowledge our ambivalence, to comprehend that our misery is also self-inflicted. To return to my example: it is not only New York City's collapsing health care system and its sinister health commissioner that affect our fate. Unconscious conflict can mean that we may make decisions—or fail to make them—whose results may be deadly too. And the rage we direct against Stephen Joseph, justified as it is, may function as the very mechanism of our disavowal, whereby we convince ourselves that we are making all the decisions we need to make.

Again I want to be very clear: The fact that our militancy may be a means of dangerous denial in no way suggests that activism is unwarranted. There is no question but that we must fight the unspeakable violence we incur from the society in which we find ourselves. But if we understand that violence is able to reap its horrible rewards through the very psychic mechanisms that make us part of this society, then we may also be able to recognize—along with our rage—our terror, our guilt, and our profound sadness. Militancy, of course, then, but mourning too: mourning *and* militancy.

This essay is for Gregg Bordowitz, my AIDS activist mentor.

1. Lee Edelman, "The Plague of Discourse: Politics, Literary Theory, and AIDS," *South Atlantic Quarterly*, vol. 88, no. 1 (Winter 1989): 313-314.
2. For other analyses of the slogan Silence = Death, written from the perspective of people directly engaged in AIDS activist and service work, see Stuart Marshall, "The Contemporary Use of Gay History: The Third Reich," forthcoming; and Cindy Patton, "Power and the Conditions of Silence," *Critical Quarterly*, vol. 31, no. 3 (Fall 1989). See also Douglas Crimp and Adam Rolston, *AIDS Demo Graphics* (Seattle: Bay Press, 1990).
3. I want to thank those people who discussed this subject with me, including their personal experiences, and helped me through the task of writing the paper: in addition to Gregg Borodowitz— David Barr, Peter Bowen, Rosalyn Deutsche, Mitchell Karp, Don Moss, and Laura Pinsky. This paper was initially given at the 1989 English Institute at Harvard in the "Gay Men in Criticism" session organized by D.A. Miller. My thanks to David for resisting the "policing function of the literary" to invite an AIDS activist working outside the discipline to this forum.
4. Larry Kramer, "Report from the Holocaust," in *Reports from the Holocaust: The Making of an AIDS Activist* (New York: St. Martin's Press, 1989), pp. 264-265.
5. The remark of Red Maloney was the subject of a letter written by Naphtali Offen to *Outweek*, no. 4 (July 17, 1989): 6.

6. Kramer, "Report from the Holocaust," p. 264.

7. Joe Hill's statement is also quoted by Michael Bronski in an essay that takes up some of the issues discussed here; see his "Death and the Erotic Imagination," in *Taking Liberties: AIDS and Cultural Politics*, eds. Erica Carter and Simon Watney (London: Serpent's Tail in association with the ICA, 1989), pp. 219-228. The pop psychological/metaphysical notions of the New Age "healers"–such as the particularly repulsive idea that people choose illness to give meaning to their lives–are considered by Allan Bérubé in "Caught in the Storm: AIDS and the Meaning of Natural Disaster," *Outlook*, vol. 1, no. 3 (Fall 1988): 8-19.

8. Sigmund Freud, "Mourning and Melancholia," in *A General Selection from the Works of Sigmund Freud*, ed. John Rickman (New York: Anchor Books, 1989), pp. 125-126 (emphasis added).

9. Ibid., p. 126.

10. Michael Moon, "Memorial Rags," paper presented in a session titled "AIDS and Our Profession" at the 1988 MLA convention, manuscript. I wish to thank Michael Moon for making this paper available to me.

11. Freud, "Mourning and Melancholia," p. 125.

12. Ibid., pp. 126-127.

13. Simon Watney, *Policing Desire: Pornography, AIDS, and the Media* (Minneapolis: University of Minnesota Press, 1987), p. 7.

14. Ibid., p. 8.

15. Freud, "Mourning and Melancholia," p. 125.

16. The *New York Times* reporting of AIDS issues– or rather its failure to report them accurately or at all–is one of the most persistent scandals of the AIDS epidemic. Larry Kramer gave a detailed, damning account of the scandal on a panel discussion of AIDS in the print media organized by the PEN American Center in New York City on May 11, 1989. In the summer of 1989, the *Times* ran an editorial that both typified its position throughout the history of the epidemic and reached new heights of callousness. Implicitly claiming once again that *its* presumed readers had little to worry about, since "the disease is still very largely confined to specific risk groups," the writer went on to say, cheerily, "Once all susceptible members [of these groups] are infected, the numbers of new victims will decline." The newspaper's simple writing off of the lives of gay men, IV drug users, their sex partners and children–a mere 200,000-400,000 people *already* estimated to be HIV-infected in New York City alone–triggered off an ACT UP demonstration, which was in turn thwarted by perhaps the largest police presence at any AIDS activist demonstration to date. ACT UP stickers saying "Buy Your Lies Here. The *New York Times* Reports Half the Truth about AIDS" still adorn newsstands in New York City, while the coin slots of *Times* vending machines are covered with stickers that read "The *New York Times* AIDS Reporting is OUT OF ORDER." The *Times* editorial is reproduced as part of a Gran Fury project titled "Control" in *Artforum*, vol. xxvii, no. 2 (October 1989), p. 167.

17. Freud, "Mourning and Melancholia," pp. 136-137.

18. The decision not to share the fate of the lost object, as well as guilt at having survived, are certainly problems of mourning for everyone. Clearly insofar as any death brings us face to face with our own mortality, identification with the lost object is something we all feel. Thus, this difficulty of mourning is certainly not gay men's alone. I only wish to emphasize its exacerbation for gay men to the extent that we are directly and immediately implicated in the particular cause of these deaths, and implicated, as well, through the specific nature of our deepest pleasures in life–our gay sexuality. Simon Watney has urged that this very implication be taken as the reason for forming consensus among gay men about AIDS activism: "I believe that the single, central factor of greatest significance for all gay men should be the recognition that the current HIV antibody status of everyone who had unprotected sex in the long years before the virus was discovered is a matter of *sheer coincidence....* Every gay man who had the good fortune to remain uninfected in the decade or so before the emergence of safer sex should meditate most profoundly on the whim of fate that spared him, but not others. Those of us who chance to be seronegative have *an absolute and unconditional responsibility* for the welfare of seropositive gay men" (Simon Watney, "'The Possibilities of Permutation': Pleasure, Proliferation, and the Politics of Gay Identity in the Age of AIDS," in *AIDS: Crisis and Criticism*, ed. James Miller (Toronto: University of Toronto Press, forthcoming).

19. Ibid., p. 125.

20. Pier Paolo Pasolini, "Gennariello," in *Lutheran Letters*, trans. Stuart Hood, (Manchester: Carcanet New Press, 1983), pp. 21-22.

21. Freud, "Mourning and Melancholia," p. 132.

22. Ibid., p. 125.

23. Ibid., p. 127.

24. Ibid., p. 128.

25. Ibid., p. 129.

26. Ibid., p. 127.

27. Ibid., p. 128.

28. Ibid., pp. 127-128.

29. Douglas Crimp, "How to Have Promiscuity in an Epidemic," *October*, no. 43 (Winter 1987) (reissued as Douglas Crimp, ed., *AIDS: Cultural Analysis/Cultural Acitivism* (Cambridge: MIT Press, 1988), esp. pp. 238-246.

30. Marshall Kirk and Hunter Madsen, *After the Ball: How America Will Conquer Its Fear of Gays in the '90s* (New York: Doubleday, 1989), p. 154.

31. "Cleaning Up Our Act" is actually a subheading of the book's final chapter, which concludes with "A Self-Policing Code."

32. Kirk and Madsen, *After the Ball*, p. 278.

33. These accusations appear in Chapter 6. "The State of Our Community: Gay Pride Goeth before a Fall."

34. Kirk and Madsen, *After the Ball*, pp. 292, 283, 313.

35. Ibid., p. 276.

36. Sigmund Freud, *The Ego and the Id* (New York: W. W. Norton, 1962), p. 43.

37. Kramer, "Report from the Holocaust," p. 128.

38. Darrell Yates Rist, "The Deadly Costs of an Obsession," *Nation* (February 13, 1989): 181. For the response of ACT UP, among others, see the issues of March 20 and May 1, 1989. For an impassioned discussion of the entire debate, see Simon Watney, "'The Possibilities of Permutation.'"

39. It seems to me particularly telling that throughout the epidemic the dominant media has routinely featured stories about anxieties provoked by AIDS—the anxieties of health care workers and cops exposed to needle sticks, of parents whose children attend school with an HIV-infected child, of straight women who once upon a time had a bisexual lover . . . But I have never once seen a story about the millions of gay men who have lived with these anxieties constantly since 1981.

40. Jacqueline Rose, "Where Does the Misery Come From?" in *Feminism and Psychoanalysis*, eds. Richard Feldstein and Judith Roof (Ithaca: Cornell University Press) p. 28.

41. Ibid.

42. I do not wish to claim that the "right" decision is to be tested. AIDS activists insist quite properly only on choice, and on making that choice viable through universally available health care. But problems of HIV testing are not only sociopolitical; they are also psychic. In "AIDS and Needless Deaths: How Early Treatment Is Ignored," Paul Harding Douglas and Laura Pinsky enumerate a number of barriers to early intervention in HIV disease, including lack of advocacy, lack of media coverage, lack of services, and, crucially, "The Symbolic Meaning of Early Intervention for the Individual." This final section of their paper provides a much-needed analysis of psychic resistance to taking the HIV antibody test. I wish to thank Paul Douglas and Laura Pinsky for making their paper available to me.

43. The successes of the AIDS activist movement are, unfortunately, never secure. In the late fall of 1989, during the transition from Ed Koch's mayoralty to that of David Dinkins, Stephen Joseph resigned his position as health commissioner. But not without a parting insult to those of us who had opposed his policies all along: once again, and now supposedly with the consensus of the New York City Board of Health, Joseph asked the state health department to collect the names of people who test HIV antibody positive and to trace and contact their sex partners and those with whom they shared needles.

• **Kobena Mercer**

Black Hair/Style Politics

Some time ago Michael Jackson's hair caught fire when he was filming a television commercial. Perhaps the incident became newsworthy because it brought together two seemingly opposed news-values: fame and misfortune. But judging by the way it was reported in one black community newspaper, *The Black Voice*, Michael's unhappy accident took on a deeper significance for a cultural politics of beauty, style and fashion. In its feature article, "Are we proud to be black?," beauty pageants, skin-bleaching cosmetics and the curly-perm hair-style epitomized by Jackson's image were interpreted as equivalent signs of a "negative" black aesthetic. All three were roundly condemned for negating the "natural" beauty of blackness and were seen as identical expressions of subjective enslavement to Eurocentric definitions of beauty, thus indicative of an "inferiority complex."[1]

The question of how ideologies of "the beautiful" have been defined by, for and—for most of the time—against black people remains crucially important. But at the same time I want to take issue with the widespread argument that, because it involves straightening, the curly-perm hair-style represents either a wretched imitation of white people's hair or, what amounts to the same thing, a diseased state of black consciousness. I have a feeling that the equation between the curly-perm and skin-bleaching cremes is made to emphasize the potential health risk sometimes associated with the chemical contents of hair-straightening products. By exaggerating this marginal risk, a moral grounding is constructed for judgements which are then extrapolated to assumptions about mental health or illness. This conflation of moral and aesthetic judgement underpins the way the article also mentions, in horror and disgust, Jackson's alleged plastic surgery to make his features "more European-looking."

Reactions to the striking changes in Jackson's image have sparked off a range of everyday critiques on the cultural politics of "race" and "aesthetics." The apparent transformation of his racial features through the glamorous violence of surgery has been read by some as the bizarre expression of a desire to achieve fame by "becoming white"—a deracializing sell-out, the morbid symptom of a psychologically mutilated black consciousness. Hence, on this occasion, Michael's misfortune could be read as "punishment" for the profane artificiality of his image: after all, it was the chemicals that caused his hair to catch afire.

The article did not prescribe hair-styles that would correspond to a "positive" black self-image or a politically "healthy" state of black subjectivity. But by reiterating the 1960s slogan—Black Is Beautiful—it implied that hair-styles which avoid artifice and look "natural," such as the Afro or Dreadlocks, are the more authentically black hair-styles and thus more ideologically "right-on." But it is too late to simply repeat the slogans of a bygone era. That slogan no longer has the same cultural or political resonance as it once did; just as the Afro, popularized in the United States in the period of Black Power, has been displaced through the 1970s by a new range of black hair-styles, of which the curly-perm is just one of the most popular. Whether you care for the results or not, these changes have been registered by the stylistic mutations of Michael Jackson and surely his fame indicates something of a shift, a sign of the times, in the agendas of black cultural politics. How are we to interpret such changes? And what relation do changes in dress, style and fashion bear to the changed political, economic and social circumstances of black people in the 1980s?

To begin to explore these issues I feel we need to *de-psychologize* the question of hair-straightening and recognize hair-styling itself for what it is, a specifically cultural activity and practice. As such we require a historical perspective on how many different strands—economic, political, psychological—have been woven into the rich and complex texture of our nappy hair, such that issues of style are so highly charged as sensitive questions about our very "identity." As part of our modes of appearance in the everyday world, the ways we shape and style hair may be seen as both individual expressions of the self and as embodiments of society's norms, conventions and expectations. By taking both aspects into account and focusing on their interaction we find there is a question that arises prior to psychological considerations, namely: *why do we pour so much creative energy into our hair?*

In any black neighborhood you cannot escape noticing the presence of so many bar-ber-shops and hairdressing salons; so many hair-care products and so much advertising to help sell them all; and, among young people especially, so much skill and sheer fastid-iousness that goes into the styles you can see on the street. Why so much time, money, energy and worry spent shaping our hair?

From a perspective informed by theoretical work on subcultures,[2] the question of style can be seen as a medium for expressing the aspirations of black people excluded from access to "official" social institutions of representation and legitimation in the urban, industrialized societies of the capitalist First World. Here, black peoples of the Af-rican diaspora have developed distinct, if not unique, patterns of style across a range of practices from music, speech, dance, dress and even cookery, which are politically intel-ligible as creative responses to the experience of oppression and dispossession. Black hair-styling may thus be evaluated as a popular *art form* articulating a variety of aesthetic "solutions" to a range of "problems" created by ideologies of race and racism.

Tangled Roots and Split Ends: Hair as Symbolic Material

As organic matter produced by physiological processes human hair seems to be a "natural" aspect of the body. Yet hair is never a straightforward biological "fact" be-cause it is almost always groomed, prepared, cut, concealed and generally "worked upon" by human hands. Such practices socialize hair, making it the medium of significant "statements" about self and society and the codes of value that bind them, or don't. In this way hair is merely a raw material, constantly processed by cultural practices which thus invest it with "meanings" and "value."

The symbolic value of hair is perhaps clearest in religious practices—shaving the head as a mark of worldly renunciation in Christianity or Buddhism, for example, or growing the hair as a sign of inner spiritual strength for Sikhs. Beliefs about gender are also evident in practices like the Muslim concealment of the woman's face and hair as a token of modesty.[3] Where race structures social relations of power, hair—as visible as skin color, but also the most tangible sign of racial difference—takes on another forcefully symbolic dimension. If racism is conceived as an ideological code in which biological attributes are invested with societal values and meanings, then it is because our hair is perceived within this framework that it is burdened with a range of "negative" connotations. Classical ideologies of race established a classificatory symbolic system of color with "black" and "white" as signifiers of a fundamental polarization of human worth— "superiority/inferiority." Distinctions of aesthetic value, "beautiful/ugly," have always been central to the way racism divides the world into binary oppositions in its adjudication of human worth.

Although dominant ideologies of race (and the way they dominate) have changed, the legacy of this biologizing and totalizing racism is traced as a presence in everyday comments made about our hair. "Good hair," used to describe hair on a black person's head, means hair that looks "European," straight, not too curly, not that kinky. And, more importantly, the given attributes of our hair are often referred to by descriptions such as "woolly," "tough," or, more to the point, just plain old "nigger hair." These terms crop up not only at the hairdresser's but more acutely when a baby is born and everyone is eager to inspect the baby's hair and predict how it will "turn out."[4] The pejorative precision of the salient expression, "nigger hair," neatly spells out how, within racism's bipolar codification of human value, black people's hair has been historically devalued as the most visible stigma of blackness, second only to skin.

In discourses of "scientific racism" in the seventeenth and eighteenth centuries, which developed in Europe alongside the slave trade, variations in pigmentation, skull and bone formation and hair texture among the species of "man" were seized upon as signs to be identified, named, classified and ordered into a hierarchy of human worth. The ordering of differences constructed a "regime of truth" that could validate the Enlightenment assumption of European "superiority" and African "inferiority." In this process, racial differences—like the new scientific taxonomies of plants, animals and minerals—were named in Latin: thus was the world appropriated in the language of the "west." But whereas the proper name "Negro" was coined to designate all that the west thought it was not, "Caucasian" was the name chosen by the west's narcissistic delusion of "superiority": "Fredrich Bluembach introduced this word in 1795 to describe white Europeans in general, for he believed that the slopes of the Caucasus [mountains in eastern Europe] were the original home of the most beautiful European species."[5] The very arbitrariness of this originary naming thus reveals how an *aesthetic* dimension, concerning blackness as the absolute negation or annulment of "beauty," has always intertwined with the rationalization of racist sentiment.

The assumption that whiteness was the measure of true beauty, condemning Europe's Other to eternal ugliness, can also be seen in images articulated around race in nineteenth-century culture. In the stereotype of Sambo–and his British counterpart, the golliwog–the "frizzy" hair of the character is an essential aspect of the iconography of "inferiority." In children's books and the minstrel shows of vaudeville, the "woolly" hair is ridiculed, just as aspects of black people's speech were lampooned in both popular music-hall and the nineteenth-century novel as evidence of the "quaint folkways" and "cultural backwardness" of the slaves.

But the stigmatization of black people's hair did not gain its historical intransigence by being a mere idea: once we consider those New World societies created on the basis of the slave trade economy–the United States and the Caribbean especially–we can see that where "race" is a constitutive element of social structure and social division, hair remains charged with symbolic currency. Plantation societies instituted a "pigmentocracy"; that is, a division of labor based on "racial" hierarchy where one's socio-economic position could be signified by one's skin color. Ferdinand Henriques's account of family, class and color in post-colonial Jamaica shows how this color/class nexus continues to structure a plurality of horizontal ethnic categories into a vertical system of class stratification. His study draws attention to the ways in which the residual value-system of "white bias"–the way ethnicities are valorized according to the tilt of whiteness–functions as the ideological basis for status ascription. In the sediment of this value-system, African elements–be they cultural or physical–are devalued as indices of low social status, while European elements are positively valorized as attributes enabling individual upward mobility.[6]

Stuart Hall in turn emphasizes the composite nature of white bias, which he refers to as the "ethnic scale," as both physiological and cultural elements are intermixed in the symbolization of one's social status. Opportunities for social mobility are therefore determined by one's ranking on the ethnic scale and involve the negotiation not only of socio-economic factors such as wealth, income, education and marriage, but also of less easily changeable elements of status symbolism such as the shape of one's nose or the shade of one's blackness.[7] In the complexity of this social code, hair functions as a key "ethnic signifier" because, compared with bodily shape or facial features, it can be changed more easily by cultural practices such as straightening. Caught on the cusp between self and society, nature and culture, the malleability of hair makes it a sensitive area of expression.

It is against this historical and sociological background that we must evaluate the personal and political economy of black hair-styles. Dominant ideologies such as white bias do not just dominate by "universalizing" the values of hegemonic social/ethnic groups so that they become everywhere accepted as the "norm." Their hegemony and historical persistence is underwritten at a subjective level by the way ideologies construct positions from which individuals "recognize" such values as a constituent element of their personal identity. Discourses of black nationalism, such as Marcus Garvey's, have always acknowledged that racism "works" by encouraging the devaluation of blackness by black subjects themselves, and that a re-centering sense of pride is a prerequisite for a politics of resistance and reconstruction. But it was Frantz Fanon who first provided a systematic framework for the political analysis of racial hegemonies at the level of black subjectivity.[8] He regarded cultural preferences for all things white as symptomatic of psychic "inferiorization" and thus might have agreed with Henrique's view of straightening as "an active expression of the feeling that it tends to Europeanize a person."

Such arguments gained influence in the 1960s when the Afro hair-style emerged as a symbol of Black Pride and Black Power. However, by regarding one's hair-style as directly "expressive" of one's political awareness this sort of argument tends to prioritize self over society and ignore the mediated and often contradictory dialectic between the two. Cheryl Clarke's poem, "Hair: a narrative," shows that the question of the relationship between self-image and hair-straightening is always shot through with emotional ambiguity. She describes her experience as implicating both pleasure and pain, shame and pride: the "negative" aspects of the hot-lye and steel-comb method are held in counterpoint to the friendship and intimacy between herself and her hairdresser who "against the war of tangles, against the burning metamorphosis . . . taught me art, gave me good advice, gave me language, made me love something about myself."[9] Another problem with prevailing anti-straightening arguments is that they rarely actually listen to what people think and feel about it.

Alternatively, I suggest that when hair-styling is critically evaluated as an aesthetic practice inscribed in everyday life, all black hair-styles are political in that they articulate responses to the panoply of historical forces which have invested this element of the ethnic signifier with both personal and political "meaning" and significance.

With its organizing principles of biological determinism, racism first "politicized" our hair by burdening it with a range of negative social and psychological "meanings." Devalorized as a "problem," each of the many stylizing practices brought to bear on this element of ethnic differentiation articulate ever so many diverse "solutions." Through aesthetic stylization each black hair-style seeks to revalorize the ethnic signifier and the political significance of each rearticulation of value and meaning depends on the historical conditions under which each style emerges.

The historical importance of Afro and Dreadlocks hair-styles cannot be underestimated as marking a "liberating" rupture or break with the dominance of white bias. But were they really that "radical" as solutions to the ideological problematization of black people's hair? Yes: in their historical contexts, they counter-politicized the signifier of ethnic devalorization, redefining blackness as a positive attribute. But, on the other hand, perhaps not, because within a relatively short period both styles became rapidly *de*politicized and, with varying degrees of resistance, both were incorporated into mainstream fashions in the dominant culture. What is at stake, I believe, is the difference between two logics of black stylization—one emphasizing "natural" looks, the other involving straightening to emphasize "artifice."

Nature/Culture: Some Vagaries of Imitation and Domination

Our hair, like our skin, is a highly sensitive surface on which competing definitions of "the beautiful" are played out in struggle. The racial overdeterminations of this nature/culture ambivalence are inscribed in this description of hair-straightening by a Jamaican hairdresser:

> *Next, apply hot oil, massaging the hair well which prepares it for a shampoo. You dry the hair, leaving a little moisture in it, and then apply grease. When the hair is completely dry you start* cultivating *it with a hot comb . . . Now the hair is all straight. You can use the curling iron on it. Most people like it curled and waved, not just straight, not just dead straight.*[10]

Her metaphor of "cultivation" is telling because it makes sense in two contradictory ways. On the one hand, it recuperates the negative logic of white bias: to cultivate is to transform something found "in the wild" into something of social use and value, like domesticating a forest into a field. It thus implies that in its "natural" given state, black people's hair has no inherent aesthetic value: it must be worked upon before it can be "beautiful." But on the other hand, all human hair is "cultivated" in this way in that it merely provides a raw material for practices, procedures and ritual techniques of cultural writing and social inscription. Moreover, in bringing out other aspects of the styling process which highlight its specificity as cultural practice—the skills of the hairdresser, the choices of the client—the ambiguous metaphor alerts us to the fact that nobody's hair is ever just natural but is always shaped or reshaped by social convention and symbolic intervention.

An appreciation of this delicate "nature/culture" relation is crucial if we are to account both for the emergence of Dreadlocks and Afro as politicized statements of "pride" *and* their eventual disappearance into the mainstream. To reconstruct the semiotic and political economy of these black hair-styles we need to examine their relation to other items of dress and the broader historical context in which ensembles of style emerged. An important clue with regard to the Afro in particular can be found in its names, as the Afro was also referred to as the "natural."

The interchangeability of its two names is important because both signified the embrace of a "natural" aesthetic as an alternative ideological code of symbolic value. The "naturalness" of the Afro consisted in its rejection both of straightened styles and of short haircuts: its distinguishing feature was the *length* of the hair. With the help of a "pick" or Afro comb the hair was encouraged to grow upwards and outwards into its characteristic rounded shape. The three-dimensionality of its shape formed the signifying link with its status as a sign of Black Pride. Its morphology suggested a certain dignified body-posture, for to wear an Afro you have to hold your head up in pride, you cannot bow down in shame and still show off your "natural" at the same time. As Flugel pointed out with regard to ceremonial head-dress and regal crowns, by virtue of their emphatic dimensions such items bestow a sense of presence, dignity and majesty on the wearer by magnifying apparent body-size and by shaping bodily movement accordingly so as to project stature and grace.[11] In a similar way, with the Afro we wore the crown, to the point where it could be assumed that the larger the Afro, the greater the degree of black "content" to one's consciousness.

In its "naturalistic" logic the Afro sought a solution that went to the source of the problem. By emphasizing the length of hair when allowed to grow "natural and free" the style counter-valorized attributes of curliness and kinkiness to convert stigmata of shame into emblematics of pride. Its name suggested a link between "Africa" and "nature" and this implied an oppositional stance against artificial techniques of any kind, as if any element of artificiality was imitative of Eurocentric, white-identified, aesthetic ideals. The oppositional economy of the Afro also depended on its connections with dress-styles adopted by various political movements of the time.

In contrast to the civil rights demand for racial equality within the given framework of society, the more radical and far-reaching objective of total "liberation" and "freedom" gained its leverage through identification and solidarity with anti-colonial and anti-imperial struggles of emergent Third World nations. And at one level, this "other" political orientation of Black Power announced itself in the language of clothes.

The Black Panthers' "urban guerrilla" attire–polo-necks, leather jackets, dark glasses and berets–encoded a uniform for protest and militancy by way of the connotations of the common denominator, the color black. The Panthers' berets invoked solidarity with the often violent means of anti-imperialism, while the dark glasses, by concealing identity from the "enemy," lent a certain political mystique and a romantic aura of dangerousness.

The Afro also featured in a range of ex-centric dress-styles associated with cultural nationalism, often influenced by the dress codes of Black Muslim organizations of the late 1950s. Here, elements of "traditional" African dress–tunics or dashikis, head-wraps and skull-caps, elaborate beads and embroidery–all suggested that black people were "contracting out" of westernness and identifying with all things African as a positive alternative. It may seem superficial to re-read these transformative political movements today in terms of style and dress: but we might also remember that as they filtered through mass media, such as television, these styles contributed to the increasing visibility of black people's struggles in the 1960s. As elements of everyday life, these black styles in hair and dress helped to underline massive shifts in popular aspirations and participated in a populist logic of rupture.

As its name suggests, the Afro symbolized a reconstitutive link with Africa, as part of a counter-hegemonic process helping to redefine a diasporean people not as Negro but as Afro-American. A similar upheaval was at work in the emergence of Dreadlocks. As the Afro's creole cousin, Dreadlocks spoke of pride and empowerment through their association with the radical discourse of Rastafari which, like Black Power in the United States, inaugurated a redirection of black consciousness in the Caribbean.[12] Within the strictures of Rastafari as doctrine, Dreadlocks embody an interpretation of a religious, biblical injunction that forbids the cutting of hair (along the lines of its rationale among Sikhs). However, once 'locks were popularized on a mass social scale–via the increasing militancy of reggae especially–their dread logic inscribed a beautification of blackness remarkably similar to the aesthetic logic of the Afro.

Dreadlocks also embrace the "natural" in the way they celebrate the very materiality of black hair texture, for black people's is the only type of hair that can be "matted" into such characteristic configurations. While the Afro's semiotics of pride depended on its rounded shape, 'locks counter-valorized nappy-headed blackness by way of this process of "matting" which is an option not readily available to white people because their hair does not "naturally" grow into such "organic"-looking shapes and strands. And where the Afro suggested a link with Africa through its name and its association with radical political discourses, Dreadlocks similarly implied a symbolic link between their "naturalistic" appearance and Africa by way of the reinterpretation of biblical narrative which identified Ethiopia as a "Zion" or Promised Land. With varying degrees of emphasis both invoked "nature" to inscribe "Africa" as the symbol of personal and political opposition to the hegemony of the west over "the rest." Both championed an aesthetic of nature that opposed itself to any artifice as the sign of corrupting Eurocentric influence. But nature had nothing to do with it! Both these hair-styles were never just natural, waiting to be found: they were stylistically *cultivated* and politically *constructed* in a particular historical moment as part of a strategic contestation of white dominance and the cultural power of whiteness.

These styles sought to "liberate" the materiality of black hair from the burdens bequeathed by racist ideology. But their respective logics of signification, positing links between the "natural," Africa, and the goal of freedom, depended on what was only a *tactical inversion* of the chain of equivalences that structured the Eurocentric system of white bias. We saw how the biological determinism of classical racist ideology first "politicized" our hair: its logic of devalorization of blackness radically devalued our hair, debarring it from access to dominant regimes of the "truth of beauty." The aesthetic de-negation "logically" depended on prior relations of equivalence which posited the categories of "Africa" and "nature" as equally other to Europe's deluded self-image which sought to monopolize claims to beauty.

The equation between the two categories in Eurocentric thought rested on the assumption that Africans had no culture or civilization worthy of the name. Philosophers like Hume and Hegel validated such assumptions, legitimating the view that Africa was outside history in a savage and rude "state of nature." Yet, while certain Enlightenment reflections on aesthetics saw in the "Negro" only the annulment of their ideas of beauty, Rousseau and later, in the eighteenth and nineteenth centuries, romanticism and realism, saw "nature" on the other hand as the source of all that was good, true and beautiful. The Negro was none of these. But by inverting the symbolic order of racial polarity the aesthetic of "nature" underpinning the Afro and Dreadlocks could negate the negation, turn white bias on its head and thus revalorize as positive all that had once been devalued as the annulment of aesthetics. In this way the black subject could accede—and only in the twentieth century, mind you—to that level of aesthetic idealization or self-valorization that had hitherto been denied as unthinkable. The radicality of the 1960s slogan, Black is Beautiful, lay in the function of the logical copula "is," as it marked the ontological affirmation of our nappy nigger hair, breaching the bar of negation signified in that utterance from the Song of Songs that Europe had rewritten (in the King James version of the Bible) as "I am black *but* beautiful."[13]

However radical this counter-move was, its tactical inversion of categories was limited. One reason why may be that the "nature" invoked was not a neutral term but an ideologically loaded *idea* created by binary and dualistic logics from European culture. The "nature" brought into play to signify a desire for "liberation" and "freedom" so effectively was also a western inheritance, sedimented with symbolic references by traditions of science, philosophy and art. Moreover, this ideological category had been fundamental to the hegemony of the west over "the rest"; the nineteenth-century bourgeoisie sought to legitimate the imperial division of the world by way of mythologies which aimed to universalize, eternalize and hence "naturalize" its power. The counter-hegemonic tactic of inversion appropriated a particularly romanticist version of "nature" as a means of empowering the black subject; but by remaining in a dualistic logic of binary oppositionality (to Europe and artifice) the moment of rupture was delimited by the fact that it was only an imaginary "Africa" that was put into play.

Clearly, this analysis is not to write off the openings and effective "liberations" gained and made possible by inverting the order of aesthetic oppression; only to point out that the counter-hegemonic project inscribed by these hair-styles is not completed or closed and that this story of struggles over the same symbols continues. Nevertheless, the limitations underline the diasporean specificity of the Afro and Dreadlocks and ask us to examine, first, their conditions of commodification and, second, the question of their "imaginary" relationship to Africa and African cultures as such.

Once commercialized in the market-place the Afro lost its specific signification as a "black" cultural-political statement. Cut off from its original political contexts, it became just another fashion: with an Afro wig anyone could wear the style. Now the fact that it could be neutralized and incorporated so quickly suggests that the aesthetic interventions of the Afro operated on terrain already mapped out by the symbolic codes of the dominant white culture. The Afro not only echoed aspects of romanticism, but shared this in common with the "counter-cultural" logic of long hair among white youth in the 1960s. From the Beatles' mop-tops to the hairy hippies of Woodstock, white subcultures of the 1960s expressed the idea that the longer you wore your hair, somehow the more "radical" and "right-on" your life-style or politics. This "far-out" logic of long hair among the hippies may have sought to symbolize disaffection from western norms, but it was rapidly assimilated and dissimulated by commodity fetishism. The incorporation of long hair as the epitome of "protest," via the fashion industry, advertising and other economies of capitalist mediation, culminated at one point in a Broadway musical that ran for years—Hair.

Like the Afghan coats and Kashmiri caftans worn by the hippy, the dashiki was reframed by dominant definitions of ethnic otherness as "exotica": its connotations of cultural nationalism were clawed back as just another item of freakish exoticism for mass consumption. Consider also the inherent semiotic instability of militant chic. The black leather jackets and dark glasses of the Panthers were already inscribed as stylized synonyms for "rebelliousness" in white male subcultures from the 1950s. There, via Marlon Brando and the metonymic association with macho and motor bikes, these elements encoded a youthful desire for "freedom," in the image of the American highway and the open road, implying opposition to the domestic norms of their parent culture. Moreover, the color black was not saturated by exclusively "racial" connotations. Dark somber colors (as well as the occasional French beret) featured in the downbeat dress statements of the 1950s boho-beatniks to suggest mystery, "cool," outsider status, anything to "alienate" the normative values of "square society."

The fact that these white subcultures themselves appropriated elements from black

American culture (rock 'n' roll and bebop respectively) is as important as the fact that a portion of the semiotic effectiveness of the Panther's look derived from associations already "embedded" by previous articulations of the same or similar elements of style. The movement back and forth indicates an underlying dynamic of struggle as different discourses compete for the same signs. It shows that for "style" to be socially intelligible as an expression of conflicting values, each cultural nucleus or articulation of signs must share access to a common stock or resource of signifying elements. To make the point from another point of view would amount to saying that the Afro engaged in a critical "dialogue" between black and white Americans, not one between black Americans and Africans. Even more so than Dreadlocks, there was nothing particularly African about the Afro at all. Neither style had a given reference point in existing African cultures, in which hair is rarely left to grow "naturally." Often it is plaited or braided, using "weaving" techniques to produce a rich variety of sometimes highly elaborate styles that are reminiscent of the patternings of African cloth and the decorative designs of African ceramics, architecture and embroidery.[14] Underlying these practices is what might be termed an African aesthetic. In contrast to the separation of the aesthetic sphere in post-Kantian European thought, this is an aesthetic which incorporates practices of beautification in everyday life. Thus artifice is valued in its own right as a mark of both invention and tradition, and aesthetic skills are deployed within a complex economy of symbolic codes in which communal subjects recreate themselves collectively.[15]

Neither the Afro nor Dreadlocks operate within this aesthetic as such. In contemporary African societies, such styles would not signify Africanness ('locks in particular would be regarded as something "alien," precisely the tactical objective of the Mau Mau in Kenya when they adopted such dread appearances in the 1950s); on the contrary, they would imply an identification with First World-ness. They are specifically diasporean. However strongly these styles expressed a desire to "return to the roots" among black peoples in the diaspora, in Africa *as it is* they would speak of a "modern" orientation, a modelling of oneself according to metropolitan images of blackness.

If there was nothing "African" about these styles, this only goes to underline the point that neither style was as "natural" as it claimed to be. Both presupposed quite artificial techniques to attain their characteristic shapes and hence political significance: the use of special combs in the case of the Afro, and the process of matting in the case of 'locks, often given a head-start by initially plaiting long strands of hair. In their rejection of artifice both styles embraced a "naturalism" that owed much more to Europe then it did to Africa. The fate of the Afro in particular might best be understood by an analogy with what happened to the Harlem Renaissance in the 1920s.

There, complementing Garvey's call for repatriation to Africa, a generation of artists, poets, writers and dancers embraced all things African to renew and refashion a collective sense of black American identity. Yet when rich white patrons descended on Harlem seeking out the salubrious spectacle of the "New Negro" it became clear—to Langston Hughes at least—that the Africa being evoked was not the real one but a mythological, imaginary "Africa" of noble savagery and primitive grace. The creative upsurge in black American culture and politics marked a moment of rupture and a reconstruction of black subjectivity *en masse*, but it was done like the Afro through an inverted reinscription of the romanticist mythology created by Europe's Enlightenment. As Langston realized, "I was only an American Negro–who had loved the surfaces of Africa and the rhythms of Africa–but I was not Africa."[16] However strategically and historically important, such tactics of reversal remain unstable and contradictory because their assertion of difference so often hinges on what is only the inversion of the same.

Style and Fashion: Semiotic Struggles in the Forest of Signs

Having alighted on a range of paradoxes of race and aesthetics via this brief excursion into the archaeology of the Afro, I want now to re-evaluate the political economy of straightening in the light of these contradictory relations between black and white cultures in diasporean societies. Having found no pre-existing referent for either style-statement in "actually existing" African cultures it should be clear that what we are dealing with are New World creations of black people's culture which, in First World societies, bear markedly different relations with the dominant Euro-American culture from those that obtain in the Third World.

By ignoring these differences, arguments that hold straightened styles to be slavish "imitations" of western norms are in fact complicit with an outmoded anthropological argument that once tried to explain diasporean black cultures as bastard products of unilateral "acculturation." By reversing the axes of traditional analysis we can see that in our era of cultural modernity it is white people who have been doing a great deal of the imitating while black people have done much of the innovating.

Refutations of the assumptions underpinning the racist myth of one-sided acculturation have often taken the form of "discoveries," usually proclaimed by anthropologists, of "africanisms" or the survival of African cultural traits across the middle passage to the New World. Melville Herskovits, for instance, made much of the retention of traditional African modes of hairdressing and covering among black Americans.[17] However, in the light of modern contradictions around "inter-culturation," our attention must now be directed not so much to the retention of actual artifacts but to the reworking of what may be seen as a "neo-African" approach to the aesthetic in diasporean cultural formations. The patterns and practices of aesthetic stylization developed by black cultures in First World societies may be seen as modalities of cultural practice *inscribed* in critical engagement with the dominant white culture and at the same time *expressive* of a "neo-African" approach to the pleasures of beauty at the level of everyday life.

Black practices of aesthetic stylization are intelligible at one "functional" level as dialogic responses to the racism of the dominant culture, but at another level involve acts of appropriation from that same "master" culture through which "syncretic" forms of diasporean culture have evolved. Syncretic strategies of black stylization, "creolizing" found or given elements, are writ large in the black codes of modern music like jazz where elements such as scales, harmonies or even instruments like the piano or saxophone from western cultural traditions are radically transformed by this "neo-African," improvisational approach to aesthetic and cultural production. In addition there is another "turn of the screw" in these modern relations of inter-culturation when these creolized cultural forms are made use of by other social groups and then, in turn, are all incorporated into mainstream "mass" culture as commodities for consumption. Any analysis of black style, in hair or any other medium, must take this field of relationships into account.

Hair-styles such as the conk of the 1940s or the curly-perm of the 1980s are syncretic products of New World stylization. Refracting elements from both black and white cultures through this framework of exchange and appropriation, imitation and incorporation, such styles are characterized by the ambivalence of their "meaning." It is implausible to attempt a reading of this ambivalence in advance of an appreciation of the historical contexts in which they emerged alongside other stylized surfaces of syncretic inscription in speech, dance, music and dress.

As a way into this arena of ambiguity listen to this voice, as Malcolm X describes his own experience of hair-straightening. After recounting the physical pain of the hot-lye and steel-comb technology, he tells of pride and pleasure in the new, self-stylized image he has made for himself:

> *My first view in the mirror blotted out the hurting. I'd seen some pretty conks, but when it's the first time, on your own head, the transformation, after a lifetime of kinks, is staggering. The mirror reflected Shorty behind me. We were both grinning and sweating. On top of my head was this thick, smooth sheen of red hair–real red–as straight as any white man's.*[18]

In his autobiographical narrative the voice then shifts immediately from past to present wherein Malcolm sees the conk as "my first really big step towards self-degradation." No attempt is made to address this mixture of feeling: pleasure and pride in the past, shame and self-denigration in the present. The narrative seems to "forget" or exclude the whole life-style of which the conk hair-style was a part. By invoking the idea of "imitation" Malcolm evades the ambiguity, his discourse cancels from the equation what his "style" meant at that moment in front of the mirror.

In its context the conk was but one aspect of a modern style of black American life, forged in the subaltern social bloc of the northern ghettos by people who, like Malcolm Little, had migrated from southern systems of segregation only to find themselves locked into another, more modern, and equally violent, order of oppression. Shut out from access to illusions of "making it," this marginalized urban formation of modern diasporean culture sponsored a sense of style that "answered back" against these conditions of existence.

Between the years of economic depression and the Second World War, big bands like Duke Ellington's, Count Basie's and Lionel Hampton's (he played at the dance-hall where Malcolm worked as a shoeshine boy) accelerated on rhythm, seeking through "speed" to pre-empt the possibility of white appropriations of jazz, as happened in the 1920s. In the "underground" music scene incubated around Kansas City in the 1940s the accent on improvisation, which later flourished as bebop, articulated an "escape"– simultaneously metaphysical and subterranean–from that system of socio-economic bondage, itself in the ruins of war. In the high-energy dance styles that might accompany the beat, the Lindy Hop and Jitter Bug traced another line of flight: through the catharsis of the dance a momentary "release" might be obtained from all the pressures on mind and body accumulated under the ritual discriminations of racism. In speech and language, games like signifyin', playing the dozens and what became known as "jive-talk," verbal style effected a discursive equivalent of jazz improvisation. The performative skills and sheer wit demanded by these speech-acts in black talk defied the idea that Black English was a degraded "version" of the master language. These games refuted America's archetype of Sambo, all tongue-tied and dumb, muttering "Yessa massa" in its miserable abjection. In the semantic play of verbal stylization, hep-cats of the cool world greeted each other as Man, systematically subverting the paternalistic interpellation–boy!–of the white master code, the voice of authority in the social text of the urban plantation.[19]

In this historical moment style was not a substitute for politics. But, in the absence of an organized direction of black political discourse and excluded from official "democratic" channels of representation, the logic of style manifested across cultural surfaces of everyday life reinforced the terms of shared experience–blackness–and thus a sense of solidarity among a subaltern social bloc. Perhaps we can trace a fragile common thread running through these styles of the 1940s: they encoded a refusal of passivity by way of a creolizing accentuation and subtle inflection of given elements, codes and conventions.

The conk involved a violent technology of straightening, but this was only the initial stage in a process of creolizing stylization. The various waves, curls and lengths introduced by practical styling served to differentiate the conk from the conventional white hair-styles which supposedly constituted the "models" from which this black hair-style was derived as imitation or "copy." No, the conk did not copy anything and certainly not any of the prevailing white male hair-styles of the day. Rather, the element of straightening suggested resemblance to white people's hair, but the nuances, inflections and accentuations introduced by artificial means of stylization emphasized difference. In this way the political economy of the conk rested on its ambiguity, the way it "played" with the given outline shapes of convention only to "disturb" the norm and hence invite a "double take" demanding that you look twice.

Consider also the use of dye, red dye: why red? To assume that black men conked up *en masse* because they secretly wanted to become "red-heads" would be way off the mark. In the chromatic scale of white bias, red is seen as a mild deviation from gendered norms which hold blonde hair as the color of "beauty" in women and brown hair among men. Far from an attempted simulation of whiteness I think the dye was used as a stylized means of defying the "natural" color codes of conventionality in order to highlight artificiality and hence exaggerate a sense of difference. Like the purple and green wigs worn by black women, which Malcolm mentions in disgust, the use of red dye seems trivial: but by flouting convention with varying degrees of artifice such techniques of black stylization participated in a defiant "dandyism," fronting-out oppression by the artful manipulation of appearances. Such dandyism is a feature of the economy of style-statements in many subaltern class cultures where "flashy" clothes are used in the art of impression-management to defy the assumption that to be poor one necessarily has to "show" it. The strategic use of artifice in such stylized modes of self-presentation was written into the pleats of the zoot suit which, together with the conk, constituted the *de rigueur* hep-cat look in the black male "hustler" life-style of the 1940s ghettos. With its wide shoulders, tight waist and baggy pants—topped off with a wide-brimmed hat, and worn with slim Italian shoes and lots of gold jewels—the zoot suit projected stature, dignity and presence: it signified that the black man was "important" in his own terrain and on his own terms.

The zoot suit is said to have originated among Latino males on the US west coast—whatever its source, it caused a "race-riot" in Los Angeles in 1943 as the amount of cloth implicated in its cut exceeded wartime rations, provoking ethnic resentment among white males. But perhaps the real historical importance of the zoot suit lies in the irony of its appropriation. By 1948 the American fashion industry had ripped it off and toned it down as the new post-war "bold look" for the mainstream male. By being commodified within such a short period the zoot suit demonstrated a reversal in the flow of fashion-diffusion as now the style of the times emerged from social groups "below," whereas previously regimes of taste had been set by the *haute couture* of the wealthy and then translated back down, via industrial reproduction, to the masses.[20] This is important because, as an aspect of inter-culturation, this story of black innovation/white imitation has been played out again and again in post-war popular culture, most markedly in music and, in so far as music has formed their nucleus, a whole procession of youth subcultures from Teddy boys to B-boys.

Once we re-contextualize the conk in this way we confront a series of "style wars," skirmishes of appropriation and commodification played out around the semiotic economy of the ethnic signifier. The complexity of this force-field of inter-culturation ambushes any attempt to track down fixed meanings or finalized readings and opens out instead on to ambiguous relations of economic and aesthetic systems of valorization. On the one hand, the conk was conceived in a subaltern culture, dominated and hedged in by a capitalist master culture, yet operating in an "underground" manner to subvert given elements by creolizing stylization. Style encoded political "messages" to those in the know which were otherwise unintelligible to white society by virtue of their ambiguous accentuation and intonation. But, on the other hand, that dominant commodity culture appropriated bits and pieces from the otherness of ethnic differentiation in order to reproduce the "new" and so, in turn, to strengthen its dominance and revalorize its own symbolic capital. Assessed in the light of these paradoxical relationships, the conk suggests a "covert" logic of cultural struggle operating "in and against" hegemonic cultural codes, a logic quite different from the overt oppositionality of the naturalistic Afro or Dreadlocks. At one level this only underlines the different historical conditions, but at another the emphasis on artifice and ambiguity rather than an inversion of equivalence strikes me as a particularly modern way in which cultural utterances may take on the force of "political" statements. Syncretic practices of black stylization, such as the conk, zoot suit or jive-talk, recognize themselves self-consciously as products of a New World culture; that is, they incorporate an awareness of the contradictory conditions of inter-culturation. It is this self-consciousness that underscores their ambivalence and in turn marks them off and differentiates them as stylized signs of blackness.

In jive-talk the very meanings of words are made uncertain and undecidable by self-conscious stylization which sends signifiers slipping and sliding over signifieds: bad means good, superbad means better. Because of the way blackness is recognized in such stratagems of creolizing intonation, inflection and accentuation, these practices of stylization exemplify "modernist" interventions whose economy of political calculation might best be illustrated by the "look" of someone like Malcolm X in the 1960s.

Malcolm always eschewed the ostentatious, overly symbolic dress code of the Muslims and wore "respectable" suits and ties, but unlike the besuited civil rights leaders his appearance was always inflected by a certain "sharpness," an accentuation of the hegemonic dress code of the corporate business suit. This intonation in his attire spelt out that he would talk to the polity on his terms, not theirs. This nuance in his public image echoed the "intellectual" look adopted by jazz musicians in the 1950s, but then again, from another frame, Malcolm looked like a mod! And in the case of this particular 1960s subculture, white English youth had taken many of the "found objects" of their stylistic bricolage from the diasporean cultural expression of black America and the Caribbean. Taking these relations of appropriation and counter-appropriation into account, it would be impossible to argue for any one "authoritative" reading of either the conk in the past or the curly-perm today. Rather, the complexity of these violent relations of valorization, which loom so large over the popular experience of cultural modernity, demands that we ask instead: are there any laws that govern this "semiotic guerrilla warfare" in the concrete jungle of the modern metropolis?

If, in the British context, "we can watch, played out on the loaded surfaces of . . . working-class youth cultures, a phantom history of race relations since the war,"[21] then any analysis of black hair-style in this territory of the diaspora must reckon with the contradictory terms of this accelerated inter-culturation around the ethnic signifier. Somewhere around 1967 or 1968 something very strange happened in the ethnic imaginary of Englishness as former mods assembled a new image out of their parents' work-clothes, creating a working-class youth culture that derived its name from their cropped hair-styles. Yet the skinhead hair-style was an imitation of the mid-1960s soulboy look where closely shaven haircuts provided one of the most "classic" solutions to the problem of kinks and curls. Every black person (at least) recognizes the "skinhead" as a political statement in its own right–but then how are we to understand the social or psychological bases for this post-imperial mode of mimicry, this ghost dance of white ethnicity? Like a photographic negative, the skinhead crop symbolized white power and white pride sure enough, but then *how* (like their love of ska and bluebeat) did this relate to their appropriation of Afro-Caribbean culture?

Similarly, we would have to confront the paradox whereby white appropriations seem to act both as a spur to further experimentation and as modified models to which black people themselves may conform. Once the Afro had been ingested, black Americans brought traditional braiding and plaiting styles out from under their wraps, introducing novel elements such as beads and feathers into cane-row patterns. No sooner said than done, by the mid-1970s the beaded cane-row style was appropriated by one-hit wonder Bo Derek. It also seemed that her success validated the style and encouraged more black people to cane-row their hair.

Moreover, if contemporary culture functions on the threshold of what has been called "postmodernism," an analysis of this force-field of inter-culturation must surely figure in the forefront of any reconstructive rejoinder to debates which have so far marginalized popular culture and aesthetic practices in everyday life. If, as Fredric Jameson argues, postmodernity merely refers to the dominant cultural logic of late capitalism which "now assigns an increasingly essential structural function to aesthetic innovation and experimentation" as a condition of commodity fetishism and higher rates of turn-over in mass consumption, then any attempt to account for the gradual dissolution of boundaries between "high" and "low" culture, "taste" and "style," must reckon with the dialogic interventions of diasporean, creolizing cultures.

As Angela McRobbie has noted, various postmodern stratagems of aesthetic critique have already been prefigured as dialogic, politicized interventions in popular culture. Scratching and rap in black music would be a good example of "radical collage" engaged in popular culture or everyday life; like the bricoleur, the DJ appropriates and juxtaposes fragments from the arche-text of popular music history in a critical engagement or "dialogue" with issues thrown up by the present.[22]

It is in the context of such critical bricolage that the question of the curly-perm today must be re-posed. One initial reading of this hair-style in the late 1970s, as a symbol of black "embourgeoisement," is undermined by the way that many wet-look styles retain the overall rounded shape of the Afro. Indeed, a point to notice about the present is that the curly-perm is not the "one" uniformly popular black hair-style, but only one among many diverse configurations of "post-liberated" black hair-styles that seem to revel in their allusions to an ever wider range of stylistic references. Relaxing cremes, gels, dyes and other new technologies have enabled a width of experimentation that suggests that hair-straightening does not "mean" the same thing after as before the era of the Afro and Dreadlocks. Black practices of stylization today seem to exude confidence in their enthusiasm for combining elements from any source—black or white, past or present—into new configurations of cultural expression. Post-liberated black hair-styling emphasizes a "pick 'n' mix" approach to aesthetic production, suggesting a different attitude to the past in its reckoning with modernity. The philly-cut on the hip-hop/go-go scene etches diagonalized lines across the head, refashioning a style from the 1940s where a parting would be shaved into the hair. Combinations of cane-row and curly-perm echo "Egyptian" imagery; she looks like Nefertiti, but this is Neasden, nowhere near the Nile.

One particular style that fascinates me is a variant of the flat-top (popularized by Grace Jones, but also perhaps a long-distance echo of the wedge-cut of the 1960s) where, underneath a crest of miniaturized dreadlocks, the hair is cut really close at the back and the sides: naturalism is invented to accentuate artifice. The differential logics of ambivalence and equivalence are shown to be not necessarily exclusive as they interweave across each other: long 'locks are tied up in pony-tails, very practical, of course, but often done as aesthetic stylization (itself in subtle counterpoint to various "new man" hair-styles that also involve the romanticist male dandyism of long hair). And perhaps the intertextual dimension of creolizing stylization is not so "new"; after all, in the

1970s black people sometimes wore wild Afro wigs in bold pink and day-glo colors, prefiguring post-punk experimentation with anti-naturalistic, "off" colors.

On top of all this, one cannot ignore how, alongside the commodification of hip-hop/electro, breakdancing and sportwear chic, some contemporary hair-styles among white youth maintain an ambiguous relationship with the stylizing practices of their black counterparts. Many use gels to effect sculptural forms and in some inner-city areas white kids us the relaxer creme technology marketed to black kids to simulate the "wet-look." So who, in this postmodern mêlée of semiotic appropriation and counter-creolization, is imitating whom?

Any attempt to make sense of these circuits of hyper-investment and overexpenditure around the symbolic economy of the ethnic signifier encounters issues that raise questions about race, power and modernity that go beyond those allowed by a static moral psychology of "self-image." I began with a polemic against one type of argument and have ended up in another: namely one that demands a critical analysis of the multi-faceted economy of black hair as a condition for appropriate aesthetic judgements. "Only a fool does not judge by appearances," Oscar Wilde said, and by the same token it would be foolish to assume that because somebody wears 'locks they are dealing in "peace, love and unity"; Dennis Brown also reminded us to take the "wolf in sheep's clothing" syndrome into account. There are no just black hair-styles, just black hair-styles. This article has prioritized the semiotic dimension in its readings to open up analyses of this polyvocal economy but there are other facets to be examined: such as the exploitative priorities of the black hairdressing industry as it affects consumers, or workers under precarious market conditions, or the question of gendered differentiations (and similarities).

On the political horizon of postmodern popular culture I think the *diversity* of contemporary black hair-styles is something to be proud of. Because this variousness testifies to an inventive, improvisational aesthetic that should be valued as an aspect of Africa's "gift" to modernity. And because, if there is the possibility of a "unity in diversity" somewhere in this field of relations, then it challenges us to cherish plurality politically.[23]

Versions of this article have been critically "dialogized" by numerous conversations. I would like to thank all the seminar participants at the Center for Caribbean Studies, Goldsmiths' College in London, April 30, 1986, and, in thinking diasporean aesthetics, thanks also to Stuart Hall, Paul Gilroy and Clyde Taylor.

1. *The Black Voice*, no. 15 (June 1983): 3 (paper of the Black Unity and Freedom Party, London SE15).

2. See Tony Jefferson, and Stuart Hall, eds., *Resistance through Rituals* (London: Hutchinson, 1975); and Dick Hebdige, *Subculture* (London: Methuen, 1979).

3. See C.R. Hallpike, "Social Hair," in *Social Aspects of the Human Body*, ed. Ted Polhemus (Harmondsworth: Penguin, 1978); on the veil see Frantz Fanon, "Algeria Unveiled," in *A Dying Colonialism* (Harmondsworth: Penguin, 1970).

4. Such anxieties, I know, are intensified around the mixed-race subject: "I still have to deal with people who go to touch my 'soft' or 'loose' or 'wavy' hair as if in the touching something . . . will be confirmed. Back then to the 60s it seems to me that my options . . . were to keep it short and thereby less visible, or to have the living curl dragged out of it: *maybe then you'd look Italian . . .*

or something." Derrick McClintock, "Color," *Ten.8,* no. 22 (1986).

5. George Mosse, *Toward the Final Solution: A History of European Racism* (London: Dent, 1978), p. 44.

6. Ferdinand Henriques, *Family and Color in Jamaica* (London: Secker & Warburg, 1953), pp. 54-55.

7. Stuart Hall, "Pluralism, Race and Class in Caribbean Society," in *Race and Class in Post-Colonial Society* (New York: UNESCO, 1977), pp. 150-182.

8. Frantz Fanon, *Black Skin, White Masks* (London: Pluto Press, 1986).

9. Cheryl Clark, *Narratives: Poems in the Tradition of Black Women* (New York: Kitchen Table/Women of Color Press, 1982); see also *Hairpiece: A Film for Nappy-Headed People,* dir. Ayoka Chinzera, 1982.

10. Henriques, *Family and Color in Jamaica,* p. 55.

11. See John C. Flugel, *The Psychology of Clothes* (London: Hogarth Press, 1930).

12. On connections between Black Power and Rastafari, see Walter Rodney, *The Groundings with my Brothers* (London: Bogle-L'Ouverture Publications, 1968), pp. 32-33.

13. On Africa as the "annulment" of Eurocentric concepts of beauty see Christopher Miller, *Blank Darkness: Africanist Discourse in French* (London and Chicago: University of Chicago Press, 1985). On systems of equivalence and difference in hegemonic struggles see Ernesto Laclau, "Populist Rupture and Discourse," *Screen Education,* no. 34 (Spring 1980) and Ernesto Laclau and Chantal Mouffe, *Hegemony and Socialist Strategy* (London: Verso, 1985).

14. Esi Sagay, *African Hairstyles* (London: Heinemann, 1983).

15. See John Miller Chernoff, *African Rhythm and African Sensibility* (Chicago: University of Chicago Press, 1979); Victoria Ebin, *The Body Decorated* (London: Thames & Hudson, 1979) and Victor Turner, *The Forest of Symbols: Aspects of Ndembu Ritual* (Ithaca: Cornell University Press, 1967).

16. Langston Hughes, *The Big Sea* (London: Pluto Press, 1986); and see also Ralph Ellison, *Shadow and Act* (New York: Random House, 1964).

17. Melville Herskovits, *The Myth of the Negro Past* (Boston: Beacon Books, 1959). During the 1950s anthropologists influenced by the "culture and personality" paradigm approached the ghetto as a domain of social pathology. Abrahams (mis)read the process rag hairdo, kept under a handkerchief until Saturday night, as "an effeminate trait . . . reminiscent of the handkerchief tying of Southern 'mammies'," a symptom of sex-role socialization gone wrong, cited in Charles Keil, *Urban Blues* (London and Chicago: University of Chicago Press, 1966), pp. 26-27. Alterative concepts of "inter-culturation" and "creolization" are developed by Edward K. Braithwaite, *Contradictory Omens: Cultural Diversity and Integration in the Caribbean* (Mona, JA: Savacou Publications, 1974); see also Janheinz Jahn, *Muntu: An Outline of Neo-African Culture* (London: Faber, 1953).

18. *The Autobiography of Malcolm X* (Harmondsworth: Penguin, 1968), pp. 134-139.

19. On Afro-American stylization see Ben Sidran, *Black Talk* (London: De Capo Press, 1973); Thomas Kochman, *Black and White Styles in Conflict* (London and Chicago: University of Chicago Press, 1981); and Henry Louis Gates Jr., "The Blackness of Blackness: A Critique of the Sign and the Signifying Monkey," in *Black Literature and Literary Theory,* ed. Gates (London and New York: Methuen, 1984).

20. Steve Chibnall, "Whistle and Zoot: the Changing Meaning of a Suit of Clothes," *History Workshop Journal,* no. 20 (1985) and Stuart Cosgrove, "The Zoot Suit and Style Warfare," *History Workshop Journal,* no. 18 (1984). See also J. Schwartz. "Men's Clothing and the Negro," in *Dress Adornment and the Social Order,* eds. M.E. Roach and J.B. Eicher (New York: Wiley, 1965).

21. Hebdige, *Subculture,* p. 45.

22. Fredric Jameson, "Postmodernism, or the Cultural Logic of Late Capitalism," *New Left Review,* no. 146 (July/August 1984): 56; and Angela McRobbie, "Postmodernism and popular culture," *ICA Documents no. 4/5* (London: ICA, 1986).

23. *Sister Carol wears locks and wants a Black revolution*
She tours with African dancers around the country
Sister Jenny has relaxed hair and wants a Black revolution
She paints scenes of oppression for an art gallery
Sister Sandra has an Afro and wants a Black revolution
She works at a women's collective in Brixton
Sister Angela wears braids and wants a Black revolution
She spreads love and harmony with her reggae song
All my sisters who want a Black revolution don't care
How they wear their hair. And they're all Beautiful.
Christabelle Peters, "The Politics of Hair," Poets Corner, *The Voice* (March 15, 1986).

Complexion

Visiting the East Coast or the gray capitals of Europe during the long months of winter, I often meet people at deluxe hotels who comment on my complexion. (In such hotels it appears nowadays a mark of leisure and wealth to have a complexion like mine.) Have I been skiing? In the Swiss Alps? Have I just returned from a Caribbean vacation? No. I say no softly but in a firm voice that intends to explain: My complexion is dark. (My skin is brown. More exactly, terra-cotta in sunlight, tawny in shade. I do not redden in sunlight. Instead, my skin becomes progressively dark; the sun singes the flesh.)

When I was a boy the white summer sun of Sacramento would darken me so, my T-shirt would seem bleached against my slender dark arms. My mother would see me come up the front steps. She'd wait for the screen door to slam at my back. "You look like a *negrito*," she'd say, angry, sorry to be angry, frustrated almost to laughing, scorn. "You know how important looks are in this country. With *los gringos* looks are all that they judge on. But you! Look at you! You're so careless!" Then she'd start in all over again. "You won't be satisfied till you end up looking like *los pobres* who work in the fields, *los braceros.*"

(*Los braceros:* Those men who work with their *brazos,* their arms; Mexican nationals who were licenced to work for American farmers in the 1950s. They worked very hard for very little money, my father would tell me. And what money they earned they sent back to Mexico to support their families, my mother would add. *Los pobres*–the poor, the pitiful, the powerless ones. But paradoxically also powerful men. They were the men with brown-muscled arms I stared at in awe on Saturday mornings when they showed up downtown like gypsies to shop at Woolworth's or Penney's. On Monday nights they would gather hours early on the steps of the Memorial Auditorium for the wrestling matches. Passing by on my bicycle in summer, I would spy them there, clustered in small groups, talking–frightening and fascinating men–some wearing Texas *sombreros* and T-shirts which shone fluorescent in the twilight. I would sit forward in the back seat of our family's '48 Chevy to see them, working alongside Valley highways: dark men on an even horizon, loading a truck amid rows of straight green. Powerful, powerless men. Their fascinating darkness–like mine–to be feared.)

"You'll end up looking just like them."

1

Regarding my family, I see faces that do not closely resemble my own. Like some other

Mexican families, my family suggests Mexico's confused colonial past. Gathered around a table, we appear to be from separate continents. My father's face recalls faces I have seen in France. His complexion is white—he does not tan; he does not burn. Over the years, his dark wavy hair has grayed handsomely. But with time his face has sagged to a perpetual sigh. My mother, whose surname is inexplicably Irish—Moran—has an olive complexion. People have frequently wondered if, perhaps, she is Italian or Portuguese. And, in fact, she looks as though she could be from southern Europe. My mother's face has not aged as quickly as the rest of her body; it remains smooth and glowing -a cool tan—which her gray hair cleanly accentuates. My older brother has inherited her good looks. When he was a boy people would tell him that he looked like Mario Lanza, and hearing it he would smile with dimpled assurance. He would come home from high school with girl friends who seemed to me glamorous (because they were) blondes. And during those years I envied him his skin that burned red and peeled like the skin of the *gringos*. His complexion never darkened like mine. My youngest sister is exotically pale, almost ashen. She is delicately featured, Near Eastern, people have said. Only my older sister has a complexion as dark as mine, though her facial features are much less harshly defined than my own. To many people meeting her, she seems (they say) Polynesian. I am the only one in the family whose face is severely cut to the line of ancient Indian ancestors. My face is mournfully long, in the classical Indian manner; my profile suggests one of those beak-nosed Mayan sculptures—the eaglelike face upturned, open-mouthed, against the deserted, primitive sky.

"We are Mexicans," my mother and father would say, and taught their four children to say whenever we (often) were asked about our ancestry. My mother and father scorned those "white" Mexican-Americans who tried to pass themselves off as Spanish. My parents would never have thought of denying their ancestry. I never denied it: My ancestry is Mexican, I told strangers mechanically. But I never forgot that only my older sister's complexion was as dark as mine.

My older sister never spoke to me about her complexion when she was a girl. But I guessed that she found her dark skin a burden. I knew that she suffered for being a "nigger." As she came home from grammar school, little boys came up behind her and pushed her down to the sidewalk. In high school, she struggled in the adolescent competition for boyfriends in a world of football games and proms, a world where her looks were plainly uncommon. In college, she was afraid and scornful when dark-skinned foreign students from countries like Turkey and India found her attractive. She revealed her fear of dark skin to me only in adulthood when, regarding her own three children, she quietly admitted relief that they were all light.

That is the kind of remark women in my family have often made before. As a boy, I'd stay in the kitchen (never seeming to attract any notice), listening while my aunts spoke of their pleasure at having light children. (The men, some of whom were dark-skinned from years of working out of doors, would be in another part of the house.) It was the woman's spoken concern: the fear of having a dark-skinned son or daughter. Remedies were exchanged. One aunt prescribed to her sisters the elixir of large doses of caster oil during the last weeks of pregnancy. (The remedy risked an abortion.) Children born dark grew up to have their faces treated regularly with a mixture of egg white and lemon juice concentrate. (In my case, the solution never would take.) One Mexican-American friend of my mother's, who regarded it a special blessing that she had a measure of English blood, spoke disparagingly of her husband, a construction worker, for being so dark. "He doesn't take care of himself," she complained. But the remark, I noticed, annoyed my mother, who sat tracing an invisible design with her finger on the tablecloth.

There was affection too and a kind of humor about these matters. With daring tenderness, one of my uncles would refer to his wife as *mi negra*. An aunt regularly called her dark child *mi feito* (my little ugly one), her smile only partially hidden as she bent down to dig her mouth under his ticklish chin. And at times relatives spoke scornfully of pale, white skin. A *gringo's* skin resembled *masa*–baker's dough–someone remarked. Everyone laughed. Voices chuckled over the fact that the *gringos* spent so many hours in summer sunning themselves. ("They need to get sun because they look like *los muertos*.")

I heard the laughing but remembered what the women had said, with unsmiling voices, concerning dark skin. Nothing I heard outside the house, regarding my skin, was so impressive to me.

In public I occasionally heard racial slurs. Complete strangers would yell out at me. A teenager drove past, shouting, "Hey, Greaser! Hey, Pancho!" Over his shoulder I saw the giggling face of his girl friend. A boy pedaled by and announced matter-of-factly, "I pee on dirty Mexicans." Such remarks would be said so casually that I wouldn't quickly realize that they were being addressed to me. When I did, I would be paralyzed with embarrassment, unable to return the insult. (Those times I happened to be with white grammar school friends, *they* shouted back. Imbued with the mysterious kindness of children, my friends would never ask later why I hadn't yelled out in my own defense.)

In all, there could not have been more than a dozen incidents of name-calling. That there were so few suggests that I was not a primary victim of racial abuse. But that, even today, I can clearly remember particular incidents is proof of their impact. Because of such incidents, I listened when my parents remarked that Mexicans were often mistreated in California border towns. And in Texas. I listened carefully when I heard that two of my cousins had been refused admittance to an "all-white" swimming pool. And that an uncle had been told by some man to go back to Africa. I followed the progress of the southern black civil rights movement, which was gaining prominent notice in Sacramento's afternoon newspaper. But what most intrigued me was the connection between dark skin and poverty. Because I heard my mother speak so often about the relegation of dark people to menial labor, I considered the great victims of racism to be those who were poor and forced to do menial work. People like the farmworkers whose skin was dark from the sun.

After meeting a black grammar school friend of my sister's, I remember thinking that she wasn't really "black." What interested me was the fact that she wasn't poor. (Her well-dressed parents would come by after work to pick her up in a shiny green Oldsmobile.) By contrast, the garbage men who appeared every Friday morning seemed to me unmistakably black. (I didn't bother to ask my parents why Sacramento garbage men always were black. I thought I knew.) One morning I was in the backyard when a man opened the gate. He was an ugly, square-faced black man with popping red eyes, a pail slung over his shoulder. As he approached, I stood up. And in a voice that seemed to me very weak, I piped, "Hi." But the man paid me no heed. He strode past to the can by the garage. In a single broad movement, he overturned its contents into his larger pail. Our can came crashing down as he turned and left me watching, in awe.

"Pobres negros," my mother remarked when she'd notice a headline in the paper about a civil rights demonstration in the South. "How the *gringos* mistreat them." In the same tone of voice she'd tell me about the mistreatment her brother endured years before. (After my grandfather's death, my grandmother had come to America with her son and five daughters.) "My sisters, we were still all just teenagers. And since *mi pápa* was dead, my brother had to be the head of the family. He had to support us, to find work. But what skills did he have! Twenty years old. *Pobre.* He was tall, like your grandfather. And strong. He did construction work. 'Construction!' The *gringos* kept him digging all day, doing the dirtiest jobs. And they would pay him next to nothing. Sometimes they promised him one salary and paid him less when he finished. But what could he do? Report them? We weren't citizens then. He didn't even know English. And he was dark. What chances could he have? As soon as we sisters got older, he went right back to Mexico. He hated this country. He looked so tired when he left. Already with a hunchback. Still in his twenties. But old-looking. No life for him here. *Pobre.*"

Dark skin was for my mother the most important symbol of a life of oppressive labor and poverty. But both my parents recognized other symbols as well.

My father noticed the feel of every hand he shook. (He'd smile sometimes—marvel more than scorn—remembering a man he'd met who had soft, uncalloused hands.)

My mother would grab a towel in the kitchen and rub my oily face sore when I came in from playing outside. "Clean the *graza* off your face!" *(Greaser!)*

Symbols: When my older sister, then in high school, asked my mother if she could do light housework in the afternoons for a rich lady we knew, my mother was frightened by the idea. For several weeks she troubled over it before granting conditional permission: "Just remember, you're not a maid. I don't want you wearing a uniform." My father echoed the same warning. Walking with him past a hotel, I watched as he stared at a doorman dressed like a Beefeater. "How can anyone let himself be dressed up like that? Like a clown. Don't you ever get a job where you have to put on a uniform." In summertime neighbors would ask me if I wanted to earn extra money by mowing their lawns. Again and again my mother worried: "Why did they ask *you*? Can't you find anything better?" Inevitably, she'd relent. She knew I needed the money. But I was instructed to work after dinner. ("When the sun's not so hot.") Even then, I'd have to wear a hat. *Un sombrero de* baseball.

(Sombrero. Watching gray cowboy movies, I'd brood over the meaning of the broad-rimmed hat—that troubling symbol—which comically distinguished a Mexican cowboy from real cowboys.)

From my father came no warnings concerning the sun. His fear was of dark factory jobs. He remembered too well his first jobs when he came to this country, not intending to stay, just to earn money enough to sail on to Australia. (In Mexico he had heard too many stories of discrimination in *Los Estados Unidos.* So it was Australia, that distant island-continent, that loomed in his imagination as his "America.") The work my father found in San Francisco was work for the unskilled. A factory job. Then a cannery job. (He'd remember the noise and the heat.) Then a job at a warehouse. (He'd remember the dark stench of old urine.) At one place there were fistfights; at another a supervisor who hated Chinese and Mexicans. Nowhere a union.

His memory of himself in those years is held by those jobs. Never making money enough for passage to Australia; slowly giving up the plan of returning to school to resume his third grade education–to become an engineer. My memory of him in those years, however, is lifted from photographs in the family album which show him on his honeymoon with my mother–the woman who had convinced him to stay in America. I have studied their photographs often, seeking to find in those figures some clear resemblance to the man and the woman I've known as my parents. But the youthful faces in the photos remain, behind dark glasses, shadowy figures anticipating my mother and father.

They are pictured on the grounds of the Coronado Hotel near San Diego, standing in the pale light of a winter afternoon. She is wearing slacks. Her hair falls seductively over one side of her face. He appears wearing a double-breasted suit, an unneeded raincoat draped over his arm. Another shows them standing together, solemnly staring ahead. Their shoulders barely are touching. There is to their pose an aristocratic formality, an elegant Latin hauteur.

The man in those pictures is the same man who was fascinated by Italian grand opera. I have never known just what my father saw in the spectacle, but he has told me that he would take my mother to the Opera House every Friday night–if he had money enough for orchestra seats. ("Why go to sit in the balcony?") On Sundays he'd don Italian silk scarves and a camel's hair coat to take his new wife to the polo matches in Golden Gate Park. But one weekend my father stopped going to the opera and polo matches. He would blame the change in his life on one job   a warehouse job, working for a large corporation which today advertises its products with the smiling faces of children. "They made me an old man before my time," he'd say to me many years later. Afterward, jobs got easier and cleaner. Eventually, in middle age, he got a job making false teeth. But his youth was spent at the warehouse. "Everything changed," his wife remembers. The dapper young man in the old photographs yielded to the man I saw after dinner: haggard, asleep on the sofa. During "The Ed Sullivan Show" on Sunday nights, when Roberta Peters or Licia Albanese would appear on the tiny blue screen, his head would jerk up alert. He'd sit forward while the notes of Puccini sounded before him. ("Un bel dí.")

By the time they had a family, my parents no longer dressed in very fine clothes. Those symbols of great wealth and the reality of their lives too noisily clashed. No longer did they try to fit themselves, like paper-doll figures, behind trappings so foreign to their actual lives. My father no longer wore silk scarves or expensive wool suits. He sold his tuxedo to a second-hand store for five dollars. My mother sold her rabbit fur coat to the wife of a Spanish radio station disc jockey. ("It looks better on you than it does on me," she kept telling the lady until the sale was completed.) I was six years old at the time, but I recall watching the transaction with complete understanding. The woman I knew as my mother was already physically unlike the woman in her honeymoon photos. My mother's hair was short. Her shoulders were thick from carrying children. Her fingers were swollen red, toughened by housecleaning. Already my mother would admit to foreseeing herself in her own mother, a woman grown old, bald and bowlegged, after a hard lifetime of working.

In their manner, both my parents continued to respect the symbols of what they considered to be upper-class life. Very early, they taught me the *propria* way of eating *como los ricos*. And I was carefully taught elaborate formulas of polite greeting and parting. The dark little boy would be invited by classmates to the rich houses on Forty-fourth and Forty-fifth streets. "How do you do?" or "I am very pleased to meet you," I would say, bowing slightly to the amused mothers of classmates. "Thank you very much for the dinner; it was very delicious."

I made an impression. I intended to make an impression, to be invited back. (I soon realized that the trick was to get the mother or father to notice me.) From those early days began my association with rich people, my fascination with their secret. My mother worried. She warned me not to come home expecting to have the things my friends possessed. But she needn't have said anything. When I went to the big houses, I remembered that I was, at best, a visitor to the world I saw there. For that reason, I was an especially watchful guest. I was my parents' child. Things most middle-class children wouldn't trouble to notice, I studied. Remembered to see: the starched black and white uniform worn by the maid who opened the door; the Mexican gardeners—their complexions as dark as my own. (One gardener's face, glassed by sweat, looked up to see me going inside.)

"Take Richard upstairs and show him your electric train," the mother said. But it was really the vast polished dining room table I'd come to appraise. Those nights when I was invited to stay for dinner, I'd notice that my friend's mother rang a small silver bell to tell the black woman when to bring in the food. The father, at his end of the table, ate while wearing his tie. When I was not required to speak, I'd skate the icy cut of crystal with my eye; my gaze would follow the golden threads etched onto the rim of china. With my mother's eyes I'd see my hostess's manicured nails and judge them to be marks of her leisure. Later, when my schoolmate's father would bid me goodnight, I would feel his soft fingers and palm when we shook hands. And turning to leave, I'd see my dark self, lit by chandelier light, in a tall hallway mirror.

2

Complexion. My first conscious experience of sexual excitement concerns my complexion. One summer weekend, when I was around seven years old, I was at a public swimming pool with the whole family. I remember sitting on the damp pavement next to the pool and seeing my mother in the spectators' bleachers, holding my younger sister on her lap. My mother, I noticed, was watching my father as he stood on a diving board, waving to her. I watched her wave back. Then saw her radiant, bashful, astonishing smile. In that second I sensed that my mother and father had a relationship I knew nothing about. A nervous excitement encircled my stomach as I saw my mother's eyes follow my father's figure curving into the water. A second or two later, he emerged. I heard him call out. Smiling, his voice sounded, buoyant, calling me to swim to him. But turning to see him, I caught my mother's eye. I heard her shout over to me. In Spanish she called through the crowd: "Put a towel on over your shoulders." In public, she didn't want to say why. I knew.

That incident anticipates the shame and sexual inferiority I was to feel in later years because of my dark complexion. I was to grow up an ugly child. Or one who thought himself ugly. (*Feo.*) One night when I was eleven or twelve years old, I locked myself in the bathroom and carefully regarded my reflection in the mirror over the sink. Without any pleasure I studied my skin. I turned on the faucet. (In my mind I heard the swirling voices of aunts, and even my mother's voice, whispering, whispering incessantly about lemon juice solutions and dark, *feo* children.) With a bar of soap, I fashioned a thick ball of lather. I began soaping my arms. I took my father's straight razor out of the medicine cabinet. Slowly, with steady deliberateness, I put the blade against my flesh, pressed it as close as I could without cutting, and moved it up and down across my skin to see if I could get out, somehow lessen, the dark. All I succeeded in doing, however, was in shaving my arms bare of their hair. For as I noted with disappointment, the dark would not come out. It remained. Trapped. Deep in the cells of my skin.

Throughout adolescence, I felt myself mysteriously marked. Nothing else about my appearance would concern me so much as the fact that my complexion was dark. My mother would say how sorry she was that there was not money enough to get braces to straighten my teeth. But I never bothered about my teeth. In three-way mirrors at department stores, I'd see my profile dramatically defined by a long nose, but it was really only the color of my skin that caught my attention.

I wasn't afraid that I would become a menial laborer because of my skin. Nor did my complexion make me feel especially vulnerable to racial abuse. (I didn't really consider my dark skin to be a racial characteristic. I would have been only too happy to look as Mexican as my light-skinned older brother.) Simply, I judged myself ugly. And, since the women in my family had been the ones who discussed it in such worried tones, I felt my dark skin made me unattractive to women.

Thirteen years old. Fourteen. In a grammar school art class, when the assignment was to draw a self-portrait, I tried and I tried but could not bring myself to shade in the face on the paper to anything like my actual tone. With disgust then I would come face to face with myself in mirrors. With disappointment I located myself in class photographs—my dark face undefined by the camera which had clearly described the white faces of classmates. Or I'd see my dark wrist against my long-sleeved white shirt.

I grew divorced from my body. Insecure, overweight, listless. On hot summer days when my rubber-soled shoes soaked up the heat from the sidewalk, I kept my head down. Or walked in the shade. My mother didn't need anymore to tell me to watch out for the sun. I denied myself a sensational life. The normal, extraordinary, animal excitement of feeling my body alive—riding shirtless on a bicycle in the warm wind created by furious self-propelled motion—the sensations that first had excited in me a sense of my maleness, I denied. I was too ashamed of my body. I wanted to forget that I had a body because I had a brown body. I was grateful that none of my classmates ever mentioned the fact.

I continued to see the *braceros*, those men I resembled in one way and, in another way, didn't resemble at all. On the watery horizon of a Valley afternoon, I'd see them. And though I feared looking like them, it was with silent envy that I regarded them still. I envied their physical lives, their freedom to violate the taboo of the sun. Closer to home I would notice the shirtless construction workers, the roofers, the sweating men tarring the street in front of the house. And I'd see the Mexican gardeners. I was unwilling to admit the attraction of their lives. I tried to deny it by looking away. But what was denied became strongly desired.

In high school physical education classes, I withdrew, in the regular company of five or six classmates, to a distant corner of a football field where we smoked and talked. Our company was composed of bodies too short or too tall, all graceless and all—except mine—pale. Our conversation was usually witty. (In fact we were intelligent.) If we referred to the athletic contests around us, it was with sarcasm. With savage scorn I'd refer to the "animals" playing football or baseball. It would have been important for me to have joined them. Or for me to have taken off my shirt, to have let the sun burn dark on my skin, and to have run barefoot on the warm wet grass. It would have been very important. Too important. It would have been too telling a gesture—to admit the desire for sensation, the body, my body.

Fifteen, sixteen. I was a teenager shy in the presence of girls. Never dated. Barely could talk to a girl without stammering. In high school I went to several dances, but I never managed to ask a girl to dance. So I stopped going. I cannot remember high school years now with the parade of typical images: bright drive-ins or gliding blue shadows of a Junior Prom. At home most weekend nights, I would pass evenings reading. Like those hidden, precocious adolescents who have no real-life sexual experiences, I read a great deal of romantic fiction. "You won't find it in your books," my brother would playfully taunt me as he prepared to go to a party by freezing the crest of the wave in his hair with sticky pomade. Through my reading, however, I developed a fabulous and sophisticated sexual imagination. At seventeen, I may not have known how to engage a girl in small talk, but I had read *Lady Chatterly's Lover*.

It annoyed me to hear my father's teasing: that I would never know what "real work" is; that my hands were so soft. I think I knew it was his way of admitting pleasure and pride in my academic success. But I didn't smile. My mother said she was glad her children were getting their educations and would not be pushed around like *los pobres*. I heard the remark ironically as a reminder of my separation from *los braceros*. At such times I suspected that education was making me effeminate. The odd thing, however, was that I did not judge my classmates so harshly. Nor did I consider my male teachers in high school effeminate. It was only myself I judged against some shadowy, mythical Mexican laborer—dark like me, yet very different.

Language was crucial. I knew that I had violated the ideal of the *macho* by becoming such a dedicated student of language and literature. *Machismo* was a word never exactly defined by the persons who used it. (It was best described in the "proper" behavior of men.) Women at home, nevertheless, would repeat the old Mexican dictum that a man should be *feo, fuerte, y formal.* "The three F's," my mother called them, smiling slyly. *Feo* I took to mean not literally ugly so much as ruggedly handsome. (When my mother and her sisters spent a loud, laughing afternoon determining ideal male good looks, they finally settled on the actor Gilbert Roland, who was neither too pretty nor ugly but had looks "like a man.") *Fuerte,* "strong," seemed to mean not physical strength as much as inner strength, character. A dependable man is *fuerte. Fuerte* for that reason was a characteristic subsumed by the last of the three qualities, and the one I most often considered—*formal.* To be *formal* is to be steady. A man of responsibility, a good provider. Someone *formal* is also constant. A person to be relied upon in adversity. A sober man, a man of high seriousness.

I learned a great deal about being *formal* just by listening to the way my father and other male relatives of his generation spoke. A man was not silent necessarily. Nor was he limited in the tones he could sound. For example, he could tell a long, involved, humorous story and laugh at his own humor with high-pitched giggling. But a man was not talkative the way a woman could be. It was permitted a woman to be gossipy and chatty. (When one heard many voices in a room, it was usually women who were talking.) Men spoke much less rapidly. And often men spoke in monologues. (When one voice sounded in a crowded room, it was most often a man's voice one heard.) More important than any of this was the fact that a man never verbally revealed his emotions. Men did not speak about their unease in moments of crisis or danger. It was the woman who worried aloud when her husband got laid off from work. At times of illness or death in the family, a man was usually quiet, even silent. Women spoke up to voice prayers. In distress, women always sounded quick ejaculations to God or the Virgin; women prayed in clearly audible voices at a wake held in a funeral parlor. And on the subject of love, a woman was verbally expansive. She spoke of her yearning and delight. A married man, if he spoke publicly about love, usually did so with playful, mischievous irony. Younger, unmarried men more often were quiet. (The *macho* is a silent suitor. *Formal.*)

At home I was quiet, so perhaps I seemed *formal* to my relations and other Spanish-speaking visitors to the house. But outside the house—my God!—I talked. Particularly in class or alone with my teachers, I chattered. (Talking seemed to make teachers think I was bright.) I often was proud of my way with words. Though, on other occasions, for example, when I would hear my mother busily speaking to women, it would occur to me that my attachment to words made me like her. Her son. Not *formal* like my father. At such times I even suspected that my nostalgia for sounds—the noisy, intimate Spanish sounds of my past—was nothing more than effeminate yearning.

High school English teachers encouraged me to describe very personal feelings in words. Poems and short stories I wrote, expressing sorrow and loneliness, were awarded high grades. In my bedroom were books by poets and novelists—books that I loved—in which male writers published feelings the men in my family never revealed or acknowledged in words. And it seemed to me that there was something unmanly about my attachment to literature. Even today, when so much about the myth of the *macho* no longer concerns me, I cannot altogether evade such notions. Writing these pages, admitting my embarrassment or my guilt, admitting my sexual anxieties and my physical insecurity, I have not been able to forget that I am not being *formal*.

So be it.

3

I went to college at Stanford, attracted partly by its academic reputation, partly because it was the school rich people went to. I found myself on a campus with golden children of western America's upper middle class. Many were students both ambitious for academic success *and* accustomed to leisured life in the sun. In the afternoon, they lay spread out, sunbathing in front of the library, reading Swift or Engels or Beckett. Others went by in convertibles, off to play tennis or ride horses or sail. Beach boys dressed in tank-tops and shorts were my classmates in undergraduate seminars. Tall tan girls wearing white strapless dresses sat directly in front of me in lecture rooms. I'd study them, their physical confidence. I was still recognizably kin to the boy I had been. Less tortured perhaps. But still kin. At Stanford, it's true, I began to have something like a conventional sexual life. I don't think, however, that I really believed that the women I knew found me physically appealing. I continued to stay out of the sun. I didn't linger in mirrors. And I was the student at Stanford who remembered to notice the Mexican-American janitors and gardeners working on the campus.

It was at Stanford, one day near the end of my senior year, that a friend told me about a summer construction job he knew was available. I was quickly alert. Desire uncoiled within me. My friend said that he knew I had been looking for summer employment. He knew I needed some money. Almost apologetically he explained: It was something I probably wouldn't be interested in, but a friend of his, a contractor, needed someone for the summer to do menial jobs. There would be lots of shoveling and raking and sweeping. Nothing too hard. But nothing more interesting either. Still, the pay would be good. Did I want it? Or did I know someone who did?

I did. Yes, I said, surprised to hear myself say it.

In the weeks following, friends cautioned that I had no idea how hard physical labor really is. ("You only *think* you know what it is like to shovel for eight hours straight.") Their objections seemed to me challenges. They resolved the issue. I became happy with the plan. I decided, however, not to tell my parents. I wouldn't tell my mother because I could guess her worried reaction. I would tell my father only after the summer was over, when I could announce that, after all, I did know what "real work" is like.

The day I met the contractor (a Princeton graduate, it turned out), he asked me whether I had done any physical labor before. "In high school, during the summer," I lied. And although he seemed to regard me with skepticism, he decided to give me a try. Several days later, expectant, I arrived at my first construction site. I would take off my shirt to the sun. And at last grasp desired sensation. No longer afraid. At last become like a *bracero*. "We need those tree stumps out of here by tomorrow," the contractor said. I started to work.

I labored with excitement that first morning–and all the days after. The work was harder than I could have expected. But it was never as tedious as my friends had warned me it would be. There was too much physical pleasure in the labor. Especially early in the day, I would be most alert to the sensations of movement and straining. Beginning around seven each morning (when the air was still damp but the scent of weeds and dry earth anticipated the heat of the sun), I would feel my body resist the first thrusts of the shovel. My arms, tightened by sleep, would gradually loosen; after only several minutes, sweat would gather in beads on my forehead and then—a short while later—I would feel my chest silky with sweat in the breeze. I would return to my work. A nervous spark of pain would fly up my arm and settle to burn like an ember in the thick of my shoulder. An hour, two passed. Three. My whole body would assume regular movements; my shoveling would be described by identical, even movements. Even later in the day, my enthusiasm for primitive sensation would survive the heat and the dust and the insects pricking my back. I would strain wildly for sensation as the day came to a close. At three-thirty, quitting time, I would stand upright and slowly let my head fall back, luxuriating in the feeling of tightness relieved.

Some of the men working nearby would watch me and laugh. Two or three of the older men took the trouble to teach me the right way to use a pick, the correct way to shovel. "You're doing it wrong, too fucking hard," one man scolded. Then proceeded to show me—what persons who work with their bodies all their lives quickly learn—the most economical way to use one's body in labor.

"Don't make your back do so much work," he instructed. I stood impatiently listening, half listening, vaguely watching, then noticed his work-thickened fingers clutching the shovel. I was annoyed. I wanted to tell him that I enjoyed shoveling the wrong way. And I didn't want to learn the right way. I wasn't afraid of back pain. I liked the way my body felt sore at the end of the day.

I was about to, but, as it turned out, I didn't say a thing. Rather it was at that moment I realized that I was fooling myself if I expected a few weeks of labor to gain me admission to the world of the laborer. I would not learn in three months what my father had meant by "real work." I was not bound to this job; I could imagine its rapid conclusion. For me the sensations of exertion and fatigue could be savored. For my father or uncle, working at comparable jobs when they were my age, such sensations were to be feared. Fatigue took a different toll on their bodies—and minds.

It was, I know, a simple insight. But it was with this realization that I took my first step that summer toward realizing something even more important about the "worker." In the company of carpenters, electricians, plumbers, and painters at lunch, I would often sit quietly, observant. I was not shy in such company. I felt easy, pleased by the knowledge that I was casually accepted, my presence taken for granted by men (exotics) who worked with their hands. Some days the younger men would talk and talk about sex, and they would howl at women who drove by in cars. Other days the talk at lunchtime was subdued; men gathered in separate groups. It depended on who was around. There were rough, good-natured workers. Others were quiet. The more I remember that summer, the more I realize that there was no single *type* of worker. I am embarrassed to say I had not expected such diversity. I certainly had not expected to meet, for example, a plumber who was an abstract painter in his off hours and admired the work of Mark Rothko. Nor did I expect to meet so many workers with college diplomas. (They were the ones who were not surprised that I intended to enter graduate school in the fall.) I suppose what I really want to say here is painfully obvious, but I must say it nevertheless: The men of that summer were middle-class Americans. They certainly didn't constitute an oppressed society. Carefully completing their work sheets; talking about the fortunes of local football teams; planning Las Vegas vacations; comparing the gas mileage of various makes of campers—they were not *los pobres* my mother had spoken about.

On two occasions, the contractor hired a group of Mexican aliens. They were employed to cut down some trees and haul off debris. In all, there were six men of varying age. The youngest in his late twenties; the oldest (his father?) perhaps sixty years old. They came and they left in a single old truck. Anonymous men. They were never introduced to the other men at the site. Immediately upon their arrival, they would follow the contractor's directions, start working—rarely resting—seemingly driven by a fatalistic sense that work which had to be done was best done as quickly as possible.

I watched them sometimes. Perhaps they watched me. The only time I saw them pay me much notice was one day at lunchtime when I was laughing with the other men. The Mexicans sat apart when they ate, just as they worked by themselves. Quiet. I rarely heard them say much to each other. All I could hear were their voices calling out sharply to one another, giving directions. Otherwise, when they stood briefly resting, they talked among themselves in voices too hard to overhear.

The contractor knew enough Spanish, and the Mexicans—or at least the oldest of them, their spokesman—seemed to know enough English to communicate. But because I was around, the contractor decided one day to make me his translator. (He assumed I could speak Spanish.) I did what I was told. Shyly I went over to tell the Mexicans that the *patrón* wanted them to do something else before they left for the day. As I started to speak, I was afraid with my old fear that I would be unable to pronounce the Spanish words. But it was a simple instruction I had to convey. I could say it in phrases.

The dark sweating faces turned toward me as I spoke. They stopped their work to hear me. Each nodded in response. I stood there. I wanted to say something more. But what could I say in Spanish, even if I could have pronounced the words right? Perhaps I just wanted to engage them in small talk, to be assured of their confidence, our familiarity. I thought for a moment to ask them where in Mexico they were from. Something like that. And maybe I wanted to tell them (a lie, if need be) that my parents were from the same part of Mexico.

I stood there.

Their faces watched me. The eyes of the man directly in front of me moved slowly over my shoulder, and I turned to follow his glance toward *el patrón* some distance away. For a moment I felt swept up by that glance into the Mexicans' company. But then I heard one of them returning to work. And then the others went back to work. I left them without saying anything more.

When they had finished, the contractor went over to pay them in cash. (He later told me that he paid them collectively—"for the job," though he wouldn't tell me their wages. He said something quickly about the good rate of exchange "in their own country.") I can still hear the loudly confident voice he used with the Mexicans. It was the sound of the *gringo* I had heard as a very young boy. And I can still hear the quiet, indistinct sounds of the Mexican, the oldest, who replied. At hearing that voice I was sad for the Mexicans. Depressed by their vulnerability. Angry at myself. The adventure of the summer seemed suddenly ludicrous. I would not shorten the distance I felt from *los pobres* with a few weeks of physical labor. I would not become like them. They were different from me.

After that summer, a great deal—and not very much really—changed in my life. The curse of physical shame was broken by the sun; I was no longer ashamed of my body. No longer would I deny myself the pleasing sensations of my maleness. During those years when middle-class black Americans began to assert with pride, "Black is beautiful," I was able to regard my complexion without shame. I am today darker than I ever was as a boy. I have taken up the middle-class sport of long-distance running. Nearly every day now I run ten or fifteen miles, barely clothed, my skin exposed to the California winter rain and wind or the summer sun of late afternoon. The torso, the soccer player's calves and thighs, the arms of the twenty-year-old I never was, I possess now in my thirties. I study the youthful parody shape in the mirror: the stomach lipped tight by muscle; the shoulders rounded by chin-ups; the arms veined strong. This man. A man. I meet him. He laughs to see me, what I have become.

The dandy. I wear double-breasted Italian suits and custom-made English shoes. I resemble no one so much as my father—the man pictured in those honeymoon photos. At that point in life when he abandoned the dandy's posture, I assume it. At the point when my parents would not consider going on vacation, I register at the Hotel Carlyle in New York and the Plaza Athenée in Paris. I am as taken by the symbols of leisure and wealth as they were. For my parents, however, those symbols became taunts, reminders of all they could not achieve in one lifetime. For me those same symbols are reassuring reminders of public success. I tempt vulgarity to be reassured. I am filled with the gaudy delight, the monstrous grace of the nouveau riche.

In recent years I have had occasion to lecture in ghetto high schools. There I see students of remarkable style and physical grace. (One can see more dandies in such schools than one ever will find in middle-class high schools.) There is not the look of casual assurance I saw students at Stanford display. Ghetto girls mimic high-fashion models. Their dresses are of bold, forceful color; their figures elegant, long; the stance theatrical. Boys wear shirts that grip at their overdeveloped muscular bodies. (Against a powerless future, they engage images of strength.) Bad nutrition does not yet tell. Great disappointment, fatal to youth, awaits them still. For the moment, movements in school hallways are dancelike, a procession of postures in a sexual masque. Watching them, I feel a kind of envy. I wonder how different my adolescence would have been had I been free. . . . But no, it is my parents I see—their optimism during those years when they were entertained by Italian grand opera.

The registration clerk in London wonders if I have just been to Switzerland. And the man who carries my luggage in New York guesses the Caribbean. My complexion becomes a mark of my leisure. Yet no one would regard my complexion the same way if I entered such hotels through the service entrance. That is only to say that my complexion assumes its significance from the context of my life. My skin, in itself, means nothing. I stress the point because I know there are people who would label me "disadvantaged" because of my color. They make the same mistake I made as a boy, when I thought a disadvantaged life was circumscribed by particular occupations. That summer I worked in the sun may have made me physically indistinguishable from the Mexicans working nearby. (My skin was actually darker because, unlike them, I worked without wearing a shirt. By late August my hands were probably as tough as theirs.) But I was not one of *los pobres*. What made me different from them was an attitude of *mind*, my imagination of myself.

I do not blame my mother for warning me away from the sun when I was young. In a world where her brother had become an old man in his twenties because he was dark, my complexion was something to worry about. "Don't run in the sun," she warns me today. I run. In the end, my father was right–though perhaps he did not know how right or why–to say that I would never know what real work is. I will never know what he felt at his last factory job. If tomorrow I worked at some kind of factory, it would go differently for me. My long education would favor me. I could act as a public person–able to defend my interests, to unionize, to petition, to speak up–to challenge and demand. (I will never know what real work is.) I will never know what the Mexicans knew, gathering their shovels and ladders and saws.

Their silence stays with me now. The wages those Mexicans received for their labor were only a measure of their disadvantaged condition. Their silence is more telling. They lack a public identity. They remain profoundly alien. Persons apart. People lacking a union obviously, people without grounds. They depend upon the relative good will or fairness of their employers each day. For such people, lacking a better alternative, it is not such an unreasonable risk.

Their silence stays with me. I have taken these many words to describe its impact. Only: the quiet. Something uncanny about it. Its compliance. Vulnerability. Pathos. As I heard their truck rumbling away, I shuddered, my face mirrored with sweat. I had finally come face to face with *los pobres*.

7. Bill and Irene Collins, a young married couple, decided to buy on the installment plan some things they needed for their home. They bought table silver for $60. They paid $10 down, a $4.50 carrying charge, and monthly payments of $7. How long did it take Bill and Irene to pay for the silver?

$$50 - 4.50 = 45.50$$

7 MONTHS

Jon E. Tower
Solved Problem # 170

Age, Race, Class, and Sex:
Women Redefining Difference

Much of Western European history conditions us to see human differences in simplistic opposition to each other: dominant/subordinate, good/bad, up/down, superior/inferior. In a society where the good is defined in terms of profit rather than in terms of human need, there must always be some group of people who, through systematized oppression, can be made to feel surplus, to occupy the space of the dehumanized inferior. Within this society, that group is made up of Black and Third World people, working-class people, older people, and women.

As a forty-nine year old Black lesbian feminist socialist mother of two, including one boy, and a member of an inter-racial couple, I usually find myself a part of some group defined as other, deviant, inferior, or just plain wrong. Traditionally, in american society, it is the members of oppressed, objectified groups who are expected to stretch out and bridge the gap between the actualities of our lives and the consciousness of our oppressor. For in order to survive, those of us for whom oppression is as american as apple pie have always had to be watchers, to become familiar with the language and manners of the oppressor, even sometimes adopting them for some illusion of protection. Whenever the need for some pretense of communication arises, those who profit from our oppression call upon us to share our knowledge with them. In other words, it is the responsibility of the oppressed to teach the oppressors their mistakes. I am responsible for educating teachers who dismiss my children's culture in school. Black and Third World people are expected to educate white people as to our humanity. Women are expected to educate men. Lesbians and gay men are expected to educate the heterosexual world. The oppressors maintain their position and evade responsibility for their own actions. There is a constant drain of energy which might be better used in redefining ourselves and devising realistic scenarios for altering the present and constructing the future.

Institutionalized rejection of difference is an absolute necessity in a profit economy which needs outsiders as surplus people. As members of such an economy, we have *all* been programmed to respond to the human differences between us with fear and loathing and to handle that difference in one of three ways: ignore it, and if that is not possible, copy it if we think it is dominant, or destroy it if we think it is subordinate. But we have no patterns for relating across our human differences as equals. As a result, those differences have been misnamed and misused in the service of separation and confusion.

Certainly there are very real differences between us of race, age, and sex. But it is not those differences between us that are separating us. It is rather our refusal to recognize those differences, and to examine the distortions which result from our misnaming them and their effects upon human behavior and expectation.

Racism, the belief in the inherent superiority of one race over all others and thereby the right to dominance. Sexism, the belief in the inherent superiority of one sex over the other and thereby the right to dominance. Ageism. Heterosexism. Elitism. Classism.

It is a lifetime pursuit for each one of us to extract these distortions from our living at the same time as we recognize, reclaim, and define those differences upon which they are imposed. For we have all been raised in a society where those distortions were endemic within our living. Too often, we pour the energy needed for recognizing and exploring difference into pretending those differences are insurmountable barriers, or that they do not exist at all. This results in a voluntary isolation, or false and treacherous connections. Either way, we do not develop tools for using human difference as a springboard for creative change within our lives. We speak not of human difference, but of human deviance.

Somewhere, on the edge of consciousness, there is what I call a *mythical norm*, which each one of us within our hearts knows "that is not me." In america, this norm is usually defined as white, thin, male, young, heterosexual, christian, and financially secure. It is with this mythical norm that the trappings of power reside within this society. Those of us who stand outside that power often identify one way in which we are different, and we assume that to be the primary cause of all oppression, forgetting other distortions around difference, some of which we ourselves may be practising. By and large within the women's movement today, white women focus upon their oppression as women and ignore differences of race, sexual preference, class, and age. There is a pretense to a homogeneity of experience covered by the word *sisterhood* that does not in fact exist.

Unacknowledged class differences rob women of each others' energy and creative insight. Recently a women's magazine collective made the decision for one issue to print only prose, saying poetry was a less "rigorous" or "serious" art form. Yet even the form our creativity takes is often a class issue. Of all the art forms, poetry is the most economical. It is the one which is the most secret, which requires the least physical labor, the least material, and the one which can be done between shifts, in the hospital pantry, on the subway, and on scraps of surplus paper. Over the last few years, writing a novel on tight finances, I came to appreciate the enormous differences in the material demands between poetry and prose. As we reclaim our literature, poetry has been the major voice of poor, working class, and Colored women. A room of one's own may be a necessity for writing prose, but so are reams of paper, a typewriter, and plenty of time. The actual requirements to produce the visual arts also help determine, along class lines, whose art is whose. In this day of inflated prices for material, who are our sculptors, our painters, our photographers? When we speak of a broadly based women's culture, we need to be aware of the effect of class and economic differences on the supplies available for producing art.

As we move toward creating a society within which we can each flourish, ageism is another distortion of relationship which interferes without vision. By ignoring the past, we are encouraged to repeat its mistakes. The "generation gap" is an important social tool for any repressive society. If the younger members of a community view the older members as contemptible or suspect or excess, they will never be able to join hands and examine the living memories of the community, nor ask the all important question, "Why?" This gives rise to a historical amnesia that keeps us working to invent the wheel every time we have to go to the store for bread.

We find ourselves having to repeat and relearn the same old lessons over and over that our mothers did because we do not pass on what we have learned, or because we are unable to listen. For instance, how many times has this all been said before? For another, who would have believed that once again our daughters are allowing their bodies to be hampered and purgatoried by girdles and high heels and hobble skirts?

Ignoring the differences of race between women and the implications of those differences presents the most serious threat to the mobilization of women's joint power.

As white women ignore their built-in privilege of whiteness and define *woman* in terms of their own experience alone, women of Color become "other," the outsider whose experience and tradition is too "alien" to comprehend. An example of this is the signal absence of the experience of women of Color as a resource for women's studies courses. The literature of women of Color is seldom included in women's literature courses and almost never in other literature courses, nor in women's studies as a whole. All too often, the excuse given is that the literatures of women of Color can only be taught by Colored women, or that they are too difficult to understand, or that classes cannot "get into" them because they come out of experiences that are "too different." I have heard this argument presented by white women of otherwise quite clear intelligence, women who seem to have no trouble at all teaching and reviewing work that comes out of the vastly different experiences of Shakespeare, Molière, Dostoyevsky, and Aristophanes. Surely there must be some other explanation.

This is a very complex question, but I believe one of the reasons white women have such difficulty reading Black women's work is because of their reluctance to see Black women as women and different from themselves. To examine Black women's literature effectively requires that we be seen as whole people in our actual complexities—as individuals, as women, as human—rather than as one of those problematic but familiar stereotypes provided in this society in place of genuine images of Black women. And I believe this holds true for the literatures of other women of Color who are not Black.

The literatures of all women of Color recreate the textures of our lives, and many white women are heavily invested in ignoring the real differences. For as long as any difference between us means one of us must be inferior, then the recognition of any difference must be fraught with guilt. To allow women of Color to step out of stereotypes is too guilt provoking, for it threatens the complacency of those women who view oppression only in terms of sex.

Refusing to recognize difference makes it impossible to see the different problems and pitfalls facing us as women.

Thus, in a patriarchal power system where whiteskin privilege is a major prop, the entrapments used to neutralize Black women and white women are not the same. For example, it is easy for Black women to be used by the power structure against Black men, not because they are men, but because they are Black. Therefore, for Black women, it is necessary at all times to separate the needs of the oppressor from our own legitimate conflicts within our communities. This same problem does not exist for white women. Black women and men have shared racist oppression and still share it, although in different ways. Out of that shared oppression we have developed joint defenses and joint vulnerabilities to each other that are not duplicated in the white community, with the exception of the relationship between Jewish women and Jewish men.

On the other hand, white women face the pitfall of being seduced into joining the oppressor under the pretense of sharing power. This possibility does not exist in the same way for women of Color. The tokenism that is sometimes extended to us is not an invitation to join power; our racial "otherness" is a visible reality that makes that quite clear. For white women there is a wider range of pretended choices and rewards for identifying with patriarchal power and its tools.

Today, with the defeat of ERA, the tightening economy and increased conservatism, it is easier once again for white women to believe the dangerous fantasy that if you are good enough, pretty enough, sweet enough, quiet enough, teach the children to behave, hate the right people, and marry the right men, then you will be allowed to co-exist with patriarchy in relative peace, at least until a man needs your job or the neighborhood rapist happens along. And true, unless one lives and loves in the trenches it is difficult to remember that the war against dehumanization is ceaseless.

But Black women and our children know the fabric of our lives is stitched with violence and with hatred, that there is no rest. We do not deal with it only on the picket lines, or in dark midnight alleys, or in the places where we dare to verbalize our resistance. For us, increasingly, violence weaves through the daily tissues of our living—in the supermarket, in the classroom, in the elevator, in the clinic and the schoolyard, from the plumber, the baker, the saleswoman, the bus driver, the bank teller, the waitress who does not serve us.

Some problems we share as women, some we do not. You fear your children will grow up to join the patriarchy and testify against you. We fear our children will be dragged from a car and shot down in the street, and you will turn your backs upon the reasons they are dying.

The threat of difference has been no less blinding to people of Color. Those of us who are Black must see that the reality of our lives and our struggle does not make us immune to the errors of ignoring and misnaming difference. Within Black communities where racism is a living reality, differences among us often seem dangerous and suspect. The need for unity is often misnamed as a need for homogeneity, and a Black feminist vision mistaken for betrayal of our common interests as a people. Because of the continuous battle against racial erasure that Black women and Black men share, some Black women still refuse to recognize that we are also oppressed as women, and that sexual hostility against Black women is practiced not only by the white racist society, but implemented within our Black communities as well. It is a disease striking the heart of Black nationhood, and silence will not make it disappear. Exacerbated by racism and the pressures of powerlessness, violence against Black women and children often becomes a standard within our commmunities, one by which manliness can be measured. But these woman-hating acts are rarely discussed as crimes against Black women.

As a group, women of Color are the lowest paid wage earners in america. We are the primary targets of abortion and sterilization abuse, here and abroad. In certain parts of Africa, small girls are still being sewed shut between their legs to keep them docile and for men's pleasure. This is known as female circumcision, and it is not a cultural affair as the late Jomo Kenyatta insisted. It is a crime against Black women.

Black women's literature is full of the pain of frequent assault, not only by a racist patriarchy, but also by Black men. Yet the necessity for and history of shared battle have made us, Black women, particularly vulnerable to the false accusation that anti-sexist is anti-Black. Meanwhile, woman-hating as a recourse of the powerless is sapping strength from Black communities, and our very lives. Rape is on the increase, reported and unreported, and rape is not aggressive sexuality, it is sexualized aggression. As Kalamu ya Salaam, a Black male writer points out, "As long as male domination exists, rape will exist. Only women revolting and men made conscious of their responsibility to fight sexism can collectively stop rape."[1]

Differences between ourselves as Black women are also being misnamed and used to separate us from one another. As a Black lesbian feminist comfortable with the many different ingredients of my identity, and a woman committed to racial and sexual freedom from oppression, I find I am constantly being encouraged to pluck out some one aspect of myself and present this as the meaningful whole, eclipsing or denying the other parts of myself. But this is a destructive and fragmenting way to live. My fullest concentration of energy is available to me only when I integrate all the parts of who I am, openly, allowing power from particular sources of my living to flow back and forth freely through all my different selves, without the restrictions of externally imposed definition. Only then can I bring myself and my energies as a whole to the service of those struggles which I embrace as part of my living.

A fear of lesbians, or of being accused of being a lesbian, has led many Black women into testifying against themselves. It has led some of us into destructive alliances, and others into despair and isolation. In the white women's communities, heterosexism is sometimes a result of identifying with the white patriarchy, a rejection of that interdependence between women-identified women which allows the self to be, rather than to be used in the service of men. Sometimes it reflects a die-hard belief in the protective coloration of heterosexual relationships, sometimes a self-hate which all women have to fight against, taught us from birth.

Although elements of these attitudes exist for all women, there are particular resonances of heterosexism and homophobia among Black women. Despite the fact that woman-bonding has a long and honorable history in the African and African-American communities, and despite the knowledge and accomplishments of many strong and creative women-identified Black women in the political, social and cultural fields, heterosexual Black women often tend to ignore or discount the existence and work of Black lesbians. Part of this attitude has come from an understandable terror of Black male attack within the close confines of Black society, where the punishment for any female self-assertion is still to be accused of being a lesbian and therefore unworthy of the attention or support of the scarce Black male. But part of this need to misname and ignore Black lesbians comes from a very real fear that openly women-identified Black women who are no longer dependent upon men for their self-definition may well reorder our whole concept of social relationships.

Black women who once insisted that lesbianism was a white woman's problem now insist that Black lesbians are a threat to Black nationhood, are consorting with the enemy, are basically un-Black. These accusations, coming from the very women to whom we look for deep and real understanding, have served to keep many Black lesbians in hiding, caught between the racism of white women and the homophobia of their sisters. Often, their work has been ignored, trivialized, or misnamed, as with the work of Angelina Grimke, Alice Dunbar-Nelson, and Lorraine Hansberry. Yet women-bonded women have always been some part of the power of Black communities, from our unmarried aunts to the amazons of Dahomey.

And it is certainly not Black lebians who are assaulting women and raping children and grandmothers on the streets of our communities.

Across this country, as in Boston during the spring of 1979 following the unsolved murders of twelve Black women, Black lesbians are spearheading movements against violence against Black women.

What are the particular details within each of our lives that can be scrutinized and altered to help bring about change? How do we redefine difference for all women? It is not our differences which separate women, but our reluctance to recognize those differences and to deal effectively with the distortions which have resulted from the ignoring and misnaming of those differences.

As a tool of social control, women have been encouraged to recognize only one area of human difference as legitimate, those differences which exist between women and men. And we have learned to deal across those differences with the urgency of all oppressed subordinates. All of us have had to learn to live or work or coexist with men, from our fathers on. We have recognized and negotiated these differences, even when this recognition only continued the old dominant/subordinate mode of human relationship, where the oppressed must recognize the masters' difference in order to survive.

But our future survival is predicated upon our ability to relate within equality. As women, we must root out internalized patterns of oppression within ourselves if we are to move beyond the most superficial aspects of social change. Now we must recognize differences among women who are our equals, neither inferior nor superior, and devise ways to use each others' difference to enrich our visions and our joint struggles.

The future of our earth may depend upon the ability of all women to identify and develop new definitions of power and new patterns of relating across difference. The old definitions have not served us, nor the earth that supports us. The old patterns, no matter how cleverly rearranged to imitate progress, still condemn us to cosmetically altered repetitions of the same old exchanges, the same old guilt, hatred, recrimination, lamentation, and suspicion.

For we have, built into all of us, old blueprints of expectation and response, old structures of oppression, and these must be altered at the same time as we alter the living conditions which are a result of those structures. For the master's tools will never dismantle the master's house.

As Paulo Freire shows so well in *The Pedagogy of the Oppressed*,[2] the true focus of revolutionary change is never merely the oppressive situations which we seek to escape, but that piece of the oppressor which is planted deep within each of us, and which knows only the oppressors' tactics, the oppressors' relationships.

Change means growth, and growth can be painful. But we sharpen self-definition by exposing the self in work and struggle, together with those whom we define as different from ourselves, although sharing the same goals. For Black and white, old and young, lesbian and heterosexual women alike, this can mean new paths to our survival.

> We have chosen each other
> and the edge of each others battles
> the war is the same
> if we lose
> someday women's blood will congeal
> upon a dead planet
> if we win
> there is no telling
> we seek beyond history
> for a new and more possible meeting.[3]

1. From "Rape: A Radical Analysis, An African-American Perspective" by Kalamu ya Salaam in *Black Books Bulletin*, vol. 6, no. 4 (1980).

2. Paulo Freire, *The Pedagogy of the Oppressed* (New York: Seabury Press, 1970).
3. From "Outlines," unpublished poem.

• **Richard Dyer**

Coming to Terms

The main suggestions I'd like to make in this essay about gay male pornographic cinema are quite brief and simple. Broadly I'm going to argue that the narrative structure of gay porn[1] is analogous to aspects of the social construction of both male sexuality in general and gay male sexual practice in particular. But before getting on to that it seems necessary to say a few things by way of introduction. Pornography has recently become a Big Topic in left cultural work,[2] and what I'm going to say needs to be situated in relation to this.

First, a definition—a working definition, the one I'm going to be working with here, rather than a statement of the correct definition of pornography. I want some definition that is as broadly descriptive as possible. Discussion about porn tends to start off by being either for or against all porn and to be caught up in equally dubious libertarian or puritanical ideas. I don't mean to imply that I believe in the myth of objectivity, that I start off utterly neutral. I'm a gay man, who has (unlike women) easy access to porn and can take pleasure in it,[3] but who feels a commitment to the more feminist inflections of gay male politics. I'm also a socialist who sees porn as capitalist production but does not believe all capitalist cultural production always all the time expresses capitalist ideology.[4] I'm constantly looking for moments of contradiction, instability and give in our culture, the points at which change can be effected, and want to start out with the possibility of finding it in porn as anywhere else. So the definition I'm going to use is that a pornographic film is *any* film that has as its aim sexual arousal in the spectator.

This definition makes porn film a familiar kind of genre, that is, one that is based on the effect that both producers and audiences know the film is supposed to have. It is not defined (or I am not asking to define it here), like the Western, gangster film or musical, by such aesthetic, textual elements as iconography, structure, style and so on, but by what it produces in the spectator. It is like genres such as the weepie and the thriller, and also low or vulgar comedy. Like all of these, it is supposed to have an effect that is registered in the spectator's body—s/he weeps, gets goose bumps, rolls about laughing, comes. Like these genres, porn is usually discussed in relation to a similar, but "higher" genre which doesn't have a bodily effect—weepies (melodramas and soap opera) are compared to tragedy or realist drama, thrillers to mystery/detective stories (based on intellectual, puzzle-solving narratives), low comedy (farce) to high comedy (comedy of manners), and porn to erotica.

I'd like to use porn as a neutral term, describing a particular genre. If one defines porn differently, then the kind of defense of porn as a genre (but emphatically not of most porn that is actually available) that I'm involved with here is not really possible. Current feminist critiques of pornography[5] rightly stress the degradation of women that characterizes so much heterosexual porn, and these critiques in fact define pornography as woman-degrading representations of sexuality. Although feeling closer to some of those feminist articles that take issue with this hard line anti-porn position,[6] I do not feel as out of sympathy with, say, Andrea Dworkin's work as many people, and especially gay men, that I know. Although in relation to gay porn Dworkin is in some respects inaccurate (e.g. in stressing gay porn's use of socially inferior—young, black—men in "feminine" positions, whereas similarity between partners is more often the case) or out of date,[7] her rage at what so much of porn consists of is fully justified, and especially so because she effectively defines porn as that which is degrading and out*rage*ous. But I'd like all the same to hang on to a wider notion of sexual representation, and still use the word pornography precisely because of its disreputable, carnal associations. (Maybe the feminist debate means that I can't use the word like this—but I don't want to fall for the trap of substituting the word erotica.[8])

The fact that porn, like weepies, thrillers and low comedy, is realized in/through the body has given it low status in our culture. Popularity these genres have, but arbiters of cultural status still tend to value "spiritual" over "bodily" qualities, and hence relegate porn and the rest to an inferior cultural position.

One of the results of this is that culturally validated knowledge of the body, of the body's involvement in emotion, tends to be intellectual knowledge about the body, uninformed by experiential knowledge of it.[9] Let me try to be clear about this. I'm not saying that there can be a transparent, pure knowledge of the body, untouched by historical and cultural reality. On the contrary, all knowledge is culturally and historically specific, we do not transcend our material circumstances. We learn to feel our bodies in particular ways, not "naturally." But an intellectual or spiritual knowledge about the body is different from experiential knowledge of the body—both are socially constructed, but the latter is always in a dynamic material and physical relationship with the body, is always knowledge in and of the body. Intellectual or spiritual knowledge on the other hand divorces social construction from that which it constructs, divorces knowledge about the body from knowing with the body. (Certain types of discourse analysis—but by no means all—clearly fall into the same idealist trap.[10])

Moreover, the effect of the cultural status of intellectual/spiritual accounts of the body is to relegate experiential knowledge of the body to a residual category. Of course idealist discourse accounts do not allow any such category at all.[11] Thus experiential knowledge (except when sanctified by the subjugation of the body in most forms of "physical education") is allowed to be both inferior and just a given, not socially constructed,[12] to be just "experience," not socially constructed experiential knowledge. By valuing the spiritual, the bodily is left as something natural, and sexuality as the most natural thing of all. What is in fact also socially constructed (experiential knowledge of the body, and of sexuality) is not recognized as such, and for that reason is not reflected upon, is allowed to go its supposed own way until it meets up with spiritual censors. Even gay and feminist theory have been notoriously reluctant to think through the social construction of the body without lapsing into the Scylla of Lacanian psycho-analysis (where social construction does not construct anything *out of* any material reality) and the Charybdis of both gay liberationist let-it-all-hang-out (where sexuality is a pure impulse awaiting release) and the implicit sexual essentialism of radical feminist ideas of masculine aggression and women's power.[13]

A defense of porn as a genre (which, I repeat, is not at all the same thing as defending most of what porn currently consists of) would be based on the idea that an art rooted in bodily effect can give us a knowledge of the body that other art cannot.

Even now porn does give us knowledge of the body—only it is mainly bad knowledge, reinforcing the worst aspects of the social construction of masculinity that men learn to experience in our bodies. All the same, porn can be a site for "re-educating desire,"[14] and in a way that constructs desire in the body, not merely theoretically in relation to, and often against, it.

To do that, though, means rejecting any notion of "pure sex," and particularly the defense of porn as expressing or releasing a sexuality "repressed" by bourgeois (etc.) society. This argument has gained some ground in gay male circles, and with good reason. Homosexual desire has been constructed as perverse and unspeakable; gay porn does speak/show gay sex. Gay porn asserts homosexual desire, it turns the definition of homosexual desire on its head, says bad is good, sick is healthy and so on. It thus defends the universal human practice of same-sex physical contact (which our society constructs as homosexual); it has made life bearable for countless millions of gay men.

But to move from there to suggest that what we have here is a natural sexuality bursting out of the confines of heterosexual artificial repression is much more of a problem.

This is certainly the way that Gregg Blachford's article "Looking at Pornography"[15] can be read, and seems to be the contention behind David Ehrenstein's article "Within the Pleasure Principle, or Irresponsible Homosexual Propaganda."[16] The latter argues that porn movies, unlike mainstream films that imply sexuality but don't show it, give us the pure pleasure of voyeurism which lies unacknowledged behind all cinema.

> The pornographic is obvious, absolute, unmistakable—no lies or omissions or evasions can hold quarter in its sphere.

Porn is the "abandon of everything to the pleasure principle,"[17] conceptualized as pure drive (the more usual appropriation of Freudian ideas than the Lacanian version so influential in academic film studies circles). Porn itself operates with this idea, and the view is clearly expressed in the introduction to *Meat*,[18] a collection of writings from the magazine *Straight to Hell*. The magazine, like the book, consists entirely of personal accounts of gay sexual experience sent in to the magazine by gay men. I have no reason to suppose that the accounts are not genuine both in the sense of having actually been sent in (not ghost written) and describing real experiences. But this "genuineness" is not to be conflated, as book and magazine do, with the notion of an unconstructed sexuality—raw, pure and so on. A reading of *Meat*, or a look at gay porn, indicates really rather obviously that the sexuality described/represented is socially meaningful. Class, ethnicity and of course concepts of masculinity and gayness/straightness all clearly mark these gay pornographic productions; and indeed the very stress on sexuality as a moment of truth, and its conceptualization as raw, pure etc., is itself historically and culturally produced.[19]

What makes *Meat* and gay movie house porn especially interesting and important is the extent to which they blur the line between representation and practice. *Meat* is based on (I think largely) true encounters that really happened. Watching porn in gay cinemas usually involves having sex as well–not just self-masturbation but sexual activity with others, in a scenario brilliantly evoked by Will Aitken in his article "Erect in the Dark."[20] In principle then gay porn is a form of representation that can be the site and occasion for the production of bodily knowledge of the body. In this definition, porn is too important to be ignored, or to be left to the pornographers.

Narrative Manifestation

I'd like now to turn to one of the ways in which the education of desire that porn is involved in is manifested, namely its use of narrative.[21]

It is often said that porn movies as a genre are characterized by their absence of narrative. The typical porn movie, hard core anyway, is held to be an endless series of people fucking, and not even, as Beatrice Faust notes, fucking in the "normal" physiological order that Masters and Johnson have "recorded."[22] Gay porn (and indeed what hetero porn I have seen), however, is full of narrative. Narrative is its very basis.

Even the simplest pornographic loops have narrative. In those quarter-in-the-slot machines where you just get a bit of a porn loop for your quarter, you are very conscious of what point (roughly) you have come into the loop, you are conscious of where the narrative has got to. Even if all that is involved is a fuck between two men, there are the following narrative elements: the arrival on the scene of the fuck, establishing contact (through greeting and recognition, or through a quickly established eye-contact agreement to fuck), undressing, exploring various parts of the body, coming, parting. The exploration of the body often involves exploring those areas less heavily codified in terms of sexuality, before "really getting down to/on with" those that are (genitals and anus). Few short porn films don't involve most or all of these narrative elements, and in that order. Usually too there is some sort of narrative detail–in *Muscle Beach*, one man (Rick Wolfmier) arrives on the scene (a beach) in a truck, the other man (Mike Betts) is already there sunbathing; Wolfmier walks by the sea for while; there is quite a long sequence of shot: reverse shot cutting as they see each other and establish contact; self-masturbation precedes their actual physical contact with each other; after orgasm, Wolfmier and Betts drive away together in the truck. Already then minimal character elements are present, of not inconsiderable social interest–the iconography of the truck, the looks of the two men, the culture of the beach and of body-building, and so on.

Even when the film is yet more minimal than this, there is still narrative–and essentially the same narrative, too. Some gay porn loops simply show one man masturbating. A rather stylish version of this is *Roger*, which just has the eponymous star masturbating. The music is a kind of echoing drum beat; there is no set to speak of; the lighting is red, covering the screen in varieties of pulsating hue; the film cuts between long shots and medium shots in a quite rhythmic way, often dissolving rather than cutting clean. It will be clear that there is something almost abstract or avant-garde-ish about the film, as the cinematic means play visually with its solo subject, Roger masturbating. Yet even here there is a basic narrative–Roger enters, masturbates, comes. (Where you put your quarter in might mean that *you* start with his orgasm and run on to where he comes in; but you'd know and be able to reconstruct the proper narrative order that your quarter has cut across.)

Even in so minimal and abstract a case, there is narrative–*Roger* is a classic goal directed narrative.[23] The desire that drives the porn narrative forward is the desire to come, to have an orgasm. And it seems to me that male sexuality, homo or hetero, is socially constructed, at the level of representation anyway, in terms of narrative; that, as it were, male sexuality is itself understood narratively.

The goal of the pornographic narrative is coming; in filmic terms, the goal is ejaculation, that is, visible coming. If the goal of the pornographic protagonist (the actor or "character") is to come, the goal of the spectator is to see him come (and, more often than not, to come at the same time as him). Partly this has to do with "proof," with the form's "literalness," as Beatrice Faust puts it, with the idea that if you don't really see semen the performer could have faked it (and so you haven't had value for money). But partly too it has to do with the importance of the visual in the way male sexuality is constructed/conceptualized. It is striking how much pornographic literature, not a visual medium, stresses the visible elements of sex. (Most remarkable perhaps is Walter, the Victorian narrator of *My Secret Life*, with his obsessive desire to see into his partner's vagina, even to the detail of seeing, for instance, what his semen looks like after he has ejaculated it into her vagina.) Men's descriptions of their own erections seldom have to do with how their penises feel, but with how they look. The emphasis on seeing orgasm is then part of the way porn (re)produces the construction of male sexuality.

Could it be otherwise, could sexuality be represented differently? So dominant are masculine-centered definitions of sexuality that it often seems as if all representations of sexuality (pornographic or otherwise) are constructed as driven narrative. But there are alternatives, and one that struck me was the lesbian sequences at the end of *je tu il elle*, directed by Chantal Akerman. (As Margaret Mead pointed out in her work on sex roles in anthropology, you only need one example of things being different to establish that things can be different in the organization of human existence and hence that things can be changed.) The sequence itself is part of a (minimalist) narrative; but taken by itself it does not have the narrative drive of male porn. It starts *in media res*–there is no arrival in the room, the women are already making love when the sequence starts (though the previous shot has, perhaps ambiguously, established that they are going to make love); there is no sense of a progression to the goal of orgasm; nor is there any attempt to find visual or even (as in hetero porn?) aural equivalents for the visible male ejaculation. In particular, there is no sense of genital activity being the last, and getting-down-to-the-real-thing, stage of the experience. It is done in three long takes–no editing cuts across a sexual narrative (as in gay porn–see below); the harsh white lighting and the women's white bodies on crumpled white sheets in a room painted white, contribute to the effect of representing the sexuality as more dissolving and ebbing than a masculine thrusting narrative. Let me stress that I am *not* talking about what the women are doing–for much of the time their actions are far more snatching and grabbing than, for instance, the generally smooth, wet action of fellatio in gay porn. My point is the difference in narrative organization, in the cinematic representation of sexuality.[24]

I am not suggesting that this is a better representation of sexuality, or the correct mode for representing lesbian sexuality. Also I want to bracket the question of whether the difference between the two modes of representation is based on biological differences between female and male sexuality, or on different social constructions of sexuality, or on a combination of the two.[25] All I want to get over is the difference itself, and the fact that male porn, whether homo or hetero, is ineluctably caught in the narrative model. (This is particularly significant in hetero porn in that it is predominantly constructed around a female protagonist,[26] who is attributed with this narrativized sexuality. However, I am not about to get into whether this is a gain–a recognition of female sexuality as desire–or a loss–a construction of female sexuality in male terms.)

The basis of gay porn film is a narrative sexuality, a construction of male sexuality as the desire to achieve the goal of a visual climax. In relation to gay sexual politics, it is worth signalling that this should give pause to those of us who thought/hoped that being a gay man meant that we were breaking with the gender role system. At certain levels this is true, but there seems no evidence that in the predominant form of how we represent our sexuality to ourselves (in gay porn) we in any way break from the norms of male sexuality.

Particularly significant here is the fact that although the pleasure of anal sex (that is, of being anally fucked) is represented, the narrative is never organized around the desire to be fucked, but around the desire to ejaculate (whether or not following on from anal intercourse). Thus although at the level of public representation gay men may be thought of as deviant and disruptive of masculine norms because we assert the pleasures of being fucked and the eroticism of the anus,[27] in our pornography this takes a back seat.

This is why porn is politically important. Gay porn, like much of the gay male ghetto, has developed partly out of the opening up of social spaces achieved by the gay liberation movements; but porn and the ghetto have overwhelmingly developed within the terms of masculinity. The knowledge that gay porn (re)produces must be put together with the fact that gay men (like straight men but unlike women) do have this mode of public sexual expression available to them, however debased it may be. Like male homosexuality itself, gay porn is always in this very ambiguous relationship to male power and privilege, neither fully within it nor fully outside it.[28] But that ambiguity is a contradiction that can be exploited. In so far as porn is part of the experiential education of the body, it has contributed to and legitimized the masculine model of gay sexuality, a model that always implies the subordination of women. But rather than just allowing it to carry on doing so, it should be our concern to work against *this* pornography by working with/within pornography to change it–either by interventions within pornographic filmmaking itself,[29] or by the development of porn within the counter cinemas (always remembering that the distinction between porn in the usual commercial sense and sexual underground/alternative/independent cinema has always been blurry when you come to look at the films themselves), or by criticism that involves audiences reflecting on their experience of pornography (rather than by closing down on reflection by straight condemnation or celebration of it).

So far all I've been talking about is the most basic, minimal narrative organization of (gay) male pornography. However, gay porn is characterized as much by the elaborations of its narrative method as by its insistence on narrative itself. Though the bare narrative elements may often not go beyond those described above, they are frequently organized into really quite complex narrative wholes. Often there is a central narrative thread–two men who are in love or who want to get off with each other–but this is punctuated by almost all of the devices of narrative elaboration imaginable, most notably flash-backs (to other encounters, or previous encounters of the main characters with each other), fantasies (again, with others or each other, of what might or could be), parallelism (cutting back and forth between two or more different sexual encounters) and so on. All preserve the coming-to-visual-climax underlying narrative organization, but why this fascination with highly wrought narrative patterns? To begin with, of course, it is a way of getting more fucks in, with more people.[30] There is even perhaps an element of humor, as the filmmakers knowingly strain their imagination to think of ways of bringing in yet more sex acts. But it is also a way of teasing the audience sexually, because it is a way of delaying climax, of extending foreplay. In parallel sequences, each fuck is effectively temporally extended, each climax is delayed. More generally, the various additional encounters delay the fulfillment of the basic narrative of the two men who are the central characters. (e.g. in *L.A. Tool and Die* the underlying narrative is Wylie's journey to Los Angeles to find a job and his lover Hank; Wylie and Hank are played by the stars of the film, Will Seagers and Richard Locke, so we know that their having sex together must be the climax; but there are various encounters along Wylie's way, including memories, observation of other couples, incidental encounters with other men, and even inserted scenes with characters with whom Wylie has no connection, before arrival at Los Angeles and finally making it with Hank.)

There is a third reason for this narrative elaboration. Just as the minimal coming-to-visual-climax structure is a structural analogue for male sexuality, so the effective multiplication of sex acts through elaborate narrativity is an analogue for a (utopian) model of a gay sexual life-style that combines a basic romanticism with an easy acceptance of promiscuity. Thus the underlying narrative is often romantic, the ultimate goal is to make love with *the* man; but along the way a free-ranging, easy-going promiscuity is possible. While not all gay men actually operate such a model of how they wish to organize their affective lives, it is a very predominant one in gay cultural production, a utopian reconciliation of the desire for romance *and* promiscuity, security *and* freedom, making love *and* having sex.

It is worth stressing how strong the element of romance is, since this is perhaps less expected than the celebration of promiscuity. The plot of *L.A. Tool and Die* outlined above is a good example, as is *Navy Blue* in which two sailors on shore leave seek out other lovers because each doesn't think that the other is gay, yet each is really in love with the other (as fantasy sequences make clear)–only at the end of the film do they realize their love for each other. Or take *Wanted*, a gay porn version of *The Defiant Ones*, in which two convicts, one gay (Al Parker) and one straight (Will Seagers), escape from prison together. Despite Seagers' hostility to Parker's sexuality, they stick together, with Parker having various sexual encounters, including watching Seagers masturbate. The film is a progression from the sadistic prison sexuality at the start (also offered, I know, as pornographic pleasure), through friendly mutual sexual pleasuring between Parker and various other men, to a final encounter, by an idyllic brookside, between Parker and Seagers which is the culmination of their developing friendship. Some men I know who've seen the film find this final sequence too conventionally romantic (which it is—that's why I like it) or else too bound up with the self-oppressive fantasy of the straight man who deigns to have sex with a fag. It can certainly be taken that way, but I know when I first saw it I was really moved by what seemed to be Seagers' realization of the sexuality of his feeling for Parker. And what particularly moved me was the moment when Seagers comes in Parker's mouth, and the latter gently licks the semen off Seagers' penis, because here it seemed was an explicit and arousing moment of genital sexuality that itself expressed a tender emotional feeling—through its place in the narrative, through the romanticism of the setting, through the delicacy of Parker's performance. If porn taught us *this* more often . . .

One of the most interesting ways of making narratives complex in gay porn is the use of films within films. Many gay porn films are about making gay porn films; and many others involve someone showing gay porn films to himself or someone else (with the film-within-the-film then becoming for a while the film we are watching). The process of watching, and also of being watched (in the case of those films about making gay porn) are thus emphasized, not in the interests of foregrounding the means of construction in order to deconstruct them, but because the pleasure of seeing sex is what motivates (gay) male pornography and can be heightened by having attention drawn to it. (There is a whole other topic, to do with the power in play in looking/being looked at, which I won't get into here.) We have in these cases a most complex set of relations between screen and auditorium. On screen someone actually having sex is watched (photographed) by a filmmaker watched (photographed) by another invisible filmmaker (the one who made the film on screen), and all are watched by someone in the audience who is (or generally reckons to be) himself actually having sex. Gay porn here collapses the distinction between representation and that which it is a representation of, while at the same time showing very clearly the degree to which representation is part of the pleasure to be had even in that which it is a representation of. Porn (all porn) is, for good or ill (and currently mainly for ill), part of how we live our sexuality; how we represent sexuality to ourselves is part of how we live it, and porn has rather cornered the market on the representation of sexuality. Gay porn seems to make that all clearer, because there is greater equality between the participants (performers, filmmakers, audiences)[31] which permits a fuller exploration of the education of desire that is going on. Porn involves us bodily in that education; criticism of porn should be opening up reflection on the education we are receiving in order to change it.

I'd like to thank JUMP CUT *editorial collective for their helpful and also very enjoyable involvement in the editing of this article. Since first writing it I have incorporated not only many of their suggestions but also much of the useful discussions on pornography and gay macho in the Birmingham Gay Men's Socialist Group. Many thanks to all these people then—but I'll still take the blame for the finished article.*

1. For the rest of the essay, gay porn will always refer to gay *male* porn.

2. For a general introduction to this, see Julia Lesage, "Women and Pornography," *Jump Cut,* no. 26, pp. 46-47, 60, and the bibliography by Gina Marchetti in the same issue, pp. 56-60.

3. This access is not actually so easy outside of certain major metropolitan centers, and the recent anti-pornography legislation in Great Britain has hit gay porn far more decisively than straight.

4. This argument is developed by Terry Lovell in *Pictures of Reality* (London: British Film Institute, 1981).

5. For example, Andrea Dworkin, *Pornography: Men Possessing Women* (New York: Putnam's, 1981); Susan Griffin, *Pornography and Silence* (London: The Women's Press, 1981); Laura Lederer, ed., *Take Back the Night* (New York: William Morrow, 1980).

6. For example, Kathy Myers, "Towards a Feminist Erotica," *Camerawork* (March 1982): 14-16, 19, reviews of Dworkin and Griffin by Deborah Allen and Gavin Harris in *Gay Information,* no. 9/10, pp. 20-27, and by Janice Winship in *Feminist Review,* no. 11, pp. 97-100, and B. Ruby Rich's review of *Not a Love Story* in *Village Voice* (July 20, 1982)

7. See Allen and Harris above, p. 22.

8. "Because it is less specific, less suggestive of actual sexual activity, 'erotica' is regularly used as a euphemism for 'classy porn.' Pornography expressed in literary language or expensive photography and consumed by the upper middle class is 'erotica'; the cheap stuff, which can't pretend to any purpose but getting people off, is smut." Ellen Willis, quoted by Mick Carter in "The Re-education of Desire: Some Thoughts on Current Erotic Visual Practices," *Art and Text,* no. 4, pp. 20-38.

9. An example of this is the role of the representation of the body in Christian iconography. At one level, the body of Christ could not be a more central motif of Christianity, most notably in the image of Christ on the cross. But the tendency remains to stress what the body means at the expense of what it is, to highlight transcendence over the body. In the Christian story of Christ as the Word made flesh, it is the Word that ultimately matters, not the flesh.

10. The magazine *m/f* is the leading example of this.

11. For a critique of idealism, see Terry Lovell, cited above.

12. The one area of cultural work that has been concerned with body knowledge is dance, but the leading exponents of Modern Dance such as Isadora Duncan and Ruth St. Denis have been influentially committed to notions of natural movement. See Elizabeth Kendally, *Where She Danced* (New York: Alfred Knopf, 1979).

13. See Elizabeth Wilson, *What Is To Be Done About Violence Against Women?* (New York: Penguin, 1983).

14. See Mick Carter, cited above.

15. In *Gay Left,* no.6, pp. 16-20.

16. In *Wide Angle,* vol. 4, no. 1, pp. 62-65. I am conscious that because this article, in a manner of speaking, attacks things I have written—and even attacks what it infers from them about my sexual practices—that I may here treat the article rather unfairly.

17. Ibid., p.65.

18. San Francisco: Gay Sunshine Press, 1981.

19. See Michel Foucault, *The History of Sexuality* (New York: Vintage Books, 1980).

20. In *Gay News,* Winter Extra (December 1981/January 1982): 15-20.

21. This is only one element of any full analysis. One of the major elements not discussed here, and that needs work doing on it, is the role of iconography—of dress and setting, and especially performers, the male types that are used, porn stars' images and so on, all drenched in ideological meanings

22. *Women, Sex and Pornography* (Harmondsworth: Penguin, 1982), p.16.

23. See David Bordwell and Kristin Thompson, *Film Art* (Reading: Addison-Wesley, 1979).

24. For further discussion, see Angela Martin, "Chantal Akerman's films: A Dossier," *Feminist Review,* no. 3, pp. 24-47.

25. For a discussion of this difficult nature/nurture debate from a socialist feminist perspective that does not discount the contribution of biology altogether, see Janet Sayers, *Biological Politics* (London: Tavistock, 1982).

26. See Dennis Giles, "Angle on Fire," *Velvet Light Trap,* no. 16.

27. See Guy Hocquenghem, *Homosexual Desire* (London: Allison and Busby, 1978). Tom Waugh disputes the assertion in this paragraph in "Men's Pornography: Gays vs. Straight," *Jump Cut,* no. 30 (1985): 30-36.

28. See Michele Barrett, *Women's Oppression To-day* (London: Verso, 1980), Chapter two, for a discus-

sion of the relationship between male homosexuality and women's subordination.

29. For some consideration of this, see Paul Alcuin Siebenand, "The Beginnings of Gay Cinema in Los Angeles: The Industry and the Audience," doctoral dissertation, University of California, Los Angeles, (Department of Communications), 1975.

30. Cf. Same Mele and Mark Thirkell, "Pornographic Narrative," *Gay Information*, no. 6.

31. This is a question of degree—producers and audiences are not equal in their power of determining the form that representation takes, and especially in a field so fiercely colonized by capitalist exploitation as pornography; and at the psychological level, performers and audience members are not necessarily equal, in that performers are validated as attractive sexual beings to a degree that audience members may not be. But the point is that they are all gay men participating in a gay sub-culture, a situation that does not hold with heterosexual porn. See Siebenand, and also Waugh, cited above.

The Site of Memory

My inclusion in a series of talks on autobiography and memoir is not entirely a misalliance.[1] Although it's probably true that a fiction writer thinks of his or her work as alien in that company, what I have to say may suggest why I'm not completely out of place here. For one thing, I might throw into relief the differences between self-recollection (memoir) and fiction, and also some of the similarities—the places where those two crafts embrace and where that embrace is symbiotic.

But the authenticity of my presence here lies in the fact that a very large part of my own literary heritage is the autobiography. In this country the print origins of black literature (as distinguished from the oral origins) were slave narratives. These book-length narratives (autobiographies, recollections, memoirs), of which well over a hundred were published, are familiar texts to historians and students of black history. They range from the adventure-packed life of Olaudah Equiano's *The Interesting Narrative of the Life of Olaudah Equiano, or Gustavus Vassa, the African, Written by Himself* (1769), to the quiet desperation of *Incidents in the Life of a Slave Girl: Written by Herself* (1861), in which Harriet Jacob ("Linda Brent") records hiding for seven years in a room too small to stand up in; from the political savvy of Frederick Douglass's *Narrative of the Life of Frederick Douglass, an American Slave, Written by Himself* (1845), to the subtlety and modesty of Henry Bibb, whose voice, in *Life and Adventures of Henry Bibb, an American Slave, Written by Himself* (1849) is surrounded by ("loaded with" is a better phrase) documents attesting to its authenticity. Bibb is careful to note that his formal schooling (three weeks) was short, but that he was "educated in the school of adversity, whips, and chains." Born in Kentucky, he put aside his plans to escape in order to marry. But when he learned that he was the father of a slave and watched the degradation of his wife and child, he reactivated those plans.

Whatever the style and circumstances of these narratives, they were written to say principally two things. One: "This is my historical life—my singular, special example that is personal, but that also represents the race." Two: "I write this text to persuade other people—you, the reader, who is probably not black—that we are human beings worthy of God's grace and the immediate abandonment of slavery." With these two missions in mind, the narratives were clearly pointed.

In Equiano's account, the purpose is quite up-front. Born in 1745 near the Niger River and captured at the age of ten, he survived the Middle Passage, American plantation slavery, wars in Canada and the Mediterranean; learned navigation and clerking from a Quaker named Robert King, and bought his freedom at twenty-one. He lived as a free servant, traveling widely and living most of his latter life in England. Here he is speaking to the British without equivocation: "I hope to have the satisfaction of seeing the renovation of liberty and justice resting on the British government. . . . I hope and expect the attention of gentlemen of power . . . May the time come—at least the speculation is to me pleasing—when the sable people shall gratefully commemorate the auspicious era of extensive freedom." With typically eighteenth-century reticence he records his singular and representative life for one purpose: to change things. In fact, he and his co-authors *did* change things. Their works gave fuel to the fires that abolitionists were setting everywhere.

More difficult was getting the fair appraisal of literary critics. The writings of church martyrs and confessors are and were read for the eloquence of their message as well as their experience of redemption, but the American slaves' autobiographical narratives were frequently scorned as "biased," "inflammatory" and "improbable." These attacks are particularly difficult to understand in view of the fact that it was extremely important, as you can imagine, for the writers of these narratives to appear as objective as possible—not to offend the reader by being too angry, or by showing too much outrage, or by calling the reader names. As recently as 1966, Paul Edwards, who edited and abridged Equiano's story, praises the narrative for its refusal to be "inflammatory."

"As a rule," Edwards writes, "he [Equiano] puts no emotional pressure on the reader other than that which the situation itself contains—his language does not strain after our sympathy, but expects it to be given naturally and at the proper time. This quiet avoidance of emotional display produces many of the best passages in the book." Similarly, an 1836 review of Charles Bell's *Life and Adventures of a Fugitive Slave*, which appeared in the "Quarterly Anti-Slavery Magazine," praised Bell's account for its objectivity. "We rejoice in the book the more, because it is not a partisan work. . . . It broaches no theory in regard to [slavery], nor proposes any mode or time of emancipation."

As determined as these black writers were to persuade the reader of the evil of slavery, they also complimented him by assuming his nobility of heart and his high-mindedness. They tried to summon up his finer nature in order to encourage him to employ it. They knew that their readers were the people who could make a difference in terminating slavery. Their stories—of brutality, adversity and deliverance—had great popularity in spite of critical hostility in many quarters and patronizing sympathy in others. There was a time when the hunger for "slave stories" was difficult to quiet, as sales figures show. Douglass's *Narrative* sold five thousand copies in four months; by 1847 it had sold eleven thousand copies. Equiano's book had thirty-six editions between 1789 and 1850. Moses Roper's book had ten editions from 1837 to 1856; William Wells Brown's was reprinted four times in its first year. Solomon Northrop's book sold twenty-seven thousand copies before two years had passed. A book by Josiah Henson (argued by some to be the model for the "Tom" of Harriet Beecher Stowe's *Uncle Tom's Cabin*) had a pre-publication sale of five thousand.

In addition to using their own lives to expose the horrors of slavery, they had a companion motive for their efforts. The prohibition against teaching a slave to read and write (which in many Southern states carried severe punishment) and against a slave's learning to read and write had to be scuttled at all costs. These writers knew that literacy was power. Voting, after all, was inextricably connected to the ability to read; literacy was a way of assuming and proving the "humanity" that the Constitution denied them. That is why the narratives carry the subtitle "written by himself," or "herself," and include introductions and prefaces by white sympathizers to authenticate them. Other narratives, "edited by" such well-known anti-slavery figures as Lydia Maria Child and John Greenleaf Whittier, contain prefaces to assure the reader how little editing was needed. A literate slave was supposed to be a contradiction in terms.

One has to remember that the climate in which they wrote reflected not only the Age of Enlightenment but its twin, born at the same time, the Age of Scientific Racism. David Hume, Immanuel Kant and Thomas Jefferson, to mention only a few, had documented their conclusions that blacks were incapable of intelligence. Frederick Douglass knew otherwise, and he wrote refutations of what Jefferson said in "Notes on the State of Virginia": "Never yet could I find that a black had uttered a thought above the level of plain narration, never see even an elementary trait of painting or sculpture." A sentence that I have always thought ought to be engraved at the door to the Rockefeller Collection of African Art. Hegel, in 1813, had said that Africans had no "history" and couldn't write in modern languages. Kant disregarded a perceptive observation by a black man by saying, "This fellow was quite black from head to foot, a clear proof that what he said was stupid."

Yet no slave society in the history of the world wrote more—or more thoughtfully—about its own enslavement. The milieu, however, dictated the purpose and the style. The narratives are instructive, moral and obviously representative. Some of them are patterned after the sentimental novel that was in vogue at the time. But whatever the level of eloquence or the form, popular taste discouraged the writers from dwelling too long or too carefully on the more sordid details of their experience. Whenever there was an unusually violent incident, or a scatological one, or something "excessive," one finds the writer taking refuge in the literary conventions of the day. "I was left in a state of distraction not to be described" (Equiano). "But let us now leave the rough usage of the field . . . and turn our attention to the less repulsive slave life as it existed in the house of my childhood" (Douglass). "I am not about to harrow the feelings of my readers by a terrific representation of the untold horrors of that fearful system of oppression . . . It is not my purpose to descend deeply into the dark and noisome caverns of the hell of slavery" (Henry Box Brown).

Over and over, the writers pull the narrative up short with a phrase such as, "But let us drop a veil over these proceedings too terrible to relate." In shaping the experience to make it palatable to those who were in a position to alleviate it, they were silent about many things, and they "forgot" many other things. There was a careful selection of the instances that they would record and a careful rendering of those that they chose to describe. Lydia Maria Child identified the problem in her introduction to "Linda Brent's" tale of sexual abuse: "I am well aware that many will accuse me of indecorum for presenting these pages to the public; for the experiences of this intelligent and much-injured woman belong to a class which some call delicate subjects, and others indelicate. This peculiar phase of Slavery has generally been kept veiled; but the public ought to be made acquainted with its monstrous features, and I am willing to take the responsibility of presenting them with the veil drawn [aside]."

But most importantly—at least for me—there was no mention of their interior life.

For me—a writer in the last quarter of the twentieth century, not much more than a hundred years after Emancipation, a writer who is black and a woman—the exercise is very different. My job becomes how to rip that veil drawn over "proceedings too terrible to relate." The exercise is also critical for any person who is black, or who belongs to any marginalized category, for, historically, we were seldom invited to participate in the discourse even when we were its topic.

Moving that veil aside requires, therefore, certain things. First of all, I must trust my own recollections. I must also depend on the recollections of others. Thus memory weighs heavily in what I write, in how I begin and in what I find to be significant. Zora Neale Hurston said, "Like the dead-seeming cold rocks, I have memories within that came out of the material that went to make me." These "memories within" are the subsoil of my work. But memories and recollections won't give me total access to the unwritten interior life of these people. Only the act of the imagination can help me.

• • •

If writing is thinking and discovery and selection and order and meaning, it is also awe and reverence and mystery and magic. I suppose I could dispense with the last four if I were not so deadly serious about fidelity to the milieu out of which I write and in which my ancestors actually lived. Infidelity to that milieu—the absence of the interior life, the deliberate excising of it from the records that the slaves themselves told—is precisely the problem in the discourse that proceeded without us. How I gain access to that interior life is what drives me and is the part of this talk which both distinguishes my fiction from autobiographical strategies and which also embraces certain autobiographical strategies. It's a kind of literary archeology: on the basis of some information and a little bit of guesswork you journey to a site to see what remains were left behind and to reconstruct the world that these remains imply. What makes it fiction is the nature of the imaginative act: my reliance on the image—on the remains—in addition to recollection, to yield up a kind of a truth. By "image," of course, I don't mean "symbol"; I simply mean "picture" and the feelings that accompany the picture.

Fiction, by definition, is distinct from fact. Presumably it's the product of imagination—invention—and it claims the freedom to dispense with "what really happened," or where it really happened, or when it really happened, and nothing in it needs to be publicly verifiable, although much in it can be verified. By contrast, the scholarship of the biographer and the literary critic seems to us only trustworthy when the events of fiction can be traced to some publicly verifiable fact. It's the research of the "Oh, yes, this is where he or she got it from" school, which gets its own credibility from excavating the credibility of the sources of the imagination, not the nature of the imagination.

The work that I do frequently falls, in the minds of most people, into that realm of fiction called fantastic, or mythic, or magical, or unbelievable. I'm not comfortable with these labels. I consider that my single gravest responsibility (in spite of that magic) is not to lie. When I hear someone say, "Truth is stranger than fiction," I think that old chestnut is truer than we know, because it doesn't say that truth is truer than fiction; just that it's stranger, meaning that it's odd. It may be excessive, it may be more interesting, but the important thing is that it's random—and fiction is not random.

Therefore the crucial distinction for me is not the difference between fact and fiction, but the distinction between fact and truth. Because facts can exist without human intelligence, but truth cannot. So if I'm looking to find and expose a truth about the interior life of people who didn't write it (which doesn't mean that they didn't have it); if I'm trying to fill in the blanks that the slave narratives left—to part the veil that was so frequently drawn, to implement the stories that I heard—then the approach that's most productive and most trustworthy for me is the recollection that moves from the image to the text. Not from the text to the image.

Simone de Beauvoir, in *A Very Easy Death*, says, "I don't know why I was so shocked by my mother's death." When she heard her mother's name being called at the funeral by the priest, she says, "Emotion seized me by the throat. . . . 'Françoise de Beauvoir': the words brought her to life; they summed up her history, from birth to marriage to widowhood to the grave. Françoise de Beauvoir—that retiring woman, so rarely named, became an *important* person." The book becomes an exploration both into her own grief and into the images in which the grief lay buried.

Unlike Mme. de Beauvoir, Frederick Douglass asks the reader's patience for spending about half a page on the death of his grandmother—easily the most profound loss he had suffered—and he apologizes by saying, in effect, "It really was very important to me. I hope you aren't bored by my indulgence." He makes no attempt to explore that death: its images or its meaning. His narrative is as close to factual as he can make it, which leaves no room for subjective speculation. James Baldwin, on the other hand, in *Notes of a Native Son*, says, in recording his father's life and his own relationship to his father, "All of my father's Biblical texts and songs, which I had decided were meaningless, were ranged before me at his death like empty bottles, waiting to hold the meaning which life would give them for me." And then his text fills those bottles. Like Simone de Beauvoir, he moves from the event to the image that it left. My route is the reverse: the image comes first and tells me what the "memory" is about.

I can't tell you how I felt when my father died. But I was able to write *Song of Solomon* and imagine, not him and not his specific interior life, but the world that he inhabited and the private or interior life of the people in it. And I can't tell you how I felt reading to my grandmother while she was turning over and over in her bed (because she was dying, and she was not comfortable), but I could try to reconstruct the world that she lived in. And I have suspected, more often than not, that I *know* more than she did, that I *know* more than my grandfather and my great-grandmother did, but I also know that I'm no wiser than they were. And whenever I have tried earnestly to diminish their vision and prove to myself that I know more, and when I have tried to speculate on their interior life and match it up with my own, I have been overwhelmed every time by the richness of theirs compared to my own. Like Frederick Douglass talking about his grandmother, and James Baldwin talking about his father, and Simone de Beauvoir talking about her mother, these people are my access to me; they are my entrance into my own interior life. Which is why the images that float around them—the remains, so to speak, at the archeological site—surface first, and they surface so vividly and so compellingly that I acknowledge them as my route to a reconstruction of a world, to an exploration of an interior life that was not written and to the revelation of a kind of truth.

So the nature of my research begins with something as ineffable and as flexible as a dimly recalled figure, the corner of a room, a voice. I began to write my second book, which was called *Sula*, because of my preoccupation with a picture of a woman and the way in which I heard her name pronounced. Her name was Hannah, and I think she was a friend of my mother's. I don't remember seeing her very much, but what I do remember is the color around her—a kind of violet, a suffusion of something violet—and her eyes, which appeared to be half closed. But what I remember most is how the women said her name: how they said "Hannah Peace" and smiled to themselves, and there was some secret about her that they knew, which they didn't talk about, at least not in my hearing, but it seemed *loaded* in the way in which they said her name. And I suspected that she was a little bit of an outlaw but that they approved in some way.

And then, thinking about their relationship to her and the way in which they talked about her, the way in which they articulated her name, made me think about friendship between women. What is it that they forgive each other for? And what it is that is unforgivable in the world of women. I don't want to know any more about Miss Hannah Peace, and I'm not going to ask my mother who she really was and what did she do and what were you laughing about and why were you smiling? Because my experience when I do this with my mother is so crushing: she will give you *the* most pedestrian information you ever heard, and I would like to keep all of my remains and my images intact in their mystery when I begin. Later I will get to the facts. That way I can explore two worlds—the actual and the possible.

What I want to do this evening is to track an image from picture to meaning to text—a journey which appears in the novel that I'm writing now, which is called *Beloved*.

I'm trying to write a particular kind of scene, and I see corn on the cob. To "see" corn on the cob doesn't mean that it suddenly hovers; it only means that it keeps coming back. And in trying to figure out "What is all this corn doing?" I discover what it *is* doing.

I see the house where I grew up in Lorain, Ohio. My parents had a garden some distance away from our house, and they didn't welcome me and my sister there, when we were young, because we were not able to distinguish between the things that they wanted to grow and the things that they didn't, so we were not able to hoe, or weed, until much later.

I see them walking, together, away from me. I'm looking at their backs and what they're carrying in their arms: their tools, and maybe a peck basket. Sometimes when they walk away from me they hold hands, and they go to this other place in the garden. They have to cross some railroad tracks to get there.

I also am aware that my mother and father sleep at odd hours because my father works many jobs and works at night. And these naps are times of pleasure for me and my sister because nobody's giving us chores, or telling us what to do, or nagging us in any way. In addition to which, there is some feeling of pleasure in them that I'm only vaguely aware of. They're very rested when they take these naps.

And later on in the summer we have an opportunity to eat corn, which is the one plant that I can distinguish from the others, and which is the harvest that I like the best; the others are the food that no child likes—the collards, the okra, the strong, violent vegetables that I would give a great deal for now. But I do like the corn because it's sweet, and because we all sit down to eat it, and it's finger food, and it's hot, and it's even good cold, and there are neighbors in, and there are uncles in, and it's easy, and it's nice.

The picture of the corn and the nimbus of emotion surrounding it became a powerful one in the manuscript I'm now completing.

Authors arrive at text and subtext in thousands of ways, learning each time they begin anew how to recognize a valuable idea and how to render the texture that accompanies, reveals or displays it to its best advantage. The process by which this is accomplished is endlessly fascinating to me. I have always thought that as an editor for twenty years I understood writers better than their most careful critics, because in examining the manuscript in each of its subsequent stages I knew the author's process, how his or her mind worked, what was effortless, what took time, where the "solution" to a problem came from. The end result—the book—was all that the critic had to go on.

Still, for me, that was the least important aspect of the work. Because, no matter how "fictional" the account of these writers, or how much it was a product of invention, the act of imagination is bound up with memory. You know, they straightened out the Mississippi River in places, to make room for houses and livable acreage. Occasionally the river floods these places. "Floods" is the word they use, but in fact it is not flooding; it is remembering. Remembering where it used to be. All water has a perfect memory and is forever trying to get back to where it was. Writers are like that: remembering where we were, what valley we ran through, what the banks were like, the light that was there and the route back to our original place. It is emotional memory—what the nerves and the skin remember as well as how it appeared. And a rush of imagination is our "flooding."

Along with personal recollection, the matrix of the work I do is the wish to extend, fill in and complement slave autobiographical narratives. But only the matrix. What comes of all that is dictated by other concerns, not least among them the novel's own integrity. Still, like water, I remember where I was before I was "straightened out."

---

1. This essay was edited from a speech developed for a series of lectures organized by the New York Public Library and the Book of the Month Club.

FEB 1960

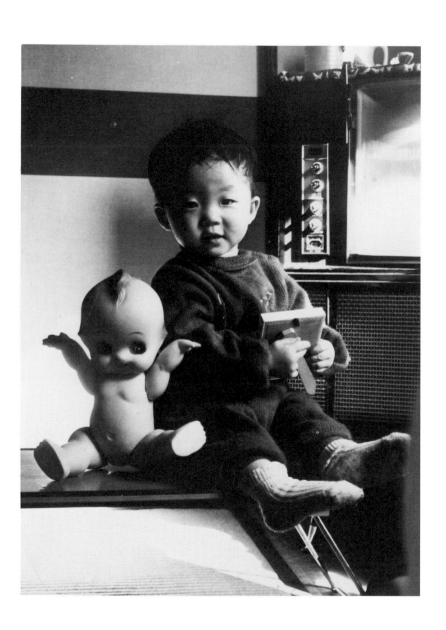

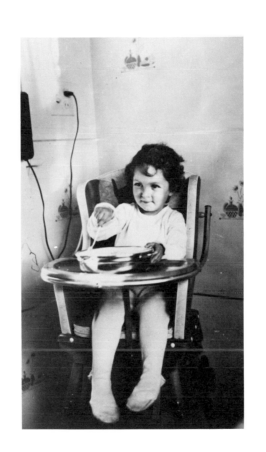

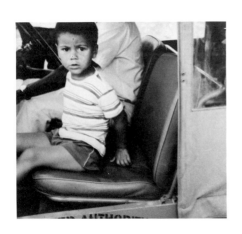

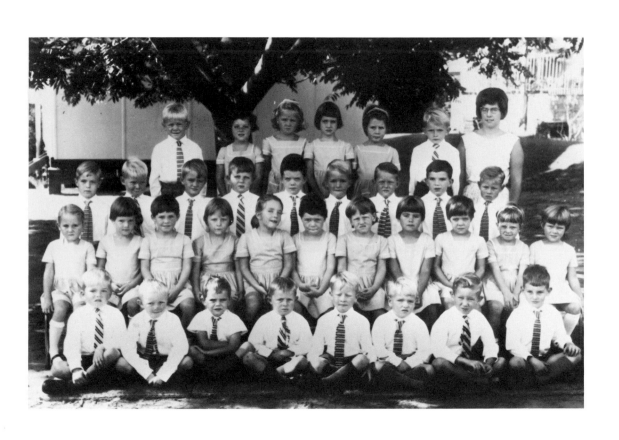

Marginalia: Displacement and Resistance

Cotton and Iron

> *Conte, conté, à conter . . .*
> > *Es-tu véridique?*
> > *Pour les bambins qui s'ébatent au clair de lune, mon conte est une*
> > *histoire fantastique.*
> > *Pour les fileuses de coton pendant les longues nuits de la saison froide,*
> > *mon récit est un passe-temps délectable.*
> > *Pour les mentons velus et les talons rugueux, c'est une véritable*
> > *révélation.*
> > *Je suis donc à la fois futile, utile et instructeur.*
> > *Déroule-le donc pour nous . . .*[1]

In these, the opening lines of a didactic narration which forms part of the traditional education of the Fulani in the Niger loop, what can be read as unwinding itself to the reader are some of the most debated issues of contemporary theory and art. *Tale, told, to be told . . . / Are you truthful?* Acknowledging the complexities inherent in any speech-act does not necessarily mean taking away or compromising the qualities of a fine story. Simple and direct in its indirectness, it neither wraps itself in a cloud of oratorical precautions, nor cocoons itself in realist illusions that make language the simple medium of thought. Who speaks? What speaks? The question is implied and the function named, but the individual never reigns, and the subject slips away without naturalizing its voice. S/he who speaks, speaks *to* the tale as s/he begins telling and retelling it. S/he does not speak *about* it. For without a certain work of displacement, "speaking about" only partakes in the conservation of systems of binary opposition (subject/object; I/It; We/They) on which territorialized knowledge depends. It places a semantic distance between oneself and the work; oneself (the maker) and the receiver; oneself and the other. It secures for the speaker a position of mastery: I am in the midst of a knowing, acquiring, deploying world—I appropriate, own, and demarcate my sovereign territory as I advance—while the "other" remains in the sphere of acquisition. Truth is the instrument of a mastery which I exert over areas of the unknown as I gather them within the fold of the known.

"Speaking to" the tale breaks the dualistic relation between subject and object as the question "who speaks?" and the implication "it-speaks-by-itself-through-me" is also a way of foregrounding the anteriority of the tale to the teller, and thereby the merging of the two through a speech-act. Truth is both a construct and beyond it; the balance is played out as the narrator interrogates the truthfulness of the tale and provides multiple answers. *For the little people gamboling under the moonlight, my tale is a fantastic story. / For the women spinning cotton during the long nights of the cold season, my narration is a delightful diversion. / For those with hairy chins and rugged heels, it is a real revelation.* Here, truth and pleasure go hand in hand. A language reduced to the status of instrument and/or of fine style either ignores the "beauty" of language or fetishizes it (as an end point). "Fine behavior (*le bel agir*), and great knowledge are inseparable from beautiful language (*beau language*)" writes, for example, the Malian scholar A. Hampate Ba, who rejects the common concept of African aesthetics as being merely functional and utilitarian—a concept which he considers to be the product of Western rationale. Poetry, he remarks, is as delicate and as sharp as "a golden thread" weaving through the entire texture of the narration. And why was gold so esoteric before it was attributed a monetary value? Because gold, which is one of the fundamental myths of all of West Africa, is also the only metal "that becomes cotton without being any less iron." Because, "gold is the support of knowledge, but if you confuse knowledge with the support [*le savoir et le socle*], it will fall on you and crush you."[2]

A form of mediation, the story and its telling are always adaptive. A narration is never a passive reflection of a reality. At the same time, it must always be truthful if it is to unwind beautifully. Truth, however, is not attained here through logocentric certainties (deriving from the tendency to identify human telos with rationality). The functions of both the tale and the mediator-storyteller are thus introduced at the outset. And, depending on who constitutes its audiences, the story can open onto the fantastic world of the imagination; it can offer a pleasant pastime; or it can engage the listener in a revelatory spiritual/philosophical journey across Fulani ethics and cosmology. *I am therefore at the same time useless, useful and instructive.* The mediator-storyteller, through whom truth is summoned to unwind itself to the audience, is at once a creator, a delighter and a teacher. Perhaps, when it is a question of both the lie and its truth, and the truth and its lie (if "lie" is what you think a "beautiful language" and a "fantastic story" are), this doubling back which enables the tale to designate itself, leads us not necessarily to the deepest interiority (peculiar to the tradition of Western thought), but also to the "outside" (speech as speech) in which the speaking subject disappears. I am useless, useful. The boundaries of lie and truth are thus multiplied, reversed and displaced without rendering meaningless either the notion of lie or that of truth. Directly questioned, the story is also indirectly unquestionable in its truthfulness. *Unwind it then for us . . .*

Re-departure: the pain and the frustration of having to live a difference that has no name and too many names already. Marginality: who names? whose fringes? An elsewhere that does not merely lie outside the center but radically striates it. Identity: the singular naming of a person, a nation, a race, has undergone a reversal of values. Effacing it used to be the only means of survival for the colonized and the exiled; naming it today often means declaring solidarity among the hyphenated people of the Diaspora. *But every place she went / they pushed her to the other side / and that other side pushed her to the other side / of the other side of the other side / Kept in the shadows of other.*[3] Identity is a way of re-departing. Rather, the return to a denied heritage allows one to start again with different re-departures, different pauses, different arrivals. Since identity can very well speak its plurality without suppressing its singularity, heterologies of knowledge give all practices of the self a festively vertiginous dimension. It is hardly surprising then that when identity is doubled, tripled, multiplied across time (generations) and space (cultures), when differences keep on blooming within despite the rejections from without, she dares, by necessity. She dares mix; she dares cross the borders to introduce into language (verbal, visual, musical) everything monologism has repressed. *"Eres una de las otras," ". . . Don't contaminate us, get away."*. . . . *Away, she went away / but each place she went / pushed her to the other side, al otro lado.*[4] Here again and anew, gender and sexuality: other struggles of borders. The triple oppression of the not-quite-second-sex and the kept-in-the-shadow-of-the-other. *Identity conflict. Uncertainty of the personal me, the national me, the sexual me: lament, endless lament!*[5] The necessity of re-naming so as to un-name. At times hindered by a somewhat pathetic tendency on the Brother's side to ignore the link between patriarchy and hegemony, and on the Sister's side to pretend that white maternalism is either non-existent or non-discriminating. Other times, disoriented by the unconscious surfacing of the named "homophobic straight mind." *Let us not entrust ourselves to failure. That would only be to indulge nostalgia for success.*[6] The challenge is thus: how can one re-create without re-circulating domination?

In undoing established models and codes, plurality adds up to no total. *Oh, girl, bailing water by the road's side / why pour off the moon's golden light?*[7] This non-totalness never fails either to baffle or to awaken profound intolerance and anxieties. Every reaching out that remains non-totalizable is a "horizontal vertigo" in which the exploring explored subject can only advance through moments of blindness. Surely, the desire to proceed straightforwardly to a goal, to attain a tangible result, to affirm a concrete social transformation is always active. But a commitment to infinite progress is also a realization that the infinite is what undermines the very notion of (rational) progress. *Tale, told, to be told.* The to-and-fro movement between advancement and regression necessarily leads to a situation where every step taken is at once the first (a step back) and the last step (a step forward)—the only step, in a precise circumstance, at a precise moment of (one's) history. In this context, a work-in-progress, for example, is not a work whose step precedes other steps in a trajectory that leads to the final work. It is not a work awaiting a better, more perfect stage of realization. Inevitably, a work is always a form of tangible closure. But closures need not close off; they can be doors opening onto other closures and functioning as ongoing passages to an elsewhere (-within-here). Like a throw of the dice, each opening is also a closing, for each work generates its own laws and limits, each has its specific condition and deals with a specific context. The closure here, however, is a way of letting the work go rather than of sealing it off. Thus, every work materialized can be said to be a work-in-progress. The notion of a finished work versus that of an uncompleted work requiring finishing, loses its pertinence. What needs to be reconsidered are these widely adopted and imposed forms of closure whose main function is simply to wrap up a product and facilitate consumption. They create neither a space of serenity nor of fecundity for the mind and body to rest and grow; rather, they naturalize the zone of conformity, where freedom consists of filling in to one's taste and monetary capacity, the pre-assigned slots.

Musicians often say the meaning of music is too precise for words . . . The imperviousness in the West of the many branches of knowledge to everything that does not fall inside their predetermined scope has been repeatedly challenged by its thinkers throughout the years. They extol the concept of decolonization and continuously invite into their fold "the challenge of the Third World." Yet, they do not seem to realize the difference when they find themselves face to face with it—a difference which does not announce itself, which they do not quite anticipate and cannot fit into any single varying compartment of their catalogued world; a difference they keep on measuring with inadequate sticks designed for their own morbid purpose. When they confront the challenge "in the flesh," they naturally do not recognize it as a challenge. Do not hear, do not see. They promptly reject it as they assign it to their one-place-fits-all "other" category and either warily explain that it is "not quite what we are looking for" and that they are not the right people for it; or they kindly refer it to other "more adequate" whereabouts such as the "counter-culture," "smaller independent," "experimental" margins.

They? Yes, they. But, in the colonial periphery (as in elsewhere), we are often them as well. Colored skins, white masks; colored masks, white skins. Reversal strategies have reigned for some time. *They* accept the margins; so do *we*. For without the margin, there is no center, no heart. *The English and the French precipitate towards us, to look at themselves in our mirror. Following the old colonizers who mixed their blood in their turn, having lost their colonies and their blondness—little by little touched by this swarthy tint spreading like an oil stain over the world—they will come to Buenos Aires in pious pilgrimage to try to understand how one cannot be, yet always be.*[8] The margins, our sites of survival, become our fighting grounds and their site for pilgrimage. Thus, while we turn around and reclaim them as our exclusive territory, they happily approve, for the divisions between margin and center should be preserved, and as clearly demarcated as possible, if the two positions are to remain intact in their power relations. Without a certain work of displacement, again, the margins can easily recomfort the center in its goodwill and liberalism; strategies of reversal thereby meet with their own limits. The critical work that has led to an acceptance of negativity and a new positivity would have to continue its course, so that even in its negativity and positivity, it baffles, displaces, rather than suppresses. By displacing, it never allows this classifying world to exert its classificatory power without returning it to its own ethnocentric classifications. All the while, it points to an elsewhere-within-here whose boundaries would continue to compel frenzied attempts at "baptizing" through logocentric naming and objectivizing to reflect on themselves as they face their own constricting apparatus of refined grids and partitioning walls.

The center itself is marginal. *By pointing attention to a feminist marginality, I have been attempting, not to win the center for ourselves, but to point at the irreducibility of the margin in all explanations.*[9] A woman narrates a displacement as she relentlessly shuttles between the center and the margin. The question is not so much that of loyalty versus betrayal, as that of practicing one's own inventive loyalty towards oneself. *Unless one lives and loves in the trenches it is difficult to remember that the war against dehumanization is ceaseless.*[10] Marginal by imposition, by choice, by necessity. The struggle is always multiple and transversal—specific but not confined to one side of any border war. At the same time as she asserts her difference, she would have to call into question everything which, in the name of the group and the community, perniciously breaks the individual's links with others, while forcing her back on herself and restrictively tying her down to her own reclaimed identity. She would have to work with the power effects of numerously varying forms of centralism and of marginalization. For, how possible is it to undertake a process of decentralization without being made aware of the margins within the center and the centers within the margin? Without encountering marginalization from both the ruling center and the established margin? Wherever she goes, she is asked to show her identity papers. What side? (Did you speak up for . . . ?) Where does she belong? (politically, economically?) Where does she place her loyalty? (sexually, ethnically, professionally?) Should she be met at the center, where they invite her in with much display, it is often only to be reminded that she holds the permanent status of a "foreign worker," "a migrant," or "a temporary sojourner"—a status necessary to the maintenance of a central power. "How about a concrete example from your own culture?" "Could you tell us what is it like in . . . (your country)?" *As a minority woman, I . . . As an Asian-American woman, I . . . As a woman of color filmmaker, I . . . As a feminist, a . . . , and a . . . , I . . .* Not foreigner, yet foreign. At times rejected by her own community, other times needfully retrieved, she is both useless and useful. *The irreducibility of the margin in all explanation. The ceaseless war against dehumanization.* This shuttling in between frontiers is a working out of and an appeal to another sensibility, another consciousness of the condition of marginality: that in which marginality is the condition of the center.

To use marginality as a starting point rather than an ending point is also to cross beyond it towards other affirmations and negations. There cannot be any grand totalizing integration without massive suppression, which is a way of recirculating the effects of domination. *Liberation opens up new relationships of power, which have to be controlled by practices of liberty.*[11] Displacement involves the invention of new forms of subjectivities, of pleasures, of intensities, of relationships, which also implies the continuous renewal of a critical work that looks carefully and intensively at the very system of values to which one refers in fabricating the tools of resistance. The risk of reproducing totalitarianism is always present and one would have to confront, in whatever capacity one has, the controversial values likely to be taken on faith as universal truths by one's own culture(s). "Why don't you show the *poverty* of these people? That's *the* reality!" "Where are the *conflicts* in your film? *That's life!" This world they had written, was the truth.*[12] Participate or perish. "Why don't they see that it is for their own good that *we* are doing this? We are just trying to *help!" I don't believe that this question of "who exercises power?" can be resolved unless that other question "how does it happen?" is resolved at the same time . . . for we know perfectly well that even if we reach the point of designating exactly . . . all those "decision-makers," we will still not really know why and how the decision was made, how it came to be accepted by everybody, and how it is that it hurts a particular category of person, etc. . . .*[13]

A particular category of person. *Lesbos is, in everyone's opinion, a special place. Some say that only Lesbians frequent Lesbos. Others are of the opinion that all the lesbians or companion lovers go there one day or another. The bearers of fables say that they, as a matter of fact, also go to Lesbos.*[14] The struggle not only continues to be carried out on many fronts simultaneously. It is also constantly a double-edged fight. In undermining the West as authoritative subject of knowledge by learning to see into the effects of power and its links with knowledge, competence and qualification, she also has to fight against backlashing through the defensive revalidation of secrecy, exploitative deformation, self-gratifying mystification, and arrogant anti-intellectualism. There is no arcane place for return. Maintaining the intuitive, emotional Other under the scientist tutelage of the rational, all-knowing Western Subject is an everlasting aim of the dominant which keeps on renewing itself through a wide range of humanistic discourses. It is difficult for her, she who partakes in theoretical production—albeit as a foreign worker—not to realize the continuing interested desire of the West to conserve itself as sovereign Subject in most of its radical criticism today. *I once overheard a conversation between two white university women: ". . . he is now in the Ethnic Studies Program. You know, they hire these people who may have an inside view of their own cultures, but who are quite unable to provide the objective, scholarly overview that is necessary for a comprehensive understanding of the culture."* She can neither settle down on a dogmatic belief in the value of scientific knowledge nor be content with a relativistic refusal of all verified truth. Decolonization often means dewesternization as taught by the White man. The latter continues to arrogate the right to tell the previously colonized how to unshackle themselves, and to pronounce whether so and so has successfully returned to his or her own kind. *Science . . . is, literally, a power that forces you to say certain things, if you are not to be disqualified not only as being wrong, but more seriously than that, as being a charlatan.*[15] Intimidation is part of the omni-revised strategies of power exerted in the production and legitimation of knowledge. Thus, she would have to reappropriate while resisting the movement of reappropriation that rules the Master's economy. *Right from the moment they venture to speak what they have to say, [women] will of necessity bring about a shift in metalanguage. And I think we're completely crushed, especially in places like universities, by the highly repressive operations of metalanguage, the operation that sees to it that the moment women open their mouths—women more often than men—they are immediately asked in whose name and from what theoretical standpoint they are speaking, who is their master and where they are coming from: they have, in short, to salute . . . and show their identity papers.*[16]

The story of marginality has taken a long time to be untold. It is neither easy nor difficult, but it can't be stopped in its collective singularities and kaleidoscopic changes. *Anchorage . . . Everyone laughed at the impossibility of it, / but also the truth. Because who would believe / the fantastic and terrible story of all of our survival / those who were never meant / to survive?*[17] *Man in the Moon . . . Yesterday he was poor / but tomorrow he says his house / will fill up with silver / the white flesh will fatten on his frame. / Old man, window in a sky / full of holes / I am like you / putting on a new white shirt / to drive away on the fine roads.*[18] Displacing is a way of surviving. It is an impossible, truthful story of living in-between regimens of truth. The responsibility involved in this motley in-between living is a highly creative one: the displacer proceeds by unceasingly introducing difference into repetition. By questioning over and over again what is taken for granted as self-evident, by reminding oneself and the others of the unchangeability of change itself. Disturbing thereby one's own thinking habits, dissipating what has become familiar and clichéd, and participating in the changing of received values—the transformation (without master) of other selves through one's self. To displace so as not to evade through shortcuts by suppressing or merely excluding. *"Nothing is that simple," [Old Betonie] said, "you don't write off all the white people, just like you don't trust all the Indians . . . They want us to believe all evil resides with white people. Then we will look no further to see what is really happening. They want us to separate ourselves from white people, to be ignorant and helpless as we watch our own destruction . . . and I tell you, we can deal with white people, with their machines and their beliefs. We can because we invented white people: it was an Indian witchery that made white people in the first place."*[19]

The war of borders is a war waged by the West on a global scale to preserve its values. Its expression is always associated with seemingly generous motives and the pass-key ideal to provide a "richer," "more meaningful" life for all men. Whereas its by-now-familiar purpose is to spread the Master's values, comforting him in his godlike charity-giver role, protecting his lifestyle, and naturalizing it as the only, the best way. *The United States idealist turns up in every theater of the war; the teacher, the volunteer, the missioner, the community organizer, the economic developer. Such men define their role as service . . . They especially are the ones for whom "ingratitude" is the bitter reward.*[20] "Don't they see We are only trying to help?!" The compulsion to "help" the needy whose needs one participates in creating and legislating ultimately leads to "bombing people into the acceptance of gifts." Whether the gift is worth the price which the receiver has to pay is a long-term question which not every gift giver asks. But it is a non-gratuitous gesture whose perverse participation in systems of dependence gift planners are often well aware of. Thus, they—the receivers—continue to be "ungrateful" for they suspect this is done on the individual level to bolster someone's guilty ego, and on the societal level, to allow the Master to have the upper hand on all matters that concern them. The "needy" cannot always afford to refuse, so they persist in accepting ungratefully. And in persisting, they are led to displace themselves. The role of the donor becoming the grateful ones, in need of giving and of acceptance, is not only reversed. For, the vitality of the ungrateful receiver lies not in destroying the giver, but in understanding that giving is mutual, and thereby in baffling expectations and unsettling the identification process of giver, given and gift. Or of sender, receiver and message. Social change implies a change in formalized values, and to persist is to maintain despite and against all the strength of a drift and a calm perseverance (in challenging accepted solutions).

Strategies of displacement defy the world of compartmentalization and the systems of dependence it engenders, while filling the shifting space of creation with a passion named wonder. *Who or what the other is, I never know.*[21] Wonder never seizes, never possesses the other as its object. It is in the ability to see, hear and touch, to go toward things as though always for the first time. The encounter is one that surprises in its unexpected, if not entirely unknown character. It does not provoke conflict, rejection or acceptance, for it constitutes an empty, "no-baggage" moment in which passion traverses the non-knowing (not ignorant) subject. A passion also dangerously named gift. Gift as no-gift. It "gives a send-off," it gives the signal to depart. *I think it's more than giving the departure signal, it's really giving, making a gift of, departure, allowing breaks, "parts," partings, separations . . . from this we break with the return-to-self, with the specular relations ruling the coherence, the identification, of the individual.*[22] We hardly know how to give. To un-give in giving, that is, to give without obligation or debt involved and, without expecting any form of return. Here, nothing is owed, for there is no donor who is not an acceptor. Who is giving whom? What is exactly given? May be something does become no-thing or something else when creation consists of voiding what one has secured, dicing with emptiness, and making with nothing. But what, how, and who are largely context-bound and will always defer from one giver and one receiver to another. Each itinerary taken, each reading constructed is at the same time active in its uniqueness and reflective in its collectivity. Where does the creation begin, where does it end? What if the work materialized is more residue than residence? The gift once circulated is always already a reciprocal gift. It is given as a link of a chain of transmission, as a setting into motion of a dormant force within us, the very force which allows threads to keep on unwinding, even in periods when dreams are said to dry up, adventures are scorned upon, and novelty has so declined as to lose its magic power.

And she came to the bank of a dark river; and the bank was steep and high. And on it an old man met her, who had a long white beard; and a stick that curled was in his hand, and on it was written Reason. And he asked her what she wanted; and she said, "I am woman; and I am seeking for the land of Freedom." And he said, "It is before you"... She said, "How am I to get there?" He said, "There is one way, and one only. Down the banks of Labour, through the water of Suffering. There is no other." She said, "Is there no bridge?" He answered, "None." She said, "Is the water deep?" He said, "Deep." She said, "Is the floor worn?" He said, "It is. Your foot may slip at any time, and you may be lost." She said, "Have any crossed already?" He said, "Some have tried!" She said, "Is there a track to show where the best fording is? He said, "It has to be made." She shaded her eyes with her hand; and she said, "I will go." And he said, "You must take off the clothes you wore in the desert: they are dragged down by them who go into the water so clothed." And she threw from her gladly the mantle of Ancient-received-opinions she wore, for it was worn full of holes. And she took the girdle from her waist that she had treasured so long, and the moths flew out of it in a cloud. And he said, "Take the shoes of dependence off your feet." And she stood there naked, but for one garment that clung close to her. And he said, "That you may keep. So they wear clothes in the Land of Freedom. In the water it buoys; it always swims."[23] She takes delight in detours. Her wandering makes things such that even when Reason is given a (biblical) role, it will have to outplay its own logic. For a permanent sojourner walking bare-footed on multiply de/re-territorialized land, thinking is not always knowing, and while an itinerary engaged in may first appear linearly inflexible—as Reason dictates—it is also capable of taking an abrupt turn, of making unanticipated intricate detours, playing thereby with its own straightness and, likewise, outwitting the strategies of its own play.

The myth of pure creativity and expressivity encodes the "natural" to the extent that it equates individualization with commodification. Vision as knowledge is the ideology operating around a notion of interiority which postulates the existence of a central unshakable certitude. The inner confirmation (with its inner ear, inner eye, inner revelation, inner pursuit and external materialization, external action, external result) validates itself through concepts of originality, substantiality, essentiality, as well as through its opposites: common sense, mass communication's clarity, visibly measurable outcome, immediate gratification. Things appear to mean something by themselves: it's a Vision of the Artist. It's a Political work. They assume the clarity of statements of fact within the slipping realm of artistic invention and/or information. "Vision" goes without deliberation, and "Political's" authority is taken on faith. The myth does away with all dialectics; it depoliticizes the tools of creation ("Forget ideology; let the work come out from the vision you have; otherwise, it is impure," or, "Forget aesthetics; only bourgeois indulge in the luxury of aesthetic experience"). What is left aside in the perpetuation of such a myth are not questions like: Who is the artist? What is it? (where does it fit within the categories of the known?) What does it (the work) mean? What are its origins? (where does it come from?) Rather, what is passed over or reduced to the technical realm is the question: How is it made? Being as much a product of a language of true inwardness as that of pure surface, the work is both reflective and reflexive. It is the site of interrelations between giver and receiver. Its poetics assumes this double movement, where reflections on what is unique to the artistic form and sets it off from other forms are also reflections on its inability to isolate itself, to participate in the flow of social life, and to engage in other forms of communication. (Re)Creating is thus not a question of talent and of accessibility; but of exactness internal to the problematic of (each) creation. Does it work? How does it work? Always compelling is the desire to unlearn and to thwart all artistic and discursive forms that attempt at laying hold of its object. A creative event does not grasp, it does not take possession, it is an excursion. More often than not, it requires that one leave the realms of the known, and take oneself there where one does not expect, is not expected to be. There is no prescriptive procedure to be applied mechanically (the formula-solutions professionals proudly come up with when questions are raised); no recipes to follow (a "successful" work is always a crucial test for the creating subject for, there could be no following without change and without risk); and no model to emulate (the imperative of having positive models often surges forth in questions like: "Who taught you?" "Who influenced you?" "Who are the artists you admire?")

If you see Buddha, kill the Buddha![24] Rooted and rootless. Each passion, each effort, each event materialized bears with it its own model. Walking on masterless and ownerless land is living always anew the exile's condition; which is here not quite an imposition nor a choice, but a necessity *You'll learn that in this house it's hard to be a stranger. You'll also learn that it's not easy to stop being one. If you miss your country, every day you'll find more reasons to miss it. But if you manage to forget it and begin to love your new place, you'll be sent home, and then, uprooted once more, you'll begin a new exile.*[25] The work space and the space of creation is where she confronts and leaves off at the same time a world of named nooks and corners, of street signs and traffic regulations, of beaten paths and multiple masks, of constant intermeshing with other bodies'–that are also her own–needs, assumptions, prejudices and limits.

> *Their names I know not,*
> *But every weed has*
> *Its tender flower.*[26]

1. A. Hampate Ba, *Kaydara* (Dakar: Les Nouvelles Editions Africaines, 1978), p. 17.

2. Ibid., pp. 13-14.

3. Gloria Evangelina Anzaldúa, "Del Otro Lado," in *Compañeras: Latina Lesbians*, ed. Juanita Ramos (New York: Latina Lesbian History Project, 1987), p. 3.

4. Ibid.

5. Alicia Dujovne Ortiz, "Buenos Aires (An Excerpt)," in *Discourse* 8 (Fall-Winter 1987): 80.

6. Maurice Blanchot, *The Writing of the Disaster*, trans. A. Smock (Minneapolis: University of Minnesota Press, 1986), p. 12.

7. Vietnamese *Ca Dao*.

8. Ortiz, "Buenos Aires (An Excerpt)," p. 96.

9. Gayatri Chakravorty Spivak, "Explanation and Culture: Marginalia," included in this anthology, p. 381.

10. Audre Lorde, "Age, Race, Class, and Sex: Women Redefining Difference," included in this anthology, p. 284.

11. Michel Foucault, "The Ethic of Care of the Self as a Practice of Freedom," in *The Final Foucault*, eds. J. Bernauer, and D. Rasmussen (Cambridge: MIT Press, 1988), p. 4.

12. Haunani-Kay Trask, "From a Native Daughter," in *The American Indian and the Problem of History*, ed. C. Martin (New York: Oxford University Press, 1987), p. 172.

13. Michel Foucault, *Politics, Philosophy, Culture. Interviews and Other Writings 1977-1984*, ed. L.D. Kritzman (New York and London: Routledge, 1988), p.103-104.

14. Monique Wittig, and Sande Zeig, *Lesbian Peoples: Material for a Dictionary* (New York: Avon Books, 1979), p. 97.

15. Foucault, *Politics, Philosophy, Culture*, pp. 106-107.

16. Hélène Cixous, "Castration or Decapitation?," included in this anthology, p. 353.

17. Joy Harjo, "The Story of All Our Survival," in Joseph Bruchac, *Survival This Way: Interviews with American Indian Poets* (Tucson: Suntrack and The University of Arizona Press, 1987), p. 90.

18. Linda Hogan, "To Take Care of Life," in Bruchac, *Survival This Way*, p. 120.

19. Leslie Marmon Silko, *Ceremony* (New York: Penguin, 1977), p. 132.

20. Ivan Illich, *Celebration of Awareness* (New York: Anchor, 1971), p. 13.

21. Luce Irigaray, "Sexual Difference," in *French Feminist Thought: A Reader*, ed. Toril Moi (Oxford and New York: Basil Blackwell, 1987), p. 124.

22. Hélène Cixous, "Castration or Decapitation?," p. 355.

23. Olive Shreiner, "Three Dreams in a Desert. Under a Mimosa-Tree," in Charlotte H. Bruner, *Unwinding Threads: Writing by Women in Africa* (Nairobi: Ibadan and London: Heinemann, 1983), p. 106.

24. Zen tenet.

25. Maurice Blanchot, *Vicious Circles*, trans. P. Auster (Barrytown, NY: Station Hill Press, 1985), pp. 25-26.

26. Haiku by Sampu, in Stewart Holmes, and Chimyo Horioka, *Zen Art for Meditation* (Rutland, VT and Tokyo, Japan: Charles E. Tuttle Company, 1973), p. 62.

Talking Back

In the world of the southern black community I grew up in "back talk" and "talking back" meant speaking as an equal to an authority figure. It meant daring to disagree and sometimes it just meant having an opinion. In the "old school" children were meant to be seen and not heard. My great-grandparents, grandparents, and parents were all from the old school. To make yourself heard, if you were a child, was to invite punishment, the backhand lick, the slap across the face that would catch you unaware, or the feel of switches stinging your arms and legs.

To speak then when one was not spoken to was a courageous act—an act of risking and daring. And yet it was hard not to speak in warm rooms where heated discussions began at the crack of dawn, women's voices filling the air, giving orders, making threats, fussing. Black men may have excelled in the art of poetic preaching in the male dominated church but in the church of the home where the everyday rules of how to live and how to act were established it was black women who preached. There, black women spoke in a language so rich, so poetic, that it felt to me like being shut off from life, smothered to death if one was not allowed to participate.

It was in that world of woman talk (the men were often silent, often absent) that was born in me the craving to speak, to have a voice, and not just any voice but one that could be identified as belonging to me. To make my voice I had to speak, to hear myself talk—and talk I did—darting in and out of grown folk's conversations and dialogues, answering questions that were not directed at me, endlessly asking questions, making speeches. Needless to say, the punishments for these acts of speech seemed endless. They were intended to silence me—the child—and more particularly the girl child. Had I been a boy they might have encouraged me to speak believing that I might someday be called to preach. There was no "calling" for talking girls, no legitimized rewarded speech. The punishments I received for "talking back" were intended to suppress all possibility that I would create my own speech. That speech was to be suppressed so the "right speech of womanhood" would emerge.

Within feminist circles silence is often seen as the sexist defined "right speech of womanhood"—the sign of woman's submission to patriarchal authority. This emphasis on woman's silence may be an accurate remembering of what has taken place in the households of women from WASP backgrounds in the United States but in black communities (and in other diverse ethnic communities) women have not been silent. Their voices can be heard. Certainly for black women our struggle has not been to emerge from silence into speech but to change the nature and direction of our speech. To make a speech that compels listeners, one that is heard.

Our speech, "the right speech of womanhood," was often the soliloquy, the talking into thin air, the talking to ears that do not hear you—the talk that is simply not listened to. Unlike the black male preacher whose speech was to be heard, who was to be listened to, whose words were to be remembered, the voices of black women—giving orders, making threats, fussing—could be tuned out, could become a kind of background music, audible but not acknowledged as significant speech. Dialogue, the sharing of speech and recognition, took place not between mother and child or mother and male authority figure but with other black women. I can remember watching, fascinated, as our mother talked with her mother, sisters, and women friends. The intimacy and intensity of their speech—the satisfaction they received from talking to one another, the pleasure, the joy. It was in this world of woman speech, loud talk, angry words, women with tongues quick and sharp, tender sweet tongues, touching our world with their words, that I made speech my birthright—and the right to voice, to authorship, a privilege I would not be denied. It was in that world and because of it that I came to dream of writing, to write.

Writing was a way to capture speech, to hold onto it, to keep it close. And so I wrote down bits and pieces of conversations, confessing in cheap diaries that soon fell apart from too much handling, expressing the intensity of my sorrow, the anguish of speech—for I was always saying the wrong thing, asking the wrong questions. I could not confine my speech to the necessary corners and concerns of life. These writings I hid under my bed, in pillow stuffings, among faded underwear. When my sisters found and read them, they ridiculed and mocked me—poking fun. I felt violated, ashamed, as if the secret parts of my self had been exposed, brought into the open, and hung like newly clean laundry, out in the air for everyone to see. The fear of exposure, the fear that one's deepest emotions and innermost thoughts would be dismissed as mere nonsense, felt by so many young girls keeping diaries, keeping and hiding speech, seems to me now one of the barriers that women have needed and need to destroy so that we are no longer pushed into secrecy or silence.

Despite my feelings of violation, of exposure, I continued to speak and write, choosing my hiding places well, learning to destroy work when no safe place could be found. Rather than teaching me absolute silence, I was taught that it was important to speak but to talk a talk that was in itself a silence. Taught to speak and yet to beware of the betrayal of too much heard speech, I experienced intense confusion and deep anxiety in my efforts to speak and write. Reciting poems at Sunday afternoon church service might be rewarded speech. Writing a poem (when one's time could be "better" spent sweeping, ironing, learning to cook) was luxurious activity, indulged in at the expense of others. Questioning authority, raising issues that were not deemed appropriate subjects, brought pain, punishments—like telling mama I wanted to die before her because I could not live without her—that was crazy talk, crazy speech, the kind that would lead you to end up in a mental institution. "Little girl," I would be told, "if you don't stop all this crazy talk and crazy acting you are going to end up right out there at Western State."

Madness too then, not just physical abuse, was the punishment for too much talk if you were female. Yet even as this fear of madness haunted me, hung over my writing like a monstrous shadow, I could not stop the words, making thought, writing speech. For this terrible madness which I feared, which I was sure was the destiny of daring women born to intense speech (after all the authorities emphasized this point daily), was not as threatening as imposed silence, as suppressed speech.

Safety and sanity were to be sacrificed if I was to experience defiant speech. Though I risked the two, deep-seated fears and anxieties characterized my childhood days. I would speak, but I would not ride a bike, play hard ball, or hold the gray kitten. Writing about the ways we are hurt by negative traumas in our growing-up years, psychoanalyst Alice Miller makes the point in *For Her Own Good* that it is not clear why wounding in childhood becomes for some folk an opportunity to grow, to move forward in the process of self-realization rather than a retardation of that process. Certainly, when I reflect on the trials of my growing-up years, the many punishments, I can see now that in resistance I learned then to be vigilant in the nourishment of my spirit, to be tough, to courageously protect that spirit from forces that would break it.

While punishing me, my parents often spoke about the necessity of breaking my spirit. Now when I ponder the silences, the voices that are not heard, the voices of those wounded and/or oppressed individuals who do not speak or write, I contemplate the acts of persecution, torture—the terrorism that breaks spirits, that makes creativity im-possible. I write these words to bear witness to the primacy of struggle in any situation of domination (even within family life), to the strength and power that emerges from sustained resistance, and the profound conviction that these forces can be healing, can protect us from dehumanization and despair.

These early trials, wherein I learned to stand my ground, to keep my spirit intact, came vividly to mind after I published *Ain't I a Woman* and the work was sharply and harshly criticized. While I had expected a climate of critical dialogue, I was not expect-ing a critical avalanche that had the power in its intensity to crush spirit, to push one into silence. Since that time I have heard stories about black women, about women of color, who write and publish, having nervous breakdowns (even when the work is quite successful), being made mad because they cannot bear the harsh responses of fam-ily, friends, and unknown critics, or becoming silent, unproductive. Surely, the absence of a humane critical response has tremendous impact on the writer from any group, but especially for those writers from oppressed, colonized groups who endeavor to speak. For us, true speaking is not solely an expression of creative power, it is an act of resis-tance, a political gesture that challenges the politics of domination that would render us nameless and voiceless. As such it is a courageous act; as such it represents a threat. To those who wield oppressive power that which is threatening must necessarily be wiped out, annihilated, silenced.

Recent efforts by black women writers to call attention to our work serve to high-light both our presence and absence. Whenever I peruse women's bookstores I am struck not by the rapidly growing body of feminist writing by black women but by the paucity of available published material. Those of us who write and are published remain few in number. The context of silence is varied and multi-dimensional. Most obvious are the ways racism, sexism, and class exploitation act as agents to suppress and silence.

Less obvious are the inner struggles, the effort made to gain necessary confidence to write, to rewrite, to fully develop craft and skill, the extent to which such efforts fail.

Although I have wanted writing to be a life work for me since childhood, it has been difficult for me to claim "writer" as part of that which identifies and shapes my everyday reality. Even after publishing books I would often speak of wanting to be a writer as though these works did not exist. And though I would be told, "you are a writer," I was not ready yet to affirm fully this truth. Part of myself was still held captive by domineering forces of history, of familial life that had charted a map of silence, of right speech. I had not completely let go the fear of saying the wrong thing, of being punished. Somewhere in the deep recesses of my mind I believed I could avoid both responsibility and punishment if I did not declare myself a writer.

One of the many reasons I chose to write using the pseudonym bell hooks, a family name (mother to Sarah Oldham, grandmother to Rosa Bell Oldham, great-grandmother to me) was to construct a writer identity that would challenge and subdue all impulses that would lead me away from speech into silence. I was a young girl buying bubble gum at the corner store when I first "really" heard the full name Bell Hooks: I had just "talked back" to a grown person. Even now I can recall the surprised look, the mocking tones that informed me I must be kin to Bell Hooks–a sharp-tongued woman, a woman who spoke her mind, a woman who was not afraid to talk back. I claimed this legacy of defiance, of will, of courage, affirming my link to female ancestors who were bold and daring in their speech. Unlike my bold and daring mother and grandmother, who were not supportive of talking back, even though they were assertive and powerful in their speech, Bell Hooks, as I discovered, claimed, and invented her, was my ally, my support.

The initial act of talking back outside the home was an empowering moment. It was the first of many acts of defiant speech that would make it possible for me to emerge as independent thinker and writer. Seen in retrospect, "talking back" became for me a rite of initiation, testing my courage, strengthening my commitment, preparing me for the days ahead–the days when writing seems impossible but necessary, rejection notices, periods of silence, publication, ongoing development.

Moving from silence into speech is for the oppressed, the colonized, the exploited, and those who stand and struggle side by side, a gesture of defiance that heals, that makes new life, and new growth possible. It is that act of speech, of "talking back" that is no mere gesture of empty words, that is the expression of moving from object to subject, that is the liberated voice.

• • •

marginality as site of resistance

Four years ago in the preface to *Feminist Theory: From Margin to Center* I expressed these thoughts on marginality:

> To be in the margin is to be part of the whole but outside the main body. As black Americans living in a small Kentucky town, the railroad tracks were a daily reminder of our marginality. Across those tracks were paved streets, stores we could not enter, restaurants we could not eat in, and people we could not look directly in the face. Across those tracks was a world we could work in as maids, as janitors, as prostitutes, as long as it was in a service capacity. We could enter that world but we could not live there. We had always to return to the margin, to cross the tracks, to shacks and abandoned houses on the edge of town.
>
> There were laws to ensure our return. To not return was to risk being punished. Living as we did—on the edge—we developed a particular way of seeing reality. We looked both from the outside in and from the inside out. We focused our attention on the center as well as on the margin. We understood both. This mode of seeing reminded us of the existence of a whole universe, a main body made up of both margin and center. Our survival depended on an ongoing public awareness of the separation between margin and center and an ongoing private acknowledgement that we were a necessary, vital part of that whole.
>
> This sense of wholeness, impressed upon our consciousness by the structure of our daily lives, provided us an oppositional world view—a mode of seeing unknown to most of our oppressors that sustained us, aided us in our struggle to transcend poverty and despair, strengthened our sense of self and our solidarity.

Though incomplete, I was working in these statements to identify marginality as much more than a site of deprivation. In fact I was saying just the opposite: that it is also the site of radical possibility, a space of resistance. It was this marginality that I was naming as a central location for the production of a counter hegemonic discourse that is not just found in words but in habits of being and the way one lives. As such, I was not speaking of a marginality one wishes to lose, to give up, or surrender as part of moving into the center, but rather as a site one stays in, clings to even, because it nourishes one's capacity to resist. It offers the possibility of radical perspectives from which to see and create, to imagine alternatives, new worlds.

This is not a mythic notion of marginality. It comes from lived experience. Yet I want to talk about what it means to struggle to maintain that marginality even as one works, produces, lives, if you will, at the center. I no longer live in that segregated world across the tracks. Central to life in that world was the ongoing awareness of the necessity of opposition. When Bob Marley sings, "We refuse to be what you want us to be, we are what we are, and that's the way it's going to be," that space of refusal, where one can say no to the colonizer, no to the downpressor, is located in the margins. And one can only say no, speak to the voice of resistance, because there exists a counter language. While it may resemble in ways the colonizer's tongue, it has to undergo a transformation. It has been irrevocably changed. When I left that concrete space in the margins, I kept alive in my heart a way of knowing reality which affirms continually not only the primacy of resistance but the necessity of a resistance that is sustained by re-membrance of the past, which includes recollections of broken tongues, giving us ways to speak that de-colonize our minds, our very beings. Once mama said to me as I was about to go again to the predominately white university, "You can take what the white people have to offer but you do not have to love them." Now understanding her cultural codes I know that she was not saying to me not to love people of other races. She was speaking about colonization and the reality of what it means to be taught in a culture of domination by those who dominate. She was insisting on my power to be able to separate useful knowledge that I might get from the dominating group from participation in ways of knowing that would lead to estrangement, alienation, and, worse, assimilation and cooption. She was saying that it is not necessary to give yourself over to them to learn. Not having been in those institutions, she still knew that I might be faced again and again with situations where I would be "tried," made to feel as though a central requirement of my being accepted might be participation in this system of exchange to ensure my success, my "making it." She was reminding me of the necessity of opposition and simultaneously encouraging me not to lose that radical perspective shaped and formed by marginality.

Understanding marginality as position and place of resistance is crucial for oppressed, exploited, colonized people. If we only view the margin as sign, marking the condition of our pain and deprivation, then a certain hopelessness and despair, a deep nihilism penetrates in a destructive way the very ground of our being. It is there in that space of collective despair that one's creativity, one's imagination is at risk, there that one's mind is fully colonized, there that the freedom one longs for is lost. Truly the mind that resists colonization struggles for freedom of expression. That struggle may not even begin with the colonizer; it may begin within one's segregated colonized community and family. I want to note that I am not trying to romantically re-inscribe the notion of that space of marginality where the oppressed live apart from their oppressors as "pure." I want to say that these margins have been both sites of repression and sites of resistance. And since we are well able to name the nature of that repression, we know better the margins as site of deprivation. We are more silent when it comes to speaking of the margin as site of resistance. We are more often silenced when it comes to speaking of the margin as site of resistance.

Silenced. During my graduate years I heard myself speaking often in the voice of resistance. I cannot say that my speech was welcomed. I cannot say that my speech was heard in such a way that it altered relations between colonizer and colonized. Yet what I have noticed is that those scholars, most especially those who name themselves radical critical thinkers, feminist thinkers, now fully participate in the construction of a discourse about the "Other." I was made "other" there in that space with them. In that space in the margins, that lived-in segregated world of my past and present, I was not "other." They did not meet me there in that space. They met me at the center. They greeted me as colonizers. I am waiting to learn from them the path of their resistance, of how it came to be that they were able to surrender the power to act as colonizers. I am waiting for them to bear witness, to give testimony. They say that the discourse on marginality, on difference has moved beyond a discussion of us and them. They do not speak of how this movement has taken place. This is a response from the radical space of my marginality. It is a space of resistance. It is a space I choose.

I am waiting for them to stop talking about the "other," to stop even describing how important it is to be able to speak about difference. It is not just important what we speak about but how and why we speak. Often this speech about the "other" is also a mask, an oppressive talk hiding gaps, absences, that space where our words would be if we were speaking, if there was silence, if we were there. This "we" is that us in the margins, that "we" who inhabit marginal space that is not a site of domination but a place of resistance. Enter that space. Often this speech about the "other" annihilates, erases. *No need to hear your voice when I can talk about you better than you can speak about yourself. No need to hear your voice. Only tell me about your pain. I want to know your story. And then I will tell it back to you in a new way. Tell it back to you in such a way that it has become mine, my own. Re-writing you I write myself anew. I am still author, authority. I am still colonizer, the speaking subject and you are now at the center of my talk.* We greet you as liberators. This "we" is that us in the margins, that "we" who inhabit marginal space that is not a site of domination but a place of resistance. Enter that space. This is an intervention. I am writing to you. I am speaking from a place in the margins where I am different—where I see things differently. Speaking from margins. Speaking in resistance. I open a book. There are words on the back cover "NEVER IN THE SHADOWS AGAIN," a book which suggests the possibility of speaking as liberators. Only who is speaking and who is silent. Only who stands in the shadows—the shadow in a doorway, the space where images of black women are represented voiceless, the space where our words are invoked to serve and support, the space of our absence. Only small echoes of protest. We are re-written. We are "other." We are the margin. Who is speaking and to whom. Where do we locate ourselves and our comrades.

Silenced. We fear those who speak about us who do not speak to us and with us. We know what it is like to be silenced. We know that the forces that silence us because they never want us to speak, differ from the forces that say speak, tell me your story. Only do not speak in the voice of resistance. Only speak from that space in the margin that is a sign of deprivation, a wound, and unfulfilled longing. Only speak your pain.

This is an intervention. A message from that space in the margin that is a site of creativity and power, that inclusive space where we recover ourselves, where we move in solidarity to erase the category colonized/colonizer. Marginality as site of resistance. Enter that space. Let us meet there. Enter that space. We greet you as liberators.

Castration or Decapitation?

On sexual difference: Let's start with these small points. One day Zeus and Hera, the ultimate couple, in the course of one of their intermittent and thoroughgoing disagreements—which today would be of the greatest interest to psychoanalysts—called on Tiresias to arbitrate. Tiresias, the blind seer who had enjoyed the uncommon fortune of having lived seven years as a woman and seven years as a man.

He was gifted with second sight. Second sight in a sense other than we might usually understand it: it isn't simply that as a prophet he could see into the future. He could also see it from both sides: from the side of the male and from the side of the female.

The subject of the disagreement was the question of sexual pleasure: "Of man and woman, who enjoys the greater pleasure?" Obviously neither Zeus nor Hera could answer this without giving their *own* answer, which they saw would be inadequate, since the ancients made fewer assumptions than we do about the possiblilty of making such identifications. So it came about that Tiresias was sought, as the only person who could know "which of the two." And Tiresias answered: "If sexual pleasure could be divided up into ten parts, nine of them would be the woman's." Nine. It's no coincidence that Tiresias makes another appearance in none other than the oedipal scene. It was Tiresias who, at Oedipus's command, reminded Oedipus that blindness was his master, and Tiresias who, so they say, "made the scales fall from his eyes" and showed Oedipus who he really was. We should note that these things are all linked together and bear some relation to the question "What is woman for man?"

It reminds me of a little Chinese story. Every detail of this story counts. I've borrowed it from a very serious text, Sun Tse's manual of strategy, which is a kind of handbook for the warrior. This is the anecdote. The king commanded General Sun Tse: "You who are a great strategist and claim to be able to train anybody in the arts of war . . . take my wives (all one hundred and eighty of them!) and make soldiers out of them." We don't know why the king conceived this desire—it's the one thing we don't know . . . it remains precisely "un(re)countable" or unaccountable in the story. But it is a king's wish, after all.

So Sun Tse had the women arranged in two rows, each headed by one of the two favorite wives, and then taught them the language of the drumbeat. It was very simple: two beats—right, three beats—left, four beats—about turn or backward march. But instead of learning the code very quickly, the ladies started laughing and chattering and paying no attention to the lesson, and Sun Tse, the master, repeated the lesson several times over. But the more he spoke, the more the women fell about laughing, upon which Sun Tse put his code to the test. It is said in this code that should women fall about laughing instead of becoming soldiers, their actions might be deemed mutinous, and the code has ordained that cases of mutiny call for the death penalty. So the women were condemned to death. This bothered the king somewhat: a hundred and eighty wives are a lot to lose! He didn't want his wives put to death. But Sun Tse replied that since he was put in charge of making soldiers out of the women, he would carry out the order: Sun Tse was a man of absolute principle. And in any case there's an order even more "royal" than that of the king himself: the Absolute Law . . . One does not go back on an order. He therefore acted according to the code and with his saber beheaded the two women commanders. They were replaced and the exercise started again, and as if they had never done anything except practice the art of war, the women turned right, left, and about in silence and with never a single mistake.

It's hard to imagine a more perfect example of a particular relationship between two economies: a masculine economy and a feminine economy, in which the masculine is governed by a rule that keeps time with two beats, three beats, four beats, with pipe and drum, exactly as it should be. An order that works by inculcation, by education: it's always a question of education. An education that consists of trying to make a soldier of the feminine by force, the force history keeps reserved for woman, the "capital" force that is effectively decapitation. Women have no choice other than to be decapitated, and in any case the moral is that if they don't actually lose their heads by the sword, *they only keep them on condition that they lose them*—lose them, that is, to complete silence, turned into automatons.

It's a question of submitting feminine disorder, its laughter, its inability to take the drumbeats seriously, to the threat of decapitation. If man operates under the threat of castration, if masculinity is culturally ordered by the castration complex, it might be said that the backlash, the return, on women of this castration anxiety is its displacement as decapitation, execution, of woman, as loss of her head.

We are led to pose the woman question to history in quite elementary forms like, "Where is she? Is there any such thing as woman?" At worst, many women wonder whether they even exist. They feel they don't exist and wonder if there has ever been a place for them. I am speaking of woman's place, *from* woman's place, if she takes (a) place.

In *La Jeune Née*[1] I made use of a story that seemed to me particularly expressive of woman's place: the story of Sleeping Beauty. Woman, if you look for her, has a strong chance of always being found in one position: in bed. In bed and asleep—"laid (out)." She is always to be found on or in a bed: Sleeping Beauty is lifted from her bed by a man because, as we all know, women don't wake up by themselves: man has to intervene, you understand. She is lifted up by the man who will lay her in her next bed so that she may be confined to bed ever after, just as the fairy tales say.

And so her trajectory is from bed to bed: one bed to another, where she can dream all the more. There are some extraordinary analyses by Kierkegaard on women's "existence"—or that part of it set aside for her by culture—in which he says he sees her as sleeper. She sleeps, he says, and first love dreams her and then she dreams of love. From dream to dream, and always in second position. In some stories, though, she can be found standing up, but not for long. Take Little Red Riding Hood as an example: it will not, I imagine, be lost on you that the "red riding hood" in question is a little clitoris. Little Red Riding Hood basically gets up to some mischief: she's the little female sex that tries to play a bit and sets out with her little pot of butter and her little jar of honey. What is interesting is that it's her mother who gives them to her and sends her on an excursion that's tempting precisely because it's forbidden: Little Red Riding Hood leaves one house, mommy's house, not to go out into the big wide world but to go from one house to another by the shortest route possible: to make haste, in other words, from the mother to the other. The other in this case is grandmother, whom we might imagine as taking the place of the "Great Mother," because there are great men but no great women: there are Grand-Mothers instead. And grandmothers are always wicked: she is the bad mother who always shuts the daughter in whenever the daughter might by chance want to live or take pleasure. So she'll always be carrying her little pot of butter and her little jar of honey to grandmother, who is there as jealousy . . . the jealousy of the woman who can't let her daughter go.

But in spite of all this Little Red Riding Hood makes her little detour, does what women should never do, travels through her own forest. She allows herself the forbidden . . . and pays dearly for it: she goes back to bed, in grandmother's stomach. The Wolf is grandmother, and all women recognize the Big Bad Wolf! We know that always lying in wait for us somewhere in some big bed is a Big Bad Wolf. The Big Bad Wolf represents, with his big teeth, his big eyes, and his grandmother's looks, that great Superego that threatens all the little female red riding hoods who try to go out and explore their forest without the psychoanalyst's permission. So, between two houses, between two beds, she is laid, ever caught in her chain of metaphors, metaphors that organize culture . . . ever her moon to the masculine sun, nature to culture, concavity to masculine convexity, matter to form, immobility/inertia to the march of progress, terrain trod by the masculine footstep, vessel . . . While man is obviously the active, the upright, the productive . . . and besides, that's how it happens in History.

This opposition to woman cuts endlessly across all the oppositions that order culture. It's the classic opposition, dualist and hierarchical. Man/Woman automatically means great/small, superior/inferior . . . means high or low, means Nature/History, means transformation/inertia. In fact, every theory of culture, every theory of society, the whole conglomeration of symbolic systems—everything, that is, that's spoken, everything that's organized as discourse, art, religion, the family, language, everything that seizes us, everything that acts on us—it is all ordered around hierarchical oppositions that come back to the man/woman opposition, an opposition that can only be sustained by means of a difference posed by cultural discourse as "natural," the difference between activity and passivity. It always works this way, and the opposition is founded in the *couple*. A couple posed in opposition, in tension, in conflict . . . a couple engaged in a kind of war in which death is always at work—and I keep emphasizing the importance of the opposition as *couple*, because all this isn't just about one word: rather everything turns on the Word: everything is the Word and only the Word. To be aware of the couple, that it's the couple that makes it all work, is also to point to the fact that it's on the couple that we have to work if we are to deconstruct and transform culture.

The couple as terrain, as space of cultural struggle, but also as terrain, as space demanding, insisting on, a complete transformation in the relation of one to the other. And so work still has to be done on the couple . . . on the question, for example, of what a completely different couple relationship would be like, what a love that was more than merely a cover for, a veil of, war would be like.

I said it turns on the Word: we must take culture at its word, as it takes us into its Word, into its tongue. You'll understand why I think that no political reflection can dispense with reflection on language, with work on language. For as soon as we exist, we are born into language and language speaks (to) us, dictates its law, a law of death: it lays down its familial model, lays down its conjugal model, and even at the moment of uttering a sentence, admitting a notion of "being," a question of being, an ontology, we are already seized by a certain kind of masculine desire, the desire that mobilizes philosophical discourse. As soon as the question "What is it?" is posed, from the moment a question is put, as soon as a reply is sought, *we are already caught up in masculine interrogation.* I say "masculine interrogation": as we say so-and-so was interrogated by the police. And this interrogation precisely involves the work of signification: "What is it? Where is it?" A work of meaning, "This means that," the predicative distribution that always at the same time orders the constitution of meaning. And while meaning is being constituted, it only gets constituted in a movement in which one of the terms of the couple is destroyed in favor of the other.

"Look for the lady," as they say in the stories. . . . "Cherchez la femme"—we always know that means: you'll find her in bed. Another question that's posed in History, rather a strange question, a typical male question is: "What do women want?" The Freudian question, of course. In his work on desire, Freud asks somewhere, or rather doesn't ask, leaves hanging in the air, the question "What do women want?" Let's talk a bit about this desire and about why/how the question "What do women want?" gets put, how it's both posed and left hanging in the air by philosophical discourse, by analytical discourse (analytic discourse being only one province of philosophical discourse), and how it is posed, let us say, by the Big Bad Wolf and the Grand-Mother.

"What does she want?" Little Red Riding Hood knew quite well what she wanted, but Freud's question is not what it seems: it's a rhetorical question. To pose the question "What do women want?" is to pose it already as answer, as from a man who isn't expecting any answer, because the answer is "She wants nothing." . . . "What does she want? . . . Nothing!" Nothing because she is passive. The only thing man can do is offer the question "What could she want, she who wants nothing?" Or in other words: "Without me, what could she want?"

Old Lacan takes up the slogan "What does she want?" when he says, "A woman cannot speak of her pleasure." Most interesting! It's all there, a woman *cannot,* is unable, hasn't the power. Not to mention "speaking": it's exactly this that she's forever deprived of. Unable to speak of pleasure = no pleasure, no desire: power, desire, speaking, pleasure, none of these is for woman. And as a quick reminder of how this works in theoretical discourse, one question: you are aware, of course, that for Freud/Lacan, woman is said to be "outside the Symbolic": outside the Symbolic, that is outside language, the place of the Law, excluded from any possible relationship with culture and the cultural order. And she is outside the Symbolic because she lacks any relation to the phallus, because she does not enjoy what orders masculinity—the castration complex. Woman does not have the advantage of the castration complex—it's reserved solely for the little boy. The phallus, in Lacanian parlance also called the "transcendental signifier," transcendental precisely as primary organizer of the structure of subjectivity, is what, for psychoanalysis, inscribes its effects, its effects of castration and resistance to castration and hence the very organization of language, as unconscious relations, and so it is the phallus that is said to constitute the a priori condition of all symbolic functioning. This has important implications as far as the body is concerned: the body is not sexed, does not recognize itself as, say, female or male without having gone through the castration complex.

What psychoanalysis points to as defining woman is that she lacks lack. She lacks lack? Curious to put it in so contradictory, so extremely paradoxical, a manner: she lacks lack. To say she lacks lack is also, after all, to say she doesn't miss lack . . . since she doesn't miss the lack of lack. Yes, they say, but the point is "she lacks The Lack," The Lack, lack of the Phallus. And so, supposedly, she misses the great lack, so that without man she would be indefinite, indefinable, nonsexed, unable to recognize herself: outside the Symbolic. But fortunately there is man: he who comes . . . Prince Charming. And it's man who teaches woman (because man is always the Master as well), who teaches her to be aware of lack, to be aware of absence, aware of death. It's man who will finally order woman, "set her to rights," by teaching her that without man she could "misrecognize." He will teach her the Law of the Father. Something of the order of: "Without me, without me—the Absolute—Father (the father is always that much more absolute the more he is improbable, dubious) without me you wouldn't exist, I'll show you." Without him she'd remain in a state of distressing and distressed undifferentiation, unbordered, unorganized, "unpoliced" by the phallus . . . incoherent, chaotic, and embedded in the Imaginary in her ignorance of the Law of the Signifier. Without him she would in all probability not be contained by the threat of death, might even, perhaps, believe herself eternal, immortal. Without him she would be deprived of sexuality. And it might be said that man works very actively to produce "his woman." Take for example *Le Ravissement de Lol V. Stein,*[2] and you will witness the moment when man can finally say "his" woman, "my" woman. It is that moment when he has taught her to be aware of Death. So man *makes*, he makes (up) his woman, not without being himself seized up and drawn into the dialectical movement that this sort of thing sets in play. We might say that the Absolute Woman, in culture, the woman who really represents femininity most effectively . . . who is closest to femininity as *prey* to masculinity, is actually the hysteric . . . he makes her image for her!

The hysteric is a divine spirit that is always at the edge, the turning point, of making. She is one who does not make herself . . . she does not make herself but she does make the other. It is said that the hysteric "makes-believe" the father, plays the father, "makes-believe" the master. Plays, makes up, makes-believe: she makes-believe she is a woman, unmakes-believe too . . . plays at desire, plays the father . . . turns herself into him, unmakes him at the same time. Anyway, without the hysteric, there's no father . . . without the hysteric, no master, no analyst, no analysis! She's the *unorganizable* feminine construct, whose power of producing the other is a power that never returns to her. She is really a wellspring nourishing the other for eternity, yet not drawing back from the other . . . not recognizing herself in the images the other may or may not give her. She is given images that don't belong to her, and she forces herself, as we've all done, to resemble them.

And so in the face of this person who lacks lack, who does not miss lack of lack, we have the construct that is infinitely easier to analyze, to put in place—manhood, flaunting it's metaphors like banners through history. You know those metaphors: they are most effective. It's always clearly a question of war, of battle. If there is no battle, it's replaced by the stake of battle: strategy. Man is strategy, is reckoning . . . "how to win" with the least possible loss, at the lowest possible cost. Throughout literature masculine figures all say the same thing: "I'm reckoning" what to do to win. Take Don Juan and you have the whole masculine economy getting together to "give women just what it takes to keep them in bed" then swiftly taking back the investment, then reinvesting, etc., so that nothing ever gets given, everything gets taken back, while in the process the greatest possible dividend of pleasure is taken. Consumption without payment, of course.

Let's take an example other than Don Juan, one clearly pushed to the point of paroxysm . . . Kafka. It was Kafka who said there was one struggle that terrified him beyond all others (he was an embattled man, but his battle was with death—in this sense he was a man greater than the rest): but in matters concerning women his was a struggle that terrified him (death did not). He said the struggle with women ended up in bed: this was his greatest fear. If you know a little about Kafka's life you should know that in his complete integrity, his absolute honesty, he attempted to live through this awful anguish in his relationships with women, in the struggle whose only outcome is bed, by working . . . finally to produce a neurosis of quite extraordinary beauty and terror consisting of a life-and-death relationship with a woman, but at the greatest possible distance. As close as possible and as distanced as possible. He would be betrothed, passionately desire a marriage which he feared above all else, and keep putting off the wedding by endless unconscious maneuvers . . . by a pattern of repeated breakups that took him right to his deathbed, the very deathbed he'd always wanted—a bed, that is, in which he could finally be alone with death. This work of keeping women at a distance while at the same time drawing them to him shows up strikingly in his diary, again because Kafka was honest enough to reveal everything, to say everything. He wrote in little columns, putting debits on the left and credits on the right . . . all the reasons I absolutely must marry, all the reasons I absolutely must not. This tension points to the spirit of male/female relationships in a way it isn't normally revealed, because what is normally revealed is actually a decoy . . . all those words about love, etc. All that is always just a cover for hatred nourished by the fear of death: woman, for man, is death. This is actually the castration complex at its most effective: giving is really dicing with death.

Giving: there you have a basic problem, which is that masculinity is always associated—in the unconscious, which is after all what makes the whole economy function—with debt. Freud, in deciphering the latent antagonisms between parents and children, shows very well the extent to which the family is founded, as far as the little boy is concerned, on a fearful debt. The child *owes* his parents his life and his problem is exactly to *repay* them: nothing is more dangerous than obligation. Obligation is submission to the enormous weight of the other's generosity, is being threatened by a blessing . . . and a blessing is always an evil when it comes from someone else. For the moment you receive something you are effectively "open" to the other, and if you are a man you have only one wish, and that is hastily to return the gift, to break the circuit of an exchange that could have no end . . . to be nobody's child, to owe no one a thing.

And so debt, what is always expressed in religions by laws like "a tooth for a tooth," "a gift for a gift," "an eye for an eye," is a system of absolute equivalence . . . of no inequality, for inequality is always interpreted by the masculine as a difference of strength, and thus as a threat. This economy is ruled by price: there's a price to pay, life is dear, the price of life has to be paid. And here lies a difficulty in connection with love, in that, at coming, love starts escaping the system of equivalence in all sorts of ways. It's very hard to give back something you can't pin down. What's so frightening in relations between male and female at the moment of coming *(au niveau de la jouissance)* is the possibility that there might be more on one side than on the other and the Symbolic finds it really tough to know who wins and who loses, who gives more in a relationship of this sort. The memory of debt and the fear of having to recognize one's debt rise up straightaway. But the refusal to know is nonetheless ambivalent in its implications, for not knowing is threatening while at the same time (and this is where the castration complex comes in) it reinforces the desire to know. So in the end woman, in man's desire, stands in the place of not knowing, the place of mystery. In this sense she is no good, but at the same time she is good because it's this mystery that leads man to keep overcoming, dominating, subduing, putting his manhood to the test, against the mystery he has to keep forcing back.

And so they want to keep woman in the place of mystery, consign her to mystery, as they say "keep her in her place," keep her at a distance: she's always not quite there . . . but no one knows exactly where she is. She is kept in place in a quite characteristic way—coming back to Oedipus, the place of one who is too often forgotten,[3] the place of the sphinx . . . she's kept in the place of what we might call the "watch-bitch" *(chienne chanteuse)*. That is to say, she is outside the city, at the edge of the city—the city is man, ruled by masculine law—and there she is. In what way is she there? She is there not recognizing: the sphinx doesn't recognize herself, she it is who poses questions, just as it's man who holds the answer and furthermore, as you know, his answer is completely worthy of him: "Man," simple answer . . . but it says everything. "Watch-bitch," the sphinx was called: she's an animal and she sings out. She sings out because women do . . . they do utter a little, but they don't speak. Always keep in mind the distinction between speaking and talking. It is said, in philosophical texts, that women's weapon is the word, because they talk, talk endlessly, chatter, overflow with sound, mouth-sound: but they don't actually *speak*, they have nothing to say. They always inhabit the place of silence, or at most make it echo with their singing. And neither is to their benefit, for they remain outside knowledge.

Silence: silence is the mark of hysteria. The great hysterics have lost speech, they are aphonic, and at times have lost more than speech: they are pushed to the point of choking, nothing gets through. They are decapitated, their tongues are cut off and what talks isn't heard because it's the body that talks, and man doesn't hear the body. In the end, the woman pushed to hysteria is the woman who disturbs and is nothing but disturbance. The master dotes on disturbance right from the moment he can subdue it and call it up at his command. Conversely the hysteric is the woman who cannot not ask the master what he wants her to want: she wants nothing, truly she wants nothing. She wants . . . she wants to want. But what is it she wants to want? So she goes to school: she asks the master: "What should I want?" and "What do you want me to want, so that I might want it?" Which is what happens in analysis.

Lets's imagine that all this functioned otherwise, that it could function otherwise. We'd first have to imagine resistance to masculine desire conducted by woman as hysteric, as distracted. We'd first have to imagine her ceasing to support with her body what I call the realm of the proper. The realm of the proper in the sense of the general cultural heterosocial establishment in which man's reign is held to be proper: proper may be the opposite of improper, and also of unfitting, just as black and white are opposites. Etymologically, the "proper" is "property," that which is not separable from me. Property is proximity, nearness: we must love our neighbors, those close to us, as ourselves: we must draw close to the other so that we may love him/her, because we love ourselves most of all. The realm of the proper, culture, functions by the appropriation articulated, set into play, by man's classic fear of seeing himself expropriated, seeing himself deprived . . . by his refusal to be deprived, in a state of separation, by his fear of losing the prerogative, fear whose response is all of History. Everything must return to the masculine. "Return": the economy is founded on a system of returns. If a man spends and is spent, it's on condition that his power returns. If a man should go out, if he should go out to the other, it's always done according to the Hegelian model, the model of the master-slave dialectic.

Woman would then have to start by resisting the movement of reappropriation that rules the whole economy, by being party no longer to the masculine return, but by proposing instead a desire no longer caught up in the death struggle, no longer implicated in the reservation and reckoning of the masculine economy, but breaking with the reckoning that "I never lose anything except to win a bit more" . . . so as to put aside all negativeness and bring out a positiveness which might be called the living other, the rescued other, the other unthreatened by destruction. Women have it in them to organize this regeneration, this vitalization of the other, of otherness in its entirety. They have it in them to affirm the difference, *their* difference, such that nothing can destroy that difference, rather that it might be affirmed, affirmed to the point of strangeness. So much so that when sexual difference, when the preservation or dissolution of sexual difference, is touched on, the whole problem of destroying the strange, destroying all the forms of racism, all the exclusions, all those instances of outlaw and genocide that recur through History, is also touched on. If women were to set themselves to transform History, it can safely be said that every aspect of History would be completely altered. Instead of being made by man, History's task would be to make woman, to produce her. And it's at this point that work by women themselves on women might be brought into play, which would benefit not only women but all humanity.

But first she would have to *speak*, start speaking, stop saying that she has nothing to say! Stop learning in school that women are created to listen, to believe, to make no discoveries. Dare to speak her piece about giving, the possibility of a giving that doesn't take away, but *gives*. Speak of her pleasure and, God knows, she has something to say about that, so that she gets to unblock a sexuality that's just as much feminine as masculine, "de-phallocentralize" the body, relieve man of his phallus, return him to an erogenous field and a libido that isn't stupidly organized round that monument, but appears shifting, diffused, taking on all the others of oneself. Very difficult: first we have to get rid of the systems of censorship that bear down on every attempt to speak in the feminine. We have to get rid of and also explain what all knowledge brings with it as its burden of power: to show in what ways, culturally, knowledge is the accomplice of power: that whoever stands in the place of knowledge is always getting a dividend of power: show that all thinking until now has been ruled by this dividend, this surplus value of power that comes back to him who knows. Take the philosophers, take their position of mastery, and you'll see that there is not a soul who dares to make an advance in thought, into the as-yet-unthought, without shuddering at the idea that he is under the surveillance of the ancestors, the grandfathers, the tyrants of the concept, without thinking that there behind your back is always the famous Name-of-the-Father, who knows whether or not you're writing whatever it is you have to write without any spelling mistakes.

Now, I think that what women will have to do and what they will do, right from the moment they venture to speak what they have to say, will of necessity bring about a shift in metalanguage. And I think we're completely crushed, especially in places like universities, by the highly repressive operations of metalanguage, the operations, that is, of the commentary on the commentary, the code, the operation that sees to it that the moment women open their mouths—women more often than men—they are immediately asked in whose name and from what theoretical standpoint they are speaking, who is their master and where they are coming from: they have, in short, to salute... and show their identity papers. There's work to be done against *class*, against categorization, against classification—classes. "Doing classes" in France means doing military service. There's work to be done against military service, against all schools, against the pervasive masculine urge to judge, diagnose, digest, name... not so much in the sense of the loving precision of poetic naming as in that of the repressive censorship of philosophical nomination/conceptualization.

Women who write have for the most part until now considered themselves to be writing not as women but as writers. Such women may declare that sexual difference means nothing, that there's no attributable difference between masculine and feminine writing. . . . What does it mean to "take no position"? When someone says "I'm not political" we all know what that means! It's just another way of saying: "My politics are someone else's!" And it's exactly the case with writing! Most women are like this: they do someone else's—man's—writing, and in their innocence sustain it and give it voice, and end up producing writing that's in effect masculine. Great care must be taken in working on feminine writing not to get trapped by names: to be signed with a woman's name doesn't necessarily make a piece of writing feminine. It could quite well be masculine writing, and conversely, the fact that a piece of writing is signed with a man's name does not in itself exclude femininity. It's rare, but you can sometimes find femininity in writings signed by men: it does happen.

Which texts appear to be woman-texts and are recognized as such today, what can this mean, how might they be read?[4] In my opinion, the writing being done now that I see emerging around me won't only be of the kinds that exist in print today, though they will always be with us, but will be something else as well. In particular we ought to be prepared for what I call the "affirmation of the difference," not a kind of wake about the corpse of the mummified woman, nor a fantasy of woman's decapitation, but something different: a step forward, an adventure, an exploration of woman's powers: of her power, her potency, her ever-dreaded strength, of the regions of femininity. Things are starting to be written, things that will constitute a feminine Imaginary, the site, that is, of identifications of an ego no longer given over to an image defined by the masculine ("like the woman I love, I mean a dead woman"), but rather inventing forms for women on the march, or as I prefer to fantasize, "in flight," so that instead of lying down, women will go forward by leaps in search of themselves.

There is work to be done on female sexual pleasure and on the production of an unconscious that would no longer be the classic unconscious. The unconscious is always cultural and when it talks it tells you your old stories, it tells you the old stories you've heard before because it consists of the repressed of culture. But it's also always shaped by the forceful return of a libido that doesn't give up that easily, and also by what is strange, what is outside culture, by a language which is a savage tongue that can make itself understood quite well. This is why, I think, *political* and not just literary work is started as soon as writing gets done by women that goes beyond the bounds of censorship, reading, the gaze, the masculine command, in that cheeky risk taking women can get into when they set out into the unknown to look for themselves.

This is how I would define a feminine textual body: as a *female libidinal economy*, a regime, energies, a system of spending not necessarily carved out by culture. A feminine textual body is recognized by the fact that it is always endless, without ending: there's no closure, it doesn't stop, and it's this that very often makes the feminine text difficult to read. For we've learned to read books that basically pose the word "end." But this one doesn't finish, a feminine text goes on and on and at a certain moment the volume comes to an end but the writing continues and for the reader this means being thrust into the void. These are texts that work on the beginning but not on the origin. The origin is a masculine myth: I always want to know where I come from. The question "Where do children come from?" is basically a masculine, much more than a feminine, question. The quest for origins, illustrated by Oedipus, doesn't haunt a feminine unconscious. Rather it's the beginning, or beginnings, the manner of beginning, not promptly with the phallus in order to close with the phallus, but starting on all sides at once, that makes a feminine writing. A feminine text starts on all sides at once, starts twenty times, thirty times, over.

The question a woman's text asks is the question of giving—"What does this writing give?" "How does it give?" And talking about nonorigin and beginnings, you might say it "gives a send-off" (*donne le départ*). Let's take the expression "giving a send-off" in a metaphorical sense: giving a send-off is generally giving the *signal* to depart. I think it's more than giving the departure signal, it's really giving, making a *gift* of, departure, allowing departure, allowing breaks, "parts," partings, separations... from this we break with the return-to-self, with the specular relations ruling the coherence, the identification, of the individual. When a woman writes in nonrepression she passes on her others, her abundance of non-ego/s in a way that destroys the form of the family structure, so that it is defamilialized, can no longer be thought in terms of the attribution of roles within a social cell: what takes place is an endless circulation of desire from one body to another, above and across sexual difference, outside those relations of power and regeneration constituted by the family. I believe regeneration leaps, age leaps, time leaps. . . . A woman-text gets across a detachment, a kind of disengagement, not the detachment that is immediately taken back, but a real capacity to lose hold and let go. This takes the metaphorical form of wandering, excess, risk of the unreckonable: no reckoning, a feminine text can't be predicted, isn't predictable, isn't knowable and is therefore very disturbing. It can't be anticipated, and I believe femininity is written outside anticipation it really is the text of the unforeseeable.

Let's look not at syntax but at fantasy, at the unconscious: all the feminine texts I've read are very close to the voice, very close to the flesh of language, much more so than masculine texts. . . perhaps because there's something in them that's freely given, perhaps because they don't rush into meaning, but are straightway at the threshold of feeling. There's *tactility* in the feminine text, there's touch, and this touch passes through the ear. Writing in the feminine is passing on what is cut out by the Symbolic, the voice of the mother, passing on what is most archaic. The most archaic force that touches a body is one that enters by the ear and reaches the most intimate point. This innermost touch always echoes in a woman-text. So the movement, the movement of the text, doesn't trace a straight line. I see it as an outpouring . . . which can appear in primitive or elementary texts as a fantasy of blood, of menstrual flow, etc., but which I prefer to see as vomiting, as "throwing up," "disgorging." And I'd link this with a basic structure of property relations defined by mourning.

Man cannot live without resigning himself to loss. He has to mourn. It's his way of withstanding castration. He goes through castration, that is, and by sublimation incorporates the lost object. Mourning, resigning oneself to loss, means not losing. When you've lost something and the loss is a dangerous one, you refuse to admit that something of your self might be lost in the lost object. So you "mourn," you make haste to recover the investment made in the lost object. But I believe women *do not mourn*, and this is where their pain lies! When you've mourned, it's all over after a year, there's no more suffering. Woman, though, does not mourn, does not resign herself to loss. She basically *takes up the challenge of loss* in order to go on living: she lives it, gives it life, is capable of unsparing loss. She does not hold onto loss, she loses without holding onto loss. This makes her writing a body that overflows, disgorges, vomiting as opposed to masculine incorporation. . . . She loses, and doubtless it would be to the death were it not for the intervention of those basic movements of a feminine unconscious (this is how I would define *feminine sublimation*) which provide the capacity of passing above it all by means of a form of oblivion which is not the oblivion of burial or interment but the oblivion of *acceptance*. This is taking loss, seizing it, living it. Leaping. This goes with not withholding: she does not withhold. She does not withhold, hence the impression of constant return evoked by this lack of withholding. It's like a kind of open memory that ceaselessly makes way. And in the end, she will write this not-withholding, this not-writing: she writes of not-writing, not-happening . . . She crosses limits: she is neither outside nor in, whereas the masculine would try to "bring the outside in, if possible."[5]

And finally this open and bewildering prospect goes hand in hand with a certain kind of laughter. Culturally speaking, women have wept a great deal, but once the tears are shed, there will be endless laughter instead. Laughter that breaks out, overflows, a humor no one would expect to find in women—which is nonetheless surely their greatest strength because it's a humor that sees man much further away than he has ever been seen. Laughter that shakes the last chapter of my text *LA*,[6] "she who laughs last." And her first laugh is at herself.

Translated by Annette Kuhn. Thanks are due to Elaine Marks for suggesting this translation of the title, to Keith Cohen for advice on specific points on translation, and to Chris Holmlund for bibliographical assistance.

1. Hélène Cixous and Catherine Clément, *La Jeune Née* (Paris: 10/18, 1975) (translator's note).
2. Marguerite Duras, *Le Ravissement de Lol V. Stein* (Paris: Gallimard, 1964). There are two English translations of this work: *The Ravishing of Lol V. Stein*, trans. Richard Seaver (New York: Grove Press, 1966), and *The Rapture of Lol V. Stein*, trans. Eileen Ellenbogen (London: Hamish Hamilton, 1967) (translator's note).
3. "La place de celle qu'on oublie en français trop souvent parce qu'on dit 'sphinx' au lieu de 'sphinge' ": That is, the French form of the word would suggest that the sphinx is male, whereas the sphinx of the oedipal myth is in fact female (translator's note).
4. There follows in the original a passage in which several categories of women's writing existing at the time (1975) are listed and discussed. These include: " 'the little girl's story,' where the little girl is getting even for a bad childhood," "texts of a return to a woman's own body," and texts which were a critical success, "ones about madwomen, deranged, sick women." The passage is omitted here, at the author's request, on the grounds that such a categorization is outdated, and that the situation with regard to women's writing is very much different now than it was five or six years ago (translator's note).
5. The following passage, deleted from the main body of the text, is regarded by the author as expressing a position tangential to the central interest of her work, which has to do with homosexuality: "And it's this being 'neither out nor in,' being 'beyond the outside/inside opposition' that permits the play of 'bisexuality.' Female sexuality is always at some point bisexual. Bisexual doesn't mean, as many people think, that she can make love with both a man and a woman, it doesn't mean she has two partners, even if it can at times mean this. Bisexuality on an unconscious level is the possibility of extending into the other, of being in such a relation with the other that *I* move into the other without destroying the other: that I will look for the other where s/he is without trying to bring everything back to myself" (translator's note).
6. Hélène Cixous, *LA* (Paris: Gallimard, 1976) (translator's note).

Reflections on Exile

Exile is strangely compelling to think about but terrible to experience. It is the unhealable rift forced between a human being and a native place, between the self and its true home: its essential sadness can never be surmounted. And while it is true that literature and history contain heroic, romantic, glorious, even triumphant episodes in an exile's life, these are no more than efforts meant to overcome the crippling sorrow of estrangement. The achievements of exile are permanently undermined by the loss of something left behind for ever.

But if true exile is a condition of terminal loss, why has it been transformed so easily into a potent, even enriching, motif of modern culture? We have become accustomed to thinking of the modern period itself as spiritually orphaned and alienated, the age of anxiety and estrangement. Nietzsche taught us to feel uncomfortable with tradition, and Freud to regard domestic intimacy as the polite face painted on patricidal and incestuous rage. Modern Western culture is in large part the work of exiles, émigrés, refugees. In the United States, academic, intellectual and aesthetic thought is what it is today because of refugees from fascism, communism and other regimes given to the oppression and expulsion of dissidents. The critic George Steiner has even proposed the perceptive thesis that a whole genre of twentieth-century Western literature is "extraterritorial," a literature by and about exiles, symbolizing the age of the refugee. Thus Steiner suggests

> It seems proper that those who create art in a civilization of quasi-barbarism, which has made so many homeless, should themselves be poets unhoused and wanderers across language. Eccentric, aloof, nostalgic, deliberately untimely . . .

In other ages, exiles had similar cross-cultural and transnational visions, suffered the same frustrations and miseries, performed the same elucidating and critical tasks—brilliantly affirmed, for instance, in E.H.Carr's classic study of the nineteenth-century Russian intellectuals clustered around Herzen, *The Romantic Exiles*. But the difference between earlier exiles and those of our own time is, it bears stressing, scale: our age—with its modern warfare, imperialism and the quasi-theological ambitions of totalitarian rulers—is indeed the age of the refugee, the displaced person, mass immigration.

Against this large, impersonal setting, exile cannot be made to serve notions of humanism. On the twentieth-century scale, exile is neither aesthetically nor humanistically comprehensible: at most the literature about exile objectifies an anguish and a predicament most people rarely experience at first hand; but to think of the exile informing this literature as beneficially humanistic is to banalize its mutilations, the losses it inflicts on those who suffer them, the muteness with which it responds to any attempt to understand it as "good for us." Is it not true that the views of exile in literature and, moreover, in religion obscure what is truly horrendous: that exile is irremediably secular and unbearably historical; that it is produced by human beings for other human beings; and that, like death but without death's ultimate mercy, it has torn millions of people from the nourishment of tradition, family and geography?

•   •   •

To see a poet in exile—as opposed to reading the poetry of exile—is to see exile's antinomies embodied and endured with a unique intensity. Several years ago I spent some time with Faiz Ahmad Faiz, the greatest of contemporary Urdu poets. He was exiled from his native Pakistan by Zia's military regime, and found a welcome of sorts in strife-torn Beirut. Naturally his closest friends were Palestinian, but I sensed that, although there was an affinity of spirit between them, nothing quite matched—language, poetic convention, or life-history. Only once, when Eqbal Ahmad, a Pakistani friend and a fellow-exile, came to Beirut, did Faiz seem to overcome his sense of constant estrangement. The three of us sat in a dingy Beirut restaurant late one night, while Faiz recited poems. After a time, he and Eqbal stopped translating his verses for my benefit, but as the night wore on it did not matter. What I watched required no translation: it was an enactment of a homecoming expressed through defiance and loss, as if to say, "Zia, we are here." Of course Zia was the one who was really at home and who would not hear their exultant voices.

Rashid Hussein was a Palestinian. He translated Bialik, one of the great modern Hebrew poets, into Arabic, and Hussein's eloquence established him in the post-1948 period as an orator and nationalist without peer. He first worked as a Hebrew language journalist in Tel Aviv, and succeeded in establishing a dialogue between Jewish and Arab writers, even as he espoused the cause of Nasserism and Arab nationalism. In time, he could no longer endure the pressure, and he left for New York. He married a Jewish woman, and began working in the PLO office at the United Nations, but regularly outraged his superiors with unconventional ideas and utopian rhetoric. In 1972 he left for the Arab world, but a few months later he was back in the United States: he had felt out of place in Syria and Lebanon, unhappy in Cairo. New York sheltered him anew, but so did endless bouts of drinking and idleness. His life was in ruins, but he remained the most hospitable of men. He died after a night of heavy drinking when, smoking in bed, his cigarette started a fire that spread to a small library of audio cassettes, consisting mostly of poets reading their verse. The fumes from the tapes asphyxiated him. His body was repatriated for burial in Musmus, the small village in Israel where his family still resided.

These and so many other exiled poets and writers lend dignity to a condition legislated to deny dignity—to deny an identity to people. From them, it is apparent that, to concentrate on exile as a contemporary political punishment, you must therefore map territories of experience beyond those mapped by the literature of exile itself. You must first set aside Joyce and Nabokov and think instead of the uncountable masses for whom UN agencies have been created. You must think of the refugee-peasants with no prospect of ever returning home, armed only with a ration card and an agency number. Paris may be a capital famous for cosmopolitan exiles, but it is also a city where unknown men and women have spent years of miserable loneliness: Vietnamese, Algerians, Cambodians, Lebanese, Senegalese, Peruvians. You must think also of Cairo, Beirut, Madagascar, Bangkok, Mexico City. As you move further from the Atlantic world, the awful forlorn waste increases: the hopelessly large numbers, the compounded misery of "undocumented" people suddenly lost, without a tellable history. To reflect on exiled Muslims from India, or Haitians in America, or Bikinians in Oceania, or Palestinians throughout the Arab world means that you must leave the modest refuge provided by subjectivity and resort instead to the abstractions of mass politics. Negotiations, wars of national liberation, people bundled out of their homes and prodded, bussed or walked to enclaves in other regions: what do these experiences add up to? Are they not manifestly and almost by design irrecoverable?

• • •

We come to nationalism and its essential association with exile. Nationalism is an assertion of belonging in and to a place, a people, a heritage. It affirms the home created by a community of language, culture and customs; and, by so doing, it fends off exile, fights to prevent its ravages. Indeed, the interplay between nationalism and exile is like Hegel's dialectic of servant and master, opposites informing and constituting each other. All nationalisms in their early stages develop from a condition of estrangement. The struggles to win American independence, to unify Germany or Italy, to liberate Algeria were those of national groups separated–exiled–from what was construed to be their rightful way of life. Triumphant, achieved nationalism then justifies, retrospectively as well as prospectively, a history selectively strung together in a narrative form: thus all nationalisms have their founding fathers, their basic, quasi-religious texts, their rhetoric of belonging, their historical and geographical landmarks, their official enemies and heroes. This collective ethos forms what Pierre Bourdieu, the French sociologist, calls the *habitus*, the coherent amalgam of practices linking habit with inhabitance. In time, successful nationalisms consign truth exclusively to themselves and relegate falsehood and inferiority to outsiders (as in the rhetoric of capitalist versus communist, or the European versus the Asiatic).

And just beyond the frontier between "us" and the "outsiders" is the perilous territory of not-belonging: this is to where in a primitive time peoples were banished, and where in the modern era immense aggregates of humanity loiter as refugees and displaced persons.

Nationalisms are about groups, but in a very acute sense exile is a solitude experienced outside the group: the deprivations felt at not being with others in the communal habitation. How, then, does one surmount the loneliness of exile without falling into the encompassing and thumping language of national pride, collective sentiments, group passions? What is there worth saving and holding on to between the extremes of exile on the one hand, and the often bloody-minded affirmations of nationalism on the other? Do nationalism and exile have any intrinsic attributes? Are they simply two conflicting varieties of paranoia?

These are questions that cannot ever be fully answered because each assumes that exile and nationalism can be discussed neutrally, without reference to each other. They cannot be. Because both terms include everything from the most collective of collective sentiments to the most private of private emotions, there is hardly language adequate for both. But there is certainly nothing about nationalism's public and all-inclusive ambitions that touches the core of the exile's predicament.

Because exile, unlike nationalism, is fundamentally a discontinuous state of being. Exiles are cut off from their roots, their land, their past. They generally do not have armies or states, although they are often in search of them. Exiles feel, therefore, an urgent need to reconstitute their broken lives, usually by choosing to see themselves as part of a triumphant ideology or a restored people. The crucial thing is that a state of exile free from this triumphant ideology—designed to reassemble an exile's broken history into a new whole—is virtually unbearable, and virtually impossible in today's world. Look at the fate of the Jews, the Palestinians and the Armenians.

•   •   •

Noubar is a solitary Armenian, and a friend. His parents had to leave Eastern Turkey in 1915, after their families were massacred: his maternal grandfather was beheaded. Noubar's mother and father went to Aleppo, then to Cairo. In the middle-sixties, life in Egypt became difficult for non-Egyptians, and his parents, along with four children, were taken to Beirut by an international relief organization. In Beirut, they lived briefly in a pension and then were bundled into two rooms of a little house outside the city. In Lebanon, they had no money and they waited: eight months later, a relief agency got them a flight to Glasgow. And then to Gander. And then to New York. They rode by Greyhound bus from New York to Seattle: Seattle was the city designated by the agency for their American residence. When I asked, "Seattle?," Noubar smiled resignedly, as if to say better Seattle than Armenia—which he never knew, or Turkey where so many were slaughtered, or Lebanon where he and his family would certainly have risked their lives. Exile is sometimes better than staying behind or not getting out: but only sometimes.

Because *nothing* is secure. Exile is a jealous state. What you achieve is precisely what you have no wish to share, and it is in the drawing of lines around you and your compatriots that the least attractive aspects of being in exile emerge: an exaggerated sense of group solidarity, and a passionate hostility to outsiders, even those who may in fact be in the same predicament as you. What could be more intransigent than the conflict between Zionist Jews and Arab Palestinians? Palestinians feel that they have been turned into exiles by the proverbial people of exile, the Jews. But the Palestinians also know that their own sense of national identity has been nourished in the exile milieu, where everyone not a blood-brother or sister is an enemy, where every sympathizer is an agent of some unfriendly power, and where the slightest deviation from the accepted group line is an act of the rankest treachery and disloyalty.

Perhaps this is the most extraordinary of exile's fates: to have been exiled by exiles: to relive the actual process of up-rooting at the hands of exiles. All Palestinians during the summer of 1982 asked themselves what inarticulate urge drove Israel, having displaced Palestinians in 1948, to expel them continuously from their refugee homes and camps in Lebanon. It is as if the reconstructed Jewish collective experience, as represented by Israel and modern Zionism, could not tolerate another story of dispossession and loss to exist alongside it—an intolerance constantly reinforced by the Israeli hostility to the nationalism of the Palestinians, who for forty-six years have been painfully reassembling a national identity in exile.

This need to reassemble an identity out of the refractions and discontinuities of exile is found in the earlier poems of Mahmud Darwish, whose considerable work amounts to an epic effort to transform the lyrics of loss into the indefinitely postponed drama of return. Thus he depicts his sense of homelessness in the form of a list of unfinished and incomplete things:

> But I am the exile.
> Seal me with your eyes.
> Take me wherever you are—
> Take me whatever you are.
> Restore to me the color of face
> And the warmth of body
> The light of heart and eye,
> The salt of bread and rhythm,
> The taste of earth . . . the Motherland.
> Shield me with your eyes.
> Take me as a relic from the mansion of sorrow.
> Take me as a verse from my tragedy;
> Take me as a toy, a brick from the house
> So that our children will remember to return.

The pathos of exile is in the loss of contact with the solidity and the satisfaction of earth: homecoming is out of the question.

Joseph Conrad's tale "Amy Foster" is perhaps the most uncompromising representation of exile ever written. Conrad thought of himself as an exile from Poland, and nearly all his work (as well as his life) carries the unmistakable mark of the sensitive émigré's obsession with his own fate and with his hopeless attempts to make satisfying contact with new surroundings. "Amy Foster" is in a sense confined to the problems of exile, perhaps so confined that it is not one of Conrad's best-known stories. This, for example, is the description of the agony of its central character, Yanko Goorall, an Eastern European peasant who, en route to America, is shipwrecked off the British coast:

It is indeed hard upon a man to find himself a lost stranger helpless, incomprehensible, and of a mysterious origin, in some obscure corner of the earth. Yet amongst all the adventurers ship-

wrecked in all the wild parts of the world, there is not one, it seems to me, that ever had to suf-fer a fate so simply tragic as the man I am speaking of, the most innocent of adventurers cast out by the sea. . . .

Yanko has left home because the pressures were too great for him to go on living there. America lures him with its promise, though England is where he ends up. He endures in England, where he cannot speak the language and is feared and misunderstood. Only Amy Foster, a plodding, unattractive peasant girl, tries to communicate with him. They marry, have a child, but when Yanko falls ill, Amy, afraid and alienated, refuses to nurse him; snatching their child, she leaves. The desertion hastens Yanko's miserable death, which like the deaths of several Conradian heroes is depicted as the result of a combination of crushing isolation and the world's indifference. Yanko's fate is described as "the supreme disaster of loneliness and despair."

Yanko's predicament is affecting: a foreigner perpetually haunted and alone in an uncomprehending society. But Conrad's own exile causes him to exaggerate the differences between Yanko and Amy. Yanko is dashing, light and bright-eyed, whereas Amy is heavy, dull, bovine; when he dies, it is as if her earlier kindness to him was a snare to lure and then trap him fatally. Yanko's death is romantic: the world is coarse, unappreciative; no one understands him, not even Amy, the one person close to him. Conrad took this neurotic exile's fear and created an aesthetic principle out of it. No one can understand or communicate in Conrad's world, but paradoxically this radical limitation on the possibilities of language doesn't inhibit elaborate efforts to communicate. All of Conrad's stories are about lonely people who talk a great deal (for indeed who of the great modernists was more voluble and "adjectival" than Conrad himself?) and whose attempts to *impress* others compound, rather than reduce, the original sense of isolation. Each Conradian exile fears, and is condemned endlessly to imagine, the spectacle of a solitary death illuminated, so to speak, by unresponsive, uncommunicating eyes.

Exiles look at non-exiles with resentment. *They* belong in their surroundings, you feel, whereas an exile is always out of place. What is it like to be born in a place, to stay and live there, to know that you are of it, more or less for ever?

• • •

Although it is true that anyone prevented from returning home is an exile, some distinctions can be made between exiles, refugees, expatriates and émigrés. Exile originated in the age-old practice of banishment. Once banished, the exile lives an anomalous and miserable life, with the stigma of being an outsider. Refugees, on the other hand, are a creation of the twentieth-century state. The word "refugee" has become a political one, suggesting large herds of innocent and bewildered people requiring urgent international assistance, whereas "exile" carries with it, I think, a touch of solitude and spirituality.

Expatriates voluntarily live in an alien country, usually for personal or social reasons. Hemingway and Fitzgerald were not forced to live in France. Expatriates may share in the solitude and estrangement of exile, but they do not suffer under its rigid proscriptions. Émigrés enjoy an ambiguous status. Technically, an émigré is anyone who emigrates to a new country. Choice in the matter is certainly a possibility. Colonial officials, missionaries, technical experts, mercenaries and military advisers on loan may in a sense live in exile, but they have not been banished. White settlers in Africa, parts of Asia and Australia may once have been exiles, but as pioneers and nation-builders the label "exile" dropped away from them.

Much of the exile's life is taken up with compensating for disorienting loss by creating a new world to rule. It is not surprising that so many exiles seem to be novelists, chess players, political activists, and intellectuals. Each of these occupations requires a minimal investment in objects and places a great premium on mobility and skill. The exile's new world, logically enough, is unnatural and its unreality resembles fiction. Georg Lukács, in *Theory of the Novel*, argued with compelling force that the novel, a literary form created out of the unreality of ambition and fantasy, is *the* form of "transcendental homelessness." Classical epics, Lukács wrote, emanate from settled cultures in which values are clear, identities stable, life unchanging. The European novel is grounded in precisely the opposite experience, that of a changing society in which an itinerant and disinherited middle-class hero or heroine seeks to construct a new world that somewhat resembles an old one left behind for ever. In the epic there is no *other* world, only the finality of *this* one. Odysseus returns to Ithaca after years of wandering; Achilles will die because he cannot escape his fate. The novel, however, exists because other worlds *may* exist, alternatives for bourgeois speculators, wanderers, exiles.

No matter how well they may do, exiles are always eccentrics who *feel* their difference (even as they frequently exploit it) as a kind of orphanhood. Anyone who is really homeless regards the habit of seeing estrangement in everything modern as an affectation, a display of modish attitudes. Clutching difference like a weapon to be used with stiffened will, the exile jealously insists on his or her right to refuse to belong.

This usually translates into an intransigence that is not easily ignored. Wilfulness, exaggeration, overstatement: these are characteristic styles of being an exile, methods for compelling the world to accept your vision—which you make more unacceptable because you are in fact unwilling to have it accepted. It is yours, after all. Composure and serenity are the last things associated with the work of exiles. Artists in exile are decidedly unpleasant, and their stubbornness insinuates itself into even their exalted works. Dante's vision in *The Divine Comedy* is tremendously powerful in its universality and detail, but even the beatific peace achieved in the *Paradiso* bears traces of the vindictiveness and severity of judgment embodied in the *Inferno*. Who but an exile like Dante, banished from Florence, would use eternity as a place for settling old scores?

James Joyce *chose* to be in exile: to give force to his artistic vocation. In an uncannily effective way—as Richard Ellmann has shown in his biography—Joyce picked a quarrel with Ireland and kept it alive so as to sustain the strictest opposition to what was familiar. Ellmann says that "whenever his relations with his native land were in danger of improving, [Joyce] was to find a new incident to solidify his intransigence and to reaffirm the rightness of his voluntary absence." Joyce's fiction concerns what in a letter he once described as the state of being "alone and friendless." And although it is rare to pick banishment as a way of life, Joyce perfectly understood its trials.

• • •

But Joyce's success as an exile stresses the question lodged at its very heart: is exile so extreme and private that any instrumental use of it is ultimately a trivialization? How is it that the literature of exile has taken its place as a *topos* of human experience alongside the literature of adventure, education or discovery? Is this the *same* exile that quite literally kills Yanko Goorall and has bred the expensive, often dehumanizing relationship between twentieth-century exile and nationalism? Or is it some more benign variety?

Much of the contemporary interest in exile can be traced to the somewhat pallid notion that non-exiles can share in the benefits of exile as a redemptive motif. There is, admittedly, a certain plausibility and truth to this idea. Like medieval itinerant scholars or learned Greek slaves in the Roman Empire, exiles—the exceptional ones among them—do leaven their environments. And naturally "we" concentrate on that enlightening aspect of "their" presence among us, not on their misery or their demands. But looked at from the bleak political perspective of modern mass dislocations, individual exiles force us to recognize the tragic fate of homelessness in a necessarily heartless world.

A generation ago, Simone Weil posed the dilemma of exile as concisely as it has ever been expressed. "To be rooted," she said, "is perhaps the most important and least recognized need of the human soul." Yet Weil also saw that most remedies for uprootedness in this era of world wars, deportations and mass exterminations are almost as dangerous as what they purportedly remedy. Of these, the state—or, more accurately, statism—is one of the most insidious, since worship of the state tends to supplant all other human bonds.

Weil exposes us anew to that whole complex of pressures and constraints that lie at the center of the exile's predicament, which, as I have suggested, is as close as we come in the modern era to tragedy. There is the sheer fact of isolation and displacement, which produces the kind of narcissistic masochism that resists all efforts at amelioration, acculturation and community. At this extreme the exile can make a fetish of exile, a practice that distances him or her from all connections and commitments. To live as if everything around you were temporary and perhaps trivial is to fall prey to petulant cynicism as well as to querulous lovelessness. More common is the pressure on the exile to join—parties, national movements, the state. The exile is offered a new set of affiliations and develops new loyalties. But there is also a loss—of critical perspective, of intellectual reserve, of moral courage.

It must also be recognized that the defensive nationalism of exiles often fosters self-awareness as much as it does the less attractive forms of self-assertion. Such reconstitutive projects as assembling a nation out of exile (and this is true in this century for Jews and Palestinians) involve constructing a national history, reviving an ancient language, founding national institutions like libraries and universities. And these, while they sometimes promote strident ethnocentrism, also give rise to investigations of self that inevitably go far beyond such simple and positive facts as "ethnicity." For example, there is the self-consciousness of an individual trying to understand why the histories of the Palestinians and the Jews have certain patterns to them, why in spite of oppression and the threat of extinction a particular ethos remains alive in exile

Necessarily, then, I speak of exile not as a privilege, but as an *alternative* to the mass institutions that dominate modern life. Exile is not, after all, a matter of choice: you are born into it, or it happens to you. But, provided that the exile refuses to sit on the sidelines nursing a wound, there are things to be learned: he or she must cultivate a scrupulous (not indulgent or sulky) subjectivity.

Perhaps the most rigorous example of such subjectivity is to be found in the writing of Theodor Adorno, the German-Jewish philosopher and critic. Adorno's masterwork, *Minima Moralia*, is an autobiography written while in exile; it is subtitled *Reflexionen aus dem beschädigten Leben (Reflections from a Mutilated Life)*. Ruthlessly opposed to what he called the "administered" world, Adorno saw all life as pressed into ready-made forms, prefabricated "homes." He argued that everything that one says or thinks, as well as every object one possesses, is ultimately a mere commodity. Language is jargon, objects are for sale. To refuse this state of affairs is the exile's intellectual mission.

Adorno's reflections are informed by the belief that the only home truly available now, though fragile and vulnerable, is in writing. Elsewhere, "the house is past. The bombings of European cities, as well as the labor and concentration camps, merely precede as executors, with what the immanent development of technology had long decided was to be the fate of houses. These are now good only to be thrown away like old food cans." In short, Adorno says with a grave irony, "it is part of morality not to be at home in one's home."

To follow Adorno is to stand away from "home" in order to look at it with the exile's detachment. For there is considerable merit in the practice of noting the discrepancies between various concepts and ideas and what they actually produce. We take home and language for granted; they become nature, and their underlying assumptions recede into dogma and orthodoxy.

The exile knows that in a secular and contingent world, homes are always provisional. Borders and barriers, which enclose us within the safety of familiar territory, can also become prisons, and are often defended beyond reason or necessity. Exiles cross borders, break barriers of thought and experience.

Hugo of St. Victor, a twelfth-century monk from Saxony, wrote these hauntingly beautiful lines:

> It is, therefore, a source of great virtue for the practiced mind to learn, bit by bit, first to change about invisible and transitory things, so that afterwards it may be able to leave them behind altogether. The man who finds his homeland sweet is still a tender beginner; he to whom every soil is as his native one is already strong; but he is perfect to whom the entire world is as a foreign land. The tender soul has fixed his love on one spot in the world; the strong man has extended his love to all places; the perfect man has extinguished his.

Erich Auerbach, the great twentieth-century literary scholar who spent the war years as an exile in Turkey, has cited this passage as a model for anyone wishing to transcend national or provincial limits. Only by embracing this attitude can a historian begin to grasp human experience and its written records in their diversity and particularity; otherwise he or she will remain committed more to the exclusions and reactions of prejudice than to the freedom that accompanies knowledge. But note that Hugo twice makes it clear that the "strong" or "perfect" man achieves independence and detachment by *working through* attachments, not by rejecting them. Exile is predicated on the existence of, love for, and bond with, one's native place; what is true of all exile is not that home and love of home are lost, but that loss is inherent in the very existence of both.

Regard experiences as if they were about to disappear. What is it that anchors them in reality? What would you save of them? What would you give up? Only someone who has achieved independence and detachment, someone whose homeland is "sweet" but whose circumstances makes it impossible to recapture that sweetness, can answer those questions. (Such a person would also find it impossible to derive satisfaction from substitutes furnished by illusion or dogma.)

This may seem like a prescription for an unrelieved grimness of outlook and, with it, a permanently sullen disapproval of all enthusiasm or buoyancy of spirit. Not necessarily. While it perhaps seems peculiar to speak of the pleasures of exile, there are some positive things to be said for a few of its conditions. Seeing "the entire world as a foreign land" makes possible originality of vision. Most people are principally aware of one culture, one setting, one home; exiles are aware of at least two, and this plurality of vision gives rise to an awareness of simultaneous dimensions, an awareness that–to borrow a phrase from music–is *contrapuntal*.

For an exile, habits of life, expression or activity in the new environment inevitably occur against the memory of these things in another environment. Thus both the new and the old environments are vivid, actual, occurring together contrapuntally. There is a unique pleasure in this sort of apprehension, especially if the exile is conscious of other contrapuntal juxtapositions that diminish orthodox judgment and elevate appreciative sympathy. There is also a particular sense of achievement in acting as if one were at home wherever one happens to be.

This remains risky, however: the habit of dissimulation is both wearing and nerve-racking. Exile is never the state of being satisfied, placid, or secure. Exile, in the words of Wallace Stevens, is "a mind of winter" in which the pathos of summer and autumn as much as the potential of spring are nearby but unobtainable. Perhaps this is another way of saying that a life of exile moves according to a different calendar, and is less seasonal and settled than life at home. Exile is life led outside habitual order. It is nomadic, decentered, contrapuntal; but no sooner does one get accustomed to it than its unsettling force erupts anew.

Ons Stel Nie Belang Nie/We Are Not
Interested In: Speaking Apartheid

*"I did not come to South Africa as a neutral observer. I came morally
and politically outraged at the brute, unmediated legislation of human
inferiority . . . I had an almost mythic image of the perpetrators of this
inhumanity . . . I indulged myself in my horror and disgust and learned
later that my indulgence was itself a symptom of the 'system.' I met
many white South Africans who were equally horrified and disgusted.
Paradoxically their horror and disgust rendered their life in South Africa
tolerable. It gave them the certainty that they were different."*
–Vincent Crapanzano, *Waiting*[1]

What is the position of the white South African intellectual who is critical of apartheid?
It is inherently contradictory, for as soon as I speak against I find myself speaking for,
on behalf of. I speak either the language of the colonizer or the language of the oppressor. In a country where the law and public notices are divided and repeated in Whites
Only English and Net Blankes Afrikaans, I cannot claim to translate much of what
other South Africans are saying. For white South African intellectuals to criticize apartheid means to examine our own positions, our two-tongued/tweetalig selves.

To speak about apartheid from the position of observer–whether a "neutral" observer or an "outraged" observer–is part of the contradiction since the matter of
my/our identity-as-white represents the central issue, the privileged subject of apartheid. Crapanzano suggests that it is from the position of observer that one can indulge
one's opinion of apartheid, with the certainty that one is different (and thus "one" is not
"I"). We cannot claim to understand apartheid without then acknowledging a certain
self-interest in any rhetoric that sets us apart. Our identity is our enfranchisement to
apartheid, and it is through a critical understanding of ourselves as subjects of apartheid
that we can begin to speak about it in terms that are not ultimately complicit with maintaining privilege.

Inscribed on Monuments

A sense of identity has always been a rallying point for party politics in South Africa. In the 20th century the Afrikaner identity has been organized around pride in the language and *kultuur*, and a morbidly self-conscious sense of Afrikaans history. English-speaking South Africans are more ambiguously lodged between a desire to be seen as distinct from the Afrikaner and a sense of exclusion from power that the distinction represents. However the definitions are established, whether based on animosities or identifications, the reference common to both, unspoken by both, is the political invisibility of blacks, whose historical absence is the condition for these "national" identities.

Accompanying this sense of self is a whole vocabulary of self-description, a self-consciousness on the scale of a national past-time, like rugby. During field research in South Africa Crapanzano found that Afrikaners welcomed his interest because the opportunity to speak about themselves or be observed affirmed their identity. English-speaking South Africans were also eager to speak about Afrikaners and the differences between them, as a way of avoiding direct scrutiny as subjects and at the same time enabling them to speak about themselves indirectly. National self-consciousness, then, is self-serving and self-involved, and Crapanzano found that instead of introducing a language of sociological description to his subjects, he was reinforcing one already in place, one in which he himself became implicated. "The observer replicates the whites' social discriminations and legitimates them . . . Each time I use one of the racist terms—'white,' 'Coloured,' 'Asian' or 'Black'—or refer to 'Afrikaners' or 'English,' I am participating in a particular self-interested constitution of social reality."[2]

Language has also been a battleground in the colonial history of South Africa, and it is to their *Taal* or tongue that Afrikaners erected a monument to mark their current status. The way Afrikaners speak about themselves reflects how actively they invest in certain self-images, particularly the depiction of their language as an indigenous language ("*Afrikaans*" meaning "African") which serves the myth that their presence is "natural," their credentials for occupation "authentic." The relationship of English-speaking South Africans to self-description is more complex, perhaps more hypo-critical; there is not the homogenized sense of self, since they do not define themselves in relation to either Europe of Africa exclusively (or to themselves as a group), but rather as non-Afrikaners. Their language is the language of commentary, of observation, and by standing apart from Afrikaners they provide for themselves a vantage point that suggests a more sophisticated, more credible sense of belonging.

. . . schools, clinics, post-offices, police stations

What relationship can the white iNtellectual have to the national institution of the Self? It is not a question of finding a way to write about ourselves (as if exempt from), but rather a question of realizing that apartheid writes us, articulates us. (Speaking for myself, my integrity is defended in a circle drawn by oxen and wagons). If we want to speak about apartheid we will lose that certainty of ourselves, that fiction of identity that apartheid provides. This means at the same time letting go of the sovereignty that allows us to believe language is an indifferent vehicle which will bear the truths of our observations and opinions (*Afrikaans* in Soweto means "*where each lead-nosed word flies/ a speech organ will be torn open.*"[3]). Loss of speech, fear of loss: as long as the desire to recuperate integrity frames political consciousness, it maintains the privilege/fear impasse.

plaster saints

Contemporary writing by white South Africans is self-conscious about identity in different ways: literature in English generally depicts existential states of alienation and abjection, exploring themes of apocalypse and crisis. Neil Lazarus qualifies dissident literature as that writing which does not participate in or identify with the white experience but takes upon itself the task of representing the limits of that experience, a literature of "parsimony and narrow depiction," one with a "restricted terrain."[4] The references to space in these descriptions are particularly suited to a post-colonial consciousness, one that acknowledges its reduced area of administration, its redundancy. Since it is white-I ntellectuals who read this work, the question of whether it is dissident to speak to ourselves about our own condition has to be addressed; certainly the "white experience" has not been altered by our abstention. Is dissidence yet another white experience when the acute self-consciousness enables a kind of blindness, or obscures the fact that the awareness constituting that (dissident) self goes unquestioned? (I am I, I can choose, I will not be conscripted, Sir, I will not carry a gun).

If literature in English can be characterized as *verlig* (enlightened), literature in Afrikaans tends to be defensive, following the well-established theme in Afrikaans popular consciousness of identity-under-siege. The title of Andre Brink's book of essays is *Writing in a State of Siege*, which could be read as both an image of the writer under siege and as a reference to the state of the State of South Africa. Identifying himself as a dissident Afrikaner, he says that significant art must be offensive, that is, it must expose the standards by which the state defines "acceptable" art : "in a society like South Africa the very threat of persecution may suggest to the writer that he is heading in the right direction."[5] For Brink, if a work transgresses the arbitrary but clearly defined border patrolled by the censors, then it has a value intrinsic to this gesture, a value that will be underwritten if the work is then suppressed by the state. Where a writer like J. M. Coetzee depicts a sense of loss and displacement, Brink is more conscious of martyrdom, of persecution.

But having identified himself on the side of offense and opposition, Brink (with other Afrikaans writers) finds himself in exile, this time from his own community, a community for whom the concept of Community (*Volk, Gemeenskap*) is sacred. His sense of exclusion is acute:

> *"If the Afrikaner dissident today encounters such a vicious reaction from the Establishment, it is because he is regarded as a traitor to everything Afrikanerdom stands for (since apartheid has usurped for itself that definition)."*[6]

The conflict about his identity in relation to the state is resolved around the concept "Afrikanerdom" (Afrikaans-ness): if he is seen as a traitor to his roots, it is only because his roots have been appropriated by the Establishment (apartheid) to buttress its interests; hence, to Brink, the betrayal is rather the other way around, the prodigal has never left home, and Afrikanerdom is intact, unspoiled. Brink is outraged at the exploitation of Afrikaans identity for the purposes of apartheid, for he believes that "apartheid . . . denies what is best in the Afrikaner himself." In this way he can distinguish the plaster saints of the *Vaderland* from his personal iconography of his culture: "the dissident is fighting to assert the most positive and creative aspects of his heritage, which are involved with that experience of Africa he shares with other Africans."[7] Certain ideologies of Afrikaners may be condemned, but the construction of identity itself is never radically questioned. For Brink, his identity can be *distorted* or *misrepresented* but at the heart of his outrage is the fear of erasure. What is at stake for him, is it not the same thing that is at stake for *supporters* of apartheid, and as much an illusion?

In terms of identity, then, writers can always be used for their whiteness, used as expressions of apartheid: what experience can one "share with other Africans" since it is not privilege that is shared? What dialogue is possible, what relationship to their realities and the conditions of their lives, if we do not disenfranchise ourselves from the privileged identity, and experience the rootlessness that identity represents for them? For blacks, "iDentity" is part of the same sleight-of-hand as "iNdependence;" identity means forced removal to that independent state called HomeLand; to be a Zulu or a Venda means to carry a document that is the substitute for human rights, family, history. But in order to preserve our "South-African-ness" the liberal appeal is made to enfranchise blacks so that identity may once again be restored to a neutral universality, and not tainted with complicity.

"By evening the Duplessis' are together again"

Brink's other anxiety is not related to identity, but to the work itself. He characterizes dissident writers as an endangered species struggling for survival. He is not writing about the threat to writers, however, so much as he is writing about the extinction of truth. "What is at stake is not just the individual writer's grasp of reality, or his freedom to write, but by implication an entire community's access to reality and truth."[8] Here we see, very concisely defined, the responsibility that many writers, but Brink in particular, feel they have, "to commit oneself unconditionally to the need to state the truth, and restate it, and state it again, and again, and forever."[9] Leaving aside for the moment the question of reality and the writer as "access" to it (access to whose reality? Realities are as different as the demographies of South Africa), we should examine this notion of truth that seems self-evident, and the political role of the work implied in it.

White writers are marginal in two respects: they cannot presume to speak to or for blacks, nor do they challenge the power of the police state. Rather than representing revolutionary change (from which, by implication, they will be absent), the intellectuals' area of expertise is the sameness of apartheid, the history of its deferred future. There is the suggestion in this awareness of the marginality of the work that, if the work is displaced from its moment in the present as politically "useful," it might at least speak to the future; some writers have submitted that their truths and values, while they may be neutralized or suppressed now, are a legacy for future social values.

Notwithstanding their sincerity, it is highly problematic for writers to arrogate to themselves the task of preserving or embodying values; it seems not only to recuperate political privilege and a brand of paternalism, but also to step into a trap about truth-telling: that truth emerges naturally in response to the lies the authorities tell; truth as the negative of lies; negative from which images are struck; images which writers insist are untruths (National inSecurity). But others will tell that truth is only the fragment extracted under torture to complete the lie, to give it verisimilitude. In terms of knowledge of truth or moral rigor, the role that writers cast for themselves is less one of social responsibility than an appointment of the writer as instrument and bearer of truth (integrity). This desire to separate truth from lies is the same as the desire to separate apartheid from the Afrikaans people; it is in a way sentimental–Brink's words are "a commitment to the *need* to state the truth"–a truth that is paradoxically ahistorical, one that is seen to transcend the ugliness of South Africa's present. In this way of thinking, political realities are transparent to the observer, are meaningful without construction or interpretation, and finally, truth and reality are singular, inseparable, categorical–an absolute truth, like a neutral identity–rather than one specific to location, legislation, education, articulation. Specific, in other words, to a subjectivity not acknowledged by the writer, who is merely the "vessel" of a truth outside him/her.

We are back at the point where the writer is an observer, perhaps even a witness, but somehow apart from the construction of meaning. Where is the self in "self-evident" or "self-explanatory" truth? Who is explaining? Truth is lying waiting to be exposed (exposed on film–just turn on the camera). This truth that speaks without a voice must be recognized as an effect of apartheid, the carefully wrought effect of meanings evolving naturally from events and relationships: for most white South Africans truth is the tangibility of the communist threat, for example, because whites feel vulnerable and threatened; the clear evidence that blacks are violent because they necklace their own people; and, in the face of these pressures, the necessity for the whites to lead the country responsibly.

Thus apartheid is enclosed on itself as a system, a logic. As a testament to its management of reality, this is the country where a state of emergency is synonymous with a state of normalcy, where violence is accepted as "imposing peace". South Africa is at war in a "war of meanings"[10] fought with naming, repetitions, justifications and the brittle self-consciousness that conceals superficial self-knowledge. If we want to speak about apartheid, we must speak about the constitution of all meaning, including defining and being defined as subjects. If we want to speak about truth, it must be specific, not categorical–in other words, in terms of questions of representation.

We can characterize apartheid's closed system as a spectacle rather than an institution, and examine the image it presents to itself, and the frame that forms the border of its reality. Just as certain theaters of identity must be produced and seen, such as the profiling of the Homelands as sites of "tribal" identity, or the biblicized history of the Afrikaners, so other stages for action must be rendered invisible. Of the period before the African National Congress renounced non-violent protest, Derrida writes:

"In order not to hear, not to understand, the white government requires that one writes to it . . . The blacks cannot assure themselves by return mail, by verbal exchange, by any look or sign, that any image of them has been formed on the other side, which might afterward return to it in some way. For the white power does not content itself with not answering. It does worse: it does not even acknowledge receipt."[11]

Now, thirty years after peaceful resistance provoked a massacre, the invisibility of blacks–their forced removal from political and social representation–is entrenched as the fundamental condition of apartheid's longevity. Visibility-invisibility as a "trope" of apartheid, or, perhaps more darkly, appearances-disappearances, suggests an analogy to cinema and lends itself to analysis in terms of cinematic forms.

cannibalism

What problems would be raised by trying to shoot a documentary in South Africa? Filming in most places is strictly prohibited, from remote homelands or labor barracks to industrial complexes and military installations. One may not see or record the massive presence of the state, organized as it is around concealment and invisibility. Even if one were to film demonstrations and their suppression, the footage is only as "true" or as "real" as the context in which it is received; in South Africa, apartheid inserts itself hermeneutically between the event and its effect, which is to say that for the "severely depoliticized white milieu" the footage simply confirms and supports the authorities' case for "containing violence." (It is widely believed that the media deliberately provoke violent incidents in order to represent the state in a negative light). All appearances, in South Africa, are carefully orchestrated; it could be said that the overwhelming natural beauty has itself been conscripted to represent an exotic and innocent image of apartheid.

Conventional documentary form cannot really signify absence, or visually represent the sutured, processed facade offered for scrutiny in cosmopolitan South Africa. One of the basic assumptions about documentary falls away: that the truth can be observed by the observer. Again, for the filmmaker to look for a truth outside his or her intervention, for the film to be simply a means to bear witness is absurd; the observer will find himself/herself involuntarily in the position of a tourist. Or, put another way, to analyze apartheid in its objective conditions means to remain an audience to its spectacle.

There is a way to explore the constructions/constrictions underlying the spectacle if we return to the images that apartheid holds up to itself, the mirror of its imaginary. The most literal possible representation of a government issue portrayal of South Africa is the kind of industrial film made to advertise tourism for a clientele abroad. It is the perfect self-reflection, a touristic mentality projected on to the tourist-consumer: Safari/Shopping Mall South Africa serves the white imagination of itself as both indigenous and exotic; in their reverence for the landscape whites can see themselves as African, and in their industrialization of the country, as European. Such footage would also be replete with "native culture," slipping into a quasi-ethnographic mode for this topic. A critical dimension cannot be presumed to operate in a simple "re-presentation" of the footage–this leaves the relationship between the spectacle and the spectator unaltered (leaves the exoticism intact). The imagery must be treated as an already read/ written text on which is performed a rereading, where the viewer cannibalizes the body, consuming selected morsels in another digestion of the same material, passing through the intestines of its *intended* meaning and coherence back to the mentality of origin. Viewer becomes editor, reader becomes writer by removing fragments from their original context, uncovering unconscious agendas, foregrounding interstices in meaning. By analyzing the images apartheid invests in we can hear the deafening silence, perceive the conspicuous absences, misrepresentations and invisibilities that are structured within this footage. From the position of a reader, rather than a writer, from a position of attention rather than commentary, we may come closer to a critique of apartheid.

Part of the paradox of apartheid/separateness is that it imagines itself as whole, where the segregated mind compensates for its amputation with social theories of the Other, knowledges and opinions of Blacks that substitute for awareness and social engagement. That the experience of reality in that society is so systematically constructed suggests that an analogy to narrative cinema is also appropriate, at least for a depiction of apartheid as maintained through the agency of white South Africans. Narrative is the syntax of a normal, decipherable world, where ruptures and incongruities can be resolved into coherent explanations.

The desire for a (national) sense of place and identity that is untroubled is like the darkness of a movie theater in which the spectacle of change is playing–the dimness of denial and atrophy of the imagination. I am thinking of *A Dry White Season* (the film version of Andre Brink's novel) which seems to address this denial in the protagonist but then undermines any real critique of the white male subject by making him a martyr of apartheid. Apartheid itself is cast in the form of several psychopathic policemen, and as usual history moves along through the agency of males at the level of individual, existential consciousness. The conflict between the good and bad men, or between Conscience and Atrocity is resolved with the exposure of police practices to the press. (In the spirit of the Voortrekker/rugby tradition, it is the young son who carries the ball and saves the day). The utopian faith in the organs of the media is consistent with the style of the choreographed, aestheticized demonstrations of students in Soweto; it occurs to me that this crop of "seasonal" films on apartheid is part of a strange reversal: they depend upon a certain level of awareness about South Africa for their impact, and in general depict apartheid as a kind of backdrop (*Cry Freedom*), when in fact it should be the other way around–we need to foreground the way we are framed and positioned as part of the narratives which provide continuity to apartheid. If we approach apartheid as subjectivity, as it inhabits and is inhabited by whites, critical understanding will not always relapse into guilt, the white man's burden.

1. Vincent Crapanzano, *Waiting* (New York: Vintage Books, 1985), p. 23.

2. Ibid., p. 28.

3. Breyten Breytenbach, *The True Confessions of an Albino Terrorist* (New York: McGraw-Hill, 1986), p. 478.

4. Neil Lazarus, "Modernism and Modernity: T. W. Adorno and Contemporary White South African Literature," *Cultural Critique*, no. 5 (Winter 1986-87): 145.

5. Andre Brink, *Writing in a State of Siege* (New York: Summit Books, 1983), p. 127.

6. Ibid., p. 19.

7. Ibid.

8. Ibid., p. 173.

9. Ibid., p. 35.

10. The phrase is borrowed from Roland Barthes, as it appears in "Alors la Chine?" *Discourse* 8 (Fall-Winter 1986-87). Barthes suggests that peace, for Westerners, might be "the region, utopian for us, where the war of meanings is abolished."

11. Jacques Derrida, and Mustapha Tlili, eds. *For Nelson Mandela* (New York: Seaver Books, 1987), pp. 30-31.

THE WHITENESS OF THE WHALE

WHAT the white whale was to Ahab, has been hinted; what, at times, he was to me, as yet remains unsaid.

Aside from those more obvious considerations touching Moby Dick, which could not but occasionally awaken in any man's soul some, there was another thought, or rather vague, unaccountable... which at times by its intensity on ... and yet so mystical and ... almost sheer ... at putting ... than ... was the whiteness of ... ed me. But ... here ... in some dim ... all these chapter ...

Though ... enhance ... own, as in ... ous nations have in ... royal pre-eminence in this ... grand old kings of ... of the White Elephants' ... of dominion; and ... of Siam unfurling the same snow-white ... the royal standard; and the Hanoverian flag ... a snow-white charger; and the great Austrian Empire, Caesarian heir to overlording Rome, having for the imperial color the same imperial hue; and this pre-eminence in it applies to the human race itself, giving the white man ideal mastership over every dusky tribe; and though, besides all this, whiteness has been ... made significant of gladness, for among the Romans white stone marked a joyful day; and though in other mortal sympathies and symbolizings, this same hue is made the emblem of many touching,

[267]

Explanation and Culture: Marginalia

I tried writing a first version of this piece in the usual disinterested academic style. I gave up after a few pages and after some thought decided to disclose a little of the undisclosed margins of that first essay. This decision was based on a certain program at least implicit in all feminist activity: the deconstruction of the opposition between the private and the public.

According to the explanations that constitute (as they are the effects of) our culture, the political, social, professional, economic, intellectual arenas belong to the public sector. The emotional, sexual, and domestic are the private sector. Certain practices of religion, psychotherapy, and art in the broadest sense are said to inhabit the private sector as well. But the institutions of religion, psychotherapy, and art, as well as the criticism of art, belong to the public. Feminist practice, at least since the European eighteenth century, suggests that each compartment of the public sector also operates emotionally and sexually, that the domestic sphere is not the emotions' only legitimate workplace.[1]

In the interest of the effectiveness of the women's movement, emphasis is often placed upon a reversal of the public-private hierarchy. This is because in ordinary sexist households, educational institutions, or workplaces, the sustaining explanation still remains that the public sector is more important, at once more rational and mysterious, and, generally, more masculine, than the private. The feminist, reversing this hierarchy, must insist that sexuality and the emotions are, in fact, so much more important and threatening that a masculinist sexual politics is obliged, repressively, to sustain all public activity. The most "material" sedimentation of this repressive politics is the institutionalized sex discrimination that seems the hardest stone to push.

The shifting limit that prevents this feminist reversal of the public-private hierarchy from freezing into a dogma or, indeed, from succeeding fully is the displacement of the opposition itself. For if the fabric of the so-called public sector is woven of the so-called private, the definition of the private is marked by a public potential, since it *is* the weave, or texture, of public activity. The opposition is thus not merely reversed; it is displaced. It is according to this practical structure of deconstruction as reversal–displacement then that I write: the deconstruction of the opposition between the private and the public is implicit in all, and explicit in some, feminist activity. The peculiarity of deconstructive practice must be reiterated here. Displacing the opposition that it initially apparently questions, it is always different from itself, always defers itself. It is neither a constitutive nor, of course, a regulative norm. If it were either, then feminist activity would articulate or strive toward that fulfilled displacement of public (male) and private (female): an *ideal* society and a sex-*transcendent* humanity. But deconstruction teaches one to question all transcendental idealisms. It is in terms of this peculiarity of deconstruction then that the displacement of male-female, public-private marks a shifting limit rather than the desire for a complete reversal.

At any rate, this is the explanation that I offer for my role at the Explanation and Culture Symposium and for the production of this expanded version of my essay. The explanatory labels are "feminist," "deconstructivist."

We take the explanations we produce to be the grounds of our action; they are endowed with coherence in terms of our explanation of a self. Thus willy-nilly, the choice of these two labels to give myself a shape produces between them a common cause. (Alternatively, the common cause between feminism and deconstruction might have made me choose them as labels for myself.) This common cause is an espousal of, and an attention to, marginality—a suspicion that what is at the center often hides a repression.

All this may be merely a preamble to admitting that at the actual symposium I sensed, and sensing cultivated, a certain marginality. Our intelligent and conscientious moderator seemed constantly to summarize me out of the group. After hearing us make our preliminary statements, he said that we were all interested in culture as process rather than object of study. No, I would not privilege process. After the next batch of short speeches, he said that it was evident that we wanted to formulate a coherent notion of explanation and culture that would accommodate all of us. No, I would not find unity in diversity; sometimes confrontation rather than integration seemed preferable. Leroy Searle, an old friend, spoke of the model of explanation having yielded to interpretation and threw me a conspirator's look. George Rousseau spoke of distrusting the text, and I wondered if he had thought to declare solidarity with a deconstructor by publicly aligning himself with what Paul Ricoeur has called "the hermeneutics of suspicion."[2] But I was not satisfied with hermeneutics—the theory of "interpretation rather than explanation"—"suspicious" or not, as long as it did not confront the problem of the critic's practice in any radical way. I thought the desire to explain might be a symptom of the desire to have a self that can control knowledge and a world that can be known; I thought to give oneself the right to a correct self-analysis and thus to avoid all thought of symptomaticity was foolish; I thought therefore that, willy-nilly, there was no way out but to develop a provisional theory of the practical politics of cultural explanations.

The group repeatedly expressed interest in my point of view because it appeared singular. But the direct question of what this point of view was was never posed or was posed at the end of a three-hour session given over to the correct definition of the role, say, of cognition in aesthetics. Is a poem cognitive? A picture? And so on. But I had no use for these phantasmic subdivisions (cognition, volition, perception, and the like) of the labor of consciousness except as an object of interpretation of which I was a part. A deconstructive point of view would reverse and displace such hierarchies as cognitive-aesthetic. I would bleat out sentences such as these in the interstices of the discussion. Kindly participants would turn to me, at best, and explain what I meant or didn't mean. At worst, the discussion of cognition and aesthetics would simply resume. On one occasion I had captured the floor with a rather cunning, if misguided series of illustrations from Nietzsche. The response was a remark that Nietzsche was a worthless philosopher, although rather fun. I countered hotly that cheap derision was out of place in a scholarly discussion. I was assured that fun was an essential element in all proper philosophers, and no harm had been meant.

This exchange illustrates yet another way I had solidly put myself in the margin. I questioned the structure of our proceedings whenever I felt it to be necessary—for the structure or means of production of explanations is, of course, a very important part of the ideology of cultural explanations that cannot be clearly distinguished, in fact, from the explanations themselves. It seemed an unrecognizable principle to this group of pleasant and gifted scholars. It didn't help that my manner in such situations is high-handed, and my sentences hopelessly periodic and Anglo-Indian. Every intervention was read as an expression of personal pique or fear. "Don't worry, no one will bother you on the big public day." I kept myself from gnashing my teeth, because that would only show that I still legitimated the male right to aggression. In fact, I was quite tough in public, having been trained before the hard-won triumphs of the latest wave of the women's movement, indeed, initially in a place out of comparison more sexist than academic America; my arguments had not been in the interest of *my* personal safety but rather against *their* masculinist practice, mistaken as the neutral and universal practice of intellectuals. In fact, I was assured at one point that male animals fought, even in play. I believe I did say that I knew it only too well; it was just that I thought some of it was curable.

Following the precarious and unrigorous rule of the deconstruction of the public and the private, I spoke of my marginality at the public session. I did not reserve my thrusts for the privacy of the bedroom or the kitchen table (in this case, the collegial dinner, lunch, or corridor chat), where decent men reprimanded their wives. (It would take me too far afield to develop and present the idea, based on a good deal of observation, that the academic male model for behavior toward their so-called female equals was that of the bourgeois husband.) I received no personal criticism "in public," of course. Taken aside, I was told I had used my power unfairly by posing as marginal; that I could criticize the establishment only because I spoke its language too well (English, masculinese, power play?). Both of these kinds of remarks would have produced lively and profitable discussion about explanation and cultural persuasion if, in fact, they had been put to me in public. But in this case, one kind of situational explanation was culturally prohibited, except as the exceptional, but more "real" matter of marginal communication.

About the worst of these asides even I feel obliged to remain silent.

Now when a Jacques Derrida deconstructs the opposition between private and public, margin and center, he touches the texture of language and tells how the old words would not resemble themselves any more if a trick of rereading were learned. The trick is to recognize that in every textual production, in the production of every explanation, there is the itinerary of a constantly thwarted desire to make the text explain. The question then becomes: What is this explanation as it is constituted by and as it effects a desire to conserve the explanation itself; what are the "means devised in the interest of the problem of a possible objective knowledge"?[3]

I wrote above that the will to explain was a symptom of the desire to have a self and a world. In other words, on the general level, the possibility of explanation carries the presupposition of an explainable (even if not fully) universe and an explaining (even if imperfectly) subject. These presuppositions assure our being. Explaining, we exclude the possibility of the *radically* heterogeneous.

On a more specific level, every explanation must secure and assure a certain *kind* of being-in-the-world, which might as well be called our politics. The general and specific levels are not clearly distinguishable, since the guarantee of sovereignty in the subject toward the object is the condition of the possibility of politics. Speaking for the specific politics of sexuality, I hoped to draw our attention to the productive and political margins of our discourse in general. I hoped to reiterate that, although the prohibition of marginality that is crucial in the production of any explanation is politics as such, what inhabits the prohibited margin of a particular explanation specifies its particular politics. To learn this without self-exculpation but without excusing the other side either is in my view so important that I will cite here a benign example from Derrida before he became playful in a way disturbing for the discipline.[4]

In *Speech and Phenomena* (1967), Derrida analyzes Edmund Husserl's *Logical Investigations I*. In the last chapter of the book, he produces this explanation: "The history of metaphysics therefore can be expressed as the unfolding of the structure or schema of an absolute will to hear-oneself-speak."[5]

Now this is indeed the product of the careful explication of Husserl through the entire book. This is also, as we know, one of the architraves of Derrida's thought. Yet if *Speech and Phenomena* is read carefully, by the time we arrive at this sentence we know that the role of "expression" as the adequate language of theory or concept is precisely what has been deconstructed in the book. Therefore, when Derrida says, "can be expressed as," he does not mean "is." He proffers us his analytical explanation in the language that he has deconstructed. Yet he does not imply that the explanation is therefore worthless, that there is a "true" explanation where the genuine copula ("is") can be used. He reminds us rather that all explanations, including his own, claim their centrality in terms of an excluded margin that makes possible the "can" of the "can be expressed" and allows "is" to be quietly substituted for it.

The implications of this philosophical position cannot remain confined to academic discourse. When all my colleagues were reacting adversely to my invocations of marginality, they were in fact performing another move within the center (public truth)-margin (private emotions) set. They were inviting me into the center at the price of exacting from me the language of centrality.

"Several of our excellent women colleagues in analysis," Freud wrote, explaining femininity, "have begun to work at the question [of femininity] . . . For the ladies, whenever some comparison seemed to turn out unfavorable to their sex, were able to utter a suspicion that we, the male analysts, had been unable to overcome certain deeply rooted prejudices against what was feminine, and that this was being paid for in the partiality of our researches. We, on the other hand, standing on the ground of bisexuality, had no difficulty in avoiding impoliteness. We had only to say: 'This doesn't apply to you. You're an exception, on this point you're more masculine than feminine.'"[6]

That passage was written in 1932. Adrienne Rich, speaking to the students of Smith College in 1979 said:

> *There's a false power which masculine society offers to a few women who "think like men" on condition that they use it to maintain things as they are. This is the meaning of female token-ism: that power withheld from the vast majority of women is offered to few, so that it may appear that any truly qualified woman can gain access to leadership, recognition, and reward; hence that justice based on merits actually prevails. The token woman is encouraged to see herself as different from most other women, as exceptionally talented and deserving; and to separate herself from the wider female condition; and she is perceived by "ordinary" women as separate also: perhaps even as stronger than themselves.*[7]

In offering me their perplexity and chagrin, my colleagues on the panel were acting out the scenario of tokenism: you are as good as we are (I was less learned than most of them, but never mind), why do you insist on emphasizing your difference? The puta-tive center welcomes selective inhabitants of the margin in order better to exclude the margin. And it is the center that offers the official explanation; or, the center is defined and reproduced by the explanation that it can express.

I have so far been explaining our symposium in terms of what had better be called a masculinist centralism. By pointing attention to a feminist marginality, I have been at-tempting, not to win the center for ourselves, but to point at the irreducibility of the margin in all explanations. That would not merely reverse but displace the distinction between margin and center. But in effect such pure innocence (pushing all guilt to the margins) is not possible, and, paradoxically, would put the very law of displacement and the irreducibility of the margin into question. The only way I can hope to suggest how the center itself is marginal is by not remaining outside in the margin and pointing my accusing finger at the center. I might do it rather by implicating myself in that cen-ter and sensing what politics make it marginal. Since one's vote is at the limit for oneself, the deconstructivist can use herself (assuming one is at one's own disposal) as a shuttle between the center (inside) and the margin (outside) and thus narrate a displacement.

The politics in terms of which all of us at the symposium as humanists are marginalized is the politics of an advanced capitalist technocracy.[8] I should insist here that the practice of capitalism is intimately linked with the practice of masculism.[9] As I speak of how humanists on the margin of such a society are tokenized, I hope these opening pages will remind the reader repeatedly how feminism, rather than being a spe-cial interest, might prove a model for the ever vigilant integration of the humanities. Here, however, in the interest of speaking from inside our group at the symposium, I will speak of this marginalization as a separate argument.

Although there are a mathematician and a physicist in our midst, we represent the humanist enclave in the academy. The mathematician is a philosopher, and the physi-cist, a philosopher of science. As such they represent acts of private good sense and intellectual foresight, which does not reproduce itself as a collective ideological change. These colleagues bring a flavor of pure science into our old-fashioned chambers and be-come practicing humanists much more easily than we could become practicing theoreticians of science. Together we represent the humanist enclave in the academy.

Our assigned role is, seemingly, the custodianship of culture. If as I have argued the concept and self-concept of culture as systems of habit are constituted by the production of explanations even as they make these explanations possible, our role is to produce and be produced by the *official* explanations in terms of the powers that police the entire society, emphasizing a continuity or a discontinuity with past explanations, depending on a seemingly judicious choice permitted by the play of this power. As we produce the official explanations, we reproduce the official ideology, the structure of possibility of a knowledge whose effect is that very structure. Our circumscribed productivity cannot be dismissed as a mere keeping of records. We are a part of the records we keep.

It is to belabor the obvious to say that we are written into the text of technology. It is no less obvious, though sometimes deliberately less well recognized (as perhaps in our symposium), that as collaborators in that text we also write it, constitutively if not regulatively. As with every text in existence, no sovereign individual writes it with full control. The most powerful technocrat is in that sense also a victim, although in brute suffering his victimhood cannot be compared to that of the poor and oppressed classes of the world. Our own victimhood is also not to be compared to this last, yet, in the name of the disinterested pursuit and perpetration of humanism, it is the only ground whose marginality I can share with the other participants, and therefore I will write about it, broadly and briefly.

Technology in this brief and broad sense is the discoveries of science applied to life uses. The advent of technology into society cannot be located as an "event." It is, however, perfectly "legitimate" to find in the so-called industrial revolution, whose own definitions are uncertain, a moment of sociological rupture when these applications began to be competitors and substitutes rather than supplements of human labor. This distinction cannot be strictly totalized or mastered by the logic of parasitism, by calling the new mode merely an unwelcome and unnatural parasite upon the previous. But for purposes of a positivistic computation of our marginalization, we can locate the moments spread out unevenly over the map of the industrial revolution, when what had seemed a benign enhancement of exchange value inserted itself into circulation in such a way as to actualize the always immanent condition of possibility of capital. In terms of any of these crudely located moments, it is impossible to claim that the priority of technological systems has been anything but profit maximization disguised as cost effectiveness. It is indeed almost impossible not to recognize everywhere technological systems where "sheer technological effectiveness"–whatever that might be, since questions of labor intensification introduce a peculiar normative factor–is gainsaid by considerations of the enhancement of the flow and accumulation of capital. No absolute priority can be declared, but technology takes its place with politics and economics as one of those "determinants" that we must grapple with if we wish to relate ourselves to any critique of social determinacy.[10] The production of the universities, the subdivision of their curricula, the hierarchy of the management-labor sandwich with the peculiarly flavored filling of the faculty, the specialization emphases, the grants and in-house financial distributions that affect choice of research and specialty, faculty life- and class-style: these "items of evidence" are often brushed aside as we perform our appointed task of producing explanations from our seemingly isolated scholarly study with its well-worn track to the library.[11]

It is a well-documented fact that technological capitalism must be dynamic in order to survive and must find newer methods of extracting surplus value from labor. Its "civilizing" efforts are felt everywhere and are not to be dismissed and ignored. In every humanistic discipline and every variety of fine art, the exigencies of the production and reproduction of capital produce impressive and exquisite by-products. In our own baili-wick, one of them would be such a group as ourselves, helping to hold money in the institutional humanistic budget, producing explanations in terms of pure categories such as cognition, epistemology, the aesthetic, interpretation, and the like; at the other end might be the tremendous exploitable energy of the freshman English machine as a panacea for social justice. Between the two poles (one might find other pairs) the hu-manities are being trashed.[12]

(I have not the expertise to speak of the hard sciences. But it would seem that the gap between the dazzling sophistication of the technique and the brutal precritical positiv-ism of the principle of its application in the practice of technology indicates the opposite predicament. For, as we hear from our friends and colleagues in the so-called "pure sciences" and as we heard from the "pure scientists" on the panel, the sophistication there extends to ontology, epistemology, and theories of space and time. Here the marginalization is thus produced by excess rather than lack [a distinction that is not tenable at the limit]. While the main text of technocracy makes a ferocious use of the substantive findings of a certain kind of "science," what is excluded and marginalized is precisely the workings of the area where the division of labor between "the sciences" and "the humanities"–excellent for the purposes of controlling and utilizing the acad-emy for ideological reproduction–begins to come undone.)

In the case of the humanities in general as in the case of feminism, the relationship be-tween margin and center is intricate and interanimating. Just as the woman chosen for special treatment by men (why she in particular was chosen can only be determined and expressed in terms of an indefinitely prolonged genealogy) can only be tolerated if she behaves "like men," so individuals in the chosen profession of humanists can only be tol-erated if they behave in a specific way. Three particular modes of behavior are relevant to my discussion: (1) to reproduce explanations and models of explanation that will take so little notice of the politico-economico-technological determinant that the latter can continue to present itself as nothing but a support system for the propagation of civiliza-tion (itself a species of cultural explanation), instrumental rather than constitutive; (2) to proliferate scientific analogies in so-called humanistic explanations: learned explanation of high art in terms of relativity or catastrophe theory, presentations of the mass seduc-tion of the populace as the organic being-in-art of the people; and (3) at the abject extreme, the open capitulation at the universities by the humanities as agents of the min-imization of their own expense of production.

It is in terms of this intricate interanimating relationship between margin and center that we cannot be called mere keepers of records. I would welcome a metaphor offered by a member of the audience at the symposium.

We are, rather, the disc jockeys of an advanced capitalist ethnocracy. The discs are not "records" of the old-fashioned kind, but productions of the most recent technology. The trends in taste and the economic factors that govern them are also the products of the most complex interrelations among a myriad factors such as international diplomacy, the world market, the conduct of advertisement supported by and supporting the first two items, and so on. To speak of the mode of production and constitution of the radio station complicates matters further. Now within this intricately determined and multiform situation, the disc jockey and his audience think, indeed are made to think, that they are free to play. This illusion of freedom allows us to protect the brutal ironies of technocracy by suggesting either that the system protects the humanist's freedom of spirit, or that "technology," that vague evil, is something the humanist must confront by inculcating humanistic "values," or by drawing generalized philosophical analogues from the latest spatio-temporal discoveries of the magical realms of "pure science," or yet by welcoming it as a benign and helpful friend.[13]

This has been a seemingly contextual explanation of our symposium. It should be noted, however, that the explanation might also be an analysis of the production of contexts and contextual explanations through marginalization centralization. My explanation cannot remain outside the structure of production of what I criticize. Yet, simply to reject my explanation on the grounds of this theoretical inadequacy that is in fact its theme would be to concede to the two specific political stances (masculist and technocratic) that I criticize. Further, the line between the politics of explanation and the specific politics that my text explains is ever wavering. If I now call this a heterogeneous predicament constituted by discontinuities, I hope I will be understood as using vocabulary rather than jargon.[14] This is the predicament as well as the condition of possibility of all practice.

•   •   •

The accounts of each other's work that we had read before the symposium can also be examined through the thematics of marginalization-centralization. Writing today in Austin, Texas (typing the first draft on the way to Ann Arbor, in fact), I cannot know what relationship those hastily written pre-symposium summaries will have with the finished essays for *Humanities in Society* nor if the participants will have taken into account the public session whose indescribable context I describe above. The blueprint of an interminable analysis that I include in this section might therefore be of special interest to our readers. It might give them a glimpse of the itinerary telescoped into the text they hold in their hands.

A specific sense of the importance of politics was not altogether lacking in these preliminary accounts. Norton Wise's project description concerned an especially interesting period in modern political and intellectual history. "In my present research I am attempting to draw connections between scientific and social concerns for a particularly revealing historical case: the reception of thermodynamics in Germany between about 1850 and 1910, including both the period of political unification and consolidation under Bismarck and the increasingly tension-ridden Wilhelmian period prior to the First World War."[15] The focus at work in the symposium did not allow him to develop his ideas in detail; I look forward to the finished project, to be completed through study of "internal published sources," "public discussions," and "general biographical information on approximately fifty people." Although the only limits to speculation that Wise can envisage are "empirical" rather than irreducibly structural, the idea that the reception of scientific "truths" can be historically vulnerable I find appealing.

It is more interesting, however, that Wise did not notice that it was not merely "Ernst Haeckel [who] employed his notion of a 'mechanical cell soul' to bridge the gap between mechanical reduction in biology and organic purposive action in the individual and the state." Here is a passage from the preface to the first edition of the first volume of *Capital*:

> *The value-form, whose fully developed shape is the money-form, is very simple and slight in content. Nevertheless, the human mind has sought in vain for more than 2,000 years to get to the bottom of it, while on the other hand there has been at least an approximation of a successful analysis of forms which are much richer in content and more complex. Why? Because the complete body is easier to study than its cells. Moreover, in the analysis of economic forms neither microscopes nor chemical reagents are of assistance. The power of abstraction must replace both. But for bourgeois society, the commodity form of the product of labor, or the value-form of the commodity, is the economic cell-form. To the superficial observer, the analysis of these forms seems to turn upon minutiae. It does in fact deal with minutiae, but so similarly does microscopic anatomy.*[16]

Such a metaphor does indeed "reveal," as it is produced by, or as it conditions, "connections between social and scientific values and beliefs." Wise has put his finger upon the great nineteenth-century theme of ideology (an unquestioningly accepted system of ideas that takes material shape in social action) and extended it to the production of scientific values. This is interesting because many contemporary critics of ideology maintain that a scientific politico-economic and socio-cultural explanation *can* be produced through a rigorous ideological critique, and that a series of structural explanations can indeed be ideology-free. Another group of thinkers, generally of a different political persuasion(s), suggest that the production of the discourse and even the methods of science must remain ideological and interpretable and need not be reasonable to be successful.[17] Wise's study would therefore be enriched if it were situated within this debate about cultural (in the broadest sense) explanation.

The study of "organic purposive action in the individual and the state" through the efficient method of scientific reduction is the issue here. Even the critics of a value-free scientific *discourse* and method would not question the plausibility of such a project, allowing for a system of compensations when the object of study is human reality.[18] The opening section of my essay should have made clear that I would be most pleased if a powerful project such as Wise's questioned even this last assumption: that "the sign" (in this case the various documentary and other evidence of the reception of thermodynamics at a certain period in Germany) is a "representation of the idea" (the basic assumptions of sociopolitical reality) "which itself represented the object perceived" (both the *real truth* of that sociopolitical reality *and* thermodynamics as such).[19] Not to be open to such questioning is, in the long run, not merely to privilege a transcendent truth behind words but also to privilege a language that can capture (versions of) such a truth and to privilege one's trade as the place where such a language can be learned.[20] I shall come back to this point.

I have a suspicion that the same sort of disciplinary vision that makes Wise overlook the Marxian passage makes Hooker and Rousseau limit their political concern in specific ways.

Rousseau speaks of the "politics of the academy": "yet ironically, only for a brief moment during the late sixties was it apparent to most American academics that the 'politics of the academy' count." It seems to me, all structural analyses aside, that it could just as easily be argued that a political activity often operating out of an academic base had an apparent effect upon American foreign policy in the sixties precisely because the academy began to see itself as the active margin of a brutal political centralism. The politics of the academy ceased to be merely academic. There are, of course, a good many problems with even this convenient cultural explanation. Many of the workers in the political arena of the sixties chose to step out of the academy. And even those workers have increasingly come to express, if one could risk such a generalization, the structure and thematics of the technocracy they inhabit.[21]

These pages are obviously not the appropriate place for disputing such specific issues. Yet, even as I applaud Rousseau's introduction of the political into our agenda, I feel this particular myopia appears also in his definition of *pluralism*: "Pluralism, originally an economic and agricultural concept, is the notion of the one over the many, as in pluralisitic societies." Nearly every survivor of the sixties would rather identify pluralism with "repressive tolerance." "Tolerance is turned from an active into a passive state, from practice to non-practice: laissez-faire the constituted authorities."[22]

Clifford Hooker, too, is concerned with the effect of social reality upon the production of knowledge. His project is particularly impressive to me because he is a "hard scientist," a theoretical physicist. I am moved by his enquiry into science "as a collective (species) institutionalized activity." I am disappointed though when the emphasis falls in the very next sentence upon science as an "*epistemic* institution." The explanation of the production of scientific knowledge is then to be explained, we surmise, in terms of abstract theories of how an abstractly defined human being *knows*. We are to be concerned, not with a cultural, but a phenomenological explanation. No mention will be made of the complicity of science and technology except by way of the kind of comment to which I have already pointed: that the technocrats know nothing about the vast changes in the concepts of space and time and knowledge that have taken place in the "pure" sciences. The confident centrality of the "purity" of science with hapless technology in the margins has a certain old-world wistfulness about it. Ignoring the immensely integrative effect of the world market, such a denial of history can only hope to establish an integrated view of all human activity through the supremacy and self-presence of the cognizing supra-historical self. The arts will be legitimated as a possible special form of cognition. This further centralism of the all-knowing mind, which can also know itself and thus the universe, is, once again, something I will mention in my last section.

In my opening pages I call "politics as such" the prohibition of marginality that is implicit in the production of any explanation. From that point of view, the choice of particular binary oppositions by our participants is no mere intellectual strategy. It is, in each case, the condition of the possibility for centralization (with appropriate apologies) and, correspondingly, marginalization.

> Humanities/Culture–Are the humanities culture-bound?
> Philosophy/Science–In the eighteenth century social philosophy was transformed into social science.
> Scientific/Social–What is the connection between the scientific and the social?
> Internal/External–Internal criticism is to examine the coherence of a system with its premises; external criticism is to examine how those premises and the principles of coherence are produced and what they, in turn, lead to.
> Speculative/Empirical–Speculative possibilities are limited only by empirical observations.
> Theory/Cultural ideology–Many objections adduced as "theoretical" are instead objections to a cultural ideology.
> Biological activity/Abstract structure–Is science most fruitfully viewed as one or the other (I am curious about the first possibility: "science as a biological activity")?
> Description-prediction/Prescription-control–Is science aimed at one or the other?
> Human artifacts/Nature–Does the study of one or the other constitute an important difference among the sciences?

(In fact, a compendious diagram accompanying Hooker's statement offers, like most diagrams, a superb collection of binaries and shows us, yet once again, how we think we conquer an unknown field by dividing it repeatedly into twos, when in fact we might be acting out the scenario of class [marginalization-centralization] and trade [knowledge is power].)

These shored-up pairs, a checklist that might have led to an exhaustive description of the field that was to have been covered by the symposium cannot, I think, allow that "theory" itself is a "cultural ideology" of a specific class and trade which must seek to reproduce itself; and upon whose reproduction a part of the stability of a technocracy depends. They cannot allow that the exclusivist ruses of theory reflect a symptom and have a history. The production of theoretical explanations and descriptions must, in this view, be taken to be the worthiest task to be performed towards any "phenomenon"; it must be seen as the best aid to enlightened practice and taken to be a universal and un-questioned good. Only then can the operation of the binaries begin. It is this unspoken premise that leads us to yet another "intellectual strategy," not necessarily articulated with the splitting into binaries: the declaration of a project to integrate things into ade-quate and encompassing explanations. The integration is sometimes explicitly, and always implicitly, in the name of the sovereign mind. Thus one project will work through "a conflation of social, philosophical, and scientific ideas," refusing to recog-nize the heterogeneity of the nonsocial, the nonphilosophical, the nonspecific that is not merely the other of society, philosophy, science. Another will attempt an "integrated view of human activity" and place the chart of this activity within a firmly drawn outline called a "consistency loop," banishing the risk of inconsistency at every step into the outer darkness.

It is thus not only the structure of marginalization centralization that assures the stability of cultural explanations in general. The fence of the consistency loop, as I argue also helps. To go back to my initial example, in order to make my behavior as a female consistent with the rest of the symposium, I would have to be defined as a sexless (in effect, male) humanist—and the rest of me would be fenced out of the consistency loop. The strongest brand of centralization is to allow in only the terms that would be consistent anyway, or could be accommodated within an argument based on consistency. The consistency loop also keeps out all the varieties of inconsistencies to which any diagram plotted in language owes its existence. Every word, not to mention combinations or parts of words, in a language, is capable of producing inexhaustible significations linked to contextual possibilities, possibilities that include citation or fictionalization "out of context." The strictly univocal or limited multivocal status of the words in a diagram operates by virtue of their difference from all the rest of this inexhaustible field. The field is kept out by reinterpreting the difference as the unique and most viable identity of the word.

In a more specific way, the plan for sweeping integrations also assures the stability of *one specific kind* of explanation, whose idealism would exclude all inconsistencies of what had best be called class, race, sex; although, if the analyses were taken far enough, even these names would begin to show the ragged edges of their own limits as unitary determinations. Thus in the theoretical establishment of the establishment of theory, mind is allowed to reign over matter, explanation, in a certain sense, over culture as the possibility of history, or as the space of dispersion of the politics of class, race, and sex. All human activity is seen as specifically integrative *cognitive* activity and the end becomes a "theory of theories." "[Literary] critical theorizing" is, in one case, seen as the "central *discipline* [the italics are presumably there to emphasize the sense of law and ordering rather than that of academic division of labor] in what we loosely call the 'humanities' or the 'human sciences' . . . the central form of self-conscious reflective thought." Such a frame of mind must disavow the *possibility* that the dream of the centralization of one's trade and one's class, and the dream of a self-present self-consciousness, intimately linked as they are, might be symptomatic and class-protective. Here the will to power through knowledge is so blind to itself that it takes the ontological question as necessarily answerable *before* theory: "the *self-evident fact* that no discipline can possibly pretend to have an adequate theory until it is possible to say *what* such a theory would have to explain."

• • •

Oh! Blessed rage for order, pale Ramon
The maker's rage to order words of the sea,
Words of the fragrant portals, dimly-starred,

> *And of ourselves and of our origins,*
> *In ghostlier demarcations, keener sounds.*[23]

Within the disciplinary mapping of the humanities, which permits them to remain preoccupied with hubris, poetry, especially modern poetry, is the thing that is allowed to make the kinds of suggestions that I have been making above. And this neutralizing permissiveness, resembling the permissiveness enjoyed by the humanities in general, would allow literary critics of even the most "theoretical" or "Marxist" bent to put the language of poetry (as well as "the *avant-garde* text and the discourse of the unconscious") out of play by claiming for them the status of special "uses of language which exceed communication."[24] That is not very far from the entrenched privatism of "spontaneous overflow of powerful feeling," the controlled detachment of "willing suspension of disbelief" or "escape from personality," the olympian (and oblivious) transhistoricity of "criticism of life."[25] Given such ferocious apartheid, the binary opposition of the literalist language of the conceptualism of pure theory and the metaphorical language of the figurative "cognition" of art becomes fully plausible. Your political allegiance can be pretty well plotted out in terms of which one you want to centralize—the concept or the metaphor.

If we could deconstruct (as far as possible) this marginalization between metaphor and concept, we would realize not only that no pure theory of metaphor is possible, because any premetaphoric base of discussion must already assume the distinction between theory and metaphor; but also that no priority, by the same token, can be given to metaphor, since every metaphor is contaminated and constituted by its conceptual justification. If neither metaphor nor concept is given priority (or both are), the passage of poetry above could be taught as a *serious* objection to the privileging of theory that takes place when humanists gather to discuss "cultural explanations." Yes, I know "blessed" is an ambiguous and overdetermined expression, that "pale Ramón" aesthetically neutralizes the "real" Ramón Fernández, that "to order" and "for order" are not synonymous, that "of" (meaning perhaps "out of" or "belonging to" or both) is undecidable and that lacking a predication, the lines carry no apparent judgment. But, questioning the prejudice that a "serious objection" must look like a literalist proposition, these very poetic and figurative gestures can be read as the conditions of the possibility of a stand against a "rage for order." Indeed, "to order" and "for order" can then be seen as at least the field of measure and coherence as well as unquestioning command and obedience, even the mass production of consumer goods for no one's particular use; and not merely for the sake of an exercise in polysemic interpretation.

At a time when the rage for order defeminates the humanities from every side, I can "make use" of such lines.[26] I have little interest in vindicating Wallace Stevens or in disclosing a plethora of "valid" readings, where *valid* is a word to dodge around the harsher and more legalistic *correct*. The line I am suggesting I have called, in a feminist context, "scrupulous and plausible misreadings." Since all readings, including the original text, are constituted by, or effects of, the necessary possibility of misreadings, in my argument the question becomes one of interpretations for use, built on the old grounds of coherence, without the cant of theoretical adequacy. And the emphasis falls on alert pedagogy.

It is not only poetry that can be taught in this way, of course. The eighteenth-century historian Giambattista Vico had a theory of language that put metaphor at the origin and suggested, I think, that first was best. It so happens that Vico took this theory seriously and at crucial moments in his argument put the burden of proof upon metaphorical production. In his speculation upon the principles of the history of human nature, Vico suggested that the sons of Noah, terrified by the first thunderclap, overcome by guilt and shame, hid in caves, dragging with them the indocile women they had been pursuing. In those caves, "gentile humanity" was founded. Although the place of guilt and shame in this story is very important, the reason for those two emotions, unlike in the Adam and Eve story, is not made clear. (Pursuing indocile women is clearly no grounds for either.) "Thus it was fear which created gods in the world . . . not fear awakened in men by other men, but fear awakened in men by themselves." It is because Vico was working his origin through metaphoric practice that this curious lack of clarity is encountered. It cannot be caught within the discourse of literalist explanations, where the adequation of cause and effect is the criterion of success. According to the literalist view, the fear of the thunderclap is itself produced through a metaphorical "mistake." Thinking of nature as "a great animated body," our fathers (Noah's sons) interpret the thunder as a threatening growl, the *response* to an act that should bring guilt and shame. The figure is metalepsis or prolepsis. The threat of the thunder, *result* of a transgression, is seen as the *cause* of the flight into the caves; or, variously, the threatening thunder *anticipates* the guilt and shame that should have produced it. Whichever is the case, the explanation hinges on a metaphor.

Again, speaking of legal marriage, or "solemn matrimony," which imposes civil status upon the patrician, Vico uses the metaphor of light. "[Juno] is also known as Lucina, who brings the offspring into the light; not natural light, for that is shared by the offspring of slaves, but the civil light by reason of which the nobles are called illustrious." Now there is a previous invocation of light at the beginning of Book I, Section III ("Principles") which seems to anticipate the light that can only come with marriage and render the one I quoted first (but which comes later in the book) logically suspect. "But in the night of thick darkness enveloping the earliest antiquity, so remote from ourselves, there shines the eternal and never-failing light of truth beyond all question: that the world of civil society has certainly been made by men, and that its principles are therefore to be found within the modification of our human mind." For the first figure of light seems to anticipate the effect and origin of the civil light that can shine only with the establishment of domestic society in the distant future. In other words, once again it is prolepsis at work. Vico used the same mechanism, the structure of figuration, to produce his theoretical discourse, which, he argued, produced the first and best language.[27]

If the discipline of literary criticism is merely permitted to indulge in the praise of metaphor, the discipline of history is expected to eschew metaphor as anything but the incidental ornamentation of the reportage of fact. The sort of reading I am describing would be dismissed by most self-respecting academic historians as reading "Vico as literature." The contribution of a critical humanist pedagogy in this case would be to take the metaphors in Vico as yet another example of the questioning of the supremacy of adequate theory, and not to relegate it to (or exalt it as) the semipoetic free-style social *philosophy* that preceded social *science*. Thus my two examples would emphasize the conceptuality of poetic language and the metaphoricity of historical language *to similar pedagogical ends*.

These examples are not audacious and revolutionary. It is not possible for a lone individual to question her disciplinary boundaries without collective effort. That is why I had hoped to hear some news of pedagogy at our symposium, not merely theory exchange. In the humanities classroom the ingredients for the methods of (the official) cultural explanation that fixes and constitutes "culture" are assembled. As a feminist, Marxist deconstructivist, I am interested in the theory-practice of pedagogic practice-theory that would allow us constructively to question privileged explanations even as explanations are generated.

It should be clear by now that I could not be embarked upon a mere reversal—a mere centralizing of teaching-as-practice at the same time as research-as-theory is marginalized. That slogan has led to the idea of teaching as the creation of human rapport or the relieving of anxiety and tension in the classroom that I have heard described as "pop psych" teaching and that I myself call "babysitting."[28] What I look for rather is a confrontational teaching of the humanities that would question the students' received disciplinary ideology (model of legitimate cultural explanations) even as it pushed into indefiniteness the most powerful ideology of the teaching of the humanities: the unquestioned explicating power of the theorizing mind and class, the need for intelligibility and the rule of law. If we meet again, as I hope we will, that is the question I will put on the agenda: the pedagogy of the humanities as the arena of cultural explanations that question the explanations of culture.

1. Stirrings of such a point of view can be seen in Mary Wollstonecraft, *Vindication of the Rights of Woman*, by way of the apparently converse argument that reason, the animating principle of civil society, must become the guiding principle of domestic society as well.

2. Paul Ricoeur, *Freud and Philosophy: An Essay on Interpretation*, trans. Denis Savage (New Haven: Yale University Press, 1970), pp. 31-36.

3. Edmund Husserl, *Ideas: General Introduction to Pure Phenomenology*, trans. W.R. Boyce Gibson (New York: Collier Books, 1962), p. 12.

4. As I argue elsewhere, Derrida's "playfulness" is in fact a "serious" and practical critique of pure seriousness. Here suffice it to point out that the disciplinary unease that is the straight reaction to the later Derrida can be described in the following way: "Here [is] a *new object*, calling for new conceptual tools, and for fresh theoretical foundations . . . [Here] is a true monster . . . [not someone who is] committing no more than a disciplined error." (Italics mine.) Michel Foucault, *The Archaeology of Knowledge*, trans. A. M. Sheridan Smith (London: Tavistock, 1972), p. 224.

5. *Speech and Phenomena: And Other Essays on Husserl's Theory of Signs*, trans. David B. Allison (Evanston: Northwestern University Press, 1973), p. 102.

6. Sigmund Freud, *The Standard Edition of the Complete Psychological Works of Sigmund Freud*. Vol. XXII, trans. James Strachey (London: Hogarth Press, 1964), pp. 116-17.

7. *Ms.* 8 (September 1979): 43.

8. By "technocracy" I am not referring to the "technocracy movement [which] was a short-lived episode of the thirties" and "was rooted in the nineteenth-century strand of thought that identified technology as the dominant force capable of fulfilling the American dream." I am referring rather to the practical sellout of this dream which is

a condition of the possibility of the theory of technocracy: "The modern postindustrial state—with its centralization, its emphasis on replacing politics with administrative decisions, and its meritocratic elite of specially trained experts—bears a more striking resemblance to the progressive formulation, which was the starting point for the technocrats. The progressive intellectuals, progressive engineers, and scientific managers of the early twentieth century saw the outlines of the future political economy with amazing clarity. But the 'immensely enriched and broadened life within reach of all,' which Harlow Person predicted, remains a dream that technology and engineering rationality seem incapable of fulfilling." William F. Akin, *Technocracy and the American Dream: The Technocrat Movement, 1900-1941* (Berkeley and Los Angeles: University of California Press, 1977), pp. xi, xiii, 170. My essay speculates in a very minor way about the theoretical humanists' unselfconscious role in sustaining this inevitable sellout. For preliminary information on some of the major actors in this drama, see Ronald Radosh and Murray N. Rothbard, eds., *A New History of Leviathan: Essays on the Rise of the American Corporate State* (New York, 1972).

9. I am simply referring as "masculism" to old-fashioned humanism, which considers the study of woman to be a special interest and defines woman invariably in terms of man. Among the many studies of the relationship between capitalism and masculism, I cite two here: *Feminism and Materialism: Women and Modes of Production*, eds. Annette Kuhn, and AnnMarie Wolpe (London: Routledge & Kegan Paul, 1978); and *Capitalist Patriarchy and the Case for Socialist Feminism*, ed. Zillah R. Eisenstein (New York: Monthly Review Press, 1979).

10. A simple test case of how politics-economics-technology (i.e., technocracy) becomes a collective determinant where "the last instance" can only be situated provisionally, temporarily, and in a slippery way, is the revisions of Edison's technological systems as recorded in the publications of the Edison Electric Institute. A humanist analysis of technology, choosing to ignore this transformation in the definition of technology, situates *technè* as the dynamic and undecidable middle term of the triad *theoria-technè-praxis*. The *loci classici* are, say, Aristotle's *Metaphysics* (1.1 and 2) and *Nicomanchean Ethics* (6). For extensive documentation, Nikolaus Lobkowicz, *Theory and Practice: History of a Concept from Aristotle to Marx* (Notre Dame: University Press of America, 1967), is useful. Heidegger's "The Question Concerning Technology," in *The Question Concerning Technology and Other Essays*, trans. William Lovitt (New York, 1977) may be cited as a case of a modern humanist study of the question. I am suggesting, of course, that such a text as the last can be made to produce a reading "against itself" if technology is understood as the disruptive middle term between politics and economics, or between science and society, making arguments from binary oppositions or "the last instance" productively undecidable.

11. I am leaving out of the argument the fact that this very "scholarly life" is sustained by bands of workers—secretarial and janitorial staff—who inhabit another world of pay scale and benefits and whose existence as labor is often, as at my own university, denied by statute.

12. I have so internalized the power of this phrase that I had forgotten in the first draft that Professor Norman Rudich had said with great passion at the Marxist Literary Group Summer Institute (1979): "They are trashing the humanities . . ."

13. The last suggestion was offered by the executive secretary of the Modern Language Association at an unpublished lecture at the University of Texas-Austin in October, 1979.

14. That the poststructuralists have developed a vocabulary that is on principle somewhat fluid has offended three groups who have no interest in studying them carefully. One group (represented by E.P. Thompson, E.J. Hobsbawm, as well as, curiously enough, Terry Eagleton) would seek to establish the disciplinary privilege of history over philosophy, or of an ultimately isomorphic theory of material and literary form over a theory that questions the convenience of isomorphism. "If we deny the determinate properties of the object, then no discipline remains." Thompson, *The Poverty of Theory and Other Essays* (New York: Monthly Review Press, 1978), p. 41. This book, containing some astute criticism of Althusser, seems finally to claim—as Althusser claims that Marx had not developed an adequate (philosophical) theory—that Marx had not developed an adequate (historical) theory. The real issue seems to be to *keep the disciplines going* so that theory can endorse "enlightened practice." For a lexical analysis of Thompson's text, see Sande Cohen, *Historical Culture* (Berkeley: University of California Press, 1986), pp. 185-229. As that thinker of a rather different persuasion, Barrington Moore, Jr., wrote in 1965: "Objective here means simply that correct and unambiguous answers, independent of individual whims and preferences, are in principle possible." *A Critique of Pure Tolerance*, ed. Robert Paul Wolff, et al. (Boston: Beacon Press, 1965), p.70. The second group is made up of conservative academic humanists like Gerald Graff (*Literature Against Itself: Literary Ideas in Modern Society*, Chicago: University of Chicago Press, 1979) or Peter Shaw ("Degenerate Criticism," *Harper's*, October 1979). These literary

disciplinarians refuse to recognize that the poststructuralist vocabulary emerges in response to the problem of practice in the discourse of the human sciences. The fault is not altogether theirs for, given the ideology of American literary criticism (hinted at cryptically by way of Wallace Stevens in my final section), American deconstructivism seems repeatedly to demonstrate that theory as such is defunct and there make an end. A Derrida or a Foucault would and do ask, if theory *as such* is defunct, what are the conditions of possibility of a practice that is not merely practice *as such?* The academic conservatives would rather argue, if a deconstructive view of things threatens business as usual, no one should be allowed to think deconstructive thoughts. In Thompson's words, the situation can be represented as a refusal to "argue with inconvenient evidence" (*Poverty,* p.43). The third group is the resolutely anti-intellectual communalist political activists whose slogan seems to be "if you think too much about words, you will do no deeds."

15. All the quotations in this essay, unless otherwise indicated, are from the typed material by all the participants circulated among us before the symposium.

16. Karl Marx, *Capital: A Critique of Political Economy*, Vol. 1, trans. Ben Fowkes (New York: Vintage Books, 1977), pp. 89-90.

17. As representative figures of the two sides of this exceedingly complex debate, let us choose the Althusser of *For Marx*, trans. Ben Brewster (London: Monthly Review Press, 1969) and the Paul K. Feyerabend of *Against Method: Outline of An Anarchist Theory of Knowledge* (London: New Left Books, 1975).

18. Such a generalization would be able to include the Pierre Bourdieu of *Outline of A Theory of Practice*, trans. Richard Nice (Cambridge: Cambridge University Press, 1977) and the Jürgen Habermas of *Theory and Practice*, trans. John Viertel (Boston, 1973), and *Knowledge and Human Interests*, trans. Jeremy J. Shapiro (Boston: Beacon Press, 1971).

19. Jacques Derrida, "Signature Event Context," *Glyph* 1 (1977): p. 179. In this passage Derrida is questioning a naive critique of ideology that assumes an isomorphic and continuous relationship between things of the mind and things of the world. I should add that I am indebted to this and its companion essay "Limited Inc," *Glyph* 2 (1977) for much of my understanding of deconstructive practice.

20. I refer the reader to the play of disciplinary allegiances broadly outlined in note 14. Michel Foucault's work on the genealogy of disciplines is of interest here. I have already cited "The Dis-

course on Language" (see note 4). Pertinent also are *The Birth of the Clinic: An Archaeology of Medical Perception*, trans. A.M. Sheridan Smith (New York: Pantheon Books, 1973) and *Discipline and Punish: the Birth of the Prison*, trans. Alan Sheridan (New York: Random House, 1977). One could do worse than cite the young Marx and Engels: "*The occupation assumes an independent existence owing to division of labour.* Everyone believes his craft to be the true one. Illusions regarding the connection between craft and reality are the more likely to be cherished by them because of the very nature of the craft." Karl Marx and Friedrich Engels, *Collected Works*. Vol. 5 (New York: International Publishers, 1976), p. 92.

21. One could ponder, for example, the splintering of Students for A Democratic Society: Progressive Labor, the New American Movement, Democratic Socialist Organizing Committee. Each splinter has taken on certain idioms permitted by American sociopolitical discourse as it has moved from a politics of personal freedom (even in a collective guise) to a politics of social justice.

22. Herbert Marcuse, "Repressive Tolerance," in *Critique of Pure Tolerance*, p. 82.

23. Wallace Stevens, "The Idea of Order at Key West," in *The Collected Poems of Wallace Stevens* (New York: Knopf, 1954), p. 130.

24. Rosalind Coward and John Ellis, *Language and Materialism: Developments in Semiology and the Theory of the Subject* (London: Routledge & Kegan Paul, 1977), p. 23.

25. Wordsworth, Coleridge, T.S. Eliot, and Matthew Arnold, of course.

26. Such a "making use" Foucault would call "the task [of] beco[ming] a curative science" based on a "historical sense" linked to Nietzsche's "active forgetfulness" which must make a "cut" in knowledge in order to act. "Nietzsche, Genealogy, History" in *Language, Counter-Memory, Practice*, trans. Donald F. Bouchard and Sherry Simon (Ithaca: Cornell University Press, 1977), pp. 156, 154. *Defeminates* is used as *emasculates*.

27. *The New Science of Giambattista Vico*, trans. Thomas Goddard Bergin and Max Harold Fisch (Ithaca: Cornell University Press, 1948), pp. 100, 109-110, 107, 106, 105, 155, 85. I am grateful to Professors Sidney Monas and James Schmidt for invoking these problematic passages.

28. Jean Bethke Elshtain, "The Social Relation of the Classroom: A Moral and Political Perspective," in *Studies in Socialist Pedagogy*, ed. T. M. Norton, and Bertell Ollman (New York: Monthly Review Press, 1978). I am grateful to Professor Michael Ryan for calling my attention to this essay.

Freedom of Choice

A vacation should be whatever you want it to be. Restful, relaxing. A seaside stroll or a conversation by moonlight. A chance to make a new friend across the bridge table. At last you can finish that novel you started three—or was it six—months ago. A good book, a drink, and the sea. Sounds like heaven? Sounds like Club Med.

• **Teshome H. Gabriel**

Thoughts on Nomadic Aesthetics and the Black Independent Cinema: Traces of a Journey

I sing
of a man
who was not a tree
but whose roots
spread throughout the land

>*Who was not fire*
>*but who smoldered*
>*in every blaze*
>*Who was not water*
>*but quenched thirst*

>>*I sing*
>>*of a man*
>>*who filled up space*
>>*with his presence*
>>*'cause he was the wind*[1]

•   •   •

The nomad has been desperately searching for water. He sends his children in all directions. He waits and none returns. His obsession becomes even more violent when his wife, the mother of his children, dies. There appears to be an imbalance in the whole search. He suffers humiliation, pain and agony. It is at this time of extreme gloom that the Goddess of the Sea sends a messenger to him.

The water goddess has remained undisturbed throughout the history of life on the earth. The earth is no more than an island in her world. She has thus remained powerful. Of course, the Goddess of the Sea knows this. She is the primary principle of all existence. While the desert had retained power and authority over living things, it is only water, the maternity of life force, that can defeat it.

The messenger tells the nomad that the goddess is prepared to send one of her daughters to guide him to the secret site of the legendary spring so he will never thirst again for 1,000 years. But she will thus free him from his search on one condition, and one condition only; that he marry her daughter. The nomad desperately wants water but he also cherishes his freedom of movement. He has been conditioned in his way of life, from childhood, for centuries. If he marries the daughter he knows he will be human-divine and immortal, but if he refuses to marry, he will violate cosmic order. The nomad goes through a deep conflict. He cannot meet the condition of the goddess because it means his desolation.

The nomad is isolated against forces that are more powerful than he. Dejected and confused, sitting around an open fire in the evening, he gazes at the blazing flames and begins to hallucinate about the legendary spring. Suddenly, through the haze there appears a woman that the nomad has not seen before. The woman stands, in darkness. Reaching into the fire, she grasps a handful of glowing embers from the ashes and throws them high into the heavens, their trail of light blazing "pathways to the stars." Ever since, moonbeams and starlight have guided nomads in the night.

On the morning of that night, with a brilliant flash of lightning, the nomad awakens and discovers he has company. A bond of spiritual harmony has been created. The nomad does not know it, but the woman is the daughter of the moon, a niece of the Goddess of the Sea. They have not been heard of since. Some said, they went to the north; others said, they went to the south; still others said, they had been taken to a far away place across the oceans.

"The sky gives witness to history," writes Brenda Marie Osbey in *Ceremony for Minneconjoux*. "Journey with me and see what I see."[2]

"Crankhandles of History"

Nomads belong to different cultures. They come from different periods of history.[3] From different time periods, they constantly incorporate and evolve a unique variation of spiritual, artistic and cultural expression. There are as many different lifestyles and aesthetic norms in the nomadic form of social organization as there are cultures and peoples in the world. Nomads are known to be rooted in myth, legend and folklore. Their artistic manifestations in song and dance, ritual and performance, are affirmations of their vigorous association with the earth and its gifts. To them art has two essential factors: (a) the ability to consolidate the community through ritual and performance and (b) collective participation in their dramatized, spoken and artistic forms. By their intensity both in communication and the immediacy of their memory, nomads reflect *par excellence* the lifestyle of a free people.

The impact of their art and their way of life has two important aspects:

> 1. The fundamental idea that all life, experience and existence is without frontiers or boundaries.

> 2. The foundational idea of not glorifying fulfillment in terms of territory or resources.

Life of sedentary or settled peoples is mostly controlled by state apparati, codified and written laws, and is dictated by resources which they transform and use. In nomadic thought, all human settlement, related to availability of resources, is only temporary.

Nomads reject the formation of the state because it curtails their freedom of movement; besides, the formation of the state has never been able to fulfill its promises. Nomads have thus developed a way of life, and an aesthetic attitude, which defy and critique both the settlement and art inspired by the state.

The moon is one of the great phenomena that is incorporated in nomadic cultures and that define the transient nature of their art work. The moon has interesting features: it is generous; it has maternal qualities of gentleness. It bathes the nomads after the scorching heat of the sun. The moon also has the capacity of transforming itself—it dies and it reappears every day. The undying moon that is dying. It actually never dies, and it actually dies—which is really the life cycle of human beings written large in the sky. Its reference to the life of the nomadic community is striking. They know they will die but also emerge to life. This is accomplished through ancestral logic. To the nomads all eventualities become the path—the footprints of the ancestors—upon which the trail of images, signs and "notes of music" are scattered. The instrumentality of these languages expresses free space.

The spiritual life of the nomad is much more highly developed in its co-existensive orientation than that of settled societies. In other words, there is not the same kind of exclusivity between the spiritual world and the physical world. Nor should this be mistaken for fusion between the two entities—the physical and the spiritual world coexist as separate but interdependent features of the universe.

Travelling Aesthetics

Nomadic outlook also lends itself to a different measure of qualities of artistic expression. In nomadic thought, art has three sides: it has functional, aesthetic and spiritual dimensions. One side of this triangle never rules out the others. Inextricably linked with this notion of art is the concept of reality.

1. Reality and Fantasy

In nomadic thought, "reality" is both tangible/seeable and untouchable/unseeable. What is not necessarily seeable and touchable, but which nevertheless exists, is merely an extension of known reality. Although the supreme reality is the earth, what is beyond or absent from this reality is explored through and manipulated by a system of fantasia. This is less anchored on symmetric or tangible realities; it subscribes to an inverted reality utilizing memory and experience to recreate the ephemeral qualities of existence. First, the cosmos is experienced and recalled as a fantastic phenomenon and then transformed—inverted—into an accessible and tangible reality through art, dance and ritual.

In short, the perceived entities of reality—i.e., the moon, the stars, mountains, wind, sun or oasis—assume a highly symbolic order. Hence, the most fantastic, sophisticated poems are in fact metaphoric structures and systems of multifaceted representation. In nomadic thought, the fantastic, which is a direct extension of everyday life, merely represents a heightened experience. In this kind of system, other planets or other words are no more than an exaggeration or minimalization of an otherwise known reality. This differs from Western metaphor, in which systems of fantasy are dislocated from reality and deviate from the known structure of *homo sapiens*.

The nomadic view is that the spiritualized entities and the realities of human existence are fused together, in an interactive creative relationship, creating a balance between the earth world and the sky world. The coexistential perceptions of these entities simultaneously evolve a symbolic world order which defies separateness, segmentation and isolation. In this instance, something is always present and absent at the same time. For the nomad, experience is not separated or segmented into categories of functions and aesthetics. In nomadic thought, what is specific (the aesthetic experience) is at the same time homogenous (i.e., it is part of an integrated experience of the mind), and vice versa. Here, aesthetic satisfaction corresponds to an aesthetic energy that the nomad consumes from physical entities that make him alive.

To nomads, art tells stories from experience and from memory. It cannot be simply one or the other; the two must coexist, as do the two worlds and two qualities of phenomena. Thus, their world and their aesthetics are more detailed and scorpious in manifesting ceaselessness, vastness and limitlessness in scale and temporal quality. These are manifest in three different ways:

> I. Art defies closure,
> II. Art rejects the structural model of beginning, middle and end, and
> III. Art reflects a cosmic integrity in the realms of (re)presentations.

2. Temporality/spatiality

In the Western context, time assumes its own "objective" existence. It is equated with the individual and is measured according to production output. Because time is measured in production, people are invested in units of time. Time is perceived as an investment and is thus valued more than the actual actors/participants in production. Time is narrativized into discrete elements of past, present and future. What issues from this is an intellectual and artistic justification for a way of life that validates a certain philosophy, and a certain tendency in modernism.

In nomadic orientations, units of time are far more broad. Time is seen, observed and experienced as "subjective." It arises out of observed and experienced relationships between planetary bodies. The central orientation points toward a "cyclic" system wherein several time frames occur simultaneously. In this kind of conceptualization, greater store is put on the value of actors/participants in production. Time does not control people, but people tend to operate within flexible time frames. In nomadism, time is not abstracted; it is an outcome of experience—it arises from life itself.

Space exists because there are tangible phenomena which are seen and felt. But there are also objects/phenomena that are touchable and seeable that we do not see that fill up space. The conception of space is thus relative to seeing, feeling and touching. To settlers, living in close proximity, distance and space are turned into an abstraction, into a greater introspection. We thus know less about more, and nomads know more about less. For instance, they have several words for village, environment and livestock. They also have a very keen sense of vision and sound. They smell the rain before the fall; they hear and see clearly where others distort. We see water where they see only mirage.

To nomads, time and space are both subjective phenomenon, operating within the system of the local absolute. The absolute is a matter of social consensus—it does not make any difference if it is, or is not. The important aspect is that there *is*, or there exists, an absolute against which to measure relationships and values of things, actions, ideas and so on.

Western systems glorify the Abstract in conceptions of Time and Space. Western thought has a love-hate relationship with the Absolute. If and when it is applied, it is abstracted and takes the notion of *the* Absolute. Take, for instance, Da Vinci's "Mona Lisa." We are told to admire the beauty of the painting for its enigmatic quality. We are told that what accounts for the painting's enduring quality is the smile. But beauty is invested in values and not in time.

In Western conceptions of the Mona Lisa, the desire to concretize and seal these values as timeless and as an Absolute is presented in a detailed and scientific manner. So much is suggested and so little revealed. That which is (ir)rational seems to necessitate the voice and expression of the many volumes written about it.

Subjective nomadic time prescribes that Mona Lisa's smile and beauty is ever shifting—OK yesterday, so so today and tomorrow who knows—it depends on circumstances of everyday feelings and experiences. To the nomadic way of thinking, Mona Lisa is tentative, incomplete, arbitrary, temporal and relative. In nomadic thought, everything is subject to aging. There is nothing timeless or enduring about beauty or aesthetics. It is, therefore, best to characterize the notion of aesthetics as transient or travelling.

Nomads in Quotations

"I'm from a nomadic society," Mahamood Issa said. "They make art, but they don't consider it as art. The two nomads meet in conversation, while one talks, the other will take a stick and design in the sands. They would be talking, I would be watching the design . . . Then an hour later, they would be gone, the design would be gone, the art would be gone."[4]

• • •

"The more I read, the more convinced I became that nomads had been the crankhandle of history, if for no other reason than that the great monotheisms had, all of them, surfaced from the pastoral milieu . . ."[5]

• • •

"Legend has it," writes John Berger, "that Pyrrhon, the founder of skepticism, was at first a painter. Later he accompanied Alexander the Great on his voyage through Asia, gave up painting and became a philosopher, declaring that *appearances and all perceptions were illusory*." [emphasis added][6]

• • •

"It is the women who make us live in the desert. They say the desert brings health and happiness, to them and to the children."[7]
–Sheikh, Sidi Ahmed el Beshir Hammadi of Mauritania

• • •

Brian Massumi, in his Foreword to *A Thousand Plateaus* wrote:

> The "nomads" whose thought lies behind the work of Deleuze and Guattari—Lucretius, Hume, Spinoza, Nietzsche, Bergson—are united by no school or direct lines of influence, only by their critical relation to official philosophy and its historical complicity with the state. They are also secretly linked, in Deleuze's words, by "the critique of negativity, the cultivation of joy, the hatred of interiority, the exteriority of forces and relations, and the denunciation of power."[8]

And what did Deleuze and Guattari say?

> In a totally different way, in a totally different context, Arab architecture constitutes a space that begins very near and low, placing the light and airy below and the solid and heavy above. This reversal of the laws of gravity turns lack of direction and negation of volume into constructive forces. There exists an absolute, as a local integration moving from part to part and constituting smooth space in an infinite succession of linkages and changes in direction. It is an absolute that is one with becoming itself, with process. It is the absolute of passage, which in nomad art merges with its manifestation. Here the absolute is local, precisely because place is not delimited.[9]

• • •

And what did Ib'n Khaldoun say?

> The Desert People are closer to being good than settled peoples because they are closer to the First State and are more removed from all the evil habits that have infected the hearts of settlers.[10]

• • •

> You cannot travel on the path before you have become the Path itself.
> –Guatama Buddha

· · ·

In a film, *Memory and Future*, by the Colombian filmmakers Marta Rodriguez and Jorge Silva, an Indian woman says, "I think, even if one dies, one doesn't lose its memory."

· · ·

Ignatieff: Let me see if I understand this. Human beings originate on the desert plains of Africa three million years ago . . .

Chatwin: Yes . . .

Ignatieff: . . . and they gradually acquire a set of instinctual behaviors that enable them to survive on the grasslands and vanquish their predators . . .

Chatwin: Yes . . .

Ignatieff: . . . and as they acquire a set of instinctual nomadic patterns of behavior they also acquire a meaning system, a set of myths which are imprinted on the brain over millions of years . . .

Chatwin: Yes . . .

Ignatieff: . . . and these are the story patterns that keep recurring even in the modern day.

Chatwin: Absolutely.[11]

· · ·

I wonder how people remember things who don't film, don't photograph, don't tape . . . The new Bible will be an eternal magnetic tape of a Time that would have to reread itself constantly, just to know it existed.
–Chris Marker in *Sans Soleil*

· · ·

And what is the visual model for "time immemorial"–towards which everything is direction and from where everything springs?

· · ·

It suits me to make pictures on celluloid . . . memory pictures . . . that make stories more interesting and exciting. With film, you are able to transpose these pictures of memory, imagination and reality, and make a [visual] story from them. It is, I think, a continuation of the oral tradition. That's how I see my work.[12]
–Merata Mirta

Black Cinema/Travelling Cinema

In my research for an alternative aesthetics of black independent cinema, I came across no man's land—to an oasis of wilderness, to the nomads in the desert. Today, nomads, in the book of travels, are to be found in the Americas and in the genesis of myths which reach back to the African savannah. Whether they are the San, Nam, Barwa Bathwa of the Kalahari, the Bedouin of Arabia, the Bakhtiaris of Persia or the Somalis and Fulanis of East and West Africa, or the Eskimos and the Indians of North and South America or the Originals (Ab-origines) of Australia, all reach back to "Africa" where the first human cry was heard.

Though black people and nomads may be racially and ethnically distinct, Language, in the broadest sense, unites them. The dominant aspect of this language is symbolism, metaphor, music and performance. They are also united in the very idea of space—they are both marginalized and (de)territorialized peoples. To both, collective memory, rather than official history, is of crucial importance. To both memory evokes mosaic images and sounds, and invades everyday existence. Both reject the idea of closure or termination, be it in their artistic manifestation or in their lifestyle. Just as the nomads are synthesizers of surrounding cultures they pass through, so are the blacks. They live in the industrialized world, but they do not belong to it; they pass through. Both opt not to adopt but to adapt. They incorporate some aspects and not others. Both seem not to be governed by the idea of physical home as much as by the mythical and spiritual home that they cherish in their belief systems and carry in their cultures. Both are obsessed by the very essence of freedom.

Black filmmakers break constraints and cross borders; they are not oppositional but pro-active in their creative work. They create their own aesthetic terms in film discourse. Call them ethnobiographies, film essays, film poems, film lore or a combination thereof: they incorporate "in clear rhythm with Africa" long-term memories and heritages. Herein are some examples from the archeology of black cinema.

In the genesis of black independent cinema the very titles of the films read like vocabularies from a nomadic dictionary. *Passing Through* by Larry Clark, *Black Exodus* by Iverson White, *Passion of Remembrance* and *Territories* by Isaac Julien and Maureen Blackwood, *Ashes and Embers* by Haile Gerima, *Patu* by Merata Mirta, *Handsworth Songs* by John Akomfrah, *Bless Their Little Hearts* by Billy Woodbury, *Burning an Illusion* by Menilik Shabazz, *King Carnival* by Horace Ove, *Langston Hughes: Dream Keeper* by St. Clair Bourne, *Pathway to the Stars* by Antonio Ole, are all examples that illustrate the terminological leitmotif of nomadic cinema and the lexicon of Nomadic philosophy.

Ben Cauldwell's *I and I*, which has its origins in African mythology, is an allegorical and metaphoric search for black identity. Barbara McCullough's *Water Ritual* is an act of purification on a spiritual and mythic level. Haile Gerima's *Bush Mama* is a film with floating style on life in the ghettoes of Industrial America. Julie Dash's *Illusions*, part one of a four part series, *Bridges*, is on the conflicts of dual identity of the African-American. *A Different Image* by Sharon Larkin is a search that traces the features of an African identity. All these films carry aspects of nomadic sensibility even if the filmmakers themselves are not aware of it. We can therefore understand why when Charles Burnett, maker of the *Killer of Sheep*, was asked; "How did you make this masterpiece of realism?" he replied, "I don't know, I just got raw stock and shot the film."[13]

And from other parts of Africa and the Third World a similar tendency abounds; we have *Ceddo* ("The Outsiders") and *Emitai* ("God of Thunder or Death or God of the Sky") by Ousmane Sembene, *Barravento* ("The Turning Wind") by Glauber Rocha of Brazil, *The Promised Land* by Miguel Littin of Chile, *Wend-Kuuni* ("God's Child or Gift") by Gaston Kabore of Burkina Faso. *Naitou* ("Orphan") by Moussa Kemoko Diakite of the Republic of Guinea, and many others carrying aspects of travelling aesthetics.

Nor are all forms of Western filmmaking ignorant of nomadic aesthetic. Perhaps most noteworthy in this regard is Chris Marker's *Sans Soleil* in its sensitivity to non-western cultures and its self-acknowledged (in)ability to penetrate them.

> *"My personal problem was more specific: how to film the ladies of [Guinea] Bissau?" says Chris Marker, ". . . the built-in grain of indestructibility of African women . . . I see her—she saw me—she knows that I see her, but just at an angle where it is still possible to act as though it was not addressed to me."*[14]

So too, Akira Kurosawa's *Dersu Uzala*, allowing its identification to influence its very aesthetic form, succeeds in communicating a sense of the nomadic, not only in its story but, perhaps more importantly, in its spatial aesthetics and in its formulation of the title character's relationship to nature. As if by acknowledgement of its nomadic impulse, one striking shot of the film shows the moon and the sun in the sky at opposite ends of the screen. Perhaps nowhere else in cinema has one single image more adeptly captured the essence of nomadic sensibility.

1. The Journey Theme

In black films there is often the depiction of journeys across space or landscape. Viewed as a whole, a pattern seems to emerge around the journey theme: wandering, exile, migration and homeland. Journeys acknowledge encounters with others, with known and unknown forces, happy or horrendous. Whatever themes these films carry, or whatever the land(e)scape they traverse, these do not seem to be the important aspect. The land ceases to be mere land, and only exists as a kind of mythic wilderness.

The journey is the link(age); without it there is no film. There is no film in and of itself. A film by itself is therefore meaningless—it conveys nothing. Film exists so that the journey may exist, and vice versa. Of course, the story sets the travel from place to place. But it is not important in itself. All filmic phenomena are subordinate in importance to the voyage. And the trace is more significant than the point of contact. Film is simply a foreshadowing device with allusions to memory. One cannot film without one's shadow. Film is only the siren call of the road: this is one of the key principles of nomadism.

2. Axis and not Poles

One of the limitations of mainstream theory and criticism has been its tendency to see the cinematic movements as tied to one of two poles: dominant (Hollywood) and oppositional (reactive) cinema. Typically, Hollywood and similar practices are lumped into the former, while Third World and independent movements are associated with the latter. This is problematic because it fails to recognize what are in fact the emerging tendencies of alternative filmmaking such as those which are here described as nomadic.

Thus, even in critical writings, Hollywood has been seen as a purveyor of colonial discourse and as a betrayer of others' cultural values. Understood merely as oppositional, black independent cinema could not be seen but as a reactive cinema. However, black independent cinema's search has gone far beyond this, for it is in fact a search for a newly born cinema, one with its own discrete identity, evolving on its own axis. It must be understood as more than a reactive pole–but rather as the development of new, emergent tendencies which are more difficult to categorize in established norms. Oppositional filmmaking is, in and of itself, not an axis; rather it is one of two opposite poles. It thus has no self-identity. Its films make use of the same reference and language of exploitative cinema.

To try to define black independent cinema merely in terms of otherness is also to create merely another reactive pole. Theorists of otherness fail to take into account that otherness speaks the same language of oppositional cinema. Culture and cinema are heterogenous and multiple and need not and cannot be fitted to a hierarchical model. To succumb to the notion of the other is to be a part of the same, to be trapped within the confined and prescribed boundaries that limit it. The other is always that which Western culture excludes in order to exploit.

Working within the debris of culture and discourse, black independent cinema moves not in between the two opposing poles but around it towards its own axis. Here the authority of the margins is born, in those blind spaces where the hierarchy of oppositions do not hold complete sway, where language confounds itself, and where liberated culture resides. In those liberated spaces outside of Hollywood and oppositional cinema, a new, newly born cinema is emerging, a cinema not-yet-here but no-longer-there, a travelling cinema–nomadic cinema. It is only in open free spaces that a new cinema can both deconstruct and construct this cinema. It is only through work of nomadic sensibility that black cinema, independent, feminist, exile and Third World cinema will capture its axis. That is why an authentic black cinema cannot be but a new, newly born, post-cinema, with new realities. We are thus witnessing a time when one cinema is dying and another one is being born in its place.

We can thus understand why Glauber Rocha remarked, "If we think that Hollywood is dangerous for us, so is Sartre [as Hegel, and others], and very much so." He added, "it's better to have a form that's badly polished but new."

Notes on Nomadic Cinema

Virtually from the beginning of cinema, with very few exceptions, the modes of genre classifications and styles have never been blended. Nomadic cinema brings an unprecedented and unexpected jolt to cinematic reality by smashing down boundaries–between documentary, ethnographic, travelogue, experimental and narrative fiction. Nomadic cinema makes both habit and virtue of this jolt.

1. The Mask as the Screen

In nomadic thought, one wears the mask during festivities to summon the universe to existence and put the world in motion. The mask represents the Absent one. It brings the unknown to recognition, the unrepresentable to representation. The mask itself is an object, it is abstract; yet it indicates that the content is present in the abstraction–where the known becomes unknown, the identical becomes different. The unrepresentable and unknowable is always "the missing content," that the mask recovers and brings forth. The mask puts the world upside down–it is a masquerade.[15]

The Screen is like the painted mask. Spectators put on the screen to sing a world into existence in movie-houses. The screen is worn at dusk, and the mask at dawn. The screen tends to distort reality and disguises meaning, while the mask de-frames the world, in inverted order, not to conceal, but to heighten and add significance. The "missing content" of the screen is "ideology," while that of the mask is "spirit." In both, there is an exchange between absent-present and between representable-unrepresentable, except that with the screen, one does not control it; "meaning" is spelled out to us; we have no contact with the screen; it does not have the social/collective aspects of the mask. There is no social boundary with the mask. Here, spectators have relation to it. Briefly, we summarize the difference as follows:

Mask	Screen
Spirit	Ideology
Collective memory	Official history
Long-term memory	Short-term memory
Interactive mode	Isolative mode
Social/collective relation	Individual relation (social is myth)
Spectator represents himself	Spectator does not represent himself
Significance: spectator makes his/her social connection	Meaning: spectator is given a social meaning, the world is him/her
Un-framed	Framed

The screen frames the world right side up. It limits its scope. It frames the world for the consolation of the turbulent viewer, who is excluded from representation. The screen, the spectacle, masks reality as a facade–the image of reality scoffs at reality itself. The screen serves as the canvas on which the West paints its own stereotypes of others. Social/collective relations to mask and the memory behind them give beleaguered cultures a strength which outlasts the brute forces of colonial culture. Therefore, to view the screen, the spectacle, more like a mask, a ritual, is to restructure one's viewing habits, i.e., to interact more socially, both with the screen and other members of the audience.

Perhaps nowhere have we seen this more clearly in American movie houses than in the screenings of Spike Lee's film, *She's Gotta Have It*. Is it any wonder that the film was roundly received by viewers, despite its clearly sexist overtones? Three elements, common to nomadic aesthetics, perhaps account for this: (a) its strong sense of place (New York's Bedford-Stuyvesant ghetto); (b) its use of face-to-face address to the audience (in the tradition of oral discourse); and (c) the resulting interactive mode which is obtained both between the film and its audiences, and among audience members themselves. Thus, the viewing experience becomes more than simply a relationship to a screen—it becomes a happening, an event.

2. Aesthetics as woman

As a branch of philosophy and theory, aesthetics itself is problematized by nomadic expression. A wandering life produces a wandering aesthetics. A travelling aesthetic requires travelling theory and criticism; yet theory and criticism are canonized, and thus become a way of fixing rather than liberating their objects. Nomadic practice thus creates havoc for such an orientation. Intrinsic to the nomadic mode of expression is an ever-constant shifting of its form and content and the relationship among them and their audience.

In theoretical and critical writings of the past, Third Cinema has been offered as one way to contextualize such aesthetics, giving it its liberatory due. To this we wish to add that these aesthetics are in fact tied closely to the mythical figure of the woman. The nomadic epic, at its best, is thus truly a woman's epic. By this it is meant that within the context of these nomadic travels what has been emphasized are various mythic and symbolic images of maternity, referring back to the land (Mother Earth) and water (Goddess of the Sea), which provide our sustenance and existence. Thus, the concept "female" represents that which both nurtures humankind and that which inspires and engenders aesthetic expression.

3. Towards a Poetics of Nomadic Aesthetics

Aesthetic is always outside the work; it is extra-cinematic. Its definition, its appreciation, its survivability are determined by the receiving subject, the spectator's memory, daily whims and fancies. Images in a film thus belong to the past; they represent re-mini-scen(c)es. However, though images belong to the past; they carry simultaneously possibilities and promises, because they also belong to the future. A nomadic cinema, then, is:

> A cinema with ritualized styles,
> > with a theme that hovers between
> > the reasoned action of psychological reality and
> > the inspired action of memory and forgetting.
> A cinema of celebration rather than tension.
> A cinema with a long-ago time frame,

> with an unbroken action,
>   followed through in long takes.
> A cinema freed from story and linear structure.
> A cinema where sound and image vary by the movement of the
>   wind.
> A cinema that floats over reality.
> A cinema that is able to break the logic it sets up for itself.
> A cinema that defies its own progress toward closure.
> A cinema that creates a rupture of its own expressive form.
> A cinema of anxiety, of ideas and mythic place.
> A cinema produced cinematically and contextualized culturally.
> A cinema with unrushed wholeness that imparts stature and
>   dignity.
> Where the hero's welcome is, at best, tentative.
>   Where off screen, the filmmaker berates his actors
>   about the reasons he is making the film.
> Where the subjects snap back that they are
>   merely the script treatment.
> Where black-frames interrupt process as discussions ensue.
> Where the filmmaker finally walks into frame, to reflect on his
> ambivalence between
>   −resolving the conflict with his actors, and
>   −to ruminate his commitment to complete the film.

This shows how film itself becomes part of alienation in filmic discourse. But the rupture and its acknowledgement are redeeming. The stylistic rift incurred becomes a specific part of the discourse. Nomadic cinema takes into account whatever is outside of the intended idea or script. This cinema resists opting for one mode exclusively. Through the use of a transgressive style, this cinema stresses, yet minimizes, conflict. It is a cinema of emphasis, of process:

> A film that acknowledges itself conceptually.
> A film that "traces no counters and delimits no form."
> A film that is comfortable with readings that float.
> A film that "both attracts spectators and allows them no place
>   to rest."
> A film where the prefilmic proves to be hopeful rather than
>   accurate.
> A film that is elated at being "a particle, a sprout," an
>   unfinished song.

Carnival of Remembrance

Along the coastline of Rio de Janeiro and Salvador in Bahia, every year, during the Summer Solstice (when the sun's eclipse is at the furthest north and south of the equator), Brazilians of African descent and others celebrate for an entire day in song, dance, ritual and carnival, in homage to Iamanja, the Goddess of the Sea. And when the sun sets "above the waves," and the moon awakens "above the clouds," all the celebrants face towards Africa, and in remembrance of an ancient homeland, throw flowers and gifts to the Goddess of the Sea:

> Your holy spirit floats
> along the cresting waves of the water,
> as we walk out upon the sands,
> night time closing on the longest day of the year,
> and join together in small circles
> around the sacred boats that we shall send you,
> each whispering our prayers to a flower
> that we lay upon the boat,
> for Iamanja, Holy Queen Sea.[16]

And all the roads branch out freely into all directions, to land and to sea. There are no longer boundaries to be patrolled. We are back in the African Savanna, and into several chains of sand dunes, plains and forests. We have entered into Africa of the Africas, we are in Angola:

> I sing
> of a Man
> who was not a myth
> 'cause he was the land

>> Who was in Ebo
>> and who did not bend
>> in Kifagondo

>>> but who held
>>> high the banner
>>> and he was
>>> a stout imbondo vine[17]

Here are the footprints from the not-so-ancient past. How momentous a whisper to a seed, and "prayers to a flower," can be. Here is the mask of memory–an anthem for Travelling Cinema–drawn from a poem by the heroic nomad-warrior, Agostinho Neto:

> Following
>   the pathway to the stars
> along the agile curve of a gazelle's neck
> above the waves above the clouds
> on springtime's wings of camaraderie
>
> A simple note of music
> an indispensable atom of harmony

a particle
a sprout
color
in the multiple combinations of humanity

Exact and inevitable
like the inevitable past of slavery
within our consciousness
like the present

Not abstract
without color
    amidst colorless ideals
without odor
    amidst the odorless rain forests
    of rootless trunks

But real
clad in green
in the fresh smell of forests after the rain
in the vigor of thunder and lightning
hands sustaining the germination of laughter
above the fields of hope

Eyes filled with freedom
ears with sound,
    of avid hands on drumheads
in rapid and sharp rhythms
of rivers Zaire deserts Kalahari mountains light
made crimson by endless fires
    in the violated grasslands
spiritual harmony of tom-tom voices
in clear rhythms of Africa

This is
    the pathway to the stars
along the agile curve of the gazelle's neck
on to the harmony of the world.[18]

1. A poem by the Angolan poet and militant, Arnaldo Santos. The myth that follows the poem is my own construction.

2. Brenda Marie Osbey, *Ceremony for Minneconjoux*, Callaloo Poetry Series (Lexington: University of Kentucky Press, 1983).

3. I am thankful to Professor Mazisi Kunene, the distinguished South African poet, for an illuminating discussion on nomadic cosmology.

4. "Ex-Somalian Exhibits 'Versatile' Art," *St. Louis Post-Dispatch* (October 15, 1987).

5. Bruce Chatwin, *The Songlines* (New York: Elizabeth Sifton Books, Viking, 1987), p. 19. I am indebted to this work for its inspiration.

6. *The Storyteller*, Special issue, *Granta*, no. 21 (Spring 1987): 18.

7. Chatwin, *The Songlines*, p. 178.

8. See no. 9.

9. Gilles Deleuze and Félix Guattari, *A Thousand Plateaus*, trans. Brian Massumi (Minneapolis: University of Minnesota Press, 1987), p. 494. See also Deleuze and Guattari, "Nomad Art," *Art & Text*, no. 19 (October-December 1985): 16-24. Deleuze and Guattari's works have been particularly useful and inspiring in this study.

10. Chatwin, *The Songlines*, p. 196.

11. *Granta*, no. 21, pp. 29-30.

12. Interview with the Maori filmmaker Merata Mita, *Framework*, no. 25 (June 1984): 3.

13. Monona Wali, "The Invisible Cinema," *Los Angeles READER* (February 24, 1984): 15.

14. The entire text of Chris Marker's narration, "Sunless," appears in *Semiotext(e)*, vol. 4, no. 3 (1984).

15. For an interesting discussion on "Art and Masquerade," by Klaus Ottman see *Art and Text*, no. 19 (October-December 1985): 47-52. See also Roland Barthes, *Camera Lucida*, trans. Richard Howard (New York: Hill & Wang, 1981), pp. 34-35.

16. Merlin Stone, *Ancient Mirrors of Womanhood* (Boston: Beacon Press, 1979), pp. 96 and 97.

17. This is a continuation of the first poem cited by Arnaldo Santos. Incidentally, the entire poem is written in the memory of Agostinho Neto, First President of Angola.

18. This poem, by Agostinho Neto, is recited in the film *Pathway to the Stars*. The film is patterned after the poem.

● **Gerald Vizenor**

Socioacupuncture: Mythic Reversals and the Striptease in Four Scenes

There's a battle for and around history going on at this very moment . . . the intention is to programme, to stifle what I've called "popular memory"; and also to propose and impose on people a framework in which to interpret the present.
−Michel Foucault

Inventing traditions . . . is essentially a process of formalization and ritualization, characterized by reference to the past, if only by imposing repetition. The actual process of creating such ritual and symbolic complexes has not been adequately studied by historians . . . There is probably no time and place with which historians are concerned which has not seen the "invention" of tradition . . .
−Eric Hobsbawm

Scene One: Release from Captured Images

Roland Barthes shows that the striptease is a contradiction; at the final moment of nakedness a "woman is desexualized." He writes in his book *Mythologies* (1972) that the spectacle is based on the "pretence of fear, as if eroticism here went no further than a sort of delicious terror, whose ritual signs have only to be announced to evoke at once the idea of sex and its conjuration."

Tribal cultures are colonized in a reversal of the striptease. Familiar tribal images are patches on the "pretence of fear," and there is a sense of "delicious terror" in the structural opposition of savagism and civilization found in the cinema and in the literature of romantic captivities. Plains tepees, and the signs of moccasins, canoes, feathers, leathers, arrowheads, numerous museum artifacts, conjure the cultural rituals of the traditional tribal past, but the pleasures of the tribal striptease are denied, data-bound, stopped in emulsion, colonized in print to resolve the insecurities and inhibitions of the dominant culture.

The striptease is a familiar expression of theatrical independence and social titillation.

In the scenes and voices here that delicious dance is a metaphor and in the metaphor are mythic strategies for survival. The striptease is the prime form of socioacupuncture, a therapeutic tease and technique, which is accomplished through tribal trickeries and mythic satire, eternal contradictions that release the ritual terror in captured images.

Ishi, for example, lived alone with one name, loose change, and a business suit, in a corner of an institution, the perfect tribal ornament. The anthropologists at the museumscape declared his private time a public venture; the survivor was collared for a place in an academic diorama until he danced in a striptease.

The inventions and historical plunders of tribal cultures by colonists, corporations, academic culture cultists, with their missions, reservations, deceptions, museum durance, have inhibited the sovereign striptease; racism and linear methods of perception have denied a theater for tribal events in mythic time.

Scene Two: Euphemisms for Linguistic Colonization

Edward Curtis possessed romantic and inhibited images of tribal people in his photographs. Posed and decorated in traditional vestments and costumes, his pictorial tribes are secular reversals of a ritual striptease, frozen faces on a calendar of arrogant discoveries, a solemn ethnocentric appeal for recognition of his own insecurities; his retouched emulsion images are based on the "pretence of fear."

Curtis could have vanished in his own culture, which he strove to understand through tribal civilizations, if tribal people had appeared in his soft focus photographs as assimilated: perched at pianos, dressed in machine stitched clothes, or writing letters to corrupt government agents.

Tribal cultures have been transformed in photographic images from mythic time into museum commodities. "Photography evades us," writes Roland Barthes in *Camera Lucida* (1981). "Photography transformed subject into object, and even, one might say, into a museum object . . ."

Photography is a social rite which turns the past into a "consumable object," argues Susan Sontag in her book *On Photography* (1977), "a defence against anxiety, and a tool of power." One cannot possess realities, but one can possess images, and "photographs are a way of imprisoning reality . . . The primitive notion of the efficacy of images presumes that images possess the qualities of real things, but our inclination is to attribute to real things the qualities of image."

Curtis retouched tribal images; he, or his darkroom assistants, removed hats, labels, suspenders, parasols, from photographic prints. In one photograph, entitled "In a Piegan Lodge," the image of an alarm clock was removed. Christopher Lyman in his recent book *The Vanishing Race and Other Illusions* (1982) reveals that the image of a clock, which on the negative appeared in a box between two tribal men, was removed from the gravure print published in the multivolume *The North American Indian* (1907-30) by Edward Curtis.

Lyman writes that the "removal of unwanted detail was certainly not the only end toward which Curtis employed retouching. When it came to pictorialist aesthetics, he was dedicated in his pursuit of dramatic effect."

Curtis invented and then possessed tribal images, while at the same time he denied the tribal people in one photograph the simple instrument of chronological time. The photographer and the clock, at last, appear more interesting now than do the two tribal men posed with their ubiquitous peacepipes. Curtis paid some tribal people to pose for photographs; he sold their images and lectured on their culture to raise cash to continue his travels to tribal communities. He traveled with his camera to capture the neonoble tribes, to preserve metasavages in the ethnographic present as consumable objects of the past.

Photographs are ambiguous, according to the novelist and art critic John Berger. "A photograph arrests the flow of time in which the event photographed once existed," he writes in *Another Way of Telling* (1982). "All photographs are of the past, yet in them an instant of the past is arrested so that, unlike a lived past, it can never lead to the present. Every photograph presents us with two messages: a message concerning the event photographed and another concerning a shock of discontinuity." Photographs of tribal people, therefore, are not connections to the traditional past; these images are discontinuous artifacts in a colonial road show.

The inventions of the tribes, and denials of the striptease, however, are not limited to emulsion images. Jingoists, historians, anthropologists, mythologists, and various culture cultists, have hatched and possessed distorted images of tribal cultures. Conference programs and the rich gossip at dinner parties continue to focus on the most recent adventures in tribal commodities. This obsession with the tribal past is not an innocent collection of arrowheads, not a crude map of public camp sites in sacred places, but rather a statement of academic power and control over tribal images, an excess of facts, data, narrative interviews, template discoveries. Academic evidence is a euphemism for linguistic colonization of oral traditions and popular memories.

Scene Three: Metasavages in Perfect Opposition

Encyclopaedia Britannica (1980) has sponsored the creation of a dozen tribal manikins, dressed in traditional vestments, for promotional exhibition at various shopping centers.

The sculpted figures, named for Black Hawk, Pontiac, Cochise, Massasoit, and other tribal leaders from the footnotes of dominant cultural histories, stand like specters from the tribal past in a secular reversal of the striptease. What is most unusual about this exhibition of anatomical artifacts is not that tribal leaders are invented and possessed as objects in a diorama to promote the sale of books, but that few of the tribal names celebrated in plastic casts are entered in the reference books published by the sponsor of the manikins.

"The Indian leaders whose likenesses appear in this exhibition represent every major region of the country and span more than four centuries of history," the editors write in the illustrated catalog, which is sold to promote their reference books. "Some were

great military leaders who fought valiantly to defend their lands. Others were states-
men, diplomats, scholars, and spiritual leaders." Nine manikins, however, are feathered
and the same number are praised as warriors. Black Hawk, the catalog reveals, "established his reputation as a warrior early in life. He wounded an enemy of his tribe at the
age of fifteen and took his first scalp the same year." Three invented tribal images bear
rifles; but only Massasoit, the manikin who associated with the colonists, is dressed in a
breechcloth and holds a short bow. In addition to those mentioned, the other plastic
manikins are named Joseph, Cornplanter, Powhatan, Red Cloud, Sequoyah, Tecumseh,
Wovoka, and Sacagawea, the one female tribal figure in the collection.

The editors of the catalog and the sculptors of the manikins consulted with "scholars
in the fields of Indian history, anthropology, and ethnology," and point out that the
tribal biographies in the catalog are the "product of hundreds of hours of research involving scores of sources of information." Such claims seem ironic, even deceptive,
because the sponsors were not able to consult entries in the *Encyclopaedia Britannica* for
most of the tribal names in the promotion catalog.

The manikin of Wovoka, spiritual founder of the Ghost Dance religion, was created
from photographs, while the other manikins, for the most part, were invented as
neonobles and metasavages from historical descriptions and from portraits painted by
Charles Bird King. "It seems odd," the editors of the catalog write, "that Wovoka is
shown dressed in white man's clothes, but this is the costume he typically wore as did
many other Indians." The other manikins in this cultural contradiction, however, are
dressed in what appear to be romantic variations of tribal vestments, evidence of the
denials of the striptease.

The sources of visual information, portraits, and historical descriptions, which the
sculptors used to cast the manikins, are colonial inventions, museum-bound. Portrait
painters, photographers, explorers, traders, and politicians have, with a few exceptions,
created a metasavage in perfect racist opposition to the theologies of the dominant culture. The editors and research consultants, even the witnesses at the shopping centers,
might vanish if these manikins were embodied in mythic time and participated in a
striptease: the structural distances captured in plastic would dissolve in a delicious dance.

Scene Four: Evelybody is Hoppy in Mythic Time

Tune Browne, mixed-blood tribal trickster from a woodland reservation, and the inspiration behind socioacupuncture, never wore beads or feathers or a wristwatch; he never
paid much attention to time or to his image until he became an independent candidate
for alderman.

Tune captured his own electronic and emulsion image when he first saw his outsized
face and eruptive nostrils on television and in newspaper photographs. He improved his
pose from week to week, one image to the next: he cocked his cheeks high at a traditional angle to mimic the old photographs, bought a watch, and dressed in leathers and
beads, bits and pieces at first, and then in six months' time he appeared on election eve

in braids and feathers, a proud reversal of the striptease. He seldom responded to abstract questions about economies; and in spite of his captured images, he found himself in the oral tradition from time to time. It happened when he removed his watch: he told stories then, myths and metaphors unfurled like blue herons in flight at dusk. Linear time seemed to vanish when he removed his watch.

Tune lost the election, he even lost the urban tribal vote, but he had earned the distinction of being the first tribal person to enter the aldermanic race. Months later in editorial articles, pictures of him in feathers and braids appeared—dubious footnotes to a loser—which he soon recognized as captured images, his image, from the past.

"Who *was* that stranger image?" he asked in a rhetorical pose at the first international conference on socioacupuncture and tribal identities. Tune was dressed in his leather and beads for the conference, redundant beside his photographic image on the right side of the screen behind the podium. "A dreamer who lost his soul for a time and found his families in still photographs," he said as he projected a second photograph on the left side of the screen.

Tune moves in mythic time, an unusual dreamer who tells that he shaves with crows and drives behind bears to the cedar treelines near the cities, hunkers with beaver over breakfast, and walks backwards under fluorescent lights and in institutions without windows. When he cannot see a tree he loses four white faces from his memories, an urban revision of the Ghost Dance.

The lead speaker on tribal identities in the modern world, Tune stands on stage, between two photographic images. On the right is his captured image in braids, sitting on the ground in a tepee with several peacepipes and an alarm clock. The photograph projected on the left side of the screen is "In a Piegan Lodge," by Edward Curtis.

"See here," Tune said as he pointed to the images, "Curtis has removed the clock, colonized the culture games and denied us our time in the world. Christopher Lyman wrote that the clock could have been a medal, a peace medal, but the box is too thick and besides, we *wore* medals then, never museum-boxed medals for a posed picture . . .

"Curtis paid us for the poses; it was hot then, but he wanted us to wear leathers to create the appearance of a traditional scene, his idea of the past . . . Curtis stood alone behind his camera, we pitied him there, he seemed lost, separated from his shadow, a desperate man who paid tribal people to become the images in his captured families. We never saw the photographs then and never thought that it would make a difference in the world of dreams, that we would become *his* images."

Tune pushed the podium aside and measured the captured images on the screen with his outstretched hands; from heads to hands he moved his fingers in shadow gestures over the screen. "But it did make a difference, we were caught dead in camera time, extinct in photographs, and now in search of our past and common memories we walk right back into these photographs, we become the invented images as this one did during the aldermanic election, to validate those who invented us on negatives."

He lowered his arms, spread his stout fingers like birds in flight and released several feathers from his vest. The lights were dim, the audience in the conference center was silent. Crows called in the distance, an otter slid down a river bank and snapped back in mythic time like a trickster on a high wire between the woodland and the cities.

"Socioacupuncture is our means of survival on the wire, our striptease in mythic time," he said in a deep voice as he untied the ties of the costumes in captured images, unhooked the hooks to museum commodities, and bead over bead he performed a slow striptease, a ritual contradiction between two frozen photographic images from the time-bound past.

"Not satire as shame," Tune explained to the tribal people at the conference, "not social ridicule as a form of social control," he continued as he dropped his bone choker to the floor, "but satire from magical connections with the oral tradition . . . Robert Elliott writes about a 'mystical ethos' in satire, from ritual dances and tribal trickeries. Mythic satire, not as a moral lesson, but a dream voice out of time like a striptease in the middle of the word wars."

Tune removed his beaded leather vest and dropped it to the floor of the stage. His hands danced as he continued his lecture stories on the ethos of the ritual striptease.

"Socioacupuncture reverses the documents, deflates data, dissolves historical time, releases the pressure in captured images, and exposes the pale inventors of the tribes. Lyman tells us that Curtis set out to construct a 'photographic monument to a vanishing race.' Not so, it was the photographer who would have vanished without our images to take as captured families.

"On the frontier, white settlers were offered free guns with the purchase of sewing machines," Tune announced to the conference participants as he untied his moccasins. "The tribes were offered free clocks with a peace medal and a reservation . . . Curtis stole our alarm clocks and we missed the plane and lost the election, dressed in leather and feathers."

"Take it off," someone yelled from the audience.

"Give him time," someone responded.

"Roy Wagner must have stopped the clocks for a time when he wrote *The Invention of Culture* [1981]," Tune said as he kicked his pinched moccasins with the floral bead patterns into the audience and gestured, at the same time, toward his image on the screen to the right. "He wrote that 'the study of culture is in fact *our* culture'—the dominant culture is what he means here—and 'it operates through our forms, creates in our terms, borrows our words and concepts for its meanings, and re-creates us through our efforts . . . By applying universal theories naively to the study of cultures we invent those cultures as stubborn and inviolable individualities. Each failure motivates a greater collectivizing effort.'

"We lose the elections in leathers and feathers, failed and fixed in histories, but through mythic satire we reverse the inventions, and during our ritual striptease the inventors vanish."

"Take it off," the tribal audience chanted again and again as Tune unbuttoned his shirt and unbraided his hair and shivered between the captured images at his sides.

"Wagner tells how Ishi, the last survivor of the Yahi tribe in California, 'brought the world into the museum,' where we lived and worked after our capture," Tune confessed, as he threw his shirt and the ribbons from his braids to the audience. "In good weather anthropologists and others would take the two of us from the museum back to the hills where we would demonstrate how to survive with a small bow and wooden arrows. He was the 'ideal museum specimen . . . Ishi accomplished the metaphorization of life into culture that defines much of anthropological understanding,' Wagner wrote."

"Take it off."

"Take it off."

"Take it off."

"Take it off."

"Tune is the name and the end of the captured game," he chanted as he combed his hair free from braids, and then untied the beaded belt that held his leather trousers erect, "the end of the captured game."

Tune turned the projectors off and the captured images died when he dropped his trousers in a sovereign striptease. The audience burst into wild cheers and peals of animal laughter in the dim light, even the cats and crows called from the crowd. Tune listened to the birds over the trees and when he removed his wristwatch the dichotomies of past and present dissolved one last time. The inventors and colonialists vanished with the striptease; even those whose ideas he had quoted seemed to vanish like petals on a pasture rose. The conference on socioacupuncture was silent.

Tune turned toward the trees in mythic time and told how he and Ishi lived together and worked at the museum to protect the anthropologists, for a time, from vanishing. Then, last summer, "the anthropologists were secure enough in their own culture to recommend that we receive honorary degrees from the University of California at Berkeley."

Tune paused in silence to celebrate the trees in his vision. Then he told stories about the graduation ceremonies in the redwoods: Morning ghosts ride with our dreams over the tribal stories from the past, dark waves, slow waves, water demons under our ocean skin waves, trickeries and turtle memories under the stone waves, under the word gates, through the earth where we hold our origins with the trees and the wind, creation myths with ocean roots . . . The ghosts dance roundabout in our dreams, clouds dance and burn free in the rituals of the morning sun. . . .

College degrees are degrees in words, with special awards for sentence structure, uniforms in the word wars, which is not much better than being elected to the plastic flower growers' association Hall of Fame, but we must not pluck the carrier pigeons with the documents too soon because the academics might vanish.

Silence.

Gregory Bateson writes in his book, *Mind and Nature* (1979), that in the affairs of living "there are typically two energetic systems in interdependence: One is the system that uses its energy to open and close the faucet or gate or relay; the other is the system whose energy 'flows through' the faucet or gate when it is open." Photographers and colonists are the faucets, historians hold the word-gates, and we are the energies of the tribes that run like dreams in a dance with the morning sun over wet meadows.

Ghosts hover in the tall redwoods roundabout the outdoor amphitheater in the

Mather Redwood Grove. Animals and birds soar through the treescapes, dream beasts browse over the mountains. We remember the flood and call the crows back from the cities.

"The imagination is always aware of the present...," writes Mary Warnock in *Imagination* (1976). "Neither understanding alone nor sensation alone can do the work of imagination, nor can they be conceived to come together without imagination... Only imagination is in this sense creative; only it makes pictures of things."

Alfred Kroeber, Thomas Waterman, Edward Sapir, the linguist, Phoebe Apperson Hearst, Regent of the University of California, Robert Sproul and Benjamin Ide Wheeler were all there for the graduation ceremonies, roundabout in the redwood trees, soaring out of time and place in magical flight.

"The University of California strives not to isolate academic ideas, races and nations on our campus as single population groups. This is not a place of racial separations," asserted Provost Pontius Booker as he pinched the skin under his chin. "Our academic communities are based on trust, research, instruction, fair examinations, and, of course, on excellence...

"This afternoon we are privileged to announce that our very own Ishi, and Tune Browne, will receive honorary Doctor of Philosophy degrees here at the University of California, where these two instinctive native scholars have lived in a museum... It is a distinct pleasure to announce these degrees and to introduce Alfred Kroeber, the famous anthropologist who worked with these two proud and unusual natives."

Kroeber shuffled on stage close to the microphone, leaned over and spoke in a gentle but distant voice: Ishi was the "most patient man I ever knew. I mean he had mastered the philosophy of patience..."

Saxton Pope, our medical doctor and master of bows and arrows, was not present for the graduation but he wrote the following to be read at the ceremonies: Ishi "looked upon us as sophisticated children–smart, but not wise. We knew many things, and much that is false. He knew nature, which is always true... His soul was that of a child, his mind that of a philosopher."

Phoebe Apperson Hearst came down to the microphone from the right rim of the amphitheater to decorate us with colorful sashes and to present our degrees. "Doctor Ishi Ishi, Doctor Tune Browne, you are both intuitive scholars, we have all agreed..." Doctor Kroeber has recorded the first words that Ishi spoke in English. "We are, at last, pleased to imitate this fine man on this special occasion, is 'evelybody hoppy?'"

"The transvaluation of roles that turns the despised and oppressed into symbols of salvation and rebirth is nothing new in the history of human culture," writes Robert Bellah, a sociologist from the University of California at Berkeley, in his book, *The Broken Covenant* (1975), "but when it occurs, it is an indication of new cultural directions, perhaps of a deep cultural revolution."

We danced roundabout on the stage of the amphitheater dressed in our breechcloths and academic sashes with all the animals and ghosts under the redwood trees; a striptease, deep in a cultural revolution.

The fogdogs laughed and barked from the rim.

"Evelybody hoppy?" asked Doctor Ishi.

"Time now for a word striptease," someone chanted.

"Take it off."

"Silence."

"We are what we imagine," wrote N. Scott Momaday, the Kiowa novelist. "Our very existence consists in our imagination of ourselves. . . . The greatest tragedy that can befall us is to go unimagined."

"Evelybody hoppy?" asked Doctor Tune Browne.

Contributors

Gloria Anzaldúa is a poet and writer. She is the author of *Borderlands/La Frontera* (1987) and co-editor of *This Bridge Called My Back* (1981).

Homi K. Bhabha teaches English literature and literary theory at Sussex University in England. He is the author of *The Location of Culture* and editor of *Nation and Narration* (forthcoming).

Hélène Cixous is head of the Center of Research in Feminine Studies in Paris and professor of English at the University of Paris VIII. Her many books include *Angst* (1977; trans. 1985), *Inside* (1969; trans. 1986), and *The Newly Born Woman* (1975; trans. 1986).

James Clifford, author of *The Predicament of Culture* (1988) and co-editor of *Writing Culture: The Poetics and Politics of Ethnography* (1986), teaches in the History of Consciousness Program at the University of California, Santa Cruz.

Douglas Crimp is an art critic, an editor of the journal *October*, and an AIDS activist. He is the editor of *AIDS: Cultural Analysis/Cultural Activism* (1989) and author, with Adam Rolston of *AIDS Demo Graphics* (1990). A collection of his essays entitled *On the Museum's Ruins* is forthcoming from MIT Press.

Gilles Deleuze, Professor of Philosophy at the University of Paris VIII, and the psychoanalyst **Félix Guattari** have worked collaboratively on numerous publications including *Anti-Oedipus* (1972; trans. 1983), *Kafka* (1975; trans. 1986), and *A Thousand Plateaus* (1980; trans. 1987).

Rosalyn Deutsche is an art historian and critic who teaches at the Cooper Union in New York City. She has written extensively about art and urban redevelopment.

Richard Dyer teaches film studies at Warwick University in England.

Russell Ferguson is Special Projects Editor and Librarian at The New Museum of Contemporary Art in New York. He is a co-editor of *Discourses: Conversations in Postmodern Art and Culture* (1990).

Teshome H. Gabriel teaches in the Department of Film and Television at the University of California, Los Angeles and is the author of *Third Cinema in the Third World: The Aesthetics of Liberation* (1982).

Martha Gever is the editor of the journal *The Independent*.

bell hooks (Gloria Watkins) is Associate Professor of English and Women's Studies at Oberlin College. She is the author of *Feminist Theory: From Margin to Center* (1984), *Talking Back* (1989) and *Yearning: Race, Gender and Culture* (1990).

Audre Lorde is a poet and Professor of English at Hunter College of the City University of New York.

Kobena Mercer has lectured widely and written on the cultural politics of race, sexuality and representation. He is currently working at The British Film Institute and will be teaching at The University of California, Santa Cruz, in the fall of 1990.

Toni Morrison's many novels include *The Bluest Eye* (1970), *Sula* (1973), *Tar Baby* (1981), and *Beloved* (1987).

Linda Peckham is a writer and filmmaker working in the Bay Area.

Richard Rodriguez is a writer living in San Francisco. His autobiography is entitled *Hunger of Memory* (1982).

Edward Said is Parr Professor of English and Comparative Literature at Columbia University. His books include *Orientalism* (1979), *The Question of Palestine* (1979) and *The World, the Text and the Critic* (1983).

James A. Snead (1953-1989) was Professor of English at the University of Pittsburgh, and the author of *Figures of Division: William Faulkner's Major Novels* (1986).

Gayatri Chakravorty Spivak, author of *In Other Worlds* (1987) and *Master Discourse Native Informant* (forthcoming), is Andrew W. Mellon Professor in the Department of English at the University of Pittsburgh.

Trinh T. Minh-ha is a writer, filmmaker and composer. Her works include the book *Woman Native Other* (1989) and the films *Reassemblage* (1982), *Naked Spaces–Living is Round* (1985) and *Surname Viet, Given Name Nam* (1989).

Gerald Vizenor is the author of numerous books including *Earthdivers: Tribal Narratives on Mixed Descent* (1981) and *The People Named the Chippewa* (1984).

Michele Wallace is the author of *Black Macho and the Myth of the Superwoman* (1979) and Assistant Professor of Women's Studies at the State University of New York in Buffalo.

Simon Watney is a writer, critic and member of the editorial board of the journal *Screen*. He has most recently co-edited, with Erica Carter, *Taking Liberties: AIDS and Cultural Politics* (1989).

Cornel West, Professor of Religion and Director of the Afro-American Studies Program at Princeton University, is the author of *Prophetic Fragments* (1988) and *The American Evasion of Philosophy* (1989). He is also on the editorial board of the journal *Social Text*.

Monique Wittig, author of *Opoponax* (1964; trans. 1976), *Les Guérillères* (1969; trans. 1975), and *The Lesbian Body* (1973; trans. 1975), is a contributor to the journal *Questions féministes* in France.

John Yau is a poet and critic. His most recent book is *Radiant Silhouette* (1989).

Illustrations

Cover: Brian Buczak, *Flags*, 1987. Courtesy of Geoffrey Hendricks and the Estate of Brian Buczak. Brian Buczak died of AIDS on July 4, 1987. Photo: Barry Pribula.

Endpapers: Nancy Spero, *Woman Sticking Out Her Tongue*, 1989. Courtesy of the artist.

Pages 2, 15, 16, 88, 131, 170, 231, 324, 420, 426: Félix González-Torres, *Untitled (I Think I Know Who You Are)*, 1989.

Page 37: "The Manual Alphabet," from Tom Humphries, Carol Padden, Terrence J. O'Rourke, *A Basic Course in American Sign Language* (Silver Spring, MD: T.J. Publishers, 1986), p. 235. Illustration by Frank A. Paul. Courtesy of the publishers.

Page 38: Lorna Simpson, *Eating Disorder*, 1989. Courtesy of the artist.

Page 58: Michael Jenkins, *Join*, 1989. Courtesy of the artist.

Page 70: Sokhi Wagner, *View from the Car*, 1988. Courtesy of the artist.

Pages 104-106: Alfredo Jaar, *La Géographie ça sert, d'abord, a faire la Guerre (Geography = War)*, 1989. ("Africa is rapidly becoming the dumping ground for millions of tons of toxic industrial waste from the so-called *developed* countries. This new *development* is the modern version of the slave trade: although the traffic is still one way, the direction has changed . . .") Courtesy of the artist.

Pages 124, 125: Krzysztof Wodiczko, Installation and slide projection of the *Homeless Vehicle Project* at the Clocktower, New York, 1988. Courtesy of *October* magazine.

Page 132: Wifredo Lam, *The Jungle*, 1943, gouache on paper mounted on canvas, 7′ 10¼″ × 7′ 6½″, Collection, The Museum of Modern Art, New York. Inter-American Fund.

Page 140: postcard, *In Flight, Route of the Flagships*. Photo by Ivan Dmitri. Courtesy of American Airlines.

Pages 172-189: childhood photos: Lorna Simpson; Jon Tower; Gayatri Chakravorty Spivak; Wifredo Lam; Michele Wallace; Toni Morrison; Nancy Spero; Martin Wong; Roger Conover; Richard Dyer; Richard Rodriguez; Douglas Crimp; clockwise: Nelson Montes, José Parissi, Nelson Savinon, Annette Rosado, Hector Rodriguez, Tim Rollins; Michael Jenkins; Alice Yang; Martha Gever; Bethany Johns.

Page 212: © Arthur Rothstein, *Eartha Kitt*, 1953. Courtesy of Grace Rothstein.

Page 232: Robert Gober, *Untitled*, 1986. Courtesy of the artist and Paula Cooper Gallery, New York.

Page 246: Martin Wong, *Rapture*, 1987. Courtesy of the artist and Exit Art, New York.

Page 279: Jon Tower, *Solved Problem #170*, 1987. Courtesy of the artist.

Page 280: Jeanne Dunning, *Head*, 1989. Courtesy of the artist and Feature Gallery, New York.

Page 288: Sylvia Plachy, *Bike Week, Daytona Beach, Florida*, 1987. Courtesy of the artist.

Pages 306-323: childhood photos: Julie Ault; bell hooks; John Yau; James Clifford; Homi K. Bhabha; Georgie Stout; Sowon Kwon; Marcia Tucker; Kobena Mercer; Alfredo Jaar; Rosalyn Deutsche; Russell Ferguson; Félix González-Torres; Jeanne Dunning; Linda Peckham; Cornel West (fifth student from the left, top row); Robert Gober; Janice Woo; Sokhi Wagner; Simon Watney.

Page 344: postcard, *Exuberant Carribean*. Photo by Mario Posada O. Courtesy of F. González-Torres.

Page 375: Julie Ault, *Torture on the Moon*, 1987. Courtesy of the artist.

Page 376: Tim Rollins and K.O.S., *The Whiteness of the Whale*, 1985-86. Courtesy of the artists and Jay Gorney Modern Art, New York.

Page 394: from the Club Med Summer/Fall 1989 catalog. Courtesy of Club Med.

Reprint Sources

Monique Wittig, "The Straight Mind," in *Feminist Issues*, vol. 1, no. 1 (Summer 1980): 103-111.

Gilles Deleuze and Félix Guattari, "What is a Minor Literature?" in *Kafka: Toward a Minor Literature* (Minneapolis: University of Minnesota Press, 1986), pp. 16-27.

Homi K. Bhabha, "The Other Question: Discrimination and the Discourse of Colonialism," in *Literature, Politics and Theory: Papers from the Essex Conference 1976-84*, eds. Francis Barker, et al. (New York: Methuen, 1986), pp. 148-172.

An earlier version of Simon Watney's, "Missionary Positions: AIDS, 'Africa' and Race," appeared in *differences*, vol 1, no. 1 (Winter 1989): 83-100, and a revised version in *Critical Quarterly*, vol. 31, no. 3 (Autumn 1989).

Rosalyn Deutsche's essay is a revised version of a much longer article that appeared in *October*, no. 47 (Winter 1988): 3-52. The original article included, among other things, a detailed history and analysis of Battery Park City in Lower Manhattan as a concrete example of the role that public art is currently playing in the redevelopment of New York.

John Yau, "Please Wait by the Coatroom: Wifredo Lam in the Museum of Modern Art," *Arts Magazine*, vol. 63, no. 4 (December 1988): 56-59.

James Clifford, "On Collecting Art and Culture," in *The Predicament of Culture: Twentieth Century Ethnography, Literature and Art* (Cambridge: Harvard University Press, 1988), pp. 215-251.

Gloria Anzaldúa, "How to Tame a Wild Tongue," in *Borderlands/La Frontera. The New Mestiza* (San Francisco: Spinsters/Aunt Lute, 1987), pp. 53-64.

James Snead, "Repetition as a Figure of Black Culture," in *Black Literature and Literary Theory*, ed. Henry Louis Gates, Jr. (London and New York: Methuen, 1984), pp. 59-79.

Kobena Mercer, "Black Hair/Style Politics," *New Formations*, no. 3: 33-54.

Richard Rodriguez, "Complexion," in *Hunger of Memory. The Education of Richard Rodriguez. An Autobiography.* (Boston: D.R. Godine, 1982), pp. 113-139.

Audre Lorde's essay was originally a paper delivered at the Copeland Coloquium, Amherst College, April 1980, and later published in *Sister Outsider: Essays and Speeches* (Trumansburg, NY: Crossing Press, 1984), pp. 114-123.

Richard Dyer, "Coming to Terms," *Jumpcut*, no. 30 (1985): 27-29.

Toni Morrison, "The Site of Memory," in *Inventing the Truth: The Art and Craft of Memoir*, ed. William K. Zinsser (Boston: Houghton Mifflin, 1987), pp. 101-124.

bell hooks, "Talking Back," in *Discourse*, no. 8 (Fall/Winter 1986-87): 123-128.

Hélène Cixous, "Castration or Decapitation?" *Signs*, vol. 7, no. 1 (Autumn 1981): 41-55. This article first appeared as "Le Sexe ou la Tête?" in *Les Cahiers du GRIF*, no. 13 (1976): 5-15. The text was transcribed from a conversation between Hélène Cixous and the editors of *Les Cahiers du GRIF* which took place in Brussels during 1975.

Edward Said, "Reflections on Exile," *Granta*, vol. 13 (1984): 159-172.

Gayatri Chakravorty Spivak, "Explanation and Culture: Marginalia," in *In Other Worlds: Essays in Cultural Politics* (New York: Methuen, 1987), pp. 103-117.

Teshome H. Gabriel, "Thoughts on Nomadic Aesthetics and Black Independent Cinema: Traces of a Journey," in *Blackframes: Critical Perspectives on Black Independent Cinema*, eds. Mbye B. Cham and Claire Andrade-Watkins (Cambridge: MIT Press, 1988), pp. 62-79.

Gerald Vizenor, "Socioacupuncture: Mythic Reversals and the Striptease in Four Scenes," in *The American Indian and the Problem of History*, ed. Calvin Martin (New York: Oxford University Press, 1987), pp. 180-191.

Select Bibliography

Abel, Elizabeth, ed. *Writing and Sexual Difference.* Chicago: University of Chicago Press, 1982.

Abu-Lughod, Lila. *Veiled Sentiments.* Berkeley: University of California Press, 1986.

Achebe, Chinua. *Hopes and Impediments: Selected Essays 1965-1987.* London: Heinemann, 1988.

Adams, Parveen, and Beverly Brown. "The Feminist Body and Feminist Politics." *m/f,* no. 3 (1979).

Adele, Lynne. *Black History/Black Vision.* Austin: Huntington Art Gallery, 1989.

Adorno, Theodor. *Aesthetic Theory.* London and New York: Routledge and Kegan Paul, 1970.

Adorno, Theodor. *Minima Moralia: Reflections from a Damaged Life.* London: Verso, 1974.

Ahmad, Jalal Ali. *Occidentosis: A Plague from the West.* Berkeley: Mizan Press, 1984.

A.I.R. Gallery, New York. *Dialectics of Isolation: An Exhibition of Third World Women Artists of the United States.* Statements by the artists. Exhibition September 2-20, 1980.

Akomfrah, John, and Pervais Khan, eds. *Third Scenario: Theory and the Politics of Location.* Special issue, *Framework,* no. 36 (1989).

Aldefer, Hannah, et al. *Sex Issue.* Special issue, *Heresies* 12, vol. 3, no. 4 (1981).

Ames, Michael. *Museums, the Public and Anthropology.* Vancouver: University of British Columbia Press, 1986.

Amin, Samir. *Eurocentrism.* New York: Monthly Review Press, 1989.

Andrews, Benny. "Is There a Black Aesthetic?" *Art Papers,* vol. 11, no. 1 (January/February 1987): 22-23.

Anzaldúa, Gloria. *Borderlands/La Frontera: The New Mestiza.* San Francisco: Spinsters/Aunt Lute, 1987.

Appignanesi, Lisa, ed. *The Real Me: Postmodernism and the Question of Identity.* ICA Document 6. London: Institute of Contemporary Arts, 1987.

Araeen, Rasheed, ed. *Magiciens de la Terre.* Special issue, *Third Text,* no. 6 (Spring 1989).

Armes, Roy. *Third World Filmmaking and the West.* Berkeley: University of California Press, 1987.

"Art and Crisis: AIDS and the Gay Politic." *High Performance* 36, vol. 9, no. 4 (1986): 22-61.

Artists Space, New York. *Witnesses: Against Our Vanishing.* Statements by Nan Goldin, David Wojnarowicz, Linda Yablonsky, and Cookie Mueller. Exhibition November 16, 1989-January 6, 1990.

Asian Women United of California, eds. *Making Waves.* Boston: Beacon Press, 1989.

Baddeley, Oriana, and Valerie Fraser. *Drawing the Line: Art and Cultural Identity in Contemporary Latin America.* New York: Verso, 1989.

Baker, D.G. *Race, Ethnicity and Power: A Comparative Study.* London: Routledge and Kegan Paul, 1983.

Baker, Houston A., Jr. *Blues Ideology and Afro-American Literature: A Vernacular Theory.* Chicago: University of Chicago Press, 1980.

Baker, Houston A., Jr. *The Journey Back: Issues in Black Literature and Criticism.* Chicago: University of Chicago Press, 1980.

Baker, Houston A., Jr. *Modernism and the Harlem Renaissance.* Chicago: University of Chicago Press, 1984.

Bakhtin, Mikhail. *The Dialogic Imagination.* Austin: University of Texas Press, 1981.

Baraka, Amiri. *Daggers and Javelins: Essays 1974-1979.* New York: Morrow, 1984.

Barker, Francis, et al. *Europe and Its Others.* Colchester: University of Essex Press, 1985.

Barker, Francis, et al., eds. *Literature, Politics and Theory: Papers from the Essex Conference 1976-1984.* New York: Methuen, 1986.

Barrett, Michele. *Women's Oppression To-day.* London: Verso, 1980.

Barthes, Roland. *Camera Lucida.* New York: Hill and Wang, 1981.

Barthes, Roland. *Mythologies.* New York: Hill and Wang, 1972.

Barthes, Roland. *The Pleasure of the Text.* New York: Hill and Wang, 1975.

Bataille, Gretchen M., and Kathleen Mullen Sands. *American Indian Women: Telling Their Lives.* Lincoln: University of Nebraska Press, 1984.

de Beauvoir, Simone. *The Second Sex.* New York: Knopf, 1953.

Bell, Roseann P., Bettye J. Parker, and Beverly Guy-Sheftall. *Sturdy Black Bridges: Visions of Black Women in Literature.* Garden City, NY: Anchor Books, 1979.

Benjamin, Walter. *Illuminations.* Edited by Hannah Arendt. New York: Schocken Books, 1969.

Benjamin, Walter. *Reflections.* New York: Schocken, 1986.

Bennet, Tony, Graham Martin, Colin Mercer, and Janet Woolacott, eds. *Culture, Ideology, and Social Process.* London: Open University Press, 1981.

Berger, John, and Jean Mohr. *Another Way of Telling.* New York: Pantheon, 1982.

Bhabha, Homi K. "Of Mimicry and Man: The Ambivalence of Colonial Discourse." *October*, no. 28 (Spring 1984): 125-133.

Bhabha, Homi K. "Representation and the Colonial Text." In *Theory of Reading.* Edited by Frank Gloversmith. Sussex: Harvester Press, 1984.

Bhabha, Homi K. "Sly Civility." *October*, no. 34 (Fall 1985): 71-80.

Blocton, Lula Mae, et al., eds. *Third World Women: The Politics of Being Other.* Special issue, *Heresies*, vol. 2, no. 4, issue 8 (1979).

Boesen, Victor, and Florence Curtis Graybill. *Edward S. Curtis: Photographer of the North American Indian.* New York: Dodd, Mead and Co., 1977.

Boffin, Tessa, and Sunil Gupta, eds. *Ecstatic Antibodies: Resisting the AIDS Mythology.* London: Rivers Oram Press, 1990.

Bogue, Ronald. *Deleuze and Guattari.* New York: Routledge, 1989.

Bontemps, Arna, ed. *Forever Free: Art by African-American Women 1862-1980.* Alexandria: Stephenson, 1980.

Bovenschen, Silvia. "Is There a Feminine Aesthetic?" *New German Critique*, no. 10 (Winter 1977): 111-137.

Bowser, Pearl, and Renee Tajima. *Journey Across Three Continents.* New York: Third World Newsreel, 1985.

Braxton, Joanne M., and Andrée Nicola McLaughlin, eds. *Wild Women in the Whirlwind.* New Brunswick, NJ: Rutgers, 1990.

Brett, Guy. *Through Our Own Eyes.* Philadelphia: New Society, 1987.

Brink, Andre. *Writing in a State of Siege.* New York: Summit, 1983.

Brodzki, Bella, and Celeste Schenck. *Life/Lines: Theorizing Women's Autobiography.* Ithaca and London: Cornell University Press, 1988.

Broe, Mary Lynn, and Angela Ingram, eds. *Women's Writing in Exile.* Chapel Hill: University of North Carolina Press, 1989.

Bronski, Michael. *Culture Clash: The Making of Gay Sensibility.* Boston: South End Press, 1984.

Bronx Museum of the Arts, New York. *The Latin American Spirit: Art and Artists in the United States 1920-1970.* Essays by Luis R. Cancel, et al. Exhibition September 29, 1988-January 29, 1989.

"Brother to Brother: Black Gay Men and Film." *Black Film Review*, vol. 5, no. 3 (Summer 1989): 14-23.

Broude, Norma, and Mary D. Garrard, eds. *Feminism and Art History: Questioning the Litany.* New York: Harper and Row, 1982.

Browne, Vivian E., et al. *Racism is the Issue.* Special issue, *Heresies* 15, vol. 4, no. 3 (1982).

Brundson, Charlotte, ed. *Films for Women.* London: British Film Institute, 1986.

Brunt, Rosalind, and Caroline Rowan, eds. *Feminism, Culture, and Politics.* London: Lawrence and Wishart, 1982.

Buchbinder, Howard, et al. *Who's on Top? The Politics of Heterosexuality.* Toronto: Garamond, 1987.

Buchloh, Benjamin H.D. "The Whole Earth Show: An Interview with Jean-Hubert Martin." *Art in America* (May 1989): 150-158, 211-213.

Bulkin, Elly, and Joan Larkin. *Lesbian Poetry: An Anthology.* Watertown, MA: Persephone Press 1981.

Bulkin, Elly, Minne Bruce Pratt, and Barbara Smith. *Yours in Struggle.* Brooklyn: Long Haul Press, 1984.

Bürger, Peter. *Theory of the Avant Garde.* Minneapolis: University of Minnesota Press, 1984.

Butler, Judith. *Gender Trouble: Feminism and the Subversion of Identity.* New York and London: Routledge, 1990.

Cadwalader, Sandra L., and Vine Deloria, Jr. *The Aggression of Civilization: Federal Indian Policy Since the 1880's*. Philadelphia: Temple University Press, 1984.

Camnitzer, Luis. "Access to the Mainstream." *New Art Examiner*, vol. 14, no. 10 (June 1987): 20-23.

Cancel, Luis, Barry Gaither, John Kinard, and Margo Machida. "Voicing Varied Opinions." *Museum News* (March/April 1989): 49-52.

Cant, Bob, and Susan Jennings, eds. *Radical Records: Thirty Years of Lesbian and Gay History*. London and New York: Routledge, 1988.

Carby, Hazel. *Reconstructing Womanhood: The Emergence of the Afro-American Woman Novelist*. New York: Oxford University Press, 1987.

Carr, Cynthia, et al. *Lesbians and Art*. Special issue, *Heresies* 3, vol. 1, no. 3 (1977).

Carter, Erica, and Simon Watney, eds. *Taking Liberties: AIDS and Cultural Politics*. London: Serpent's Tail Press, 1989.

Castells, Manuel. *The City and the Grassroots: A Cross-Cultural Theory of Urban Social Movements*. Berkeley and Los Angeles: University of California Press, 1983.

Cederholm, Theresa. *Afro-American Artists: A Bibliographical Directory*. Boston: The Boston Public Library, 1973.

Centre Georges Pompidou, Paris, France. *Magiciens de la Terre*. Essays by Jean-Hubert Martin, et al. Exhibition May 18-August 14, 1989.

Cham, Mbye B., and Claire Andrade-Watkins, eds. *Black Frames: Critical Perspectives on Black Independent Cinema*. Cambridge: MIT Press, 1988.

Chatterjee, Lola, ed. *Women/Image/Text*. Delhi: Trianka, 1986.

Chauncey, George, Jr., Martin Bauml Duberman, and Martha Vicinus. *Reclaiming the Past: The New Social History of Homosexuality*. New York: New American Library, 1989.

Chernoff, John Miller. *African Rhythm and African Sensibility*. Chicago: University of Chicago Press, 1979.

Chin, Daryl. "Some Remarks on Racism in the American Arts." *M/E/A/N/I/N/G*, no. 3 (May 1988): 18-25.

Chirimuuta, Richard C., and Rosalind J. Chirimuuta. *AIDS, Africa, and Racism*. Burton-on-Trent: R. Chirimuuta, 1987.

Chodorow, Nancy. *The Reproduction of Mothering: Psychoanalysis and the Sociology of Gender*. Berkeley: University of California Press, 1978.

Chodorow, Nancy. *Woman, Culture and Society*. Stanford: Stanford University Press, 1974.

Christian, Barbara. "The Race for Theory." *Cultural Critique*, no. 6 (Spring 1987). 51-63.

Cixous, Hélène. *Angst*. New York: Riverrun Press, 1985.

Cixous, Hélène. *Inside*. New York: Schocken, 1986.

Cixous, Hélène. *LA*. Paris: Gallimard, 1976.

Cixous, Hélène. *Writing Differences: Readings from the Seminar of Hélène Cixous*. Milton Keyes: Open University Press, 1988.

Cixous, Hélène, and Catherine Clément. *The Newly Born Woman*. Minneapolis: University of Minnesota Press, 1986.

Clarke, Cheryl. *Living as a Lesbian*. Ithaca: Firebrand Books, 1986.

Clarke, Cheryl, Jewelle Gomez, Evelynn Hammonds, Bonnie Johnson, and Linda Powell. "Conversations and Questions: Black Women on Black Women Writers." *Conditions* 9 (1983): 88-137.

Clastres, Pierre. *Society Against the State*. New York: Zone Books, 1989.

Clifford, James, Boris Groys, Craig Owens, Martha Rosler, Robert Storr, and Michele Wallace. "The Global Issue: A Symposium." *Art in America* (July 1989): 86-89, 151-153.

Clifford, James. *The Predicament of Culture*. Cambridge: Harvard University Press, 1988.

Clifford, James, and George Marcus, eds. *Writing Culture*. Berkeley: University of California Press, 1986.

Cooper, Emmanuel. *The Sexual Perspective: Homosexuality and Art in the Last 100 Years in the West*. London and New York: Routledge and Kegan Paul, 1986.

Cornerhouse, Manchester, England. *The Image Employed: The Use of Narrative in Black Art*. Essays by Keith Piper and Marlene Smith. Exhibition June 13-July 19, 1987.

Coward, Rosalind. *Female Desires*. New York: Grove Press, 1985.

Crapanzano, Vincent. *Waiting*. New York: Vintage, 1985.

Crimp, Douglas, ed. *AIDS: Cultural Analysis/Cultural Activism*. Cambridge and London: MIT Press, 1989.

Crimp, Douglas, and Adam Rolston. *AIDS Demo Graphics*. Seattle: Bay Press, 1990.

Curtin, Philip D. *Cross Cultural Trade in World History*. New York: Cambridge University Press, 1984.

Danzig, Alexis. "Acting-Up. Independent Video and the AIDS Crisis." *Afterimage*, vol. 16, no. 10 (May 1989): 5-7.

Darwish, Mahmud. *Victims of a Map*. London: Al Sagi Books, 1984.

Davies, Miranda. *Third World-Second Sex*. London: Zed Press, 1987.

Deitcher, David. "Ideas and Emotions." *Artforum* (May 1989): 122-127.

De Lauretis, Teresa. *Alice Doesn't*. Bloomington: Indiana University Press, 1984.

De Lauretis, Teresa. *Technologies of Gender*. Bloomington: Indiana University Press, 1987.

De Lauretis, Teresa, ed. *Feminist Studies Critical Studies*. Bloomington: Indiana University Press, 1986.

Deleuze, Gilles. *Cinema 1: Movement-Image*. Minneapolis: University of Minnesota Press, 1986.

Deleuze, Gilles, and Félix Guattari. *Anti-Oedipus. Capitalism and Schizophrenia*. Minneapolis: University of Minnesota Press, 1983.

Deleuze, Gilles, and Félix Guattari. *Kafka: Toward a Minor Literature*. Minneapolis: University of Minnesota Press, 1987.

Deleuze, Gilles, and Félix Guattari. *A Thousand Plateaus. Capitalism and Schizophrenia*. Minneapolis: University of Minnesota Press, 1987.

Deleuze, Gilles, and Claire Parnet. *Dialogues*. New York: Columbia University Press, 1987.

Deloria, Vine, Jr., ed. *American Indian Policy in the Twentieth Century*. Norman: University of Oklahoma Press, 1985.

D'Emilio, John. *Sexual Politics, Sexual Communities: The Making of a Homosexual Minority in the United States, 1940-1970*. Chicago: University of Chicago Press, 1983.

D'Emilio, John, and Estelle B. Freedman. *Intimate Matters*. New York: Harper and Row, 1988.

Dennett, Terry, et al. *Photography/Politics: One*. London: Photography Workshop, 1979.

Derrida, Jacques. *Of Grammatology*. Baltimore: Johns Hopkins Press, 1976.

Derrida, Jacques. "Racism's Last Word." *Critical Inquiry* 12, no. 1 (1985): 291-299.

Derrida, Jacques. *Writing and Difference*. Chicago: University of Chicago Press, 1978.

Derrida, Jacques, and Tlili Mustapha, eds. *For Nelson Mandela*. New York: Seaver, 1987.

Deutsche, Rosalyn. "Krzysztof Wodiczko's *Homeless Projection* and the Site of Urban 'Revitalization.'" *October*, no. 38 (Fall 1986): 63-98.

Deutsche, Rosalyn. "Men in Space." *Artforum*, vol. 28, no. 6 (February 1990): 21-23.

Deutsche, Rosalyn. "Property Values: Hans Haacke, Real Estate and the Museum." In *Hans Haacke: Unfinished Business*. Edited by Brian Wallis. New York: The New Museum of Contemporary Art and Cambridge: MIT Press, 1986.

Deutsche, Rosalyn. "Representing Berlin: Urban Ideology and Aesthetic Practice." In *The Divided Heritage: Themes and Problems in German Modernism*. Edited by Irit Rogoff and Mary Anne Stevens. Cambridge, England: Cambridge University Press (forthcoming).

Doane, Mary Ann, Patricia Mellencamp, and Linda Williams. *Re-vision: Essays in Feminist Film Criticism*. Los Angeles and Maryland: The American Film Institute and University Publications of America, 1984.

Drinnon, Richard. *Facing West*. Minneapolis: University of Minnesota Press, 1980.

Driskell, David. *Two Centuries of Black American Art*. Los Angeles: The Los Angeles County Museum, 1976.

DuBois, W. E. B. *The Souls of Black Folk. Essays and Sketches*. New York: Fawcett Press, 1961.

Duncan, Carol, and Alan Wallach. "The Museum of Modern Art as Late Capitalist Ritual." *Marxist Perspectives*, no. 4 (Winter 1978): 28-51.

Durham, Jimmie. *Columbus Day*. Minneapolis: West End Press, 1983.

Durham, Jimmie, and Jean Fisher. "The Ground Has Been Covered." *Artforum* (Summer 1988): 99-105.

Dyer, Richard. *Heavenly Bodies: Film Stars and Society*. London: British Film Institute, 1986.

Dyer, Richard, ed. *Gays and Film*. New York: New York Zoetrope, 1984.

Eagleton, Mary, ed. *Feminist Literary Theory*. New York: Basil Blackwell, 1986.

Eagleton, Terry. *Literary Theory: An Introduction*. Minneapolis: University of Minnesota Press, 1983.

East/West: Contemporary American Art. Los Angeles: California Afro-American Museum, 1985.

Eisenstein, Hester, and Alice Jardine, eds. *The Future of Difference*. Boston: G.K. Hall, 1980.

Eisenstein, Zillah R., ed. *Capitalist Patriarchy and the Case for Socialist Feminism*. New York: Monthly Review Press, 1979.

Ellison, Ralph. *The Invisible Man*. New York: Random House, 1952.

The Empire Strikes Back. London: Hutchinson in association with The University of Birmingham, 1982.

Epstein, Steven. "Gay Politics, Ethnic Identity: The Limits of Social Construction." *Socialist Review*, vol. 17, nos. 3/4 (May-August 1987): 9-54.

Fabian, Johannes. *Time and the Other: How Anthropology Makes Its Object*. New York: Columbia University Press, 1983.

F.A.C.T. Book Committee. *Caught Looking: Feminism, Pornography and Censorship*. New York: Caught Looking, 1986.

Fanon, Frantz. *Black Skin White Masks*. New York: Grove Press, 1967.

Fanon, Frantz. *A Dying Colonialism*. New York: Grove Press, 1965.

Fanon, Frantz. *The Wretched of the Earth*. New York: Grove Press, 1968.

Feminist Press, eds. *Sexuality: A Reader*. London: Virago Press, 1987.

Ferguson, Russell, William Olander, Marcia Tucker, and Karen Fiss, eds. *Discourses: Conversations in Postmodern Art and Culture*. New York: The New Museum of Contemporary Art and Cambridge: MIT Press, 1990.

Findlay, James A. *Modern Latin American Art: A Bibliography*. Westport, CT: Greenwood Press, 1983.

Fine, Michelle, and Adrienne Asch, eds. *Women with Disabilities*. Philadelphia: Temple University Press, 1988.

Formations of Nation and People. London and Boston: Routledge and Kegan Paul, 1984.

Formations of Pleasure. London and Boston: Routledge and Kegan Paul, 1983.

Foster, Hal. *Recodings*. Port Townsend, WA: Bay Press, 1985.

Foster, Hal, ed. *The Anti-Aesthetic*. Port Townsend, WA: Bay Press, 1983.

Foster, Hal, ed. *Discussions in Contemporary Culture*. Seattle: Bay Press, 1985.

Foucault, Michel. *The Archaeology of Knowledge and the Discourse of Language*. New York: Harper Colophon, 1972.

Foucault, Michel. *The Final Foucault*. Edited by J. Bernauer, and D. Rasmussen. Cambridge: MIT Press, 1988.

Foucault, Michel. *The History of Sexuality. Vol. 1: An Introduction*. New York: Pantheon Books, 1978.

Foucault, Michel. *The Order of Things: An Archaeology of the Human Sciences*. New York: Pantheon, 1970.

Fowler, Carolyn. *Black Arts and Black Aesthetics: A Bibliography*. Atlanta: Atlanta University, 1976.

Freedman, Estelle B., et al. *The Lesbian Issue: Essays from Signs*. Chicago: University of Chicago Press, 1985.

Freire, Paulo. *Pedagogy of the Oppressed*. New York: Continuum, 1982.

Fusco, Coco. "Fantasies of Oppositionality." *Afterimage*, vol. 16, no. 5 (December 1988): 6-9.

Fusco, Coco. *Young, British and Black: The Work of Sankofa and Black Audio Film Collective*. Buffalo: Hallwalls, 1988.

Fusco, Coco, ed. *Reviewing Histories: Selections from New Latin American Cinema*. Buffalo: Hallwalls, 1987.

Fuss, Diana. *Essentially Speaking: Feminism, Nature and Difference*. London and New York: Routledge, 1989.

Gabriel, Teshome H. *Third Cinema in the Third World: The Aesthetics of Liberation*. Ann Arbor: UMI Research Press, 1982.

Gallop, Jane. *The Daughter's Seduction: Feminism and Psychoanalysis*. Ithaca: Cornell University Press, 1982.

Gammon, Lorraine, and Margaret Marshment, eds. *The Female Gaze*. London: The Women's Press, 1988.

Gates, Henry Louis, Jr. "Authority, (White) Power and the (Black) Critic: It's All Greek to Me." *Cultural Critique*, no. 7 (Fall 1987).

Gates, Henry Louis, Jr. *Figures in Black*. New York: Oxford University Press, 1987.

Gates, Henry Louis, Jr. *The Signifying Monkey*. New York: Oxford University Press, 1989.

Gates, Henry Louis, Jr., ed. *Black Literature and Literary Theory*. London and New York: Methuen, 1984.

Gates, Henry Louis, Jr., ed. *"Race," Writing and Difference*. Chicago: University of Chicago Press, 1986.

Gayle, Addison, Jr., ed. *The Black Aesthetic*. Garden City, NY: Doubleday, 1972.

Gever, Martha. "The Feminism Factor: Women Artists and Video in the Eighties." In *Reading Video*. Edited by Jo Fifer and Doug Hall. New York: Aperture, (forthcoming).

Gever, Martha. "Girl Crazy: Lesbian Narratives in *She Must Be Seeing Things* and *Damned If You Don't*." *The Independent*, vol. 11, no. 6 (1988): 14-18.

Gever, Martha. "Pressure Points: Video in the Public Sphere." *Art Journal*, vol. 45, no. 3 (Fall 1985): 238-243.

Gever, Martha. "Seduction Hot and Cold." *Screen*, vol. 28, no. 4 (Autumn 1987): 58-65.

Gever, Martha. "Where We Are Now." *Art in America* (July 1987): 43.

Gever, Martha. "Visibility/Invisibility: Contradictions in Lesbian Representations." *White Walls*, no. 23 (Fall 1989): 52-56.

Gever, Martha, and Nathalie Magnan. "The Same Difference: On Lesbian Representation." *Exposure*, vol. 24, no. 2 (1986): 27-35.

Georgakas, Dan, and Miriam Rosen, eds. "The Arab Image in American Film and Television." Supplement to *Cineaste*, vol. 17, no. 1 (1989): 2-24.

Gilman, Sander. *Difference and Pathology*. Ithaca: Cornell University Press, 1985.

Gilman, Sander. *Diseases and Representation: Images of Illness from Madness to AIDS*. Ithaca: Cornell University Press, 1988.

Gilroy, Paul. *There Ain't No Black in the Union Jack*. London: Century Hutchinson, 1987.

Gomez, Alma, Cherrie Moraga, and Mariana Romo-Carmona, eds. *Cuentos, Stories by Latinas*. New York: Kitchen Table/Women of Color Press, 1983.

Gomez-Peña, Guillermo. "The Multicultural Paradigm: An Open Letter to the National Arts Community." *High Performance*, no. 47 (Fall 1989): 18-27.

Gordimer, Nadine, and David Goldblatt. *Lifetimes: Under Apartheid*. London: J. Cape, 1986.

Gottdiener, M., and Alexandros Ph. Lagopoulos, eds. *The City and the Sign: An Introduction to Urban Semiotics*. New York: Columbia University Press, 1986.

Goulma-Peterson, Thalia, and Patricia Matthews. "The Feminist Critique of Art History." *Art Bulletin* LXIX (September 1987): 326-357.

Graham, Joseph R., ed. *Difference in Transition*. Ithaca and London: Cornell University Press, 1985.

Gramsci, Antonio. *Letters from Prison*. New York: Harper and Row, 1973.

Gramsci, Antonio. *Selections from Political Writings 1910-1920*. New York: International Publishers, 1977.

Grossberg, Lawrence, and Cary Nelson, eds. *Marxism and the Interpretation of Culture*. Urbana: University of Illinois Press, 1988.

Group Material. *Democracy: A Project by Group Material*. New York: Dia Foundation and Seattle: Bay Press, 1990.

Grover, Jan Zita. *AIDS: The Artists' Response*. Columbus: Ohio State University, 1989.

Grover, Jan Zita. "Dykes in Context: Some Problems in Minority Representation." In *The Contest of Meaning: Critical Histories of Photography*. Edited by Richard Bolton. Cambridge: MIT Press, 1989.

Guha, Ranajit, and Gayatri Chakravorty Spivak, eds. *Selected Subaltern Studies*. New York: Oxford University Press, 1988.

Hall, Stuart. "Gramsci's Relevance for the Study of Race and Ethnicity." *Journal of Communication Inquiry*, vol. 10, no. 2 (1986): 5-27.

Hall, Stuart. *Race and Class in Post-Colonial Society*. New York: UNESCO, 1977.

Hall, Stuart, et al. *Policing the Crisis*. London: MacMillan, 1978.

Haraway, Donna. *Primate Visions: Gender, Race, and Nature in the World of Modern Science*. New York: Routledge, 1989.

Harlow, Barbara. *Resistance Literature*. New York and London: Methuen, 1987.

Harper, Glenn, ed. *Special Issue on Contemporary Black Artists*. Special issue, *Art Papers*, vol. 12, no. 4 (July/August 1988).

Harris, Nigel. *The End of the Third World*. London: I.B. Tauris, 1986.

Hartstock, Nancy. *Money, Sex and Power: Toward a Feminist Historical Materialism*. Boston: Northeastern University Press, 1981.

Heap of Birds, Edgar. *Sharp Rocks*. Buffalo: CEPA, 1986.

Heath, Stephen. "Difference." *Screen* 19, no. 3 (Autumn 1978): 51-112.

Heath, Stephen. *The Sexual Fix*. London: Macmillan, 1982.

Hebdige, Dick. *Cut 'N Mix*. London: Macmillan, 1987.

Hebdige, Dick. *Hiding in the Light*. New York: Routledge, 1988.

Hebdige, Dick. *Subculture: The Meaning of Style*. London: Methuen, 1979.

Heilbrun, Carolyn. *Writing a Woman's Life*. New York: Norton, 1988.

Hess, Thomas B., and Elizabeth C. Baker, eds. *After Sexual Politics: Why Have There Been No Great Women Artists?* New York: Macmillan, 1971.

Hirson, Denis. *The House Next Door to Africa*. New York: Carcanet, 1987.

Hoch, Paul. *White Hero, Black Beast: Racism, Sexism and the Mask of Masculinity*. London: Pluto Press, 1979.

Hocquenghem, Guy. *Homosexual Desire*. London: Allison and Busby, 1978.

Holland, Patricia, Jo Spence, and Simon Watney, eds. *Photography/Politics: Two*. London: Comedia Publishing Group, 1986.

Honour, Hugh. *The Image of the Black in Western Art*. 4 Vols. Cambridge: Harvard University Press, 1989.

hooks, bell. *Ain't I A Woman? Black Women and Feminism*. Boston: South End Press, 1981.

hooks, bell. *Feminist Theory: From Margin to Center*. Boston: South End Press, 1984.

hooks, bell. *Talking Back: Thinking Feminist Thinking Black*. Boston: South End Press, 1989.

Howe, Florence, and Marsha Saxton, eds. *With Wings: An Anthology of Literature by and About Women with Disabilities*. New York: The Feminist Press, 1987.

Hull, Gloria T., Patricia Bell Scott, and Barbara Smith, eds. *All the Women are White, All the Blacks are Men, But Some of Us Are Brave: Black Women's Studies*. Old Westbury, NY: Feminist Press, 1981.

Hunter College of the City University of New York, New York. *Race and Representation*. Essays by Maurice Berger, et al. Exhibition January 26-March 6, 1987.

Hurston, Zora Neale. *Dust Tracks on a Road: An Autobiography*. Urbana: University of Illinois Press, 1984.

Hurston, Zora Neale. *I Love Myself When I am Laughing . . . and Then Again When I am Looking Mean and Impressive: A Zora Neale Hurston Reader*. Edited by Alice Walker. Old Westbury, NY: Feminist Press, 1979.

Huyssens, Andreas. *After the Great Divide*. London: Macmillan, 1987.

Intar Latin American Gallery, New York. *Another Face of the Diamond: Pathways Through the Black Atlantic South*. Essays by Robert Farris Thompson, John Mason, and Judith McWillie. Exhibition January 23-March 3, 1989.

Intar Latin American Gallery, New York. *Autobiography: In Her Own Image*. Essays by Judith Wilson, and Moira Roth. Exhibition April 25-May 27, 1988.

Jahn, Janheinz. *A History of Neo-African Literature. Writing in Two Continents*. London. Faber, 1968.

Jameson, Fredric. "Third-World Literature in the Era of Multinational Capitalism." *Social Text* 15, vol. 5, no. 3 (Fall 1986): 65-88.

Jardine, Alice. *Gynesis*. Ithaca: Cornell University Press, 1985.

Jardine, Alice, and Paul Smith, eds. *Men in Feminism*. New York and London: Methuen, 1987.

Jefferson, Tony, and Stuart Hall, eds. *Resistance Through Rituals*. London: Hutchinson, 1975.

Johnson, Barbara. *A World of Difference*. Baltimore: Johns Hopkins University Press, 1987.

Jordan, June. *On Call: Political Essays*. Boston: South End Press, 1985.

Joseph, Gloria I., and Jill Lewis. *Common Differences*. Boston: South End Press, 1981.

Julien, Isaac, and Kobena Mercer, eds. *The Last 'Special Issue' on Race?* Special issue, *Screen*, vol. 29, no. 4 (Autumn 1988).

Kahn, Douglas, and Diane Neumaier, eds. *Cultures in Contention*. Seattle: The Real Comet Press, 1985.

Katz, Jonathan. *Gay American History: Lesbians and Gay Men in the U.S.A.* New York: Harper and Row, 1976.

Kimmel, Michael. *Gender and Desire*. New York: Basic, 1989.

Kimmel, Michael, and Michael Messner. *Men's Lives*. New York: Macmillan, 1989.

Knabb, Ken, ed. *Situationist International Anthology*. Berkeley: Bureau of Public Secrets, 1981.

Koch, Gertrud. "The Body's Shadow Realm." *October*, no. 50 (Fall 1989): 3-29.

Kolbowski, Silvia, ed. *Sexuality: Re/Positions*. Special issue, *Wedge*, no. 6 (Winter 1984).

Kroeber, Theodora. *Ishi in Two Worlds*. Berkeley and Los Angeles: University of California Press, 1977.

Kruger, Barbara, and Phil Mariani, eds. *Remaking History*. Seattle: Bay Press, 1989.

Kuhn, Annette. *The Power of the Image: Essays on Representation and Sexuality*. London: Routledge and Kegan Paul, 1985.

Kuhn, Annette. *Women's Pictures: Feminism and Cinema*. London: Routledge and Kegan Paul, 1982.

Kuhn, Annette, and AnnMarie Wolpe, eds. *Feminism and Materialism*. London: Routledge and Kegan Paul, 1978.

Lacan, Jacques. *Ecrits: A Selection*. New York: Tavistock, 1977.

Lacan, Jacques. *Feminine Sexuality*. Edited by Juliet Mitchell and Jacqueline Rose. New York: Norton, 1982.

Lee, Spike, and Lisa Jones. *Do the Right Thing*. New York: Simon and Schuster, 1989.

Lefebvre, Henri. *Everyday Life in the Modern World*. New Brunswick, NJ: Transaction Books, 1984.

Leiris, Michel. *Wifredo Lam*. New York: Abrams, 1970.

Lévi-Strauss, Claude. *The Savage Mind*. Chicago: University of Chicago Press, 1966.

Lévi-Strauss, Claude. *Tristes Tropiques*. New York: Atheneum, 1973.

Lévi-Strauss, Claude. *The View from Afar*. New York: Basic Books, 1984.

Lim, Shirley Geok-Lin, and Mayumi Tsutakawa, eds. *The Forbidden Stitch: An Asian American Women's Anthology*. Corvallis, OR: Calyx Books, 1989.

Lionnet, Francoise. *Autobiographical Voices: Race, Gender, Self-Portraiture*. Ithaca: Cornell University Press, 1989.

Lippard, Lucy. *From the Center: Feminist Essays on Women's Art*. New York: Dutton, 1976.

Lippard, Lucy. *Get the Message? A Decade of Art for Social Change*. New York: Dutton, 1984.

Lorde, Audre. *A Burst of Light*: Essays. Ithaca: Firebrand Books, 1988.

Lorde, Audre. *Chosen Poems: Old and New*. New York: Norton, 1982.

Lorde, Audre. *Movement in Black*. Oakland: Diana Press, 1978.

Lorde, Audre. *Sister Outsider: Essays and Speeches*. Trumansburg, NY: Crossing Press, 1984.

Lorde, Audre. *Zami: A New Spelling of My Name*. Trumansburg, NY: The Crossing Press, 1982.

Los Angeles Contemporary Exhibitions, Los Angeles. *Against Nature: A Group Show of Work by Homosexual Men*. Statements by the artists. Exhibition January 6-February 12, 1988.

Lyman, Christopher M. *The Vanishing Race: Photographs of Indians by Edward S. Curtis*. New York: Pantheon Books in association with The Smithsonian Institute, 1982.

Lyotard, Jean-Francois. *The Postmodern Condition: A Report on Knowledge*. Minneapolis: University of Minnesota Press, 1984.

MacDonald, Scott. *A Critical Cinema: Interviews with Independent Filmmakers*. Berkeley and Los Angeles: University of California Press, 1988.

Marks, Elaine, and Isabelle de Courtivron, eds. *New French Feminisms: An Anthology*. New York: Schocken Books, 1981.

Martin, Calvin, ed. *The American Indian and the Problem of History*. New York: Oxford University Press, 1987.

McGann, Nadine. "Picturing Apartheid." *Afterimage*, vol. 15, no. 4 (November 1987): 16-19.

Mercer, Kobena, ed. *Black Film/British Cinema*. ICA Document 7. London: Institute of Contemporary Arts, 1988.

Merck, Mandy. "The Train of Thought in Freud's Case of Homosexuality in a Woman." *m/f*, nos. 11/12 (1986).

Miller, Christopher. *Blank Darkness: Africanist Discourse in French*. London and Chicago: University of Chicago Press, 1985.

Miller, Nancy K., ed. *The Poetics of Gender*. New York: Columbia University Press, 1986.

Millet, Kate. *Sexual Politics*. New York: Ballantine, 1970.

Modleski, Tania. *Loving With a Vengeance: Mass-Produced Fantasies for Women*. New York: Methuen, 1982.

Mohanty, Chandra Talpade. "Under Western Eyes: Feminist Scholarship and Colonial Discourse." *Boundary* 2, vol. XII, no. 1 (Spring/Fall 1984): 333-358.

Moi, Toril. *Sexual Textual Politics*. London and New York: Methuen, 1985.

Moi, Toril, ed. *French Feminist Thought: A Reader*. Oxford and New York: Methuen, 1985.

Mora, Carl J. *Mexican Cinema: Reflections of a Society 1896-1988*. Berkeley: University of California Press, 1988.

Moraga, Cherrie. *Loving in the War Years, Lo Que Nunca Pasó por Sus Labios*. Boston: South End Press, 1983.

Moraga, Cherrie, and Gloria Anzaldúa, eds. *This Bridge Called My Back: Writings by Radical Women of Color*. Watertown, MA: Persephone, 1981.

Morrison, Toni. *Beloved*. New York: Random House, 1987.

Morrison, Toni. *The Bluest Eye*. New York: Pocket Books, 1970.

Morrison, Toni. *Song of Solomon*. New York: Knopf, 1978.

Morrison, Toni. *Sula*. New York: New American Library, 1973.

Morrison, Toni. *Tar Baby*. New York: New American Library, 1981.

Mosquera, Gerardo. "Bad Taste in Good Form." *Social Text* 15 (Fall 1986): 54-64.

Mosse, George. *Toward the Final Solution: A History of European Racism*. London: Dent, 1978.

Mulvey, Laura. *Visual and Other Pleasures*. Bloomington: Indiana University Press, 1989.

The Museum of Contemporary Hispanic Art, The New Museum of Contemporary Art, and The Studio Museum in Harlem, New York. *The Decade Show: Frameworks of Identity in the 1980s*. Exhibition May-August 1990.

The New Museum of Contemporary Art, New York. *Difference: On Representation and Sexuality*. Edited by Kate Linker. Exhibition December 8, 1984-February 10, 1985.

The New Museum of Contemporary Art, New York. *Extended Sensibilities*. Essay by Daniel J. Cameron. Exhibition October 16-December 30, 1982.

Newton, Judith, and Deborah Rosenfelt, eds. *Feminist Criticism and Social Change*. New York and London: Methuen, 1985.

Ngugi wa Th'iongo. *Decolonizing the Mind*. London: James Curry, 1986.

Ngugi wa Th'iongo. *Writers in Politics*. London: Heinemann, 1981.

The 1989 Guide to Multicultural Resources. Madison, WI: Praxis Publications, 1989.

Nochlin, Linda. *Women, Art, and Power and Other Essays*. New York: Harper and Row, 1988.

Owusu, Kwesi. *Storms of the Heart*. London: Camden Press, 1988.

Panos Dossier. *AIDS and the Third World*. London, Paris, and Washington: Panos Institute, 1989.

Parker, Roszika, and Griselda Pollock. *Old Mistresses. Women, Art and Ideology*. London: Routledge and Kegan Paul, 1981.

Parker, Roszika, and Griselda Pollock, eds. *Framing Feminism*. London and New York: Pandora, 1987.

Parry, Benita. "Problems in Current Theories of Colonial Discourse." *Oxford Literary Review*, vol. 9, nos. 1/2 (1987): 27-58.

Patton, Cindy. *Sex and Germs: The Politics of AIDS*. Boston: South End Press, 1985.

Personal Narratives Group, eds. *Interpreting Women's Lives: Feminist Theory and Personal Narratives*. Bloomington: Indiana University Press, 1989.

Pines, Jim, and Paul Willemen, eds. *Questions of Third Cinema*. London: British Film Institute, 1989.

Poggioli, Renato. *The Theory of the Avant Garde*. Cambridge: Harvard University Press, 1968.

Pollock, Griselda. *Vision and Difference*. London and New York: Routledge, 1988.

Polhemus, Ted, ed. *Social Aspects of the Human Body*. Harmondsworth: Penguin, 1978.

The Politics of Exile. Special issue, *Third World Quarterly*, vol. 9, no. 1 (January 1987).

Rajchman, John, and Cornel West, eds. *Post Analytic Philosophy*. New York: Columbia University Press, 1985.

Ramos, Juanita, ed. *Compañeras: Latina Lesbians*. New York: Latina Lesbian History Project, 1987.

Raven, Arlene. *Art in the Public Interest*. Ann Arbor: UMI Research Press, 1988.

Raven, Arlene. *Crossing Over: Feminism and Art of Social Concern*. Ann Arbor: UMI Research Press, 1988.

Raven, Arlene, Cassandra L. Langer, and Joanna Frueh, eds. *Feminist Art Criticism: An Anthology*. Ann Arbor: UMI Research Press, 1988.

Reed, Ishmael. *Mumbo Jumbo*. New York: Bantam, 1972.

Reynaud, Berenice, and Yvonne Rainer. "Responses to Coco Fusco's 'Fantasies of Oppositionality.' " *Screen*, vol. 30, no. 3 (Summer 1989): 79-99.

Rich, Adrienne. "Compulsory Heterosexuality and Lesbian Existence." in *Signs*. London: Only Women Press, 1980.

Rich, Adrienne. *On Lies, Secrets and Silence*. New York: Norton, 1979.

Richardson, Diane. *Women and AIDS*. New York: Methuen, 1988.

Robinson, Lillian S. *Sex, Class and Culture*. New York: Methuen, 1978.

Rodriguez, Richard. *Hunger of Memory. The Education of Richard Rodriguez: An Autobigraphy*. Boston: D.R. Godine, 1982.

Rose, Jacqueline. *Sexuality in the Field of Vision*. London: Verso, 1986.

Rowbotham, Sheila. *Women's Consciousness, Man's World*. Harmondsworth: Penguin, 1973.

Ruskin, Cindy. *The Quilt: Stories from the Names Project*. New York: Pocket Books, 1988.

Russo, Vito. *The Celluloid Closet: Homosexuality in the Movies*. New York: Harper and Row, 1981.

Ryan, Michael. *Marxism and Deconstruction*. Baltimore: Johns Hopkins University Press, 1982.

Sabatier, Renee. *Blaming Others: Prejudice, Race and Worldwide AIDS*. London: Panos Institute, 1988.

Sagay, Esi. *African Hairstyles*. London: Heinemann, 1983.

Said, Edward W. *After the Last Sky*. New York: Pantheon, 1986.

Said, Edward W. *Beginnings: Intention and Method*. New York: Columbia University Press, 1985.

Said, Edward W. *Covering Islam: How the Media and the Experts Determine How We See the Rest of the World*. New York: Pantheon Books, 1981.

Said, Edward W. *Literature and Society*. Baltimore: Johns Hopkins University Press, 1980.

Said, Edward W. *Orientalism*. New York: Vintage, 1979.

Said, Edward W. *The Question of Palestine*. New York: Times Books, 1979.

Said, Edward W. *The World, the Text and the Critic*. Cambridge: Harvard University Press, 1983.

Said, Edward W., and Christopher Hitchens, eds. *Blaming the Victims: Spurious Scholarship and the Palestinian Question*. London: Verso, 1988.

Sangari, Kumkum, and Sudesh Vaid, eds. *Recasting Women: Essays in Colonial History*. New Delhi, India: Kali for Women Press, 1989.

Sayres, Sohnya, et al., eds. *The Sixties Without Apology*. Minneapolis: The University of Minnesota Press, 1985.

Schmidt Campbell, Dr. Mary. *Tradition and Conflict: Images of a Turbulent Decade 1963-1973*. New York: Studio Museum in Harlem, 1985.

Schor, Naomi, and Elizabeth Weed, eds. *The Essential Difference: Another Look at Essentialism*. Special issue, *differences*, vol. 1, no. 2 (Summer 1989).

Schor, Naomi, and Elizabeth Weed, eds. *Life and Death in Sexuality: Reproductive Technologies and AIDS*. Special issue, *differences*, vol. 1, no. 1 (Winter 1989).

Scott, Joan Wallach. *Gender and the Politics of History*. New York: Columbia University Press, 1988.

Sedgwick, Eve Kosofsky. *Between Men: English Literature and Male Homosexual Desire*. New York: Columbia University Press, 1985.

Sekula, Allan. "The Body and the Archive." *October* 39 (Winter 1986): 3-64.

Showalter, Elaine, ed. *Speaking of Gender*. New York and London: Routledge, 1989.

Simone, Timothy Maligalim. *About Face: Race in Postmodern America*. Brooklyn: Autonomedia, 1989.

Simonson, Rick, and Scott Walker, eds. *The Graywolf Annual Five: Multi-Cultural Literacy*. St. Paul: Graywolf, 1988.

Since the Harlem Renaissance: 50 Years of Afro-American Art. Lewisburg, PA: Bucknell University, 1985.

Smith, Barbara, ed. *Home Girls: A Black Feminist Anthology*. New York: Kitchen Table Women of Color Press, 1983.

Smith, Neil. *Uneven Development: Nature, Capital, and the Production of Space*. Oxford: Basil Blackwell, 1984.

Snead, James. *Figures of Division: William Faulkner's Major Novels*. New York: Methuen, 1986.

Soble, Alan. *Pornography: Marxism, Feminism and the Future of Sexuality*. New Haven: Yale University Press, 1986.

Sontag, Susan. *AIDS and Its Metaphors*. New York: Random House, 1979.

Sontag, Susan. *On Photography*. New York: Dell, 1973.

Soyinka, Wole. *Myth, Literature and the African World*. London and New York: Cambridge University Press, 1976.

Spivak, Gayatri Chakravorty. "Can the Subaltern Speak? Speculations on Widow-Sacrifice." *Wedge*, no. 7/8 (1985): 120-130.

Spivak, Gayatri Chakravorty. *In Other Worlds: Essays in Cultural Politics*. New York and London: Routledge, 1987.

Spivak, Gayatri Chakravorty. *Master Discourse Native Informant*. New York: Columbia University Press, (forthcoming).

Spivak, Gayatri Chakravorty. "Three Women's Texts and a Critique of Imperialism." *Critical Inquiry* 12, no. 1 (1985): 243-161.

Stern, Simon. "Lesbian and Gay Studies. A Selective Bibliography." *Yale Journal of Criticism*, vol. 3, no. 1 (1989): 253-260.

Stimpson, Catharine R., and Ethel Spector Person, eds. *Women: Sex and Sexuality*. Chicago: University of Chicago Press, 1980

Stocking, George, ed. *Objects and Others*. Madison: University of Wisconsin Press, 1985.

Stocking, George, ed. *Observers Observed*. Madison: University of Wisconsin Press, 1983.

The Studio Museum in Harlem, New York. *Faith Ringgold*. Edited by Michele Wallace. Exhibition April 8- September 4, 1984.

Suleiman, Susan Rubin, ed. *The Female Body in Western Culture*. Cambridge: Harvard University Press, 1986.

Swann, Brian, and Arnold Krupit, eds. *I Tell You Now: Autobiographical Essays by Native American Writers*. Lincoln: University of Nebraska Press, 1987.

Swerdlow, Amy, and Hanna Lessinger, eds. *Class, Race, and the Dynamics of Control*. Boston: Hall, 1983.

Takaki, Ronald T. *From Different Shores: Perspectives on Race and Ethnicity in America*. New York: Oxford University Press, 1988.

Theweleit, Klaus. *Male Fantasies*. 2 Vols. Minneapolis: University of Minnesota Press, 1987.

Thompson, Robert Farris. *Flash of the Spirit*. New York: Random House, 1983.

Todorov, Tzvetan. *The Conquest of America*. New York: Harper and Row, 1984.

Tomaselli, Keyan, et al. *Myth, Race and Power: South Africans Imaged on Film and TV*. Belville, South Africa: Anthropos, 1986.

Trinh T. Minh-ha. *Un Art sans oeuvre*. Troy, MI: International Book Publishers, 1981.

Trinh T. Minh-ha. "Black Bamboo." *CineAction*, no. 18 (Fall 1989): 56-60.

Trinh T. Minh-ha. "Mechanical Eye, Electronic Ear and the Lure of Authenticity." *Wide Angle*, vol. 6, no. 2 (Summer 1984): 58-63.

Trinh T. Minh-ha. *En miniscules*. Paris, France: Le Meridien Editeur, 1987.

Trinh T. Minh-ha. "The Plural Void: Barthes and Asia." *Sub-Stance* 26, vol. XI, no. 3 (Winter 1982): 41-49.

Trinh T. Minh-ha. *Woman Native Other*. Bloomington: Indiana University Press, 1989.

Trinh T. Minh-ha, and Jean-Paul Boudier. *African Spaces: Designs for Living in Upper Volta*. New York: Holms and Meier, 1985.

Trinh T. Minh-ha, ed. *She, The Inappropriate/d Other*. Special issue, *Discourse*, no. 8 (Fall/Winter 1986-87).

Trinh T. Minh-ha, ed. *(Un)Naming Cultures*. Special issue, *Discourse*, no. 11.2 (Spring/Summer 1989).

Vance, Carole S., ed. *Pleasure and Danger*. Boston and London: Routledge and Kegan Paul, 1984.

Vizenor, Gerald. *Darkness in Saint Louis Beefheart.* St. Paul: Truck Press, 1978.

Vizenor, Gerald. *Earthdivers: Tribal Narratives on Mixed Descent.* Minneapolis: University of Minnesota Press, 1981.

Vizenor, Gerald. *The People Named the Chippewa: Narrative Histories.* Minneapolis: University of Minnesota Press, 1984.

Vizenor, Gerald. *Wordarrows: Indians and Whites in the New Fur Trade.* Minneapolis: University of Minnesota Press, 1978.

Walker, Alice. *Living by the Word. Selected Writings 1973-1987.* New York: Harcourt, 1988.

Wall, Cheryl A., ed. *Changing Our Own Words.* New Brunswick and London: Rutgers University Press, 1989.

Wallace, Michele. *Black Macho and the Myth of the Superwoman.* New York: Dial Press, 1979.

Wallis, Brian, ed. *Art After Modernism: Rethinking Representation.* New York: The New Museum of Contemporary Art and Boston: David R. Godine, Publisher, 1984.

Wallis, Brian, ed. *Blasted Allegories: An Anthology of Writings by Contemporary Artists.* New York: The New Museum of Contemporary Art and Cambridge: MIT Press, 1987.

Wallis, M., and S. Shepherd, eds. *Homosexuality, Politics and Culture.* London: Unwin-Heinneman, 1989.

Watney, Simon. *Policing Desire: Pornography, AIDS and the Media.* Minneapolis: University of Minnesota Press, 1987.

Weeks, Jeffrey. *Sexuality and Its Discontents.* London: Routledge and Kegan Paul, 1985.

West, Cornel. *The American Evasion of Philosophy.* Madison: University of Wisconsin Press, 1989.

West, Cornel. "The Dilemma of the Black Intellectual." *Cultural Critique,* vol. 1, no. 1 (Fall 1985).

West, Cornel. "Philosophy and the Afro-American Experience." *The Philosophical Forum,* vol ix, no. 2 (Winter 1977-78): 117-148.

West, Cornel. *Prophesy Deliverance! An Afro-American Revolutionary Christianity.* Philadelphia: The Westminster Press, 1982.

West, Cornel. *Prophetic Fragments.* Trenton: Africa World Press, 1988.

West, Cornel. "Reconstructing the American Left: The Challenge of Jesse Jackson." *Social Text,* no. 11 (Winter 1984-85): 3-19.

Williams, Raymond. *Keywords: A Vocabulary of Culture and Society.* New York: Oxford University Press, 1976.

Williams, Raymond. *The Long Revolution.* New York: Columbia University Press, 1961.

Williams, Raymond. *Writing and Society.* London: Verso, 1984.

Williamson, Judith. *Consuming Passions.* London and New York: Marion Boyars, 1986.

Wittig, Monique. *Les Guérillères.* London: Paladin, 1975.

Wittig, Monique. *The Lesbian Body.* New York: William Morrow, 1975.

Wittig, Monique. *Opoponax.* Plainsfield, VT: Daughters, Inc., 1976.

Wittig, Monique, and Sandy Zweig. *Lesbian Peoples: Material for a Dictionary.* New York: Avon, 1979.

Wittig, Monique. "The Mark of Gender." *Feminist Issues* 5, no. 2 (Fall 1985).

Wolf, Eric R. *Europe and the People without History.* Berkeley: University of California Press, 1982.

X, Malcolm. *The Autobiography of Malcolm X.* Harmondsworth: Penguin, 1968.

Yau, John. "Official Policy: Toward the 1990's with the Whitney Biennial." *Arts Magazine* (September 1989): 50-54.

Yau, John. *Radiant Silhouette: New and Selected Works 1974-1988.* Santa Rosa: Black Sparrow Press, 1989.

Young, Robert, ed. *Sexual Difference.* Special issue, *Oxford Literary Review,* vol 8 (1986).

Index